The Professional Chef®

Prepared by The Culinary Institute of America and the
Editors of Institutions Magazine

FOURTH EDITION

LeRoi A. Folsom, B.S., Editor and Text Author
Vice President, Industry Relations, The Culinary Institute
of America, Formerly Chef-Instructor

A CBI Book
Published by Van Nostrand Reinhold Company
New York

A CBI Book
(CBI is an imprint of Van Nostrand Reinhold Company Inc.)

Copyright © 1974 by the Culinary Institute of America, Inc.

Library of Congress Catalog Card Number 73-19070

ISBN 0-8436-0571-5

Printed in the United States of America

Published by Van Nostrand Reinhold Company Inc.
115 Fifth Avenue
New York, New York 10003

Van Nostrand Reinhold Company Limited
Molly Millars Lane
Wokingham, Berkshire RG11 2PY, England

Van Nostrand Reinhold
480 La Trobe Street
Melbourne, Victoria 3000, Australia

Macmillan of Canada
Division of Canada Publishing Corporation
164 Commander Boulevard
Agincourt, Ontario M1S 3C7, Canada

16 15 14 13 12

About this book

In 1962, The Culinary Institute of America and Institutions/VF Magazine joined forces to present *The Professional Chef,* a comprehensive study of professional cookery. For the first time, the complex artistry of the chef was detailed with scientific accuracy. Information on equipment, formulas and techniques revealed the chef's secrets to the apprentice cook.

In the second edition, the material presented in the original book was refined, and the material was cross-referenced. Also, a Dessert Section was added to make this the most complete professional cookbook available.

Because International Cuisine has become a subject of growing interest in the years since *The Professional Chef* was first published, menus and recipes based on the cuisine of 13 international food areas were added to the third edition. Menus from some 20 countries, and the 154 formulas needed to reproduce the dishes listed on these menus, were added in a special section. For this fourth revised edition, the recipes in all sections of the book have been set up in a more easily used format. Directions for the preparation of the recipes have been updated with changes made to conform to new techniques, equipment and products. The glossary, bibliography and the many charts have all been reviewed and, where desirable, have been updated to provide the most pertinent information available.

In some cases, formulas are given in this book for items that are often purchased completely or partly prepared. These are included because we feel every cook should know how to prepare these foods, although in actual practice he may rarely do it. This knowledge will give him a yardstick by which to measure the quality of the products he buys.

On pages 423 through 437 are the Basic and Advanced Menus on which the Culinary Institute bases its two-year training program. The formulas covered in the Basic Menus were selected after extensive research into the most often ordered menu items in American food operations. The formulas covered in the Advanced Menus continue this program and progress to classical cookery and more advanced food preparation. The two phases have been closely correlated to include some method review in important areas.

Where possible, menus have been planned so that soup, vegetable and salad will be related to the entree. However, in order to provide the widest range of training, greatest emphasis has been placed on incorporating as many essential and useful dishes as possible into each menu.

Although the progression of menus has been selected to coordinate the training program at the Culinary Institute, menus may be rearranged to satisfy the needs of any operation.

The bulk of the formulas included in the Basic Menus are based on 50 portions. But interspersed are formulas of varying proportions to ready the student for the Advanced Menus he will encounter during his second year.

Quantities in the formulas covered in the Advanced Menus are more variable, to give the student experience in "a la carte" conditions, which he will encounter working in the field. In this manner, he also learns to convert formulas to greater or lesser amounts as required.

An important step toward learning to cook is learning to taste. The student is urged to taste all food that is prepared, regardless of personal dislikes or previous eating habits. It is only by tasting properly prepared food that he can develop his palate so he can recognize when foods are properly cooked and seasoned and when they are not. This cannot be taught through a book. It is only learned by experience.

As an additional aid to operators, recipes presented in this text are available on standard 5 by 8 inch recipe cards.

The formulas and text contained in this book were prepared by the staff of the Culinary Institute with LeRoi Folsom acting as editor and coordinator. Murray Schuman, Director of Curriculum, has supervised the preparation of this revised fourth edition with special assistance from Chef Aldo Graziotin and Chef Eric Saucy. Joseph Amendola prepared the material contained in the Dessert Section. Recipes in the International Section were prepared by Chef Bruno Ellmer and Arno Schmidt. The staff of Institutions/VF Magazine supervised photography, final editing and graphic presentation of material. All formulas were tested in the kitchen of the Culinary Institute of America, Hyde Park, N. Y.

Acknowledgments

Special acknowledgment should be given the following people for their assistance in providing the original material for The Professional Chef:

Joseph Amendola, Vice President, Culinary Institute of America, formerly Pastry Chef-Instructor, *Dessert Section*
Chef Theodore Baun
Chef Pierre Berard, Washington, D.C., *Formulas*
Chef Herman Breithaupt, formerly Chadsey High School, Detroit, *Technical Assistance*
Chef Paul Brunet, formerly The Palmer House, Chicago, *Formulas*
Mary Carter, Research Kitchen, Sheraton Hotel Corporation, *Technical Assistance*
Chef Emile DeLorme
Chef Aldo Graziotin
Margaret Johnson, formerly University of Illinois, Chicago Campuses, *Technical Assistance*
Chef Arthur Jones
Eric Mood, New Haven Board of Health. *Technical Assistance*
Chef Howard Partridge, Culinary Institute of America, *Editorial Assistant*
Antonios Pronoitis, Art Director, INSTITUTIONS/VF Magazine
Chef Paui Troescher
Jane Young Wallace, Editor, INSTITUTIONS/VF Magazine
John Welch, Missouri Restaurant Association, *Technical Assistance*
Jule Wilkinson, Contributing Editor, INSTITUTIONS/VF Magazine

Special acknowledgement for encouragement and support in the original preparation and subsequent revisions of The Professional Chef:

Frances L. Roth, Director, The Culinary Institute of America, 1946-1965
Jacob Rosenthal, President, The Culinary Institute of America, 1965-1974

Preparation and formulas in the International Cuisine Section, which appeared for the first time in the third edition, contributed by:

Bruno Ellmer, Chef-Instructor, Culinary Institute of America
Arno Schmidt, former Chef Supervisor, Culinary Institute of America

Revised Fourth Edition prepared under the supervision of Murray Schuman, Vice President, Educational Services, The Culinary Institute of America

with special assistance from
Chef Aldo Graziotin
Chef Eric Saucy
Jule Wilkinson

Grants to assist in the original preparation of the book were received by the Culinary Institute of America from:

The Trustees of the Statler Foundation
The Educational Institute of The American Hotel and Motel Association
Hotel and Restaurant Employees and Bartenders International Union, AFofL/CIO

Contents

A Chef Is
Many Things

In past years, when labor and food costs were low, there was ample time and opportunity to develop artistic culinary talent. The Chef was often a creative figure in the kitchen. His concern was the development of new dishes and of varied and often complicated methods of preparing and presenting foods in grand fashion to patrons who were appreciative of this type of service and who were willing and able to spend the time and money for it. In that era the Chef's business was food—and that was his immediate and prime responsibility.

Changing Role Today, the Chef's business is still food—but his responsibilities have changed. They have grown to varied and gigantic proportions. The creative spirit is still required, but it seeks different channels.

The Chef has taken on a new and challenging role. Knowing how to cook is only one part of the background a chef needs. Today, he must be an organizer, a personnel man and often also a buyer. He should have some knowledge of nutrition and diet and should employ this knowledge in planning menus and instructing his personnel in food preparation. He should have some background in kitchen layout and design—knowledge of equipment and of the various elements required to operate and maintain it.

Background Necessary He must have a good basic foundation in mathematics and be able to calculate food and labor costs quickly and accurately.

A good background in English is a prerequisite. Today's Chef must not only write menus, but he is often responsible for letters, reports and written instructions. He often deals with other executive personnel and must be able to communicate effectively.

It is vital that he have a good understanding of people and that he be able to get along well with them. He must have the ability to instill in his employees a desire to do their best, for his employees are often a reflection of himself; and the work that they perform is the structure of his reputation.

Personality Traits He should be of even temperament and disposition. Food service is a difficult and pressing business. Too often the holder of the title, "Chef," presumes a carte blanche to any variation of mood or temper. To hold people together, to make them a team, does not allow for this dubious privilege.

It is said that "the speed of the leader is the speed of the team." This refers not only to physical activity but to mental outlook and attitude. Working with people is one of the most important areas for creativity.

A Chef, to function effectively, must be of good physical and mental health and possess great stamina. Long hours, hard work and great responsibility demand no less than excellent health.

His knowledge and ability do not come overnight. Experience is a great teacher. Good training is of extreme importance, but it becomes valuable only when supplemented by actual experience. This means hard work in the field.

The Chef is responsible for organizing all of the vital elements discussed; for putting them together in a manner that will result in a smoothly functioning, effective and profitable operation.

Wide Responsibility Today's Chef is a businessman. His responsibility does not end with serving the finest food possible or making money for his employer. He is also responsible to the people that work for him and to the public which he serves. Above all, he is responsible to himself.

Food Service Occupations

Jobs in the food service industry are briefly described in this section. In many establishments, two or more of the jobs described may be combined; for example, the Second Cook may do all the work usually assigned to the Soup, Sauce, Roast and Broiler Cooks. The work of the Fry Cook and Broiler Cook may be combined. Nevertheless, it is important for the professional food training program to prepare the student so that he or she may advance to any or all of these positions.

Chef The Chef is the person in authority in a kitchen. He has complete charge of all food preparation and supervises the serving of foods for the dining rooms, banquets and all other functions. He may have one of the following titles: Executive Chef, Head Chef, Chef Steward, or Working Chef.

Executive Chef The Executive Chef is in charge of the kitchen in the larger hotels, with a full staff at his command. He plans and writes the menus and coordinates all activities pertaining to the kitchen.

He attends daily conferences with the manager and other heads of departments related to the food service, such as the purchasing agent, steward, maitre d'hotel and wine steward. It is his responsibility to see that all food served from the various kitchens in the establishment is prepared and served according to the standards and practices of the hotel.

Sous-Chef The Sous-Chef is second in command and is responsible for the physical aspect of the kitchen operation, including supervision of kitchen personnel as well as the preparation and serving of food.

Chef Steward The position of Chef Steward is established in medium-sized hotels as an economy factor. In addition to discharging the regular duties of a Chef, the Chef Steward also purchases all the food supplies. This requires a few hours each morning away from the kitchen. In his absence, either the Sous-Chef or Second Cook is in charge. During meal hours and banquet service, the Chef Steward acts in a supervisory capacity.

Working Chef The Working Chef is in charge in smaller hotels, restaurants and cafeterias. Since production is on a smaller scale, the kitchen staff is smaller and the Working Chef himself takes over part of a station or an entire station. He may perform such tasks as cutting the meats; making the soups, entrees and sauces; assisting all station men; preparing dishes that require special attention. During the meal hours he performs the same duties as other Chefs, except that he both works and supervises.

In order to be a competent Chef, regardless of the size of establishment, a Chef must have worked on all the stations in the kitchen. He should have a thorough knowledge of food and food combinations to be able to write and construct well-balanced menus. The Chef must know food and labor costs and have a good background in employer-employee relationships. He must be able to please the discriminating public and at the same time show a profit for his department.

Chef de Partie This is the person in charge of a department, such as the fry station, broil station, etc.

Night Chef The Night Chef takes complete charge of the kitchen immediately after the Executive Chef and Sous-Chef are gone for the day. Otherwise, he acts as alternate for the Cold Meat Man. (See Garde Manger.) Either the Sous-Chef or the Banquet Chef supervises and checks dishes or dinner menus to assure continued service until the end of the dinner hour. He supervises the preparation of all orders, including sandwiches and dishes from the pantry.

Banquet Chef The Banquet Chef has full charge of breakfast, luncheon, dinner and buffet parties; he is responsible for all stations to which banquet work has been assigned; he is under direct supervision of the Executive Chef; he is in full authority when the Head Chef is absent.

Second Cook The Second Cook makes all stocks, soup, bouillons, jellied consommes and sauces. He also prepares boiled dishes, such as boiled beef, corned beef, chicken, tongue, boiled and sauteed fish; all stewed, braised and smothered dishes, such as goulash, swiss steak, pot roast, beef a la mode; all combination creamed dishes, such as creamed chipped beef, ham and mushrooms; all special a la carte and chafing dish orders, such as breast of chicken, sweetbreads and mushrooms under bell, chicken a la king and lobster newburg.

Soup Cook All soup stocks, soup consommes and bouillons are made by the soup cook. He also boils hens for chicken broth and makes fish stock for chowder. This job may be combined with the Second Cook's.

Broiler Cook The broiler cook broils steaks, chops, chicken, fish, lobsters, bacon, ham, liver, sweetbreads, tomatoes, mushrooms, mixed grill, veal kidneys and chicken livers en brochette. Quite often the roast and broiler stations are combined and the cook who is assigned to either must be thoroughly trained for both jobs.

Fry Cook The Fry Cook's work centers around deep fat frying, omelettes, eggs, fritters, all kinds of potatoes, au gratin dishes, spaghetti, special pancakes and crepes suzette. All fresh and frozen vegetables are cooked on this station if there is no Vegetable Cook on the staff. Cooking vegetables not only requires special knowledge, but also constant attention if color, vitamins and minerals are to be retained.

Usually the Fry Cook station is in the center of the range, facing the hot stove on one side and the steam table on the other. The Fry Cook, therefore, must have energy and endurance to work in the temperature of his station.

The assistant, after he has gained a thorough knowledge of the station routine, is eligible to become a Head Fry Cook, or he proceeds to other stations. The Head Fry Cook may remain in that position, or, if he wishes to advance and knows the fundamentals and routine of a higher station, may become Second Cook, Cold Meat Man or Night Chef.

Vegetable Cook The Vegetable Cook directs the preparation, cleaning and cooking of all vegetables. He is responsible to the Chef.

Cook's Helper The Cook's Helper assists in preparing and serving food. Some of his specific duties are:
- Cleaning and preparing fruits and vegetables
- Setting up relish dishes
- Making cream sauces
- Placing food on plates and similar duties

The job of Cook's Helper affords an excellent opportunity for the beginner to learn how food is prepared and served in a particular establishment. He may be promoted to Vegetable Cook or Fry Cook.

Swing Cook-Roundsman-Relief Cook The duty of the Swing Cook is to relieve all cooks on all stations one day each week. He must, therefore, be an all-around experienced man, able to handle the responsibilities of all stations.

The head Swing Cook relieves the cooks on the major stations, and the assistants relieve those on minor stations. The Swing Man must maintain the current supplies for the menus and keep up the routine of the day. He must plan and do advance work for the menus of the following day as if he were the regular station man who will be on the job the next day.

The usual procedure for promotion of Head Swing Man is to Second Cook. However, if he has all the necessary experience, he is eligible for advancement to Cold Meat Man, Night Chef or Banquet Chef.

Garde Manger (Cold Meat Department) The cold meat department is under the supervision of the Head Cold Meat Man or Garde Manger. He oversees the breading of meats, fish, croquettes and seafoods, such as oysters, scallops and frog legs. He prepares salad dressings, cocktail sauce and all other cold sauces; he prepares meat, fish and seafood salads; parboils sweetbreads; cooks shrimp; prepares and decorates all cold food for buffet service; makes appetizers, canapes and sandwiches. In a large hotel or restaurant some of these duties are performed in the pantry.

Pastry Chef The Pastry Chef supervises the pastry department, writes the dessert menus, requisitions materials, schedules the work for his assistants, decorates cakes, makes ornamental pieces, works on new recipes and figures production costs.

Assistant Pastry Chef The first Assistant Pastry Chef is under the direct supervision of the Pastry Chef and is in full charge of production. He makes all cakes, cookies, pies, puddings, French pastry and other items which are found on the dessert menu.

Baker The Head Baker bakes all the breads, rolls, hot breads and muffins. He regulates temperature of ovens, sets and punches the dough and has full responsibility for the operation of the bakery department.

Baker's Helper The Baker's Helper assists the Baker in scaling off ingredients; prepares bake sheets, muffin tins and bread pans; keeps bread cloths and bread boxes clean and keeps the bake shop in sanitary condition.

Butcher The Head Butcher cuts and bones all beef, lamb, pork and veal; cares for and cleans associated meat products and smoked meats.

Fish Butcher The Fish Butcher takes care of and cleans fresh and salt water fish, lobster, shrimp, oysters and other seafood.

Chicken Butcher The Chicken Butcher cleans and prepares poultry: chickens, turkeys, capons, ducks, geese, hens and game birds.

Oyster Man The Oyster Man cares for and opens shell oysters and clams; takes care of bulk oysters and cuts and prepares lobsters and shell seafood for cooks.

Other Opportunities Additional jobs directly associated with the preparation and service of food include: Sandwich Maker, Salad Maker, Pantry Worker, Cake Decorator, Food Checker, Food Purchaser or Buyer.

Hygiene and Sanitation

Sanitation and hygiene have become practically synonymous, referring to preservation of health, although hygiene is defined specifically as that science which deals with sanitation and the system of principles and rules applied to health preservation.

We think of personal hygiene as cleanliness practiced by an individual, that is, his personal grooming and habits. Sanitation is usually interpreted in a more general sense as the principles of hygiene and cleanliness applied to all.

Importance for Food Service Worker The subjects of personal hygiene and sanitation are of extreme importance to the food service worker. He is a vital link in the prevention of food-borne disease.

Bacteria are everywhere, particularly in our breath, body discharges, on our hands and skin, in our mouths, on clothing and in our hair. No matter how clean we are or how carefully we handle food, some bacteria are bound to be present. This means that we must do two things: 1) Minimize the bacteria that get into food by practicing good personal hygiene and sanitation procedures, and 2) keep the food under such conditions that the bacteria which do get in it or are already present in it, do not have

Check list of 50 factors which can make your appearance seem poor to others—Explanation: We frequently offend others unknowingly. This list was made up from hundreds of answers to the question: "What factors keep people from presenting the best appearance of which each is capable?" Directions: Place a check mark before each factor which applies to you now. Less than five check marks—your appearance aids your personality. From 5 to 10—you should be more careful about your appearance. Between 10 and 15—you will have the reputation of being physically unattractive. Over 15—you are in bad shape!

1. *How you look*
   A. Your head:
      ( ) Need a haircut or hairdo ( ) Hair greasy
      ( ) Dandruff ( ) Dirty ears
      ( ) Hair not combed ( ) Dirty neck

   B. Your face:
      ( ) No shave today
      ( ) Too much make-up
      ( ) Powder smears or dabs
      ( ) Visible blackheads
      ( ) Pimples on face
      ( ) Greasy skin
      ( ) Yellow or unclean teeth
      ( ) Food showing between teeth

   C. Your hands:
      ( ) Dirty hands
      ( ) Dirty fingernails
      ( ) Ragged, broken fingernails
      ( ) Gaudy colored fingernails

2. *How you smell:*
   ( ) Body odor
   ( ) Need a bath
   ( ) Too much or too strong perfume
   ( ) Bad breath

3. *How you act:*
   ( ) Awkward posture
   ( ) Stooped shoulders
   ( ) Slouchy or shuffling walk

4. *How you dress:*
   ( ) Inappropriate clothes
   ( ) Soiled suit or dress
   ( ) Clothes poorly fitted
   ( ) Wrinkled suit or dress
   ( ) Trousers or skirt baggy
   ( ) Dirty shirt
   ( ) Dirty collar or cuffs
   ( ) Collar wrinkled or wilted
   ( ) Tie poorly or carelessly tied
   ( ) Tie crooked
   ( ) Tie wrinkled or dirty
   ( ) Soiled underclothing
   ( ) Missing buttons
   ( ) Visible runs in hose
   ( ) Hose seams crooked
   ( ) Unshined shoes
   ( ) Broken shoestring
   ( ) Run-over heels on shoes
   ( ) Too much or gaudy jewelry
   ( ) Dirty gloves
   ( ) Torn gloves
   ( ) Soiled or dirty purse
   ( ) Dirty handkerchief

   Number of checks_____

Every one of these defects can be avoided—*with great advantage to your personal appearance—and your own satisfaction in being well groomed!*

Appearance and professional attitudes are the basis on which people form their first impressions. If these are unattractive, most people will not be motivated to look beyond them and to discover valuable aspects of your personality that are not immediately evident.

the conditions under which they best grow and multiply.

Our bodies have certain built in mechanisms for destroying or getting rid of some harmful bacteria. One of the most effective of these is the elimination of waste. Body wastes are highly contaminated. That is why it is important to *wash your hands often, using soap and a fingernail brush, particularly after every trip to the toilet.*

Many nose, mouth and throat bacteria are spread by coughing and sneezing. *Cover your nose and mouth when sneezing or coughing.* When possible, use disposable tissues or a handkerchief. *Then wash your hands at once.*

Other mechanisms act to push out invading bacteria from cuts and infected sores or boils. The pus and other poisons that are discharged from infected areas are highly contaminated with the very type of bacteria that cause a large percentage of food poisoning. *Avoid handling food when you have open cuts, sores or boils on your hands.*

Touching open sores on other parts of the body, or the hair, nose or mouth—then touching food, transfers bacteria to the food. Wash your hands often, particularly after touching the hair or any body opening.

Wearing soiled or dirty uniforms, wiping utensils with soiled towels or rags, laying food on soiled tables or counters and bringing food in contact with any soiled or dirty surface brings danger of bacterial contamination. The food contaminated through your carelessness may be the food you eat, as well as the guests' food.

Cleanliness Pays The practice of personal hygiene and cleanliness has many advantages other than the obvious. People are largely judged by their appearance. If their appearance is neat, clean and in good taste, the impressions will be favorable. It is an important step in establishing friendship and popularity. A sloppy, dirty appearance will discourage people from wanting to know you better, regardless of what other good qualities you may have.

When you apply for a position in food service your prospective employer will look you over carefully. If you are clean and neat, he will probably assume that your work will be clean and neat. If you are slovenly about your appearance, he can only believe that you will be the same way about your work.

A person is judged by the company he keeps. Make sure that the company you keep has the same high standards that you set for yourself. Your school or place of employment may also be judged by your appearance. Let each represent the other properly by good personal hygiene and sanitation.

Check list of 50 factors which can make your appearance seem poor to others—Explanation: We frequently offend others unknowingly. This list was made up from hundreds of answers to the question: "What factors keep people from presenting the best appearance of which each is capable?" Directions: Place a check mark before each factor which applies to you now. Less than five check marks—your appearance aids your personality. From 5 to 10—you

should be more careful about your appearance. Between 10 and 15—you will have the reputation of being physically unattractive. Over 15—you are in bad shape!

The problems of food poisoning are easier to understand when we know something about how bacteria grow and multiply. Their growth is fast and simple. They multiply by dividing in two, like this:

GERM OR BACTERIUM	⬭	NOW TWO BACTERIA	⬭ ⬭
STARTS TO DIVIDE	⬭⬭	EACH DIVIDE	⬭⬭
PARTLY DIVIDED	⬭ ⬭		⬭⬭
COMPLETED DIVISION	⬭ ⬭	NOW FOUR BACTERIA	⬭ ⬭ ⬭ ⬭

Under favorable conditions, germs—or bacteria, as we will call them from now on—divide once every 20 minutes. In eight hours, one bacterium, under favorable conditions, can multiply into over 35,000,000,000,000 (thirty-five trillion)! And they multiply day and night, without stopping.

Note, however, that they multiply this fast under *favorable* conditions. The conditions they like are the same that we like for comfort. They are:

Warmth—bacteria grow most rapidly at the temperature of your body

Food—they like the same foods you eat

Moisture—needed both to live and to expand and grow

Since we are most concerned with the bacteria which are already in or which get into food, where moisture is also usually present, our principal weapon against them is temperature.

Bacteria grow slowly at temperatures below 40°F. and little if any at 0°F. and below. They grow very slowly at temperatures over 140°F. and are killed rapidly by temperatures over 170°F.

So our first lesson is: *Get hot foods over 140°F. as fast as possible and keep them there!*

Get cold foods below 40°F. as fast as possible and keep them there!

Keep foods at temperatures between 40°F. and 140°F. as short a time as possible and for preparation only.

Besides the bacteria which may be in food—and some usually are—food which is left exposed receives more bacteria from outside sources. Therefore, food should always be covered and protected.

Salmonella Infection This is a common type of food infection characterized by gastro-intestinal disturbances or upsets. The disease is spread by the ingestion of the meat in infected animals, by human carriers and by the excreta of mice and rats. Although it is often prevalent in low acid foods, nearly any kind of food may be involved.

The disease is also spread by raw or improperly cooked foods; by foods that are left unrefrigerated, giving the organisms opportunity to grow, and by uncovered foods, left exposed to excreta of rodents.

Preventive measures are: 1) good personal hygiene habits, and 2) constant practice of cleanliness and sanitation in the kitchen. This includes proper handling, cooking, storage and refrigeration of foods.

These facts are important to you as a food service employee:

THE SPREAD OF FOOD BORNE DISEASE

Germs Causing These Diseases	Reaching Customer Through	What You Can Do to Stop It
Food Poisoning	Food contaminated by unwashed hands. Unrefrigerated perishables. Food contaminated by rodents.	Wash hands frequently. Keep foods cold (below 40°F.) Control rodents and pests.
Typhoid Fever	Water, milk, shellfish contaminated at source. Food contaminated by unwashed hands or by flies.	Purchase and serve approved food products. Wash hands. Control flies.
Dysentery	Water contaminated at source. Defective plumbing. Food contaminated by unwashed hands or by flies.	Use approved water supply. Check faulty plumbing. Wash hands. Control flies.
Trichinosis	Underdone pork. Ham cuts and products.	Cook all pork and pork products to not less than 170°F.
Botulism	Home-canned foods, improperly prepared.	Serve canned foods properly prepared.
Septic Sore Throat Scarlet Fever	Raw milk contaminated at the source.	Buy and serve only pasteurized milk.
Diphtheria	Dishes or silverware contaminated by a carrier—sneezing, coughing and spitting.	Approved warewashing and pot washing procedures. Good personal hygiene.
Brucellosis	Infected milk.	Buy and serve only pasteurized milk.

FOOD-BORNE DISEASE ROUTES

Source (Bacteria)	May Travel In or On	To You
	MAN	
	AIR	
DISEASED PERSON	RODENTS	
	INSECTS	
	FOOD	
CARRIER	MILK	
	WATER	
	EQUIPMENT	
	UTENSILS	
DISEASED ANIMAL		

Staphylococcus Food Poisoning This type of poisoning is caused by a toxin produced by staphylococcus bacteria. The food may be contaminated by boils, cuts or abcesses on the skin, nose or mouth of a food handler. Improper storage procedures and inadequate refrigeration allow bacteria to grow and toxins to be formed. Heating may destroy the growth or the organisms but not the toxin, as the toxin is heat resistant.

Gastro-intestinal disturbances are often associated with eating contaminated foods such as eclairs, cream puffs, some cake fillings, salad dressing and other foods containing starch thickening. Proper and immediate refrigeration of these and other foods may prevent food poisoning.

Sanitation Measures that Prevent Food-Borne Diseases Rats, mice, roaches and flies are carriers of germs and disease and all food and equipment should be safeguarded from these sources of contamination. Whenever you see one of these pests, be assured there are others. They live in colonies. There is no such thing as a few.

Rats are one of man's worst enemies.

They are filthy; they contaminate and spoil food with their feces and urine. They are infested with fleas. These fleas carry disease to man. The bubonic plague is a rat-flea carried disease. Rats are the source of trichinosis, the worm which makes it necessary to cook pork well done. (Hogs eat rats which infect the hogs; then man eats the infected hog.)

Here is how we must get rid of rats and mice and keep them out:
1) Keep everything clean, neat and free from trash and places where rodents can hide.
2) Block up their entrances.
 a. Close all wall cracks and openings.
 b. Use metal or cement, through which they can't gnaw; close all openings of ½ inch or more.
 c. Rat-proof all foundations with metal, cement.
3) Starve them out.
 a. Rats live only where they can get food; use tight garbage containers, and *keep the lids on them.*
 b. Keep the floors clean in every room and passageway: kitchen, dining room, store room, toilet, locker rooms and all others.
 c. Cover and protect all food, particularly at night and in places where there is little human activity during the day.
 d. Store foods and supplies at least 12 inches above the floor.
4) Trap and destroy any rodents which may get in.
Flies and roaches are also filthy pests. They live and breed in filth, carry it on their feet and in their intestines and deposit it on food. Bacteria also thrive on filth. They live in it on the feet of flies and roaches and in their intestines. When deposited on food, these bacteria grow and multiply.

Controlling Flies and Roaches Flies and roaches are particularly good at passing on such diseases as typhoid fever and summer diarrhea.

Here is what we must do to get rid of flies and roaches and keep them out:
1) Keep everything in the food service establishment clean.
2) Keep all foods covered; this will starve out flies and roaches.

3) Keep all garbage cans tightly closed.
4) Close all openings; use screens; fill cracks and crevices where pests might hide and breed.
5) Get rid of food wastes at once; dispose of garbage daily.
6) Search for and get rid of breeding places.
7) Make all doors self-closing.
8) Use insect sprays, traps, fly paper and insecticides to kill pests that get in.
9) Upon delivery, look over vegetables, fruits and groceries for roaches before storing.
10) If infestation gets beyond your control, call in a professional exterminator. Follow his advice.

Control with Heat and Cold We have found that the best and surest way of reducing bacterial action is by the control of heat and cold. The scale we use to measure heat is temperature and the instrument used for its measurement is the thermometer.

Because cooked food has been held at a temperature which will kill bacteria during the cooking process, food right off the range is generally safe. Therefore, food should be prepared as near serving time as possible. *Long storage during which bacteria can grow should be avoided.*

When we have to keep hot foods over long serving periods, they should be kept HOT—above 140°F.—in some type of a hot food storage unit, such as a steam table. *Never let food stand for any appreciable time at room temperature.*

Even foods cooked until sterile can be quickly reinfected and will become dangerous under improper storage conditions. If food has to be left at room temperature—even for a few minutes—*cover it* to prevent contamination.

Temperatures ranging from 60°F. to 100°F. are most favorable for the growth and multiplication of the bacteria associated with food service. This is sometimes termed the incubation range. The shorter the time of exposure at these temperatures, the less time bacteria have in which to develop. This reduces the possibility of spoilage or the creation of poisons known as toxins.

While these are the optimum, or most favorable, temperatures for bacterial growth, bacteria will survive in a far wider range of temperatures. It is most important to reduce the exposure time of foods to room temperatures and to refrigerate them properly. Thus follows this vital rule: *Cool hot foods as quickly as possible. Reheat cold foods as quickly as possible.*

Many bacteria are killed or inactivated by bringing a liquid to the boiling point (212°F.).

Some Guides to Safe Food Service
1) Purchase federally inspected meat and poultry.
2) Buy pasteurized milk.
3) Serve only shellfish taken from inspected and approved beds.
4) Avoid bulging cans.
5) Wash all fruits and vegetables.
6) Work with as small quantities of food as possible.
7) Avoid alternate refrigeration and heating.
8) Total accumulated exposure time (within the danger range) of preparation, or pre-preparation, and of service, must never exceed four hours.
9) Treat all left-overs with great care.
10) Use all left-overs within 24 hours *or* discard.
11) Avoid refreezing defrosted food items.

Safe Food for Good Health
1) Keep it hot or keep it cold.
2) Always keep it covered.
3) When in doubt, throw it out.

Some Critical Temperatures

Let's set up a scale of critical temperatures beside a thermometer:

212°	Water boils at sea level. Most resistant bacteria killed within 2 minutes.
195°	Water above this point sprayed from dish washing machine rinse nozzles vaporizes so readily that rinse action is reduced.
180°	Water at this temperature in rinse line of the dishwasher will give 170°F.—killing temperature—at the utensil.
170°	Practically all common disease producing bacteria killed at this temperature.
160°	Some foods start to cook on utensils here.
140°	Bacterial growth practically stopped. May die.
98.6°	Body temperature. Bacteria's most rapid growth.
70°	Room temperature. Bacteria grow fast.
50°	Bacterial growth slowed greatly; almost stopped below this point.
38°) to 33°)	Walk-in refrigerator temperature range for most foods. Near freezing temperature in ice recommended for fish.
32°	Freezing point of water. Practically no bacterial growth.
10° and below	Recommended for storage of frozen foods.

TO GET THE BEST FROM YOUR REFRIGERATOR

What To Do	Why You Do It
1) Pack food loosely; allow air to circulate.	1) To get cooler air in contact with food.
2) Hang raw meats away from walls with drip trays underneath	2) Cold air needs to circulate to keep food from spoiling.
3) Cover food with waxed paper or other covering.	3) To prevent contamination by dripping from other foods.
4) Discard things not needed.	4) To prevent crowding and increase circulation.
5) Place new purchases at back.	5) Use older things first.
6) Wash refrigerator frequently.	6) It must be kept clean.
7) Defrost before ¼ in. frost gathers.	7) Frost slows cooling process.
8) Open door only when necessary.	8) Open door raises the temperature.

Tools and Equipment

No cook will be able to prepare the recipes given in this book unless he or she has a thorough knowledge of kitchen tools and equipment. These are discussed in this section.

Knives and Hand Tools To the experienced cook, knives are of the greatest importance. For speed and for the professionally finished appearance of his or her work, cuts must always be clean and accurate.

For this reason most good cooks purchase their own personal set of knives. They mark them plainly, take meticulous care of them themselves and permit no one else to use them.

There is an almost infinite variety of styles and types of knives, hand tools and cooking utensils. Those presented here are, however, the most generally encountered types.

FRENCH KNIFE—Most used of all. Wide, functionally curved, pointed blade. Used for slicing, chopping and mincing food. Most popular size for a french knife is a 12 in. blade.

ROAST BEEF SLICER—Long (14 in.) round-nosed blade which will slice completely across the largest cooked roast beef.

CHEF'S SLICER—A shorter (12 in.) pointed blade knife for slicing other cooked meats, where point may be needed around bones.

BUTCHER KNIFE—A slightly curved, pointed, heavy bladed knife used in sectioning raw, carcass meat.

CIMETER OR STEAK KNIFE—A distinctly curved, pointed blade knife used in making accurate cuts, as cutting steaks from a loin. Gives clean, professional cut.

BONING KNIFE—A short (6 in. blade), very thin, pointed blade knife used in separating raw meat from bone with minimum waste. A boning knife may have stiff or flexible blade.

FRUIT AND SALAD KNIFE—A short (6 in.) pointed blade knife for pantry use in preparing salad greens, coring lettuce, paring and sectioning fruits. Various shapes for individual preference.

PARING KNIFE—A very short (2½ to 3½ in.), pointed blade knife. Used for paring fruit and vegetables. Point used for eyeing and removing blemishes.

SPATULAS—Wide, flexible, blunt-nosed blade knives for scraping utensils or spreading. Sizes range from 3½ in. blade butter spreader to 12 in. Rated as semi-flexible (frosting spreaders), regular and highly flexible (bowl knives). Also termed palette knife.

HOT CAKE OR MEAT TURNER—Wide, offset, chisel edge blade. Used to slip under and support hot cakes, fried eggs, hamburgers, etc., while turning on griddle, broiler or oven sheet.

OFFSET SPATULA—Same uses as hot cake or meat turner.

PIE AND CAKE KNIVES—Wide bladed, offset knives with blades shaped as pie or cake wedges. Used to slip under individual pieces after cutting to remove from pan or stand without breaking.

FORKS—Insulated handle cook's forks used for holding meats while slicing, turning and handling roasts and serving. Many sizes and types.

STEEL—For maintaining cutting edge of knives. Magnetically treated. Removes burrs to keep knives sharp.

CLEAVERS—An extra wide, heavy blade, square-nosed knife. Used to chop through medium bone and heavy cartilage, such as the backbone structure of chops.

MEAT SAWS—Bow mounted, thin, fine-toothed blade saws for sawing through heavy bone structure, such as shank, thigh and shoulder bones in carcass meat.

OYSTER KNIFE—Short with thin tapering end for opening oysters.

CLAM KNIFE—Flat blade with sharp edge for opening clams.

Pots, Pans and Equipment

STOCK POTS—Large round, high-walled pots with loop handles for lifting on and off the stove. May be equipped with a draw-off faucet or strainer. Well fitting covers and inside racks to hold certain foods off the bottom should be available. Used for boiling and simmering, where a large amount of water in relation to solids is used, as in making stocks, soups and boiling certain vegetables. Sizes graduated from about 2½ gal. to 40 gal. capacity.

SAUCE POTS—Large, round, medium-deep pots with loop handles for lifting on and off the stove. Used for stove top cooking where the ratio of solid to liquid is higher and stirring or whipping is necessary. Sizes graduated from about 8½ to 60 qt.

BRAZIERS—Large, round, shallow-walled pots with loop handles for lifting on and off the stove. Very heavy to resist warping under high heat when used dry, as for searing meat. Used for searing, braising and stewing. Sizes graduated from 12 qt. to 28 qt.

SAUCE PANS—Smaller, shallower, lighter versions of the sauce pot. Have a single, long handle for lifting. Same uses as sauce pot, but for smaller quantities of food. Sizes range from 3 to 6 in. deep and from 1½ qt. to 11½ qt. capacity. Should have well-fitting covers available.

SAUTOIRS—Large, round, shallow, straight walled pans with long handle for lifting. (Largest sizes also have one loop handle.) Used for sautéing or cooking food in shallow fat. Heavy construction to withstand warping at high temperatures. Sizes range from about 2½ to 4½ in. deep and from about 10 to 20 in. inside diameter.

SAUTE PAN (SAUTEUSE)—Smaller, round, shallow pans with sloping sides, for the quick frying of food in a minimum amount of fat. One long handle for lifting. Sizes range from inside bottom diameter of about 5 in. to 11 in.

SKILLET—Iron, heavy, for pan-broiling or frying. Holds heat well. May be used for varying temperatures. Many sizes.

FRYING PAN—For light work (fried potatoes, omelettes). All sizes.

DOUBLE BOILERS—Consist of a lower section very similar to a stock pot, in which water is boiled, and an upper section for food which must be cooked at temperatures below that of boiling water. The upper section is suspended in the boiling water by means of shoulders which rest on the rim of the lower section, preventing contact between the bottoms of the upper and lower containers. Sizes range from upper section capacities of 4 qt. to 40 qt. Covers are provided for upper sections.

ROASTING PANS—Large, rectangular, medium high-walled pans, with or without covers. Several sizes to fit standard large quantity ranges and separate roasting ovens. Check your oven sizes before ordering roasting pans.

BAKE PANS—Large, rectangular, shallow pans without covers. Used for baking. Sizes of bake pans are similar to roast pans.

SHEET PANS—Rectangular, very shallow (1-in.) pans in varying sizes. Used for baking sweet goods, oven frying and baking such products as cookies and melba toast.

COUNTER OR SERVICE PANS—Shallow pans with wide rims designed to fit standard steam table openings, usually about 12 by 20 in. Used 1) for baking or steaming some foods in the same pan in which served, or 2) as a transfer pan from cooking utensil to hot storage. May be obtained perforated for steaming some foods. Also available in ½, ⅓, ¼ and ⅛ sizes for insertion in one opening through use of adaptors. Several depths, though standard depth is about 2½ in. Sometimes called hotel pans.

STRAINERS—Perforated metal bowl with long handle and hook for hanging across pot. Used for draining such foods as spaghetti, rice, spinach and other leafy vegetables. Several sizes available, depending upon size of pots used.

COLANDERS—Perforated metal bowls with foot and loop handles. Used for draining salad greens, fruits and raw garnish or salad vegetables after washing. Several sizes.

CHINA CAP STRAINER AND ROLLER—A pointed, extra strong, perforated metal strainer. Has long handle and hook for hanging on side of pot. Used to strain sauces and semi-solids which can be forced through perforations with roller. One of the most used kitchen utensils.

SIEVES—Round metal frames with mesh bottoms. May be obtained in several diameters and with several mesh sizes. Used to sift flour and other dry ingredients.

SKIMMER—Flat ladle with small holes for removing scum from simmering liquids or cooked items from deep fat fryer.

SCOOP—Metal, usually aluminum, of specific capacity, (1 lb., 2 lb.). For scooping flour, rice, meals, etc.

WHIPS—Loops of wire with ends formed into a handle. Much more efficient in stirring or whipping quantities of food than spoons.

SPOONS—All sizes. Used in same manner as in home kitchen. Slotted or perforated spoons used to drain liquid in serving.

FOOD TONGS—For handling food without touching with hands. Spring type metal, formed in elongated "U" shape, with sawtooth like gripping fingers on each end.

GRATER—Used to shred cheese, vegetables, rinds in varying degrees of fineness.

RICER—Device used to force cooked potatoes through small holes.

PIE AND CAKE MARKERS—Circular metal frames, mounted with wire guide bars for accurate marking, to place over pie or cake. Available in various diameters and portion sizes. A must for uniformity and portion control.

DOUGH CUTTERS—Wide rectangular blade with top mounted handle. Used for cutting or dividing rolled out or batch doughs, lifting doughs from board and scraping dough board.

PUREE SIEVE OR FOOD MILL—Designed for one purpose only, to puree cooked foods such as fruits, potatoes and other vegetables.

WOODEN PADDLES—Various lengths. To stir foods in stock pots and steam kettles.

Measuring Devices

URN CUPS—Round, lipped, cool handled measuring containers for the accurate measurement of boiling water, so important in making good coffee. Usually 1 gal. capacity, with graduations showing quarts.

MEASURES—Round, lipped, side handled measuring containers, accurately graduated, usually in quarters. For the accurate measurement of liquids and some dry ingredients. Available in gallon, half gallon, quart, pint and half pint (cup) sizes.

MEASURING CUPS — Round, handled, accurately calibrated cups. Hold one standard cup (½ pt.) when level full. Graduated in quarters.

MEASURING SPOONS — Accurately calibrated spoons, usually five to a set, linked together: tablespoon, teaspoon, ½ teaspoon, ¼ teaspoon and ⅛ teaspoon. Parallel edges for accurate leveling.

LADLES—Metal bowls or cups of known capacity attached to long handles with hooks at opposite end to prevent dippers from slipping into container. Used to measure liquids for service and portion control. Also to stir, mix and dip.

SCOOPS (ice cream dippers)—Bowl of known capacity on rigid handle. Has thumb operated rotating vane to release semi-solid contents. Used both to measure and shape contents in serving and portion control.

Numbers and approximate capacities and scoop sizes commonly used in portion control:

Scoop Sizes

Number	Measure	Approx. Weight
30	2 tbsp.	1–1½ oz.
24	2⅔ tbsp.	1½–1¾ oz.
20	3 tbsp.	1¾–2 oz.
16	4 tbsp.	2–2¼ oz.
12	5 tbsp.	2½–3 oz.
10	6 tbsp.	4–5 oz.
6	10 tbsp.	6 oz.

Brushes and Scrapers

VEGETABLE BRUSHES—Used to scrub root vegetables in preparation for cooking or for use in salad preparation.

POT AND PAN BRUSHES—Handled brushes for removing food residues from and for scraping pots and pans. Stiff bristles, usually of palmetto fiber. Sometimes called gong brushes.

POT HOOK—Metal hook for lifting pots and pans from boiling sterilizing rinse water.

COFFEE URN AND GAUGE GLASS BRUSHES—A must for keeping coffee urns clean and sanitary.

TUBE BRUSHES—For cleaning wash and rinse tubes of dishwashing machine. Original brush usually furnished with machine.

BLOCK SCRAPER—Bristles of spring steel with chisel points, set in wooden block. Used to scrape wooden butcher's block surface after cutting meat. *Never* use water to scrub a block. Scrape well, remove scrapings and cover with salt.

Kitchen Equipment Since each kitchen is different and there is such a wide range of kitchen equipment and machinery, your instructor will explain and demonstrate to you the equipment with which you will work while you are in his kitchen.

Some items, such as the mixer, have many attachments which will be demonstrated to you as you have occasion to use them.

It will pay dividends to give particular attention to the instruction on the use, care, precautions and maintenance procedure described for kitchen equipment. You can save much time and extra work by using and caring for this equipment properly.

Safety

Accidents are caused 1) by not knowing the right way to do things, or 2) by deliberately or thoughtlessly doing things the wrong way.

Here are the right ways to do many of the food service tasks that you will encounter.

Receiving and Storing Operations

1) When opening boxes, crates, etc., remove the nails. Don't bend them down.
2) Always store heavy materials on bottom shelves, medium weight next above, light weight on top. *Don't* put things on locker tops or other high storage places.
3) Keep food containers covered except when in actual use.
4) When opening anything, keep at a distance from food containers which might catch pieces of wire, splinters, bits of paper wrapping, straw, dirt, etc., and pass them on to guests.
5) Get rid of all dirt, grease and trash promptly to reduce fire hazard. Eliminate hiding-breeding places for rats and roaches.
6) Be sure the light bulbs are guarded. *Don't* store any material within 18 inches of any bulb.
7) Use ladders—not boxes, crates or chairs—to get things from high shelves. And see that the ladder is safe, too. Avoid losing your balance by overreaching.
8) Avoid lifting or carrying too heavy objects; and when you lift a heavy object, keep your back straight and lift with your legs. *Don't* carry bulky objects too big for you to see over or around.

Food Preparation Operations

1) Use only dry cloths, towels, to handle hot cooking utensils.

2) Lift edge of cover on side of pot away from you first—so that steam will escape that way, not blast into your face. Stand far enough back when removing cover so steam cannot reach you. *Don't* try to peek into open steam jacketed kettles.

3) Keep stove top and hood free from grease to avoid dangerous fires.

4) Keep handles of pans away from stove and out of the aisle so that utensils won't be brushed off stove. Take care that handle is not near an open flame.

5) Get help in moving heavy, hot containers. Be sure work area is clear when swinging them out.

6) When drawing hot water or coffee from an urn, turn spigot slowly to avoid rush-and-splash. Check that all valves and spigots are in proper position before filling an urn.

7) Keep oven doors closed—out of aisle—when not in use.

8) Ventilate a gas oven several minutes before lighting. Strike matches away from clothing or flammable matter. Place match at gas jet before turning on gas. Open gas gradually to avoid blowing out match.

9) Don't clean oven or stove until it has cooled.

10) Protect food from foreign substances. If you break an article near open food containers, report this immediately to your supervisor so that the food can be taken out of service.

11) Avoid over-filling containers with hot liquids or foods. Make sure edges are free from foods. Warn service people of hot dishes.

Drawers and Doors

1) Be careful in closing drawers—they have a trick of pinching fingers and hands. Keep them closed, out of the way.

2) Open and close doors by handles or knobs. Avoid crushed fingers.

Handling Knives

1) Don't daydream with a knife in your hand. Pay attention to what you are doing.

2) Cut away from your body—and away from fellow workers.

3) When drying a knife, keep the sharp edge away from you.

4) Use a cutting board—*never* a knife edge against metal.

5) Keep all knives in proper storage place when not in use.

6) *Don't* leave knives in sink or in water or any place where they can't be seen easily.

7) A sharp knife is *safer* than a dull one. It cuts more easily, takes less pressure, has less danger of slippage. The proper way to sharpen knives should be decided by the kitchen supervisor.

8) After honing knives, place on the steel to remove burrs. Then wipe knives with a cloth or towel to remove any additional particles that may be present.

9) If a knife falls, get out of the way! *Don't* try to grab it.

10) Use the knife for the operation for which it is intended. (See section on Tools and Equipment.) No knife or cleaver is a can opener! *Never* use them that way!

11) Be careful in reaching for knives, forks or other sharp objects. Pick them up by handles, *not* by blade or tines.

Machines Used for Food Preparation

1) *Never* use any machine you have not been trained to use. Be sure that all safety devices are in place before using.

2) Pull plug or throw switch to "off" position before cleaning or adjusting any machine. Keep fingers, hands, spoons, etc., away from moving parts. Wait until machine stops before moving food.

3) Check all switches on electric appliances to see that they are "off" before plugging into the outlet.

4) Particular care must be exercised in cleaning the slicing machine. To clean this machine: a) Pull the plug. b) Turn the gauge to zero. This position masks the cutting edge of the blade on most machines. c) Don't touch the edge of the cutting blade. d) Clean the blade from the center out. e) While cleaning one side of the blade, hold a protective cloth in the other hand to use in rotating the blade.

5) *Don't* start a mixing machine until the bowl or kettle is locked in place and the attachment securely fastened. *Do not* operate the grinder and the mixer at the same time. *Always* read instructions if posted on or near machine.

6) Always use the proper tool for pushing food into a grinder. Tampers or pestles are made of special wood or metal. Tamping foods in the grinder with other tools or instruments is dangerous. Wooden handles may splinter and mix with the food. Metals may damage the equipment or injure you.

China and Glassware

1) Use care in handling glasses and dishes.

2) Use pan and broom to sweep up large pieces of broken glass or china. Use a dampened paper towel or cloth to pick up slivers. Put broken glass or china in a special container. *Do not place in waste baskets or garbage or refuse cans.*

3) Drinking glasses or other glassware or china that are chipped or cracked should be discarded.

4) Glasses and metal pots do not mix. Keep glass and china out of the pot sink.

5) If you suspect that there is broken glass or dishware in soapy water, drain the water first, then remove pieces carefully with a cloth.

6) *Don't* use a glass for an ice scoop. It may break in your hand or may leave pieces of glass in the ice.

Floors

1) Keep floors clean and dry. If you spill anything or see spilled liquids or foods, wipe them up immediately. In cleaning, wet mop first, then rinse and dry mop, doing one small area at a time.

2) Tile floors may be slippery when weather is humid and muggy. Be careful at such times to avoid falls.
3) Walk—don't run or slide—across the floor.
4) *Never* leave utensils on the floor. Someone is sure to trip over them—maybe *you.*

Refuse Disposal

1) Place food scraps in protected sanitary containers.
2) Don't overflow containers.
3) Don't stack refuse containers.
4) Report broken or defective refuse containers.
5) Keep hands out of mechanized garbage disposal machines.

Safe Clothing

1) Wear a safe shoe with closed toe for added protection; keep neatly laced to prevent tripping over untied shoelaces. A sensible heel provides balance; good strong support provides comfort. Heels kept in good repair prevent slipping.
2) Do not wear excessively loose clothing. Sleeves, ties and aprons may easily get caught when working with or near grinders, mixers and other moving machinery.
3) Keep uniforms free of pins and gadgets which might drop in food or cause scratches.

Fire Safety

1) Smoke only in designated areas.
2) Immediately report any fire, no matter how small, so that the fire department may be called.
3) Know where the fire extinguishers are located and how each should be used. If you find an extinguisher partially used that needs recharging, or one with its seal broken, report it to your supervisor immediately.
4) Know the fire exits and how to use them and be prepared to show them to guests should need arise.
5) Know your station and duties on the organization's "Fire Instructions."
6) Keep fire doors, fire exits and fire stairs clear of material and equipment. Use only in the event of emergency or fire drill.
7) Don't let grease accumulate on grill canopies and filters. Fires started in these areas are major causes of kitchen damage.

For extinguishing fires, keep in mind the following:

Fires are divided into 3 classifications. Learn these classifications so you will be able to use the right material to extinguish a fire.

Class A: Rubbish, wood, paper, etc. *Use water to extinguish.*

Class B: Oil. *Use foam to extinguish or a box of baking soda kept handy may be used.*

Class C: Electrical. *Use CO_2 to extinguish.*

TYPES OF ACCIDENTS	HOW TO AVOID
1) Cuts	1) Use knives properly. Keep knives in plain sight. Don't grab at knives. Pick up broken glass properly. Avoid using glass or china for things which may result in the pieces breaking in your hand. Don't "fish" for broken glass or china.
2) Burns	2) Assume that every pot and pan is hot. Use dry side towels only for handling hot pots and pans. Wet towels will transfer the heat from the pot to your hands. Keep handles away from aisles. Dry wet foods before deep fat frying. Open hot water faucets carefully to avoid splash. Tip pot covers open at rear (away from you). Learn how to operate steam kettles and steamers and follow safety precautions with them. Get assistance in handling heavy, hot utensils.
3) Falls	3) Keep floors clean. Wipe up spilled foods, grease, etc., at once. Keep floors and aisles clear of obstructions of all kinds—including open oven doors. Don't stand on boxes, tables or chairs to reach objects. Use a safe ladder. Don't over-reach from a ladder. Don't block your view. . . Be sure that you see where you are going.
4) Strains	4) Don't try to carry too heavy loads. Lift properly with the leg muscles, NOT the back. Don't turn or twist the body while lifting—move your feet instead.

Food Cost

Food represents the largest single item of expenditure in the food service business, from 35 to 50 per cent of the total income. It is the commodity on which the entire business is based. Although careful and intelligent purchasing of food is necessary, it is equally, or perhaps even more, important that great care, planning, skill and wisdom be used in its storage, preparation and service.

Percentages Vary Food cost percentages vary in different eating establishments, depending on the type of operation, the clientele and the menu. Many establishments aim at a 40 per cent food cost. This means that the total cost of all foodstuffs purchased by that business is equal to 40 per cent of the sales. A meal or an item that sells for $1 has a raw food cost of approximately 40¢. A meal that costs $2 would have a raw food cost of 80¢.

It is not always possible for every item on the menu to be sold or merchandised at the same percentage of food cost. Some items may permit a higher mark-up than others, depending on many factors, such as habit or custom, general availability of the product, competition, clientele and luxury of service and surroundings.

Some items, expensive in cost alone, may not allow a high enough mark-up to be profitable items. However, they still may be carried on the menu, perhaps as a convenience to guests, as a necessary item because of competition or seasonal demand, or simply for a change to add variety. This is why food costs must be averaged, to arrive at an average raw food cost.

Calculating Food Cost To maintain a 40 per cent food cost, the selling price of a meal or item should average 2½ times the cost of the raw food. Thus we can arrive at a selling price in this manner:

The raw cost is 40¢; 2½ times 40¢ is $1. $1 becomes the selling price, based on a 40 per cent food cost. If the establishment operates on a 50 per cent food cost, the selling price should be twice the cost of the raw food.

The table above right shows sales prices for foods at 40, 45 and 50 per cent food costs (prices are rounded off to the nearest figure):

In order to know the cost of each item on a menu, it is necessary to know the yield of each food. Either definite portion sizes must be determined, based on yield and the price range of the menu, or the menu price may be determined by portion cost. It is often difficult to disassociate the two. It should be readily recognized at this point, that *portion control is a determining factor in the financial success of any food business.*

Portions may be regulated by the use of scales, ladles, measuring cups, scoops or any means by

Food cost per portion	Selling prices per portion		
	50% Food Cost	45% Food Cost	40% Food Cost
$0.10	$0.20	$0.23	$0.25
.11	.22	.25	.28
.12	.24	.27	.30
.13	.26	.30	.33
.14	.28	.32	.35
.15	.30	.34	.38
.16	.32	.36	.40
.17	.34	.39	.43
.18	.36	.41	.45
.19	.38	.43	.47
.20	.40	.45	.50

which definite and accurate measurement may be made.

Standardized Recipes Standardization of recipes is also important. Standardization assures the guest of the same product each time he orders it, and assures the operator that his food cost remains stable. It is also helpful in enabling the operator to calculate yield and costs with a greater degree of accuracy.

Many operations keep a physical record of recipes, recipe cost, portion cost, etc. These recipes, usually part of a card system, are dated and maintained by management. Variations and improvements may be made from time to time, properly recording any changes or variations. This offers a system of close control.

Recipes may be costed in the manner shown in the chart below:

It is not the intention of this text to teach food cost, but to create an awareness of its existence and its importance, and to develop an interest and a challenge to further study. Many excellent articles and books on the subject of food cost are available.

FRUIT SALAD

YIELD: 3¼ gallons or 100 portions.
EACH PORTION: ½ cup or 4 oz. or No. 10 scoop.

Ingredient	Weight	Measure	Unit Cost	Total Cost
Fruit Dressing		2½ qt.	$0.50	$1.25
Pineapple, canned chunks	6½ lb.	1 No. 10	1.56	1.56
Oranges, washed	11 lb.	approx. 27	.16	1.10
Bananas, A.P.	6 lb.	18	.11	.66
Apples, unpeeled, washed	6 lb.	19	.14	.84
Dates, pitted	1 lb.		.40	.40
Marshmallows	1 lb.		.19	.19
Total cost $6.00				$6.00
Cost per serving .06				

Converting
Recipes

The basic formula for converting recipes to provide different numbers of servings is given below.

Divide the required number of servings by the original number the recipe is for:

$$or\ \frac{\text{Required Number}}{\text{number recipe is for}} = ?$$

Then
multiply each ingredient by the resultant answer:

$$\frac{\text{Required Number}}{\text{number recipe is for}} = ?$$

? times each ingredient = the required amount of each ingredient.

Example: 50 Portions:
Rice (raw) 1¾ lb. (28 oz.)
Ham (cooked) 8 lb.
Cheese Sauce 5 qt.

$$\frac{\text{Required Number}}{\text{number recipe is for}} = ?$$

? times each ingredient = the required amount of that ingredient.

To change the recipe to 30 portions
(*round figures*):

$$\frac{30}{50} = .60$$

.60 × 28 oz. = 16.80 oz. or 17 oz. or 1 lb., 1 oz.
.60 × 8 lb. = 4.80 lb. or 4 lb., 13 oz.
.60 × 5 qt. = 3.00 qt. or 3 qt.

New recipe . . . . *serving 30 portions:*
Rice (raw) . . . . .1 lb., 1 oz.
Ham (cooked) . . . . .4 lb., 13 oz.
Cheese Sauce . . . . .3 qt.

Appetizers

An appetizer may be defined as a small portion of food or drink served before a meal. Appetizers include a variety of food combinations designed to whet or stimulate the appetite. They afford an opportunity to introduce colorful and refreshing foods that will add interest. Appetizers include:

1) Seafood
2) Meats and Poultry
3) Fruits
4) Vegetables
5) Juices
6) Dairy Products
7) Any combination of these foods

The characteristics of properly prepared appetizers are much the same as those of salads:

1) Eye appeal
2) Taste appeal
3) Stimulating ingredients
4) Easy to eat (bite size)
5) Hot appetizers must be piping hot
6) Cold appetizers must be well chilled

Simplicity, harmony of color, pleasing contrasts, attractive arrangement and presentation are the key points. Over-garnishing can be unattractive and costly.

In this country, there are five basic categories:

1) Cocktails (served at the table)
2) Appetizer salads, such as antipasto, (served at the table)
3) Hors d'oeuvre
4) Canapes
5) Relishes

Cocktails Cocktails are made of the following: shrimp, lobster, crabmeat, shellfish, fruits and vegetables. Fruit and vegetable juices are also included in this group. They are generally served well-chilled and are most appropriate when tangy or tartly flavored rather than sweet.

When appetizers of a sweet nature are served, they should precede foods of light character. Heavy or rich entrees call for light, stimulating appetizers.

Appetizer Salads Appetizer salads include pickled herring, chopped chicken livers, smoked salmon and stuffed eggs.

Hors d'oeuvre Hors d'oeuvre and canapes are a specific type of appetizer. While often served preceding a meal, they are sometimes served as the only food at cocktail parties and other functions involving alcoholic beverages. Canapes and hors d'oeuvre are most often served buffet style.

Hors d'oeuvre should be small enough to be eaten with the fingers, with a toothpick or with a small fork when served at the table. They may be hot or cold.

It is important to remember that hot hors d'oeuvre must be piping hot, cold hors d'oeuvre well chilled.

Hors d'oeuvre may be any combination of the foods included under appetizers: rolled or stuffed meats, glazed shrimp, miniature sausages or pizza, angels on horseback (oysters wrapped in bacon), bite size cheese or meats, spiced fruits and vegetables, various meatballs.

Canapes Canapes are tiny open-faced sandwiches. They should be bite size and are usually highly flavored or tangy. They may be made of any of the same combinations or mixes as hors d'oeuvre, but are always served on a base, such as bread, toast or crackers.

Canapes include: smoked salmon, anchovies, caviar, various cheeses—hot and cold, cold or hot meats and various fish, meat or dairy paste preparations.

Canapes and hors d'oeuvre provide an area of advantageous food cost and may be extremely profitable *if* the labor cost is kept at a minimum. The person preparing these foods should be able to produce something attractive and appetizing out of very little. These foods should be prepared and presented as artistically as possible within the limits of the labor budget.

The skill is not merely preparing quality products, but producing them in a minimum of time. In large operations, this task falls to the garde manger department. In some operations, the chef may take care of this area of preparation. It may be the responsibility of the salad department or the person in charge of that department.

Relishes Relishes include radish roses, carrot curls, scallions, vegetable sticks, hearts of celery, stuffed olives, ripe olives, pickles, chopped vegetables and pickle combinations.

Appetizers

Seafood Cocktail

YIELD: 50 portions	EACH PORTION: 2 oz. seafood, 1¼ oz. sauce.	
INGREDIENTS	*QUANTITY*	*METHOD*
Lettuce, washed, cleaned and trimmed	4 heads	1. Place a lettuce leaf in each sherbet glass. Shred additional lettuce and put in center of each glass on top of lettuce leaf.

Crabmeat, cooked, flaked
Halibut, cooked, broken in
  small pieces
Scallops, cooked, cut in
  medium pieces
Shrimp, cooked, peeled and deveined
Cocktail Sauce (p. 323)
Parsley
Lemon Wedges (optional)
	1 lb.
	2 lb.
	
	1 lb.
	
	50
	2 qt.
	to garnish
	50
		2. Arrange seafood on shredded lettuce, dividing portions evenly. Place shrimp on last.
		3. Dress with 1 tbsp. Cocktail Sauce (p. 323), leaving a portion of the seafood exposed.
		4. Garnish with fresh parsley. A lemon wedge may be cut and placed on the rim of the glass or served separately.

Cider Shrub

YIELD: 12 portions	EACH PORTION: 4 oz. with sherbet	
INGREDIENTS	*QUANTITY*	*METHOD*
Apples, small dice Apple Cider, sweet, chilled Sherbet, frozen Fresh Mint	2 oz. 1½ qt. 1 pt. for garnish	1. Marinate apples in acid juice or salted water to prevent discoloration. Drain diced apples well and divide evenly into 6 oz. chilled fruit glasses. 2. Pour 4 oz. cider into each glass. Place a No. 40 scoop of orange or lemon sherbet in each glass. Garnish with a sprig of mint. Serve immediately.
NOTE: Rims of glasses are sometimes dipped in lightly beaten egg white and colored sugar and placed in freezer prior to filling. Any fruit juice may be substituted for cider and combined with any choice of sherbet. The shrub then takes its name from those ingredients.		

Baked Grapefruit au Sherry

YIELD: 50 portions	EACH PORTION: ½ grapefruit	
INGREDIENTS	*QUANTITY*	*METHOD*
Grapefruit	25	1. Cut grapefruit in half. Trim ends so they will stay in place. Remove core and section.
Honey	1 lb.	2. Place on sheet pan and brush with honey. Bake at 350°F. until warm all the way through.
Sherry Brown Sugar	1 pt. 1 lb.	3. Remove grapefruit from oven and sprinkle with Sherry and brown sugar. Hold for service. 4. To serve place under broiler until lightly browned. 5. Serve with mint leaf in center, if available.
VARIATION: Grapefruit au Rum—substitute light rum for sherry.		

Fresh Fruit Cup

YIELD: 25 portions		EACH PORTION: 5 oz.
INGREDIENTS	QUANTITY	METHOD
Grapefruit Sections, bite size Orange Sections Pineapple, diced (½ in.)	1 qt. 1 qt. 1 qt.	1. Place grapefruit, orange and pineapple in a stainless steel bowl. Strain juice into a second stainless steel bowl. Sweeten to taste.
Apples, diced (½ in.) Bananas, sliced	1 pt. 1 pt.	2. Add juice to apples and bananas to prevent discoloration.
		3. Add drained fruit mixing carefully using a folding motion.
		4. Arrange fruit in sherbet glasses or supreme cups Add small amount of juice to maintain moisture.
Fruit for garnish	as needed	5. Garnish as desired and chill well before serving.

NOTE: Any colorful and contrasting fruit in season may be used for garnish (fresh strawberries, blueberries, grapes, melon balls, etc.). Sherbet is also often used with fruit cups. Mint leaves provide a refreshing additional garnish. Selection of fruit may vary. One gallon of fruit will yield about 25 to 30 standard portions.

Beverages

Coffee comes from the green or roasted seeds or beans obtained from the berrylike fruit of an evergreen shrub. Most of the coffee consumed in the United States comes from South and Central America.

Brazil is probably one of the largest exporters of coffee to this country. These coffees include Rio, Santos and Bourbon Santos. Colombia exports what are known as milds. Bogotá produces a coffee of that name, the better grades of which have excellent flavor. Coffees from other countries are Java, Mocha and Maracaibo.

Coffee beans from different sources contribute different qualities or characteristics, such as: 1) flavor, 2) color, 3) aroma and 4) strength. As many as 15 different kinds of coffee may be blended to produce one brand.

The green or unroasted coffee bean has little or no flavor or aroma. It is during the roasting process that these characteristics are developed. Roasts are classified according to color: 1) light, a cinnamon-brown, 2) medium, a deep chestnut—most used in this country, 3) dark.

An element known as caffeol, formed during roasting, contributes flavor and aroma to coffee, but is water soluble and may become chemically destroyed or extremely sharp or volatile during prolonged heating.

The caffeine in coffee is a mild stimulant. Tannins are the bitter substance found in both coffee and tea. These substances are soluble at high temperatures, and prolonged heating, coupled with excessive temperatures, results in an over-extraction that results in unpleasant bitterness.

Although a few establishments grind their own coffee, most food service operations purchase ground coffee. Exposure to air and moisture contributes greatly to staleness. Coffee should be kept in a cool, dry place and supplies rotated carefully so that the old is always used first. Frequent deliveries are recommended. Dating individual coffee packets at time of delivery insures their use in proper rotation.

How to Make Good Coffee

1) *Clean Equipment*
2) *Freshly Boiled Water*
3) *Fresh Coffee*

How to Brew in An Urn

1) Never guess. Accurate measurement is the most important step in brewing good coffee.
2) Spread fresh coffee evenly on filter. An even coffee

bed is important to even extraction.

3) Use fresh boiling water. Start with cold water to insure freshness.

4) Pour water in slow circular motion. Make sure you wet all grounds evenly. (Total exposure time should be 4 to 6 minutes when using urn or drip grind.)

5) Remove grounds immediately after all the water has dripped through.

6) Mix brew. Draw off heavy coffee from bottom of batch and pour back into brew for uniform mixing. Urns equipped with an agitator do not require this procedure.

7) Hold coffee at 185°F. to 190°F. Never boil.

8) Serve fresh coffee. Make fresh coffee every hour.

9) Good coffee must have flavor, strength and aroma.

How to Brew in a Vacuum Maker

1) Never guess. Accurate measurement is the most important step in brewing good coffee.

2) Fill lower bowl with cold, fresh water. Fill to water level mark. If bowl is unmarked, leave at least an inch at the top for water expansion.

3) Adjust clean filter in upper bowl. If cloth filter is used, rinse in cold water; also store in cold water.

4) Put coffee in upper bowl. Never guess, measure the correct amount.

5) Set upper bowl on lower bowl only when water in lower bowl is boiling briskly.

6) Stir water in upper bowl 30 seconds. Total exposure time 2 to 4 minutes with fine or vacuum grind.

7) Turn off heat.

8) Remove upper bowl. Rinse upper bowl and filter.

9) Good coffee must have flavor, strength and aroma.

Cleaning and Care of Urns

1) Always clean urn immediately after each use.

2) Add small quantity of hot water, brush sides and rinse with hot water until it runs clean. Urn is now ready for next batch.

3) At the end of each day clean and brush urn several times, then rinse thoroughly with hot water.

4) Remove clean-out cap at end of coffee faucet (or take apart faucets which have no caps) and scrub pipe leading to center of urn.

5) Scrub the spigot, then rinse it thoroughly with hot water.

6) Place several gallons of fresh water in urn until next use. Leave cover partly open.

7) Always remember to empty and rinse the urn with boiling water before using again. This eliminates off flavors or odors caused by rancid coffee oils.

Semi-Weekly Cleaning Procedure

1) Be sure outer jacket is ¾ full of water.

2) Turn off heat and fill urn jar ¾ full of water; use only urn cleaning compounds, following manufacturer's directions; mix thoroughly and let stand about 30 minutes.

3) Clean gauge glasses, faucet pipe, plugs, etc., using long thin brush. Use urn cleaning solution for scrubbing. Take faucet valve apart and clean thoroughly. Clean all tubes well.

4) Scrub inside of urn and inside of cover with long-handled brush.

5) Rinse inside of urn three or four times with hot water—scrubbing each time. Also rinse parts well. Repeat until all traces of foreign odor and cleaning solution are removed.

6) Leave a few gallons of fresh water in urn with cover partly open until next use. If cold water is used, allow urn to cool to prevent cracking liner.

7) Urn baskets may be scoured with scouring powder or stiff brush and urn cleaner. Rinse thoroughly and let dry. Never use steel wool. Spray-heads should be checked to see that all holes are open. If any are clogged, use stiff wire to open.

Important Things to Remember

1) Use fresh coffee. As ground coffee ages it loses its flavor, strength and aroma which are important assets.

2) Store coffee in a cool, dry place. Heat and moisture cause coffee to stale rapidly. Coffee picks up outside odors very quickly.

3) Use proper grind for equipment. Too fine a grind for the equipment used is the chief cause of astringent and bitter coffee. Too coarse a grind produces weak, unflavorful coffee.

4) Use cold fresh water. Hot water has a tendency to be flat and stale. This can make the coffee taste the same. Never use water that you wouldn't drink.

5) Spread coffee evenly. To obtain an even extraction from your ground coffee, the layer should be even in depth. (Filter bed should be about an inch in depth.)

6) Remove grounds immediately. After the grounds have released their flavor, strength and aroma-bearing properties, all that remains are astringent and bitter substances which will make coffee strong and bitter if allowed to mix with it.

7) Mix brew. When coffee is first made in an urn, the heaviest concentration is at the bottom. Drawing this heavy coffee off and pouring it back into the brew mixes it and gives a uniform strength throughout.

8) Hold coffee at 185° to 190°F. Holding the brew in the urn at temperatures lower than 185°F. to 190°F. makes it too cool for drinking. Holding at higher temperatures causes the brew to lose its flavor and become more astringent in taste.

9) Serve it fresh in warm cups. The longer brewed coffee is held, the less desirable it becomes. It loses flavor and aroma as it becomes older.

10) Rinse urn with boiling water after each batch of coffee is removed from the urn; a thin layer of old coffee remains, coating all exposed surfaces. Rinsing removes this layer, preventing it from affecting the next brew.

11) Rinse urn bag and cloth filters in hot water. Hot water removes more of the old coffee deposits than cold. Do not use soap, bleaches or detergents. They will affect the flavor of the following brews.

12) Store urn or cloth filters in cold water when not

in use. This prevents them from becoming sour and rancid or picking up food odors.

13) Replace urn bags at least once a week. If used frequently, bags become badly stained and should be replaced.

14) Use correct size urn bag. If the bag is too large, it may hang in the brew and cause the coffee to lie in a ball rather than in an even layer. This condition interferes with proper extraction.

15) Do not set the upper bowl on lower bowl until water in lower bowl is boiling. This may start the water into the upper bowl before it is hot enough.

Servings Per Pound It is difficult to state how many servings per pound you will get out of any specific urn or pound of coffee because number of servings vary as cup sizes vary. However, brewing according to the recommendations of the Coffee Brewing Institute (2½ gal. water to 1 lb. of coffee), the average servings will be:

52 4½-oz. servings (average serving in a 6-oz. cup).

47 5-oz. servings (average serving in a 6½-oz. cup).

43 5½-oz. servings (average serving in a 7-oz. cup).

39 6-oz. servings (average serving in an 8-oz. cup).

Grinds Because grinds are directly related to exposure time of coffee and water, the following recommendations are for evenly distributed water at or about 200°F.

Fine or Vacuum (2 to 4 minutes)
Drip or Urn   (4 to 6 minutes)
Regular   (6 to 8 minutes)

The grind specifications are those contained in simplified practice recommendations R231-48 U. S. Dept. of Commerce.

Cream Good coffee suggests good cream. The butter fat content of the cream bears direct relation to cost so that one standard cannot fit the requirements of all food operations. Light coffee cream may not be less than 18 per cent butterfat, according to federal standards, but good cream may run up to 20 to 22 per cent. Extra light cream is used in many operations that are restricted by budget. Extra light cream, or half and half, is classified as a milk and cream mixture and contains approximately 12 per cent butter fat. Excellent cream substitutes are also on the market.

Other Coffees Café au lait is coffee served with hot milk.

Café noir is heavy black coffee, usually served in a demitasse after dinner.

French coffee is finely pulverized with chicory.

Turkish coffee is a strong, unstrained, extremely heavy coffee made from finely pulverized coffee. It often appears quite thick or muddy. It is usually prepared in small pots designed specifically for this use.

Decaffeinated coffee has a large part of the caffeine removed and is often requested by persons for health reasons. Prepare by mixing with near-boiling water.

Coffee substitutes derived from cereal are prepared for service in the same manner as instant coffee.

Coffee for iced coffee should be double strength as ice dilutes flavor as it melts.

Tea is prepared from the leaves of an oriental shrub native to China. Today teas are imported from Ceylon, Taiwan, India, Java and other warm climate countries.

There are three major types of tea: 1) black tea, 2) green tea and 3) oolong tea. The differences in these teas result primarily from processing.

Black tea, principally used in the United States, is fermented, which gives it the black color and rich flavor.

Green tea is unfermented, green in appearance and has a light color when brewed.

Oolong tea is semi-processed or semi-fermented so that its leaves are partly brown and partly green. Oolong tea also has a light color.

Many other teas are available, such as jasmine and orange blossom tea; but these are usually used only for special functions.

Most teas in commercial operations are preportioned in individual tea bags or larger bags for quantity service or the preparation of iced tea. Instant tea has made great strides and is used extensively in preparing iced tea.

Tea tannins react intensely when in contact with certain metals. This is one reason why teapots are made of china. China also holds the heat. You will notice that silver teapots are china-lined. Most of the aluminum alloys used in today's cooking equipment do not affect tea adversely. However, when making tea for iced tea, a glass or crockery iced tea container with spigot is best.

The chemical composition of tea is similar to coffee and the brewing procedures are similar.

Infusion, or steeping of tea, should not exceed four to five minutes as the tannin reacts to prolonged steeping in the same manner as prolonged heating of coffee. Fresh cold water, brought to a rolling boil, makes the best tea.

Tea for iced tea should also be made double strength to allow for dilution by melting ice. Iced tea is best prepared by making a concentrate (that is by using a portion of the total required liquid for the infusion). When the tea bag is removed, the remaining required water may be added, cold. Iced tea is served in chilled glasses filled with ice cubes. A slice of lemon and sweeteners may be added as desired.

When making hot tea in pots for individual service, the pot should be preheated by filling with hot water for a few minutes and dumping the water before making the tea. Milk, cream or lemon may be served with hot tea as the guest requests.

Breakfast Cookery

Breakfast cookery is an important area that is too often overlooked. Knowledge of breakfast cookery involves a varied background in many phases of cookery including meats, fish, potatoes, various batters, eggs, preparation of fruits and other products.

Breakfast is important nutritionally because it is the first food eaten for a period of nearly 12 hours. The body requires a balanced breakfast to function at top efficiency, particularly in starting a new day.

Most people are fussier about breakfast than other meals, especially where egg cookery is involved.

Eggs, like milk, constitute one of the most important food components in the daily meal. Eggs are a complete protein food, containing the essential amino acids. The yolk is high in fat and iron. Eggs are also important for their vitamin content. Ease of digestion depends greatly on cooking methods. Eggs, in addition to being a breakfast item, are also an excellent meat substitute and are frequently used at luncheon and dinner as a main course. Eggs are also an excellent food cost item.

Eggs may be used in a variety of ways:
1) Clarifying agent   Example: Preparing consommé
2) Binding agent   Example: Preparing meat loaf
3) Emulsifying agent   Example: Preparing mayonnaise
4) Thickening agent   Example: Preparing custard liaison
5) Adhesive agent   Example: Preparing breading
6) Glazing agent   Example: Eggwash on baked products
7) Table service   Example: Breakfast cookery

Egg shells are porous. Some of the dirt and fecal matter from nests may, through the process of cleaning and storing, find its way under the shell. While the thin membrane inside the shell often protects the enclosed egg, these highly infected accumulations may remain in the shell. *Shells should not be used for cooking under any circumstances.* It has been proved that egg shells do not perform the exaggerated claims of clarification and other benefits that are often mistakenly attributed to them. *If benefits were* derived, the danger of bacterial infections and possible illness would nullify their use.

It has also been proved conclusively that the color of the shell has no bearing on the cooking and baking performance or nutritive value of the egg.

It may be seen in the table above right that there is a 3-ounce difference between classes. It is easy

U. S. Weight Classes, Consumer Grades for Eggs in the Shell

Size or Weight Class	Minimum Net Weight per dozen
Jumbo	30 oz.
Extra Large	27 oz.
Large	24 oz.
Medium	21 oz.
Small	18 oz.
Peewee	15 oz.

to remember by establishing large as 24 ounces and adding or subtracting 3 ounces in steps to determine proper weights for other classes.

Egg Grades

The quality of eggs depends on flavor and appearance. Eggs are graded according to appearance and size. There are four U. S. Grades of quality: AA, A, B and C. AA are the finest quality. Grade A eggs are suitable for all table use. Grade B eggs are primarily for baking. Grade C are strictly for baking.

Storage

Eggs should be refrigerated covered as they pick up strong odors easily because of their porous shells. Varied temperatures are recommended, but practicability suggests holding at normal refrigerator or walk-in temperatures.

Egg Cookery Cooking eggs changes their flavor and consistency and makes them more palatable. Raw egg white is difficult to digest. Cooking aids digestion when proper procedures are followed.

The popular methods of cooking eggs are: coddled, fried, scrambled, country style, omelettes, boiled and poached. Eggs are also shirred and french fried for garnishing.

Coddled Eggs Prepared in special coddlers.

Poaching Acid toughens albumen. Slightly acidifying the water used for poaching helps to set the white firmly around the yolk. Eggs with thick whites do not present a problem. If eggs with thin whites are used, water may be acidified by adding 1 tablespoon *distilled* vinegar to 1 quart of water. In dilute quantities the acid will not affect the flavor of the eggs.

Fill a reasonably shallow pan with enough salted water (or acidified water) so that the eggs will be entirely covered. Bring to a boil and keep at simmering point. Break egg in saucer or nappy (vegetable dish) and slide gently into water. Cook as desired. Remove with skimmer and drain well before placing on hot buttered toast. For quantity cooking, poach eggs rapidly in acidified salted water just until the white is set and the egg is firm enough to remove from the water. Place immediately in cold water to prevent further cooking. Reheat in salted hot water as needed. This method is not recommended for maximum nutritive retention, but there are times when other considerations are also important.

Simmering Boiling is a misnomer as eggs should never be boiled vigorously, but simmered. Simmering is recommended for higher nutritive value, better color and better texture. Prolonged cooking, cooking at high temperatures and improper cooling often result in the formation of a green film around the outside of the yolk. This is caused by the combination of chemicals in the eggs: the sulphur of the white and the iron of the yolk. The green ring may be eliminated by plunging the eggs in cold water immediately after proper cooking. This releases the pressure on the outside of the egg whites and allows the gases causing discoloration to escape.

Cooking time and temperatures will vary with the size of the eggs, the volume or number of eggs in relation to water and the temperature of the eggs. Simmering temperatures are usually between 185°F. and 195°F. Temperature may be checked with a thermometer.

Guide to Simmering Eggs

METHOD 1—Place eggs in boiling water. Return to simmer and cook to desired doneness.

Soft-cooked eggs require about 3 to 5 minutes, medium cooked, 7 to 8 minutes; hard cooked, about 12-15 minutes.

METHOD 2—Place eggs in cold water. Bring to boil, reduce heat to simmer and cook to desired doneness. Soft cooked eggs require about 1 minute; medium cooked, 3 to 5 minutes; hard cooked, 8 to 10 minutes.

If eggs are too cold they may crack when placed in boiling water, therefore, use eggs at room temperature or temper them by placing in warm water just prior to cooking. Another method to hard cook eggs is to place eggs in cold water, bring to a boil and remove from heat. Let stand covered 25 to 30 minutes.

Fried Eggs

Common faults in preparing fried eggs:
1) Cooking at too high a temperature so that egg burns and is tough
2) Cooking at too low a temperature so that the egg white spreads
3) Cooking with too much fat so that egg is greasy
4) Cooking with too little fat so that the product sticks

Highest quality eggs should be used for frying. Eggs may be fried in butter, margarine, shortening or bland oil.

Bland-flavored agents should be used unless guests request bacon fat or other products with characteristic flavor. The fat should be hot enough to set the eggs in a few minutes but not hot enough to brown the whites. If desired, the egg may be basted by dripping a little hot fat over it or placing a cover over it until cooked. Clarified butter, from which the milk solids are removed, is often used for egg cookery as it does not burn as quickly as regular butter. Break eggs one at a time into small dish and slip them into hot greased pan or onto a greased griddle. Cook as requested by guest. Over-light eggs are turned over and cooked briefly on the other side. Sunny-side up eggs are not turned. Use slotted spatula to remove eggs from skillet or griddle. This will allow excess grease to drain off eggs.

Country style eggs may be served with corned beef hash, ham, bacon or dried chipped beef that has been freshened by soaking. Ham or bacon must be pre-cooked. The meat item is placed in a greased pan and heated or browned on one side and turned. The eggs are placed on top of the meat item in the same manner as fried eggs and cooked covered on top of the range until the whites are set and a cooked coating appears over the yolk. The pan may be removed to the oven for finishing.

Deep Fat Fried Eggs Break egg into small dish. Slide egg into sufficiently heated fat to cover. Carefully stirring the fat in a whirl before the egg is dropped will aid in effecting the ball shape usually associated with this method of cookery. Gathering the egg white over the yolk with two wooden spatulas aids in forming the desired shape. Used primarily as a garnish. Drain well on paper towels before serving.

Scrambled Eggs Break eggs in bowl. Beat slightly with fork or wire whip. Add small amount of cold water, cream or milk if desired (about 1 tablespoon to 2 eggs). If excess liquid is used the eggs may weep after serving. Place the eggs in heated and buttered pan so egg begins to coagulate when it hits the pan. Stir gently with a wooden spoon or palette knife until desired consistency. Remove to service plate. Eggs continue to cook after removal from the heat. They should be slightly under the desired finished consistency when taken from the range. Soft, fluffy scrambled eggs require very little cooking. Overcooked eggs become dry and hard. Cook scrambled eggs soft unless requested otherwise.

If using large quantities of eggs for scrambling, eggs may be broken out of shell the night before or previous to service period and put through a china cap to remove all shell particles and to break the eggs down. Eggs may be beaten further with a wire whip and measured for individual portions at cooking time.

When preparing large quantities of scrambled eggs, the beaten eggs can be cooked either in a large skillet, on a griddle or, preferably, in a large sauce pan over a bain marie or double boiler. The eggs should be stirred constantly to insure uniform cooking and to avoid formation of large masses. They should be cooked just until they have reached a creamy consistency and should be transferred immediately into another container that is warm but not hot.

For added creaminess and for extended holding

before service, a small amount of cream or half-and-half can be added and mixed into the scrambled eggs. This also serves the purpose of quickly reducing the temperature of the eggs, therefore stopping the cooking process.

Shirred Eggs Break eggs into small dish. Transfer two eggs to heated, buttered shirred egg dishes. Place on top of range and cook gently until whites are set. Place in oven and finish cooking. Eggs should not be cooked hard. Shirred egg dishes may be placed directly in the oven without cooking on the range. Cooked chicken livers, sausages or bacon slices are often placed around the edge of the shirred egg dish before serving. Foods served in this manner make excellent luncheon and supper items.

Omelettes Many variations may be developed from the plain omelette with the addition of cooked meats, fish, fruit, berries, vegetables, sauces, jelly, cheese and other dairy products. The omelette then takes the name of the garnish or accompanying item: cheese omelette, jelly omelette or spanish omelette (with spanish sauce). Omelettes are also served as luncheon and dinner items. Dinner omelettes are usually made with three eggs, breakfast and luncheon with two.

Omelettes made with jelly, fruit or other delicate garnishes are usually made pancake style and folded in half. Fruit should be well-drained before adding to an omelette that has started to firm. It may then be folded and cooking completed.

Omelettes should be made to order and served immediately. They quickly lose their light fluffiness and long holding makes them tough and rubbery. Omelettes may be started on the range and transferred to the oven for finishing.

There are three basic methods of preparing omelettes.
1) Folded three ways like a business letter: Omelette should have pointed ends. Break eggs into mixing bowl. Whip lightly adding small amount of liquid if desired. Place in a well greased hot frying pan. Pull egg slightly away from side of pan with palette knife as it coagulates, tilting pan and letting the remaining liquid portion run to the sides. When still wet on top but firmly set, fold nearest side ⅔ over away from you. Fold far side back toward you, covering first fold and closing ends to a point to prevent any remaining liquid from flowing out. Tilt pan away from you and at an angle and slide omelette to far side and part way up the side of the pan. When lightly browned invert on serving plate so that browned side will be up. Minimum of grease should be used so that all will be absorbed when cooking of the omelette is completed.
2) Pancake style, folded in half: Place egg mixture in well greased hot frying pan. Follow above procedure until eggs are well set but still slightly moist on top. Fold in half only and brown lightly. Invert on warm plate or platter and serve.
3) Rolled like a cigar: Place egg mixture in well greased hot frying pan. Eggs should set but not as firmly as in other procedures. Start rolling egg away

from you, starting at nearest side, using palette knife and quick backward snap of frying pan. When completely rolled, follow basic procedure; let brown and invert on warm plate or platter for service.

Cereals are seeds of various grasses. The principal grains are rice, wheat, barley, oats, rye and corn. They are starch products that provide a valuable source of energy as carbohydrates. Almost all are relatively low in fat, and they vary in their protein content. Although our basic concern in this section is breakfast cookery, cereals may also be used in preparing meat loaf, croquettes, breading and toppings, in bakery products and other dishes.

Ready-to-eat cereals are the cold cereals such as corn flakes, shredded wheat and bran.

Cereals that require cooking are of two kinds: quick cooking and regular. Quick cooking cereals have been pre-cooked and do not require as long a cooking period as do regular cereals. Containers are clearly marked with small quantity cooking instructions. Many cereals are enriched or fortified to restore some of the nutritional value lost in milling and processing.

Both quick cooking and regular cereals to be cooked are of two basic forms: small granules, such as farina, cream of wheat and cornmeal; flaked or whole grain cereals such as rolled oats (oatmeal) and rice. Rice and barley are discussed in a separate section covering Rice and Farinaceous Products.

Fine Granular Cereals These cereals should be prepared in the same manner as starch to prevent lumps. The necessary amount of cereal should be combined with cold water to make a paste and then stirred into the remaining total amount of boiling liquid. The mixture will cool but should be brought back to a boil over direct heat, the heat reduced and it should be cooked covered until done. If heavy duty cookware is not available the use of a double boiler is recommended. In small amounts only, the cereal may be sprinkled gradually into boiling water, stirring constantly.

Flakes or Whole Grain Cereals Rolled oats or other flakes or coarse cereals are sprinkled gradually into the required amount of boiling salted water. Stirring may be necessary if the water stops boiling. Cereal may be cooked over low direct heat or in a double boiler. Overcooking or unnecessary stirring may result in a gummy product and loss of identity. *Always follow manufacturer's directions.* Water may be salted in ratio of 1 tablespoon to a gallon.

Meats on Breakfast Menus Sausage, bacon and ham are the most popular meat items served on the breakfast menu. These products are usually blanched or pre-cooked prior to the breakfast hour to facilitate service.

Fish are sometimes served on hotel breakfast menus in addition to the meat items. (For instructions, see Fish Section.)

Sausage is treated as a fresh pork product and should be cooked well done. Care must be taken that it is refrigerated properly. There are two types of breakfast sausage in wide use: link sausage and sausage patties. Link sausages are in casings like frankfurters and average about 12 to the pound. Sausage patties may be purchased in bulk or made in the kitchen from ground fresh pork and spices. Portion size depends on intended use. Both link sausage and sausage patties are often served as luncheon items in combination with other meats and vegetables.

Pre-Cooking Sausage Link sausage may be pre-cooked in three basic ways: 1) by blanching, 2) by baking in the oven, 3) by pan broiling.

Blanched sausage may be refrigerated for some time without spoilage. Blanching prevents splitting or breaking of the sausage casing. This process also removes excess grease and helps to retain moisture when sausages are cooked properly. Overcooking will shrink the sausages and make them excessively hard. To blanch: Place sausages in cold water and bring to a boil, remove immediately from the heat and place in the sink under cold running water until completely cooled (in much the same manner as with hard cooked eggs). Sausage links may then be easily separated and refrigerated for further use. At serving time, they are heated and browned. The major argument against this method might be possible loss of flavor and nutritive value. However, the flavor loss is small and, where sausage may be highly seasoned, it serves to make the product a little more bland. Fat losses in this method might be construed as beneficial.

Partial baking is recommended for sausages that are prepared only in sufficient quantity for one meal. Sausage prepared in this manner dries quickly if held overnight. Sausages may be placed in hotel pan or pan deep enough to hold extracted fats and baked until partially browned so that little further cooking is necessary. Pricking sausages with a fork prior to cooking reduces splitting as internal heat pressure often results in bursting of casing. Care must be taken that sausages color evenly and are not overcooked.

This same procedure is used for pan broiling in a heavy skillet on top of the range.

Blanching in water is not suitable for sausage patties as they have no casing or protective covering. Patties may be pre-cooked in the oven, on top of the range or on the griddle. Small amounts of water are sometimes added to prevent burning or drying out. Remember that overcooking by any method will lead to dryness and an excessively hard finished product.

Bacon and Ham are smoked pork products with keeping qualities in the raw state that are generally superior to sausage and other fresh pork products. Scotch ham is processed differently from smoked ham and must be treated as fresh pork. Scotch ham is usually marketed boned and rolled, raw or pre-cooked. Raw Scotch ham has an extremely high water content and is often messy and difficult to handle. Pre-cooked Scotch ham is preferred. Scotch ham has a flavor of its own and is sometimes of a salty nature.

Regular ham is marketed with the bone in, boned

and rolled or canned (pullman or pear shape). With the bone in and boned and rolled hams have superior flavor, but canned hams are often used for convenience. Pullman and pear shape refer to the shape or conformation of the hams in the can. Pullman is oblong and provides a square slice that is helpful in maintaining uniformity and portion control. Canned hams are used extensively in sandwiches.

Bacon may be purchased as slab bacon, which is marketed in large pieces or slabs, to be sliced in the kitchen, or as hotel pack which averages 20 to 22 slices of bacon to a pound. Most operations prefer the hotel pack.

Canadian bacon is cured, smoked strips of boned and rolled pork loin. It is usually extremely lean. Its flavor is similar to ham, but more delicate. It is considered expensive.

Cooking Bacon Bacon may be blanched by separating the slices and placing them on a baking sheet in a 350°F. oven. When partially cooked, drippings should be poured off. (Extreme caution is required in pouring the grease off to avoid serious burns.) Bacon can then be turned over and cooked until about half done. It is then removed from the oven, all surplus fat drained off, transferred to a smaller pan and held for service. Cooking is completed to order as needed. For additional draining of grease, the bacon strips should be placed on absorbent toweling or on slices of bread.

Suggested method of holding bacon: Place a heavy strip of cardboard or a wooden stick across a pie plate or small pan. Lay the bacon across the cardboard or stick, uniformly, so that the centers of the bacon strips are higher than both ends. This helps to further drain the bacon and prevents it from being immersed in grease and matting or sticking together. Do not pile more than a few layers high. (There are other methods of blanching bacon that are easier and less time consuming, but these will not produce as satisfactory a product.)

Separating the slices and cooking at a moderate temperature reduces shrinkage and curling and improves appearance. Reducing shrinkage is not only a factor in improving appearance but is important in food cost, too.

Potatoes Some form of potato is usually offered on the breakfast menu. There are an infinite variety of potatoes that are popular at breakfast time. Most of the breakfast potatoes are fried. (See Vegetable Section, page 210 - 218.)

Pancakes Griddle cakes (pancakes), waffles, french toast and cinnamon toast are familiar breakfast items that are often served as light snacks and luncheon items. Quality products must be cooked to order and served piping hot. Batters are mixed prior to the service hour and in some cases the night previous. When mixing ahead, loss of rising power must be considered. Batters must be refrigerated.

Varied jams, jellies and syrups are served, but maple syrup blends and substitutes are most popular. Pure maple syrup is considerably more expensive than the blends or the sugar and corn syrups. When possible from a cost standpoint, pure maple syrup is generally preferred. However, many operations may use inexpensive syrups or make their own with simple sugar syrup and maple flavoring. Any type of syrup is improved by heating and serving warm. Fresh butter should always be served. Food cost on these items should be low enough to warrant the use of butter rather than margarine.

Pastries All types of pastries are served and are usually the responsibility of the bake shop. When it is the duty of the breakfast cook to prepare any of these items, care should be exercised that proper procedures and correct weights and measures are used to assure product success and uniformity. These items are sometimes purchased. They include: doughnuts, coffee cake, english muffins, other types of muffins, danish pastry and brioche. With the exception of doughnuts, most items are improved by serving them warm when possible.

Fruits Fresh fruits in season and dried fruits such as figs, prunes and apricots, presoaked and stewed, are also served at breakfast time. Citrus fruit such as oranges and grapefruit is available year round. Melons are usually available, but the kind varies with the season. Among the kinds of melon are: honey-dew, cantaloupe, Cranshaw, Persian and Casaba melons. They may be cut in half or in wedges depending on size. Melons should be served with a slice or wedge of fresh lime or lemon. Melons should be served chilled but not cold enough to reduce flavor. They *must* be ripe.

Dried prunes and apricots must be cooked slightly in water to restore moisture. They are often cooked with sugar, lemon, stick cinnamon and seasoning. The seasoning should augment the flavor of the fruit but not overshadow it. Fruits should retain shape and reasonable texture. Overcooking can make them mushy and unattractive.

Juices Fruit and vegetable juices are a standard item, often served at all meals. Juices may be canned, fresh or frozen. They include: orange juice, grapefruit juice, tomato juice, pineapple juice, prune juice, papaya juice, apple juice and blends or mixed juices. In addition to freshly squeezed juices, many operations purchase fresh juice from dairies or juice companies or use frozen products. Frozen juices generally have better flavor when allowed to stand for a short while after mixing and before using. Juices should always be served chilled.

Continental Breakfast A continental breakfast implies a light breakfast like those served on the continent (in Europe) and is now being served extensively in this country. This breakfast is often served on modified American plan menus and is sometimes served after the kitchen is closed for regular breakfast service. It usually consists of juice or fruit, coffee, toast or light pastry and involves no heavy cooking.

Dairy Products

Milk is one of the most complete food items in the diet. Milk and its derivatives are used in a variety of ways in all types of food preparation.

State laws vary regarding the prescribed butter fat content of milk, but federal regulations set a standard of not less than 3.25 per cent butterfat for whole milk.

Most milk sold today is homogenized and pasteurized. It is heated under prescribed conditions to destroy undesirable bacteria and improve its keeping qualities. Pasteurization affects the nutritive value to a very small degree. Vitamin C losses are easily made up by the many high vitamin C foods included in the average diet. Nearly all milk is fortified with vitamin D.

Homogenized Milk is whole milk in which the fat has been broken into small globules or drops that are evenly distributed throughout the milk. Homogenization provides a permanent emulsion that prevents separation of the cream. This assures uniform fat content throughout.

Skim Milk is milk from which the butterfat has been removed. The butterfat content is, by definition, reduced to less than that of whole milk, but is usually considerably lower. Fat content is usually less than 0.1 per cent. Generally speaking, skim milk has much the same nutritive value as whole milk, without the fat.

Evaporated Milk is whole milk from which 50 to 60 per cent of the moisture has been removed. The Food and Drug Administration has prescribed standards for the product. It is usually fortified with vitamin D and may be reconstituted to a product equal in food value to whole milk by adding 50 per cent water to replace liquid removed by evaporation.

Condensed Milk is similar to evaporated milk but has a high sugar content, about 42 per cent, that gives it a creamy consistency.

Nonfat Dry Milk is skim milk with the water removed. It is easily reconstituted to a liquid product by adding water, or it may be used in dry form in many recipes, particularly in baking. It is the least expensive of all milk forms and provides excellent results when properly used.

Buttermilk There are several types of buttermilk. The source from which buttermilk is derived determines its fat content and, therefore, its caloric value. Buttermilk may be a by-product from the processing of sweet cream or sour cream in making butter. Cultured buttermilk, processed by adding favorable bacteria to skim milk or partially skim milk, is usually a low calorie food with high nutritive value.

Sour Cream is also a cultured product, but unlike buttermilk has a standard of not less than 18 per cent butterfat. It is used in various culinary preparations, including salads and appetizers.

Cream Classification of cream is based on butterfat content. Heavy or whipping cream may be not less than 32 per cent butterfat and usually contains 36 to 40 per cent. As noted in the Beverage Section, light or coffee cream must be not less than 18 per cent and extra light or half and half contains 11 to 12 per cent butterfat.

Ice Cream standards vary in different states but usually require a butterfat content of at least 10 per cent and a specific minimum weight. Average weight is 4½ to 5 lb. per gallon with higher weights and increased butterfat content for quality ice cream.

Butter Butter is the fat of cream separated from the other milk components by agitation. Butter may be made from either sweet or sour cream. Sweet cream butter is sometimes marketed unsalted for salt-free diets and for use in Jewish cuisine. Salted butter has better keeping qualities and is generally preferred. Butter is graded or scored largely on flavor, although body, color, salt and packaging are also considered. Top quality is 93 score.

Cheese There are hundreds of different varieties of cheese, processed by different methods, with varied moisture content and derived from different sources of milk, such as cow's milk or goat's milk. For practical purposes we may classify cheese in four ways:
1) Hard grating cheese, such as Romano and Parmesan
2) Hard cheese, such as Cheddar or Swiss
3) Semi-soft cheese, such as Roquefort or Blue
4) Soft cheese, such as Limburger and Cottage Cheese

Cottage cheese is a curd cheese made from cultured skim milk and is used in cooking, salads and baking. It is extremely popular with weight-conscious patrons.

Baker's cheese and pot cheese have a lower moisture content and are used for making cheesecake and other bakery products and in Jewish cooking.

Cream cheese is made from whole sweet milk

enriched with cream and is used in appetizers, sandwiches, salads and in baking.

Yoghurt is a cultured cheese from whole milk. It has no curd and is the consistency of soft custard.

Processed cheese is made from a combination of cheeses, blended together and emulsified to produce a product uniform in flavor and consistency. It melts easily for incorporation in cooked dishes and may be readily prepared as a spread for canapes and hors d'oeuvres.

There are varied standards for processed cheeses, depending on their character. Moisture content ranges from 41 to 60 per cent. Fat content is also variable.

Excessive heat and prolonged cooking cause a separation of the fat in cheese and develop a tough, rubbery product. The basic principle is use of a moderate or low temperature and a minimum of cooking time so that the proper texture is maintained in the finished dish.

Rice, Farinaceous Products

Pastas include all types of macaroni, spaghetti and noodles. They are made of water and semolina or farina flour, or both. These are hard wheat flours whose high gluten content helps to maintain their shape, form and texture when cooked. These pastas are usually named for their shape and size, with the exception of egg noodles, which must contain not less than 5.3 per cent egg in the finished product, according to government standards.

All pastas are considered macaroni products, although the term macaroni is commonly applied to a pasta shaped in a certain way. Many other products are made from basic noodle dough including ravioli and kreplach. Such products represent many different nationalities. The pastas are an extremely versatile product and are used as potato and vegetable substitutes, in salads, some desserts, appetizers, in soups and, in many instances, as a main course.

All farinaceous products (having a flour or meal base) are essentially starch foods. Starch foods are carbohydrates which are necessary for energy. Pastas are invariably associated or combined with other foods or accompanying sauces that provide them with additional nutritional value.

Pasta should nearly always be cooked "al dente," meaning "to the teeth." This denotes a firm, chewy texture rather than an overcooked and mushy item. With the exception of deep fat frying, as with some Chinese products, pastas are cooked in liquid to make them digestible, palatable and to improve their appearance.

Products like ravioli and kreplach are soft noodle doughs. That is, they are cooked while the dough is still soft. Macaroni and spaghetti are thoroughly dried before cooking so that all moisture is evaporated and the product is hard and brittle. If the soft noodle doughs are exposed to the air for any length of time, they lose their moisture and become hard like the other pasta products.

Cooking Pasta A rule of thumb in cooking pasta products is to use approximately 4 parts of salted water to 1 part pasta, for example 3 or 4 quarts of water to 1 pound spaghetti. These proportions will give approximately 3 pounds of cooked product. The water must be boiling vigorously when the pasta is added to prevent sticking together.

The product is often stirred at the beginning to separate the strands or pieces and prevent sticking on the bottom of the pot. Cooking time will vary according to the shape and size. Thin spaghetti, or vermicelli, requires little cooking time, while large shells must be cooked longer.

Here's a guide to cooking time, but it should be used with consideration: noodles, 8 to 10 minutes; spaghetti, 10 to 15 minutes; macaroni, 15 to 20 minutes. Pastas should be cooked uncovered, as they create a large head of froth that when covered often boils over on the range.

Farinaceous Products and Rice Although rice is a grain, it is considered in this section because it is widely used in much the same fashion as pastas and other farinaceous products. Rice is an excellent potato or vegetable substitute and lends itself to combination with a variety of foods in many ways. It is an inexpensive food source and, when properly prepared, is a valuable addition to the diet.

Cultivated rice is available in this country in three main varieties: long or head rice, medium grain and short grain. Fortuna and Honduras are two of the best known varieties of head rice, possessing long, slender grains. Blue Rose is the most popular of the other categories and is classified as a medium grain rice with shorter, plumper grains than head rice. There are many other varieties of rice all over the world.

Rice is subjected to a process called milling which removes part of the outer coating of the grain in order to make it digestible. The extent to which the rice is milled and the coatings removed determines to a great extent its nutritive value.

Spaghetti (and other Pasta Products)

YIELD: 50 portions	EACH PORTION: 5½ oz.	
INGREDIENTS	*QUANTITY*	*METHOD*
Water, salted Spaghetti	about 5 to 6 gal. 6 lb.	1. Place a soup pot 2/3 full of salted water on the range. Bring to boil. 2. Break spaghetti according to length required and place in boiling water, stirring with wooden paddle to separate strands. 3. When water returns to boil, reduce heat and cook until spaghetti is "al dente," (cooked but not mushy). 4. If holding for service, remove entire pot to sink and let cold water run directly into pot until spaghetti is cold. This will prevent further cooking and sticking. 5. Store well drained and covered until ready to use. 6. Reheat in boiling water and drain with china cap or drain and saute in butter or oil until hot.

NOTE: This method applies to all pasta products. Amounts will vary depending on product and intended use.

It is recommended that most pasta products be cooked slightly underdone if they are to be reheated. They continue to cook to some degree while cooling and reheating affects their degree of doneness.

If necessary to hold on steam table, butter or oil spaghetti or other pasta products lightly and mix well to prevent strands from sticking together.

Brown rice has the hull removed, but is unpolished and retains most of the bran coating and the germ. It has a higher nutritive value than other processed rice and has a nutlike flavor.

White rice or polished rice is produced when the brown coating and bran are removed, resulting in greater loss of nutritive value.

Coated rice is polished rice that has been treated with glucose and talc to improve its appearance and keeping qualities. This coating is removed when rice is washed before cooking.

Unpolished rice has less of the bran layer and germ removed in milling. Rice is often enriched to replace some of the nutritive values lost in milling.

Converted rice is processed prior to milling in such a way as to retain more of its food value than other white rice. Converted rice does not require washing or draining and retains a higher degree of nutritive value in the cooking process than many other rices. Converted rice is preferred for use as white rice because it also maintains its shape and texture well. Its superior qualities make it popular for use in all phases of professional cookery.

Pre-cooked rice is also available on the market. These products may not stand up well under heat and often do not hold their shape and texture as well as converted rice.

Wild rice is not a true rice. It is the seed of a tall grass which grows in shallow water. Wild rice has only recently been raised commercially in this country and is difficult to harvest, which may partially account for its high price. Wild rice is considered a delicacy and is used to a great extent with poultry and game.

Preparing Rice Rice is usually prepared in the kitchen by two methods: 1) the boiling-steaming method, 2) the pilaf method.

In the boiling-steaming method, the rice is cooked in excess water, 2½ to 3 parts of water to 1 part rice by volume. The rice is stirred gradually into boiling water and cooked covered until nearly tender. It is then drained and the cooking completed over very low heat in a double boiler until all excess

SCHEMATIC DIAGRAM OF KERNEL OF RICE OR GRAIN

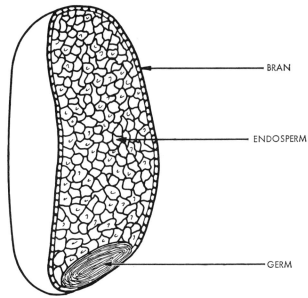

— BRAN

— ENDOSPERM

— GERM

BRAN OR OUTER COATING: *Cellulose (also protein, phosphorous, iron, thiamine, riboflavin, niacin).*
ENDOSPERM: *Primarily starch.*
GERM: *Thiamine, riboflavin, niacin, some fat.*

water has evaporated and the product is light and fluffy. Rice should not boil vigorously but simmer gently.

In the pilaf method, ratios are about 2 parts water or stock to 1 part rice by volume. This may vary, depending on the rice and the desired doneness. The rice is sautéed in a small amount of butter, margarine or other fat until all grains are well coated. (A small amount of finely chopped onion is sometimes sauteed prior to adding the rice.) Hot or boiling stock or water in the correct proportions is then added and the sauce pan or pot covered. Cooking may be completed over very low heat or in the oven. All liquid should be absorbed and the rice should be light and fluffy with each grain separate. This is a basic method of preparing many rice dishes that are used as potato substitutes or combined with meat and poultry.

The pilaf method is used to a great extent in nearly all phases of cookery, while the boiling-steaming method is more acceptable for preparing rice for custards and desserts.

Cooking time for baking in the oven varies, depending primarily on oven temperature. At 200°F., rice may take as long as 1 hour. At 375°F., about 20 minutes will be sufficient.

Brown rice and wild rice may be cooked in the same manner, although wild rice usually requires a little more liquid and longer cooking time.

To prevent overcooking and sticking, cooked rice should never be left in the container in which it is cooked. A little raw butter is added and stirred in using the tines of a cooking fork, then the cooked rice is transferred into a shallow pan which permits steam to escape and lowers the temperature. Cover with a buttered paper or piece of foil and hold for service in moderate heat to prevent overcooking. Leftover cooked rice may be used in soups, salads, croquettes, fried rice, etc.

LAMB BEEF PORK

Because America is a nation of meat lovers, meat items on the menu can make or break the reputation of a food service operation.
In this section, the keys to proper preparation and service are presented by chefs known for their mastery of meat cookery.

TECHNIQUES FOR MEAT COOKERY

Roast Tender Ham

Roast Rib of Beef au Jus

Roast Leg of Lamb, Mint Jelly

Techniques for Meat Cookery

The term "meat" is applied to the flesh of beef, pork, veal, mutton and lamb. The chief nutritional significance of meat is as a source of protein. Meat is an excellent source of vitamins and minerals and is said to be a complete protein. A complete protein contains the essential amino acids which are vital in maintaining proper body growth and repair.

Meats generally contain more connective tissue and fat than other flesh such as chicken and many kinds of fish. The texture and amount of connective tissue vary between animals and even in different parts of the same animal. The connective tissue holds together and connects the muscles, fat cells, fibers and other constituents of the flesh. In cooking, when this connective tissue is destroyed or weakened, the meat becomes tender.

Meat is highly perishable and requires refrigeration. Low temperatures retard or kill bacterial action and minimize spoilage. Quality meats are aged or ripened before purchase. The term "aging" is applied to the changes which occur in meats due to the action of enzymes (body chemicals) while the meats hang in cold storage. Aging meats improves their flavor and tenderness.

When meats are over-aged or over-ripened, they begin to spoil and become discolored, moldy and slimy. They develop an off-flavor and odor and are no longer suitable for service.

We cook meat in order to sterilize it, make it more palatable, improve its appearance and supply a valuable nutritional need.

Economically meat is one of the most important items carried on a menu as it is the most expensive and represents the highest single item of food cost with which we have to deal.

Basic Methods of Cooking Meat There are two basic methods of cooking meat: meat may be cooked by *dry heat* and by *moist heat.* Each of these methods has modifications that give a variety of cooking procedures.

The method of procedure to be used depends on: the kind of meat; the quality and grade, and the cut.

Under the moist heat method are: 1) steaming, 2) boiling, 3) poaching. Dry heat methods include: 1) roasting or baking, 2) broiling and grilling, 3) sauteing, 4) pan frying. Combinations of the two methods, dry heat and moist heat, include, 1) braising and 2) stewing the meat.

(For the purpose of this text, deep fat frying will be treated as a separate area. However, although some foods are deep fat fried from the raw stage, others are put through one or more of the previously mentioned cooking methods before they are deep fat fried. Deep fat frying is a popular way to use leftovers. If the leftovers are wholesome foods, they may either be combined with different foods or converted to present new products. There is usually some type of breading used with fried foods that aids in sealing the product. The sealing of the product helps to protect the food from excessive grease absorption and to give it a crisp, palatable coating.)

Moist Heat Methods In general, the moist heat methods or combinations are applied to the more economical cuts of meat. These meats are tougher and require moist heat to break down the connective tissues and make them tender. There are on the market tenderizing agents made from papaya juice and other ingredients containing enzymes that break down connective tissue. These are used to a great extent in commercial feeding operations with low menu prices. While these low cost meats are satisfactory for such menus, it must be remembered that there is no substitute for quality.

Steaming is not used to a great degree in meat cookery except in combination with other methods, although some steaming is done in institutional operations. In steaming, a smaller amount of liquid is used than in boiling. Steaming may be done in a covered pot on the range or in a conventional steamer or pressure cooker. Steaming is used with greater success in cooking poultry.

Boiling is a moist heat method of cookery used extensively for less tender cuts of meat. Boiling is recognized and accepted terminology, but should be amended to mean simmering. Meat should not be boiled, but simmered to retain its full nutritive value and to keep it from getting stringy. With the exception of salted or smoked meats, most other meats should be placed in a stockpot in boiling water (212°F.). Cold water aids in extracting flavor and juice and is used principally in the making of stocks.

The temperature of the water or stock will be lowered when the meat is added. When the boiling temperature is again reached, the stock should be skimmed to remove any scum and the heat reduced or the pot moved to a part of the range where it will simmer and not boil. Remember that vigorous boiling will produce cloudy stock and increase shrinkage of the meat.

If different quality or different size cuts are cooked in the same pot, butcher's twine is sometimes tied to the smaller or more tender cuts so that they may be easily checked during the cooking process and removed when cooked.

After simmered meat has become tender, it may be held on the steamtable for future service. Meat so held should either be stored in liquid or wrapped with clean wet towels so that it does not dry out in the heat of the steamtable.

Meats to be served cold, such as corned beef, may be cooled and pressed in a pan with a heavy weight on top. The weight compresses the meat which aids in slicing and produces greater yield. All meats (excluding poultry) are sliced across the grain.

Many boiled meats, because of their bland flavor, are served with tangy and savory sauces to increase their palatability and make them more appetizing. The following are examples of meats that are at their best when boiled or simmered:

Fresh Brisket of Beef	Ox Tongue, smoked or
Corned Brisket of Beef	cured
Ham, cured or smoked	Shoulder or Breast of
Short Ribs of Beef	Veal
Ham Hocks	Smoked Pork Butt or
Fresh Spareribs	Picnic
Polish Sausage	Fresh Shoulder of Beef

Poaching is a simmering process that takes place in a small amount of water. The stock or water in which the poaching is done barely bubbles. This process is used primarily with specialty items and the variety meats such as sweetbreads, brains and kidneys.

In the poaching process, items are seldom cooked well done. Poaching helps them to set or hold their shape; makes it easy to remove tough membranes or tissue, and prepares them for final cooking procedures such as sauteing or broiling. Poaching also extends keeping qualities as in variety meats which are highly perishable when raw. The poaching of kidneys also extracts the strong odor that sometimes prevails and makes them more appetizing.

Dry Heat Methods are intended for the better cuts of meat that have little connective tissue and become readily tender when cooked. The two methods are *not* interchangeable as the economical cuts of meat are never at their best when cooked by dry heat. On the other hand, it is a waste of money and food to cook tender cuts by any moist heat method. The exceptions to this rule are extremely rare, although some of the less tender cuts, such as chuck or bottom round, are often ground (as hamburger) and then cooked by the dry heat method (either grilling or broiling).

Sauteing To saute is to fry lightly and quickly in a small amount of fat. Only tender cuts are used for this method. Its use is usually restricted to thin cuts of meat that do not require extensive cooking. The smaller and thinner the cut, the more rapidly the searing and cooking should take place. When blood rises and appears on the surface, the meat should be turned over and cooked on the other side. If the product is breaded, it should be turned when the underside is golden brown.

The utensil used for sauteing should have a heavy bottom and be just large enough to hold the product to be cooked.

Nearly all sauteing of meat is done uncovered.

Many of the sauteed meats are served with sauces made from the crusts that coat the bottom of the pan in which the meat has been cooked. The excess fat is poured off and the meats removed and held in a warm place until service.

The utensil is then deglazed by scraping and swishing it with wine or stock, with the resulting liquid or "fond" allowed to boil until the remaining crusts have been entirely dissolved. A prepared sauce or gravy is sometimes added, and it may be further seasoned to produce the desired flavor. The sauce, which is usually of light consistency, may be poured over the meat or served separately with an appropriate garnish.

Examples of meats to be sauteed are:

Scallopini of Veal, Chausseur
Tenderloin Tips, Mushroom Sauce
Veal Cutlet, Milanaise
Pork Tenderloin, Saute Normand

Pan Frying This procedure differs from sauteing principally in the amount of fat used in frying. Considerably more fat is used in pan frying. This prevents the formation of crusting on the bottom of the pan.

Pan frying is not highly popular in meat cookery, but is used extensively in cooking poultry and some fish. Products that require a longer cooking time are first browned in a pan on top of the range until they acquire a golden color and then finished with lower heat, uncovered, in a slow or moderate oven.

Roasting or Baking The term roasting was originally applied to the cooking of large pieces of meats over an open fire. The meats were spitted or held over the fire by rods inserted in the ends of the meat or entirely through the body cavity. The spits were held in place by forked sticks and turned by hand to cook the meat uniformly.

This type of cooking is now referred to as open roasting or barbecuing. Marinades, or liquids in which meat is soaked prior to cooking, play an important role in barbecued foods. Spicy sauces quite often accompany foods prepared in this manner.

As now used, the terms roasting and baking refer to cooking uncovered in the oven with little or no added liquid. Roasting and baking are the same process, except that roasting is usually applied to meat cookery.

Meat to be roasted is usually placed fat side up in a shallow roasting pan that most nearly approximates the size of the roast. The roast should not be covered.

Thousands of experiments have been conducted in the research laboratories of colleges, universities and the U. S. Department of Agriculture on the cooking of meat.

These tests have proved conclusively that cooking meats at low temperatures, instead of high temperatures, results in: (1) a more tender product, (2) a more flavorful and juicier product, (3) less shrinkage, and (4) greater yields, because of the ease of carving. There is less watching of the meat during cooking, less cleaning afterward, since there is no burning on pans and equipment, and less fuel is consumed when constant low temperatures are used.

The old method of starting a roast at high temperature to sear the meat and then reducing the temperature has been corrected. It has been found that a constant temperature produces the best product if the oven is properly preheated. There are minor exceptions to this rule.

The fat content of the meat will determine whether additional fats or oils are necessary to prevent burning. Extremely lean cuts are sometimes barded or larded to permit proper cooking and to give additional flavor. (*Larding* is insertion of thin strips of salt pork along surface of meat. *Barding* is covering lean meat with thin slices of fat bacon or salt pork to prevent burning and retain moisture in cooking.)

Roasts are sometimes seasoned with spices, herbs, salt, pepper and minute slivers of garlic. Meats are usually salted on the fat side as excesses of salt tend to draw the moisture out on exposed or very lean surfaces, making the cooked meat dry.

A mirepoix consisting of carrots, onions and celery is usually added to meat, either at the beginning or during the roasting period, depending on the length of cooking time. Fresh vegetables must be used in the mirepoix to obtain good gravy. Each gravy should be derived from the meat with which it is associated. Roast beef is generally served with natural gravy called "au jus naturel."

Roasting temperatures vary from 250°F. to 375°F., although there may be exceptions. Large cuts of meat, such as steamship rounds weighing from 50 to 70 pounds, are roasted for longer periods at extremely low temperatures. A 50 lb. steamship round may cook approximately six hours to six-and-a-half hours at 300°F. for a rare roast.

Meats placed in the oven fat side up are, in some measure, self-basting or moistened by their own fat. Further occasional basting may be necessary to prevent dryness.

The back or rear of the oven is usually slightly hotter than the front because there is some heat loss at the oven door. It is sometimes necessary to change the position of the meat during the roasting period to insure uniform cooking.

Determining Doneness of Meat The degree of doneness of meat influences shrinkage. As the doneness is increased the shrinkage is increased by extraction of moisture. Pork must be well done to kill the trichina parasite, but unduly overcooking it results in a dried-out product with a high degree of shrinkage. When cooked to the correct degree of doneness, roasts are juicier, give more flavor and yield.

Degree of doneness may be determined by: (1) time-weight ratio, (2) insertion of needles, (3) applying light pressure with the fingers, (4) meat thermometer.

In the time-weight ratio, a specific number of minutes of cooking time is allowed for each pound of meat. (See pp. 41, 81, 90.)

The insertion of needles is used to test the internal temperature of the meat by placing the withdrawn metal against the cheek or other sensitive skin area. The degree of heat transmitted from the meat to the needle aids in determining the degree of doneness. The meat should not be pierced by heavy forks or tested constantly as these procedures result in bleeding and loss of moisture.

The meat may also be tested by applying light pressure with the fingers to the middle or largest portion of the meat. The springier or more yielding the meat, the lesser the degree of doneness. The less yielding or the firmer the flesh, the greater degree of doneness. However, the textures of some meats vary. A roast may sometimes feel undercooked, although it is actually overcooked, because of a peculiar spongy quality occasionally found in meat. The characteristics of different cuts of meats at different times, as well as the human trait of error, have encouraged the search for a more accurate means of determining doneness.

The research laboratory has proved that, when properly used, a meat thermometer that registers the internal temperature of the meat is the most accurate means of determining doneness. The thermometer should be inserted in the thickest portion of the meat away from bone or fat pockets with the tip penetrating just to the middle.

Heavy duty, good quality meat thermometers are available at moderate cost from food service equipment supply houses. These thermometers have visual indicators that show the exact temperature for different meats at varying degrees of doneness. The use of a meat thermometer also makes possible greater utilization of unskilled help in the kitchen.

Every cook should know how to test meats successfully manually and should gain this experience as quickly as possible, but the proven success of the use of meat thermometers should not be overlooked.

The internal heat of a roast will cause it to continue to cook even after it has been removed from the oven. This must be taken into consideration, particularly when planning rare roasts. Roast meat, therefore, should always be removed from the oven before it has reached the desired temperature.

All roasts should stand for at least a half hour before carving. This releases the heat pressure and the juices will be more evenly distributed throughout the meat. Rare beef may appear grey or well done looking if it is sliced before the red juices are redistributed. All meats should be sliced to order when possible. This is a must for roast beef if it is to retain its flavorful juices and red color.

Examples of meats to be roasted:

Ribs of beef	Leg of lamb
Sirloin of beef	Shoulder of lamb
Top Round and	Rack of lamb
Rump of beef	Loin of pork
Ham, fresh or smoked	Pork butt

Broiling and Grilling Broiling is a popular method of dry heat cookery which is done by direct heat over hot coals, such as charcoal or briquets, or under gas flame or electric units. Some electric units also have heating elements on the sides.

The intense heat used in broiling forces the blood in the meat away from the source of heat. The meat should be turned during the cooking process so that both sides will be equally done.

Only tender cuts are used for broiling. All broiling should be done to order when possible and the meat cooked to the degree of doneness specified by the guest.

For banquets or large parties meat is often broiled a few minutes ahead to facilitate service. The meat is broiled very rare and removed from the heat. It is placed in a pan and reserved until service time when it is finished in the oven or, preferably, under the broiler.

Care must be taken not to overcook foods in the broiler as they lose natural flavors, juices and nutritive value.

Poultry and fish are also popular broiler items usually cooked well done, but overcooking will make them dry.

The broiler should be preheated before cooking time. If using gas, the broiler should be heated until all the ceramics (the brick-type elements over the grill) are radiating heat. If using electricity, the reflector plates should be radiating full heat. Charcoal or briquets should be burned to glowing coals.

The intense heat of the broiler rack or grill rack will help to prevent sticking. Nearness of the broiler rack to the heat determines the cooking time of the product.

The proper location of the broiler rack can be learned only through experience. It depends upon the size and thickness of the piece to be cooked, the amount of other foods on the broiler also demanding heat and the doneness desired.

Most foods are brushed with or dipped in unseasoned oil or other suitable fat before being placed on the rack. The oil prevents sticking and affords protection to the meat. It aids in retarding dryness and cracking and helps to give the surface of the product good color.

Foods of less than moderate fat are not desirable for broiling since they tend to dry out. When very lean foods are used, fat supplement is advisable.

At one time broiling and grilling were practically synonymous. Today broiling is the acceptable term for cooking by direct heat, regardless of direction of its source.

The method of testing the degree of doneness by light pressure with the fingers, as described in the section on roasting, is the only practical method now in use for broiling. This method is used exclusively and must be mastered in order to operate a broiler successfully.

Grilling usually designates cooking on a solid grill or griddle where the product is not directly exposed to open heat. This is a form of pan broiling which utilizes the same type of heat. Some operations list items "from the grill" on menus, but are usually referring to broiled foods.

Maintenance of Broiler and Grill The broiler rack and grill must be kept clean at all times. It is necessary to clean the equipment during service as well as at closing time. Conscientious observance of this rule aids in presenting a wholesome and palatable product; makes for less work, by not letting dirt and grease accumulate, and invites inspection of the facilities at any time with assured pride in the appearance of the station. Wire brushes, scrapers and other cleaning equipment are usually provided. The drip trays and grease drawers should be cleaned at the close of service to prevent a fire hazard as well as for sanitary reasons.

Recommended tools and equipment:

1. A large range fork to turn meats. Care must be taken to insert the fork only slightly at the very edge of the meat or in the fat to prevent piercing and causing the flesh to bleed.

2. An offset spatula for grill work and for use with soft meats and fish.

3. A long handled fork or hooked rod to reach pans placed in the rear of the flash oven where it is difficult to reach.

4. A suitable pan to hold oil for dipping the foods or a brush for brushing them before placing them on the grill or broiler.

5. An empty pan in which to place partially cooked meats that will be returned to the broiler for finishing.

6. A sufficient number of hand racks or grills are necessary for proper work.

These hand racks or grills are utilized more in poultry and fish cookery but are handled by the same station unless the food operation is large enough to employ a man to cook only fish. The racks may be single or double with hinges and are used to help retain the shape of soft and flaky foods and prevent them from falling apart. They are easily handled and may be transferred to the sink for cleaning.

It is obvious that proper refrigeration and sufficient work area, benches, etc., should be provided. A sink is of great benefit near the area.

Other small equipment and dishes are used in preparing and holding the mise en place (see Glossary), such as melted butter, lemon wedges and slices, parsley and watercress, bread and cracker crumbs, paprika, etc.

Meat Grading Rigid laws and inspections by federal agencies, including grading and classification, have furnished us with specific standards by which meat may be purchased. Grading is a voluntary process at the packers' request. Meat crossing state lines must be inspected for wholesomeness only. The local houses are governed only by the city, municipality and state in which they are located. Packing houses with local distribution only are few in number today; but care should be taken, as in all good purchasing, that dealings are transacted with reputable firms whose quality and integrity are known.

The grading stamp on meat designates quality as

specified by the U. S. Dept. of Agriculture. The inspection stamp shows that the animal has been examined by government inspectors and passed as wholesome. This stamp, utilizing harmless vegetable dyes, contains the words "U. S. Inspected and Passed." All packing houses under federal inspection are assigned identifying numbers which appear on the stamp.

The higher grades of beef are more tender and usually have a better flavor than the lower grades. Certain cuts from the same carcass are often in demand because of tenderness and flavor. The most popular cuts, such as tenderloin and sirloin, usually comprise a small percentage of carcass weight. The law of supply and demand makes higher grades and popular cuts more expensive; grades and cuts less in demand, less expensive.

Many packing houses have their own brand names and their own system of grading that is not necessarily consistent with federal grades. Butcher shop and supermarket terms usually differ considerably from those used in professional cookery.

Combination Methods—Braising is a combination of dry and moist heat cookery. The meat is first seared and then subjected to moisture in order (1) to break down the connective tissues, and (2) provide a flavorful sauce. This method is applied to less expensive and less tender cuts of meat.

(The most expensive meats are often the least profitable. The less expensive cuts offer a variety of attractive menu items that may be profitable and satisfying.)

This method of cooking involves more time and care than methods used for the expensive, tender cuts. This rule applies generally to all types of cooking: the less expensive the item, the greater the time and labor involved.

Greater knowledge and versatility are also needed for the less expensive ingredients. Braised meats provide high nutritional values, as fresh vegetables usually go into the preparation of the sauces and, when skillfully and properly prepared, many of the vitamins and minerals of the meats and vegetables are retained.

Meats are usually tied individually to hold them together and aid in retaining their shape so that uniform slicing is possible. Loose or odd-shaped pieces may be tied to conform to any desired shape or size. Tying also facilitates handling of the product later.

To braise a piece of meat, first select the proper size of brazier or roast pan for which there is a suitable cover. Place mirepoix of celery, onions and carrots in bottom of pan. Place meat on top of the mirepoix. If the meat is lean a small amount of oil may be added or additional fat coverage tied on when preparing the meat. Add desired seasonings, spices and herbs. The oil will help hold them on the surface of the meat.

Place pan with meat, uncovered, in a moderately hot oven (400°F.). Brown meat on all sides, being careful that oven is not hot enough to burn vegetables. To intensify browning, meat may be dredged or sprinkled with flour. Caution must be taken here to prevent burning. The flour is not essential but a matter of preference. Occasional turning of meat is necessary.

When the meat is browned on all sides, a small amount of tomato product is added. It may be tomato paste, tomato puree or trimmings and ends of fresh or overripe tomatoes. A small amount of tomato product adds flavor and helps the color of the finished sauce. It must be added early enough to cook thoroughly and in small enough quantity so that it does not overshadow the flavor of the sauce.

In moist heat cookery the seasoning penetrates the meat to greater extent than in dry heat cookery. Discretion must be used to obtain the proper flavor. Overseasoning is worse than no seasoning at all.

Let the vegetables reach a unified brownish color, reducing heat if necessary. Add a sufficient amount of stock to cover meat by one-third. Reduce the oven temperature to about 300°F. and fit brazier with tight cover. Check on the doneness of the meat from time to time, turning when necessary to prevent the exposed portion from drying. Even though a certain degree of steaming takes place from the liquid in the bottom of the pan, a better product is obtained if meat is turned occasionally and kept covered.

Braise until tender and remove meat from pan, reserving liquid for the sauce. The entire contents of the brazier should now be transferred to a small pot or sauce pan and placed on top of the range. Bring the stock to a boil and simmer until vegetables are quite soft. Strain through a fine china cap and skim fat to make roux. Thicken to desired consistency. The sauce should be light in character. Finish with wine, if desired. Correct seasoning and color. Bring to final boil, strain through fine china cap and hold for service.

If a faster browning is desired in the beginning, the meat may be browned in a skillet or suitable pan on top of the range. However, a slow brown at low temperature is retained by the meat better than a quick brown at high temperature.

The work load is often so heavy that there is little range room during the preparation hours. Using the oven for the entire procedure leaves the range top free for other work. This does not present as great a problem in a large operation where there is ample or even excessive equipment. Unfortunately, the average operation often has less than ample equipment, and ingenuity must be exercised to facilitate work and make it more efficient.

The change that takes place during braising is a type of filtering process. The external temperature forces the blood and juices to the center of the meat (or away from the source of heat, as stated in the broiling section). When the heat reaches the center of the meat, the juices release excess water in the form of vapor which breaks down the connective tissue and allows the concentration of juices in the center to filter back through the meat where it becomes concentrated in the braising liquor. It is through this means that the braising liquor or stock gets its flavor and the meat becomes tender.

Stewing or simmering is the process of cooking food in a small amount of liquid, usually no more than required to cover the food. The proper temperature range for stewing is 185 to 190°F. The liquid is preheated to this temperature range and the temperature should be maintained until the food item is cooked.

Stewing is usually confined to the less tender cuts of meat, although some regional and nationality dishes do not follow this rule.

While stewing as suggested here is intended expressly for meat, poultry and seafood, stewing may also be applied to some fruits and vegetables—particularly dried fruits such as prunes and apricots.

Many of the same basic principles of braising apply to stewing although there are some exceptions. Meats may or may not be browned, depending on the color desired in the finished product. For white stews such as Irish Lamb Stew, the meat is not browned, but is blanched.

The meat must be carefully cut in uniform pieces and all gristle, tough membrane and excess fat removed.

Vegetables are sometimes cooked separately from the meat to retain their fresh look and either incorporated at the last minute prior to service or used as a garnish. They may be glazed by sauteing, if desired.

When vegetables are cooked with the meat, care must be taken that the meat is sufficiently cooked before adding the vegetables so that both products will finish cooking and be properly tender at the same time.

Stews may be thickened or unthickened and in some cases become thickened by their own ingredients. Old-fashioned Irish Lamb Stew is thickened with the potatoes in it rather than a roux.

In thick stews, the juices dissolved in the liquid are eaten, together with the cooked food, in the form of gravy. It is advisable, in order to serve a very appetizing and satisfactory stew, to remove or skim superfluous fats which will come to the surface.

Meat must be cut in uniform pieces, free from inedible parts, bloody tissues, fat and bones. Small amounts of fat on flank and breast, however, are a good addition to stews.

Stewing of meat is very popular. There are many dishes developed by stewing, and nearly every country has its own specialty. Stews were originally economical to prepare and highly nutritious as they retained in their liquor most of the vitamin and mineral content. They were a necessary part of the menu for people of moderate means. Our economy today does not demand the effort of preparing stews in the home and this may in part account for their popularity on away-from-home menus. The French term for stew is ragout (rahgoo). This applies principally to a thickened brown stew.

Some of the popular stews are:

Irish Lamb Stew	Hungarian Goulash
Navarin of Lamb	Curry of Veal
Beef Stew	Beef Stew (thickened)

Attractive casseroles and serving dishes add to the appeal of stews. Various starch garnitures, such as dumplings, noodles and rice, are often served as accompaniments to provide a filling and satisfying meal.

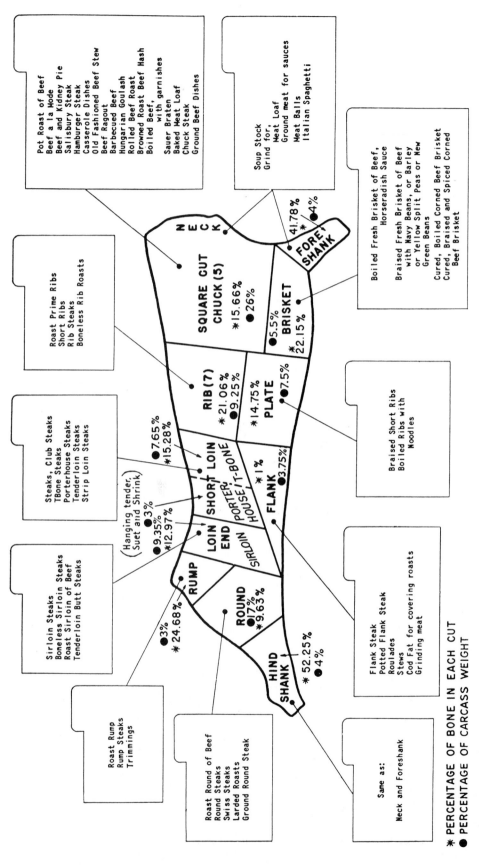

Pot Roast of Beef
Beef a la Mode
Beef and Kidney Pie
Salisbury Steak
Hamburger Steak
Casserole Dishes
Old Fashioned Beef Stew
Beef Ragout
Barbecued Beef
Hungarian Goulash
Rolled Beef Roast
Browned Roast Beef Hash
Boiled Beef,
    with garnishes
Sauer Braten
Baked Meat Loaf
Chuck Steak
Ground Beef Dishes

Soup Stock
Grind for,
    Meat Loaf
    Ground meat for sauces
    Meat Balls
    Italian Spaghetti

Boiled Fresh Brisket of Beef,
    Horseradish Sauce
Braised Fresh Brisket of Beef
    with Navy Beans, or Barley
    or Yellow Split Peas or New
    Green Beans
Cured, Boiled Corned Beef Brisket
Cured, Braised and Spiced Corned
    Beef Brisket

Roast Prime Ribs
Short Ribs
Rib Steaks
Boneless Rib Roasts

Steaks, Club Steaks
TBone Steaks
Porterhouse Steaks
Tenderloin Steaks
Strip Loin Steaks

Sirloin Steaks
Boneless Sirloin Steaks
Roast Sirloin of Beef
Tenderloin Butt Steaks

Braised Short Ribs
Boiled Ribs with
Noodles

Roast Rump
Rump Steaks
Trimmings

Flank Steak
Potted Flank Steak
Roulades
Stews
Cod Fat for covering roasts
Grinding meat

Roast Round of Beef
Round Steaks
Swiss Steaks
Larded Roasts
Ground Round Steak

Same as:

Neck and Foreshank

NECK

SQUARE CUT
CHUCK (5)
*15.66%
●26%

FORE
SHANK
41.78%
*
●4%

BRISKET
●5.5%
*22.15%

RIB (7)
21.06%
*
●9.25%

PLATE
*14.75%
●7.5%

●7.65%
*15.28%

SHORT LOIN
PORTER
HOUSE/T-BONE

FLANK
*1%
●3.75%

LOIN
END
SIRLOIN
●9.35%
*12.97%

●3%
(Hanging tender,
Suet and Shrink)

RUMP
●3%
*24.68%

ROUND
17%
*9.63%

HIND
SHANK
*52.25%
●4%

* PERCENTAGE OF BONE IN EACH CUT
● PERCENTAGE OF CARCASS WEIGHT

Above chart developed by Armour & Co.

BEEF

Chef Arthur Jones presides over an elegant table containing many of the favorite beef entrees featured in this section of The Professional Chef.

Here, artistry of the chef is detailed with scientific accuracy. Basic, intermediate and advanced information covering equipment, formulas, techniques and training methods enables the secrets of the chefs to be communicated to the cooks in any Institutions' kitchen.

London Broil, Bordelaise Sauce

Beef Pot Pie

Chopped Beefsteak Patties with Mushroom Sauce

Braised Short Ribs of Beef

Roast Sirloin of Beef, Pan Gravy

ALL-AMERICAN

Beef Stroganoff

Old Fashioned Beef Stew

Minute Sirloin Steak

Spaghetti with Meat Balls, Italian Sauce

BEEF FAVORITES

Most popular of all beef entrees, according to a survey made by food service consultants Flambert and Flambert, are hamburger, steak, prime ribs, swiss steak, pot roast and beef stew. And because a greater part of the 35 to 40 per cent of the food budget that is devoted to meat will be spent on these beef entrees, the profit picture of any operation can rise or fall depending on the care exercised in beef purchasing and preparation. For this reason, leading operators use written specifications when purchasing beef. These cover cut, grade, weight and trim desired. But even where careful purchasing techniques are employed, the cost of beef is high — often approaching an over 50 per cent food cost. Fortunately, however, the most high-priced beef entrees involve a low labor cost — around 20 per cent — making them potentially one of the biggest profit items on the menu.

German Sauerbraten

Baked Hamburg Loaf

Yankee Pot Roast of Beef

Beef round-up

Medium, rare or well-done, beef entrees are the most often selected by 37 per cent of the dining-out public. Ways to prepare these all-time favorites are given on the following pages.

Roulades of Beef

Braised Round of Beef, Jardiniere

Swiss Steak, Jardiniere

Broiled Hip Steak, French Fried Onion Rings

Techniques for
Beef Cookery

Beef Grades Although there are several official U. S. Government grades of beef, they are not all pertinent to the food service industry. The poorer grades of beef are used in commercial canning and are not found in the wholesale or retail market.

The first five grades of beef are:

1) USDA (United States Dept. of Agriculture) PRIME
2) USDA CHOICE
3) USDA GOOD
4) USDA STANDARD
5) USDA COMMERCIAL

Prime beef is, as the name implies, of highest quality and palatability. However, its high fat content makes it extremely wasteful in trimming and cooking and only eating establishments with extremely high menu prices can afford to serve it. The supply is not always abundant.

Choice beef is preferred by most quality operations because its eating characteristics are excellent and reasonably consistent. Although less costly than prime beef in terms of waste, it is still an expensive product and must be handled with care.

Good, Standard, and *Commercial* beef may be used by operations with lower menu prices and by schools, hospitals and other institutions. The nutritional values of the various grades do not differ greatly.

In 1959 the U. S. Dept. of Agriculture instituted a grade termed *Standard,* which is between good and commercial. It is not handled by many purveyors to the wholesale trade as it is not suitable for commercial food service use. It is used mostly in retail outlets. Standard beef has poor conformation and an ex-tremely thin fat covering with a high ratio of lean to fat. Many purveyors are not even aware that the Standard grade exists.

Internal Temperatures of Large Beef Roasts for Different Degrees of Doneness*

Degree of Doneness	Oven Temperature	Color of Inside Roast	Meat Thermometer Reading When Roast Comes From Oven
Rare	300°F.	Bright Pink	120° to 125°F.
Medium	300°F.	Pinkish Brown	135° to 145°F.
Well Done	300°F.	Greyish or Light Brown	150° to 160°F.

The temperatures at which color changes take place in beef as it cooks are considerably higher than the temperatures above indicate; however, large roasts continue cooking for some time after they are removed from the oven. Therefore, to prevent overcooking, roasts should be removed from the oven when the meat thermometer shows several degrees lower than the temperature at which the actual color change takes place.

TIMETABLE FOR ROASTING BEEF*

Cut	Approx. wt. of single roast lb.	Oven temper- ature	Interior temp. of roast removed from oven	Minutes per lb. based on one roast	Approx. total time
Standing rib (7 rib)	23	300°F.	125°F. (rare)	11	4 hr.
			140°F. (medium)	12	4½ hr.
			150°F. (well)	13	5 hr.
Rolled Rib (7 rib)	17	300°F.	150°F. (well)	24	6 hr.
Chuck rib	5 to 8	300°F.	150°F. to 170°F.	25 to 30	2½ to 4 hr.
Rump	5 to 7	300°F.	150°F. to 170°F	25 to 30	2½ to 3½ hr.

*Courtesy of the National Livestock and Meat Board

SAVORY SWISS STEAK

The first step in the preparation of Savory Swiss Steak is trimming bottom round and portioning into 5 ounce steaks. Then dredge steaks in seasoned flour and brown in hot oil.

Prepare sauce base from beef stock, tomato puree, soy sauce and seasoning. Sauté vegetables, then add flour to make a roux. Strain stock, stir into roux. Pour sauce over steaks as at right.

Steaks are baked in sauce at 350°F. for about two hours. Plate finished steak with appropriate vegetables and potato, then serve with 2 ounces of sauce over each portion, below right. (Recipe on facing page.)

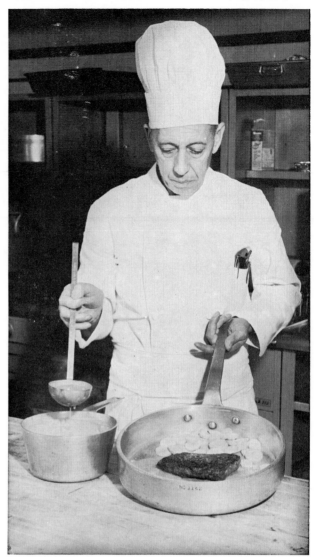

Savory Swiss Steak

YIELD: 50 portions	EACH PORTION: about 5 oz. with 2 oz. sauce	
INGREDIENTS	QUANTITY	METHOD
Bottom Round, trimmed (5 oz. steaks) Bread Flour, seasoned with salt and pepper Salad Oil	50 1 lb. 1 qt.	1. Dredge steaks in seasoned flour. Pour oil in skillet to depth of 1/8 in.; heat. Add steaks and brown on both sides. Place steaks in brazier or roast pan.
Beef Stock Tomato Puree Soy Sauce Black Pepper Whole Cloves Bay Leaves Thyme Savory	5 qt. 8 oz. 5 oz. 1 tsp. 6 2 1/2 tsp. 1/2 tsp.	2. Combine all ingredients and simmer for 20 min. to make hot stock.
Salad Oil Onions, small dice Garlic, crushed Celery, small dice Bread Flour Salt	1 pt. 1 lb. 2 cloves 1/2 lb. 12 oz. to taste	3. Saute onions, garlic and celery in oil in sauce pot until vegetables are tender. Add flour to make roux. Stir and cook for 10 min., browning lightly. 4. Strain hot stock and add gradually to roux, stirring until thickened and smooth. Adjust seasoning with salt if desired and pour sauce over steaks. Bake at 350°F. about 2 hr. or until tender. 5. Serve one steak per portion with sauce.

Beef Stew Bordelaise

YIELD: 50 portions	EACH PORTION 4 oz. cooked meat, 5 oz. sauce	
INGREDIENTS	QUANTITY	METHOD
Beef Chuck, trimmed Shortening Onions, chopped	18 lb. 8 oz. 4 lb.	1. Cut beef into 1 in. cubes. Melt shortening in fry pan or skillet; add onions, saute until tender. Reserve onions. 2. Drain shortening into brazier. Add part of meat and saute until brown. Remove browned meat to large pot. Brown remaining meat as above and add to large pot. Bake meat at 450°F. for 10 min.
Flour Paprika Salt Pepper	14¼ oz. 1 oz. to taste to taste	3. Combine flour, paprika, salt and pepper; sprinkle over meat; stir into pan drippings and return to oven until browned.

Red Wine
Tomato Puree
Beef Stock
Spice Bag:
    Crushed Black Pepper
    Caraway Seed
    Thyme
    Bay Leaves
	1 pt.
	3 pt.
	7 qt.
	
	¼ oz.
	1 tbsp.
	1 tsp.
	4
		4. Remove from oven, add onions, half the red wine and stir. Add tomato puree, beef stock and spice bag. Bring to a boil and simmer for about 3 hr. Correct seasoning and add remaining wine.

		5. Serve 4 oz. cooked meat with 5 oz. sauce per portion. Top with Mushrooms and Potato Bordelaise, p. 46.

Beef

Braised Short Ribs of Beef (recipe below)   *Beef Rouladen in Burgundy Sauce (recipe on facing page)*

Braised Short Ribs of Beef

YIELD: 50 portions		EACH PORTION: 10 oz. rib with 3 oz. sauce
INGREDIENTS	*QUANTITY*	*METHOD*
Short Ribs Onions, peeled, medium cut Carrots, scrubbed, medium cut Celery, cleaned, medium cut	50 (about 10 oz. ea.) 1½ lb. ½ lb. ½ lb.	1. Trim ribs; remove fat and tie meat to bone. 2. Put vegetables in lightly greased roasting pan and place short ribs on top.
Salad Oil Sweet Basil Sage Thyme	1 pt. 2 tsp. ½ tsp. ½ tsp.	3. Pour 1 cup oil evenly over all. Combine spices and sprinkle as evenly as possible over top. Brown in oven at 400°F., turning as necessary. Do not let vegetables burn.
Bread Flour Beef Stock, hot Tomatoes, chopped	1 lb. 6 qt. 1 No. 2½ can	4. When nicely browned add remainder of oil and flour, blending well. Cook for 5 to 10 min. Add hot stock, stirring to mix well until slightly thickened. Add tomatoes and blend. Cover, return to oven and cook 2 to 2½ hr. or until tender.
		5. When ribs are cooked, remove to clean pan. Strain sauce. Adjust seasoning and thickening. Remove excess fat. Pour sauce over ribs. 6. Hold for service in warm place but do not continue to cook. When serving, remove string. Serve one 10 oz. rib portion with 3 oz. sauce. A fresh vegetable garnish may be added.
See color picture, p. 37.		

Beef Rouladen in Burgundy Sauce

YIELD: 20 portions	EACH PORTION: 2 rolls	
INGREDIENTS	QUANTITY	METHOD
Bottom Round, trimmed	5 lb.	1. Slice beef in 2 oz. pcs (3 in. by 4 in.). Flatten with cleaver.
Bacon, chopped Lean Raw Smoked Ham Scraps, chopped Ground Beef Onions, chopped and sauteed Eggs, beaten Fine Dry Crumbs Parsley, chopped Sweet Pickle Strips, thin	1 lb. ½ lb. ¼ lb. 5 oz. 4 1½ pt. 2 tbsp. 40	2. Combine bacon, ham, ground beef, onions, eggs, bread crumbs and parsley; mix well. 3. Put 1 oz. filling and 1 pickle strip on each piece of meat. Roll up and secure with toothpicks.

Seasoned Flour:
    Flour
    Salt
    Pepper
Salad Oil
	
	for dredging
	to taste
	to taste
	for browning
		4. Dredge rolls in seasoned flour. Brown on all sides in hot oil. Place browned rolls in baking pan.

Sauce:
    Brown Sauce (p. 312)
    Dry Red Wine
    Tomato Puree
    Garlic Cloves, minced
    Garlic Cloves, whole
	
	2 qt.
	8 oz.
	8 oz.
	2
	3
		5. Combine all sauce ingredients and blend; pour over rolls. Cover tightly; braise at 350°F. 1½ hr. or until meat is tender. Turn once during braising. Strain sauce and serve over rouladen. Serve 2 rouladen per portion.

See color picture, p. 40.

Individual Beefsteak Pie with Vegetables

YIELD: 50 portions	EACH PORTION: 3 oz. meat, 4 oz. sauce	
INGREDIENTS	QUANTITY	METHOD

Bottom Round, cut (1 in. cubes)
Salad Oil
Bread Flour
Brown Stock, hot (p. 271)
Tomato Puree
Sachet Bag:
    Thyme
    Bay Leaf, large
	17 lb.
	24 oz.
	1 lb.
	7 qt.
	12 oz.
	
	1 tsp.
	1
		1. Prepare meat and sauce and bake same method as Beef Pot Pie, p. 50.

Potatoes, cut (½ in. dice) Carrots, medium dice Fresh or Frozen Peas, cooked Pearl Onions, medium Salt	2 qt. 1½ qt. 2½ qt. 50 to taste	2. Cook vegetables separately in lightly salted boiling water. 3. Distribute meat and vegetables evenly among all casseroles. Ladle about 4 oz. sauce into each casserole, leaving slight space at top for baking crust.
Pie Crusts	50	4. Prepare crust, cutting crust same shape as casserole but slightly larger to allow for shrinkage in baking. Mold crust edges to sides of casserole. Make slight gash or hole in center crust for escape of steam. Brush with egg wash. 5. Place casseroles on sheet pans and bake at 400°F. for 15 min. or until done.

NOTE: Crust may be baked separately and placed on casserole at time of service.

Beef

Beef Stroganoff
(recipe below)

Yankee Pot Roast of Beef (Braised Round of Beef, Jardiniere)
(recipe on facing page)

Beef Stroganoff

YIELD: 48 portions		EACH PORTION: about 6 oz. beef and sauce
INGREDIENTS	*QUANTITY*	*METHOD*
Tenderloin Tips	12 lb.	1. Slice tenderloin tips in very thin strips (about 2 by 1 by ¼ in.).
White Wine Vinegar Rich Brown Sauce (p. 312) Sour Cream Butter	8 oz. 8 oz. 3 qt. 24 oz. 6 oz.	2. Reduce white wine and vinegar by boiling for several minutes. Add to Brown Sauce. Add hot Brown Sauce slowly to cream, stirring constantly to prevent curdling. Add butter (not melted).
Salad Oil	for sauteing	4. Saute tenderloin strips in heavy skillet until light brown. Strain all grease off in china cap.
Mushrooms, sliced Butter Salt Pepper	24 oz. 6 oz. to taste to taste	5. Saute sliced mushrooms in butter and add to beef. Pour sauce over all and heat but do not permit to boil. Add salt and pepper to taste. Keep warm in double boiler until ready to serve. 6. Serve with ¾ cup (3½ oz.) steamed rice, noodles or spaetzli.
See color picture, p. 38.		

Mushrooms and Potato Bordelaise

YIELD: 50 portions		EACH PORTION: about 2½ oz. as garnish
INGREDIENTS	*QUANTITY*	METHOD
Olive Oil Potatoes (cut in ¾ in. cubes)	1 pt. 8 lb.	1. Pour olive oil into shallow roasting pan and heat in oven at 450°F. until it reaches smoking point. Be sure that potatoes are well-drained and dry, add to hot oil, spreading evenly in pan. Cook in oven until browned, stirring occasionally during cooking.
Butter Mushrooms, halved Onions, chopped fine Garlic, chopped Salt Chopped Parsley	4 oz. 5 lb. 2 oz. 1 tbsp. 2 tbsp. for garnish	2. Melt butter in another pan; add mushrooms and saute until brown. Add onions and garlic and saute until tender. Add salt. 3. Add mushroom mixture to potatoes, blending well. 4. Sprinkle over Beef Stew Bordelaise (see formula p. 43), before serving. Top with chopped parsley.

Yankee Pot Roast of Beef (Braised Round of Beef, Jardiniere)

YIELD: 50 portions		EACH PORTION: 4 oz. meat, 2 oz. sauce
INGREDIENTS	QUANTITY	METHOD
Bottom Round, trimmed and tied, 5 to 6 lb. pcs. Salad Oil	18 lb. 1 pt.	1. Brown meat on all sides in 8 oz. hot oil in fry or skillet. Remove meat to brazier or heavy pot. Pour oil from meat into sauce pot and add 8 oz. more oil.
Onions, medium dice Celery, medium dice Carrots, medium dice Bread Flour Beef Stock, hot Tomatoes, chopped fine Bay Leaf Thyme, ground	1 lb. 8 oz. 4 oz. 1 lb. 5 qt. 1 No. 2½ can 1 ½ tsp.	2. Add onions, celery, carrots; saute 15 min. Blend in flour and cook 10 min. If roux is too thick, add more oil. Add hot stock, stir until thickened and smooth. Add tomatoes, juice, seasonings; mix well.
		3. Pour sauce over meat. Cover and cook at 400°F. for 2½ hr. or until meat is tender. 4. Remove meat from sauce. Strain sauce and adjust seasoning, if necessary. 5. Cut meat across grain. Serve 4-oz. portion of meat with 2 oz. ladle of sauce.

NOTE: A jardiniere or fresh vegetable garnish is often served on top of sauce.
See color picture, p. 39.

Saute Tenderloin Tips with Mushrooms in Sauce

YIELD: 50 portions		EACH PORTION: about 5 oz. meat and sauce
INGREDIENTS	QUANTITY	METHOD
Tenderloin Tips, trimmed, fat free	17 lb.	1. Slice tenderloin tips on the bias.
Mushrooms Shallots Butter Brown Sauce, hot (p. 312) Burgundy Wine	3 lb. 1 lb. 3 oz. 1½ gal. 6 oz.	2. Wash mushrooms and slice thoroughly, lifting mushrooms from water rather than pouring water off. Fine particles of mushrooms will be avoided and dirt will also remain in bottom of pan. 3. Saute shallots and mushrooms in butter and combine with hot Brown Sauce. Add burgundy wine and adjust seasoning. Simmer slowly while preparing tenderloin tips.
Salad Oil	1 pt.	4. Heat oil to smoke point and cook tenderloin tips quickly in large frying pan or sautoir. Brown nicely but do not cook well done. 5. Mix cooked tips (draining oil) with mushroom sauce. Bring to boiling point without scorching; remove from heat.
Butter, melted Parsley, chopped	for toast points 6 oz.	6. Serve in casseroles. Dip small toast points in melted butter and chopped parsley. Insert toast points deep into casserole, parsley end out. Provides both garnish and accompaniment.

NOTE: Casseroles should be piping hot with adequate underliners for service.

Beef

Baked Hamburger Loaf, right (recipe below)

Baked Spanish Meat Loaf, (recipe bottom of page)

Baked Hamburger Loaf

YIELD: 50 portions		EACH PORTION: 1 slice with 2 oz. sauce
INGREDIENTS	QUANTITY	METHOD
Onions, chopped fine Celery, chopped fine Salad Oil	3 lb. 1 lb. 8 oz.	1. Saute onions and celery in oil until tender.
Bread, trimmed Milk OR Stock Eggs, whole Salt Pepper Beef, ground	1½ lb. 1 pt. 8 to taste to taste 13 lb.	2. Place bread in large mixing bowl and add milk. Mix thoroughly until smooth. 3. Add eggs, celery, onions and seasonings. 4. Add beef and mix thoroughly. If mixture is too moist, adjust consistency by adding bread or cracker crumbs. 5. Form in 3 lb. loaves. Place in lightly greased roast pan and lightly oil outside of loaves. 6. Bake in preheated oven at 350° for 1½ hr.
NOTE: For service, slice desired portion size (7 to 8 slices to loaf) and dress with 2 oz. appropriate sauce.		

Baked Spanish Meat Loaf

YIELD: 50 portions		EACH PORTION: about 5 oz.
INGREDIENTS	QUANTITY	METHOD
Beef, ground Eggs, whole Catsup Chili Sauce Parsley, chopped Chives, chopped Worcestershire Sauce Chili Powder Paprika Saffron Salt Pepper	15 lb. 8 8 oz. 8 oz. 1½ oz. 2 oz. 2 oz. ¼ oz. 1 oz. ½ tsp. to taste to taste	1. Pass beef, eggs, catsup, chili sauce, parsley, chives, worcestershire sauce and spices once through fine grinder.
Onions, chopped Rice, baked Green Peppers, chopped Pimientoes, chopped Garlic, minced	1 lb. 8 oz. 4 oz. 7 oz. 1 tbsp.	2. Combine with above mixture, mixing well. Grease 4 5-lb. loaf pans and press meat mixture into pans, leaving ¾ in. at top of pans. Cover meat with aluminum foil. 3. Bake in water bath in oven at 375°F. for 1½ hr. Remove foil. Slice and serve with Mushroom, Tomato or Brown Sauce. (See Sauce Section for formulas.)

Beef a la Deutsch, right (recipe below)

Minute Steak, far right (recipe bottom of page)

Beef a la Deutsch

YIELD: 50 portions	EACH PORTION: about 4 oz. beef	
INGREDIENTS	QUANTITY	METHOD
Onions, sliced Garlic, chopped fine Clarified Butter Mushrooms, sliced Green Peppers, thin strips	3 lb. 2 tsp. for sauteing 3 lb. 24 oz.	1. Saute onions and garlic in small amount of clarified butter. Add mushrooms and green peppers; cook for 5 min.
Claret Wine Rich Brown Sauce (p. 312) Salt Pepper Bay Leaf	8 oz. 4 qt. to taste to taste 1	2. Add claret and simmer for 5 min. Add Brown Sauce, seasoning and bay leaf. A little crushed tomato may be added to give color to sauce.
Beef Tenderloin Tips, sliced Salad Oil	12 lb. for sauteing	3. Saute tenderloin tips in hot oil until well browned. Drain oil. Season with salt and pepper. Combine with sauce. Do not boil.
NOTE: Serve in a shirred egg dish (or a silver dish) with sauce; garnish with chopped parsley.		

Minute Steak

YIELD: 50 portions	EACH PORTION: 6 oz.	
INGREDIENTS	QUANTITY	METHOD
Sirloin Strips, boneless, well trimmed, small eye Salad Oil	20 lb. to lightly coat	1. Using extreme care, cut 6 oz. portions (full cut). Use sharp knife and portion scale. Eye must be small or steaks will be too thin. 2. Chill well before cooking. Thinly cut, room temperature steaks may cook all the way through before acquiring any outside color. Thinly cut, chilled steaks are more apt to color before cooking all the way through. Steaks are never cooked well done except by request. Keep rare, if possible. 3. Place lightly oiled or buttered steaks in pan or on hot griddle. Brown on one side, turn and brown other side. Thin steaks, particularly, should be cooked to order. Steaks may be sauteed or pan-broiled. Broiling is usually reserved for thicker steaks. 4. Serve plain, with chopped parsley, au beurre or with maitre d'hotel butter.
NOTE: Griddle or pan must be very hot for thin steaks.		

Beef

Beef Steak Patties, right (recipe below)

Beef Pot Pie, far right (recipe bottom of page)

Beef Steak Patties

YIELD: 50 portions		EACH PORTION: 1 patty, 6 oz.
INGREDIENTS	*QUANTITY*	*METHOD*
Beef, ground Salad Oil	19 lb. to lightly coat	1. Scale ground meat into 6 oz. portions and form in oval patties. 2. Dip patties in oil and place on preheated broiler rack. 3. When lightly browned, turn carefully, using a spatula or meat turner. Broiler marks should show on meat. Brown second side and remove to clean bake sheet or other pan when still rare. Finish in oven or return to broiler at service time. Cook medium unless otherwise indicated.
NOTE: Patties may be served with appropriate sauce, onion rings or brushed with butter and sprinkled with fresh chopped parsley.		

Beef Pot Pie

YIELD: 50 portions		EACH PORTION: 8 oz. ladle with 3 oz. cooked meat
INGREDIENTS	*QUANTITY*	*METHOD*
Salad Oil Bottom Round, shank or chuck, cut (1 in. cubes)	1½ pt. 17 lb.	1. Heat 1/8 in. oil in fry pans; add meat, brown. Place meat in brazier or roast pan.

Bread Flour
Brown Stock, hot (p. 271)
Tomato Puree
Sachet Bag:
    Thyme
    Bay Leaf, large
	1 lb.
	7 qt.
	12 oz.
	
	1 tsp.
	1
		2. Add balance of oil and flour to make roux. Stir until well blended. Add Brown Stock; cook until slightly thickened and smooth. Add tomato puree and sachet bag. Bring to boil.
		3. Cover and bake at 350°F. for 2 hr. or until meat is tender.

Carrots, Parisienne, pcs. Potatoes, Parisienne, pcs. Pearl Onions, medium Frozen Peas, cooked	200 200 50 2½ lb.	4. Cook each vegetable separately in lightly salted boiling water.
Salt Pepper Dumplings OR Baked Pastry Cut-Outs	to taste to taste	5. When meat is cooked, remove sachet bag and add 1 pt. each onion and carrot liquid. Adjust seasoning. 6. Vegetables may either be incorporated or placed on stew as garnish. Serve 8 oz. ladle with 3 oz. cooked meat per portion. Top with dumplings or pastry cut-outs.

Boiled Fresh Beef, right (recipe below)

Swiss Steak with Sour Cream, far right (recipe bottom of page)

Boiled Fresh Beef

YIELD: 50 portions	EACH PORTION: 4 oz.	
INGREDIENTS	*QUANTITY*	*METHOD*

Fresh Brisket
   OR Rolled Chuck,
   (cut in 5 to 6 lb. pieces)
Onions (cut in large pieces,
   about 1 in.)
Carrots (cut in large pieces,
   about 1 in.)
Celery (cut in large pieces,
   about 1 in.)
Bay Leaves
Whole Cloves
Peppercorns, crushed
Salt
	22 lb.
	
	2 lb.
	
	1 lb.
	
	1 lb.
	
	2
	5
	1 tsp.
	to taste
		1. Place meat in stock pot in boiling water to cover. Return to boil and remove scum as it rises to surface. Reduce heat to simmer and add vegetables and seasonings.
		2. Simmer for 2½ to 3 hr. or until tender. Test for doneness by inserting fork. Fork should be inserted and withdrawn with ease. Do not overcook. Check each piece of meat separately.
		3. Keep the meat in cooking liquid (warm) until ready to serve.
		4. Serve 4 oz. portions, sliced 1/8 in. thick.

NOTE: Boiled beef should be accompanied by appropriate sauce, such as Horseradish Sauce (p.317) or Mustard Sauce (p.315).

   Liquid may be strained carefully and used as beef broth.

   Garnishes for beef include: boiled vegetables, such as potatoes, beets, carrots, turnips, etc.; also cabbage, spinach or kale.

   Other meats which may be boiled in the same manner are **Corned Brisket of Beef**; **Corned Rump of Beef**; **Tongues**, fresh, smoked or corned; **Short-Ribs of Beef**; **Shoulder or Breast of Veal**; **Leg of Lamb or Mutton**; **Ham**, fresh or smoked; **Fresh Pork Shoulder**; **Smoked Pork Butt**; fresh or corned **Spareribs**.

Swiss Steak with Sour Cream

YIELD: 50 portions	EACH PORTION: 6 oz. steak	
INGREDIENTS	*QUANTITY*	*METHOD*
Bottom Round Steaks Salad Oil	50 (6 oz.) 1 qt.	1. Saute steaks in 1/8 in. hot oil until well browned on both sides. Remove steaks to brazier or roast pan.
Onions, small dice Bread Flour Paprika Brown Stock, hot (p.271) Salt Pepper Worcestershire Sauce Parmesan Cheese	3 lb. 12 oz. 5/8 oz. 6 qt. to taste 1 tsp. 6 oz. 4 oz.	2. Saute onions in sauce pot in remaining oil. Cook until soft. Add flour and paprika, blending well; cook 10 min. 3. Add Brown Stock stirring until slightly thickened and smooth. Add salt, pepper, worcestershire and parmesan cheese. Pour sauce over steaks. 4. Bake covered at 350°F. for 2 hr. or until tender. Skim excess fat.
Sour Cream	1 qt.	5. Remove steaks to serving pan. Add sauce to sour cream. Adjust seasoning; strain over steaks. Heat before serving but do not boil.

Beef

Beef Tenderloin Wellington, right (recipe below)

Broiled Hip Steak, far right (recipe bottom of page)

Beef Tenderloin Wellington

YIELD: 8 portions	EACH PORTION: 1 slice (¾ in.)	
INGREDIENTS	*QUANTITY*	*METHOD*

DOUGH
  Bread Flour
  Salt
  Butter
  Shortening
  Egg Yolks
  Olive Oil
  Cold Water
	
	24 oz.
	½ tsp.
	6 oz.
	6 oz.
	3
	½ oz.
	6 to 8 oz.
		1. Sift flour. Fold remaining ingredients into flour as for pie dough. Blend lightly. Cover dough with cloth; allow to stand 1 hr.

Beef Tenderloin, whole, trimmed, peeled Liver Pate OR Foie Gras *Truffle Peelings, finely chopped	1 (5 lb.) 8 oz. 2 oz.	2. Sear tenderloin well, leaving center practically raw. Cool. Spread with liver pate or foie gras. Sprinkle with chopped truffles.
Egg Wash Salad Oil	to brush for pan	3. Roll out Pate en Croute dough 3/16 in. thick. Wrap dough around tenderloin keeping seam on bottom. Fold ends under. Decorate with cut-out made from dough trimmings. 4. Brush surface with egg wash. Place on oiled bake sheet. Bake at 350°F. about 40 min. or until dough is done. (If dough browns too quickly, shield with foil.) 5. Cut in slices about ¾ in. thick; serve 1 slice per portion. Serve Madeira Sauce (p. 63) separately in gravy boat or appropriate container.
*If foie gras or liver pate has chopped truffles, truffles may be omitted as a separate ingredient.		

Broiled Hip Steak

YIELD: 50 portions	EACH PORTION: 6 to 7 oz.	
INGREDIENTS	*QUANTITY*	*METHOD*
Sirloin Top Butt Steaks, boneless (6 to 7 oz.) Salad Oil	50 to coat	1. Dip steaks in oil and place on preheated broiler. Broiler rack should be high enough to sear steaks quickly and color them well. When partially cooked, turn without piercing meat and cook other side. Steaks may be removed when very rare and reheated or finished cooking at actual service time, or may be served directly from the broiler. Steaks would normally be cooked to order to the degree of doneness specified by the patron. 2. Serve with appropriate butter, sauce or onion rings.

Italian Meat Balls, right (recipe below)

Roulade of Beef, Farcie, far right (recipe bottom of page)

Italian Meat Balls

YIELD: 50 portions		**EACH PORTION**: 2 meat balls with pasta and Spaghetti Sauce
INGREDIENTS	*QUANTITY*	*METHOD*
Onions, finely chopped Celery, fine chopped Garlic, minced Salad Oil	3 lb. 1 lb. 2 tbsp. 8 oz.	1. Saute onions, celery, garlic in oil.
Bread, fresh, cubed Stock 　OR Milk Ground Beef (or 1/3 ea.: 　ground pork, beef, veal) Eggs, whole Parmesan Cheese, grated Parsley, finely chopped Oregano, minced Salt Pepper	1 lb. 24 oz. 12 lb. 8 4 oz. 3 oz. 1 tbsp. to taste to taste	2. Combine bread and stock or milk in large mixing bowl; mix well. Add remaining ingredients; blend thoroughly. 3. Using No. 12 ice cream scoop as measuring guide, scale 2½ oz. meat balls. Scale entire mix up, then mold all balls into round shape.
Stock, hot	1 qt.	4. Place meat balls in greased roast pan; bake ½ hr. at 350°F. Remove meat balls to smaller pan, add hot stock and cover. Keep hot for service. 5. Serve 2 meat balls on top of a portion of pasta and Spaghetti Sauce (p. 319).
See color picture, p. 38.		

Roulade of Beef, Farcie

YIELD: 50 portions		**EACH PORTION**: 4-5 oz. roulade, 2 oz. sauce
INGREDIENTS	*QUANTITY*	*METHOD*
Lean Bottom Round Slices Duxelle (p. 113)	50 (4 to 5 oz.) 3 qt.	1. Pound beef slices until thin with mallet or cleaver. Roll 2 oz. stuffing (duxelle) in each slice of beef to make roulade and fold in ends, using toothpick to hold in place. 2. Put in greased roasting pan; place in oven at 400°F. until lightly browned.
Brown Sauce (p. 312)	1 gal.	3. Pour hot Brown Sauce over roulades; cover. Lower heat to 350°F.; bake about 1½ hr., basting every half hour. 4. Serve 1 roulade per portion with 2 oz. sauce.
See color picture, p. 40.		

Beef

Sweet-Sour Stuffed Cabbage, right (recipe below)

Old Fashioned Beef Stew, far right (recipe on facing page)

Sweet-Sour Stuffed Cabbage

YIELD: 50 portions		EACH PORTION: 1 cabbage roll with 2 oz. sauce
INGREDIENTS	*QUANTITY*	*METHOD*
MEAT MIXTURE: Onions Apples Ground Beef Rice, cooked Tomatoes, canned Eggs, whole Salt White Pepper Sugar Water Fresh White Bread Crumbs	 8 oz. 8 oz. 10 lb. 16 oz. 8 oz. 6 1/2 oz. 1/8 tsp. 1/4 oz. 1-1/2 pt. 1 pt.	1. Grind onions and apples together; mix with remaining ingredients. Adjust consistency if necessary, Mixture should be moist and soft. Cover and refrigerate.
SAUCE: Tomato Puree Lemon Juice Beef Stock Paprika Salt Sugar White Pepper Cornstarch (diluted in water)	 1 No. 10 can 12 oz. 1-1/2 gal. 1/4 oz. 2 oz. 5 oz. 1/8 tsp. 3 oz.	2. Combine ingredients and bring to boil. Reduce heat and simmer lightly while preparing cabbage.
Cabbage, medium-size heads	4	3. Remove cores from cabbage heads. Cook in boiling salted water about 5 min. or until tender. Cool and drain. Separate leaves carefully. 4. Scale 4 oz. portions of refrigerated meat mixture. Place 1 portion on each flattened cabbage leaf. Fold ends of leaf toward center and roll up firmly. Leaf must be large enough to cover completely and hold securely.
Raisins	5-1/4 oz.	5. Pack rolls tightly in shallow baking pans. Chop 8 oz. small cooked cabbage leaves. Sprinkle over cabbage rolls with raisins.
		6. Bind sauce with diluted cornstarch. Pour sauce over all ingredients and cover pans securely with foil. Bake at 325°F. about 1 hr. Adjust consistency and season, if necessary. Serve 1 roll per portion with 2 oz. ladle of sauce.

Old Fashioned Beef Stew

YIELD: 50 portions	EACH PORTION: 8 oz. stew with 3 oz. meat	
INGREDIENTS	*QUANTITY*	*METHOD*
Chuck or other Boneless Beef, cut (1 in. cubes)	17 lb.	1. Brown meat in hot oil in sauce pot or in pan in oven. Stir occasionally with fork or wooden paddle. When uniformly browned on all sides, add chopped tomatoes, water and seasoning. Simmer about 2 hr. or until tender. Drain meat stock into large pot.
Salad Oil	1 pt.	
Canned Tomatoes (and juice), chopped	1 No. 2½ can	
Water	3 gal.	
Salt	to taste	
Pepper	to taste	
Turnips, yellow (½ in. dice)	3 lb.	2. Add turnips, carrots, celery and coarse cut onions. Simmer until vegetables are nearly cooked; then add potatoes.
Carrots (¾ in. dice)	5 lb.	
Celery (¾ in. diagonal pcs.)	2 b.	
Onions, coarse cut	2 lb.	
Potatoes (¾ in. dice)	7 lb.	
Pearl Onions, medium	50	3. Cook separately.
Tomatoes, canned, whole Italian style	50	4. Heat tomatoes in hotel pan (12- by 12- by 2-in.).
Frozen Green Peas	2½ lb.	5. Cook peas.
		6. When potatoes are cooked, adjust seasoning.
		7. Serve generous 8 oz. ladle of stew in large soup bowl with about 3 oz. cooked meat. Distribute vegetables as evenly as possible. Top each bowl of stew with 1 whole tomato, 1 pearl onion; sprinkle a few cooked peas over serving. Stew may be accompanied by dumplings.

Swiss Steak, Jardiniere

YIELD: 50 portions	EACH PORTION: 5 oz. steak with 2 oz. sauce	
INGREDIENTS	*QUANTITY*	*METHOD*
Salad Oil	1½ pt.	1. Heat 1/8 in. oil in fry pans or skillets; brown steaks on both sides. Place browned steaks in brazier or roast pan and hold.
Bottom Round Steak	50 (5 oz.)	
Bread Flour	12 oz.	2. Put all remaining oil in sauce pan and add flour to make roux. Stir until well blended and lightly browned.
Brown Stock	6½ qt.	3. Deglaze fry pan with 1 pt. brown stock. Add deglazing liquid, rest of brown stock and tomato puree to roux. Cook until sauce is slightly thickened and smooth. Season lightly with salt and pepper. Pour over steaks; bake at 350°F. for 2 hr. or until tender.
Tomato Puree	12 oz.	
Salt	to taste	
Pepper	to taste	
Carrots, cut (1 in. long, ¼ in.wide)	1 lb.	4. Cook carrots, onions and celery together in lightly salted boiling water. Drain and mix with cooked peas.
Onions, cut like carrots	1 lb.	
Celery, cut like carrots	½ lb.	
Frozen Peas, cooked	2½ lb.	
		5. Serve 1 steak per portion with 2 oz. sauce. Garnish with serving spoon of mixed vegetables.

Beef

Roast Sirloin of Beef, right (recipe below)

Swiss Steak in Tomato Sauce, far right (recipe bottom of page)

Roast Sirloin of Beef

YIELD: 50 portions	EACH PORTION: about 7 oz. beef	
INGREDIENTS	*QUANTITY*	*METHOD*

Sirloin of Beef, boneless
Mirepoix:
    Onions, medium cut
    Celery, medium cut
    Carrots, medium cut
Salad Oil
Salt
Pepper
	25 lb.
	
	1 lb.
	8 oz.
	8 oz.
	4 oz.
	to taste
	to taste
		1. Trim sirloin and prepare for oven; be sure to remove cartilage near edge of large part of eye of roast. Place sirloin fat side up on bed of mirepoix in oiled roast pan. Sprinkle with salt and pepper. Insert meat thermometer so bulb reaches center of largest muscle. Place in oven preheated to 350°F.
		2. Cook rare (140°F. on meat thermometer) or medium rare (150°F. on meat thermometer). Cooking time will vary; if roast is rolled and tied, more time will be required.
		3. When cooked, remove to clean pan and hold in warm place but not where meat will continue to cook. Roast should stand 30 min. before carving.

Brown Beef Stock) OR Consomme) hot	1 gal.	4. Pour fat off roast and deglaze with hot stock. Simmer vegetables lightly, keeping au jus as clear as possible. Strain; adjust seasoning. Skim off all fat before serving.
NOTE: If au jus is not required, or if serving with other sauce, mirepoix is not required and deglazing is not necessary. *See color picture, p. 37.*		

Swiss Steak in Tomato Sauce

YIELD: 50 portions	EACH PORTION: 5 oz. steak; 2 oz. sauce	
INGREDIENTS	*QUANTITY*	*METHOD*
Bottom Round Steaks Salad Oil	50 (5 oz. portions) 1½ pt.	1. Heat 1/8 in. oil in fry pans or skillets; add steaks; brown on both sides. Place steaks in brazier or roast pan.
Onions, cut (1 in. long, ¼ in. wide) Celery, cut (1/8- in. wide)	3 lb. 1 lb.	2. Saute onions and celery in remainder of oil in sauce pan 15 min.
Bread Flour Brown Stock Tomatoes, canned, chopped Tomato Puree Salt Pepper	10 oz. 4 qt. 1 No. 10 can ½ No. 10 can to taste to taste	3. Add flour to make roux; cook 5 min. Add Brown Stock and stir until slightly thickened and smooth. Add tomatoes, puree and seasonings. Blend well.
Parsley, fresh, chopped	for garnish	4. Pour sauce over steaks. Bake at 350°F. about 2 hr. or until tender. Serve 1 steak per portion with 2 oz. sauce. Garnish with fresh chopped parsley.
See color picture, p. 40.		

*Roast Ribs of Beef,
au jus, with
Yorkshire Pudding*

Roast Ribs of Beef, au jus, with Yorkshire Pudding

YIELD: 50 portions		EACH PORTION: 8 oz. beef (bone-in)
INGREDIENTS	*QUANTITY*	*METHOD*

Ribs of Beef, oven ready
 	
Mirepoix:
   Onions, medium cut
   Celery, medium cut
   Carrots, medium cut
Salt
Pepper
	2 (about 20 lb. ea., bone in)
	
	1 lb.
	8 oz.
	8 oz.
	to taste
	to taste
		1. Place ribs in roast pan fat side up. Insert meat thermometer. Roast in oven at 350°F. 2 hr. Add mirepoix; season. Cook until thermometer reads 140°F. for rare or 150°F. for medium rare, about 2½ to 3 hr.
		2. Remove to clean pan and hold in warm place. Let stand ½ hr. before serving. Stand roast in carving position on a tray that will hold meat juices until time to serve.

Brown Beef Stock) OR Consomme) hot	½ gal.	3. Pour fat off roast pan and deglaze with hot beef stock or consomme. Simmer vegetables lightly, keeping au jus as clear as possible. Strain and adjust seasoning and skim fat. Make gravy.

Yorkshire Pudding

YIELD: 50 portions		EACH PORTION: about 3 by 4 in.
INGREDIENTS	*QUANTITY*	*METHOD*
Eggs, whole Milk Bread Flour Salt Butter, melted	20 2 qt. 2 lb. 1 oz. 24 oz.	1. Break eggs in mixing bowl; beat well. Add milk; mix well. Add flour and salt; beat until smooth. Beat in melted butter.
Drippings from Roast Beef (fat only)	24 oz.	2. Place 12 oz. drippings in each of 2 15- by 18-in. baking pans. Place pans on range and when smoking hot, divide batter evenly between pans. 3. Place pans in oven at 375°F. on lower shelf or bottom of oven. Do not open oven door for 25 min.; total cooking time about 35 to 40 min. Remove from oven and drain excess fat by tipping pan to pour off excess. Cut in squares to serve, 25 portions per pan.

Beef

Roast Beef Hash, right (recipe below)

New England Boiled Dinner, far right (recipe on facing page)

Roast Beef Hash

YIELD: 25 portions	EACH PORTION: 8 oz.	
INGREDIENTS	*QUANTITY*	*METHOD*
Onions, diced fine Celery, diced fine Salad Oil	1 lb. 8 oz. 5 oz.	1. Saute onions and celery in hot oil in skillet until tender. Cool.
Potatoes, cooked, cold (3/8 in. dice) Roast Beef, cooked, coarsely chopped Salt Pepper	6½ lb. 4½ lb. to taste to taste	2. Combine onions and celery with potatoes and beef. Season to taste.
		3. Pan fry 8 oz. portions in hot frying pan with very little oil. Pan must be very hot when hash is added to prevent sticking. Form in shape of omelet by folding in thirds, edges to center. When heated through and golden brown, place on bake sheets to be reheated at service time. May be served with poached egg.

NOTE: Hash may be baked in pan in oven. For more economical service, meat may be ground and ratio of potatoes increased. Other cooked meats may be substituted for roast beef and the hash named according to the ingredients. When serving plain, or without poached eggs, hash may be sprinkled with fresh chopped parsley at serving time.

Entrecote Bercy

YIELD: 25 portions	EACH PORTION: 6 to 7 oz. steak with 1 oz. Bercy Butter	
INGREDIENTS	*QUANTITY*	*METHOD FOR PREPARING ENTRECOTE BERCY*
Boneless Rib Eye of Beef (small eye) OR Strip Loin	about 12 lb.	1. Cut 25 6 to 7 oz. steaks from rib eye. Refrigerate. 2. Immediately prior to service, remove steaks from refrigerator and saute in a hot pan or cook on a hot grill. Cook to desired doneness and place on warm individual plates or platters. 3. Place a slice of Bercy Butter (about 1 oz.) on top of hot steak and serve immediately. Garnish with a sprig of watercress or fresh parsley.
Bercy Butter: Butter Shallots, minced fine Chives, minced fine Parsley, minced fine Tarragon Leaves, minced fine	 1½ lb. 1 tbsp. 1 tsp. 1 tbsp. 1 tsp.	*METHOD FOR PREPARING BERCY BUTTER* 1. Cream butter until smooth. Add shallots, chives, parsley and tarragon. Form into a long roll about as big around as a 50¢ piece. Wrap firmly in waxed paper and refrigerate until service time.

NOTE: As indicated in text, small steaks are often kept refrigerated until immediately before cooking so that they may be cooked rare and still achieve color. If larger steaks are served (in instances where menu prices permit), this procedure is not necessary.

New England Boiled Dinner

YIELD: 50 portions	EACH PORTION: 3 oz. corned beef, 1 ea. cabbage wedge, potato, turnip slice, pearl onion, whole beet.	
INGREDIENTS	QUANTITY	METHOD
Brisket, gray cure	17 lb.	1. Place brisket in large pot; cover with cold water. Cover and simmer until done, (usually 3½ to 4 hr.), Check each piece of meat separately by inserting fork. Fork should be easy to insert and withdraw when meat is done. Do not overcook. 2. Remove brisket from pot; reserve cooking liquor. If holding for service, cool brisket in cold water, remove and cover with damp towel or foil. Refrigerate.
Beets, whole Carrots, small whole or sliced Cabbage Potatoes, whole peeled, medium Turnip Slices, yellow Pearl Onions, medium, (optional)	1 No.10 can 7 lb. 50 wedges 50 50 (about 7 lb.) 50	3. Heat beets in liquid from can; drain. 4. Cook remaining vegetables separately, using part corned beef stock and part water; drain. Cut cabbage in wedges; do not remove core as it aids in holding cabbage together during cooking. Do not overcook vegetables.
		5. Slice brisket diagonally across grain, holding carving knife at 45° angle. Because grain runs in many directions, turn piece of meat while carving to assure cutting across grain. Reheat in corned beef stock. 6. Serve generous 3 oz. portion on top of cabbage wedge, accompanied by other vegetables.
NOTE: Horseradish Sauce (p. 317) may be served with New England Boiled Dinner. Although gray cure brisket is definitely associated with New England boiled dinner, many operations are substituting Jewish corned beef which has a red cure. This would more correctly be called New York Boiled Dinner.		

Ragout of Beef

YIELD: 50 portions	EACH PORTION: 4 oz. meat, 5 oz. sauce	
INGREDIENTS	QUANTITY	METHOD
Beef, lean, cut (1-in. cubes) Salad Oil	17 lb. 24 oz.	1. Saute meat in hot oil until brown. Transfer to brazier.
Celery, cut (1 in. long, ½ in. wide) Onions, cut (1 in. long, ½ in. wide) Bread Flour Beef Stock, hot Tomato Puree	1 lb. 1 lb. 1 lb. 7 qt. 1 pt.	2. In same pans, saute celery and onions until tender but not browned; add to meat. Add flour to meat and vegetables; stir until well blended. Add hot stock and stir until slightly thickened and smooth. Add tomato puree and blend well. Cover brazier and place in oven at 350°F. about 2 hr. or until meat is tender.
Carrots, Parisienne Turnips, yellow, Parisienne Potatoes, Parisienne Onions, pearl Fresh or Frozen Green Peas Fresh or Frozen Cut Green Beans	100 pcs. 100 pcs. 150 pcs. 50 2½ lb. 2½ lb.	3. Cook remaining vegetables until just tender. Drain vegetables and glaze in butter.
Tomatoes, Italian, canned, drained	50	4. Remove meat from oven and check seasonings. Place drained tomatoes over meat and return to oven without cover for ½ hr. Use green beans as garnish when serving.
NOTE: Balance of vegetables may be kept separate and used as garnish or they may be combined with the stew.		

Beef

Braised Oxtails, right (recipe top of facing page)

London Broil, far right (recipe bottom of facing page)

Roast Top Round of Beef, au jus, right (recipe below)

Roast Top Round of Beef, au jus

YIELD: 50 portions	EACH PORTION: 4 oz.	
INGREDIENTS	QUANTITY	METHOD
Top Round, boneless	20 lb.	1. Cut top round in 2 equal pieces. Tie with butchers twine to retain shape of roast.

Mirepoix:
   Onions, coarse cut
   Celery, coarse cut
   Carrots, coarse cut
Salad Oil
Salt
Pepper
	
	1 lb.
	8 oz.
	8 oz.
	4 oz.
	to taste
	to taste
		2. Place mirepoix in roast pan. Put meat on top of mirepoix; rub with oil. Season lightly with salt and pepper. Insert meat thermometer so bulb reaches center of largest muscle.
		3. Place in oven preheated to 350°F. Turn after 1 hr. Continue cooking until meat thermometer reaches 140°F. (rare) or 150°F. (medium). Roasting will take about 2 hr. although time may vary.
		4. Remove to clean pan; cover with foil or paper. Keep warm but do not allow roast to continue cooking. Skim fat.

Brown Beef Stock OR Consomme Salt	1 gal. to taste	5. Deglaze roast pan with brown beef stock or consomme. (Chicken stock may be used if necessary.) 6. Strain through fine cheesecloth and china cap. Add salt to taste.
		7. Slice meat across grain, serving about 4 oz. per portion with a 2 oz. ladle of au jus.

Braised Oxtails

YIELD: 50 portions	EACH PORTION: 1 lb. plus garnish	
INGREDIENTS	QUANTITY	METHOD
Oxtails, cut at joints Salt Pepper Beef Suet, rendered	50 lb. 1½ oz. 1 tsp. 12 oz.	1. Wash oxtails in cold water, dry with towel. Place cut oxtail pieces in large roast pan. Season with salt and pepper. Coat with fat from rendered beef suet.
Flour Onions, chopped coarsely Carrots, chopped coarsely Celery, chopped coarsely Garlic Cloves, chopped fine	1 lb. 2 lb. 1 lb. 1 lb. 4	2. Place meat in oven heated to 350°F. Roast uncovered; turn frequently to brown evenly. Add vegetables, brown lightly. Stir flour into pan drippings. Allow flour to brown. (Watch carefully to avoid burning.)
Brown Beef Stock Tomato Puree Bouquet Garni	1½ gal. 1 No. 5 can	3. Add beef stock and tomato puree, stirring well to form a thick gravy. Add the bouquet garni and cook for another 10 to 15 min. Remove from oven.
Sherry Wine Parsley, chopped	1 pt. for garnish	4. With skimmer, transfer ox joints into braising pot. Strain sauce from roasting pan through china cap into braising pot with ox joints. Add more beef stock if needed to thin sauce or to fully cover ox joints. Cover, bring to boil; reduce heat to simmering; cook until meat is tender. 5. While ox joints are cooking skim fat from time to time. When joints are done, remove to bain marie for serving in casseroles. Add sherry wine. Sprinkle servings with chopped parsley.

VARIATIONS: A garniture of vegetables may be added to the oxtails, such as Parisienne, Bourgeoise, or button mushrooms. In some instances, glazed onions, carrots and white turnips are served. Small-tourne, boiled or Parisienne Potatoes may be served. Always sprinkle with chopped parsley.

London Broil

YIELD: 50 portions	EACH PORTION: 5 oz.	
INGREDIENTS	QUANTITY	METHOD

Flank Steaks
 	
Marinade:
  Salad Oil
  Salt
  Pepper
  Paprika
	20 lb. (1½ to 2 lb. flanks)
	
	1 qt.
	to taste
	to taste
	2 tbsp.
		1. Trim flanks very close; remove all skin, membrane and fat.
		2. Pour marinade over steaks, refrigerate and let marinate for a few hours prior to service.

		3. Flanks broil best if taken directly from refrigeration to broiler; they cook more slowly and have better outside color. Place on preheated broiler rack at highest point to assure best color. Cook 3 to 5 min. on each side, depending on thickness of meat. (London Broil is cooked rare when possible; when it is overcooked, it is no longer tender. This is the one steak guests are requested not to order in different degrees of doneness.) 4. Cut steak in very thin diagonal slices (cut across the grain).

NOTE: London Broil is usually served with a sauce such as Mushroom Sauce (p. 313) or Bordelaise Sauce (p. 312).

See color picture, p. 37.

*Braised Beef a la
Mode Parisienne*

Braised Beef a la Mode Parisienne

YIELD: 50 portions		EACH PORTION: 4 oz. with vegetables and sauce
INGREDIENTS	*QUANTITY*	*METHOD*
Salad Oil	to brown	1. Heat oil.
Beef Rounds, tied	22 lb.	2. Dredge meat in seasoned flour and brown in oil on
Flour	as needed	all sides.
Salt	to taste	3. Add mirepoix and saute until tender.
Pepper	to taste	4. Add tomatoes, beef stock, sachet bag.
Mirepoix:		5. Bring to boil, cover and bake at 400°F. for 3½ hr.
Celery, coarsely chopped	1 lb.	
Carrots, coarsely chopped	1 lb.	
Onions, coarsely chopped	1 lb.	
Tomatoes, crushed	1 No. 10 can	
Beef Stock	2 qt.	
Sachet Bag:		
Whole Peppercorns	10	
Oregano	1 oz.	
Silver Skin Onions	100	6. Parboil all vegetables, then saute in hot fat until
Potatoes, Parisienne cut	100	light brown. Place in oven until done.
Carrots, Parisienne cut	100	7. When meat is done, remove from brazier and pass
Turnips, Parisienne cut	100	sauce through china cap. Skim excess fat.
Frozen Peas	2½ lb.	8. Slice meat 1/8 in. thick. Garnish with Parisienne
		vegetables and peas.
		9. Serve with 2 oz. sauce per portion.

Tournedos Rossini

Tournedos Rossini are two 4 oz. steaks cut from the filet of beef—about 1½ in. thick.

They are prepared with a thin slice of larding pork or a slice of bacon tied around each steak.

They are sauteed in clarified butter over a brisk fire, then set on a round piece of toast. A slice of foie gras, slightly smaller than the steak, is placed on top of each steak. This is topped with a sauteed mushroom cap and garnished with 1 truffle slice. This item is placed under broiler to quickly heat foie gras.

Tournedos Rossini are accompanied by Madeira Sauce below.

Sauce Madere (Madeira Sauce)

YIELD: about 1 qt.

INGREDIENTS	QUANTITY	METHOD
Butter	1 oz.	1. Melt the butter in a thick-bottomed sauce pan, add ham and cook for a few minutes; then add onions, carrot, celery and garlic and fry briskly until light brown.
Ham)	1 tbsp.	
Onion) all	1 small	
Carrot) coarsely	1 small	
Celery) chopped	1 stalk	
Garlic)	1 clove	
Flour	½ oz.	2. Stir in the flour until lightly brown, and the beef broth and all remaining ingredients except Madeira and salt and let simmer for 30 min. During the cooking, fat will come to the surface. Remove it with a spoon, then strain. This sauce should have the consistency of cream.
Beef Broth	1 qt.	
Tomatoes, coarsely chopped	2	
Parsley, coarsely chopped	1 sprig	
Thyme, coarsely chopped	1 sprig	
Bay Leaf	¼	
Peppercorns, whole	3	
Madeira Wine	8 oz.	3. Deglaze the pan in which the Tournedos have been sauteed with the Madeira wine. Add the sauce and season to taste. Serve 1 to 2 tbsp. for Tournedos Rossini or other meat.
Salt	to taste	

Potted Swiss Steak, Smothered Onions

YIELD: 50 portions	**EACH PORTION:** 5 oz. with 4 oz. sauce and onions	
INGREDIENTS	QUANTITY	METHOD
Salad Oil	1 qt.	1. Pour 1/8 in. oil in large fry pans or skillets and heat. Add 5 oz. steaks and brown.
Bottom Round Steaks	50	2. Place browned steaks in brazier or roast pan.
Bread Flour	12 oz.	3. Put remainder of oil in sauce pot and add flour to make roux. Cook 10 min.
Brown Stock, hot (p. 271)	4 qt.	4. Add hot stock to roux and stir until thickened and smooth. Add tomato puree.
Tomato Puree	1 pt.	5. Season lightly and pour sauce over steaks. Bake at 350°F. for about 2 hr. or until tender.
Salt	to taste	
Pepper	to taste	
Onions, (sliced 1/8 in. thick)	8 lb.	6. Saute onions in butter until soft and lightly browned.
Butter	12 oz.	7. When meat is cooked, remove from oven and adjust seasoning. Spread onions evenly over top of meat and hold for service.
OR Salad Oil		8. Serve one 5 oz. steak per portion with 4 oz. sauce and serving spoon of onions.

Sauerbraten No. 1

Sauerbraten No. 1

YIELD: 50 portions		**EACH PORTION**: 4 oz. beef with 2 oz. sauce
INGREDIENTS	*QUANTITY*	*METHOD*
STEP NO. 1: Cold Water Red Wine Vinegar Onions, sliced thin Carrots, sliced thin Celery, sliced thin Brown Sugar Garlic Cloves, chopped Salt Bay Leaves Peppercorns, crushed Bottom Round of Beef, lean, trimmed, cut to size of eye of round	 6 qt. 2 qt. 2 lb. 1 lb. 8 oz. 8 oz. 8 2 oz. 6 1 tsp. 18 lb.	1. Put all ingredients in crock and stir well. Place meat in crock. Cover. Place in refrigerator and marinate for at least 72 hr.
Salad Oil OR Lard	8 oz.	2. Remove meat from marinade, wipe dry; brown in hot oil in fry pan or skillet. Remove to large heavy pot or brazier. 3. Strain marinade. Put vegetables and spices in with meat. Add 5 qt. marinade to meat. Cover. Bring to boil and simmer for 1½ hr. or until tender. When meat is done, transfer to dry pan, cover with damp cloth and keep warm.
Gingersnaps, crushed	1 lb.	4. Whip crushed gingersnaps into the sauce and let stand until gingersnaps are soft and blended with sauce. Strain and hold for service. If desired, 4 oz. burgundy wine may be added to the sauce. Adjust consistency as required. 5. Cut meat across grain the same as pot roast and serve with 2 oz. ladle of sauce. Potato Pancakes (p. 212) or Potato Dumplings (p. 217) and applesauce or braised red cabbage are often served with Sauerbraten.
See color picture, p. 39.		

Sauerbraten No. 2

YIELD: 50 portions		EACH PORTION: about 4 oz. beef
INGREDIENTS	*QUANTITY*	*METHOD*
STEP NO: 1 Cold Water Red Wine Vinegar Burgundy Wine Onions, sliced thin Carrots, sliced thin Celery, sliced thin Brown Sugar Garlic Cloves, chopped Salt Bay Leaves Peppercorns, crushed Whole Cloves Bottom Round of Beef, lean, trimmed, cut to size of eye of round	 3 qt. 1 qt. 1 qt. 2 lb. 1 lb. ½ lb. ½ lb. 6 2 oz. 6 1 tbsp. 10 18 lb.	1. Put all ingredients into crock and stir well. Place meat in crock. Cover. Place in refrigerator for at least 72 hr.
Salad Oil OR Lard	8 oz.	2. Remove meat, wipe dry; brown in hot oil in fry pan or skillet. 3. Remove to large heavy pot or brazier. Place marinade in with meat. Cover, bring to boil and simmer for 1½ hr. or until tender. When meat is done, transfer to dry pan, cover with a damp cloth and keep warm.
Gingersnaps, crushed	1 lb.	4. Whip crushed gingersnaps into liquid, stir until smooth and slightly thickened. Strain and hold for service. 5. Cut meat across grain (like Pot Roast) and serve with 2 oz. ladle of sauce. Potato Dumplings (p. 217) or Potato Pancakes (p. 212) and braised red cabbage or applesauce are often served with Sauerbraten.

LAMB CHART

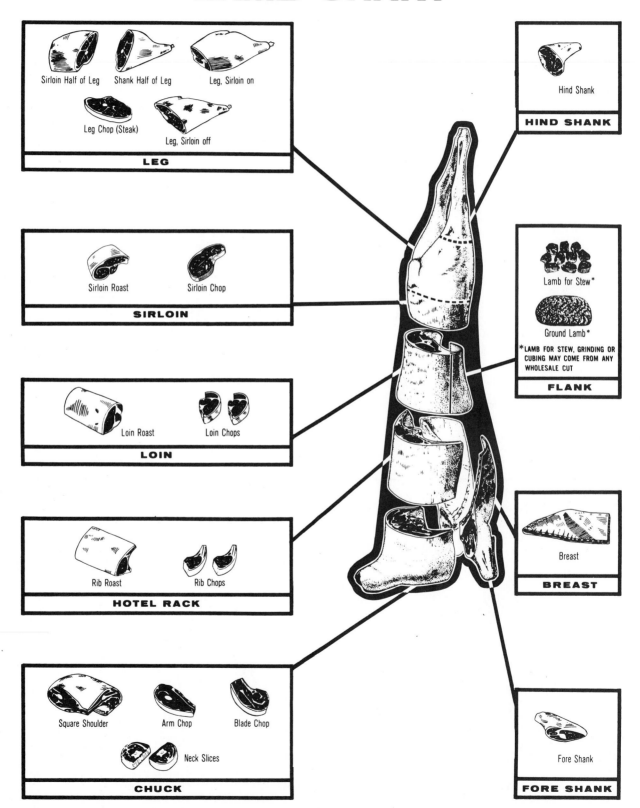

LEG
- Sirloin Half of Leg
- Shank Half of Leg
- Leg, Sirloin on
- Leg Chop (Steak)
- Leg, Sirloin off

SIRLOIN
- Sirloin Roast
- Sirloin Chop

LOIN
- Loin Roast
- Loin Chops

HOTEL RACK
- Rib Roast
- Rib Chops

CHUCK
- Square Shoulder
- Arm Chop
- Blade Chop
- Neck Slices

HIND SHANK
- Hind Shank

FLANK
- Lamb for Stew *
- Ground Lamb *

*LAMB FOR STEW, GRINDING OR CUBING MAY COME FROM ANY WHOLESALE CUT

BREAST
- Breast

FORE SHANK
- Fore Shank

Argentine Lamb Chops

Irish Lamb Stew

Osso Bucco

Navarin of Spring Lamb

Rolled Braised Shoulder of Lamb, Mint Jelly

Epigramme of Lamb

Shish Kebob

amb

The increasing popularity of lamb has brought to the fore new formulas and old time favorites utilizing a variety of the lamb cuts available. Shish Kebab, served flaming on a sword-like skewer, has long reigned in many well known establishments. Others among the dishes shown above are low cost, high profit items that also merit recognition on the menu as specialties of the house.

THE PROFESSIONAL CHEF

Techniques for Lamb Cookery

Lamb Grades Lamb is graded as PRIME, CHOICE, GOOD, COMMERCIAL. Grades lower than this are not used in commercial establishments. There is very little Prime on the market and most quality operations purchase Choice. Most lamb falls in the six weeks to ten months old bracket but may run up to one year old. Yearlings are over one year old, but less than two years old, averaging twenty months.

Mutton is usually one and a half to two years of age or older. Its protein is slightly less than beef.

Lamb is highly perishable and picks up foreign odors and flavors readily.

Some lamb cuts carry an extremely thin membrane or covering called fell. It is usually removed from chops for broiling but is left on legs and roasts to aid in maintaining their shape and moisture while roasting.

LAMB A L'INDIENNE

Sauté onions in butter, then add flour to make a roux. It is important that curry powder be cooked briefly in butter to develop full flavor and avoid a "raw" taste.

For Lamb a l'Indienne, cut lean boneless lamb into cubes. Blanch lamb in boiling salted water and drain. Cook in additional boiling salted water until lamb is tender.

Add apples, tomatoes and finely chopped ham. Strain stock from lamb into curry mixture. Cook ½ hour and skim. Pass sauce through china cap to insure smoothness.

Add cream, season to taste and serve over fluffy cooked rice. Lamb a l'Indienne should be served with a variety of condiments: chutney, chopped peanuts, coconut. (Recipe on facing page.)

Lamb a l'Indienne

YIELD: 50 portions		EACH PORTION: 4 oz. meat
INGREDIENTS	QUANTITY	METHOD
Lamb, boneless and cubed Water Salt Water Salt	17 lb. 2 gal. 2 oz. 2 gal. 2 oz.	1. Blanch cubed lamb in 2 gal. water and 2 oz. salt; drain. 2. Add the second 2 gal. water and 2 oz. salt. Cook until meat is tender. Hold lamb in warm place. 3. Reduce stock by about ½.
Butter Onions, chopped Curry Powder Flour Apples, raw, with skins, seeded Ham, chopped fine Tomatoes, medium	1 lb. 3 lb. 4 tbsp. 8 oz. 6 ¼ lb. 1 No. 2½ can	4. Melt butter in brazier. Add onions and saute. Stir in curry powder; add flour to make roux. Add apples and ham, then tomatoes. 5. Strain stock from cooked lamb into curry mixture. Cook ½ hr. and skim. Strain sauce over lamb through fine china cap.
Cream	½ gal.	6. Add cream; season to taste. 7. Serve with rice and a variety of condiments such as chutney, chopped salted peanuts, flaked coconut, lemon or lime wedges and chopped raw onion.

Roast Stuffed Shoulder of Lamb

YIELD: 50 portions		EACH PORTION: 5 oz. lamb, 1 oz. stuffing, 2 oz. gravy
INGREDIENTS	QUANTITY	METHOD
Basic Bread Stuffing (p. 113) Lamb Shoulders, boned, trimmed of excess fat	1/3 recipe 25 lb.	1. Divide stuffing equally among lamb shoulders and roll mixture inside each shoulder. Tie securely with butcher's twine.
Oil Salt Pepper Rosemary	4 oz. to taste to taste 2 tsp.	2. Place lamb in greased roasting pan; rub outside of each shoulder with oil, salt, pepper, rosemary. Roast in preheated 350°F. oven for about 2½ hr.

Mirepoix:
   Onions, coarsely chopped
   Celery, coarsely chopped
   Carrots, coarsely chopped
	
	1 lb.
	1/2 lb.
	1/2 lb.
		3. At end of 1 hr., turn lamb on opposite side and add mirepoix.
		4. When done, remove meat from pan. Cover with clean, damp towel; hold in warm place.

Bread Flour Brown Beef Stock (p. 271) OR Lamb Stock if available	10 oz. 5 qt.	5. Pour about 10 oz. oil and fat from roast pan into a saucepan and add flour to make roux. Cook 10 min. browning lightly. 6. Place pan in which meat was roasted on range and add stock. Scrape bottom of pan to loosen little brown particles known as fond. Simmer until vegetables are tender. Strain. 7. Add strained stock to cooked roux, stirring until thickened and smooth. Strain again through fine china cap, adjust seasoning and hold for service. 8. Slice across grain, so that stuffing shows in center of each slice. Serve with 2 oz. gravy.

Lamb

Shish Kebab (recipe below)

Irish Lamb Stew No. 1 (recipe on facing page)

Shish Kebab

YIELD: 20 portions	EACH PORTION: 1 skewer	
INGREDIENTS	*QUANTITY*	*METHOD*

Marinade:
  Salad Oil
  Olive Oil
  Vinegar
  Lemon Juice
  Garlic, chopped
  Salt
  Pepper
  Marjoram
  Thyme
  Oregano
Lamb Leg, boned (1-in. cubes)
	
	2 pt.
	1 pt.
	12 oz.
	4 oz.
	2 tbsp.
	2 tbsp.
	2 tsp.
	½ tsp.
	½ tsp.
	½ tsp.
	5 lb.
		1. Mix all marinade ingredients; pour over lamb and marinate several hours or overnight.

Mushroom Caps, large Salad Oil	40 pieces for sauteing	2. Saute mushroom caps slightly in oil.
Pearl Onions	40 pieces	3. Blanch onions if fresh. May use canned onions.
Green Peppers, large dice, blanched Tomatoes, fresh (¾ in. thick slices)	40 pieces 40 pieces	4. Place ingredients on long skewer as follows: (Do not crowd on skewer) tomato, lamb, mushroom, onion, lamb, pepper, onion, lamb, pepper, mushroom, lamb, tomato. Place in marinade until ready to broil. 5. Drain well and place under hot broiler about 10 min., turning as needed to cook uniformly. Do not burn. 6. Lamb should be medium unless otherwise indicated. Serve on bed of rice pilaf.
See color picture, p. 67.		

Irish Lamb Stew No. 1

YIELD: 50 portions		EACH PORTION: about 10 oz. with vegetables and sauce
INGREDIENTS	QUANTITY	METHOD
Water, boiling Lamb Fores, lean, cut (½-in. squares)	2 gal. 17 lb.	1. Place meat in 2 gal. of rapidly boiling water. Stir with wooden paddle to separate. As water returns to boil, remove scum that forms. Continue to remove scum until clear. Simmer meat for 1½ hr. or until tender.
Pearl Onions, medium Potatoes, Parisienne White Turnips, Parisienne Carrots, Parisienne	5 lb. 2 qt. 1 qt. 1 qt.	2. Cook each vegetable separately in boiling water, drain. Add liquor from cooked carrots and onions to meat.
Butter, melted Bread Flour Salt Pepper	20 oz. 20 oz. to taste to taste	3. Place butter in heavy pot and add flour to make roux. Do not brown. When meat is cooked, strain stock from meat into roux. Bring to a boil. Adjust seasoning and add vegetables, mixing gently with wooden paddle. 4. Serve in bowl or large casserole or in a soup plate.

NOTE: This stew often made with diced vegetables and without a roux and served in a bowl. It can also be thickened by making a puree of part of the potatoes and adding it to the stew.

Irish Lamb Stew No. 2

YIELD: 50 portions		EACH PORTION: 4 oz. lamb, 4 oz. vegetables
INGREDIENTS	QUANTITY	METHOD

Lean Lamb, cut in 1 in. cubes
    (from Dutch cut or shoulder
    and neck)
Salt
Pepper
	17 lb.
	
	to taste
	to taste
		1. Place meat in brazier, season with salt and pepper. cover with water, place over high heat and bring to a boil. Stir with wooden paddle and boil 5 to 8 min. Remove scum. With a clean, damp towel, wipe residue from inside of pot. Simmer 1 hr.

Potatoes, peeled, sliced thin	8 lb.	2. Wash and drain sliced potatoes.
Onions, peeled, sliced thin	6 lb.	3. In brazier, make 1 layer of sliced onions, 1 layer of meat and 1 layer of sliced potatoes. Repeat in same order until all ingredients are placed in brazier, end with a layer of potatoes nicely arranged.
Salt Pepper Water or White Stock	to taste to taste	4. Season with salt and pepper. Cover with water or white stock if available. Cover and bring to a boil; reduce heat to simmering. Cook until meat is tender, about 1 to 1½ hr. Check seasoning.
Parsley, chopped Dumplings (p. 77) (optional)	1 bunch 50	5. To serve, fill individual casseroles or portion on plates. Sprinkle with chopped parsley.

Lamb

Epigramme of Lamb, right (recipe on facing page)

Navarin of Spring Lamb (French Lamb Stew), far right (recipe bottom facing page)

Irish Lamb Stew No. 3

YIELD: 50 portions	EACH PORTION: 4 oz. meat and vegetables	
INGREDIENTS	QUANTITY	METHOD
Water, cold Lamb Fores (¾ in. cubes), blanched Potatoes, thinly sliced	2 gal. 17 lb. 6 lb.	1. Place meat in 2 gal. cold water. Stir with wooden paddle to separate. As water boils, remove scum that forms. Continue to remove scum until clear. Add sliced potatoes and simmer 1½ hr. or until meat is tender.
Pearl Onions, medium Potatoes Parisienne White Turnips (½ in. cubes) Carrots (½ in. cubes) Salt Pepper Worcestershire Sauce	100 100 1 pt. 1 qt. to taste to taste to taste	2. Cook each vegetable separately in boiling salted water and drain. 3. Adjust seasoning for meat and add vegetables, mixing gently with wooden paddle.
Parsley, chopped	6 oz.	4. Serve in bowl or large casserole or on plate. Sprinkle with chopped parsley.
NOTE: This stew is often served with dumplings, (p.77).		
See color picture, p. 67.		

Curried Lamb with Rice and Chutney

YIELD: 50 portions	EACH PORTION: 4 oz. of lamb	
INGREDIENTS	QUANTITY	METHOD

Lamb Fores, lean, cut (1-in. cubes)
Water, cold
Sachet Bag:
    Thyme
    Bay Leaf
    Cloves, whole
	18 lb.
	2 gal.
	
	1 tsp.
	1
	6
		1. Place meat in cold water. Stir with wooden paddle to separate. As water boils, remove scum that forms. Continue to remove scum until stock is clear. Add sachet bag and cover. Simmer 1½ to 2 hr.

Onions, small dice Butter, melted Bread Flour Curry Powder	2 lb. 2 lb. 1½ lb. ¾ oz.	2. Saute onions in butter in large sauce pot. Cook until tender. Add flour, curry powder; cook 10 min. 3. When meat is cooked, remove sachet bag and strain stock into roux, stirring to keep smooth. Adjust seasoning and consistency; if curry flavor is not strong enough, dissolve additional curry in cold water to remove lumps before adding to sauce.
		4. Combine meat with sauce. Serve with rice pilaf and chutney.

Epigramme of Lamb

YIELD: 10 portions	EACH PORTION: 2 triangles as described below	
INGREDIENTS	*QUANTITY*	*METHOD*
Breast of Lamb	10 lb.	1. Trim superfluous fat from breast of lamb; wash well in cold water. Do not remove bones. Blanch in boiling water for 15 min. Place in cold water until cold.

Mirepoix:
    Carrots, sliced coarsely
    Onions, sliced coarsely
    Celery, sliced coarsely
    Garlic Cloves, chopped
    Garlic Cloves, whole
Salt
Water
	
	8 oz.
	8 oz.
	4 oz.
	2
	2
	½ oz.
	2 gal.
		2. Add mirepoix and salt to water in saucepan. Bring to a fast boil. Add blanched breast of lamb; simmer until meat is tender, about 1 to 1½ hr. Remove from heat. Allow meat to cool slightly in its juices.
		3. When cool enough to handle, remove meat. Remove all bones, nerves and cooked fat from meat. Place trimmed meat in deep pan. Place another pan over meat. Add weights or a saucepan of cold water to press meat to thickness of ¾ in. Refrigerate until firm.

Flour Egg Wash Fresh White Bread Crumbs Oil	8 oz. 2 qt. 2 lb. for deep frying	4. Cut pressed meat in triangle shapes, 5 in. long, 3½ in. wide at base. Dredge in flour. Dip in egg wash; bread with fresh bread crumbs. 5. Cook in deep fat fryer until brown and crisp. Serve with Tomato Sauce, p. 318.

NOTE: One epigramme of lamb may be served with one broiled French lamb chop and grilled bacon as a combination luncheon plate. Epigramme of Veal from breast of veal may also be prepared in the same manner.

See color picture, p. 67.

Navarin of Spring Lamb

YIELD: 50 portions	EACH PORTION: 4 oz. lamb plus vegetable garnish and sauce	
INGREDIENTS	*QUANTITY*	*METHOD*
Salad Oil Lamb Fores, trimmed cut (1 in. cubes)	1 qt. 17 lb.	1. Pour 1/8 in. oil into large fry pans or skillets and heat. Add meat and brown on all sides. Place browned meat in brazier or roast pan.
Bread Flour Brown Stock, hot (p. 271) Sachet Bag	1 lb. 7 qt. 1	2. Add remaining oil. Add flour, blending well. Add hot stock. Cook on range until thickened and smooth. Add sachet bag, cover and bake at 350°F. for 1 hr.
Carrots, Parisienne Pearl Onions, medium White Turnips, Parisienne Butter	100 pieces 50 100 pieces for sauteing	3. Cook carrots, onions and turnips separately in boiling salted water until half done. Drain well and saute in butter to finish cooking.
Salt Pepper Tomatoes, canned, drained Parsley, fresh, chopped	to taste to taste 1½ No. 10 cans for garnish	4. Remove lamb stew from oven, season with salt and pepper and place tomatoes in large pieces on top of meat. Return to oven uncovered and continue cooking until meat is tender (about ¾ hr.). 5. Serve in casseroles with a piece of tomato on top accompanied by heated onion and 2 pcs. each carrots and turnip. Sprinkle with freshly chopped parsley.

NOTE: In the original recipe the vegetables are cooked with lamb which results in excellent flavor. The above method provides a more attractive product.

See color picture, p. 67.

Lamb

*Argentine Lamb
Chops, right
(recipe below)*

*Braised Shoulder
of Lamb Bretonne,
far right (recipe
bottom of page)*

Argentine Lamb Chops

YIELD: 50 portions		EACH PORTION: 11 oz.
INGREDIENTS	*QUANTITY*	*METHOD*
Lamb Racks, whole, trimmed Black Pepper, whole, ground	32 lb. to taste	1. Cut racks of lamb into 50 11 oz. portions (see note). Season with black pepper.
		2. Broil chops 7 to 8 min. on each side. Serve with Maitre d'Hotel Butter (p. 323).
NOTE: Argentine Lamb Chops are prepared by cutting across entire rack between the bones. Two chops are joined by backbone.		
See color picture, p. 67.		

Braised Shoulder of Lamb Bretonne

YIELD: 50 portions		EACH PORTION: 4 oz. lamb
INGREDIENTS	*QUANTITY*	*METHOD*
California Pea Beans Bouquet Garni	6 lb.	1. Soak beans overnight. Next day cook beans al dente with bouquet garni in 5 to 6 gal. of water.
Pesto (p. 88) Shallot Butter Onions, finely chopped Parsley, chopped Celery Hearts, chopped Garlic, minced fine White Wine	8 oz. 4 oz. 1 lb. 2¼ oz. 4 oz. 2 tbsp. 1½ pt.	2. Smother pesto and shallot butter. Add onions, cook until transparent. Add chopped parsley, celery hearts and garlic; cook 5 min. Then add wine and cook slowly ½ hr.
Whole Tomatoes Brown Sauce (p. 312) Salt Pepper Worcestershire Sauce	1 No. 10 can 1 pt. to taste to taste to taste	3. Drain tomatoes, add juice to cooked ingredients in Step 2. Add Brown Sauce and bring to a boil. 4. Cut whole tomatoes in small squares and add. Add cooked, drained pea beans. Season with salt, pepper, worcestershire sauce.
Shoulder of Lamb, boned and rolled	18 lb.	5. Roast lamb at 350°F. about 2 hr. until nearly done. Prepare pan gravy from lamb drippings in roasting pan. Reserve gravy for service.
		6. Combine all ingredients except gravy. Cover and place in oven at 400°F. until done or until beans become dry and take up liquid.
Parsley, chopped	for garnish	7. Remove lamb, slice into 1/8 in. slices. Place slices on the prepared beans. Cover lightly with pan gravy and garnish with chopped parsley.

Rolled Braised Lamb Shoulder

YIELD: 50 portions	EACH PORTION: 4 oz. lamb, 2 oz. gravy	
INGREDIENTS	*QUANTITY*	*METHOD*

Lamb Shoulders, boned, rolled, tied
Salad Oil
Mirepoix:
   Onions, coarsely chopped
   Celery, coarsely chopped
   Carrots, coarsely chopped
	18 to 20 lb.
	
	8 oz.
	
	1 lb.
	8 oz.
	8 oz.
		1. Brown meat on all sides and on ends in hot oil in fry pans or skillets. Place meat in a brazier or roast pan that has a cover. Add mirepoix and brown.

Brown Stock (p. 271) Tomato Puree Rosemary	5 qt. 8 oz. 3 tsp.	2. Add Brown Stock, tomato puree and rosemary. Cover and simmer for 2 hr. or until done (on range or in oven at 350°F.) 3. Remove meat and place in storage pan; cover and keep warm until serving time.
Bread Flour Salt	10 oz. to taste	4. Skim fat from stock in which lamb was cooked and place in saucepan. Add flour to make roux; cook for 10 min. Add enough stock from lamb (about 5 qt.)to make a slightly thickened sauce. Adjust consistency if necessary, correct seasoning and strain.

Garnish (Jardiniere):
   Frozen Peas, cooked
   Carrots, medium dice, cooked
   Celery, medium dice, cooked
	
	2 lb.
	1 lb.
	1 lb.
		5. Slice lamb 1/8 in. thick. Serve 4 oz. portion topped with 2 oz. gravy. Garnish with Jardiniere vegetables over gravy (use level serving spoon, about 3/4 oz. per portion).

See color picture, p. 67.		

Broiled Lamb Patties

YIELD: 50 portions	EACH PORTION: 1 patty (5 oz. ea.)	
INGREDIENTS	*QUANTITY*	*METHOD*
Salad Oil Onions, finely chopped Celery, finely chopped	½ pt. 12 oz. 1 lb.	1. Saute onions and celery in oil.
Bread, fresh, trimmed, cubed Milk Eggs, whole	4 oz. 1 pt. 8	2. Mix bread, milk and raw eggs thoroughly but lightly in large pan or mixing bowl until smooth.
Lamb Fores, lean, ground Oregano, crushed Parsley, chopped Salt Pepper Bacon, slices Oil	12 lb. 1 tsp. 3 oz. to taste to taste 50 4 oz.	3. Add meat, seasoning, parsley, celery and onions and blend well. 4. Form patties. 5. Wrap a slice of bacon around each patty and secure with toothpick. Place patties on lightly greased bake sheet and place under broiler, keeping rack low and down from source of heat. Brown both sides of patties. Finish patties in oven at 400°F. for about 20 min. Cook well but do not dry out.

Lamb

Roast Leg of Lamb, Boulangere, right (recipe below)

Lamb Chop Mixed Grill, far right (recipe on facing page)

Roast Leg of Lamb, Boulangere

YIELD: 50 portions	**EACH PORTION:** 3 to 3½ oz. sliced lamb with potatoes, gravy	
INGREDIENTS	*QUANTITY*	*METHOD*
Lamb Legs, bone in (about 7 lb. ea.) Marjoram Thyme Rosemary Sage Garlic, slivered	4 1 tsp. 1 tsp. 1 tsp. 1 tsp. ½ tsp.	1. Before tying, rub with marjoram, thyme, rosemary and sage; insert garlic in meat. Place in roast pan, fat side down. Bake at 350°F. for about ½ hr. Turn and roast for ½ hr.

Mirepoix:
   Onions, medium cut
   Carrots, medium cut
   Celery, medium cut
	
	1 lb.
	½ lb.
	½ lb.
		2. Add Mirepoix and continue roasting for an additional half hour.

Onions, sliced Butter Potatoes, peeled, sliced (1/8 in. thick) Salt Pepper Stock, chicken, beef or lamb (if available), hot	4 lb. 6 oz. 15 lb. to taste to taste 6 qt.	3. Saute sliced onions lightly in butter. Season raw, sliced potatoes with salt and pepper and mix well with onions. Place in 2 hotel pans. Pour about 1 qt. stock in each pan. 4. Remove lamb legs and place 2 on top of each pan of potatoes. Wire racks may be placed on top of each pan of potatoes and lamb placed on racks. 5. Bake at 350°F. about 1 to 1½ hr. or until potatoes are done and lamb is 140°F (rare); 160°F. (medium) or 180°F. (well done). Additional stock may be added to keep potatoes from drying out. Potatoes should absorb stock. 6. While lamb is cooking, deglaze original roast pan with remainder of stock and simmer until vegetables (mirepoix) are tender. Strain and remove all grease. Use as pan gravy. Gravy may be thickened with roux if desired. 7. Serve about 3 to 3½ oz. of sliced lamb with generous portion potatoes and pan gravy. Leg of Lamb slices may be placed at opposite ends of large oval casserole or on a plate. Accompany with mint jelly.
See color picture, p. 29.		

Lamb Chop Mixed Grill

YIELD: 50 portions	EACH PORTION: 1 chop, 1 sausage link, 1 slice bacon, 1 slice liver, mushroom cap, ½ tomato	
INGREDIENTS	*QUANTITY*	*METHOD*
Sausage Links	50	1. Separate sausages, place in baking pan and pierce with fork to prevent spitting. Bake at 400°F. about 15 min. Remove to clean pan and hold in warm place. Save grease from sausage for other use.
Bacon Slices	50	2. Place bacon slices on sheet pan and cook under low heat on broiler or in oven. Turn once. When cooked, remove from pan, drain well and hold for service. Reserve bacon fat.
Mushroom Caps Butter	50 for caps	3. Place mushroom caps in a greased pan, brush with butter and cook under broiler or in oven. When cooked, remove and keep hot.
Tomatoes, fresh Bread Crumbs Paprika Butter, melted	25 8 oz. for topping for topping	4. Wash tomatoes; remove stem end. Cut tomatoes in half crosswise. Place on buttered sheetpan, cut side up. Sprinkle top of tomatoes with bread crumbs and paprika and drizzle with melted butter. Place under broiler for a few minutes to brown crumbs. Then bake at 400°F. for 10 min.
Salad Oil Lamb Chops	for chops 50	5. Oil lamb chops and place on preheated grill or broiler When brown, turn and brown other side. Cook little less than medium to allow for reheating, if necessary. Remove and hold in warm place.
Calves Liver Slices Flour Bacon Fat	50 for dredging for sauteing	6. Dredge skinned and deveined liver slices in flour and saute in hot fry pan or skillet in bacon fat. Brown both sides, but do not use excessive heat as this forms a hard outer crust. If serving immediately, cook medium. If reheating, cook less than medium to start. Usually cook to guest's specifications.
Parsley	for garnish	7. Arrange all items carefully on plate. Reheat if necessary. Garnish with fresh parsley.

Dumplings for Stew, Pie, Etc.

YIELD: about 30 dumplings	EACH PORTION: 1 oz. dumpling	
INGREDIENTS	*QUANTITY*	*METHOD*
Cake Flour Baking Powder Salt	1 lb. 4 tsp. 1 tsp.	1. Combine and sift flour, baking powder and salt.
Milk Parsley, chopped (optional)	about 1 pt. 2 tbsp.	2. Add about 1 pt. milk and mix lightly. Do not over-mix. Consistency should be slightly softer than biscuit dough. 3. Drop 1 oz. portions from spoon or No. 40 scoop about 1 in. apart in hot thickened sauce. Cover and cook for 20 to 25 min.
NOTE: FOR STEAMING, reduce milk so dough is stiffer.		

Marketed in many different forms — fresh, cured and smoked, and salted — pork lends itself to many varied and popular dishes. It is available the year around, but the season of greatest abundance is in the late fall and early winter months.

As practically all pork on the market comes from young hogs, pork cuts are fairly uniform in quality. Pork from government-inspected plants is stamped "U.S. Inspected and Passed."

The lean of high quality fresh pork is a light, grayish-pink color, mottled with fat. Both the flesh and fat are firm. The bones are soft with a slight tinge of red.

Pork cuts on the market today take into consideration the demands of a "fat conscious" public for lean pork. To meet this demand, several of the principal cuts now carry a closer trim than in former years.

The demand for leaner cuts has also led to the breeding of a new meat-type hog characterized by high muscular development which yields pork cuts with a high proportion of lean to fat. The determining value of pork cuts today is the distinction between muscle and fat. To the food service operator this means a higher net yield of usable meat from the leaner cuts with a high proportion of muscle.

Since fresh or chilled pork is a perishable food, it requires careful handling. It must be kept refrigerated at temperatures ranging from 33° to 38°F. from the time it is received until it is prepared for cooking.

Because today's hams, with the exception of Smithfield and Tennessee hams, are mild cured, and not done in as salty a brine as in our grandfathers' day, they also must be kept refrigerated at all times. In storage, the original wrappings are left on the ham, and this prevents the cured and smoked odor from permeating other foods in the refrigerator.

Large canned hams should be kept refrigerated, but small hams — 1 to 3 pounds — may be kept in dry storage.

profit from pork

Barbecued Fresh Spareribs

Roast Loin of Pork

Ham Steak Hawaiian

Braised Pork Tenderloin

Tournedos Rossini

Holsteiner Schnitzel

Bacon and Eggs, Country Style

Boiled Picnic Shoulder with Cabbage

Techniques for Pork Cookery

Pork Grades Pork has a higher degree of uniformity in quality than other meats and the wholesale cutting of pork is fairly well standardized. There have been no standard grades set by the federal government for cutting and grading pork. It must be inspected, however, in packing houses engaged in interstate commerce. This is to lessen the danger of trichinosis, a disease found in infected swine. The disease is caused by a parasite in the muscle tissue of some pork and is transmissible to man. Pork must *always* be cooked well done to kill this parasite.

Scientific studies have proved that the same 170°F. internal roasting temperature that turns out well done roast beef and veal ensures complete destruction of Trichinella spiralis (trichinosis causing parasite) in infected pork. The studies confirm that this temperature is well above the temperature required to kill the parasite, if present in pork.

Pork cooked to 170°F. temperature is not only safe to eat, but it loses less juice and gives improved yield over that obtained when the 185°F. internal roasting temperature was the rule.

TIMETABLE FOR ROASTING CURED PORK*

Cut	Approx. weight of single roast (pounds)	Oven temperature	Interior temperature when removed from oven	Minutes per pound based on one roast	Approximate total time
Whole ham	10 to 14	300°F.	170°F.	15 to 18	3 to 3½ hr.
Shoulder butt	2 to 4	300°F.	170°F.	30 to 35	1 to 2 hr.
Picnic	3 to 10	300°F.	170°F.	30 to 35	2 to 5 hr.
Canadian style bacon (casing on)	7	350°F.	170°F.	10 to 12	1 to 1½ hr.

TIMETABLE FOR COOKING FRESH ROAST PORK*

Cut	Approx. weight of single roast (pounds)	Oven temperature	Interior temperature of roast when removed from oven	Minutes per pound based on one roast	Approximate total time
Loin (bone in)	11 to 15	350°F.	185°F.	15 to 18	3 to 3½ hr.
Rolled loin (two halves tied together)		350°F.	185°F.		4 hr.
Half loin (bone in)		350°F.	185°F.		4½ hr.
Center Cut loin	3 to 4	350°F.	185°F.	35 to 40	2 to 2½ hr.
End cut loin	3 to 4	350°F.	185°F.	45 to 50	2½ to 3 hr.
Shoulder	12 to 14	350°F.	185°F.	30 to 35	6½ hr.
Cushion shoulder (with stuffing)	4 to 6	350°F.	185°F.	35 to 40	3 to 3½ hr.
Rolled shoulder	4 to 6	350°F.	185°F.	35 to 40	3 to 3½ hr.
Boston butt	4 to 6	350°F.	185°F.	45 to 50	3½ to 4½ hr.
Ham (leg)	10 to 12	350°F.	185°F.	30 to 35	6 hr.
Ham (leg)	15	350°F.	185 F.	30	8 hr.
Ham (leg) boned, split, and tied in two rolls	10	350°F.	185°F.	20 to 25	4 to 5 hr.

*Courtesy of the National Live Stock and Meat Board

Barbequed Fresh Spareribs (recipe on p. 82)

Pork

Ham Steak Hawaiian

Ham Steak Hawaiian

YIELD: 50 portions	**EACH PORTION:** 4 oz. ham, 1 pineapple slice	
INGREDIENTS	*QUANTITY*	*METHOD*
Pullman Ham Steaks Salad Oil	50 for sheet pan	1. Place ham steaks on lightly oiled sheet pan. Place under broiler at high point for about 3 min. Turn ham and repeat process. Remove from broiler, keep hot.
Butter Pineapple Slices Sugar Cinnamon	for sheet pan 50 8 oz. 1 tsp.	2. Place pineapple slices on buttered sheet pan. Combine sugar and cinnamon; sprinkle over pineapple. Place pineapple under broiler and glaze.
Maraschino Cherries	50	3. Place pineapple slice on ham steak to serve. Place a maraschino cherry in center of pineapple ring.
See color picture, p. 79.		

Barbecued Fresh Spareribs

YIELD: 50 portions	**EACH PORTION:** about 12 oz. with sauce	
INGREDIENTS	*QUANTITY*	*METHOD*
Fresh Pork Spareribs (12 oz. portions) Salad Oil	50 for browning	1. Place ribs in large pot. Cover with boiling water. When water returns to boil, reduce heat and simmer for 30 min. Remove ribs from pot and place on sheet pans. Oil ribs lightly and brown both sides under broiler.
Barbecue Sauce (p. 314)	1 gal.	2. Place ribs flat in roast pans (inside of rib down) and cover with Barbecue Sauce. 3. Bake at 350°F. 1 to 1½ hr. or until tender. Turn once during cooking period and baste with sauce. 4. When serving, cut between each rib for guest's convenience. Plate or platter ribs in original form.

Boiled Corned Spareribs, right (recipe below)

Roast Loin of Pork, far right (recipe bottom of page)

Boiled Corned Spareribs

YIELD: 50 portions		EACH PORTION: 12 oz.
INGREDIENTS	*QUANTITY*	*METHOD*
Corned Spareribs Sachet Bag	50 (12 oz.)	1. Place ribs in large pot. Cover with cool water and bring to boil. Add sachet bag; reduce heat and simmer 1½ to 2 hr. or until ribs will slip from meat. 2. Serve one piece of spareribs with accompanying vegetables.

NOTE: Ribs are sometimes braised with sauerkraut for a short time before service for additional flavor.

Roast Loin of Pork

YIELD: 50 portions		EACH PORTION: about 6 oz.
INGREDIENTS	*QUANTITY*	*METHOD*
Pork Loins Salt Pepper Rosemary Sage	30 lb. to taste to taste 2 tsp. 2 tsp.	1. Remove chine bone leaving ribs in. Remove tenderloin for other dishes. Place pork in greased roasting pan; rub outside of each loin with salt, pepper, rosemary and sage. 2. Place in oven preheated to 350°F. for 1 hr.

Mirepoix:
   Onions, coarsely chopped
   Celery, coarsely chopped
   Carrots, coarsely chopped
	1 lb.
	8 oz.
	8 oz.
		3. Turn loins, add mirepoix; roast for 1½ hr. When meat is done, remove from pan and place in clean storage pan. Cover with clean, damp towel and hold in warm place.

Bread Flour Chicken OR Beef Stock, hot	10 oz. 5 qt.	4. Pour about 10 oz. fat from roast pan into a saucepan; add flour to make roux. Cook 10 min., browning lightly. 5. Place pan in which meat was roasted on range and add stock. Scrape bottom of pan to loosen little brown particles known as "fond." Simmer until mirepoix is tender. Strain and bring to boil again. Carefully skim off fat. 6. Add strained stock to cooked roux, stirring until thickened and smooth. Strain again through fine china cap and adjust seasoning. Hold for service. 7. Slice meat between ribs and serve with 2 oz. ladle of gravy poured around meat.

NOTE: Apple products are often served with pork. For Boneless Roast Loin of Pork: before roasting, separate meat, in one piece, from bones. Proceed as above to cook. Pork loins can also be made into a Crown Roast of Pork.

Pork

Baked Stuffed Pork Chops, right (recipe below)

Baked Cider Ham, far right (recipe bottom of page)

Baked Stuffed Pork Chops

YIELD: 50 portions	EACH PORTION: 6 oz. chop	
INGREDIENTS	QUANTITY	METHOD
Pork Chops	50 (6 oz.)	1. With a boning knife, cut pockets in chops.

Corn Stuffing:
   Whole Kernel Corn
   Basic Bread Stuffing (p. 113)
Oil
	1 No. 303 can
	2½ qt.
	for chops
		2. Drain corn and combine with basic stuffing.
		3. Using pastry bag and large round tube, squeeze corn stuffing into pocket of each chop. Fasten opening in chop with toothpick.
		4. Place chops in lightly greased roast pan. You will need 2 pans for 50 portions. Brush tops of chops with oil, broil to brown and bake in 375°F. oven for ½ hr. Small amount of stock may be added during baking to prevent drying.

Brown Sauce (p. 312)	1 gal.	5. Remove cooked chops from oven and deglaze roast pan. Strain deglazing liquid into hot Brown Sauce and bring to boil. 6. Serve 2 oz. ladle of sauce over each chop for single portion.
NOTE: Another method of preparing chops is to flatten with cleaver and spread stuffing on top. This makes portions look larger. Increase amount of stuffing to 4 qt. and corn to 2 No. 303 cans for this method. Varieties of sauce may be served such as Creole Sauce (p. 320) or Tomato Sauce (p. 318).		

Baked Cider Ham

YIELD: 50 portions	EACH PORTION: 5 oz.	
INGREDIENTS	QUANTITY	METHOD
Hams, smoked	30 lb.	1. Place hams in large pot. Cover with cold water; bring to boil. 2. Drain hams; recover with cold water. Return to boil and cook for 2 hr. 3. Remove hams from water and take off rinds and hocks. Trim ham for even shaping and score.
Boiled Cider Sugar, granulated Espagnole (p. 312)	1 pt. 12 oz. 1½ qt.	4. Place hams in roast pan; pour ½ pt. cider on each. Sprinkle hams evenly with sugar. Bake at 350°F. for 1 hr. 5. For sauce, remove fat from pan and deglaze with a small amount of water if needed. 6. Add deglazing liquid to Espagnole. Bring to boil; skim; strain; season to taste.

Boiled Fresh Pork Shoulder with Cabbage, right (recipe below)

Pork Chop Fermiere, far right (recipe bottom of page)

Boiled Fresh Pork Shoulder with Cabbage

YIELD: 50 portions	**EACH PORTION**: 5 oz. with cabbage wedge	
INGREDIENTS	*QUANTITY*	*METHOD*
Pork Shoulder, fresh	30 lb.	1. Place pork shoulder in soup pot and cover with boiling water. When water returns to boil, reduce heat and simmer about 2 hr. or until done. Check after 1½ hr. If the small bone located at the shank end pulls loose easily, the meat is usually cooked. 2. Remove shoulder from pot, trim skin and excess fat and prepare for carving. After trimming, shoulders may be held in warm stock for service.
Cabbage	14 lb.	3. Trim cabbage and cut in wedges. Place in soup pot. Pour boiling water and shoulder stock mixture (half and half) over cabbage to cover. Cook for 7 to 10 min. or until cabbage is tender. Drain. Hold cabbage in warm place for service. 4. Serve meat over boiled cabbage or cabbage wedges.

NOTE: Cooking water may be seasoned with garlic, salt and pepper and rosemary or other spices if desired.
Spinach is sometimes served as an accompanying vegetable in place of cabbage.

Pork Chop Fermiere

YIELD: 50 portions	**EACH PORTION**: 1 7 oz. chop	
INGREDIENTS	*QUANTITY*	*METHOD*
Pork Chops, fat trimmed	50 (7 oz.)	1. Saute pork chops on both sides, line up standing one against another in a square pan.

Celery Stalks, sliced
Carrots, sliced
Onions, diced
Mushrooms, sliced
Whole Tomatoes
Chili Sauce
Worcestershire Sauce
Sachet Bag:
    Black Pepper, crushed
    Rosemary Leaves
    Thyme
    Sweet Basil
    Coriander
    Marjoram
    Bay Leaf
	6
	6 lb.
	8 lb.
	2-1/2 lb.
	2 No. 10 cans
	24 oz.
	2-1/2 oz.
	
	1/4 oz.
	2 tsp.
	1/8 tsp.
	1/8 tsp.
	1/8 tsp.
	1/8 tsp.
	1
		2. Lightly fry vegetables in drippings from pork chops, add remaining ingredients and cook about 1 hr.
		3. Pour vegetables over pork chops, bring to boil and finish cooking in 350°F. oven, about ½ hr. or until done.

Parsley, chopped	to garnish	4. To serve, place tablespoon of vegetables on top of pork chop. Sprinkle chopped parsley over serving.

Roast Tender Ham

Roast Tender Ham

YIELD: 50 portions		EACH PORTION: about 5 oz.
INGREDIENTS	*QUANTITY*	*METHOD*
Hams, smoked	28 to 30 lb.	1. Cover hams with cool water. Bring to boil, reduce heat; simmer 1 hr. 2. Remove hams from water. Remove skin and excess fat. Place in preheated oven at 350°F. about 1 hr.
Prepared Mustard Sugar, granulated	3 oz. 4 oz.	3. Make a paste by mixing mustard and sugar. Remove hams from oven and coat well with mustard-sugar mixture. Return hams to oven and bake ½ hr. 4. Slice ham and serve with Raisin Sauce (p. 324) or other appropriate sauce. Save ham trimmings for other use.
NOTE: Cooking time may vary. Ham should be baked with mustard-sugar mix last ½ hr. Various glazes may be used with hams, usually derived from fruits and associated ingredients. Hams may be scored for display or buffet service. Whole cloves are sometimes used for additional flavor. Small amount of ground cloves may be mixed with mustard and sugar.		

Baked Stuffed Spareribs

YIELD: 12 portions		EACH PORTION: about 12 oz. plus stuffing
INGREDIENTS	*QUANTITY*	*METHOD*
Milk Bread Crumbs Onions, medium, sliced fine Shortening Celery Salt Sage Salt White Pepper Marjoram Eggs, whole, beaten	to moisten 1½ qt. 6 6 oz. 1 tbsp. 1½ tsp. 1½ tsp. 1½ tsp. 1½ tsp. 2	1. Pour milk over bread crumbs and let soak. Saute onions in shortening until tender. Mix onions, celery salt, sage, salt, pepper, marjoram and moistened crumbs together and add eggs. Mix well.
Fresh Spareribs, trimmed	9 lb.	2. Crack spareribs across the middle and place the stuffing on one half; then fold over and sew or tie together. 3. Barely cover bottom of roasting pan with water and place the ribs on a rack in the pan. Roast at 375°F. turning until the ribs are brown and crisp on both sides.
NOTE: Boston baked beans or applesauce goes well with this dish.		

YIELD: 50 portions		EACH PORTION: 3 oz. meat with cabbage wedge
INGREDIENTS	QUANTITY	METHOD
Smoked Pork Shoulder	25 lb.	1. Place shoulder in soup pot; cover with cold water. Bring to boil; reduce heat. Simmer about 2 hr. or until done. Check meat during cooking. When small bone at shank end pulls loose easily, meat is usually cooked. 2. Remove shoulders from pot, trim skin and excess fat and prepare for carving. After trimming, shoulders may be held in warm stock for service.
Cabbage	14 lb.	3. Trim cabbage and cut in wedges. Place in soup pot. Pour boiling water and shoulder stock mixture, using half of each to cover. Cook for 7 to 10 min. or until cabbage is tender. Drain excess water and hold in warm place for service.
		4. Serve 3 oz. portion with slices placed over and across cabbage wedge. Be sure cabbage is drained well before it is put on plate.

NOTE: Cooking water may be seasoned with sugar, prepared mustard and cloves, if desired. A dash of vinegar is sometimes added toward end of cooking.

Spinach is sometimes served instead of cabbage as an accompanying vegetable. Boiled or steamed potatoes sprinkled with chopped parsley may also be added. Serve with Mustard Sauce, (p. 315).

Ham Croquettes

YIELD: 50 portions		EACH PORTION: 2 croquettes, each 3 oz., with sauce
INGREDIENTS	QUANTITY	METHOD
Celery, chopped fine Onions, chopped fine Green Peppers, chopped fine Butter, melted	1 lb. 1 lb. 4 oz. 1½ lb.	1. Saute celery, onions, green peppers in butter until tender.
Bread Flour	1½ lb.	2. Add flour to make roux. Cook 8 to 10 min.
Milk, hot	2 qt.	3. Add hot milk; stir until thickened and smooth.
Dry Mustard Prepared Mustard Ham, cooked, chopped fine or ground Parsley, chopped	2 tbsp. 2 oz. 8 lb. 4 oz.	4. Blend dry and prepared mustard; add to ham and parsley. Combine all ingredients; mix thoroughly.
		5. Put mixture in greased baking pan; cover with waxed paper. Bake at 350°F. for 45 min. Cool. 6. Portion each croquette with level No. 20 ice cream scoop. Shape into cones of uniform size.
Flour Milk Eggs Bread Crumbs	2 lb. 1 qt. 6 3 lb.	7. Bread croquettes, using standard procedure. Deep fry at 350°F. until well-browned and heated.
		8. Serve order with sauce such as Cream Sauce (p. 314) or Raisin Sauce (p. 324).

YIELD: 50 portions		EACH PORTION: about 4 oz. with 2 oz. sauce
INGREDIENTS	QUANTITY	METHOD
Pork Tenderloins Salad Oil	25 1 pt.	1. Saute pork tenderloins in oil until browned on all sides. Place in a brazier or pan that has a cover.

SAUCE:
    Butter
    Shallots, finely chopped
    Bread Flour
    Mustard, dry
    Black Pepper
    Brown Stock, hot (p. 271)
    Lemon Juice
    White Wine
    Salt
    Sugar
	
	8 oz.
	2 oz.
	8 oz.
	3 tbsp.
	½ tsp.
	4 qt.
	2 oz.
	6 oz.
	to taste
	2 tbsp.
		2. Saute shallots in butter. Add flour, dry mustard and pepper. Cook 10 min., browning lightly. Add hot stock, lemon juice and wine. Stir until slightly thickened and smooth. Season with salt to taste. Add sugar and pour sauce over tenderloins.

		3. Cover pan and bake at 350°F. about 1 hr. or until pork is done. Remove tenderloins to clean pan, cover with damp towel and keep warm.
		4. Strain sauce and adjust seasoning. Adjust consistency, if necessary.
		5. Serve meat topped with sauce. (Size of tenderloin will determine size of slice—slightly less than ¼ in. thick.)

Pesto

YIELD: about 20 oz.		
INGREDIENTS	QUANTITY	METHOD
Fresh Pork Fat Salt Pork, rind removed Celery Leaves Parsley Leaves with Stalks Rosemary Sweet Basil Marjoram Oregano Thyme	10½ oz. 10½ oz. 1/3 oz. 1/3 oz. ½ tsp. ½ tsp. ½ tsp. ½ tsp. ½ tsp.	1. Dice pork fat fine and mix well with all ingredients. 2. Pass through fine grinder twice. 3. Store in refrigerator. Do not store in aluminum or copper.

NOTE: Pesto is used in Italian recipes as a cooking fat and seasoning agent. Seasoning of the pork fat adds additional flavor to such dishes as soups and sauces.

Techniques for
Veal and Variety Meats

Veal is the most delicately flavored of all meats. It combines well with other foods and rich colorful sauces. French and Italian cooking make a specialty of many intriguing and appetizing veal dishes. Scallopine of Veal, Veal Steak Paprika, Wiener Schnitzel, Veal a la Suisse and Veal Lasagne, all made famous by European cooks, are but a few of the veal dishes served extensively in this country.

Differentiation between veal and calf is made primarily on the basis of the color of the lean, although such factors as texture of the lean; character of the fat; color, shape, size, and ossification of the bones and cartilage, and the general contour of the carcass are also given consideration.

In high-quality veal, the fat is clear, firm and white. The lean is light pink with no marbling as veal contains very little fat. The texture of the lean is fine, fairly firm and velvety in appearance. Since the veal is the young of the beef, the bones are soft and porous with a reddish tinge and the ends of some will still be in the cartilage stage.

Wholesale cuts of veal resemble beef although they are from one-third to one-half the size of comparable cuts of beef.

U. S. Grades of Veal Veal is graded on a composite evaluation of three general factors—conformation, finish and quality. The U. S. Grades usually found on the market are Prime, Choice and Good. Prime or Top Choice are the recommended grades for quantity food operators. Packer's brands closely parallel government grades. Government grades of Prime, Choice and Good and/or their equivalent in packer's brands are generally stamped on these better grades. Veal from government inspected plants carries the purple inspection seal for wholesomeness.

Buy by Specification Similar to other types of meat, veal regardless of the style of purchase should be bought by specification. Such specifications should state the cut, grade, size or weight, trim, fresh or frozen, etc.

Cooking Methods Veal is lacking in fat and this differentiates it from other meats. This lack of fat is reflected in the methods of cooking. Veal also has a delicate color that becomes lighter when cooked.

The best methods of cooking veal are roasting, braising, sauteing, frying and stewing. (See pp. 30 to 35 for description of these cooking methods.) Chops and steaks are best when braised. Only high-grade loin or rib chops from more mature, fatter animals should ever be broiled. Cutlets are pan fried, sauteed or deep fat fried. Regardless of the method of cooking, veal should always be cooked well-done.

Individual cuts of frozen veal, such as chops, steaks and cutlets, may be cooked directly from the frozen state. Many authorities state that this is the preferred method. If desirable to have individual cuts of veal defrosted before cooking, the defrosting should be done in the refrigerator and not at room temperature.

Variety Meat in Entrees Edible parts, other than the regular cuts of beef, veal, pork and lamb, are called variety meats. This list includes liver, kidneys, heart, tongue, sweetbreads, tripe, brains and other meats. Long regarded as delicacies, these variety meats have in recent years stepped into the menu forefront because of their high content of essential nutrients —amino acids, vitamins and minerals.

Liver—Beef, Veal, Pork and Lamb Beef liver is the largest and least tender of the group. Veal liver comes from the milk-fed calves and is very tender and flavorful. Calves liver comes from older calves that are not milk-fed, is also tender and flavorful and is probably in the greatest demand of all liver. Pork liver is particularly high in essential nutrients. Lamb liver is milder in flavor than pork or beef. Beef and pork liver are especially well suited for braising. Veal, calf and lamb livers are well adapted for broiling, sauteing and pan-frying.

Kidneys—Beef, Veal, Pork and Lamb Beef kidneys are distinguished by their irregular lobes and deep fissures. The best beef kidneys come from steers and heifers. Veal kidneys resemble beef kidneys in appearance. Pork kidneys have a smooth appearance. Lamb kidneys are smooth and bean-shaped. Beef kidneys are the least tender of the group, and should be cooked in liquid or braised. Other kidneys are tender enough to be broiled.

Heart—Beef, Veal, Pork and Lamb Beef heart is the largest and least tender of the group. While highly nutritious, heart is one of the less tender meats. It can be made deliciously appetizing and tender by long, slow, moist cooking. When simmered or braised, beef heart requires from three to three and one-half hours of cooking time; veal, pork and lamb hearts require from two to two and one-half hours.

Brains—Beef, Veal, Pork and Lamb Brains are economical to buy, and easy to prepare and cook. There is very little difference in the flavor, texture, and tenderness of beef, veal, lamb and pork brains.

Brains are extremely perishable; if not used immediately after purchase, unfrozen brains should be precooked regardless of the type of preparation. They are washed, soaked in salted water 15 minutes, then simmered gently 20 minutes in fresh water to which has been added salt and lemon juice or vinegar. (The acidulated water helps to keep the brains white and firmer). The membrane may be removed before or after cooking. To prevent spoilage the brains should be kept well refrigerated after cooking.

Sweetbreads Only lamb and calf sweetbreads are used in fine cookery. They are white and tender. While they may be braised or fried without precooking, the usual procedure is to blanch sweetbreads whenever they are received. They are placed in cold water for a few minutes, then simmered slowly in fresh water to which has been added salt and lemon juice or vinegar. (The acid keeps the flesh white and firm.) At the end of 15 minutes, they are plunged into ice cold water. The membrane may be easily removed before or after blanching. If not used immediately, sweetbreads should be refrigerated.

Tongue—Beef, Veal, Pork and Lamb All tongue may be purchased fresh, pickled, corned or smoked. Beef and veal tongues are usually available as uncooked tongues; pork and lamb are frequently purchased ready to serve as they are small tongues. Beef tongue is in greatest demand as it is the most popular.

Smoked or pickled tongues often require soaking in fresh water for several hours. Tongue is simmered slowly in liquid (usually water) for three or four hours until tender. After it is cooked it is skinned. It may be served hot or cold.

Tripe Tripe is the muscular lining of a beef animal. Honeycomb tripe, the type most frequently found on the market, comes from the lining of the second stomach, and is considered more tender and delicate than the smooth or plain type obtained from the first stomach. Tripe may be purchased fresh, pickled or canned. Fresh tripe is usually partially cooked before marketing, but further cooking in water is preliminary to all ways of serving. To precook the tripe, simmer slowly for two hours in salted water. (Herbs and spices may be added to the water, if desired.)

PREPARING BRAISED SWEETBREADS

Soak sweetbreads in cold water to extract all blood. Wash, trim off all inedible portions and drain well.

Poach in lightly salted boiling water until tender. Add lemon slices, lemon juice or vinegar to cooking water to keep flesh firm and white. Drain dry.

Place sweetbreads over mirepoix in a sauté pan. Add demi-glaze and wine, if desired. Cover and bake. (Recipe on facing page.)

TIMETABLE FOR ROASTING VEAL

Cut	Approx. weight of single roast (pounds)	Oven temperature	Interior temperature of roast when removed from oven	Minutes per pound based on one roast	Approx. total time
Leg	16	300°F.	170°F	22	6 hr.
Leg	23	300°F.	170°F.	18 to 20	7 to 7½ hr.
Loin	4½ to 5	300°F.	170°F.	30 to 35	2½ to 3 hr.
Rack (4 to 6 ribs)	2½ to 3	300°F.	170°F.	30 to 35	1½ hr.
Shoulder	7	300°F.	170°F.	25	3 hr.
Shoulder	12 to 13	300°F.	170°F.	25	5 to 5½ hr.
Rolled shoulder	5	300°F.		40 to 45	3½ to 4 hr.

*Courtesy of the National Livestock and Meat Board

Braised Sweetbreads and Variations

YIELD: 10 portions		**EACH PORTION:** 1 sweetbread

INGREDIENTS	QUANTITY	METHOD
Sweetbreads	10	1. Soak sweetbreads overnight in cold water in order to extract all blood from them. Wash, trim and drain. Poach lightly in salted water until tender. Remove from water, drain dry.
Butter OR Fat Carrots, sliced fine Onions, sliced fine Celery, sliced fine Bay Leaf Cloves	4 oz. ½ lb. ½ lb. 6 oz. 1 2	2. Heat butter in saute pan. Over it lay the mirepoix made of carrots, onions, celery, bay leaf and cloves. Place the sweetbreads over the vegetables. Start on high heat in order to color the vegetables lightly.
Demi-glaze OR Light Brown Sauce	1 qt.	3. Pour the demi-glaze or light brown sauce over the sweetbreads; cover. Place the saute pan in oven preheated to 350°F. Braise sweetbreads for 30 to 35 min. basting them frequently with the sauce. When done, remove sweetbreads to a heat proof platter. Keep hot. 4. Strain the sauce through fine china cap. Reserve for usage in various recipes.

VARIATIONS:

Sweetbreads Carolina—Poached sweetbreads, split in two, sauteed in butter, garnished with julienne of Virginia ham, slitted browned almonds, served on hominy fritters and mushrooms with sherry wine cream sauce.

Sweetbreads St. Germain—Braised sweetbreads served on a bed of puree of green peas and chopped truffles with sherry wine and brown sauce.

Braised Sweetbreads Mary Garden—Braised sweetbreads demi-glazed with port wine, served with baked tomato stuffed with duxelle, buttered julienne green beans and asparagus tips bouquet.

Poached Sweetbread Variations:

Poached sweetbreads split in two, dipped in oil and fresh bread crumbs and grilled. Serve with grilled bacon, fried bananas, Bearnaise Sauce.

Poached sweetbreads, split in two, rolled in flour, dipped in egg wash, rolled in white bread crumbs, pan fried in butter. Serve with garniture on vegetables, on creamed spinach or buttered spaghetti.

Poached sweetbreads, scalloped in thin slices, prepared in chafing dish a la Newburg or a la King.

Poached sweetbreads, cut in dices with diced mushrooms, thick cream sauce; prepared as for cutlet.

Poached sweetbreads may be larded or pique with truffles, also stuffed with duxelle farce.

Broiled Veal Kidney with Mushroom Caps and Chateau Sauce

YIELD: 6 portions		**EACH PORTION:** 12 oz.

INGREDIENTS	QUANTITY	METHOD
Veal Kidneys, in fat Salt Pepper Butter, melted Lemon Juice Salad Oil	6 (12 oz. each) to taste to taste 2 oz. ½ lemon	1. Trim kidneys, leaving 1/8 in. fat. Butterfly lengthwise, removing center core. Season with salt and pepper. Sprinkle with butter and lemon juice. Brush open side with oil.
		2. Place kidneys in hand grill; broil until brown. (Cooking time: about 10 min. Meat should be light pink internally.)
Mushroom Caps, fluted Chateau Sauce (p. 313) Parsley, chopped		3. Arrange on serving platter, placing kidneys on trimmed toast cut diagonally. Top with 2 mushroom caps, 2 tbsp. Chateau Sauce and chopped parsley.

VEAL
and Variety Meats

Although only 7 per cent of the meat used in Institutions is veal, it can be a very important 7 per cent, since it adds variety to the menu. The rich and colorful sauces that cover veal entrees and the wines, herbs and cheeses with which they are cooked make these dishes naturals to be developed into house specialties.

Whenever developing these specialties, however, the cook should consider how the veal is to be cooked and how much will be required. For example, it takes about 30 lb. of veal round to serve 100 portions of 3-oz. veal cutlets.

Although the labor involved is likely to be greater than with other types of meat, variety meats, featured on the following page, are low enough in initial cost so they are also good candidates for specialty billing.

It is in the preparation of variety meats that the chef proves his mettle, since technique in preparing these entrees makes the difference between "innards" and gourmet delicacies.

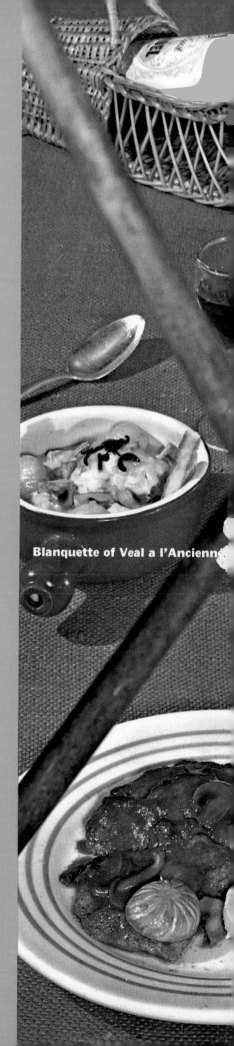

Blanquette of Veal a l'Ancienne

Sweetbread Variation

Braised Oxtails

Sweetbread Variation

Calves Liver, Saute

Veal Chops, Saute' Italienne

Breaded Veal Cutlet

Veal Paprika with Sauerkraut

Scallopine of Veal Marsala

Fricassee of Veal

YIELD: 50 portions		EACH PORTION: about 3 oz. meat, 8 oz. sauce
INGREDIENTS	*QUANTITY*	*METHOD*
Forequarter Veal, trimmed, cut (1 in. cubes) Sachet Bag: Parsley Stems Bay Leaf Thyme Peppercorns, crushed	17 lb. 4 oz. 1 1 tsp. 1 tsp.	1. Bring 2 gal. water to boil in 6 gal. heavy duty pot. Add meat to boiling water and stir with wooden paddle to separate meat. When water returns to boil, drain off water and again cover meat with cold water and bring to a boil. 2. Add sachet bag and simmer 1½ hr. Skim all scum from top of stock as soon as it starts to form. Skim until stock is clear.
Pearl Onions, medium to small	100	3. Place onions in sauce pan, cover with cold water and cook slowly until nearly tender.
Mushroom Caps, small, washed Butter Lemon Dry White Wine (optional)	100 4 oz. juice of 1 8 oz.	4. Saute mushroom caps in butter with lemon juice and wine until tender.
Butter Flour	1 lb. 1 lb.	5. In a heavy pot, make roux with butter and flour. Cook 5 min. Do not brown.
Veal Stock Salt	from cooking veal to taste	6. Remove sachet bag when meat is cooked and drain off stock. Add veal stock obtained from cooking veal for this recipe with liquor from onions and mushrooms to roux, stirring until thickened and smooth. Season with salt and adjust consistency. 7. Add meat, drained mushrooms and onions, stirring gently to combine. Hold for service. Serve 8 oz. ladle sauce containing 3 oz. cooked meat per portion.

Hungarian Veal Goulash

YIELD: 50 portions		EACH PORTION: about 4 oz. veal
INGREDIENTS	*QUANTITY*	*METHOD*
Veal, boneless, trimmed, cut (1 in. cubes) Salad Oil Onions, small dice	17 lb. 1 pt. 6 lb.	1. Saute meat in hot oil and braise with onions. Reduce liquid to 1/3.
Hungarian Paprika Bread Flour Sachet Bag: Caraway Seeds Bay Leaves Parsley Stems Brown Stock, hot (p. 271) Tomato Puree	2 oz. 1 lb. 1 tbsp. 4 6 2 gal. 1 No. 2½ can	2. Add paprika; stir; then add flour. Cook 5 min. blending well. Add sachet bag, brown stock and tomato puree. Bring to a boil. Cover and braise at 350°F. in oven about 1 hr. or until tender.
Salt Pepper Sour Cream	to taste to taste 1 qt.	3. Remove cooked meat. Adjust seasoning and hold for service. Sour cream may be served on the side as an optional accompaniment. Spaetzli is usually served with goulash.
NOTE: For Hungarian Beef Goulash, substitute 17 lb. boneless bottom round, beef shank or chuck for veal.		

Veal and Variety Meats

Breaded Veal Cutlet (recipe below)

Calves Liver, Saute (recipe top facing page)

Breaded Veal Cutlet

YIELD: 50 portions		EACH PORTION: 4 oz.
INGREDIENTS	QUANTITY	METHOD
Veal Cutlets (about 4 oz. ea.)	50	1. Using boneless leg of veal, cut uniform portions about ¼ in. thick. Place on cutting board or meat block and pound with cutlet hammer to flatten and break tissues. Do not pound hard enough to destroy meat.
Bread Flour Salt Pepper Eggs, whole Milk Bread Crumbs OR Cracker Meal	2 lb. to taste to taste 6 1 qt. 3 lb.	2. Bread according to standard procedure (p. 178) using flour, salt and pepper; egg wash made of eggs and milk; bread crumbs or cracker meal.
Salad Oil	for sauteing	3. Place ¼ in. salad oil in heavy skillet and saute cutlets until golden brown on 1 side. Turn and brown other side. Remove and drain well. In mass production, cutlets may be finished in oven on sheet pan or roast pan lined with brown paper.
NOTE: A richer egg wash can be made by doubling amount of egg and adding 1 cup oil. Oil is sometimes used to reduce browning.		
See color picture, p. 93.		

Breaded Veal Cutlet, Saute Gruyere

YIELD: 1 portion		EACH PORTION: 1 cutlet
INGREDIENTS	QUANTITY	METHOD
Veal Cutlet, breaded Salad Oil Tomato Slices, thin Swiss Cheese Slice	1 for sauteing 2 to 3 1	1. Saute breaded veal cutlet in oil until golden brown. Arrange tomato slices on cutlet; cover with slice of Swiss cheese. 2. Place dish under broiler until cheese is melted and lightly browned.
Parsley, chopped Mushroom Sauce (p. 313)	for garnish	3. Sprinkle with chopped parsley and serve with a little Mushroom Sauce.
NOTE: See standard breading procedure, p. 178.		

Calves Liver, Saute

YIELD: 50 portions		EACH PORTION: 5 oz.
INGREDIENTS	*QUANTITY*	*METHOD*
Calves Liver Flour, seasoned with salt and pepper	16 lb. as needed	1. Skin liver and remove veins. 2. Slice liver on bias, about ¼ in. thick. Dredge in seasoned flour.
Salad Oil	1 qt.	3. Saute in hot oil. Cook liver until brown on underside, then turn liver to complete cooking. Too high heat causes formation of an undesirable hard crust.

VARIATIONS: Liver may be broiled. If broiling, do not dredge with flour. Either dip liver in, or brush with, salad oil or melted butter. Liver may be served with grilled bacon, Canadian bacon, french fried onions, smothered onions, fried or baked bananas, shallot butter, parsley or lemon butter or brown butter. Liver can be served with brown butter that has been seasoned with worcestershire sauce; garnished with parsley.

See color picture, p. 94.

Blanquette de Veau a l'Ancienne

YIELD: 6 portions		EACH PORTION: about 5 oz.
INGREDIENTS	*QUANTITY*	*METHOD*
Breast of Veal, boned Water	2 lb. to cover	1. Cut veal in large pieces. Place in sauce pan; cover with cold water and parboil. Remove veal and wash in cold water.

Bouquet in cheesecloth:
  Parsley
  Celery
  Bay Leaf
  Thyme
  Garlic Cloves
  Peppercorns
Salt
Carrot, sliced
	
	1 sprig
	2 branches
	½
	½ tsp.
	2
	8
	to taste
	1
		2. Return veal to sauce pan, cover with cold water. Add bouquet and salt. Simmer about 1½ hr. or until meat is nearly tender. Add carrots and finish cooking. Remove bouquet.

Butter Flour	1 tbsp. 2 tbsp.	3. Combine butter and flour to make roux. 4. Reduce cooking liquid to about 2 cups, add to roux. Cook and stir until smooth and thickened.
Mushrooms Butter Lemon Juice Salt Pepper	1 lb. 1 tsp. ½ tsp. to taste to taste	5. While veal is cooking clean mushrooms and cook in 1 tbsp. water with 1 tsp. butter, lemon juice, salt and pepper for 5 min. Drain off juice and add to sauce. Reserve mushrooms.

Liaison:
  Egg Yolk
  Cream
Onions, pearl
	
	1
	4 oz.
	1 doz.
		6. Complete sauce by adding liaison (p. 311). Bring just to boiling but do not let boil. Strain through cheesecloth. Add cooked pearl onions and mushrooms. Correct seasoning.

Parsley, chopped	for garnish	7. Pour sauce over meat. Sprinkle with chopped parsley.

NOTE: In modern methods, boneless breast or shoulder of veal is often used. However, the old-fashioned or "a l'ancienne" method was originally prepared using the extreme ends of ribs from the breast, including cartilage. Substituting trimmed, boneless shoulder or breast in equal quantity in the above formula provides a larger serving portion.

See color picture, p. 92.

Veal and Variety Meats

Veal Chops, Saute Italienne (recipe below)

Scaloppine of Veal Marsala (recipe top facing page)

Veal Chops, Saute Italienne

YIELD: 50 portions		EACH PORTION: 1 6 oz. veal chop
INGREDIENTS	*QUANTITY*	*METHOD*
Veal Chops, trimmed (6 oz. ea.)	18¾ lb.	1. Butterfly veal chops and flatten with cleaver.
Ham Slices (1½ oz. ea.) Swiss Cheese slices (1 oz. ea.) Salt Pepper	5 lb. 3 lb. 5 oz. to taste to taste	2. Cut ham slices into triangles. Wrap 1 slice Swiss cheese around each ham triangle. 3. Place cheese-wrapped ham triangle inside chop. Season with salt and pepper.
Flour Egg Wash	for dredging for breading	4. Dredge each chop in flour and pound with hand to flatten. Dip in egg wash and drain.
Italian Breading	for breading	5. Bread chops.

Oil Mixture:
    Clarified Butter
    Salad Oil
	12 oz.
	12 oz.
		6. Heat oil mixture in saute pan and brown chops on both sides.

		7. Bake at 300°F. ½ hr. or until done.
Tomato Sauce (p. 318)	about 2 tbsp.	8. Place about 2 tbsp. Tomato Sauce under each chop when serving.
NOTE: Pork chops prepared in this manner can be featured as Pork Chops, Saute Italienne.		
See color picture, p. 93.		

Scaloppine of Veal Marsala

YIELD: 6 portions	EACH PORTION: 2 2 oz. pieces	
INGREDIENTS	*QUANTITY*	*METHOD*
Veal Leg, boned	1½ lb.	1. Slice veal very thin into 12 2 oz. pieces and pound to flatten.
Salt Pepper Flour	to taste to taste for dredging	2. To cook, season with salt and pepper and dredge in flour.
Butter	3 oz.	3. Melt butter in large skillet. When hot, place veal cutlets in skillet and brown thoroughly on both sides. Remove to serving dish.
Marsala Wine Lemon Juice Brown Sauce (p. 312) Parsley, chopped	4 oz. from ½ lemon 4 oz. 2 tbsp.	4. Deglaze pan with Marsala wine and lemon juice. Cook 1 min. scraping bottom and sides of pan until all residue is dissolved. Add brown sauce to pan, bring to boil and pour sauce over meat. Sprinkle with chopped parsley.

TO SERVE: Place veal in shirred egg dish on buttered noodles and serve with freshly cooked green peas and sauteed sliced mushrooms or caps. Add lemon slice.
NOTE: Veal tenderloin can be substituted for boneless veal leg.

See color picture, p. 93.

Veal Scaloppini with Mushrooms

YIELD: 50 portions	EACH PORTION: about 5 oz.	
INGREDIENTS	*QUANTITY*	*METHOD*

Veal Scallops
  OR Small Leg Cutlets,
    pounded thin
Seasoned Flour:
  Bread Flour
  Salt
  Pepper
Oil Mixture:
  Clarified Butter
  Salad Oil
	17 lb.
	
	2 lb.
	to taste
	to taste
	
	12 oz.
	1 qt.
		1. Dredge scaloppini in flour. Put 1/8 in. oil mixture in fry pan, skillet or sautoir and fry veal until lightly browned on both sides. Remove to roast pan or hotel pans, overlapping pieces of meat.

Mushroom Caps Garlic, minced Lemon Juice Brown Sauce (p. 312) Marsala Wine Salt	50 2 tsp. 2 oz. 3 qt. 12 oz. to taste	2. Saute mushroom caps and garlic in balance of oil mixture. Drain off oil, add lemon juice. Add brown sauce and wine; season to taste. 3. Pour sauce over meat. Place in oven at 350°F. for 15 min. before serving. Hold for service.
Parsley, chopped	8 oz.	4. Serve three 1½ oz. slices with mushroom cap for each portion. Sprinkle with chopped parsley.

VARIATIONS: There are several variations of this dish. Different provinces of Italy vary in their cooking methods.

NOTE: In a la carte service, meat is cooked to order and placed on platter or serving dish with no further cooking.

Veal and Variety Meats

Veal Paprika with Sauerkraut, right (recipe below)

Holstein Schnitzel, far right (recipe bottom of page)

Veal Paprika with Sauerkraut

YIELD: 50 portions		EACH PORTION: about 4 oz. veal
INGREDIENTS	*QUANTITY*	*METHOD*
Veal	18 lb.	1. Cut meat into 1½-in. by 1-in. pcs.
Butter Onions, sliced Garlic Cloves, minced Paprika Dry Wine White Stock (p. 271)	1 lb. 6 lb. 3 6 tbsp. 8 oz. 8 oz.	2. Melt butter in sauce kettle. Add onions and cook slowly until tender. Add garlic, cook lightly. Add paprika. Add 8 oz. dry wine and 8 oz. of white stock. Add meat and cook until meat is slightly brown.
Sauerkraut, with juice	10 lb.	3. Add sauerkraut and seasonings. Cover and simmer gently until meat is very tender, about 2 hr.
		4. Serve with thick sour cream.
NOTE: If canned sauerkraut is used, drain and wash. Substitute white stock for juice.		

Holstein Schnitzel

YIELD: 6 portions		EACH PORTION: 5 oz.
INGREDIENTS	*QUANTITY*	*METHOD*
Veal Cutlets, thinly sliced Salt Pepper Flour Egg Wash Fresh White Bread Crumbs	6 (5 oz. ea.) to taste to taste 8 oz. 8 oz. for breading	1. Flatten cutlets with a cutlet beater or meat cleaver, sprinkle well with salt and pepper and bread according to standard procedure. (p. 178).
Butter	6 oz.	2. Saute in butter slowly until golden brown.
Fried Eggs Whole Lemon, grooved and 　　cut into 6 slices Anchovy Fillets Capers Dill Pickles, small, fanned Pickled Beets, small	6 1 6 2 tbsp. 6 6	3. Place cutlets on platter. Top each with fried egg. Garnish with a slice of lemon. Top with circle of anchovy fillets with capers in center. Dill pickles, beets and sprigs of parsley may be used as additional garnishes.
Butter	3 oz.	4. Brown 3 oz. butter in a frying pan, then pour over cutlets. 5. Serve sauteed potatoes as a side dish.

*Osso Bucco
(recipe below)*

Osso Bucco

YIELD: 50 portions	EACH PORTION: 2 Ossi Bucci with sauce	
INGREDIENTS	QUANTITY	METHOD
Veal Shank Bread Flour Salad Oil Salt Pepper	30 (3 to 3½ lb. ea.) for dredging for sauteing to taste to taste	1. Cut end bones off shank, then saw shank in 3 or 4 equal pieces, about 1½ in. long. Dredge cut veal shank in seasoned flour, brown in hot oil. Remove browned Ossi Bucci to brazier.
Onions, minced Garlic Cloves	2 lb. 3	2. Saute onions and garlic in same oil used for browning shanks.
Bread Flour White Wine Tomato Puree Brown Stock (p. 271)	6 oz. 1 pt. 8 oz. 1 gal.	3. Add flour to onion mixture and make roux. Add wine and tomato puree gradually, stirring as it thickens. Bring to near boil. Incorporate hot stock into boiling mixture. Pour sauce over shanks in brazier. Cover. Bake at 350°F. for 1 hr. or until very tender.
Parsley, chopped Lemon Peel, grated Anchovy Fillets, chopped	1 oz. 2 lemons 6	4. Add parsley, lemon peel and anchovy fillets. Simmer 5 min. Serve two shanks with sauce per portion. (See picture). Accompany with pasta or rice.

Ris de Veau, Montebello

YIELD: 2 portions	EACH PORTION: 8 oz.	
INGREDIENTS	QUANTITY	METHOD
Sweetbreads Lemon Juice OR Vinegar	1 lb. 1 tbsp.	1. Soak sweetbreads about 1 hr. in cold water. Drain, put in saucepan with cold water to cover and lemon juice or vinegar; bring to a boil. Simmer for 5 min., drain; put in bowl of ice water for a few minutes. Drain; remove skin and sinew.

Seasoned Flour:
  Flour
  Salt
  Cayenne Pepper
	2 tbsp.
	to taste
	to taste
		2. Dust lightly with flour which has been seasoned with salt and cayenne pepper.

Butter	2 oz.	3. Brown quickly on both sides in hot butter and then cook slowly about 5 min. on each side. 4. Arrange on hot serving dish and keep warm until Montebello Sauce has been prepared.

NOTE: Montebello Sauce is a half serving of Tomato Sauce (p. 318) and a half serving of Hollandaise Sauce (p. 321), each thinned lightly with champagne. The most popular way of presenting this dish is to mound the sweetbreads on a toast round or rusk, then cover one-half of the top and side with Tomato Sauce and the other half with Hollandaise Sauce. Top with a slice of truffle or black olive that has been soaked in sherry wine.

Arroz con Pollo

Coq au Vin

Chicken Cacciatore

Poulet a la Kiev

Chicken Marengo

The popularity of chicken knows no national boundaries. Sauces that are prepared from ingredients associated with a particular area, unusual cooking methods, variations in garniture, accompaniments and service techniques adapt the versatile chicken to regional cuisines and tastes. Many national specialties in addition to those shown above and several American favorites are pictured, described and formulated in this section.

POULTRY

Duckling is most often roasted, although it may be broiled or served in a rich sauce as a ragout or stew. Duck is usually accompanied by sweet sauces using fruit, honey, jellies and wine. Because the flesh has an extremely high fat content, the duck should be placed on racks during roasting to eliminate grease absorption. Duckling, which is all dark meat, is most palatable when cooked until the skin is very crisp. The bird is usually cut into eight uniform pieces for service to four people. This section discusses poultry cooking methods — from the complex techniques used in the duck entrees shown here to basic information on roasting, broiling, stewing, poaching, sautéing and fricasseeing.

Roast Duckling a l'Orange

Estouffade of Duckling

Roast Young Duckling Bigarade

Rock Cornish Game Hen Palermitana

Stuffed Half Rock Cornish Game Hen

VERSATILITY
with
CHICKEN

Roast Native Capon, Chestnut Stuffing

THIS IS THE PROPERTY OF

Chicken a la King

Chicken Stew, Family Style

Chickenburgers, Sauce Chateau

Broiled Spring Chicken

Fricassee of Chicken with Buttered Noodles

Chicken Pot Pie with Tender Crust

EGGS WITH SMALL ENDS DOWN

DOZEN EGGS

EGGS

Three Variations of Fried Chicken Maryland

Fried chicken is second only to beef in popularity of all entrees served in food service establishments across the country.

The variations possible in cooking fried chicken are almost endless. Only one variation, Fried Chicken, Maryland, is shown here to prove its versatility. Recipes for other methods are included in this section.

Because chicken is plentiful most of the time, fried chicken is at home on any menu: the hospital tray (pictured at left) where low cost is important; the drive-in operation (at right) where its adaptability to merchandising — such as "Chicken in the Basket" — is the strong point; or the elegant restaurant or hotel dining room (center) where it can be sauced and garnished to tempt any gourmet — and the price can compensate for added labor involved in preparation.

Wiener Backhaenel

Rock Cornish Game Hen Palermitana

Stuffed Half Rock Cornish Game Hen

Roast Boneless Rock Cornish Game Hen

Rock Cornish Game Hens, the glamour birds of the poultry family, are chubby, fine-grained birds, practically all white meat and just large enough to provide one or two servings.

They are available to food service operators fresh and packed in ice, frozen, frozen stuffed, with bone or boneless and split into halves or whole and dressed.

Although somewhat expensive, Rock Cornish Game Hens, which are sweet with just a hint of gamey flavor, are a top-ranking favorite among patrons. Some of the many variations possible in their preparation are illustrated above.

**Turkey Mushroom Pie
with Cornbread Topping**

Techniques for
Poultry Cookery

All domestic birds that are bred and marketed for human consumption are classified as poultry. Included are chicken, turkey, capon, duck, goose, squab and Rock Cornish game hen. Game birds are generally wild birds hunted for sport and used for food, although some are now raised domestically. Game birds include pheasant, partridge, quail, wild duck and grouse.

The composition and nutritive value of poultry is similar to meat. Poultry is rich in protein, vitamins and minerals. Like pork and veal, it should be well done.

Poultry is easily digested, particularly the white meat, because of its texture and short fibers. It may be served in many ways and is usually an excellent food cost item.

Poultry Grading All poultry in interstate commerce is required to be eviscerated. Eviscerated means removal of all viscera or entrails and heads and feet off. Like meat products, poultry is government graded and inspected. The grade mark refers to quality of shape, flesh and general appearance; the inspection mark certifies its wholesomeness as a food product. Government grades are: U.S. Grade A, U.S. Grade B, and U.S. Grade C. Poultry is also state graded and inspected. Grade A birds are preferred for most food service. Poultry is further classified by weight, sex and age. These factors affect tenderness.

Cooking Techniques In general, the same cooking principles that apply to meat also apply to poultry. However, steaming is used more successfully with poultry than with meat.

Broilers and Fryers may be broiled, pan fried, roasted, boiled (simmered) for deep fat frying, stewed or braised. When broiling or pan frying, one-half bird

Fricassee of Turkey Wings

Roast Tom Turkey, Giblet Gravy

is usually served as a portion. Chicken is roasted whole and cut in halves or quarters for service.

Chickens that are steamed or boiled are cooked whole to retain shape and reduce shrinkage. They are broken down into serving portions after cooking. For other service, chicken is often disjointed before cooking. The larger birds can be cut or disjointed.

Chicken may be broken down into component parts. Breasts may be sauteed, poached, fried. Legs may be fried, stewed, fricasseed. Wings are often served boneless and sometimes are boiled before deep frying.

Roasters provide an excellent menu item and are often used where the expense of capon is prohibitive.

The method of cutting the cooked product is usually determined by the size. Small roasters may be cut in quarters. Large roasters (in the 5 lb. range) are usually sliced in the same manner as capon or turkey.

Capons are often found on higher priced menus. They are expensive and do not provide great yield. Their tenderness and palatability make them highly prized. They are cooked whole (roasted) and sliced in the same manner as turkey.

Squab are expensive and, like capon, are found only on higher priced menus. They are usually cooked and served whole. Roasting is the most popular method although squab may be broiled (after splitting), cooked en cocotte (in casserole) or sauteed. The breasts may be sauteed for special parties. Squab are usually served one to each person.

Rock Cornish Game Hens are not as expensive as squab and continue to gain in popularity because of their excellent eating qualities and light meat. They may be cooked and served in the same manner as squab. Various rice stuffings often accompany squab and Rock Cornish Game Hens.

Turkey may be boiled or roasted whole or cut into steaks and broiled, grilled or sauteed. It may be completely removed from the bone and rolled and tied before cooking. Turkey may be purchased boned, rolled and fully cooked. This is primarily for use in low cost operations and for sandwich preparation. It allows for excellent portion control and may be purchased as all white meat, all dark meat, or part white and part dark.

Young Toms are used mostly for roasting. Both hens and toms may be boiled and used for sandwiches and salads.

Turkeys under 20 lb. do not usually provide as good yield (meat to carcass ratio) as larger birds. Turkeys are purchased by sex and weight; young toms averaging 22 lb. are the most popular.

Turkey wings and sometimes the drumsticks (lower legs) are often braised and served on luncheon menus in order to utilize them. The wings are not suitable for slicing and the drumstick has considerable tendon which provides little yield as roast, yet is quite adequate for other dishes.

Turkey that is broiled or grilled must be handled

CHARACTERISTICS OF POULTRY

BROILER-FRYERS:	Tender. 1½ lb. to 3½ lb. Average 9 weeks old.
ROASTERS:	Tender. 3½ to 5 lb. 12 weeks old. Little heavier fat covering than most broilers and fryers.
CAPON:	Very tender. Castrated male chicken. Good fat covering with high proportion of light meat. Good texture. Over 4 lb. Expensive.
TURKEY:	Hens and Toms (male). 8 to 30 lb. Hens generally lighter than toms. Young toms on commercial market best weight, eviscerated, 20 to 22 lb. Beltsville turkey, recently developed breed, 4 to 9 lb. Poor ratio of meat to carcass and little fat which tends to dryness. Not generally suitable for commercial cookery.
BRO-HENS:	The laying hen of the broiler industry. 4½ to 6 lb.
SQUAB:	Very tender. Usually less than 1 lb. eviscerated. Young. About 4 weeks old. Expensive.
ROCK CORNISH GAME HEN:	Relatively new. Very young, tender. Usually under 1 lb. eviscerated. Heavy breasted. High in protein, low in fat.
DUCK:	Old ducks have tough flesh and are not suitable for general use.
DUCKLINGS:	Birds up to 16 weeks old, average 3½ lb. to 5½ lb. eviscerated. Tender meat; high fat content.
FOWL:	Also termed hens. Mature female. Less tender than most other poultry. Any weight. Range from 3 lb. to 7 lb. or more. Average 5 lb. to 6 lb. High fat content.
STAGS:	Also termed roosters. 3 lb. to 6 lb. Usually tough and stringy.

with care and is often floured or breaded before cooking to provide a protective coating. Turkey is relatively lean compared to most meats and dries quickly under heat. When dry, turkey becomes tough and stringy. Except when served cold, turkey is almost always served with a sauce. Turkey is used for pie, fricassee, sandwiches, croquettes, hash.

Fowl is almost always boiled (simmered). It is less tender than other poultry and must be cooked by moist heat. Chicken fat derived from the cooking of fowl is highly prized, especially in Jewish cuisine.

Fowl is cooked whole and removed from the bone for fricassee, chicken pie, chicken a la king, brunswick stew, salads and a variety of other dishes. Quality food operations use fowl for chicken sandwiches and salads. Fowl is also the best source of chicken stock for preparing soups and sauces. All boiled chicken or chicken parts provide stock suitable for various culinary preparations.

Giblets The livers from broilers and fryers are served as chicken livers and may be broiled, sauteed, pan fried or served en brochette (on a skewer). They are often accompanied by a light, savory sauce. Chicken livers are also prepared and served cold as appetizers and hors d'oeuvres. They may be used in finer culinary preparation in stuffings, forcemeats and paté.

Hearts and gizzards are used in gravies and prepared as luncheon dishes in some hotels and restaurants and are often used in industrial feeding. The edible trimmings, liver, hearts and gizzards, are called giblets.

Spoilage All poultry is highly perishable and rapidly develops an off-odor when not properly refrigerated or when beginning to spoil. Off-flavors are quickly recognized. It is dangerous to fool with questionable poultry. Serious food poisoning may result.

Portion Control Uniformity of size and weight is extremely important for uniform cookery and to insure portion control and customer satisfaction. Poultry is often graded by a packer or purveyor by uniformity of weight. Price per pound is slightly higher but is money well spent.

Frozen Poultry Broilers and fryers are usually purchased fresh. Fowl is often fresh but may be purchased frozen at times. Turkey is nearly always frozen and should be thawed completely before cooking. Turkey may be thawed over a two-day period at walk-in refrigerator temperatures or thawed in cold running water at room temperature. Care must be exercised in thawing at room temperature so that spoilage does not occur.

Trussing When broilers and fryers are boiled or roasted they are often tied or trussed to aid in maintaining shape. This is not necessary with ducklings because of their body contour and extremely short legs. The legs of squab and cornish hens are usually tied to maintain shape and hold stuffing. Turkeys are tied for both roasting and boiling. Maintaining shape also aids in uniform cooking and facilitates handling during and after the cooking process. It is usually not necessary to truss fowl.

Testing for Doneness Meat thermometers may be used for testing large birds such as turkeys for doneness, although hand testing is quite reliable, particularly with smaller birds. If the drumstick bone twists easily on broilers, they are usually cooked. Pressing the drumstick flesh of other birds provides an indication of doneness. When cooked, they lose the soft feel of raw meat and develop a firmness of flesh that yields easily to the bone.

Doneness may also be determined by feeling the keel or breast bone. As the meat cooks, it shrinks slightly away from the keel bone. An overcooked bird will have a definite space or separation between the flesh and the bone. Remember that overcooking any poultry makes it dry, stringy and unpalatable.

Boiling The same basic methods of boiling fowl apply to turkey. Because of the widespread use of fowl and the importance of extracting suitable stock, the following measures are recommended in their preparation, cooking and handling after cooking. This is not intended as a recipe, but as recommended procedure.

Cleaning Although all fowl is eviscerated, additional cleaning is often necessary. A short soaking period is recommended before using in order to remove all traces of blood. This is particularly true of frozen turkeys which retain a substantial quantity of blood in the body cavity. If the blood is not removed, stock may be discolored.

After removing giblets, liver and gizzard and cleaning and soaking fowl, place fowl in a suitable stockpot and cover with cool water. Place on range and bring to boiling point. Reduce heat or move pot to range area where stock will simmer. A mirepoix and a sachet bag for flavor are added while simmering.

Cooking Time There can be no general rule for the cooking time of fowl as the cooking time varies considerably depending on the characteristics, flesh and weight of the fowl. It is possible for two fowl of equal weight to have markedly different cooking times.

Testing Fowl for Doneness To test a fowl for doneness, remove it from the pot by inserting a range fork directly next to the backbone behind the wing. This will hold the fowl securely and prevent its splashing back into the pot. Safety measures should always be exercised to prevent burns. This method also prevents damage to the breast from piercing.

The actual test is made by gently squeezing the drumstick (lower leg) between the thumb and forefinger. When cooked, the meat will yield easily. When not sufficiently cooked, the meat will be firm and unyielding. The feel for this can only be learned by experience; the more experience, the greater the skill.

Each fowl in the pot should be tested to determine doneness. When the fowl are cooked, they should be removed from the stock and placed in cold running water immediately. This quick cooling serves several purposes. It prevents further cooking, reduces the possibility of spoilage and prevents the fowl from turning dark, which often occurs when birds are exposed to the air and left to cool at room temperature.

Stock and Fat When the fowl has been removed, the stock should be strained through a cheesecloth and fine china cap. If the stock is to be used immediately, it should be allowed to stand for a few minutes so that the fat will rise to the top. The fat should then be skimmed from the stock, clarified and placed in a suitable container for future use. It may be necessary to simmer the fat slowly under low heat to evaporate any stock that may have been removed in the skimming process. This will insure the quality of the fat for proper preparation of roux. This also extends its keeping qualities if it is not used immediately. Chicken fat is valuable in roux for thickening veloute and other sauces.

Use of Chicken Parts Chicken parts such as backs, necks and wings may also be used in making chicken stock. These will require much less cooking time than whole fowl and are relatively inexpensive.

Game The laws of many states prohibit the serving of game in public dining rooms. Its use has become relegated primarily to clubs and private organizations.

Most dark meat game birds, such as duck, pheasant and grouse, are often cooked rare; white meat birds, such as partridge and quail, are cooked well done. Mature game with extremely lean meat is often barded prior to roasting for additional moisture. Barding is covering breasts of poultry or game with salt pork, bacon or other fat agent to prevent drying, to augment the flavor and to provide a self-basting agent.

Game cookery is a highly specialized field, and because of its limited application will be treated only briefly in this text.

Stuffings and Dressings The terms stuffing and dressing are used interchangeably although, theoretically, stuffing could be interpreted as a product with which poultry, meat or fish is stuffed, while dressing is baked separately.

Basic Ingredients The basic ingredients in most stuffings are: 1) a starchy base, such as bread, various rices or potato; 2) onions and/or celery; 3) some form of fat in which the vegetables are sauteed; 4) seasonings, such as sage or thyme, or poultry seasoning which combines them both. Other stuffings and dressings may combine meats, oysters and other seafood, mushrooms, fruits and nuts.

Preparation Vegetables should always be cooked thoroughly prior to incorporating in a stuffing. This is particularly true of onions which spoil easily when not properly cooked. The vegetables will cook very little once incorporated. Vegetables should be cooled prior to mixing with the other ingredients, unless the dressing is to be baked immediately.

Stuffings should be light and moist. In preparing them, a minimum of handling, and care that excess liquids are not used, will prove beneficial. Always spoon stuffing lightly into cavities of poultry, meat or fish. Do not pack it in. Chicken stock and chicken fats are excellent for preparing dressings. Discretion should be used in seasoning. As previously noted, too much seasoning is worse than none at all. Bear in mind that you are not cooking for your own preference but for general acceptability.

Cooking Time Stuffed turkeys require about one more hour of cooking time than turkeys that are not stuffed. (See time tables at right above.) Many operations no longer stuff turkeys, but bake the dressing separately. This saves time and makes possible better use of carcasses for stock.

Farces and Duxelles In classical cookery, stuffings are further classified as farces and duxelles (pronounced due-sel).

Farces are made of forcemeats (finely chopped

TIMETABLE FOR ROASTING FOWL*

TURKEY-STUFFED, READY-TO-COOK WEIGHT*

Ready to Cook Weight Pounds	Oven Temperature	Total Roasting Time— Approximate Hours— Stuffed Bird	Internal Temperature
Whole Birds			
4 to 6	325°F.	3 to 3¾	190–195°F.
6 to 8	325°F.	3¾ to 4½	190–195°F.
8 to 10	325°F.	4 to 4½	190–195°F.
10 to 12	325°F.	4½ to 5	190–195°F.
12 to 14	325°F.	5 to 5¼	190–195°F.
14 to 16	325°F.	5¼ to 6	190–195°F.
16 to 18	325°F.	6 to 6½	190–195°F.
18 to 20	325°F.	6½ to 7½	190–195°F.
20 to 24	325°F.	7½ to 9	190–195°F.
Half and Quarter Turkey			
3½ to 5	325°F.	3 to 3½	190–195°F.
5 to 8	325°F.	3½ to 4	190–195°F.
8 to 12	325°F.	4 to 5	190–195°F.

It is advisable to plan work schedules so that turkeys are out of the oven 20 to 30 minutes before serving time. This gives the meat a chance to absorb the juices. It will carve more easily.

CHICKEN*

Ready to cook Weight	Oven Temperature	Approx. Time Stuffed Bird	Approx. Time Unstuffed Bird
1½ to 2½ lb.	325°F.	1¼ to 1¾ hr.	1 to 1¾ hr.
2½ to 3½ lb.	325°F.	2 to 3 hr.	1¾ to 2¾ hr.
3½ to 4¾ lb.	325°F.	3 to 3½ hr.	2¾ to 3¼ hr.
4¾ to 6 lb.	325°F.	3½ to 4 hr.	3¼ to 3¾ hr.

DUCK*

2½ to 3 lb.	325°F.	1¾ to 2 hr.	1½ to 1¾ hr.
3 to 3½ lb.	325°F.	2 to 2½ hr.	1¾ to 2¼ hr.
3½ to 4 lb.	325°F.	2½ to 3 hr.	2¼ to 2¾ hr.

GOOSE*

Ready to cook Weight	Oven Temperature	Approx. Time Stuffed Bird	Approx. Time Unstuffed Bird
6 to 8 lb.	325°F.	3 to 3½ hr.	2¾ to 3¼ hr.
8 to 10 lb.	325°F.	3½ to 3¾ hr.	3¼ to 3½ hr.
10 to 12 lb.	325°F.	3¾ to 4¼ hr.	3½ to 4 hr.

*Courtesy of Poultry and Egg National Board

or ground meat, fish or poultry), highly seasoned, with various binding ingredients. Meat, poultry or fish for farces may be raw or cooked prior to their incorporation.

Types of Farces There are two types of farces:
1) Mousseline—a very light farce, bound together with egg whites and cream.
2) Farces with a panada base. Escoffier describes these preparations as: Bread panada or Panade au Pain, prepared from cooked fresh bread crumbs and milk; Flour panada or Panade a la Farine, prepared from cooked mixture of flour, water and butter; Frangipan panada or Panade a la Frangipan, derived from a cooked mixture of flour, egg yolks, butter, milk and seasonings. Modern methods often substitute heavy cream sauce.

Use of Farces

Farces may be used in a number of different ways:
1) They may be used for stuffing meat, fish or poultry.
2) They may be combined with other products as in:
   (a) Galantines (a decorated dish of boneless poultry)
   (b) Pates (pronounced pah-tay), a pie, baked in

a casserole and having a dough topping; filled with aspic jelly when cooked and allowed to cool. Pate also refers to pastes made from meat and poultry.

(c) Terrines (like pates, but molded and often decorated) without baked dough; originally molded in a shallow, earthenware dish.

Types of Duxelles

Duxelles are of two types:

1) Dry duxelles, or duxelles seches, composed of sauteed, chopped shallots, chopped mushrooms, herbs and seasonings, which serve as a base for:
2) Duxelles with added moisture in the form of Brown Sauce, tomato products, glace de viande, fish fumet, sauces, wines and other ingredients, such as bread crumbs or ham trimmings. Duxelles may be used for stuffing mushrooms, tomatoes and other vegetables or may be combined with a variety of forcemeats to provide further varieties of stuffings and farces.

Basic Bread Stuffing

YIELD: 50 portions	EACH PORTION: 3 oz.	
INGREDIENTS	*QUANTITY*	*METHOD*
Bread, 2 to 4 days old	6 lb.	1. Trim bread, removing crusts; cube. Soak in cold water. Drain.

Celery, chopped
Onions, chopped
Butter
    OR Salad Oil
    OR Bacon Fat
	1 lb.
	3 lb.
	12 oz.
		2. Saute celery and onions in fat until tender.

Poultry Seasoning Salt Sage Parsley, chopped	¾ oz. 1½ oz. ¾ oz. 1½ oz.	3. Combine vegetables, seasonings and bread and toss lightly to blend. 4. Place in greased baking pan and cover with greased paper. Bake at 350° to 375°F. for 1 hr.

Chestnut Dressing No. 1

YIELD: 50 portions	EACH PORTION: 4 to 5 oz.	
INGREDIENTS	*QUANTITY*	*METHOD*

Celery, diced small
Onions, chopped medium
Bacon Fat
    OR Sausage Fat
Fresh Bread Crumbs
Milk
Eggs, whole, beaten
Parsley, chopped
Black Pepper
Chestnuts, cooked, peeled,
    coarsely chopped
Salt
	2 lb.
	4 lb.
	1 pt.
	
	4 qt.
	2 qt.
	8
	3 oz.
	2 tsp.
	3 lb.
	
	to taste
		1. Saute celery and onions in fat until soft. Mix crumbs, milk and eggs together. Add onions, parsley, chestnuts, salt and pepper. Mix well.
		2. Put dressing in greased baking pan and cover with a sheet of greased paper.
		3. Bake at 300°F. for 45 min.

NOTE: When using dried chestnuts soak them overnight before cooking.		
See p. 114 for Chestnut Dressing No. 2.		

ROAST DUCKLING A L'ORANGE *See recipe top of facing page.*

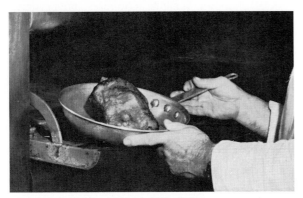

Roast ducklings in a 400°F. oven for about 1½ to 2 hr. A higher temperature is used for roasting ducks than for other poultry to extract grease and to crisp the skin.

Turn ducklings once during the roasting period so that they will brown evenly. When tender, remove to a clean pan and keep warm. Cut each duckling into eight equal portions.

Serve duckling topped with Orange Sauce. Rice is often served as an accompaniment. Plate should be attractively garnished as shown above. (Recipe on facing page.)

Chestnut Dressing No. 2

YIELD: 50 portions	EACH PORTION: about 3½ oz.	
INGREDIENTS	*QUANTITY*	*METHOD*
Onions, finely minced	4 lb.	1. Saute onions in fat until soft. Mix bread cubes, chicken stock and eggs together. Add onions, parsley, chestnuts, sage, salt and pepper.
Bacon Fat	1 pt.	
Dry White Bread, cubed	4 qt.	
Chicken Stock, hot	1½ qt.	2. Put in greased baking pan and cover with a sheet of greased paper.
Eggs, whole, beaten	6	
Parsley, chopped	3 oz.	4. Bake at 350°F. for 45 min.
Black Pepper	2 tsp.	
Sage, ground	1 tbsp.	
Chestnuts, cooked, peeled, chopped	3 lb.	
Salt	to taste	

Roast Duckling a l'Orange

YIELD: 48 portions		EACH PORTION: ¼ duck, 2 oz. sauce
INGREDIENTS	QUANTITY	METHOD
Ducklings (5 to 6 lb.) Salt Pepper	12 for seasoning for seasoning	1. Season cavity of ducks with salt and pepper. 2. Truss ducks and place breast up on racks in roast pan. 3. Roast in oven preheated to 400°F. for 1½ to 2 hr. or until done, turning as required.
Oranges Lemons	6 4	4. Peel zest from oranges and lemons. Squeeze juice from zested fruit; combine juices and reserve. 5. Cut zest in fine julienne and blanch in boiling water for 5 min. Drain well and reserve.
Sugar Vinegar, Wine Orange Juice Espagnole, strained, hot (simmered with duck trimmings)	8 oz. 8 oz. 1 pt. 4 qt.	6. Place the sugar in a saucepan. Cook over low heat until sugar is caramelized. 7. Add the vinegar and reserved fruit juices, plus 1 pt. orange juice. Reduce to half. 8. Combine with Espagnole and hold over low heat.
White Wine (dry)	1 pt.	9. When ducks are cooked, remove to clean pan and keep ducks warm. 10. Pour off all fat from pan. Deglaze pan with white wine and strain resulting liquor into sauce. Simmer sauce for about 5 min. to finish. 11. Adjust seasoning and consistency as required. 12. Cut ducks in portion size, removing small breast bones, etc. 13. For service, sprinkle each duck portion with a small amount of blanched orange and lemon zest. Serve about 2 oz. of sauce over each duck portion.

Optional:
    Red Currant Jelly
    Cointreau
	2 oz.
	8 oz.
		If using cointreau and/or currant jelly, they should be added to sauce with deglazing liquor and simmered for about 5 min. to finish sauce.

NOTE: For quantity service, fruit zest may be added directly to sauce immediately prior to serving.		
See color picture, p. 103.		

Salmis of Duckling

YIELD: 48 portions		EACH PORTION: 2 pcs. duck with sauce
INGREDIENTS	QUANTITY	METHOD
Butter, melted Onions, small dice Mushrooms, washed and cut in ½ in. pieces	1 lb. 1 lb. 3 lb.	1. Saute onions and mushrooms in butter in sauce pot until tender.
Bread Flour Brown Stock, hot (p. 271) Burgundy Wine	12 oz. 5 qt. 1 pt.	2. Add flour, blend well and cook 10 min., browning lightly. Add hot stock and stir until thickened and smooth. Incorporate wine.
Duck, roasted, cut in 8 pieces per duck	12	3. Place duck in roast pans. Pour sauce over duck. 4. Bake at 350°F. for ½ hr. 5. Remove from oven and adjust seasoning of sauce. Serve 2 pieces of duck in casserole and cover with sauce.
NOTE: Varied rices often accompany this dish.		

Poultry

FRIED CHICKEN MARYLAND *(recipe on facing page)*

Disjoint 25 2¼ to 2½ lb. chickens and clean. Dredge in seasoned flour. Dip chickens in egg wash, then in bread crumbs, following standard breading procedure (p. 178).

Heat ¼ in. oil in heavy skillets. When oil is hot, add chickens and fry until golden brown on all sides. Remove to sheet pans and complete cooking in 350°F. oven.

Ladle cream sauce on plate or platter and make a ring of tomato sauce outside around cream sauce. Place ½ disjointed chicken on sauce and top with two strips of bacon.

Add corn fritter sprinkled with powdered sugar to plate. See recipe above for other variations of fried chicken: Baltimore, Virginia, New England, Vermont, with Sour Cream Gravy.

Curried Chicken

YIELD: 50 portions	EACH PORTION: 4 oz. chicken, 4 oz. sauce	
INGREDIENTS	*QUANTITY*	*METHOD*
Chicken Meat, cooked, boned, skinned	12 lb.	1. Cut each leg in 4 pieces and each single breast in 4 pieces.
Onions, chopped fine Butter Bread Flour Curry Powder	2 lb. 1½ lb. 1½ lb. 1¾ oz.	2. Melt butter. Saute onions in butter until transparent. Add flour and curry powder and cook for 10 min. Do not brown.
Chicken Stock, hot Light Cream, hot Salt	6 qt. 1 qt. as needed.	3. Add hot stock and cream gradually, stirring until thickened and smooth. Season to taste with salt. 4. Reheat chicken meat in stock it was cooked in and drain well. 5. Place heated chicken in pans; pour sauce to cover generously in each pan. Shake pan to mix sauce well with chicken without stirring. 6. Heat in oven. Bake at 350°F. for 10 to 15 min. Serve hot.
NOTE: Curried chicken is usually served with rice pilaf or boiled rice and chutney.		

Fried Chicken Maryland

YIELD: 50 portions		EACH PORTION: ½ chicken on 2 oz. sauce with 2 strips bacon and fritter
INGREDIENTS	QUANTITY	METHOD

Chickens, whole
 	
Seasoned Flour:
  Bread Flour
  Salt
  Pepper
	25 (2¼ to
	2½ lb. ea.)
	
	2 lb.
	to taste
	to taste
		1. Disjoint and clean chicken. Season flour with salt and pepper and use to dredge chicken.

Eggs, whole Milk Bread Crumbs	6 1 qt. 2 lb.	2. Prepare egg wash by beating eggs in bowl and adding milk. Dip floured chicken in egg wash, then in bread crumbs, following standard breading procedure.
Salad Oil	1 qt.	3. Place chicken in ¼ in. hot oil in heavy skillets. Fry until golden brown on both sides. Remove and complete cooking in sheet pans or roast pans in 350°F. oven.
Cream Sauce (p. 314) Tomato Sauce (p. 318)	1 gal. 2 qt.	4. Prepare Cream Sauce and Tomato Sauce.
Bacon slices, cooked crisp Corn Fritters Powdered Sugar	100 50 for fritters	5. To serve, ladle 2 oz. Cream Sauce on plate or platter and make ring of Tomato Sauce outside around Cream Sauce. Place ½ disjointed chicken on sauce and top with 2 strips of crisp bacon, placed crossways. Sprinkle corn fritter with powdered sugar and place on plate with chicken.

VARIATIONS: **Fried Chicken Baltimore**: Serve fried chicken on chicken gravy. Garnish with rice fritters, sweet potato croquettes and bacon.

Fried Chicken Virginia: Serve on Tomato Sauce garnished with grilled ham and mushroom caps. Use Virginia ham, if available.

New England Style: Serve on light chicken gravy; do not color gravy. Garnish with slices of fried salt pork and glazed tiny onions.

With Sour Cream Gravy: 2 parts chicken gravy, 2 parts sour cream; season with vinegar to taste.

Vermont Style: Serve on chicken gravy. Garnish with baked tomato and Canadian bacon.

See color picture, p. 106.

Chicken Pot Pie with Dumplings

YIELD: 50 portions		EACH PORTION: 3 oz. cooked meat, 5 oz. sauce and 1 dumpling
INGREDIENTS	QUANTITY	METHOD
Chicken Meat, cooked, boned, skinned	10 lb.	1. Cut each chicken leg in 4 pieces and each single breast in 4 pieces.
Potatoes, Parisienne, pieces Carrots, Parisienne, pieces Pearl Onions, medium Frozen Peas, cooked	200 200 50 2½ lb.	2. Cook each vegetable separately in boiling, salted water; drain.
Chicken Veloute (p. 317) Dumplings (p. 77)	8 qt. 50	3. Reheat chicken meat in chicken stock or vegetable liquor. Drain chicken meat and combine with vegetables and Veloute, stirring gently to prevent breaking of chicken in small pieces. 4. Serve uniform portions in casseroles and top with dumpling.

NOTE: For individual service, reserve heated peas and top casserole with level serving spoonful (about ¾ oz.).

Poultry

Fricassee of Turkey Wings (recipe below)

Arroz Con Pollo (recipe on facing page)

Fricassee of Turkey Wings

YIELD: 50 portions	**EACH PORTION**: 2 wings with Veloute Sauce	
INGREDIENTS	*QUANTITY*	*METHOD*

Turkey Wings
Water
Mirepoix:
   Onions
   Carrots
   Celery
	100
	to cover
	
	1 lb.
	½ lb.
	½ lb.
		1. Place wings in stock pot, cover with cold water; bring to a boil.
		2. Drain, rinse and re-cover with cold water. Bring to a boil; skim; add mirepoix.
		3. Simmer until done, about 2 hr.

Veloute (p. 317) Salt	6 qt. to taste	4. Remove wings from pot. Pull bones from meat, leaving meat in one piece. 5. Place the wings in hotel pan and cover with Veloute. Reheat in oven at 350°F. for 15 to 20 min.
NOTE: This entree may be served with a starch product and garnished with peas.		
See color picture, p. 109.		

Chicken Fricassee

YIELD: 50 portions	**EACH PORTION**: 3 oz. chicken, 5 oz. sauce	
INGREDIENTS	*QUANTITY*	*METHOD*
Pearl Onions, medium	100	1. Place onions in cool water to cover, bring to boil and simmer until done but not soft.
Mushroom Caps, small Lemon Juice	50 from 1 lemon	2. Cook mushroom caps in small amount of boiling salted water with juice of 1 lemon.
		3. Drain onions and mushrooms well.
Chicken Meat, cooked, boned, skinned Chicken Veloute (p. 317)	10 lb. 8 qt.	4. Reheat chicken meat in stock it was cooked in; drain. 5. Combine drained vegetables and chicken meat with sauce, stirring gently to prevent breaking of chicken in small pieces. Serve with buttered noodles, if desired.
See color picture, p. 105.		

Arroz Con Pollo

YIELD: 4 portions		
INGREDIENTS	QUANTITY	METHOD
Broiler-Fryers, cut in small pieces or disjointed Olive Oil	2 2-2/3 oz.	1. Saute chicken in oil in frying pan until brown. Remove to 1½ or 2 qt. casserole.
Onion, chopped Green Pepper, diced Garlic, minced	1 3 oz. 1 clove	2. Add onion, green pepper and garlic to same frying pan and saute until tender.
Chicken Stock Rice, raw Tomatoes, peeled and quartered Pimientoes, diced Saffron Salt Pepper	12 oz. 8 oz. 4 3-1/2 oz. 1/8 tsp. to taste to taste	3. Stir stock, rice, tomatoes, pimientoes and seasonings into onion and green pepper mixture. 4. Pour over chicken. Bake, covered, at 350°F. for 30 to 35 min. or until done.
Green Peas, cooked	4 oz.	5. Serve in casserole garnished with green peas.
See color picture, p. 102.		

Chicken Marengo

YIELD: 50 portions	EACH PORTION: ½ chicken and sauce	
INGREDIENTS	QUANTITY	METHOD
Chickens, disjointed (2¼ to 2½ lb.) Salad Oil	25 2 qt.	1. Salt and pepper chickens. Saute in 1 qt. oil until golden brown. Place in brazier with chicken legs on one side of pan and breasts on the other.
Chicken Stock Shallot Butter Garlic Cloves White Wine Tomato Sauce (p. 318) Espagnole Sauce (p. 312)	1 qt. ¼ lb. 3 cloves 1 qt. ½ gal. ½ gal.	2. Deglaze the sautoirs with 1 qt. chicken stock and save for sauce. 3. Place shallot butter and 3 cloves of crushed garlic in sautoir and cook until aromatic. 4. Add the white wine and reduce to 1 qt. 5. Add Tomato Sauce and Espagnole Sauce. 6. Simmer about ½ hr. Strain through a fine china cap over the chickens.
Butter Mushrooms, washed, sliced	½ lb. 4 lb.	7. Place ½ lb. butter in sautoir and add mushrooms. Saute until done and spread over the chickens. 8. Cover brazier; bring sauce to boil on range, then finish in oven at 350°F. for 45 min. or until tender.
Eggs	50	EGGS: 1. Heat 2 to 3 in. of oil to smoking point in a heavy sauce pot. 2. Break 1 egg into small dish and slide carefully into oil. Shape egg white with wooden spoon by forming around yolk. When half done, turn egg over to finish browning. 3. Drain well and serve on top of chicken as a garnish.
NOTE: Sweetwater crayfish and croutons are sometimes used as additional garnish (see picture).		
See color picture, p. 102.		

Roast Turkey with Gravy (recipe below)   *Chicken a la King (recipe facing page)*

Roast Turkey with Gravy

YIELD: 35 portions	EACH PORTION: about 4 to 5 oz.	
INGREDIENTS	*QUANTITY*	*METHOD*

Turkey (eviscerated)
Salt
Pepper
Salad Oil
Mirepoix:
  Onions, medium chopped
  Celery, medium chopped
  Carrots, medium chopped
	24 lb.
	to taste
	to taste
	3 oz.
	
	½ lb.
	¼ lb.
	¼ lb.
		1. Lightly oil turkey. Salt and pepper inside. Place on side in roasting pan.
		2. Roast at 350°F. for 1½ hr. Turn to opposite side and cook an additional 1½ hr. Place turkey breast side up, add mirepoix and roast for 1 more hr. or until done.

Bread Flour Chicken Stock, hot	6 oz. 3 qt.	3. Remove turkey from pan. Place pan in oven or on top of range and reduce excess moisture from the fat. Blend in flour and cook about 8 to 10 min. over slow heat. 4. Add hot stock and blend well. Simmer for 15 min. Strain the gravy, adjust seasoning and hold for service (A small amount of raw butter may be worked into gravy for additional richness.)
See color picture p. 109.		

Alternate Method for Preparing Turkey Gravy

METHOD

1. Remove cooked turkey from roast pan. Place remaining contents of roast pan (above) in sauce pot and deglaze roast pan with chicken stock. Add this liquid to the sauce pot.
2. Add desired amount of chicken stock.
3. Simmer contents until vegetables become mushy. Strain through a china cap and let stock rest for a few minutes to allow turkey fat to form on top of stock. Skim off as much fat as desired for roux. (Turkey usually provides an excess of fat that is quite strong in flavor.)
4. Add flour to turkey fat to make roux. Cook 5 to 10 min. browning lightly.
5. While roux is cooking, skim balance of fat from stock. Keep stock hot. Fat may be discarded or cooked slowly to evaporate liquid and reserved for future use.
6. When roux is cooked, whip small amounts of roux

into stock. After each addition, incorporate fully and stir smooth before adding more. Add sufficient roux for flavor only. If gravy requires further thickening add a small amount of butter roux. (Use of turkey roux alone often results in a flavor that is too strong.)

7. Simmer gravy for about 5 min., beating smooth. Adjust seasoning and bring to a boil to finish.
8. For **Giblet Gravy**, add chopped or ground cooked chicken or turkey giblets (hearts and gizzards) to turkey gravy. When giblets are added, bring gravy to a boil quickly in a heavy pot. Remove to bain marie or cooling area. The fine particles and small pieces of giblets tend to stick to the bottom of the pot and burn easily if care is not taken to prevent this.

NOTE: The above procedures are more involved than other methods, but are especially well suited to preparation of large quantities.

Chicken a la King

YIELD: 50 portions	EACH PORTION: 3 oz. chicken, 5½ oz. sauce	
INGREDIENTS	*QUANTITY*	*METHOD*
Mushrooms, diced (½ in.) Butter, melted Bread Flour Chicken Stock, hot Milk, hot Light Cream, hot	2 lb. 2 lb. 16 oz. 2 qt. 3 qt. 1 qt.	1. Saute mushrooms in melted butter until soft. Add flour. Stir, and cook slowly for 10 min. Do not brown. 2. Add hot stock. Stir until slightly thickened and smooth. Add milk and cream and blend well.
Green Peppers, diced (½ in.) Pimientoes, drained, diced (½ in. square) Salt Sherry Wine	1 lb. 2 4 oz. cans to taste 6 oz.	3. Cook peppers in boiling salted water for 5 min. Drain peppers and add to sauce with pimientoes. 4. Add sherry and adjust seasoning. Reheat chicken meat in stock it was cooked in and drain.
Chicken Meat, cooked, boneless, skinless, diced (1 in.)	9 lb.	5. Combine chicken and sauce, stirring carefully to prevent breaking up pieces of chicken or vegetables.

NOTE: May be served with rice, in patty shell, on toast or en casserole with toast points.

See color picture, p. 104.

Individual Chicken Pie with Flaky Crust

YIELD: 50 portions	EACH PORTION: 3 oz. chicken, 2 oz. vegetables, 5 oz. sauce	
INGREDIENTS	*QUANTITY*	*METHOD*
Chicken Meat, cooked, boned and skinned	10 lb.	1. Cut each chicken leg in 4 pieces and each single breast in 4 pieces.
Potatoes, raw, dice (½ in.) Carrots, medium dice (about 3/8 in.) Frozen Peas, cooked Pearl Onions, small	2 qt. 1½ qt. 2½ lb. 100	2. Cook vegetables separately in boiling salted water and drain.
Chicken Veloute (p. 317)	8 qt.	3. Place casseroles on sheet pan with small amount of water at bottom of sheet pan to prevent buckling. 4. Place 3 oz. of meat in each casserole, distributing white and dark meat uniformly. 5. Divide vegetables evenly among all casseroles. 6. Ladle veloute over vegetables in each casserole, leaving slight space at top for baking crust.
Pie Crust	50 portions	7. Prepare pie crust, cutting crust same shape as casserole but slightly larger to allow for shrinkage in baking. Allow about 2 oz. crust for each pie. Mold crust edges to sides of casserole. 8. Make slight gash or hole in center crust for escape of steam. Brush with eggwash. 9. Place casseroles on sheet pans and bake at 400°F. for 15 min. or until done. Brush with melted butter or margarine. (See picture, p. 126)

NOTE: Crust may be baked separately and placed on casserole at time of service.

Poultry

Chicken Cacciatore (recipe below)

Chicken Stew, Family Style (recipe on facing page)

Chicken Cacciatore

YIELD: 50 portions	EACH PORTION: ½ chicken with 3 oz. sauce	
INGREDIENTS	*QUANTITY*	*METHOD*

Chickens, whole
Seasoned Flour:
   Bread Flour
   Salt
   Pepper
Oil
	25 (2¼ to 2½ lb.)
	
	1½ lb.
	to taste
	to taste
	1½ pt.
		1. Clean and disjoint chicken. Remove rib bones from breast. Dredge in seasoned flour.
		2. Fry chicken in 1/8 in. hot oil in fry pans or heavy skillets until lightly browned on both sides. Place in roast pans, separate white and dark meat.

Onions, cut (1 in. long, ½ in. wide) Mushrooms, cut (½ in. pieces, both caps and stems) Green Peppers, cut (1 in. long, ½ in. wide) Garlic, minced Tomatoes, crushed and juice Marsala OR Madeira Wine Oregano, crushed Salt Pepper	3 lb. 3 lb. 2 lb. 6 tbsp. 2 No. 10 cans 1 pt. 1 tsp. to taste to taste	3. Saute onions, mushrooms, green pepper and garlic in large saucepot in remainder of oil. 4. Cook 15 min.; add crushed tomatoes with juice, wine and seasoning. 5. Blend well, pour sauce over chicken and bake covered for 45 min. to 1 hr. 6. Serve ½ chicken for each portion, using both white and dark meat. Serve with 3 oz. sauce.
See color picture, p. 102.		

Breast of Chicken Saute Hongroise

YIELD: 12 portions	EACH PORTION: 1 chicken breast	
INGREDIENTS	*QUANTITY*	*METHOD*
Chicken Breasts (from 6 3½ lb. chickens) Butter	12 as needed	1. Saute breasts in butter until tender and a golden brown. Place on platter.
Shallots, finely chopped Dry White Wine Hungarian Paprika Supreme Sauce	1 tbsp. 5 oz. 2 tbsp. 1 pt.	2. In same pan, cook shallots in butter, deglaze pan with wine; reduce to 1 oz. liquid. Add paprika and supreme sauce; cook 5 min.
Light Cream Ham, lean, cooked, julienne	1½ pt. 4 oz.	3. Strain sauce through cheesecloth, add cream and julienne ham. Heat, but do not boil; pour over chicken breasts and serve with spaetzli (p. 288), rice or noodles.

Chicken Stew, Family Style

YIELD: 50 portions	EACH PORTION:	½ chicken with vegetables
INGREDIENTS	*QUANTITY*	*METHOD*
Broiler-Fryers	25	1. Cook chicken as instructed in text. Cool. 2. Remove legs. Disjoint drumsticks from upper legs. Do not remove bones. 3. Disjoint wings at breast and cut off tips. 4. Remove breasts, cut in two pieces each. 5. Skim fat from stock from cooked chickens, reserve fat for roux.
Butter Bread Flour	as needed 12 oz.	6. Add butter, if necessary, to make 12 oz. fat. 7. Prepare roux from bread flour and fat.
Peas, frozen Carrots, peeled, cut (¾ in. pieces) Potatoes, peeled, cut (¾ in. pieces) Turnips, peeled, cut (¾ in. pieces) Pearl Onions, peeled	2½ lb. 100 pieces 100 pieces 50 pieces 100	8. Cook each vegetable separately in chicken stock to cover until done. Drain, reserving all stock except that used to cook turnips. 9. Combine vegetable stock with stock from cooking chickens to make 2 gal. Add 2 gal. stock to roux. Cook and stir until smooth and thickened. Season to taste, enriching with chicken base if necessary. 10. Combine all ingredients, mixing carefully. Place in hotel pans, cover with greased paper. Bake at 350° F. 20 min. 11. Serve chicken and vegetables in equal portions.

Chicken Chow Mein

YIELD: 50 portions	EACH PORTION:	10 to 12 oz.
INGREDIENTS	*QUANTITY*	*METHOD*
Oil Celery, cleaned, trimmed, thinly sliced on bias	1 qt. 8 lb.	1. Put oil in wok or large brazier and place over very hot fire until it begins to smoke. 2. Add celery and stir. Cook for 5 min., but do not brown.
Onions, peeled, cut in half lengthwise and cut (1/8-in. thick on bias) Monosodium Glutamate	8 lb. 3 tbsp.	3. Add onions and monosodium glutamate. Cook vegetables to crispy texture, stirring briskly (7 to 8 min.). Remove from fire.
Water Chestnuts Bamboo Shoots, sliced Bean Sprouts	1 No. 2½ can 1 No. 2½ can 1 No. 10 can	4. Drain water chestnuts, bamboo shoots and bean sprouts, reserving liquid. Slice water chestnuts and bamboo shoots paper thin and heat with the bean sprouts in liquid from cans.
Cornstarch Cold Water Soy Sauce Chicken Stock, hot	1 lb. 1 pt. 4 oz. 1 gal.	5. Blend cornstarch in mixture of cold water and soy sauce. 6. Whip cornstarch mixture briskly into hot stock and heat until thickened, smooth and glossy.
Chicken Meat, cooked, skinless, boneless	6 lb.	7. Cut cooked chicken in strips 1 in. long and ¼ in. wide, reserving 1 whole breast cut in fine julienne for garnishing. 8. Add chicken strips to sauce. 9. Drain bean sprouts, water chestnuts and bamboo shoots and add to celery and onions. 10. Add sauce with the chicken meat. Mix well and adjust seasoning. Serve in casserole with fried noodles and Chinese steamed rice.

NOTE: Soy sauce is served at the table. Peanut oil is preferred for Chinese cookery.

Poultry

Turkey Mushroom Pie with Cornbread Topping, right (recipe below)

Chicken Chasseur, far right (recipe bottom of page)

Turkey Mushroom Pie with Cornbread Topping

YIELD: 50 portions		EACH PORTION: 8 to 10 oz.
INGREDIENTS	*QUANTITY*	*METHOD*
Butter Onions, minced Mushrooms, sliced Lemon Juice Sherry Wine	6 oz. 8 oz. 3 lb. to taste 8 oz.	1. Melt butter, add onions and saute until transparent. Add mushrooms and lemon juice; cook until tender. 2. Add sherry wine; reduce to one-half.
Turkey Meat, cooked, diced Turkey Veloute Sauce (p. 317) Salt Pepper Pimiento, diced	8 lb. 2 gal. to taste to taste ½ pt.	3. Add turkey meat and heat thoroughly. Add turkey veloute and bring to a boil. Adjust seasonings. Add pimiento last. 4. Ladle out individual portions into casseroles.

CORNBREAD TOPPING:
  Cornmeal
  Flour
  Sugar
  Baking Powder
  Salt
  Milk
  Eggs, well beaten
  Fat, melted
	
	14 oz.
	13 oz.
	5 oz.
	3 oz.
	1½ tsp.
	1½ pt.
	3
	3 tbsp.
		
		5. Sift dry cornbread topping ingredients together. Add milk, beaten eggs and melted fat. Mix well.
		6. Spoon Cornbread Topping over each portion. Bake at 400°F. for about 30 min., until cornbread is done.

See color picture, p. 108.		

Chicken Chasseur

YIELD: 10 portions		EACH PORTION: ½ chicken with sauce
INGREDIENTS	*QUANTITY*	*METHOD*
Chickens, disjointed (2½ to 3 lb. ea.) Salt, variable Pepper Salad Oil	5 2 tbsp. ½ tsp. 8 oz.	1. Clean and disjoint chickens. Season chicken with salt and pepper. 2. Heat oil in large saute pan. Add chicken pieces and brown carefully on all sides.

Shallots or Onions
Garlic Cloves, chopped
Mushrooms, sliced fine
White Wine
Tomatoes, fresh, peeled, seeded
  and cut in cubes
  OR Tomatoes, canned
Demi-glaze
	2 oz.
	2
	1 lb.
	8 oz.
	
	1 qt.
	1 No. 2½ can
	8 oz.
		3. To prepare sauce: Remove all but ½ cup of the oil in saute pan, add chopped shallots or onions; smother until tender; add garlic and mushrooms and saute; add white wine. Add tomatoes; if using fresh tomatoes continue to smother a few minutes. Add demi-glaze. Bring to a boil. Check the seasonings; reduce to simmering.
		4. Add the chicken, cover and continue to cook for about ½ hr. or until tender.

Fines Herbes, chopped	2 oz.	5. Sprinkle chopped fines herbes over when serving.

Roast Chicken, right (recipe below)

Broiled Chicken Half, far right (recipe bottom of page)

Roast Chicken

YIELD: 48 portions		EACH PORTION: ¼ chicken
INGREDIENTS	*QUANTITY*	*METHOD*
Oil Roasting Chickens	8 oz. 12 (4 lb. ea.)	1. Lightly oil chicken. Place on side in roasting pan in oven at 350°F.
Mirepoix: 　Onions, coarsely chopped 　Celery, coarsely chopped 　Carrots, coarsely chopped	1 lb. ½ lb. ½ lb.	2. Roast for ½ hr., then turn to opposite side and continue roasting for another ½ hr. For the last ½ hr. place chicken breast side up and add coarsely cut mirepoix. Roast until done. (Total cooking time is about 1½ hr.)
Bread Flour Chicken Stock Salt	10 oz. 1 gal. 2 oz.	3. Remove chicken from pan. Place pan in oven or on top of range to reduce excess moisture from fat. 4. Blend in the flour and cook about 8 to 10 min. over slow heat. 5. Add hot stock and blend well with roux. Simmer for about 15 min. Strain sauce, adjust seasoning and hold for service.
NOTE: A small amount of raw butter may be worked into the sauce for additional richness.		

Broiled Chicken Half

YIELD: 50 portions		EACH PORTION: ½ chicken
INGREDIENTS	*QUANTITY*	*METHOD*
Broiler-Fryers (2½ lb. each) Salad Oil Salt, variable	25 8 oz. 3 tbsp.	1. Clean and split chickens. Brush chickens with oil and season with salt. 2. Place in wire hand racks and adjust broiler rack to low point. Place chickens (in hand racks) under pre-heated broiler, skin side down. Cook several minutes until medium brown. Turn over with skin side up and cook until grill marks show and chicken begins to brown.
Butter, melted	1 lb.	3. Remove from racks and place in roast pans. Add a small amount of melted butter, if necessary, to prevent sticking. Bake at 350°F. until done. Drum stick joint should move freely when cooked. 4. Brush with melted butter at service time. 5. If necessary, chickens may be held in warm place for a short while and reheated for service.
NOTE: Drumstick joint is sometimes removed or paper frills, sometimes called "pants," are attached to end of leg bone.		

Poultry

Chicken Pot Pie, right (recipe below)

Poulet a la Kiev, far right (recipe bottom of page)

Chicken Pot Pie

YIELD: 1 portion		
INGREDIENTS	*QUANTITY*	*METHOD*
White Meat of Chicken, cooked	2 oz.	1. Cut chicken in large pieces and place in a deep pie dish with the cooked vegetables.
Dark Meat of Chicken, cooked	1 oz.	2. Pour hot Veloute over chicken and vegetables and cover with thin pastry; bake at 425°F. until crust is done.
Cooked Vegetables:		
Small White Onions	2	
Mushroom Cap	1	
Carrots, pieces	5	
Potatoes, Parisienne	5	
Green Peas	1 tbsp.	
Veloute, hot (p. 317)	¾ cup	
Pastry Cover	1	
NOTE: In quantity service, casseroles may be placed on sheet pans in water and baked to prevent pies from drying out.		
See color picture, p. 105.		

Poulet a la Kiev

YIELD: 4 portions	**EACH PORTION:** ½ chicken breast	
INGREDIENTS	*QUANTITY*	*METHOD*
Chicken Breasts (halves)	4	1. Skin chicken and remove breastbones. 2. Cut off wing tips leaving small wing bones attached to the meat as a handle. 3. Place each chicken breast butterflied between 2 sheets of waxed paper, skin side down. 4. Beat gently with wooden mallet, starting in the center, until ¼ in. thick. Remove the paper.
Sweet Butter	1/8 lb.	5. In the middle of each breast place a small finger of firm cold butter, a bit of garlic, ½ tsp. chopped chives, salt and pepper. Roll up, tuck in each end.
Garlic, minced	1 clove	6. Dust lightly with flour, brush with beaten egg and roll in bread crumbs. Fry in pan in hot fat (350°F.) until golden brown and breast is cooked. Chill before cooking for best results.
Chives	2 tsp.	
OR Marjoram, finely chopped		
Salt	to taste	
Pepper	to taste	7. Remove and drain on absorbent paper.
Flour	2-3/8 oz.	8. Put paper cutlet frills on wing bone, serve on hot platter with watercress or parsley.
Egg, beaten	1	
White Bread Crumbs	2 oz.	9. Serve with Poulette Sauce, p. 317.
Watercress	for garnish	
OR Parsley		
See color picture, p. 102.		

Chickenburgers,
(recipe below)

Turkey or Chicken
Croquettes (recipe
bottom of page)

Chickenburgers

YIELD: 50 portions	**EACH PORTION**: 7 oz. burger	
INGREDIENTS	*QUANTITY*	*METHOD*
Chicken Meat (raw), trimmed from legs and thigs Pork, raw	14 lb. 4 lb.	1. Cut up chicken and pork so that it can pass through the grinder.
Celery Onions Chicken Fat	2 lb. 1 lb. 5 oz.	2. Chop celery and onions finely and saute in chicken fat. Allow to cool before mixing with cold chicken mix.
Eggs Heavy Cream Salt Pepper Parsley, bunches	8 ½ pt. to taste to taste 2	3. Combine all ingredients and mix, then pass through medium grinder and then fine grinder. 4. Scale 7 oz. portions, then shape burgers, using oil so that they will not stick to board. 5. Place on sheet pans and pan broil or saute until done.
See color picture, p. 105.		

Turkey or Chicken Croquettes

YIELD: 50 portions	**EACH PORTION**: 2 croquettes	
INGREDIENTS	*QUANTITY*	*METHOD*
Celery, chopped fine Onions, chopped fine Butter, melted Bread Flour Milk, hot Turkey Meat, cooked, chopped fine Parsley, chopped Salt Pepper	1 lb. 1 lb. 1½ lb. 1½ lb. 2 qt. 8 lb. 3 oz. to taste to taste	1. Saute celery and onions in butter. Add flour to make roux and cook 8 to 10 min. Add hot milk, stir until thick and smooth. 2. Add turkey and parsley and mix thoroughly. Season to taste with salt and pepper.
		3. Put mixture in greased baking pan and cover top with sheet of waxed paper. Bake at 350°F. for 45 min. Remove from oven and cool.
		4. Portion each croquette with level No. 20 ice cream scoop. Form into cones of uniform size and shape. 5. Bread croquettes using standard procedure (p. 178). Deep fry at 350°F. until golden brown.
NOTE: Croquettes are usually served 2 to an order with Cream Sauce (p. 314) or Supreme Sauce (p. 317). They may be garnished with chopped parsley.		

Poultry

Chicken Tetrazzini, right (recipe top of facing page)

Roast Capon, far right (recipe bottom of facing page)

Supreme of Rock Cornish Game Hen Gourmet

YIELD: 1 portion		
INGREDIENTS	*QUANTITY*	*METHOD*
Avocado	½	1. Cut avocado in half and remove stone. 2. Scoop out 20 pearls with very small Parisienne scoop and set aside.
Lean Ham, diced Large Mushroom, diced and sauteed Truffle, diced Cream Sauce Salt Pepper	3 oz. 1 ½ 1 tbsp. to taste to taste	3. Combine ham, mushroom and truffle with Cream Sauce. Season with salt and pepper. 4. Fill cavity of avocado.
Breast of Rock Cornish Game Hen, boned Butter	½ ½ oz.	5. Saute breast of hen in butter for 5 min. until golden brown. 6. Place on half stuffed avocado.
Heavy Cream Egg Yolk Duchesse Potatoes (p. 212)	3 tbsp. 1 2 oz.	7. Combine cream with egg yolk and pour over breast. 8. Pipe a border of Duchesse Potatoes (p. 212) around the avocado with pastry bag and star cone. 9. Place the avocado pearls on border around the avocado and glaze in broiler for 1 min. 10. Heat at 300°F. in oven for 5 min. Serve hot.

Supreme (Delice) of Rock Cornish Game Hen

YIELD: 1 portion		
INGREDIENTS	*QUANTITY*	*METHOD*
Whole Breast of Rock Cornish Game Hen Lean Ham, in 1 stick Black Truffle, in stick Foie Gras (goose liver paste) Salt Pepper	1 ½ oz. ½ ½ oz. to taste to taste	1. Butterfly and stuff the breast of Rock Cornish Game Hen with the ham, truffle, goose liver and seasoning. Close with 2 toothpicks.
Flour Egg, beaten Bread Crumbs Salad Oil	as needed 1 2 oz. as needed	2. Coat with flour, egg and bread crumbs. Fry in hot oil on all sides for about 10 min. or until a golden brown.
Potato Lorette (p. 214) Oil Duxelle: chopped mushrooms (p. 113) stuffed into Tomato, halved	4 oz. for deep frying 2 tbsp. 1	3. Pipe Potato Lorette with a star cone and pastry bag on a greased sheet of paper in the form of a crown. 4. Deep fry in 400°F. fat for 2 min. 5. Drain on sheet of paper. Place breast in center of potato crown. 6. Place stuffed tomato on plate with hen as a garnish.
NOTE: Artichoke bottom stuffed with puree of green peas may be served on the side.		

Chicken Tetrazzini

YIELD: 6 portions		
INGREDIENTS	*QUANTITY*	*METHOD*

Chicken
Mirepoix:
   Onion, sliced
   Carrot, sliced
   Celery, sliced
   Salt
   Pepper
   Parsley
   Bay Leaf
	1 (6 lb.)
	
	1
	1
	1 rib
	to taste
	to taste
	1 sprig
	1
		1. Truss chicken and place in heavy sauce pan with mirepoix of sliced onion, carrot, celery, salt, pepper, parsley and bay leaf. Add just enough cold water to cover chicken and bring to a boil. Simmer chicken covered until tender. (Variable: about 2 to 2½ hr.)
		2. Remove chicken, reserving stock. Remove meat from bones and cut into strips.

Mushrooms Butter Flour Chicken Stock Cream Egg Yolk Sherry Cayenne Pepper	½ lb. ¼ lb. ¾ oz. 12 oz. 4 oz. 1 ¾ oz. to taste	3. Slice mushrooms and cook in 2 oz. butter until lightly browned. 4. In another pan, melt 2 oz. butter. Remove from heat and blend in flour, salt and a pinch of cayenne pepper. Add 1½ cups chicken stock and blend over heat. 5. Beat cream and egg yolk in a cup and add to sauce; stir until sauce is hot. Do not boil. Add sherry, chicken and mushrooms.

Thin Spaghetti
   OR Spaghettini
   OR Vermicelli
Parmesan Cheese, grated
	½ lb.
	
	5 oz.
		6. Meanwhile, boil thin spaghetti in 3 qt. water until al dente. Rinse in warm water and drain. Arrange spaghetti in individual casseroles. Place chicken mixture in center. Sprinkle with grated cheese and dot with butter. Place under broiler until golden brown. Royal Glaze (p. 322) may be used if desired.

NOTE: In quantity service, casseroles may be placed on sheet pans in water and browned in hot oven.		

Roast Capon

YIELD: 50 portions	EACH PORTION: about 6 oz.	
INGREDIENTS	*QUANTITY*	*METHOD*
Capons, eviscerated	35 lb. (total)	1. Clean and tie capons. Brush with salad oil. Sprinkle cavity of each lightly with salt. Add mirepoix. Tie legs together.

Salad Oil
Salt
Mirepoix:
   Onions, coarsely chopped
   Carrots, coarsely chopped
   Celery, coarsely chopped
	as needed
	as needed
	
	1 lb.
	8 oz.
	8 oz.
		2. Roast according to method for Roast Chicken, (p. 125), increasing the cooking time to about 2 hr.

Bread Flour Chicken Stock, hot	10 oz. 1 gal.	3. To make gravy, remove capons from pan. Reduce pan drippings by boiling for 5 to 10 min. Blend flour into drippings. Cook over low heat for 8 to 10 min. stirring constantly. Slowly incorporate hot chicken stock. Simmer 15 min. Strain.
		4. Slice capon as Turkey. Serve white and dark meat on top of a No. 12 scoop of dressing. 5. Serve with 2 oz. gravy and garnish.
NOTE: Roast capon is often served with Chestnut Dressing. Recipes are on pp. 113-114.		
See color picture, p. 104.		

Poultry

Breast of Chicken, Eugenie, right (recipe top of facing page)

Poulet Roti Farci, far right (recipe bottom of facing page)

Wiener Backhendl (Deep Fried Breaded Rock Cornish Hen)

YIELD: 1 portion

INGREDIENTS	QUANTITY	METHOD
Rock Cornish Game Hen, whole Lemon Juice Salt Pepper Flour Egg, beaten Bread Crumbs, fine, dry	1 2 oz. to taste to taste ¼ oz. 1 2 oz.	1. Cut hen in 6 parts and remove legs. 2. Cut legs in half. Cut breast in half in the center. Remove skin but not bones. 3. Dip in lemon juice seasoned with salt and pepper. 4. Roll in flour, then egg and then bread crumbs.
Salad Oil Parsley, fresh	1 qt. 3 to 4 sprigs	5. Heat oil for deep frying to 375°F., add hen and fry for 7 to 8 min., completely submerging in oil. 6. Drain on paper towels or trays with wire racks. 7. Remove stems from parsley and fry tops. Drain on paper towels. Serve hen with lemon wedge and the fried parsley.

NOTE: This dish, originally Viennese, is usually served with freshly made potato salad made with new potatoes or the typical **Viennese Kipferl'** potatoes (oil, cream and lemon dressing with salt and pepper).

See color picture, p. 107.

Breast of Rock Cornish Game Hen Palermitana

YIELD: 1 portion

INGREDIENTS	QUANTITY	METHOD
Butter Fresh Mushrooms, sliced Shallot, chopped	2 oz. 3 oz. ½	1. Saute mushrooms and shallot in 2 oz. butter.
Whole Eggplant Slice, cut lengthwise (¼ in. thick) Tomato Slice Parmesan Cheese, grated	1 1 1 tsp.	2. On top of eggplant, place slice of tomato, parmesan cheese, mushroom and shallot.
Breast of Rock Cornish Game Hen, boned, cooked Salt Pepper	1 to taste to taste	3. Place breast on top of ingredients in Step 2. 4. Season with salt and pepper.
Flour Egg, slightly beaten Bread Crumbs Butter	for breading 1 for breading 2 oz.	5. Coat entire surface with flour, egg wash and bread crumbs. 6. Pan fry in foamy butter 5 min. on each side to a golden brown.

NOTE: Diamond of red pimiento may be placed on top for garnish.

See color picture, p. 107.

Breast of Chicken, Eugenie

YIELD: 50 portions	EACH PORTION: ½ chicken breast on ham, toast with 2 oz. sauce	
INGREDIENTS	*QUANTITY*	*METHOD*
Chicken Breasts, whole (1 lb. ea.)	25	1. Place chicken breasts in pot of boiling water. Simmer gently for 10 min. after water returns to boil. 2. Remove from fire. Cool breasts in cold running water. 3. Remove skin and bones, dividing double breast in two equal, single portions.
Bread Flour Salt White Pepper	2 lb. 2 tbsp. to taste	4. Dredge in seasoned flour.
Salad Oil	1 qt.	5. Saute breasts in oil in heavy skillet until light, golden brown. Remove and keep hot; finish cooking in oven at 350°F. if necessary.
Ham Slices, pre-cooked, (about 2 in. by 4 in., 2½ oz. ea.)	50	6. Place ham slices on sheet pan under broiler. Heat through on both sides.
Bread Slices, trimmed, toasted	50	7. To serve, place slice of toast on platter or plate. Top with ham slice. Place 1 breast each, outside up, on ham slice. Dress each portion with Supreme Sauce. Place sauteed mushroom cap on top.
Supreme Sauce (p. 317) Mushroom Caps, medium	1 gal. 50	
NOTE: This entree is sometimes served under glass "bell," (termed Sous Cloche).		

Poulet Roti Farci

YIELD: 4 portions	EACH PORTION: 1/4 chicken with stuffing and gravy	
INGREDIENTS	*QUANTITY*	*METHOD*
Butter Onions, chopped	2 tbsp. 1/4 lb.	1. Melt 1 tbsp. butter in small skillet. Add onions and cook over low heat for 5 min.
Sausage Meat Mushrooms, chopped Garlic Chicken Livers, sauteed and chopped Parsley, chopped Thyme Salt Pepper	1/2 lb. 1/4 lb. 1 small clove 5 1 tbsp. 1/4 tsp. to taste to taste	2. Put 1/2 lb. sausage meat in mixing bowl and add cooked onions and mushrooms, garlic, chicken livers, chopped parsley, thyme, salt and pepper; mix thoroughly.
Chicken (3-1/2 to 4 lb.) Salad Oil White Wine Tarragon Watercress	1 for rubbing 6 oz. 1/8 tsp. as needed	3. Starting at the spine bone, completely bone the roasting chicken leaving only the wing bones. Stuff the chicken with the above mixture and secure with skewers. Rub the chicken skin completely with oil.
White Wine Tarragon Watercress	6 oz. 1/8 tsp. as needed	4. Put wine, tarragon and chicken into a roasting pan. (Sherry may be substituted for white wine and tarragon if preferred.) 5. Roast at 350°F. for 1 to 1½ hr. or until tender, basting every 15 min. or so with remaining wine. Remove chicken. Put 1/2 cup of water into roasting pan and bring to a boil. Strain gravy and serve in a separate gravy bowl. Garnish with watercress.

Estouffade of Duckling, right (recipe facing page)

Individual Chicken Pie with Flaky Crust, far right (recipe p. 121)

French Pancakes Stuffed with Creamed Chicken (Crepes a la Reine)

YIELD: 50 portions	EACH PORTION: 1 pancake filled with 2 oz. chicken and sauce	
INGREDIENTS	*QUANTITY*	*METHOD*
Chicken Meat, cooked, boned, skinned (cut in ½ in. dice) Cream Sauce, heavy (p. 314)	6 lb. 3 qt.	1. Reheat chicken meat in stock it was cooked in, drain well and combine with Cream Sauce.
French Pancakes (below) Mornay Sauce (p. 316)	50 1 gal.	2. Lay pancakes flat on sheet pan. Place generous serving spoonful of creamed chicken in center of each pancake. Fold like an envelope. 3. Cover folded pancake with Mornay Sauce and brown in oven at 475°F. or under broiler. 4. Serve immediately with desired garnish.

FRENCH PANCAKES

YIELD: 50 1-oz. pancakes		
INGREDIENTS	*QUANTITY*	*METHOD*
Eggs, whole Milk Bread Flour Salt Butter	8 1 qt. 12 oz. 1 tsp. for frying	1. Break eggs in stainless steel mixing bowl and beat well. Add milk and blend. 2. Add flour and salt and beat until smooth. 3. Fry in hot omelette pans lightly coated with melted butter. Stack on a tray until ready to use.

Le Coq au Vin Champenoise

YIELD: 4 portions	EACH PORTION: 2 pieces chicken with 2 oz. sauce	
INGREDIENTS	*QUANTITY*	*METHOD*
Chicken (3½-4 lb.)	1	1. Disjoint chicken into 8 parts, cutting each leg in two and each breast in two.
Salt Pork, cut in large dice and parboiled Garlic Clove, lightly crushed, chopped	¼ lb. 1 clove	2. Place the salt pork in a sautoir and cook over moderately high heat until partially rendered. Add garlic clove, brown lightly and then remove. 3. Dredge chicken pieces in flour seasoned with salt and pepper. Add chicken pieces to sautoir and brown well on both sides. Remove from pan and reserve.

(Recipe continued on facing page)

Estouffade of Duckling

INGREDIENTS	QUANTITY	METHOD
Long Island Ducklings	5 (5 to 6 lb. ea.)	1. Bone ducklings from the back. Leave wing bone on breast. Bone second joint of leg. Leave drum stick bone in. Remove fat, skin. Reverve bones. Cut 4 equal portions: 2 breasts, 2 legs.
Carrots, chopped Onions, chopped Celery, chopped Bay Leaves Cloves, whole Salt Pepper Flour Sherry Wine Beef Stock	½ lb. ½ lb. 6 oz. 3 4 to taste to taste ¾ lb. 1 pt. 2 gal.	2. SAUCE: Chop carcass of ducklings. Place in roasting pan. Add carrots, onions, celery, bay leaves, cloves, salt and pepper. Brown at 375°F. Remove drippings and reserve. 3. Add flour and stir. Brown 10 to 15 min. Add sherry. Stir in stock, reserving 1 qt.; blend well. Cover; cook 2 hr. Strain.
Shallots, chopped Garlic, chopped Duckling Livers, chopped fine Sausage Meat Eggs, whole Fresh Bread Crumbs Parsley, chopped Sage, crushed	3 tbsp. 2 cloves 5 1 lb. 4 1 qt. 1½ oz. 2 tbsp.	4. STUFFING: Heat ½ cup of reserve drippings. Add shallots; smother until tender. Add garlic, livers and sausage. Cook and stir for 10 to 12 min. Blend in well-beaten eggs. Add crumbs, parsley, sage. Cool.
Onions, chopped Apples, peeled, cored, chopped	1 lb. 1 lb.	5. Place No. 12 scoop of stuffing on each portion. Fold skin over stuffing, fasten with picks.
See color picture, p. 103.		6. Line brazier with onions, apples. Sprinkle with 3 to 4 tbsp. drippings. Add ducklings. 7. Add 1 qt. stock (sauce obtained from bones). Bake at 350°F. Baste frequently. Cover, braise 1½ hr. 8. Strain sauce from ducklings through fine china cap. Add to the sauce obtained from bones; boil. Skim off fat. Serve sauce over each portion.

Pearl Onions, raw, peeled
Mushroom Caps, small
  OR Whole Mushrooms,
    cut (½ in. pcs.)
Champagne
Chicken Stock
Bouquet Garni:
  Parsley
  Thyme
  Bay Leaf
Salt
Pepper
	8
	½ lb.
	
	8 oz.
	4 oz.
	
	1 sprig
	½ sprig
	¼
	to taste
	to taste
		4. Add onions and washed, drained mushrooms to pan in which chicken was sauteed and cook until lightly colored.
		5. Add wine and chicken stock, stirring gently with a wooden spoon and scraping particles from the sides of pan.
		6. When particles have been incorporated and liquid starts to boil, return chicken to pan, add bouquet garni and cover. Simmer gently for about ½ hr. or till tender; or cover, bake at 350°F.
		7. Remove bouquet garni and adjust seasoning.

		8. Serve two pieces of chicken for each portion, one piece of white (breast) and one piece of dark (leg), with pearl onions and mushroom garnish. The sauce should be thin and served sparingly as it is very rich. (2 oz. is ample.)

VARIATION: For **Le Coq au Vin Rouge,** substitute red wine for champagne.
NOTE: Covered casseroles make service more attractive and allow the guest to savor the full aroma of this French specialty. Another variation of this procedure is to disjoint each chicken half, separating leg from breast only, before starting cooking process. Further disjointing is completed after cooking. This procedure results in less shrinkage during cooking but entails additional handling at service.

*Chicken Saute
a la Pierre*

Chicken Saute a la Pierre

YIELD: about 10 portions	EACH PORTION: ½ chicken	
INGREDIENTS	*QUANTITY*	*METHOD*
Chickens (2½ lb. ea.)	5	1. Wash, trim, skin and cut chicken into 8 pieces. Remove the 2 legs, cut in two at joint. Remove the wings at joint and cut off tips. Cut breast in two at breast bone. Reserve carcass bones for future stock pot use.
Salt Pepper Flour	2 tbsp. ½ tsp. 6½ oz.	2. Season all chicken pieces with salt and pepper; dredge with flour.
Salad Oil	8 oz.	3. Heat oil in large saute pan. Add chicken pieces and saute until light brown. Place chicken in roasting pan; cover and bake at 300°F. for 30 min. or until tender. Remove chicken and hold.
Butter Green Onions (scallions), chopped Mushrooms, sliced Garlic, chopped fine	6 oz. 6 oz. 1 lb. 2 cloves	4. Pour off oil from saute pan, add butter and heat. Add green onions, mushrooms, garlic and cook for a few minutes until tender, but not browned.
Tomatoes, fresh, peeled seeded, cut in cubes Dry White Wine Meat Glaze (pp. 309-10)	1 lb. 8 oz. 1 tbsp.	5. Add tomatoes, white wine and meat glaze. Add chicken pieces. Cover and simmer 20 min.
Heavy Cream Parsley, chopped Puff Paste Crescents OR Toast Triangles	12 oz. 2 oz. 20 pieces	6. When ready to serve, arrange the chicken pieces on platter and keep warm. Bring the sauce to a fast boil while stirring. Add the juices from the roasting pan; check the seasoning carefully. Stir in the heavy cream, add the chopped parsley and remove from fire. Pour sauce over chicken. 7. Decorate the platter with baked puff paste crescents or toast triangles.

*Boneless Stuffed
Chicken with Rice*

Boneless Stuffed Chicken with Rice

YIELD: 4 portions		EACH PORTION: ¼ boneless chicken with rice stuffing
INGREDIENTS	QUANTITY	METHOD
Rice	1 cup	1. Wash rice in cold water.
Butter Onion, chopped very fine Sausage Meat, ground Cold Water OR Chicken Broth Salt	2 oz. 1 small ½ lb. 1½ pt. ½ tsp.	2. Melt butter in sauce pan; add chopped onion and brown lightly. Add ground sausage meat. Stir to break up lumps. 3. Add rice and cold water or chicken broth and salt. Stir, bring to a boil, cover and bake at 450°F. for 18 to 20 min. or until rice has absorbed all liquid.
Parsley, fresh, chopped	1 tbsp.	4. When rice is cooked, remove from sauce pan, stir in chopped parsley and let cool. Rice should be prepared early and reserved for use.
Roasting Chicken Carrot, peeled and sliced Onion, sliced Garlic, crushed Bay Leaf Clove	1 (4 lb., A.P.) 1 large 1 large 1 clove 1 1	5. Singe chicken. Cut neck, feet and wings at second joint. Make a complete incision on back of chicken with a very sharp pointed small knife, and continue to follow this incision against the bones and on both sides until the whole chicken is completely separated from the carcass. Spread chicken on table with skin underneath. 6. Place rice on chicken to take place of bones, and fold or draw the chicken around it. With a white string and trussing needle sew back of chicken.
		7. Place chicken on a bed of sliced carrot, onion, garlic, bay leaf and clove in sauce pan. Spread a little melted butter on chicken. 8. Bake at 325°F. until done and well browned, 40 to 45 min., basting once in a while and adding a little water or chicken broth to prevent vegetables from burning.
		8. To make the gravy, add chicken broth to vegetables in sauce pan and boil for a few minutes. Season to taste with salt and pepper; for thick gravy, thicken with 1 tbsp. of butter kneaded with ½ tbsp. of flour.

INDIVIDUAL PORTION CHART FOR FISH

Kind of fish	Method of cutting	Method of cooking	Luncheon weight	Dinner weight
Butterfish	Whole	Pan Fry	1 whole fish (12 to 14 oz.)	1 whole fish (12 to 16 oz.)
Cod, Finnan Haddie, Scrod	Fillets	Boiled, Steamed, Broil	5 to 6 oz.	6 to 7 oz.
Flounder (Sole)	Fillets	Deep Fry, Saute	3 oz.	4 oz.
		Poach	4½ to 5 oz.	5 to 6 oz.
Haddock	Fillets	Deep Fry, Boil	4 oz.	5 oz.
		Broil, au gratin	6 oz.	7 to 8 oz.
		Baked stuffed	5 oz.	6 to 7 oz.
Halibut	Steaks, bone in	Broil, Boil	8 to 9 oz.	9 to 11 oz.
	Steaks, boneless	Broil, Boil	6 to 7 oz.	7 to 8 oz.
Mackerel	Whole (Tinkers) (split)	Broil, Pickle	12 oz.	1 lb.
	Fillets	Broil, Pickle		
Perch	Fillets	Fry, Bake	Same as sole	Same as sole
Pompano	Whole, Split, or Fillet	Broil en Papillote	1 small, whole, split	1 small, whole, split
			1 fillet (6 to 7 oz.)	1 fillet (7 to 8 oz.)
Red Snapper	Fillets	Bake, Broil	6 to 7 oz.	7 to 8 oz.
	Steaks		8 to 9 oz.	9 to 11 oz.
Sea Bass	Fillets	Broil	6 to 7 oz.	7 to 8 oz.
Shad	Whole split Fillets	Broil, Bake	1 small, whole, split (6 to 7 oz.)	1 small, whole, split (7 to 8 oz.)
Spanish Mackerel	Whole split Fillets	Broil, Bake, Pickle	1 small, whole, split	1 small, whole, split
			1 fillet	1 fillet
Salmon	Steak (bone in)	Broil, Boil	8 to 9 oz.	9 to 11 oz.
Smelt	Whole (cleaned, heads off)	Deep fry	Varies with size 8 to 10 oz.	Varies with size 10 to 12 oz.
Swordfish	Steaks (Boneless)	Broil, Bake	6 to 7 oz.	7 to 9 oz.
Clams	Shucked	Fried, Stuffed, Chowder	4 oz. with liquor	5 oz. with liquor
Scallops	Shucked	Fried, Broil	3½ oz.	4½ oz.
		Sauteed, Poach	5 oz.	6 oz.
Oysters		Fried, Poach Bisque	Selects—6 to 7 in number	Selects—7 to 9 in number
		Stew or Escallop		
Lobster	Shucked	Newburg, thermidor, Salad, Cocktail	3 to 4 oz.	4 to 5 oz.
	In shell	Broil, Bake, Boil, Stuffed cold, or Hot Bisque	1 lb. (chicken)	1 to 2 lb. depending on guest
Shrimp	In shell	Fried, Boil Cold or Hot	(21–25's) 5 to 6 in number	(21–25's) 7 to 8 in number
		Baked stuffed Bisque	(U-10's) 2–3 depending on size	(U-10's) 3–4 depending on size
	In shell	Newburg, salad Cocktail	2 to 3 oz. cooked	3 to 4 oz. cooked
Crabmeat Soft Shell crabs	In shell In shell	Salad, au gratin	3 oz., cooked	4 oz., cooked
		Fried, Saute	5 to 1 lb. } 2 to 3	5 to 1 lb. } 3 to 4
Herring	Whole, Split, Fillet	Broil, Pan Fry, Pickle	8 oz.	1 lb.
Trout	Whole, Split, Fillet	Broil, Saute, Smoke		

In this section featuring fish, the complex artistry of the chef is detailed with scientific accuracy so that the knowledge and skills developed over many years can be passed on — insuring continuing service of fish entrees with maximum eye and appetite appeal.

Baked Finnan Haddie with border of Duchesse Potatoes

Baked Fish en Papillote

Filet de Sole Marguery

Brook Trout, Saute Meuniere

Dumpling of Pike, Venetian Sauce

Sauteed Filet of Whitefish, Maitre d'Hotel

Cooking Techniques for Shellfish

A tested method for opening oysters developed by Chef Le Roi Folsom, pictured here, and techniques to follow when preparing Coquilles St. Jacques, Mornay, are among the many secrets of the chef covered in this section of The Professional Chef.

Coquilles St. Jacques, Mornay

Classical Lobster Newburgh

Broiled Lobster

Shrimp and Rice,
Louisiana Style

Techniques for Fish Cookery

As specifically related to food service, fish may be classified in two categories: fin fish and shellfish. Fin fish include all edible salt water and fresh water fish possessing fins. Shellfish are further classified as *crustacea* which include lobsters, crayfish, shrimp and crabs; and *mollusks* which include clams, oysters and scallops.

Fish are rich in nutritive value and are excellent sources of protein, vitamins and minerals. Like meats, they are complete proteins, containing all the essential amino acids. Fish may supply any degree of fat desired, depending on variety or type selected. They are easily digested and assimilated by the body. Many fish oils are particularly high in vitamins A and D; salt water fish are valued for their iodine content.

The supply of various kinds of fish and their abundance during different seasons of the year are reflected in the market price. Although prices of some fish are high during offseason or because of scarcity, generally speaking, fish are an economical food source and can be a profitable menu item.

Handling Fish Fish are highly perishable and must be kept under refrigeration at all times. Frozen fish should be kept frozen until ready for use and should never be refrozen.

Fresh fish must be kept below 40°F. and preferably near freezing temperature. Crushed ice is the best refrigerant for fresh fish because it holds the temperature, keeps the surface of the fish moist, allows fish to hold their natural shape and reduces bruising and excessive handling which hasten deterioration.

Normal refrigeration (without ice) causes rapid surface drying and eventual dehydration and spoilage. If ice is not available, fish should be wrapped in nonabsorbent paper to retard drying and prevent odors from permeating other food products in the refrigerator. When possible, separate chests or storage areas should be provided for fish.

Determining Freshness If high standards are to be maintained, it is important to recognize the qualities that indicate freshness when fish are received from the purveyor. The following characteristics should be considered for all fin fish in determining freshness:

- Fresh smelling; free from off-odors or excessively fishy odor
- Bright, clear, bulging eyes
- Reddish-pink color around the gills
- Brightness or sheen of tightly adhering scales
- Flesh firm and elastic, springs back to shape when pressed

The Bureau of Commercial Fisheries has established a voluntary inspection service for grading and certifying many fishery products. The products are designated "U. S. Grade A" and are marked "Packed Under Continuous Inspection by the U. S. Dept. of the Interior."

Purchasing Fin Fish Fin fish may be purchased in many different forms, ranging from whole fish to portion size pieces.

When purchasing fish, knowledge of these forms and methods is important:

- Whole: just as they come from the water
- Drawn: entrails or viscera removed
- Dressed: eviscerated and usually with head, tail and fins removed
- Sections: large fish, weighing up to 400 lb. are cut in sections, depending on size of fish and demand of customers
- Fillets: fish sides, cut lengthwise from backbone
- Steaks: cross-section slices of dressed fish, large enough for one or more individual portions

Except when used for buffets and special parties, nearly all fish are cut, cooked and served in individual portions. Fish are usually cut and portion-controlled prior to cooking. This facilitates handling, decreases cooking time, ensures uniform cooking and uniform portions, reduces waste, promotes better appearance and provides for ease of service in the dining room.

Fresh Water Fish Few fresh water fish are used in commercial cookery. Carp and pike are used to some extent in Jewish cuisine, but not extensively in other areas. Whitefish is often found on hotel menus. The most popular and widely used fresh water fish is trout. Lake trout, which run as large as 10 lb. are sometimes baked for parties or special service, but brook trout and rainbow trout are in greater favor. They are raised on trout farms in this country and abroad and are usually purchased frozen. Trout ranging from 9 to 12 oz. are most popular. They may be purchased whole or drawn and are packed in 5 lb. boxes. They may be broiled, sauteed or pan fried and are usually served with heads on.

Fish Products There are many fish products including various smoked and pickled fish, salt fish and roe. Smoked fish include cod, haddock and salmon. Finnan haddie, which has a highly smoked flavor, is derived from both cod and haddock and is often served creamed and with breakfast dishes. Smoked salmon and pickled herring are used as appetizers, particularly in Jewish cuisine.

Dried salt fish, like cod, may be purchased shredded in fillets and pieces. It requires soaking and sometimes cooking to restore its moisture and extract some of the salt content. Salt cod fish is used in creamed dishes and in fish cakes.

Roe are the eggs of fish and are generally considered a delicacy. Salmon roe and caviar (derived from sturgeon roe) are used for hors d'oeuvre and canapes. Other fish roe are sometimes used in place of real caviar which is extremely expensive. Shad roe are larger and treated much the same as sweetbreads, by poaching prior to sauteing or pan frying. They are highly perishable.

Preparation Methods Because they originate in many different kinds of water, fish vary considerably in structure, shape and taste. Not all fish are suitable for all methods of preparation, and the special qualities of each usually determine the method of cooking.

Most fish require a very short cooking time because of lack of connective tissue. Intense heat and overcooking destroy their nutritive value, appearance and palatability.

The fat content of fish is a factor that is helpful in determining the cooking method. Lean fish do not usually lend themselves well to dry heat cookery unless some fatty or moistening agent is employed. High fat content fish are best broiled or baked. This aids in extracting excessive oils.

Moist heat cookery is used for nearly all types of fish. This method is not employed for tenderizing effect, but to provide variety. Remember that excessive cooking under any method—including moist heat—may toughen or disintegrate fish.

The chart on the facing page lists the most popular and widely used salt water fish and their cooking methods. Additional methods used for other types of fish include grilling, sauteing and stewing. Baking, broiling, deep fat frying, en papillote methods, boiling, poaching, steaming, grilling, pan frying, sauteing and stewing are discussed in the following pages.

Frog Legs The flesh of frog legs is similar to chicken in texture and taste, although somewhat more delicate in character. The methods of cooking frog legs follow the principles employed in cooking poultry and fish. Frog legs may be prepared by poaching and serving with a delicate sauce, but are more often sauteed, pan fried, or deep fried from the raw state. They are often marinated in lemon juice for a short time prior to cooking. Frog legs may also be prepared a la Meuniere, as in fish cookery.

Frogs are raised on frog farms; and in production the legs are carefully selected and graded for size. Only the hind legs are used for food. They are marketed by number of pairs (the hind legs joined together) to the pound. Purchased in this manner, uniformity of cooking and close portion control are maintained. They are expensive.

Deep Fat Frying Methods of deep fat frying are discussed in a separate section on that subject. When fish are deep fat fried, they are sometimes cut in sticks or "fingers" before frying. This method is

mostly used on lean type fish, although there may be a very few minor exceptions.

Most frozen breaded fish portions, which are growing in popularity in institutions because they are low in cost, eliminate kitchen labor and are extremely useful in portion control, are best when deep fat fried.

Cold sauces usually accompany fried foods. They include mayonnaise and its variations, such as remoulade or tartar sauce and cocktail sauce.

Baking is a form of dry heat cookery comparable to roasting, although fish are sometimes baked in sauce or extremely small amounts of liquid to prevent drying. Liquid is used primarily with lean fish that have no fat protection. Fish of high fat content do not usually require additional liquid.

Fish may be baked whole (with or without stuffing), as fillets cut in portioned individual servings, as turbans (small rolled fillets) or as steaks. Moderate heat is usually preferred (350°F.). Variations in temperature may occur, depending on the type and size of fish and amount of work load. Baking is often combined with other methods such as poaching or steaming to produce creamed or au gratin dishes.

Gratin refers to a food that is covered with sauce, sprinkled with crumbs or grated cheese and browned. Delicious fish dishes may be prepared in the au gratin style. Leftovers are often used in combination with mushrooms, truffles, shrimp, crabmeat and asparagus tips. This is an excellent method for preparing low food cost items when the accompanying garnish is also inexpensive. The covering sauce should be of the right consistency. Too thick a sauce makes a dry fish dish; too thin a sauce runs off the fish and does not gratin well.

Leftovers should be carefully skinned and boned and flaked; or fresh fish may be cut into portion size fillets. Fish must be cooked prior to applying the gratin, and usually is served in an individual casserole. The fish should be well covered or napped with appropriate sauce, sprinkled with bread raspings or crumbs and a few drops of butter. Grated parmesan cheese may also be used. Casseroles may then be baked on a sheet pan or in a shallow bain marie or water bath in the oven.

The crusting should be baked to a golden brown. Small amounts of paprika are sometimes used to add coloring. Au gratin dishes are often sprinkled with chopped parsley before serving. Tops may be brushed with butter before sprinkling parsley. Prior to baking, a border of Potato Duchesse may be piped around the edge of the casserole with a pastry bag and tube and brushed with egg white before browning. The dish is then called en bordure.

Broiling is particularly suitable for fish of high fat content, but is also used for some types of lean fish. Broiling may be an excellent method of preparing fish; but great care must be exercised that the fish is not over-cooked, as it then becomes extremely dry and unpalatable. Cook broiled fish to order.

Fish may be floured, crumbed or plain, depending on the type of fish; but it is always necessary, even with high fat content fish, to butter or oil fish prior to cooking. Oil is often preferred for broiling as butter burns quickly under the intense heat of the broiler.

Hand racks or grills are often employed in broiling fish to facilitate handling, eliminate breakage and hold fish together. Broiled fish are usually accompanied by melted or compound butter or sauces derived from butter. Lemon and parsley are often used as a garnish.

Partially cooked fish are sometimes removed to buttered pie plates and cooking is then finished in the oven under reduced heat to retain more moisture.

Grilling is substituted, in many instances, for broiling, but with less success. It results in a crisper outer coating and sometimes more dryness. While meat and poultry may be *broiled* at the same time as fish, particularly when using hand racks, it is difficult and often inadvisable to attempt to *grill* them together. Oils and butters used in cooking fish often run across the grill or otherwise become mixed with meat, poultry or other products being grilled, giving them an off-flavor.

Pan Frying is used in preparing small whole fish such as trout or smelt. It provides a crisp golden outer coating when fish are previously floured or crumbed. Fish must be carefully handled to prevent breaking and loss of crisp coating. Fat should be hot before fish are placed in the pan so that the heat will sear the surface, effecting a crisp coat and reducing fat absorption. Use off-set spatulas to turn fish in the pan to avoid breaking the skin.

Sauteing In addition to the standard sauteing method discussed in the meat section, an additional principle in fish cookery is a la Meuniere (pronounced mee-nee-yair).

The fish is floured and sauteed in the usual manner with a small amount of hot butter. Ordinary butter may be used if the fish is quite small. If the fish is large, butter must be clarified to prevent burning. After the fish is browned on one side, it is carefully turned for completion of cooking and browning.

It is at this point that the a la Meuniere process begins. The fish is removed whole (using an off-set spatula) to a warm platter and held in a warm place for service. A piece of butter is placed in the pan and allowed to brown lightly. At the last moment, a few drops of lemon juice and chopped parsley are sprinkled over the fish. The hot brown butter is poured over the fish, creating a bubbly froth which results from the contact of the lemon juice, butter and parsley. Serve immediately.

Stewing is not used to a great extent in cooking fish, except in specialty dishes such as Bouillabaisse (pronounced boo-yah-bays) and Matelotes (mah-teh-lot). Both of these are fish stews heavily seasoned with herbs and spices. Bouillabaisse is discussed in the Soup Section. Fish used for the Matelote are eel, carp, bream and perch. Matelotes are slightly thickened with beurre manie and are prepared with wine.

Glazing, as specifically applied to fish cookery, means the covering of a cooked fish product with a delicate sauce, usually containing eggs, cream and/or butter so that a glaze or lightly browned surface will result when the product is placed under a broiler or salamander or in a very hot oven. This is a quick finishing process used in more advanced cookery. (Note: A salamander is a smaller broiler type unit with overhead heat and is used principally for glazing and quick browning.) See Hot Glaze Royal Sauce, p. 320.

Kind of Fish	Composition	Weight in Pounds	Cooking Methods	How Purchased
Butterfish	fat	¼ to 1	broil, pan fry, bake	whole, dressed
Cod	lean	3 to 20	broil, bake, boil, chowder, steam	drawn, dressed steaks, fillets
Flounder (Sole)	lean	¼ to 5	bake, saute, poach, deep fry, steam	whole dressed, fillets
Haddock	lean	1½ to 7	broil, bake, boil, steam, chowder, deep fry, poach	whole, dressed, fillets
Halibut	lean	10 to 300	broil, bake, boil, steam, chowder, deep fry	drawn, sections, steaks
Mackerel	fat	¾ to 3	broil, bake	whole, drawn, dressed, fillets
Perch	lean	½ to 1¾	broil, pan fry	dressed, fillets
Pompano	fat	1 to 3	broil, bake, en papillote	whole
Red Snapper	lean	2 to 15	broil, bake	drawn, dressed, steaks, fillets
Sea Bass	variable	¼ to 4	broil, bake	whole, dressed, fillets
Shad	fat	½ to 7	broil, bake, pan fry	whole, drawn, fillets
Spanish Mackerel	fat	1 to 4	broil, bake, pan fry	whole, drawn, dressed, fillets
Smelt	lean	⅓ to 1	pan fry, deep fry,	whole
Swordfish	lean	60 to 700	broil, bake, deep fat	sections, steaks

Cooking en Papillote Cooking in paper or en papillote (pronounced pah-pee-yoht) embraces some of the principles used in other cooking methods, but because it is a special type of presentation, deserves separate discussion.

Cooking in paper or parchment, a non-absorbent type of paper, is most suitable for lean fish as a fat type fish may leave deposits of unpalatable fat in the bottom of the parchment. When fish are poached or pre-cooked, however, this is not a problem.

A bag is constructed of parchment by cutting a heart-shaped piece, approximately 14 in. across at its widest point, the dimensions of the heart corresponding to this measurement. An individual portion of raw fish is placed on one side of the heart with butter, lemon juice and seasoning. The other side of the heart is folded over from the center, like a book, and the edges tightly sealed. The parchment is greased on the outside to prevent burning, and the whole thing is placed in a hot oven to cook.

The fish will cook in its own juice with the lemon and butter, and when served will be delicious and moist. The bag will puff from the steam and be lightly browned. The fish is served in the paper, or "en Papillote."

Fish that is cooked in sauce in the parchment should first be poached or otherwise pre-cooked to ensure proper cooking and to avoid watering or diluting the sauce by its own juices and moisture. This method is sometimes used to add drama when serving delicate fish like pompano or oysters.

Nutritive values are best retained when cooking fish from the raw state, as nearly all of the vitamins and minerals are in the liquid in the bag. This supposes, of course, that the liquor will be consumed by the guest. The same nutritional benefits are derived if a sauce is prepared from the liquor.

Parchment may also be used in steaming clams. Clams must be free of all sand and grit. After washing they are placed in the center of a square sheet of parchment. The paper is brought up over the clams so that it forms a pear shape. It is secured near the top by tying with a piece of butcher's twine or other suitable fastener. The bag is then placed in a small amount of water, covered and steamed for about 5 to 10 minutes.

As the clams cook, they provide their own broth which is drained into a cup through a small hole that is pierced in the bottom of the parchment after removal from the cooking pot. The broth is served in a cup and the bag of clams served at the table in a large bowl with a suitable underliner or service plate. The bag retains the heat and moisture in the dining room.

Drawn butter usually accompanies this dish.

PREPARING FISH EN PAPILLOTE

To prepare Fish en Papillote, served as shown in picture above, place Pompano Supreme and sliced green onions in shallow saucepan with melted butter.

Next place sliced shrimp and fresh crabmeat over pompano. Cook pompano and prepare sauce according to directions on facing page.

To complete, spoon cooked pompano in center of white parchment paper heart as shown and bake. (Recipe on facing page.)

Pompano En Papillote

YIELD: 6 portions		
INGREDIENTS	*QUANTITY*	*METHOD*
Butter	4 oz.	1. In a shallow sauce pan, melt butter. Place the sliced green onions and the supreme of pompano in it. Over and around it, place the sliced shrimp and the fresh white crabmeat. Cover and let simmer or steam for a few minutes. At that time, sprinkle with salt and pepper, moisten with white wine and sherry wine, cover again and cook over low heat until pompano is done and firm.
Green Onions (scallions), sliced very fine	8	
Pompano, split in two, bones, heads and skins removed	3 (2 lb. ea.)	
Shrimp, fresh cooked, sliced finely	6 oz.	
Fresh White Crabmeat	12 oz.	2. Carefully remove the pompano supreme from sauce pan and reserve in a warm place while completing the sauce.
Salt	to taste	
Pepper	to taste	
Dry White Wine	5 oz.	
Sherry Wine	2 oz.	
Fish Veloute OR Cream Sauce	1½ pt.	3. To the shrimp, crabmeat and juices in sauce pan, add the fish veloute or cream sauce, bring to a fast boil while stirring. Rectify the seasoning and add a few dashes of hot pepper sauce (taste must be very sharp), then proceed as follows:
Hot Pepper Sauce	few dashes	4. Cut special white parchment paper in a heart shaped piece, about 14 in. across at its widest point. Oil the outside of paper and lay the oiled side flat on table. In center of right side of heart, place 2 tbsp. of sauce as prepared above; on it, lay the cooked pompano supreme, then cover it with 2 tbsp. of sauce.
		5. To close the paper bag, fold over the left half of paper on the pompano and roll edges of paper, starting from the left inside top of the shape, and with small even turns until envelope is firmly closed all around to the very tip of the heart shape. Turn in paper point to hold shape. Place the bag on side which has been folded on well oiled baking pan. Place pan on top of range for a few minutes or until bag begins to puff, then place pan in a very hot oven until paper bag is browned. Slide from pan on to plate and serve.
		6. At the table supply a very sharp pointed knife to cut paper, lift and uncover one of the most delicious pompano dishes that could be prepared.

NOTE: Other lean fish can be prepared in the same fashion.

See color picture, p. 138.

Boiling, Poaching and Steaming A better word for "boiling," as suggested in the section on meat cookery, is "simmering." Fish as a protein food should not be boiled. Simmering is usually associated with lean fish.

Boiling, poaching and steaming are closely related, the prime difference being in the amount of cooking liquid used. In the case of steaming, the product is also covered tightly so it is cooked by the steam generated. These three methods utilize top of range cooking in shallow pans, depending on the size or volume of the fish.

BAKED COD, BELLA VISTA

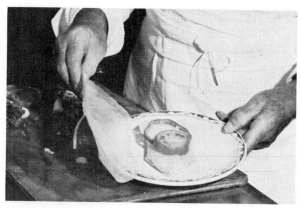

Overlap onion, green pepper and tomato slices on top of cod. Cover platter or plate with greased paper and bake at 375°F. for 15 to 20 min.

For individual portions of Baked Cod Bella Vista, place codfish portion on buttered heatproof plate or platter. Sprinkle with seasonings. Saute vegetables in butter and add wine.

After the first 10 min. of cooking, remove greased paper and baste fish with juices in platter or plate. For luncheon service, codfish portions may be reduced to 5 to 6 oz.

Poaching and steaming may also be accomplished in the oven. Steaming may also utilize conventional steam cooking equipment. The more liquid used, the less flavor (or more dilute the flavor).

In simmering, the liquid must cover the fish. Fish may be cooked in plain water or in a prepared stock called court bouillon. Court bouillon means "short boil," as applied to fish cookery. Court bouillon consists of onion, celery, carrots, water, vinegar or lemon juice or wine, bouquet garni and salt. These products are cooked for approximately one-half hour and strained. The liquid is then used for cooking fish.

Boiling or simmering, poaching and steaming may all utilize court bouillon. Whole fish, portion size fillets and steaks may be prepared by any of these methods. In simmering and poaching, it is suggested that large fish be started in cold liquid, while small or portion sized pieces should be started in hot or boiling liquid. This aids proper cooking and eliminates some breakage. The bottom of the cooking pan is usually buttered or oiled to prevent sticking.

It may sometimes be necessary to wrap fish tightly in cheesecloth to prevent flaking or breaking and to help hold its shape. This is particularly true when cooking whole fish such as fresh salmon for buffet or party work.

Additional protection, which also facilitates handling, may be achieved by tying the wrapped fish to thin boards, using wide bands of cloth to prevent cutting of the skin or flesh. This method is much like applying a splint to a broken arm or leg, the whole fish being placed on the board lengthwise and tied securely, but not so as to cut or mark the surface of the fish or to leave an impression or indentation. Overcooking by moist heat will disintegrate fish, leaving only flakes or shreds which may or may not be utilized.

Fish to be served cold should be slightly undercooked so that cooling in their own liquid (to retain moisture) will finish the cooking. Fish, particularly when moist heat methods are used, requires very little cooking time. Only small amounts should be prepared at one time to assure quality products. Fish will retain greater moisture if held in liquid until time for service.

Fish cooked by moist heat are invariably accompanied by a sauce. Piquant or highly flavored sauces are often (but not always) served. Although it has been said that the sauce makes the fish, remember that the sauce should not overpower the product that it accompanies. Delicate fish should be served with delicate sauce.

Baked Cod, Bella Vista

YIELD: 8 portions	EACH PORTION: about 6 oz.	
INGREDIENTS	*QUANTITY*	*METHOD*
Fresh Codfish	3½ lb.	1. Cut codfish in 6½ to 7 oz. portions.
Shallots, chopped Butter White Wine	2 2 oz. ¼ cup	2. Saute chopped shallots in butter. Add wine and codfish.
Green Pepper, sliced in 8 rings Onion, cut in 8 slices Tomatoes Salt	1 1 medium 8 slices to taste	3. Place one slice each of green pepper, onion and tomato overlapping on top of each portion.
		4. Cover with greased brown paper. 5. Bake at 375°F. for 15 to 20 min. After first 10 min. remove cover and baste fish.
NOTE: For luncheon dishes, reduce portion size to 5 to 6 oz.		

Fillet de Sole Marguery

YIELD: 8 portions	EACH PORTION: 4 oz. fish	
INGREDIENTS	*QUANTITY*	*METHOD*
Butter Shallots, chopped very fine Fillets of Sole (2 oz. ea) Mushrooms, cooked Shrimp, cooked and shelled Large Oysters Dry White Wine Fish Stock OR Water Lemon Juice Salt Pepper	for pan 3 16 8 caps 8 8 4 oz. 4 oz. from ¼ lemon to taste to taste	1. Butter a sauce pan well and add chopped shallots. Arrange the fillets of sole over the shallots. On each fillet place a mushroom, shrimp and an oyster. Add the white wine, fish stock, lemon juice and salt and pepper. 2. Cover with a well buttered paper and bake at 475° F. for about 12 min. Remove the fillets from the pan and arrange them on a heated platter.
Cream Sauce (p. 314) OR Fish Sauce	8 oz.	3. Reduce the juice in the pan by boiling for a few minutes. Add Cream Sauce. Stir with a wire whip to blend, cook for a few seconds and remove from heat.
Egg Yolks Light Cream Whipped Cream Truffle	2 4 oz. 3 tbsp. 8 thin slices	4. Mix egg yolks with cream and blend into the sauce. At the last minute fold in whipped cream. Strain sauce through a cheesecloth. 5. Pour sauce over the fillets, pipe on border of Duchesse Potatoes (p. 212) if desired. Place the platter in oven heated to 475°F. or under a salamander until golden brown. Garnish with a thick slice of truffle on each fillet, if desired. Serve at once.
See color picture, p. 139.		

Fish

Fried Fillet of Sole
(recipe below)

Baked Smoked Cod, Delmonico (recipe
top of facing page)

Fried Fillet of Sole

YIELD: 50 portions	EACH PORTION: 2 fillets	
INGREDIENTS	*QUANTITY*	*METHOD*
Bread Flour Salt Pepper Eggs Milk	2 lb. to taste to taste 6 1 qt.	1. Season flour. Combine eggs and milk, blend well.
Bread Crumbs OR Cracker Meal Sole Fillets (2 oz. ea.)	as needed 100	2. Follow breading procedure (p. 178). 3. Fry fillets in deep fat at 350° to 375°F., depending on volume, until golden brown. 4. Drain well on absorbent paper or fine wire rack. 5. Serve with lemon slice and tartar sauce. Garnish with parsley.

Baked Stuffed Shore Haddock, Creole Sauce

YIELD: 50 portions	EACH PORTION: about 5 oz. with sauce	
INGREDIENTS	*QUANTITY*	*METHOD*
Haddock Fillets , skin removed	50 (5 oz. ea)	1. Place haddock pieces on oiled sheet pans. Fold thin ends or pieces under to make them compact and as uniform as possible.
Bread Stuffing, cooked (p. 113) Butter, melted	3 qt. 8 oz.	2. Place a No. 20 scoop of stuffing on each portion. Mold to cover fish portion uniformly. 3. Brush with melted butter. Bake at 350°F. for about 20 min. or until fish is done but still moist.
Creole Sauce (p. 320)	1 gal.	4. Serve with 2 to 3 oz. of Creole Sauce over top.

Baked Smoked Cod, Delmonico

YIELD: 50 portions		EACH PORTION: 4 oz. fish
INGREDIENTS	*QUANTITY*	*METHOD*
Smoked Cod Medium Cream Sauce (p. 314) Hard Boiled Eggs, diced Pimientoes Worcestershire Sauce Pepper	16 lb. 2 gal. 18 12 oz. to taste to taste	1. Because of its excessive saltiness, whole fish should be blanched. Cover fish in pot with cold water. Slowly bring to a boil and simmer for a few minutes. After blanching remove, let cool, then flake fish before combining with the rest of the ingredients. 2. Put in suitable pot and stir in Cream Sauce. 3. Add diced eggs, pimientoes and seasoning.
Potatoes Duchesse (p. 212) Hollandaise Sauce (p. 321)	3 lb. 1 qt.	4. Place in individual casseroles. Pipe border of Potatoes Duchesse around edge. 5. Cover with Hollandaise Sauce and brown under broiler or in very hot oven before serving.

NOTE: Use same procedure for Baked Finnan Haddie Delmonico.

See color picture Baked Finnan Haddie, p. 138.

Dumplings of Pike, Venetian Sauce

YIELD: 6 portions		EACH PORTION: 4½ oz.
INGREDIENTS	*QUANTITY*	*METHOD*
Pike, boned and skinned Egg Whites Heavy Cream Salt Nutmeg Cayenne	1 lb. 2 8 oz. to taste to taste to taste	1. Pound the pike and rub through a fine sieve. Place in mortar or sauce pan; keep on ice. 2. Mix the egg whites into the pike with a wooden spoon, then gradually add half of the cream, stirring constantly. Add a small amount of the salt, nutmeg and cayenne. Put ½ tsp. of pike mixture into very hot salted water (not boiling) for 2 min. to test for consistency. 3. A quenelle (dumpling) is perfect when it has attained the maximum of lightness without losing its body. Add more cream until this point is reached and poach once or twice more in hot water. This tests consistency and seasoning. 4. When seasoning and consistency are correct, fill a tablespoon with the pike mixture. Dip another tablespoon in hot water, scoop up the quenelle and invert into a buttered saute pan. Repeat until the whole mixture has been divided. 5. Slowly pour a small amount of boiling water over the quenelles, season with salt, cover and let poach over very low heat for 6 to 8 min. Do not boil.

VENETIAN SAUCE:
  White Wine
  Tarragon Vinegar
  Fish Veloute Sauce (p. 317)
  Sweet Butter
    OR Hollandaise Sauce (p. 321)
  Chervil and Tarragon,
    finely chopped
	8 oz.
	8 oz.
	1 pt.
	2 oz.
	8 oz.
	½ tsp.
		6. Boil white wine and tarragon vinegar until reduced to 4 oz.
		7. Add Fish Veloute Sauce.
		8. Bring to boil and then finish away from stove with sweet butter or Hollandaise Sauce and chopped chervil and tarragon.
		9. At service time, dry the quenelles on a napkin, arrange on dish or plate and cover with Venetian Sauce.

See picture, p. 140.

Fish

Broiled Swordfish Steak, Maitre d'Hotel (recipe below)

Broiled Mackerel, Anchovy Butter (recipe top of facing page)

Broiled Swordfish Steak, Maitre d'Hotel

YIELD: 50 portions		EACH PORTION: about 6 oz.
INGREDIENTS	*QUANTITY*	*METHOD*
Swordfish, fresh or frozen	50 steaks (6 to 7 oz. ea.)	1. Cut and trim swordfish. Remove all skin and any worms that may be found. (Swordfish worms have no known effect on eating qualities of the flesh.) Trim out other undesirable areas and cut in portion size.
Salad Oil Bread Crumbs Paprika	as needed 2 lb. 2 oz.	3. Mix bread crumbs with paprika. 4. Dip steaks in oil. Dip one side lightly in bread crumb mixture, then lightly in oil. 5. Place fish, crumb side up, in hand rack and place under broiler. When lightly browned, turn over and brown other side. When both sides are lightly colored, remove from broiler and place in lightly greased pan. Bake at 375°F. A small amount of water may be added to prevent drying.
Maitre d'Hotel Butter (Lemon Butter) (p. 323)		6. When cooked, plate neatly, and serve with maitre d'hotel butter. Butter should be sufficient for fish, but not flowing on plate. 7. Garnish with lemon wedge.

Poached Salmon

YIELD: 50 portions		EACH PORTION: about 5 oz.
INGREDIENTS	*QUANTITY*	*METHOD*
Salmon, steaks or boneless Butter Court Bouillon (p. 272)	50 pieces (5 to 6 oz. ea.) 8 oz. 1 gal.	1. Place fish in bottom of buttered baking pans and barely cover with hot Court Bouillon. 2. Cover pans with sheets of buttered paper. 3. Cook slowly on top of range OR bake at 350°F. for about 20 to 25 min. Fish must barely simmer. 4. When cooked, drain well. Remove all skin and bones before serving. 5. Serve hot with appropriate sauce. May be served with Egg Sauce (p. 315), Hollandaise (p. 321) or Bearnaise Sauce (p. 322).

NOTE: If fish is not to be served immediately, it may be undercooked so that it will finish cooking in its own liquid at holding temperature. Be sure that it is fully cooked when served.

Broiled Mackerel, Anchovy Butter

YIELD: 50 portions		EACH PORTION: 1 fillet
INGREDIENTS	*QUANTITY*	*METHOD*
Salad Oil Mackerel Fillets OR Whole Tinker Mackerel	for pan 50 (under 1 lb.)	1. Lightly grease sheet pan and lay fillets on it, skin side down. 2. Rub fillets lightly on bottom of pan and turn skin side up. 3. Place under preheated broiler at point low enough to prevent burning. 4. When partly cooked and skin begins to blister lightly, turn skin side down with offset spatula or palette knife. 5. Continue cooking until done or transfer to oven preheated to 375°F. until done. 6. Serve with Anchovy Butter (p. 323) and garnish with lemon wedge and parsley.

NOTE: Mackerel is a high fat content fish and requires only sufficient oil to prevent sticking or burning. Care should be taken when plating mackerel that bottom skin is not burned or greasy. Mackerel portions must be larger than most fish portions as it is quite bony and does not yield as much meat as some other types. It also shrinks considerably due to its fat content.

New England Codfish Cakes

YIELD: 50 5 oz. cakes or 100 2½ oz. cakes		EACH PORTION: 1 5 oz. or 2 2½ oz. cakes
INGREDIENTS	*QUANTITY*	*METHOD*
Codfish, shredded	3½ lb.	1. Add water to cod to cover. Soak cod 20 to 30 min. to freshen. 2. Press or wring out in towel. Cod must be as dry as possible.
Potatoes, fresh boiled, riced White Pepper Egg Yolks Cornstarch Breading Egg Wash	12 lb. 1 tsp. 10 6 oz. for cakes for breading	3. Combine with potatoes and pepper and mix well, but do not overhandle. 4. Add egg yolks and mix lightly. 5. Add cornstarch and blend thoroughly. 6. Cod does not usually require salt, but test for seasoning. If not dry enough, a small amount of dehydrated potato may be added to bind. 7. If time permits, place in refrigerator to firm.
		8. Using No. 12 or No. 8 ice cream scoop and portion scale, make 100 2½ oz. cakes or 50 5 oz. cakes. 9. Form in uniform flat, round cakes. 10. Bread using standard procedure p. 178. Do not let stand in wash. 11. If holding for service after breading, sprinkle bread crumbs on tray and place fish cakes on top of crumbs. Sprinkle additional crumbs on top of fish cakes and refrigerate. 12. When serving, fry in deep fat at 350° to 375°F., depending on volume, until well-browned and heated through. Drain well and serve.

NOTE: May be served plain, topped with poached or fried eggs or with Tomato Sauce (p. 318).

Frog Legs, Provencale, right (recipe top of facing page)

Broiled Halibut with Lobster Newburg Sauce, far right (recipe bottom of facing page)

Poached Fillet of Sole

YIELD: 50 portions	EACH PORTION: about 4 oz.	
INGREDIENTS	*QUANTITY*	*METHOD*
Fillet of Sole, (4 to 5 oz. fillets)	50 fillets	1. Skin the fillets and roll them with "skin" side of the fillet facing up. Start rolling the tail end in first and continue to roll so that the wider part of the fish is on the outside. Fillets may be fastened with a toothpick which is removed prior to service.
Butter Court Bouillon (p. 272)	8 oz. 1 gal.	2. Place fish in buttered baking pan. Add hot Court Bouillon to barely cover fish. 3. Cover pan with sheet of buttered paper. 4. Cook slowly on top of range OR bake at 350°F. about 20 to 25 min. Fish must barely simmer. Boiling will break down the tissue and destroy flavor. 5. Drain well and serve with appropriate sauce.

Fillet of Sole, Bonne Femme

YIELD: 25 portions	EACH PORTION: 2 fillets	
INGREDIENTS	*QUANTITY*	*METHOD*
Fillets of Sole, skinless (2 oz. ea.)	50	1. Roll fish starting with small end or fold in half.
Butter	4 oz.	2. Butter two hotel pans, place fillets of sole in them.
Mushrooms, sliced	1½ lb.	3. Sprinkle the sliced mushrooms, chopped shallots, chopped parsley and white wine over the fish. Add the strained fish fumet.
Shallots	2 oz.	
Parsley, chopped	¾ oz.	4. Cut brown paper to size of hotel pans, grease and use to cover the hotel pans.
White Wine	½ pt.	
Fish Fumet	1 qt.	5. Place the pans on the range and bring to a boil; then place in oven at 400°F. and cook 5 to 6 min. or until fish is done.
Butter	3 oz.	
Flour	4 oz.	
Hollandaise Sauce	1 qt.	6. Pour off fish fumet from the pans. Strain, reserving vegetables.
Whipped Cream, unsweetened	1 pt.	7. Melt the butter; add flour and blend. Cook for 5 min. Add the fish fumet to it for a fish veloute.
		8. Add the mushrooms, shallots and chopped parsley to the veloute.
		9. Work Hollandaise into veloute; season to taste. Then fold unsweetened whipped cream into sauce.
		10. Place portion of fish on the plate and then pour sauce over it. Place under the broiler or salamander to brown lightly (glaze); serve with a Fleuron (p. 407).

Frog Legs, Provencale

YIELD: 1 portion	EACH PORTION: 2 pair legs	
INGREDIENTS	QUANTITY	METHOD
Fresh Frog Legs, 2 pair Milk Flour Olive Oil Salt Pepper	½ lb. as needed as needed 4 oz. to taste to taste	1. Dip frog legs in milk, roll in flour. 2. Heat the olive oil in a frying pan to the smoking point. Add the frog legs and fry until golden brown on one side; turn and brown other side. 3. Remove from pan and place on heated serving dish. 4. Season with salt and pepper.
Butter Lemon Juice Parsley, chopped Garlic Clove, finely chopped	1 oz. 1 tbsp. 1 tsp. ½ tsp.	5. Brown the butter in a frying pan, add lemon juice, parsley and garlic, blend well. Pour over frog legs. Serve very hot.

Broiled Halibut with Lobster Newburg Sauce

YIELD: 50 portions	EACH PORTION: 1 steak or 1 fillet	
INGREDIENTS	QUANTITY	METHOD

Halibut, fresh or frozen
(8 to 9 oz. portions, bone in;
6 to 7 oz. portions, boneless)
Salad Oil
Breading Mixture:
    Bread Crumbs
    Paprika
	50
	
	for broiling
	
	2 lb.
	2 oz.
		1. Trim and cut halibut portions. If using chicken halibut, cut in same manner as salmon steaks. If using large pieces of halibut, cut fillets; cut boneless portions from fillets, butterflying if necessary.
		2. Broil the same as salmon steaks, removing skin and bones before serving. (See recipe for **Broiled Salmon**, p. 157).
		3. When plating, care should be taken to keep portion together just as it would appear with the bone in. Top with Newburg Sauce, return to broiler and brown lightly.

NEWBURG SAUCE		
YIELD: 50 portions		
Boiled Lobster Meat Butter Paprika	3½ lb. 6 oz. 2 tbsp.	1. Cut the lobster meat in ½ in. squares. 2. Put the butter in a large saute pan; place on range, add paprika and heat butter slowly but do not brown. 3. Add the lobster meat, saute for 5 min.
Light Cream Sauce (p. 314) Dry Sherry Salt Pepper Lemon Juice Monosodium Glutamate	3 qt. 4 oz. to taste to taste from ½ lemon 1 tbsp.	4. Mix lobster meat with Cream Sauce, using a wooden paddle so lobster will not break up. Bring to boiling point; add sherry; season to taste with salt and pepper. Add the lemon juice and monosodium glutamate.

Fillet of Flounder, McBane, right (recipe below)

Brook Trout, Meuniere, far right (recipe top of facing page)

Fillet of Flounder, McBane

YIELD: 10 portions		EACH PORTION: 1 fillet, 3 oz. noodle cake
INGREDIENTS	*QUANTITY*	*METHOD*
Fillets of Flounder, flattened, trimmed Salt Pepper Fine Fish Farce (p. 112) Fish Stock	10 (large) to taste to taste 5-1/3 oz. 1 pt.	1. Season each fillet of flounder with salt and pepper. Spread about 1 tbsp. fine fish farce over each fillet; fold in two. Place in buttered pan. Pour in fish stock. 2. Cook over low heat for 10 to 15 min.
Noodle Cakes (recipe below) Shrimp, cooked, diced Mornay Sauce (p. 316) Dry Sherry Wine	10 4 oz. 1¼ pt. 4 oz.	3. Remove fillet from sauce pan. Place each fillet on noodle cake on a heated platter. 4. Reduce juices in sauce pan by boiling for a few minutes. Add the diced shrimp. Stir in Mornay Sauce and wine. Add a pinch of salt and cayenne pepper. 5. Pour this sauce over fillet of flounder and glaze in oven at 500°F. or under broiler or salamander.

NOODLE CAKES

YIELD: 10 cakes		
INGREDIENTS	*QUANTITY*	*METHOD*
Fine Egg Noodles	4 oz.	1. Break noodles into small pieces (1 to 2 in. in length). Cook in boiling salted water for 7 to 8 min. or until tender. Wash in cold water. Drain well.
Eggs, whole Milk Flour Salt	3 8 oz. 4 oz. ¼ tsp.	2. Break eggs into stainless steel bowl and whip lightly. Add milk and mix well. 3. Add flour and salt to egg mixture and mix batter smooth. Incorporate cooked, drained noodles and blend thoroughly. 4. Fry in butter at medium temperature. Use small egg pans. Measure a 3 oz. ladle of batter for each noodle cake. Cook until golden brown on both sides. Remove to trays or baking pans and hold for service. Keep warm.

Brook Trout, Meuniere

YIELD: 50 portions		EACH PORTION: about 9 oz.
INGREDIENTS	QUANTITY	METHOD
Brook Trout, fresh or frozen (thawed) (9 to 10 oz. ea.) Milk Bread Flour	50 (9-10 oz. ea.) 1 qt. 4 lb.	1. Dress and clean trout. Dip trout in milk to which salt and crushed peppercorns have been added, then in flour.
Butter, clarified OR Butter Butter Salad Oil	2 lb. 1 lb. 1 pt.	2. Place whole trout in heated clarified butter or butter-oil mixture in large frying pan or sautoir. 3. Saute about 5 to 7 min. on each side or until nicely browned. 4. Remove carefully to lightly buttered pans and keep warm in moderate oven. Finish cooking if necessary.
Butter Parsley, fresh, chopped Lemon Juice Brown Butter	3 lb. 3 oz. 6 oz.	5. Heat the 3 lb. butter in frying pan or skillet until lightly browned (Beurre noisette). 6. Remove fish from oven. Plate. Sprinkle with chopped parsley. 7. Lemon juice may be sprinkled over fish and topped with brown butter OR lemon juice may be mixed with brown butter before pouring over fish. Garnish with lemon wedge and serve immediately.

NOTE: Fillets and fish steaks may be prepared in this manner, but it is more suitable for whole fish.

See color picture, p. 140.

Broiled Salmon Steak

YIELD: 50 portions		EACH PORTION: about 8 oz.
INGREDIENTS	QUANTITY	METHOD
Salmon, fresh or frozen (8 to 9 oz. steaks)	50 steaks	1. Clean and trim salmon. 2. Cut steaks crosswise through bone until reaching tail end where steaks are too small. Reserve this end to be removed from the bone for poaching.
Salad Oil Crumb Mixture : Bread Crumbs Paprika	for coating 2 lb. 2 oz.	3. Dip steaks in oil. Then dip one side lightly in bread crumb mixture, then again lightly in oil. 4. Place fish, crumb side up, on a single hand rack and place under broiler. When lightly browned, turn, and brown other side. When both sides are lightly colored, remove from broiler. Place in lightly greased pan. Finish in oven at 350°F. A small amount of water in pan in oven prevents drying.
		5. When fish is cooked, remove skin and bones. Plate. 6. Garnish with lemon wedge and serve with melted butter and chopped fresh parsley or appropriate sauce.

Fish

White Fish
Continental, right
(recipe below)

Fillet of Haddock,
Meuniere, far right
(recipe bottom of
page)

White Fish Continental

YIELD: 10 portions	EACH PORTION: about 6 to 7 oz.	
INGREDIENTS	QUANTITY	METHOD
Butter, melted Onion, chopped finely 　OR Shallots Fresh Mushrooms, sliced, 　washed, drained White Fish	4 oz. 1 oz. ½ lb. 2 (3 to 4 lb.)	1. Heat melted butter in shallow sauce pan. Add chopped onion or shallots and sliced mushrooms. Clean and fillet the fish, cut into 10 equal portions and arrange over vegetables in pan.
Fish Farce (p. 112) Large Raw Oysters Shrimp, precooked White Wine	4 oz. 10 20 2 oz.	2. Spread fish farce evenly over white fish. Place 1 raw oyster on each portion of fish, and 2 shrimp on either side of each oyster. 3. Cover with well-buttered paper or closely fitting cover. Place on very low fire and simmer for 10 min. 4. Uncover; add the white wine. Cover again and continue to simmer for another 15 min. or until fish is done. 5. Remove fish from sauce pan, place on platter. Keep warm.
White Wine Sauce Salt Pepper Cayenne	1½ pt. to taste to taste to taste	6. Blend the White Wine Sauce with juices and mushrooms in pan. Season to taste. Bring to fast boil. Pour over fish and serve.

Fillet of Haddock, Meuniere

YIELD: 50 portions	EACH PORTION: 1 fillet	
INGREDIENTS	QUANTITY	METHOD
Haddock Fillets, skin on 　(6 to 7 oz. portions) Bread Flour Butter, clarified) Salad Oil 　　) combined	50 2 lb. 1 lb. 3 cups	1. Dredge fish in flour and saute skin side up in hot oil and clarified butter mixture in fry pan or skillet. 2. When fish is browned, turn skin side down and brown. 3. When browned on both sides, remove to sheet pan and finish in oven at 350°F.
Butter, melted Lemon Juice Parsley, fresh, chopped	2½ lb. from 8 lemons 3 oz.	4. Heat melted butter in skillet until lightly browned but not burned. 5. To serve, sprinkle a few drops of lemon juice and freshly chopped parsley over each fish portion. Pour hot browned butter over fish, creating a bubbly froth which results from contact of lemon juice, butter, parsley. Fish must be served at once.

VARIATIONS: **Saute Grenbloise:** Add capers to the butter while browning.
　Saute Amandine: Add finely sliced almonds to the butter while browning.
　Saute Doria: Peel several cucumbers; cut them in sections about 1 in. in length; cut these sections into wedges ¼ in. wide. Place the wedges in a saute pan, season with salt and pepper. Add a little melted butter, cover with a buttered paper and let simmer on side of range until tender. Serve as a garnish.

Techniques for Shellfish Cookery

Shellfish, as contrasted to fin fish, are divided into two classifications: *crustacea,* which include lobsters, crayfish, shrimp and crabs; and *mollusks,* which include clams, oysters and scallops.

All shellfish should be live when purchased in the shell unless they are pre-cooked or frozen. Live shellfish keep well in ice, but not in water. Shellfish that do not close tightly when handled are dead and no longer fit for service.

"Shucked" shellfish are those which have been removed from their shells. Clams, oysters and scallops are often marketed in this manner.

Shrimp refers to the fresh, frozen or cooked tail section of the shrimp. The head is removed in processing at the plant. ("Prawns" is the term applied to large shrimp. It generally refers to jumbo Louisiana shrimp. The only difference between shrimp and prawns is one of size.)

Shrimp in the shell are marketed by size or number to the pound. (21-25's are 21 to 25 shrimp to the pound; U-10's are under 10 to a pound.)

Shrimp are also marketed peeled and deveined (shell off and intestines removed). Shrimp may also be purchased breaded or as salad shrimp which are broken pieces, shell off. Shrimp in the shell are usually marketed frozen in 5 lb. boxes.

Raw shrimp are sometimes called "green" shrimp. They require very little cooking, and when overcooked, become tough and rubbery. They yield about one-half cooked meat by weight (1 lb. of raw or green shrimp will yield about ½ lb. of peeled cooked shrimp).

Shrimp may be boiled and used as hors d'oeuvres, in cocktails, salads, sandwiches. newburg and other dishes. They may also be deep fried, baked stuffed or sauteed. The large shrimp are usually baked stuffed. To avoid toughness in shrimp, be careful not to overcook.

Lobster Northern lobsters are taken from cold Atlantic waters, ranging from Nova Scotia, Newfoundland and Canada to Maine, Massachusetts and as far south as Carolina. They are available the year around, but are most plentiful during the summer months, starting in May.

Lobsters may be purchased live in the shell or as fresh or frozen cooked meat. Fresh meat is usually expensive, as it takes four to five chicken lobsters to make 1 lb. of meat. Frozen meat is widely marketed in 14 oz. cans and is packed in salt water brine. Canned lobster is primarily for home use.

Lobsters that weigh up to 30 lb. have been caught, but the practical size for food service operations seldom should exceed 2 lb. One-pound lobsters are called "chickens;" "quarters" weigh 1¼ lb; "selects" weigh 1½ to 2¼ lb., and lobsters weighing over 2½ lb. are called "jumbos."

In some states it is illegal for fishermen to take female lobsters that are carrying eggs. It is equally illegal for an eating establishment to cook and serve them. Although supervision of these laws is difficult, severe fines and penalties may be imposed if they are not obeyed.

Live lobsters keep best when they remain covered with seaweed or heavy paper. Excessive cold may make them appear "sleepy" when they are not. (Sleepers are lobsters that are dying and are no longer active. They are often boiled for meat.)

Lobster must be live when cooked. The flesh of dead meat flakes and falls apart when cooked. Fresh meat is firm and white with pink tinges. If the tail of a boiled lobster (in the shell) springs back when straightened out, it indicates that the lobster was live when cooked. The shells of live lobsters vary in color from dark bluish green or nearly black, to mottled shades of brown and dark green, depending on their origin. During cooking, the shells turn bright red.

Lobsters have a moulting period each year when they shed their hard shells (in order to grow) and start new ones. When in the soft shell stage, lobsters are extremely perishable, and through loss of weight, they do not have as much meat as hard shell lobsters. The moulting season varies geographically, but generally late July and early August are soft shell periods when lobsters must be handled with extreme care.

Lobsters may be broiled, baked stuffed, sauteed, steamed, boiled, deep fried and used in other culinary preparations. Lobster meat is used for salads, cocktails, sandwiches, newburgh, chowder, thermidor and bisque.

Crayfish (or crawfish) and rock lobsters are relatives of the northern lobster, but do not have large claws. The meat comes almost entirely from the broad tail. Lobster tails may be treated in the same manner as other lobsters, but are used most successfully broiled, baked and baked stuffed.

Scallops are marketed as deep sea, bay or cape scallops. They are the edible portion of the adductor muscle which opens and closes the shell. They are marketed shucked, by the gallon.

Shells may be purchased for serving scallops and other fish en coquille (pronounced ahn-koh-keel),

COQUILLES ST. JACQUES, MORNAY

To serve Coquilles St. Jacques, Mornay (recipe p. 161), fill scallop shells with sauteed scallops and pour sauce over the scallops. Next, sprinkle tops with grated cheese and brown under broiler. As an optional decoration, a border of duchess potatoes may be piped around the edge as shown in the third picture. Decoration also makes serving look more sizable.

which means in the shell.

Cape scallops are very small and considered to be the most delicate. They are expensive. Deep sea scallops are large; bay scallops are an intermediate size. They may be purchased fresh or frozen. They are served broiled, en brochette (on a skewer), sauteed, deep fried, au gratin, in chowder, newburg, soup, etc.

Snails are sometimes served in restaurants and hotels featuring French cuisine. Snails are purchased canned, with shells separate. The snails are prepared with butter and other ingredients and stuffed back into the shells to complete cooking before serving. The French term for snails is escargots (pronounced ays-kahr-go). They are served on a proper snail platter with special tongs for holding the snail shell.

Clams Hard shell clams are all members of the quahaug family, although the term quahaug is generally applied to the larger size clams used exclusively for chowder. They are not tender enough for most other uses and are often chopped or ground for chowder.

Quahaugs are sometimes used for making strips. Strips are the necks of quahaugs that are machine sliced very thinly in processing and used for deep frying. Thin slicing does not increase tenderness, but makes them easier to chew and, therefore, seem more tender.

Cherrystones and Little Necks, in order of diminishing size, are served on the half shell as appetizers. Soft shell clams are primarily served as steamers. They are purchased by the bushel or peck. They are steam cooked and served with the broth in which they were cooked and with drawn butter.

Shucked clams are purchased by the gallon as chowder clams or frying clams. They vary in size, color and quality, depending on their source.

Canned clams are also marketed. Chopped clams are packed in No. 5 cans for chowder. Clams may be fried, served as fritters, canapes, in chowder, soup, stew, stuffing and sauces.

Oysters may be purchased live in the shell or fresh and frozen shucked. Canned oysters are rarely used in commercial cooking.

Oysters in the shell are purchased by the barrel, part barrel, bushel, half-bushel, etc. They are marketed by size, blue points being preferred. Cotuit oysters are now in greater abundance than blue point oysters and are generally accepted as a substitute. They may be served raw on the half shell as appetizers, or may be baked or baked stuffed.

Shucked oysters are sold by the gallon and are used for chowder, bisque, stew, stuffing, scalloped oysters, deep fried, etc. They are classified by count or number to the gallon.

Standards are small oysters that run 301 to 500 to the gallon. Selects are 211 to 300 per gallon and are preferred for frying. Larger oysters, called extra selects or counts are also available.

Crabs Although several varieties of crabs are important to the food business as a whole, only two play an important part in professional cookery: blue crabs (from which we get our soft shell crabs—crabs in moult, as described in the Lobster section) and Alaska king crabs.

Soft shell crabs may be purchased fresh, but are available frozen year round. They are marketed by size or number to the pound. They are usually cleaned prior to freezing and may be eaten shell and all. Fresh crabs must be cleaned before cooking. Soft shell crabs may be sauteed or deep fried.

King crabs from the Pacific Ocean off Alaska weigh from 6 to 20 lb. Body meat is usually canned. Leg meat is marketed (1) frozen, (2) cooked in the shell and (3) frozen meat. Meat is packed in easy-to-handle frozen blocks. Water should be pressed out of blocks both after thawing and before use.

Crab meat may be served in newburg, salads and sandwiches, cocktails, hors d'oeuvre or crab cakes. Crab may also be served creamed, mornay or au gratin. Whole or part legs in the shell are sometimes broiled or baked. Many of the methods used in cooking meat and poultry may also be applied with some slight variation to fish cookery. In addition, there are many methods that apply exclusively to fish cookery. As previously stated, the type of fish determines the method of cooking.

Coquilles St. Jacques, Mornay

YIELD: 2 portions		EACH PORTION: about 5 oz. scallops	
INGREDIENTS		*QUANTITY*	*METHOD*
Scallops Butter Lemon Juice		10 oz. 1 oz. 3 tbsp.	1. Saute scallops in 1 oz. butter for 1 min. Add lemon juice. 2. Remove scallops and place in coquilles (shells). Keep warm.
Butter Mushrooms, sliced Shallot, chopped Dry White Wine		1 oz. 2 oz. 1 2 oz.	3. Saute sliced mushrooms and shallot in remaining 1 oz. butter; add wine and liquor from scallops. Reduce 1/3.
Egg Yolks Heavy Cream Medium Cream Sauce (p. 314) Salt Pepper		2 2 oz. 8 oz. to taste to taste	4. Incorporate blended cream and egg yolks (liaison) into hot cream sauce, tempering the liaison first. Blend hot sauce mixture into mushroom mixture. Season to taste. Do not boil.
Gruyere or Parmesan Cheese, grated		1 oz.	5. Pour sauce over scallops. Sprinkle with cheese. Brown under broiler or salamander. 6. Serve immediately.

Lobster a l'Americaine

YIELD: about 10 to 12 portions			
INGREDIENTS		*QUANTITY*	*METHOD*
Lobsters, live (1½ to 2 lb. ea.)		8 to 10	1. Split fresh live lobsters lengthwise in halves. Remove stone bag and intestinal vein. Remove and crack claws. Reserve all juices, corals and tamale and press through fine wire strainer and reserve. Cut each half lobster into three equal portions.

Salad Oil
Onions
Shallots
Garlic Cloves
Brandy
White Wine, dry
Tomatoes, fresh or canned
   crushed
Tomato Paste
Fish Veloute (p. 317)
Fish Fumet
		8 oz.
		2 oz.
		2 oz.
		3 cloves
		4 oz.
		8 oz.
		8 fresh or 1
		  No. 2½ can
		4 oz.
		4 oz.
		1½ pt.
			2. Heat oil in large saute pan. Add cut lobster pieces and season with salt and pepper. Saute until all parts of shells have turned red.
			3. Stir in the chopped onions, shallots and garlic. Cook until vegetables are tender. Add brandy, white wine, the fresh or canned crushed tomatoes (if fresh, tomatoes must be peeled, seeded and chopped) and tomato paste.
			4. Stir in fish veloute and fish fumet. Cover and continue to simmer about 25 min.

Butter Parsley, chopped Tarragon Chervil Salt Pepper Cayenne Pepper		¼ lb. 1½ oz. 1 tsp. 1 tsp. to taste to taste to taste	5. At that time, remove all lobster pieces into casserole or chafing dish. Place saute pan on high heat. Stir sauce until smooth. Stir in the pressed juices, corals and tamale (liver); then stir in the butter. Add the chopped parsley, tarragon and chervil. Adjust seasoning. Pour sauce over lobster pieces and serve.

ADDITIONAL INFORMATION:
(1) It will be noted that flaming of brandy is omitted. Flaming may burn the shells and create a bitter flavor.
(b) Juices, coral and tamale are added in time to cook, and the butter finally to enrich the flavor.
(c) Some recipes call for a base of fine diced onions, carrots and celery; others add meat or fish glaze to the sauce, and several others add sliced mushrooms.
(d) This recipe as presented is the original recipe created and served at the Restaurant Noel in Paris during the second Empire of France.

Oysters or Clams on the Half Shell

Method

1. Fill a soup plate with crushed ice. Place on an underliner.

2. Place a 2-oz. container of Cocktail Sauce (p. 323) in the center of the ice.

3. Open shellfish and loosen from the shell, being careful not to damage the flesh. (See instructions below for clams and on facing page for oysters.)

4. Place shellfish in half shells on the bed of ice. Arrange around the Cocktail Sauce.

5. Garnish with fresh lemon wedge and a sprig of fresh parsley.

Note: The number of clams or oysters served per portion may vary depending on the price structure of your menu. Most operators serve between 3 and 5 per portion.

Crackers, horseradish, worcestershire sauce and hot pepper sauce are usually offered at service time.

HOW TO OPEN CLAMS

1. Before starting, examine the shell-fish to eliminate dead or otherwise unfit clams.

2. Hold clam in left hand as indicated in photos A and B. Rinse quickly in cold running water. Do not jar or handle excessively as this causes the clam to "tighten up."

3. Hold clam knife in right hand as shown in Photos A and B. Place the sharp edge of the knife against the outside edge between shells.

4. With a firm pressure of left hand and fingers, exert sharp pressure against dull or heavy side of blade, forcing blade between shells and severing first muscle (Photo B).

5. Withdraw knife blade part way, tipping handle downward slightly so that blade rests against upper shell riding over flesh of the clam (Photo C). Turn the clam counter-clockwise, running knife around edge of shell to sever second muscle which is located opposite first muscle. Be careful not to cut or damage the flesh of the clam as this causes "watering," and the clam loses its plumpness.

6. Open clam and discard upper shell (Photo D).

7. Loosen clam from lower shell as a convenience for the guest.

8. Examine clam for shell fragments and serve as shown in Photo E.

A

B

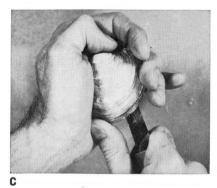

C

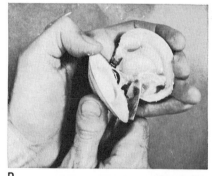

D

E

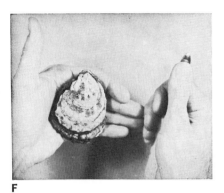

F

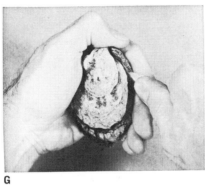

G

H

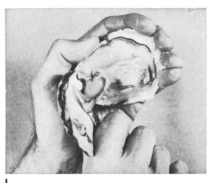

I

HOW
TO OPEN OYSTERS

1. Before starting, examine the shell-fish to eliminate dead or otherwise unfit oysters.

2. Hold oyster in left hand as indicated in Photos F and G. Rinse quickly in cold running water. Do not jar the oyster or handle excessively as this will cause oyster to "tighten up."

3. Hold oyster knife in right hand as shown in Photo F, with thumb extending toward tip of knife. Knife should be held firmly but allowing some flexibility so that the thumb may be quickly slid beyond extreme tip of knife as a protective measure. If knife hand should slip while opening oysters, the tip of the thumb will serve as a guard against a possible serious wound to the palm of the left hand.

4. Insert the tip of the knife firmly between the shells (Photo G). With a sharp clockwise twist, pry open the shell.

5. Changing the position of the handle slightly (Photo H), bring the side of the blade across the inside of the upper shell and cut the large adductor muscle close to the upper shell to which it is attached. Be careful not to cut or damage the flesh of the oyster as this causes "watering" and the oyster loses its plumpness.

6. Cut down the lower end of the same muscle (Photo I) and loosen the oyster in the deep part of the shell as a convenience to the guest.

7. Discard upper shell and examine the oyster for particles of broken shell.

8. Serve as shown in Photo J.

J

Shellfish

Baked Oysters Remick (recipe below)

Fisherman's Platter (recipe top of facing page)

Baked Oysters Remick

INGREDIENTS	QUANTITY	METHOD
YIELD: 1 portion		
Oysters White Wine Butter Stock	6 1 oz. 2 tsp. 4 oz.	1. Poach oysters in white wine, butter and stock until they curl. Do not overcook. 2. Drain and put back in half shell, placing each on a platter lined with rock salt.

SAUCE:
   Thick Mayonnaise 6 oz.
   Chili Sauce 3 oz.
   Horseradish 1 oz.
Sauce
Grated Swiss Cheese
	
	3 oz.
	1 oz.
		3. Make sauce by mixing mayonnaise, chili sauce and horseradish. Cover each oyster generously with sauce. Sprinkle with grated cheese.
		4. Broil or bake at 400°F. until golden brown.
		5. Oysters may be served with Saratoga Potato Chips (p. 182) or julienne potatoes.

Baked Oysters a l'Ancienne

INGREDIENTS	QUANTITY	METHOD
YIELD: 25 appetizer portions **EACH PORTION:** 4 oysters 12 entree portions 8 oysters		
Large Green Peppers, chopped fine Mushrooms, chopped fine Shallots, chopped fine Butter Pimientoes, chopped fine	2 5 oz. 3 oz. 1½ lb. 3 oz.	1. Saute green peppers, mushrooms, shallots in 1 lb. of the butter; cool and add the rest of butter and the pimientoes.
Oysters on Half Shell Bacon Slices, half cooked (cut 2 in. long)	100 25	2. Place a teaspoon of vegetable mixture on top of each oyster and cover with a piece of bacon. 3. Place oysters in pan of rock salt and bake at 475°F. about 15 min. 4. Serve with large section of lemon.

Fisherman's Platter

YIELD: 50 portions	**EACH PORTION**: about 8 oz.	

INGREDIENTS	QUANTITY	METHOD
Shrimp, peeled and deveined	50 (2½ lb., A.P., 21 to 25 count)	1. Bread all items except clams. (Breading procedures on page 178.) Use egg wash and breading for all items except clams.
Oysters, shucked	½ gal.	
Scallops	5 lb.	2. Deep fry at 375°F. Keep fried food hot.
Fillets of Sole (1½ oz. portions)	50 fillets (5 lb.)	3. Do not salt. Cook as near service time as possible.
Egg Wash	for breading	
Breading	for breading	
OR Bread Crumbs		
Fishmeal	for breading	
Clams, shucked	½ gal.	4. Bread clams with egg wash and fish meal. Bread and fry to order. Deep fry at 375°F.
		5. Divide all items evenly; serve 1 shrimp, 1 to 3 oysters, 2 to 4 scallops, 1 fillet of sole, 1 to 3 clams per order.
		6. Serve with Tartar Sauce (p. 324). Cocktail Sauce (p. 323) may be served with fried shrimp and other seafoods. Garnish is usually lemon wedge and parsley sprig.

NOTE: This volume of frying necessitates frying some items ahead. Clams are more demanding of fat due to high water content. Therefore, reserve clams to fry to order.

The above items are not necessarily usual seafood combinations but are chosen to increase your familiarity with all types of seafood. Nearly any reasonable combination of seafoods may be used. Four items are usually sufficient. More than this may prove difficult for service.

Wash and clean seafood products as necessary.

Boiled Lobster

METHOD

1. Plunge live lobsters head first into large pot of boiling salted water.
2. When water returns to boil simmer for 6 to 8 min. for 1 lb. lobsters. Larger lobsters may take up to 20 min. depending on weight. Meat toughens with overcooking.
3. For cold boiled lobster or to prepare lobsters for meat, cool cooked lobsters in cold running water. This also prevents further cooking.
4. For hot boiled lobster, serve directly from range.
5. Claws should be disjointed and cracked or portion of the shell removed for convenience of guest.
6. Body may be split from head to tail all the way through shell. Stomach and intestinal vein must be removed. (See recipe for Broiled Live Lobsters.) Empty cavity is sometimes filled with parsley sprigs, lobster mayonnaise and other variations OR
7. Tail may be broken from carapace (body section) and split in half lengthwise, removing intestinal vein.
8. The shell is easily pulled away from remainder of body section for removal of stomach or lady. The body section is then re-assembled and placed head up in center of platter or plate. Claws and tail sections are then placed around body section. May be served with lemon slice pierced on top of pointed head section or lemon wedge and parsley sprig. Hot drawn butter is served separately.

To prepare meat for newburg, salad and other dishes, remove all meat from shells and clean meat by removal of cartilage from large claws and intestinal vein from tail. The balance of shell is discarded. Cut meat to desired size.

To prepare **Lobster for Thermidor** and other similar dishes, place the cooked lobster ventral (belly) side down, on cutting board. Hold a sharp knife in a horizontal position (level with the board), and cut shallow slice from top of lobster starting immediately in front of, or in back of eyes, and extending to beginning of last tail segment, depending on how large a cavity is desired. The meat is removed and shell thoroughly rinsed in clear cold water and drained before filling with appropriate mixture. **Safety Precaution**: Hold folded towel opposite knife hand to maintain pressure on lobster and aid in guiding knife. Towel usually protects hand if knife slips or shell breaks.

STEAMED LOBSTER
Follow same basic procedure. Check cooking chart and instructions of manufacturer if using steam equipment.
FROZEN ROCK LOBSTER (Crawfish or Langouste)
The tails of these lobsters are used and they may be boiled, steamed, broiled or baked stuffed. Cooking time is 15 to 17 min. depending on size and origin. The lobster tails should be thawed only in time to be used, not far in advance of actual preparation.

Shellfish

Shrimp and Rice, Louisiana Style (recipe below)   *Lobster Newburg (recipe bottom of page)*

Shrimp and Rice, Louisiana Style

YIELD: 1 portion	**EACH PORTION:** 3 oz. shrimp plus sauce and garnish	
INGREDIENTS	*QUANTITY*	*METHOD*
Butter Onion, chopped fine Cooked Shrimp	1 oz. 1 tsp. 3 oz.	1. Saute onion in butter for a few minutes until transparent. 2. Add cooked shrimp and saute lightly.
Light Cream Catsup Celery Salt Cayenne Pepper Salt	3 oz. 2 oz. 1/8 tsp. to taste to taste	3. Add remaining ingredients, except rice and peas. Simmer 1 min.
Cooked Rice Green Peas, cooked	3 oz. 1 oz.	4. Serve piping hot in casserole with cooked rice. Garnish with peas.

Lobster Newburg

YIELD: 48 portions		
INGREDIENTS	*QUANTITY*	*METHOD*
Cooked Lobster Meat Butter Paprika Dry Sherry Lemon Juice	12 lb. 1 lb. ¾ oz. 6 oz. from 1 lemon	1. Cut the lobster meat into ¾ in. pieces. 2. Saute lobster meat in butter in large sautoir. Add paprika, sherry and lemon juice.
Medium Cream Sauce (p. 314) Salt Pepper	2 gal. to taste to taste	3. Blend in Cream Sauce; bring to a boil; season to taste. 4. Serve in patty shells or with rice pilaf or buttered noodles or in casseroles with toast tips.
NOTE: Amount of lobster meat used will vary with price structure of the menu.		
See color picture, p. 142.		

Seafood Newburg

	YIELD: 50 portions	EACH PORTION: about 9 oz. with sauce
INGREDIENTS	*QUANTITY*	*METHOD*
Scallops	5 lb.	1. Wash scallops and cut in ¾ in. pieces. Poach in boiling water 3 min. Drain and cover with cold water.
Shrimp, in shell Lemon, sliced Bay Leaves Cloves, whole	4 lb. 1 2 2	2. Cook shrimp in boiling water with lemon, bay leaves and whole cloves for 5 min. Drain and cool in cold water. Clean shrimp and cut in half lengthwise.
Butter Bread Flour Milk, hot	1¼ lb. 20 oz. 6 qt.	3. Melt 1¼ lb. butter in heavy sauce pot. Add flour to make roux (see p. 310). Cook 8 to 10 min. but do not brown. 4. Add scalded milk and stir until thickened and smooth.
Butter Lobster Meat, cooked Paprika	12 oz. 4 lb. 4 tsp.	5. Clean lobster meat, removing bone in large claws and long intestinal vein from the tail. Cut in chunks same size as scallops. 6. Saute lobster in butter until lobster is hot. Add shrimp and paprika. Saute until seafood is done, about 3 min.
Sherry Wine	6 oz.	7. Heat scallops to boiling. Remove from heat; drain. 8. Add all seafood to sauce. Incorporate wine. Season lightly with salt. Garnish with parsley. 9. Newburg may be served in patty shell, on toast or in casserole with toast points.

Deep Fried Soft Shell Crabs

	YIELD: 5 portions	EACH PORTION: 3 crabs, about 9 oz.
INGREDIENTS	*QUANTITY*	*METHOD*
Soft Shell Blue Crabs, frozen, cleaned	3 lb. (about 15)	1. Dress crabs by cutting off the face just back of the eyes. Remove the apron (on the under side of the body) and the spongy parts, including the gills, stomach and intestines. Rinse in cold water and drain.
Eggs, whole, beaten Milk Salt Bread Flour	4 1 pt. ½ oz. 8 oz.	2. Combine eggs, milk and salt. 3. Place crabs in egg-milk mixture for 2 or 3 min. 4. Remove and place in flour. Toss flour over crabs and pat lightly but firmly. They must be handled with care as they are quite fragile. 5. Fry in deep fat at 360°F. for 3 or 4 min. or until done. They should be golden brown. 6. Drain well and serve on toast points, garnished with lemon wedge and sprig of fresh parsley. Tartar Sauce (p. 324) may be served on the side if desired.

NOTE: The size of crabs is variable. They may be purchased by size and number to pound. Portions are determined by size of the crab.

Slightly varied breading procedures may be used. Crabs may be double-floured (placed back in egg wash and floured again). Bread crumbs may be used as in standard procedures or may be combined with flour as a breading agent. The type of breading will vary with the size of the crab as larger crabs take longer to cook and a light colored breading agent might be more desirable.

Crabs may also be prepared pan fried or sauteed Meuniere.

Shellfish

Pizzaola Sauce with Shrimp, right (recipe below)

Broiled Lobster, far right (recipe on facing page)

Pizzaola Sauce with Shrimp

YIELD: 50 portions	EACH PORTION: about 6 oz.	
INGREDIENTS	QUANTITY	METHOD

SAUCE:
    Onions, chopped
    Garlic, chopped fine
    Olive Oil
    Italian Tomatoes
    Tomato Puree
    Sugar
    Sweet Basil, crushed fine
    Oregano, crushed fine
    Salt
	2 lb.
	3 tbsp.
	1 pt.
	2 No. 10 cans
	2 No. 10 cans
	4 oz.
	4 tbsp.
	4 tbsp.
	4 tbsp.
		1. To Make Sauce: Saute onions and chopped garlic in first amount of olive oil for about 5 min. or until nearly tender. Do not brown.
		2. Add tomatoes and tomato puree. Simmer for 1 hr. stirring occasionally.
		3. Add sugar, sweet basil, oregano and salt. Simmer for 1 hr., stirring occasionally. Adjust seasoning for the sauce.

Garlic Cloves Olive Oil Shrimp, peeled, deveined and cut in half crosswise	2 1 pt. 7½ lb.	4. Saute garlic cloves in second amount of olive oil until well browned. Discard garlic, add shrimp and saute lightly for 5 min. 5. Remove shrimp and combine with sauce. Simmer 15 min. 6. Serve 5 to 6 oz. sauce over spaghetti or other paste product.
NOTE: Pizzaola Sauce without shrimp is a basic Italian sauce that has many applications in the preparation of other Italian dishes.		

Scalloped Oysters

YIELD: 8 portions	EACH PORTION: 5 oysters	
INGREDIENTS	QUANTITY	METHOD
Oysters, shucked Cracker Crumbs Butter, melted Lemon Juice Salt Pepper Oyster Liquor Cream, light	1 qt. (40 large) 1 pt. (¼ lb.) 4 oz. 1 tbsp. ¼ tsp. ¼ tsp. 4 oz. 8 oz.	1. Drain liquor from oysters, and wash oysters well. 2. Butter 8 small shirred egg dishes and cover bottoms with cracker crumbs. Arrange 5 oysters in each dish, pour melted butter and lemon juice over top and sprinkle with more cracker crumbs. Sprinkle with salt and pepper. 3. Heat oyster liquor and cream together, and pour over oysters. 4. Bake at 350°F. for 10 min.

Broiled Lobster

METHOD

1. Rinse live chicken lobsters (1 lb.) thoroughly in cold water. Chop off claws and legs.
2. Place lobsters on chopping board with back down (ventral side up). Starting at the head, insert a sharp knife and split lobster in two and open flat lengthwise, but do not cut through back shell.
3. Remove the stomach which lies just back of the head and the long intestinal vein which runs the length of the body and tail. Discard both.
4. The coral, found only in female lobsters, is often removed and used for other products. The liver or tamale may be removed and mixed with the stuffing for added flavor.
5. Place lobsters in grill rack, shell side up and place under broiler. Large claws may be baked in the oven with a little water to retain moisture.
6. Broil 3 or 4 min. or until shells are red.
7. Remove from racks and fill body cavity (but not tail) with stuffing made from bread crumbs and butter. Tamale may be added.
8. Place a few of the small legs on top of stuffing.
9. Place on bake sheets or in roast pans and finish at 400°F. in oven. Total cooking time of 15 to 18 min. is usually sufficient. Larger lobsters require slightly longer cooking time.
10. Crack claws *after* cooking, for convenience of guests. Serve lobster on platter with one claw on each side, matching claws so that one large claw, (the fighting claw) and one small claw are served with each lobster. Garnish with lemon wedge and parsley sprig. Serve with drawn butter.

VARIATION: For **Baked Stuffed Lobsters**, meat may be removed from cooked claws and placed in body cavity and covered with crumb stuffing. Seafood may also be added to the lobster stuffing. Chopped shrimp and minced cold cooked fish may be mixed with worcestershire and other seasonings such as sherry wine.

NOTE: Broiled lobsters were originally served with no stuffing. It is commonly accepted now, however, for a small amount of stuffing to be served with broiled live lobsters.

When facilities require placing lobsters in oven without pre-cooking in broiler, a weight of some kind must be placed across the bottoms of the tails to prevent curling.

See color picture, p. 142.

Crab Cakes

Crab Cakes

YIELD: 50 portions	EACH PORTION: 2 cakes	
INGREDIENTS	*QUANTITY*	*METHOD*
Butter, melted Mushrooms, chopped fine Onions, chopped fine Green Pepper, chopped fine Bread Flour Dry Mustard Paprika Cayenne Pepper Light Cream, hot	8 oz. 8 oz. 4 oz. 2 oz. 9-1/2 oz. 1/2 oz. 1/4 oz. 1/8 tsp. 1 qt.	1. Pour butter into sauce pot and heat. Add mushrooms, onions and green pepper. Cook until soft. 2. Add flour, dry mustard and paprika. Stir until smooth. Cook for 15 min. 3. Blend in cream and stir until smooth.
Crab Meat, chopped medium Fresh Bread Crumbs White Wine Parsley, chopped fine Worcestershire Sauce Salt	8 lb. 2 qt. 8 oz. 1-1/2 oz. 2 tbsp. to taste	4. Remove from heat, add all remaining ingredients except egg yolks, whites, the 2 lb. flour and oil; mix well.
Egg Yolks Egg Whites Bread Flour	6 6 2 lb.	5. Beat egg yolks until light and lemon-colored. Fold into crab mixture. 6. Beat egg whites until stiff. Fold into crab mixture. Allow mixture to cool.
Flour Salad Oil	for dredging 1 qt.	7. Portion 100 cakes, using No. 24 ice cream scoop. Shape into patties and dredge in flour. 8. Fry in oil until golden brown. (May also be fried in deep fat at 350°F. until golden brown.) 9. Remove and place on paper towels to absorb grease. Serve hot. 10. Serve with a marinara or tomato sauce.

DEEP FRYING

Well prepared deep-fried foods add variety to any menu and are especially suitable where rapid service is stressed. In this section you will find basic and advanced formulas and techniques for a variety of deep-fried dishes.

THE PROFESSIONAL CHEF

Pre-processed French Fried Potatoes—available in many forms

French Fried Zucchini

Deep Fried Scallops

French Fried Onion Rings

French Fried Eggplant

Rice Croquettes

DEEP FRYING

Deep frying takes place in one of the following mediums: liquid frying agents or oils; compounds; vegetable shortenings; lard; rendered beef fat.

No matter which medium is used, the prime concern in deep fat frying is to minimize fat absorption. This is extremely important as the extent of fat absorption determines the palatability and acceptability of the finished product as well as its digestibility.

There are several advantages to the use of deep fat frying in a food service operation. Deep fried foods lend variety and color to the menu. They are highly acceptable to the American patron. The process is suitable for many low cost food items and is an excellent way to utilize leftovers. They lend themselves to rapid service since they may be prepared (although not cooked) in advance; and the actual cooking time required is short. Deep frying also helps distribute the work load of the kitchen staff.

The prime disadvantage of deep frying is not in the medium itself, but in the application of improper cooking procedures and care and handling of food, fat and equipment.

Foods to be fried, for example, are usually coated, breaded or dipped in batter. The sudden contact of hot fat converts the coating into a resisting crust that forms a protective coating and prevents leakage of the product being fried into the frying medium.

But if the fat is not sufficiently hot, the crisp coating is not developed and the product becomes saturated with fat. Loose crumbs fall into the fat and burn, increasing the rate of decomposition.

Turkey Croquettes, Supreme Sauce

Fisherman's Plate

Corn Fritters

Techniques for Deep Frying

Edible fats are divided into two basic categories: fats—solid or near solid at room temperature; oils—liquid under the same conditions. In general, fats that are liquid at room temperature are more easily digested than those that are not.

Hydrogenization is a process by which fats and oils are treated with hydrogen to improve their keeping qualities and convert them to solid fats that will not melt at room temperature. Hydrogenated fats and natural fats are resistant to oxidation changes that contribute to decomposition.

Decomposition is the disintegration or breaking down of the chemical constituents that compose fats and oils and results in an accumulation of fatty acids that cause the product being fried to absorb fat because the fat will not maintain proper frying temperatures. Breakdown is often accompanied by the excessive smoking and irritating odors of the hot fat.

Frying fats are often selected on the basis of their resistance to decomposition at frying temperatures. However, it must be noted that regardless of the quality of fat selected, quality fried products and prolonged cooking life of the fat can only be obtained through proper care and handling of foods, fat and equipment. Proper methods and procedures will also effect appreciable dollar savings in food, labor and equipment.

Deep Fat Frying is the cooking of food, submerged, in hot fat at temperatures ranging from 325°F. to 400°F., depending on the food being cooked.

Properly prepared fried foods, eaten in moderation, are easily digested and may provide nutritional benefit. Fats serve as a concentrated fuel food and aid in hunger satisfaction, as they remain in the digestive tract for a longer period of time than do many other foods.

Recent scientific research has brought considerable controversy regarding the place of certain fats in the diet and the association of fat with heart disease. Various publications are available in public libraries and are recommended reading.

Frying Mediums

Among the various frying mediums are:
1) Lard
2) Rendered beef fat
3) Vegetable shortenings
4) Compounds
5) Vegetable oils

Lard is fat separated by heating fat tissues of the hog. Its quality depends on the part of the animal from which it was obtained and the method of processing. Leaf lard, which is obtained from the abdominal cavity, is considered to possess the best qualities. New processes have been developed to produce bland lard that is equal or superior to some vegetable shortenings for frying life.

Rendered beef fat is an inexpensive frying medium that is in wide use. Some initial odor is experienced that burns off after a little use. Beef fats may be purchased hydrogenated, which gives them a white, creamy color, or not hydrogenated, in which case they retain much of their yellow coloring.

Vegetable shortenings are often double purpose shortenings, used in deep fat frying and in baking. Generally speaking, they have a lower fatty acid content than do many other frying media. This contributes to their frying life. They have a higher smoke point than most animal fats. (Smoke point is the temperature at which fats begin to smoke.)

Compounds are made by combining a hard fat with a soft fat to give body to the product. Although they may be composed of all-animal or all-vegetable fat, they are often a combination of the two. They vary in their smoke point, but have a higher degree of fatty acids than do most vegetable shortenings.

Vegetable oils are liquid frying agents that remain fluid at room temperature. Their advantage is in ease of handling as they are packed in easy-to-handle cans. They are readily available for use as no melting is necessary. They are merely opened and poured into the deep fat fryer. Constant research and new product developments are creating liquid frying agents with longer life and less decomposition.

Breading or Batter A batter is a semi-liquid mixture of flour, eggs, milk, etc., that is used to coat or bind various culinary preparations. Foods treated with batter are exposed to hot fat in order to set them quickly and prevent leakage of the product in much the same manner as a breaded item. Breaded foods are prepared by dipping, in flour, then in beaten eggs or eggs and milk and rolling in bread crumbs, cracker meal or commercially prepared products.

Breaded products usually provide a crisper and longer lasting crust than batter-treated products.

Factors Affecting the Degree of Fat Absorption

1) Quality and condition of fat.

The quality and condition of the fat will, in great part, influence the temperature, as fat that is in the process of decomposition will not maintain necessary frying temperatures. Quality foods must begin with quality products.

2) Amount of surface area exposed.

The more surface area of a product exposed, the greater the fat absorption; the less surface exposed, the less the fat absorption.

3) Type and composition of food.

The texture and chemical composition of some foods make them more susceptible to fat absorption than others. Foods of high sugar content absorb fats more readily than foods of low sugar content. High gluten flours, such as bread flour, absorb less fat than soft wheat flour, such as cake and pastry flours. This is one of the chief reasons why bread flour is used for breading and frying. Watery foods tend to absorb more fat than foods of more solid composition.

4) Length of cooking time.

The length of cooking time varies with: (1) the temperature selected; (2) the temperature of the product before frying; (3) the state of the product, whether raw or cooked; (4) the size or volume of the product, and, again repeating, (5) the quality or condition of the fat.

Foods at room temperature will obviously require less heat than foods that are refrigerated, chilled or frozen; therefore, they will cook more rapidly. Raw or uncooked foods will require a longer cooking time than will partially cooked or fully cooked foods. It will take longer for the heat to penetrate to the center of large pieces of meat than it will for small pieces. Fat that is losing its power will require longer cooking periods to accomplish complete cooking. This obviously will result in greater fat absorption.

5) Temperature of the fat.

Principles employed in the selection of temperature are interrelated to the preceding factors affecting fat absorption. Foods that require longer cooking time should be cooked at lower temperatures to prevent burning. Foods that cook rapidly require higher temperatures to effect crisping and coloring in a short period of exposure. Large amounts of food demand more heat than do small amounts.

If the fat becomes overburdened or the ratio of food to fat is too great, the temperature will be lowered and result in greasy foods. The type of breading also influences the selection of temperature. Dark colored breading colors much more rapidly than light colored breading. Cornflakes, rolled oats, bread crumbs, cracker meal should not be cooked at the same temperature.

When fats begin to break down, they require higher than normal temperatures in order to maintain frying ability. Excessive temperatures speed decomposition. When fat has reached this stage, it is not suitable for proper frying.

Frying Temperatures Because of the various factors involving the selection of frying temperature, it should be recognized that it is impossible to state a definite single frying temperature for a product. However, we may use a temperature range that will guide us, with consideration of other factors, in selecting appropriate frying temperatures for specific products.

Fritters, scallops and other uncooked foods	350°F. to 375°F.
French fried potatoes, blanching	325°F. to 360°F.
French fried potatoes, finishing	About 375°F.
Croquettes, cutlets and cooked mixtures	350°F. to 375°F.

While 360°F. may be considered to be an excessively high temperature, it must be noted that the temperature selected and set by the automatic temperature control or thermostat is not necessarily the temperature of the fat once the food product is introduced. Any good fat fryer will maintain temperatures relatively close to the thermostat setting when cooking moderate quantities of food. However, when a large volume of food is suddenly introduced, the temperature may be reduced.

This is often true in blanching french fried potatoes where large work-baskets are sometimes used to facilitate handling of the potatoes and to allow work to be done on a production basis. The high water content of raw potatoes, when placed in the deep fat fryer in quantity, may pull the temperature of the fat down from 360°F. to 325°F. or lower in a matter of seconds. In this fashion, the blanching takes place at the lower temperature, not at 360°F.

The demand for heat from the deep fat fryer may become too great for it to recover the selected temperature until the product is removed and the demand is lessened or halted. The temperature will then recover to the selected thermostat setting. Determining the selection of proper frying temperatures must be learned through experience, and it is useless to state definite temperatures that may or may not hold true in actual practice.

Proper Care of Fat
1) Maintain even temperatures.
2) Hold to proper work load (do not overburden).
3) Shake breaded item well before placing over or in deep fat fryer.
4) Remove floating particles during the work period.
5) Strain fat daily or more often if subjected to heavy use.
6) Keep proper fat level.
7) Change fat when no longer serviceable.
8) Add new fat to old only when old fat is still serviceable.
9) Do not add suet or rendered fat in the deep fat fryer.
10) Do not salt products while frying. Salt breaks down fat.

Constant temperatures will aid in prolonging the life of fat. Continued and unwarranted fluctuations in temperature settings contribute to fat breakdown just as stop and go temperatures break down automobile oil. Playing with the thermostat will reduce its life and often results in faulty settings.

Overburdening fat results in grease saturated products and puts unnecessary strain on the deep fat fryer. Reasonable work loads will aid in producing quality foods and prolonging the life of the fat.

If food products are placed in the deep fat fryer without shaking them, excess crumbs often fall into the fat. The small particles burn easily and cause more rapid deterioration of the frying medium. Frequent skimming of floating particles aids in alleviating this problem. Fat should be strained daily to dispose

PREPARING FISHERMAN'S PLATTER

Bread all items—shrimp, oysters, scallops and fillet of sole—by dipping in seasoned flour, or breading, egg wash and breading. Bread clams at service time.

Fry at about 375°F. This volume of frying means that some items will have to be cooked in advance of service, but they should be cooked as close to service time as possible.

Nearly any reasonable combination of seafood may be used for Fisherman's Platter. The above items have been included so that you will become familiar with all types of seafood.

of crumbs and fine food particles that fall off in the frying process. Proper straining increases fat life.

Replacing Fat In the course of normal frying, foods will absorb some part of the fat during the work period. The fat that is absorbed must be replaced in the amount necessary to keep fat at the proper level.

It is good policy to change the fat as frequently as needed. Stretching the fat does not really prolong its life and can only result in inferior products and dissatisfied patrons. It is more expensive to lose customers or to have them disgruntled than to bear the comparatively small cost of dumping the old fat and replacing it with new. Old fat and fat trimmings are saved and sold to commercial rendering companies.

While fat must be kept at a proper level, it is false economy to add good fat to bad in hopes of extending its use. The same applies to adding suet or meat fats and rendering them in the deep fat fryer. The extraction of acids and impurities can only be accomplished by commercial processes and the harm that home rendering can do to fats far outweighs any hoped-for saving that might accrue by rendering them in the deep fat fryer.

To produce and maintain quality fried foods, fat must be kept in excellent condition at all times and products must be handled quickly and skillfully during their preparation and service. This includes prompt pickup from the kitchens by members of the service staff. Fried foods should be cooked to order and served immediately to the guest. Fried foods should be served piping hot on hot plates as once they start to cool they lose their eye appeal, flavor and ease of digestibility.

Care of Fryer The deep fat fryer should be drained weekly or as often as necessary, scrubbed and boiled out with baking soda or prescribed detergents and rinsed well before adding new fat. This prevents accumulation of acid products and increases the life of the deep fat fryer. It decreases maintenance costs, produces superior products and improves the keeping qualities of the new fat.

Products Often Associated with Deep Fat Frying

1) **Poultry: used extensively**
   Chicken breasts
   Boneless Chicken wings
   Chicken legs
   Croquettes (turkey and chicken)
2) **Meats: used very little in deep fat frying**
   Veal cutlets
   Croquettes (ham and other cooked ground meats)
3) **Fish: used extensively**

Frozen breaded fish portions	Haddock
Clams	Lobster
Codfish (cakes)	Scallops
Halibut (sometimes served as	Smelt
"fingers," cut in finger-size)	Sole

   Swordfish (pieces, breaded and fried)
4) **Fruit**
   Primarily fritters: apple, banana, pineapple, etc.
5) **Vegetables:**

Eggplant	Potatoes (also croquettes)
Parsley	Fritters: corn, mixed vegetables,
Zucchini	rice

Breading

Breading, in its simplest form, means the coating of a product with bread crumbs preparatory to frying. Other ingredients are also referred to as breading. They include: cracker meal, corn flakes, rolled oats, bolted corn meal and other commercially prepared products.

The object of breading is to coat a product uniformly with some type of breading agent that will form a crisp, protective covering when exposed to frying temperature.

Uniform coating is of extreme importance. Cracks or breaks in the surface or incompletely breaded spots often cause bursting or splitting of the product under heat.

Products Used in Breading There are three major products used in most breading procedures: 1) bread flour, 2) wash and 3) any of the breading agents previously noted.

Wash is a liquid agent which, in combination with flour, forms a paste to which breading will adhere. Wash may be prepared in many ways: all eggs (beaten), eggs and milk, eggs and water, evaporated milk. For general use, eggs and milk are combined in varying proportions: more eggs—greater binding power—greater expense.

An average ratio of three whole eggs to one quart of milk produces a satisfactory product. The eggs and milk may be beaten together, although it is easier to beat the eggs lightly before adding the milk.

Hotel pans are most suitable for general breading work. Stainless steel bowls may be used for holding wash. All ingredients and equipment should be assembled before starting work.

Breading Procedure:

1) Place product or products in flour, coating well.
2) Remove and shake off excess flour.
3) Immerse in wash, wetting well so that no dry or floured areas are visible.
4) Remove from wash with as little handling as possible. Heavy or excessive handling may remove part of the paste coating made of the flour and liquid and breading agent will not adhere.
5) Drain or gently shake off excess wash.
6) Place in crumbs or breading agent. Cover well before handling. Press breading gently but firmly to product for strong adhesion. Cover again with crumbs.
7) Remove from crumbs; shake off excess breading.
8) The product is now ready for frying. It may, however, be refrigerated for future use.

When breading in quantity for future service, completed products should be covered lightly with crumbs before refrigerating to reduce sweating or drying out. (Procedure will depend on whether original state of product is moist or dry.)

The same basic steps are taken in the breading of nearly all foods. Items such as veal cutlets and chicken breasts may be done singly without loss of time, provided an adequate breading set-up is arranged.

Scallops and other small items may be done in larger quantities, but in small enough volume to ensure complete coating with all breading products. Best results are obtained when a few products are processed at one time. Scallops are handled in a slightly different manner by tossing loosely when in flour and in crumbs in order to coat them evenly.

Flour and crumbs should be sifted when lumpy to prevent lumps from adhering to the product to be fried. The egg wash should be strained periodically to remove flour and bread crumbs.

Small quantities of breaded food should be taken from the refrigerator at one time. This reduces the possibility of spoilage in extremely warm weather and keeps most foods firm enough to handle without difficulty.

Foods should not be breaded too far in advance. Moist products tend to sweat. Dry foods tend to become dryer. It often becomes necessary to re-bread them; this may result in excessive breading which detracts from the product. Darker finished products may also result.

Breading Seafood Bolted corn meal or fish meal is often used for breading clams and other seafood. Products must be breaded to order when using meal as it absorbs moisture from the product rapidly and becomes sweaty. (Cornflakes also absorb moisture readily.)

Clams are of extremely wet nature and are best breaded (when using fish meal) by immersing in wash, draining and placing in fish meal where they are tossed lightly and separated. They must be used immediately. If they sit or are improperly handled, they become soggy and mat together in large globs.

Keep Hands Dry When breading food, it is suggested that one hand be kept dry. If right-handed, keep right hand dry. If left-handed, keep left hand dry.

If your hands are covered with flour and wash, the breading agent will adhere to your hands just as it does with a product to be breaded. Successive passes through the three agents—flour, wash and breading—will build up a heavy coating that is awkward to work with. Also, particles of the coating may be deposited in the breading agent which will necessitate additional sifting.

Small wire baskets simplify work and keep hands dry, eliminating unnecessary continuous washing of hands and sifting of crumbs.

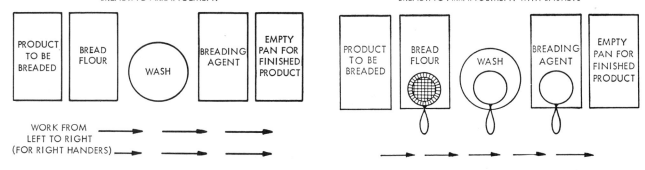

BREADING ARRANGEMENT

BREADING ARRANGEMENT WITH BASKETS

PRODUCT TO BE BREADED — BREAD FLOUR — WASH — BREADING AGENT — EMPTY PAN FOR FINISHED PRODUCT

WORK FROM LEFT TO RIGHT (FOR RIGHT HANDERS)

THE ARRANGEMENT IS REVERSED FOR LEFT-HANDERS

Onion Rings are made by slicing raw onion thin by hand or, preferably, by machine for greater uniformity and less waste. They may be prepared by breading in the manner already described or placed in batter or simply in wash and flour.

If it is necessary to bread onion rings ahead, the crumbing procedure must be used. When used in batter or wash and flour, they must be breaded to order. Superior onion rings are prepared by slicing onions very thin, placing in wash and flour and frying quickly in extremely hot fat until golden brown and crisp. They must be served immediately.

Fried foods should not be covered so that steam cannot escape as they will lose crispness and become soggy. Onion rings cut ¼-in. thick, floured and dipped in batter, recipe below, then deep fat fried can be cooked ahead of service time and kept warm for use as ordered (see color pictures pp. 172–173).

Onion Ring Batter

YIELD: 50 portions		EACH PORTION: 5 to 8 rings
INGREDIENTS	*QUANTITY*	*METHOD*
Eggs, whole Milk	4 1 qt.	1. Beat eggs, preferably in stainless steel bowl. 2. Add milk and blend.
Cake Flour Baking Powder Salt	1 lb. 4 tsp. 1 tsp.	3. Sift flour with baking powder and salt. Add to egg-milk mixture, mixing thoroughly. Batter should be be smooth.
Onions, E.P., cut (¼ in. slices), separated into rings	8 lb.	4. Dip onion rings in batter. 5. Deep fry at 325°F. until golden brown. Drain and serve hot.

Fritter Batter

YIELD: 10 portions		EACH PORTION: 3 to 4 fritters
INGREDIENTS	*QUANTITY*	*METHOD*
Eggs Flour Sugar Baking Powder Salt Milk	6 medium 1 lb. 2¼ oz. 1 oz. 2 tsp. 9 oz.	1. Beat eggs until frothy. 2. Combine flour with other dry ingredients; alternately add flour mixture and milk to eggs. Blend well after each addition.
		3. Drop by spoonfuls into hot fat, OR use a No. 24 ice cream scoop. Deep fry at 350°F. for 5 min. or until golden brown.

VARIATIONS: To basic batter add 10 oz. of any of the following—blueberries (frozen, well drained); whole kernel corn (frozen); succotash (canned); diced carrots (canned); pineapple tidbits; brown and serve sausage (diced), or fully cooked ham (diced). Fritters may be dusted with powdered sugar or served with syrup or fresh fruit.

Deep Frying

Corn Fritters (recipe below)

Fried Scallops (recipe bottom of page)

Corn Fritters

YIELD: 50 portions		EACH PORTION: 1 to 2 fritters, about 2 oz.
INGREDIENTS	*QUANTITY*	*METHOD*
Eggs, whole Whole Kernel Corn, drained Cream Style Corn	9 (1 lb.) 3 cups (1½ lb.) 3 cups (1½ lb.)	1. Separate eggs. 2. Add yolks to all of corn, mixing well.
Salt	½ tsp.	3. Whip egg whites in dry, clean, stainless steel bowl. Add salt. Whip to stiff shiny peaks.
Milk Cake Flour Baking Powder	6 oz. 1½ lb. 2 tbsp.	4. Add milk to corn mixture. 5. Add flour and baking powder, blending well. 6. Fold in beaten egg whites.
		7. Drop from No. 24 ice cream scoop into deep fat. Fry at 325°F. until golden brown and done through.
See color picture, p. 174.		

Fried Scallops

YIELD: 50 portions		EACH PORTION: 6 oz. cooked
INGREDIENTS	*QUANTITY*	*METHOD*
Scallops Eggs Milk Bread Flour Bread Crumbs OR Cracker Meal Lemon Wedges	14 lb. 6 1 qt. 2 lb. 5 lb. 50	1. Clean and remove tough membrane often found on side of scallop (particularly deep sea). Wash scallops if necessary and place in colander to drain. Cape scallops should be left intact. Sea scallops should be cut to size comparable to cape scallops. Do not slice in flat pieces. Cut as square as possible. 2. Refer to text on breading, p. 178. Combine eggs and milk for wash. Follow breading procedure. 3. Scallops should be fried in deep fat at 350°F. to 375°F. depending on volume. 4. Cook until golden brown. Drain well on absorbent paper or fine wire rack. 5. Fried scallops may be served with lemon slice and Tartar Sauce (p. 324), Cocktail Sauce (p. 323) or Remoulade Sauce. Do not salt. Leave this to the guest.
NOTE: 1 gal. scallops equals 8 lb. Average serving is 4 oz. raw; there is a slight loss in cleaning.		

French Fried Potatoes, right (recipe below)

Souffle Potatoes, far right (recipe bottom of page)

French Fried Potatoes

YIELD: 50 portions	EACH PORTION: about 5 oz.	
INGREDIENTS	QUANTITY	METHOD
Potatoes, A.P.	20 lb.	1. Wash and peel potatoes. Cut in strips 3/8 in. thick and 3 in. long or cut with french fry cutter. 2. Rinse in cold water, drain thoroughly. 3. Heat deep fat fryer to 350°F. 4. To blanch french fries: fill baskets 2/3 full and immerse slowly in hot fat. This precaution is taken so that the moisture in the potatoes does not cause the fat to spatter and boil over. 5. Shake the baskets occasionally to keep potatoes from sticking. 6. Cook until potatoes are nearly tender; should yield a little bit when squeezed between fingers. 7. Drain well and spread in pans lined with absorbent paper. 8. When ready for service, return potatoes to fry baskets in small quantities and fry at 375°F. until golden brown. Drain well and serve. Do *not* finish french fries until ready for service.
NOTE: Variations for French Fried Potatoes are given in recipe for Julienne Potatoes on p. 210.		

Souffle Potatoes

YIELD: 50 portions	EACH PORTION: about 4½ oz.	
INGREDIENTS	QUANTITY	METHOD
Potatoes, peeled, raw	15 lb.	1. Wash and peel potatoes; trim into an oval shape. 2. Do not wash after peeling, but wipe with clean kitchen towel. 3. Cut oval-shaped potatoes lengthwise in strips about 1/8 in. thick. 4. Place potato strips in deep fat at 275°F. Cook until potatoes float on top of the fat and swell up. Use a fat skimmer to turn potatoes at this stage. 5. Remove potatoes and place in baking pan lined with absorbent paper. 6. Bring temperature of the fat up to 380° to 400°F. and return potatoes to fryer as needed. When potatoes have souffled and are evenly colored to a golden brown, remove to a tray lined with absorbent paper. 7. Salt lightly. Serve on a clean napkin.
NOTE: Idaho potatoes provide most suitable product for this method of preparation because of their uniformity of shape and characteristic dry or mealy quality.		

Deep Frying

French Fried Zucchini

French Fried Zucchini

YIELD: 50 portions	EACH PORTION: 3 oz.	
INGREDIENTS	QUANTITY	METHOD
Zucchini Bread Flour Egg Wash Bread Crumbs OR Cornmeal	10 lb. 2 lb. 1 qt. 3 lb.	1. Wash zucchini and cut in finger-size pieces about ½ in. by 2 in. Cover with strong solution of salted cold water to prevent discoloration. 2. Bread according to standard procedure. 3. Fry at 350° to 375°F., depending on volume, until golden brown and tender. 4. Drain well.

NOTE: Zucchini may be served plain or with Tomato Sauce (p.318) or other sauces.
   Zucchini may be crisped by soaking in ice water prior to breading. This procedure would be more important if cutting the zucchini in another manner, such as often done with eggplant.

Saratoga Chips

YIELD: 50 portions	EACH PORTION: 4 oz.	
INGREDIENTS	QUANTITY	METHOD
Potatoes, A.P. Salt	17 lb. to taste	1. Peel and eye potatoes. Slice paper thin using "mandolin." 2. Cover with ice water and let stand for at least 30 min. Refrigerate if possible. 3. Drain well and dry between towels. 4. Fry in deep hot fat (325°F.) until golden brown. Drain on absorbent paper and salt to taste.

Rice Croquettes

Rice Croquettes

YIELD: 50 portions		EACH PORTION: 2 fritters, about 2½ oz.
INGREDIENTS	*QUANTITY*	*METHOD*
Butter Bread Flour Milk, hot	8 oz. 8 oz. 3 pt.	1. Melt butter in sauce pan. Stir in flour and cook carefully for a few minutes. Do not brown. 2. Add hot milk gradually, stirring until thickened and smooth.
Boiled Rice Salt Nutmeg White Pepper	1 gal. 4 tsp. 1 tsp. ½ tsp.	3. Add remaining ingredients, except egg yolks. Stir while cooking until mixture boils at sides of pan. Mixture should leave bottom of pan easily.
Egg Yolks, beaten	12	4. Add some hot rice mixture to egg yolk, stirring continuously. Incorporate egg yolk mixture into hot rice mixture. 5. Turn mixture out on well buttered flat pan and cover with waxed or greased paper to prevent crusting. 6. Cool and refrigerate. Mixture will handle better if thoroughly chilled.
		7. When cold, use No. 12 ice cream scoop for portions the size of egg.
Breading Materials		8. Roll into desired shape and bread, using standard procedure (see p. 164). 9. Fry in deep fat at 350°F. until golden brown and crisp.

Steaming Fresh Vegetables (5 to 6 pounds pressure)

Times given for cooking are approximate depending upon age of vegetables used and the equipment in which they are cooked. Material is available from the various manufacturers of steaming equipment that will give the recommended steaming times for their specific equipment. Salt used should be in this proportion: 1 oz. (2 tbsp.) per 10 lb. of raw vegetables. Timetable is given in terms of 5 to 6 pounds steam pressure. Steaming is not recommended for leafy greens.

Vegetable	Preparation	Type Container and Fill of Vegetables	App. Cooking time in minutes
Beans, Lima	Shell, wash	Solid (½ full)	20
Beans, String or	Wash, remove ends and strings	Solid (⅓ full)	25
Wax	Break into 1 in. pieces	Perforated (⅔ full)	20
Beets	Remove tops and wash. Do not pare or remove roots	Solid (full) or Perforated (full)	60–75 60
Broccoli	Cut off tough stalks, wash, soak in salted water to remove insects	Solid (½ full) or Perforated (⅓ full)	12 25
Carrots	Wash, pare	Solid (½ full) or Perforated (½ full)	30 20
Cauliflower	Remove green leaves, break into flowerettes Wash and drain	Solid (⅓ full) or Perforated (¼ full)	12–15 12
Corn on Cob	Remove silk, etc., wash and drain	Perforated (25 ears)	8
Kale	Sort, strip leaves from stem. Wash well	Perforated (¼ full) Solid (¼ full)	20 35
Mushrooms	Wash and dice	Perforated (full)	15
Onions	Peel, wash, quarter or dice	Solid (½ full) Perforated (⅓ full)	40 25
Parsnips	Wash, pare and quarter	Perforated (¼ full)	15
Peppers	Wash, dice	Perforated (full)	20
Potatoes	Peel, eye	Perforated (¾ full)	35
Squash (winter)	Wash, cut. Remove and peel afterward	Solid (½ full) or Perforated (½ full)	15 12
Turnips	Wash, pare and dice	Perforated (½ full)	15

Steaming Frozen Vegetables

Frozen vegetables should be cooked in their frozen state. There are a few exceptions, which are discussed on p. 188 Five-pound lots are the most that should be cooked at a time, Pans should be nonperforated shallow cafeteria pans (12 x 20 x 12½ in.) or flat, narrow steam cooker pans. Most vegetables should be steam cooked uncovered for the approximate time specified below. Broccoli should be covered, if possible, to prevent loss of color. Squash should be covered to keep out moisture which results from condensation during cooking. Material is available from equipment manufacturers giving recommended steaming times for their own equipment.

Vegetable	Cooking Time at 5 to 6 pounds pressure
Beans, baby lima	15 minutes
Beans, large lima	25 minutes
Beans, snap, green or wax	15 minutes
Broccoli spears, uncovered	10 minutes
Broccoli spears, covered	30 minutes
Cauliflower	5 minutes
Corn	4 minutes
Mixed Vegetables	15 minutes
Peas, green	5 minutes
Peas and carrots	5 minutes
Squash, hubbard (covered)	25 minutes
Succotash	15 minutes

Whole Beets in Orange Sauce

Fresh Corn on the Cob

Stewed Tomatoes

Whipped Potatoes

Braised Red Cabbage

Acorn Squash

Tomato Rice Pilaff

Vegetable Cookery

In today's food service industry, the importance of proper vegetable cookery is becoming of increasingly greater consequence. The public is developing an awareness of nutritional values. It has become necessary to know the basic principles of nutrition and to recognize the importance of food values.

As a whole, vegetables are valuable for maintenance of alkaline reserves in the body, for the vitamins and minerals they contain which contribute to bone and tooth structure and for their bulk and laxative properties.

The method of cooking vegetables determines the extent to which nutritive value, color, odor and flavor are maintained. Proper cooking methods preserve all these qualities. Improper cooking methods may destroy any or all of them.

The rules which govern vegetable cookery are discussed on the following pages.

Braised Celery

Spinach Vinaigrette

Buttered Asparagus

MENU PRESENTATION OF
VEGETABLES

Because their low food cost can help offset the high food cost of other items, vegetables should be presented on the menu in a way that will step up sales. Selection should be based on contrast in color, flavor, form and texture. Do not feature two strong flavored vegetables or two that belong to the same family (broccoli and cauliflower). Avoid too many vegetables of the same color. Vary the form as well as the style of preparation—for instance, creamed, buttered, honey-glazed. Make it a point not to list two vegetables that have the same shape or form such as sliced, julienned, diced. Descriptive wording that is appropriate and makes sense can also help increase sales.

Sauteed Zucchini

Green Peas

String Beans, Amandine

Brussels Sprouts

Broccoli Hollandaise

Cauliflower au Gratin

Carrots Vichy

Risi Bisi

Au Gratin Potatoes

Sweet Potato Patties with Coconut

Glazed Yellow Turnips with Peas

Scientific research by food technologists, dietitians and nutritionists in industry and government service has enabled us to formulate a set of rules to govern our methods of cooking vegetables. We will call them "The Laws of Proper Vegetable Cookery."

The same methods of cooking that are recommended for maximum nutritive retention also preserve the color to the highest degree; and when vegetables are cooked so that they look better and taste better, they also contain the greatest amount of food value.

Vegetables are cooked to improve their digestibility, to increase their palatability and their acceptance. The three major changes that occur in vegetables as they cook are: 1) change in flavor, 2) change in cellulose and 3) change in water content.

Many vegetables require cooking to bring out their individual flavors. However, adverse changes may be brought about by improper cooking. Overcooking decomposes vegetables, destroying their flavor and causing them to have an unappetizing appearance. This is particularly true of the strong-juiced and sulphurous vegetables which include cabbage, onions, turnips, brussels sprouts, broccoli and cauliflower.

Overcooking green vegetables that have a natural acid content, such as peas and leaf greens, causes discoloration, loss of food value and may cause caramelization.

Techniques for Vegetable Cookery

All fresh vegetables should be thoroughly washed before cooking. To assure cleanliness in preparing vegetables that may be infested, exceptionally dirty or covered with spray, it is sometimes necessary to bring them to a boil, cool and drain before completing the cooking process.

This precooking procedure is a form of blanching. It is also helpful in maintaining whiteness in vegetables such as cauliflower. Occasionally small worms may be found in cauliflower and broccoli. Blanching or a half hour soaking period in cold salted water or mild vinegar solution will remove live worms.

Fresh Vegetables Leaf vegetables should be washed several times in cold water to remove all traces of dirt and sand. Remove the greens from the water rather than the water from the greens. This allows the grit and dirt to settle to the bottom of the sink or container, not back into the greens.

Vegetables to be cooked in their skins should be well scrubbed. Other vegetables should be thinly and carefully pared to retain nutritive value and keep waste to a minimum. Clean peelings and scraps may be utilized in stock making and as garnish for preparing roasts.

Frozen Vegetables With the exception of washing, most of the rules that apply to fresh vegetables apply to frozen vegetables. Frozen vegetables should be cooked in their frozen state. A few vegetables, such as spinach and other leaf greens, are better completely thawed before they are cooked. This facilitates separation of the leaves to insure uniform cooking.

Corn on the cob should be allowed to thaw completely before cooking. Frozen squash, which is fully cooked, may be partially thawed, preferably under refrigeration. Because of its high water content the squash is a solid block when frozen and will cook unevenly.

Most vegetables will thaw at walk-in refrigerator temperatures (34°F. to 38°F.) in a few hours.

Because of the blanching process before freezing, frozen vegetables usually require less cooking time than fresh vegetables. Frozen vegetables should never be refrozen once they are thawed. The effect of blanching and freezing causes a rapid multiplication of bacteria once food is thawed. To avoid food poisoning, use thawed foods as quickly as possible, or, if necessary, cook them and hold for use as soon as possible.

Canned Vegetables Canned vegetables are fully cooked and require only reheating. They should be reheated in their own liquid and seasoned to taste before serving. Butter and salt are usually needed.

Do not overcook canned vegetables or heat in large quantities or food values may be lost.

Dried Legumes The year round availability of nearly all types of vegetables has cut down on the use of dried legumes in vegetable cookery. The legumes are the family of pod bearing vegetables such as peas and beans. They are often purchased as canned food (cooked) and used in salads, relishes and in combination with other foods.

There is still widespread use of the dried legumes in soup making and all cooks should be familiar with their treatment. Water lost in ripening and drying must be replaced. This is done by soaking the legumes in water for five to six hours or overnight. Most dried legumes absorb their own weight during soaking.

For cooking the ratio is about four to one, or one gallon of water to one pound of legumes. Soaking is not required for split peas or lentils.

Legumes should simmer but not boil since they toughen when subjected to boiling temperature.

Classification of Vegetables—Green Vegetables The natural color of green vegetables is the most appetizing color they can have. The green color is due to a substance called chlorophyll which is affected by acids and alkalies in the presence of heat.

The green color becomes more intense in an alkaline solution. Baking soda is an alkali that may intensify color. However, the use of baking soda destroys the vitamin content and flavor and tends to make the vegetable mushy and lends an artificial color. One of our important rules: do not use baking soda in green vegetable cookery. The same applies to ammonia which not only destroys the nutritive value but is also a poison.

Generally green vegetables should be cooked uncovered so that the acids may escape in the steam. Cooking them uncovered also reduces the danger of overcooking. Remember the rule: Use a minimum amount of boiling salted water and cook in as short a time as possible.

Red Vegetables In cooking red vegetables, the reactions are exactly the opposite of those that occur when cooking green vegetables. The presence of acid intensifies the red color while alkaline water creates a purple or bluish tinge.

Red vegetables are cooked covered for just the opposite reason that green vegetables are cooked uncovered; so that they may benefit from their own acid content. An exception is red cabbage which is cooked uncovered to release some of its sulphur content through evaporation.

Yellow Vegetables Yellow vegetables are not subject to much color change unless overcooked; then they may lose their intensity or brilliance. Remember that overcooking any classification of vegetable will destroy its nutritional value.

White Vegetables Overcooking white vegetables tends to give them an unattractive gray appearance. Care should be taken to cook them only until tender in as short a time as possible. This rule also applies to the strong juiced vegetables, most of which require a more generous amount of water in cooking to dilute volatile substances. Most strong juiced vegetables are cooked uncovered so that the sulphur content is released.

Vegetable Plates A vegetable plate is a combination of contrasting vegetables, usually served hot. There is no set rule for the number of vegetables to be served, but four or five vegetables or vegetable substitutes seem best. Fewer than four do not offer sufficient contrast.

Noodles, macaroni, rice and other grains may be substituted for one of the vegetables. The pasta and grain products offer infinite variety in their methods of preparation and serving.

Many food operations offer a vegetable plate as a standard item on the menu due to its increasing popularity. The vegetables should be selected each day to maintain a variety that will be appealing to the same patrons. The same vegetable may often be served in a variety of ways that make it appear new each time.

Storage of Vegetables—Fresh Potatoes, onions and winter squash should be stored in a cool, dry place. In very cool weather some other hardy vegetables may be stored in this manner, but all other fresh vegetables require refrigeration.

All cut or peeled vegetables should be refrigerated since exposure to the air causes them to deteriorate rapidly. Peeled potatoes must be stored covered with ice water or treated with chemical oxidizing agents to prevent discoloration.

Covering vegetables with clean wet towels or plastic wrap under refrigeration will minimize drying out and will prevent odors from permeating other foods. Newspaper or printed material should not be used as covering because the ink will come off.

Storage of Vegetables—Frozen The ideal storage temperature for frozen vegetables is 0°F. or below. Temperature ranges above this may reduce the storage life and possibly the quality of the product. Thawed vegetables should not be refrozen.

Storage of Vegetables—Canned Canned vegetables should be stored in a cool, dry place where they will not be exposed to direct sunlight. Spoilage is detected by swelling or distortion of can, off flavors, odors or unusual spurting when opened. *When in doubt, throw it out.*

Storage of Vegetables—Dried Legumes should be stored in a cool, dry place where they will not be exposed to direct sunlight or extremes of temperature. Rotate stocks to use old first.

Potato Varieties The potato market varies greatly with the season. Idaho-Russets are most suitable for baking and deep-frying. Maine potatoes are good for general all-purpose use. Other potatoes will be utilized in the course of the growing season. Processed potatoes, either frozen or instant (dehydrated) are available.

Cellulose in Vegetables Many raw vegetables are recommended for use in salads and relishes. Most vegetables, however, contain a high percentage of cellulose and benefit from cooking.

Cellulose, the material that holds the cells together, is roughage or bulk and aids in elimination. It is partially dissolved by cooking.

Alkali, such as baking soda, may aid in breaking down cellulose, but produces soft or mushy vegetables. Vinegar and other acids tend to firm or toughen cellulose. When these acids are added to red vegetables to retain the color, they are added near the end of the cooking period so that they will not toughen the product.

The Laws of Proper Vegetable Cookery

- Use only enough water to cover.
- Use only boiling salted water.
- Cook in as small quantities as possible and as frequently as possible.
- Cook only until tender.
- Cook as close to serving time as possible.
- Cool with cold running water if not used immediately. Drain well.
- Save pot liquor (water vegetables were cooked in) for reheating the vegetables or for use in soups, sauces and gravies.
- Drain well before serving.
- Season to taste before serving. Sugar improves the flavor of many vegetables, particularly if vegetable is over-mature. Add prior to service.
- Cut fresh vegetables uniformly for even cooking.
- Clean fresh vegetables thoroughly.
- Store and prepare fresh vegetables to maintain maximum food value.
- Don't use excessive amounts of water. This will result in loss of flavor and destruction of nutritive values.
- Don't add soda to green vegetables. The alkaline solution created destroys vitamin C, makes vegetables mushy.
- Don't overcook vegetables. Nutritive values and yield will decrease, and flavor and appearance will be poor.
- Don't let vegetables stand in hot water after cooking. Heat from water continues to cook vegetables.
- Don't cook in too large quantities. Will cause loss of food value, and color and appearance will be poor.
- Don't thaw frozen vegetables too far in advance

of cooking. Food values may be lost and there is danger of spoilage and food poisoning.

■ Don't mix newly cooked vegetables with vegetables cooked earlier. Colors and textures will vary.

Pressure Cooking In range or top of stove cooking, the boiling point of water is the highest temperature that can be reached (212°F.). In a pressure sauce pan, the pressure of live steam raises the temperature above the boiling point and forces heat through foods at a much faster rate.

These pressure sauce pans are excellent for small quantity cooking, for preparation near closing time or when vegetables are needed quickly. The

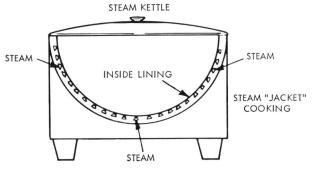

STEAM KETTLE

STEAM — INSIDE LINING — STEAM

STEAM "JACKET" COOKING

STEAM

pressure sauce pans vary in size from 1½ to 6 quarts and are equipped to operate under different pressures.

Temperatures vary from 228°F. at 5 lb. pressure to 250°F. at 15 lb. pressure. Although high temperatures are used, cooking time is minimal; the exclusion of air and light conserves vitamin content. Small amounts of water aid in retention of minerals.

Steam jacket cooking is not to be confused with steam cooking. In steam jacket cooking the food is not directly exposed to steam. The steam is circulated within the jacket and provides an equal distribution of heat around sides and bottom of kettle. Although dry heat is obtainable here, water is the usual cooking medium.

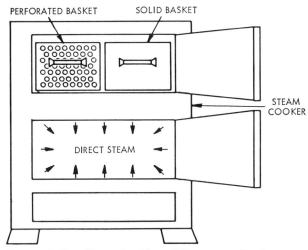

PERFORATED BASKET   SOLID BASKET

STEAM COOKER

DIRECT STEAM

General Directions for Use of Pressure Cookers

Place ¼ to ½ in. of lightly salted water in pressure cooker (depending on size of sauce pan). Place rack in bottom of sauce pan. Add vegetables. Cover the cooker and lock tightly. Start pressure by applying

heat. Average cooking time varies with degree of pressure and type of vegetable. Start timing when cooker is under full pressure. Remove vegetables when cooked and season. *Always* follow manufacturer's directions.

Large steam cookers (commercial type) work on much the same principle except that this type of unit often manufactures its own steam or is connected to a direct source of steam. These steamers often require preheating. If metal inside cooking compartment is cold, initial steam will only heat metal and result in immediate reduction of pressure.

A short time must be allowed for the steam to build up to cooking pressure (about 6 lb.). This is only necessary when the steamer has been idle long enough for the metal to become cool.

There are some countertop models that require addition of water, as with a pressure sauce pan. This type also allows for use of the cooking liquid, if desired.

Never attempt to remove the cover of a pressure sauce pan or open the hatch or door of a steam cooker until all steam has dissipated or the pressure gauge registers zero!

The proper seating and locking of covers and doors is also important as high pressure can blow cover and contents off, resulting in possible injury. If there is leakage around the cover or door, proper pressure cannot be maintained; cooking time will vary and possible damage may result to sealers and gaskets.

Most manufacturers recommend that frozen vegetables be thawed prior to steaming, although vegetables may be cooked frozen. Timing becomes less accurate, as it is difficult to determine thawing time. For small quantity preparation, vegetables may be used frozen.

Cooking Methods Suitable to Various Vegetables

Boiling:

Artichokes	
Asparagus	Parsnips
Beans, Wax and Green	Peas
Beets	Potatoes
Broccoli	Spinach
Carrots	Other Leaf Vegetables
Cabbage	Kale
Celery	Swiss Chard
Corn	Beet Greens
Eggplant	Squash
Okra	Tomatoes
Onions	Turnips

Baking:

Eggplant	Onions
Squash	Potatoes, White and Sweet

Braising:

Belgian Endive	Onions
Celery	Lettuce
Cabbage	

Frying and Sauteing:

Eggplant	Parsley
Squash	Potatoes
Tomatoes	Parsnips (parboiled)

CANDIED SWEET POTATOES

Preparation Steps: After cooking potatoes just long enough to loosen skins, place under cold running water to cool. Remove skins by scraping with knife, peeling if needed.

Orange sections or slices may be arranged over sweet potatoes before cooking, or may be poured on with syrup and placed on potatoes after cooking.

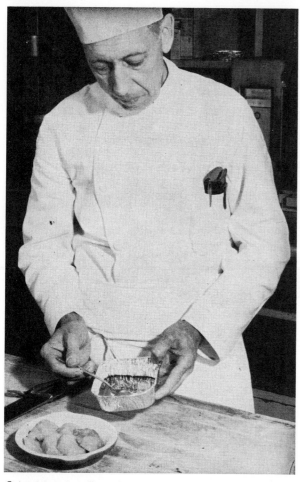

Cut potatoes to uniform sizes and place in buttered hotel pans or individual casseroles. Spoon on syrup until potatoes are three-quarters covered.(See recipe facing page.)

Bake potatoes in moderate oven for about one hour. Cooking in syrup will candy the potatoes throughout. Garnish with halved or quartered maraschino cherries.

Candied Sweet Potatoes or Yams

YIELD: 50 portions		EACH PORTION: about 6 oz.
INGREDIENTS	*QUANTITY*	*METHOD*
Sweet Potatoes, A. P.	20 lb.	1. Grade potatoes for size and wash thoroughly. Blanch potatoes of uniform size together. Blanch in more than one pot, if necessary. (Potatoes may be steamed or boiled.) Blanch potatoes for 5 to 10 min.—only enough to loosen the skin. 2. Cool potatoes in cold running water. 3. Remove skin. It should come off easily by scraping with knife, but some peeling may be necessary. 4. Remove all soft, discolored or otherwise undesirable areas; trim potatoes to as near uniform size as possible.

Syrup:
    Water, boiling
    Brown Sugar
    Granulated Sugar
    Light Corn Syrup
    Lemon Juice
    Oranges, peeled, sliced or sectioned
    Granulated Sugar
	
	1 qt.
	· 3 lb.
	2 lb.
	3 qt.
	2 oz.
	6
	
	8 oz.
		5. To Make Syrup: Combine water and all other syrup ingredients. Stir to mix well. Bring just to boiling; simmer 5 min.
		6. Place potatoes in lightly buttered hotel pan. Cover with syrup and oranges to ¾ cover. Sprinkle the 8 oz. of sugar over top.
		7. Bake at 350°F. for 1 hr. or until done. Baste frequently during cooking; turn if necessary. Do not overcook. Potatoes should retain their shape and be candied throughout.
		8. Arrange orange pieces over top of potatoes. Serve hot.

Buttered Zucchini

YIELD: 50 portions		EACH PORTION: about 4 oz.
INGREDIENTS	*QUANTITY*	*METHOD*
Zucchini Squash Butter, melted Salad Oil Salt Pepper	12 lb. 1 lb. as needed to taste to taste	1. Wash and scrub zucchini. If zucchini is small, cut straight across in 3/8 in. slices. Cut larger zucchini in half, lengthwise, then slice. 2. Melt ½ lb. butter; mix with small amount of oil. Saute zucchini in butter-oil mixture. Crispness should be retained. 3. Turn over in same manner as frying potatoes. Do not overcook. 4. When tender, add remaining butter and season to taste with salt and pepper.
See color picture, p. 187.		

Baked Zucchini

YIELD: 50 portions		EACH PORTION: 4 oz.
INGREDIENTS	*QUANTITY*	*METHOD*
Zucchini Squash, A.P. Creole Sauce (p. 320), hot	9 lb. ½ gal.	1. Wash and dry squash thoroughly. 2. Slice across ¼ in. thick. 3. Combine with Creole Sauce and place in a hotel pan. 4. Bake at 350°F. for about ½ hr. or until squash is tender.

Vegetables

Buttered Asparagus

YIELD: 50 portions	EACH PORTION: 3 oz.	
INGREDIENTS	QUANTITY	METHOD
Frozen Asparagus Spears Butter, melted Salt	10 lb. 1 lb. to taste	1. Separate stalks without breaking tips. Spread evenly in two separate hotel pans. Cover with boiling salted water. If too solidly frozen to separate without breaking, separate after covering with boiling water. 2. Cover asparagus with clean wet towel. When water returns to boil, reduce heat and simmer until tender. Move pan occasionally if necessary to insure uniform cooking. Test by squeezing near base of stalk. 3. Do not boil vigorously or overcook or tips will be destroyed. Serve from the pan with melted butter.

NOTE: To hold for service, slightly undercook. Drain and reserve cooking liquor. Cool in same pan in cold running water being careful not to let water run directly on tips, breaking them. Drain and hold. Do not handle asparagus at all. Reheat with cooking liquor in same pan asparagus was cooked in. Drain well and butter tips.

See color picture, p. 186.

Buttered Green Peas

YIELD: 50 portions	EACH PORTION: about 3 oz.	
INGREDIENTS	QUANTITY	METHOD
Frozen Green Peas Water, boiling, salted Butter Salt Pepper Sugar	10 lb. to cover 6 oz. to taste to taste to taste	1. Place 5 lb. peas each in separate pots or sauce pans. Cover with minimum amount of boiling salted water. 2. When water returns to boil, reduce heat and simmer until peas are tender (about 5 min.). Do not overcook. Drain well. 3. If serving at once, add butter and adjust seasoning. If holding peas for service, cool, drain well, refrigerate. 4. Saute in butter for service. Season to taste.

VARIATIONS: For **English Green Peas**, add 4 oz. sugar and 1 bunch fresh chopped mint leaves to each 5 lb. peas when cooking. Drain well and saute in butter. (If using dried mint, use about 1 tsp.)

For **Diced Fresh Carrots and Peas**, combine 8 lb. diced cooked carrots and 2½ lb. cooked peas. Add butter and adjust seasoning prior to service.

See color picture, p. 187.

Sauerkraut

YIELD: 50 portions	EACH PORTION: about 4 oz.	
INGREDIENTS	QUANTITY	METHOD
Onions, sliced thin Bacon Fat Caraway Seed (optional) Sauerkraut, drained White Stock, hot Ham Hocks, blanched Potatoes, raw, grated	2 lb. 8 oz. 2 tsp. 2 No. 10 cans 1 qt. 2 lb. 2 lb.	1. Saute onions in bacon fat until tender. 2. Mix caraway seed, sauerkraut and grated raw potato well and add to onions. 3. Add stock. 4. Bury ham hocks in sauerkraut. 5. Cover pot and simmer slowly 1½ to 2 hr., stirring occasionally to prevent burning. 6. Finish cooking ham hocks separately after removing sauerkraut. 7. Remove meat from hocks after cooking and dice fine. Mix with sauerkraut.

Buttered Broccoli

YIELD: 50 portions		**EACH PORTION**: 3 oz.

INGREDIENTS	QUANTITY	METHOD
Broccoli, A.P. Butter	17 lb. 1 lb.	1. Remove outer leaves and tough ends of stems. Wash thoroughly in cold water, being careful not to damage blossoms. Let stand in cold, salted water, (about 2 oz. salt to 1 gal. of water) for 20 to 30 min. 2. Remove broccoli and split stalks part way up. Peel if necessary. 3. Place broccoli in hotel pans and cover part way with boiling, salted water. Cover pans with clean, wet towels and cook on top of the range for 15 to 20 min. Do not boil vigorously or overcook as it will destroy the blossoms. 4. Test stems for doneness. 5. Drain well when serving. Dress each portion with butter at time of service.

VARIATIONS: For **Broccoli Hollandaise**, mask each portion with a generous spoonful of Hollandaise sauce at service time—about 3 qt. of sauce for 50 portions.

NOTE: To hold for service, slightly undercook. Drain liquor and reserve. Place pans in sink and cool with cold running water, being careful not to let water run directly on blossoms, breaking them. Drain and hold for service. Do not handle. Reheat in cooking liquor and serve from pan. For quantity foodservice, broccoli may be arranged in a buttered pan, covered and reheated in an oven or steamer.

Ten pounds frozen broccoli may be substituted for 17 lb. fresh.

See color picture, p. 187.

Spinach Timbales

YIELD: 50 portions		**EACH PORTION**: about 4 oz.

INGREDIENTS	QUANTITY	METHOD
Spinach, frozen Water, boiling, salted Eggs, whole, beaten Butter, melted Vinegar, cider Onions, minced Salt	15 lb. for cooking 15 8 oz. 5 oz. 3 oz. 1½ tsp.	1. Cook spinach in boiling salted water; drain well. 2. Chop spinach. Add beaten eggs. 3. Add butter, vinegar, sauteed onions and salt to spinach mixture.
Pimientoes Eggs, hard cooked, sliced	1 4-oz. can 8	4. Cut pimientoes in diamond shapes. Place in bottom of well greased or buttered individual custard cups or molds. 5. Place a slice of hard cooked egg on top of pimiento in each cup. 6. Place 3½ to 4 oz. of spinach mixture on top of egg slice in each cup. 7. Place custard cups in pan with hot water about halfway up to top of mold. 8. Bake at 350°F. for about 30 min. or until spinach is firm but not dry. 9. Remove from oven. Invert cup onto plate removing spinach intact so that pimiento-egg garnish is on top.

NOTE: If necessary, a small knife may be used to loosen sides of spinach from mold.

Garnish may be omitted and spinach timble served with Cheese Sauce (p. 316), if desired.

Greased paper or foil may be placed on top of custard cups during baking to retain greater moisture.

Vegetables

Lima Beans, Forestiere

YIELD: 50 portions		EACH PORTION: about 3 oz.
INGREDIENTS	QUANTITY	METHOD
Shallots, minced Butter Mushrooms, sliced	4 oz. 8 oz. 2 lb.	1. Saute shallots in butter for a few minutes. 2. Add mushrooms and cook until tender. Reserve.
Frozen Lima Beans Water, boiling, salted Salt Pepper	7½ lb. for cooking to taste to taste	3. Place lima beans in sauce pan; add boiling salted water. When water returns to boil, reduce heat and simmer until lima beans are tender. Drain well. 4. Combine lima beans with mushrooms and butter. Cover. 5. Let stand in warm place for about 5 min. so that flavor of mushrooms will permeate lima beans.
NOTE: "Forestiere" refers to the use of mushrooms. Other vegetables may be substituted for lima beans in the above recipe (**Peas Forestiere**, etc.).		

Horticultural Beans (Shell Beans) with Onions

YIELD: 50 portions		EACH PORTION: about 3½ oz.
INGREDIENTS	QUANTITY	METHOD
Onions, chopped Celery, diced Butter, melted Pimientoes, diced	2 lb. 6 oz. 8 oz. 1 7-oz. can	1. Saute onions and celery in butter until tender. 2. Remove from heat and combine with pimientoes.
Shell Beans	1½ No. 10 cans	3. Heat shell beans in their own juice. 4. Combine all ingredients, adding small amount of stock if necessary.
Salt Pepper	to taste to taste	5. Simmer about 5 min. Season to taste with salt and pepper.
NOTE: Any type of dried bean may be prepared in this manner. Beans must be soaked over night and simmered until tender. Amount required averages 5 to 6 lb. dry beans, depending on kind of bean selected. Other variations may be made in the garnish.		

Braised Celery

YIELD: 50 portions		EACH PORTION: 4 oz.
INGREDIENTS	QUANTITY	METHOD
Celery, A.P. Butter Bread Flour Beef Stock, hot OR Chicken Stock, hot	12 lb. 8 oz. 5 oz. about 3 qt.	1. Remove leaves and root ends of celery. 2. Wash and trim, peeling where necessary. 3. Cut lengthwise and then across in pieces about ½ in. by 1½ in. 4. Saute celery in butter until nearly tender. Add flour and blend well. Cook for a few minutes, stirring so that celery will not burn. Stir in hot stock gradually until slightly thickened and smooth. 5. Bring to a boil, transfer to lightly greased hotel pan. 6. Cover with buttered paper or foil and bake at 350°F. for 30 min. or until celery is tender and liquid is reduced and thickened. Season to taste.
NOTE: Beurre manie may be used for further thickening.		

See color picture, p. 186.

Green Peas with Tiny Pearl Onions

YIELD: 50 portions		EACH PORTION: about 3 oz.
INGREDIENTS	*QUANTITY*	*METHOD*
Green Peas, frozen	7½ lb.	1. Cook peas as for Buttered Green Peas (p. 194).
Pearl Onions, A.P. Butter Salt Pepper	3 lb. 8 oz. to taste to taste	2. Select the smallest onions possible. Follow directions for cooking pearl onions (p. 198). 3. Drain vegetables. Combine peas and onions. 4. Saute in butter until heated through and flavors are blended. Season to taste with salt and pepper.

French Green Peas

YIELD: 50 portions		EACH PORTION: 3 oz.
INGREDIENTS	*QUANTITY*	*METHOD*
Frozen Peas Lettuce, shredded outside leaves Pearl Onions Salt Pepper Sugar Butter Chicken Stock	7½ lb. 2 lb. 8 oz. ¾ oz. to taste ¾ oz. 8 oz. 1 pt.	1. Smother lettuce and onions lightly in butter in a covered sautoire. 2. Add salt, sugar and peas, mixing well. Steam for a few minutes. 3. Add boiling stock, cover and simmer until peas are tender. 4. Beurre manie may be used to thicken the liquid.

Buttered Lima Beans

YIELD: 50 portions		EACH PORTION: 3 oz.
INGREDIENTS	*QUANTITY*	*METHOD*
Frozen Lima Beans Butter Salt Pepper	10 lb. 6 oz. to taste to taste	1. Place lima beans in sauce pan with minimum amount of boiling salted water to cover. When water returns to boil, reduce heat and simmer until lima beans are tender. 2. Add butter and adjust seasoning. 3. For holding prior to service, see recipes for green peas and green beans.

Spinach

YIELD: 50 portions		EACH PORTION: 3 oz.
INGREDIENTS	*QUANTITY*	*METHOD*
Frozen Spinach Water, boiling, salted Butter	12 lb to cover 8 oz.	1. Place spinach in large pot with boiling salted water to cover. 2. Break block apart with a range fork as it begins to loosen to assure uniform cooking. 3. Cook only until tender. It should have slight crispness. Drain well. 4. Adjust seasoning and toss well with butter.

VARIATIONS: For **Spinach Vinaigrette**, drain cooked spinach well and dress with hot Vinaigrette Sauce. (See recipe in Salad Dressing Section (p. 261.) *See color picture, p. 186.*

NOTE: Frozen spinach may be partially thawed prior to cooking. If using fresh spinach, increase required amount to 22 lb. Review section on washing greens before cooking fresh spinach (p. 189). If spinach is good quality, water that remains on leaves after washing should be sufficient for cooking.

Vegetables

Brussels Sprouts

YIELD: 50 portions		EACH PORTION: 3 oz.
INGREDIENTS	QUANTITY	METHOD
Brussels Sprouts, A.P. Butter Salt Pepper	12 lb. 8 oz. to taste to taste	1. Remove wilted and discolored outer leaves and trim stem ends. Wash thoroughly. 2. Soak in cold, salted water in same manner as for broccoli. 3. Drain well and place in boiling salted water. 4. When water returns to second boil, simmer for 15 min. or until tender. 5. Add butter and seasoning before serving.

NOTE: Brussels sprouts may be drained well and sauteed in butter for a few minutes before serving. They may also be prepared creamed and au gratin.

See color picture, p. 187.

Buttered Green Beans

YIELD: 50 portions		EACH PORTION: 3 oz.
INGREDIENTS	QUANTITY	METHOD
Frozen Green Beans Water, boiling, salted Butter Salt White Pepper	10 lb. to cover 8 oz. to taste to taste	1. Divide beans between two pots and cover generously with boiling, salted water. 2. When water returns to boil, reduce heat and cook about 10 to 12 min. or until tender. 3. Add butter, salt and pepper at service time.

VARIATIONS: **Italian Green Beans:** Prepare as above.

Interesting combinations and variations may be made by combining other vegetables or by the addition of onions, shallots, scallions or pimientoes. **Green Beans Amandine** are prepared by slightly undercooking beans as above. Saute slivered almonds in butter and when butter begins to turn slightly brown, combine with green beans. Toss lightly and saute to blend flavors. Season to taste.

NOTE: If necessary to hold for service, drain cooking liquor and reserve. Rinse beans with cold running water until cool. Drain and refrigerate. Reheat in cooking liquor or saute in butter. Adjust seasoning.

Cook fresh green beans in same manner after preparing and washing thoroughly. Use generous amount of water and stir frequently for even color. Fifty portions require about 14 lb., A.P. (½ bushel).

See color picture, p. 187.

Pearl Onions

YIELD: 50 portions		EACH PORTION: 3½ oz.
INGREDIENTS	QUANTITY	METHOD
Pearl Onions, medium Butter Water, boiling, salted OR White Chicken Stock	12 lb. 4 oz. to cover	1. Cut off ends only of pearl onions. Plunge in boiling water for 1 min. to loosen skin. 2. Remove from range and run cold water directly into pot. Most skins can be slipped off easily by hand. 3. After cleaning all onions, place in salted water and simmer until tender but not overcooked. Centers will pop out if overcooked. 4. When tender, drain, add butter and serve.

VARIATIONS: For **Creamed Pearl Onions**, add Cream Sauce, (p. 314).
NOTE: If holding onions, do not add butter until service time. Onions may be drained and sauteed in butter prior to service.

Creamed Peas and Celery

YIELD: 50 portions	EACH PORTION:	about 2½ oz. vegetables, 2½ oz. sauce
INGREDIENTS	*QUANTITY*	*METHOD*
Frozen Green Peas Celery, diced Water, boiling, salted Cream Sauce, hot (p. 314)	5 lb. 3 lb. for cooking 1 gal.	1. Cook peas and celery separately in boiling salted water. Drain well. 2. Blend with Cream Sauce. Adjust seasoning.
NOTE: Vegetable liquor may be used to make Cream Sauce.		

Buttered Kale

YIELD: 50 portions	EACH PORTION:	about 3 oz.
INGREDIENTS	*QUANTITY*	*METHOD*
Kale, A.P. Water, boiling, salted Butter Salt Pepper	18 lb. about 1 gal. 12 oz. to taste to taste	1. Remove roots and tough parts of stem from kale. 2. Wash thoroughly several times in cold water. Drain, lifting greens from water. 3. Place in large pot and cover with boiling salted water to 1/3 depth of kale. 4. Cover and cook for 20 min. or until tender, turning kale over with a wooden paddle. 5. Drain, toss with butter and seasoning and serve.

NOTE: Product may be improved by dividing into two separate batches.
   Swiss Chard, Beet Greens and Dandelion Greens may be substituted using same quantities and seasonings except that kale usually requires more cooking water than do the other greens.
   Kale also requires additional cooking time. Young greens may cook in only slightly more water than is left on the leaves after washing thoroughly.		

Green Beans Panache

YIELD: 50 portions	EACH PORTION:	about 3½ oz.
INGREDIENTS	*QUANTITY*	*METHOD*
Green Beans, frozen Lima Beans, frozen	5 lb. 5 lb.	1. Cook green beans and lima beans separately; undercook slightly. Drain well.
Butter Pimientoes, drained, diced Salt Pepper	8 oz. 1 7-oz. can to taste to taste	2. Melt butter; saute all beans with pimientoes. Add salt and pepper to taste. 3. Continue to saute until vegetables are fully cooked and heated through.

Shredded Cabbage

YIELD: 50 portions	EACH PORTION:	about 4 oz.
INGREDIENTS	*QUANTITY*	*METHOD*
Cabbage, A.P. Water, boiling, salted Celery Seeds	16 lb. to cover as needed	1. Trim and wash cabbage. Cut into wedges and remove core. Shred coarsely. 2. Cook cabbage in boiling salted water to cover for about 7 min. It should retain texture. 3. Drain well and saute lightly in butter. Toss with celery seeds and serve.
VARIATIONS: For **Boiled Cabbage**, cut about 3 oz. wedges. Do not remove core. Cook in water or part stock if available. Do not overcook. Cabbage should be tender but retain some texture and shape.		

Vegetables

Cauliflower au Gratin
(recipe below)

Sweet Potato Patties with Coconut
(recipe on top of facing page)

Cauliflower au Gratin

YIELD: 50 portions	EACH PORTION: 3 oz. and sauce	
INGREDIENTS	QUANTITY	METHOD
Cauliflower, fresh, cleaned and trimmed, or frozen	12½ lb.	1. Place cauliflower in rapidly boiling salted water. When water returns to boil, reduce heat and cook until just tender. Drain. Do not overcook. Frozen vegetables do not require as long a cooking time as fresh.
Light Cheese Sauce Bread Crumbs Paprika Butter, melted	1 gal. 1 oz. 1 tbsp. 2 oz.	2. Place drained cauliflower in lightly buttered baking pan and cover with cheese sauce. Combine bread crumbs and paprika and sprinkle over sauce. Drizzle with melted butter. 3. Bake at 350°F. for 20 min. or until nicely browned and bubbly.
See color picture, p. 188.		

Cauliflower Polonaise

YIELD: 50 portions	EACH PORTION: 3 oz.	
INGREDIENTS	QUANTITY	METHOD
Cauliflower, fresh or frozen, trimmed White Pepper	12½ lb. to taste	1. Clean and section cauliflower and cook. 2. Drain cooked cauliflower and place in a buttered hotel pan. Sprinkle with white pepper and cover with damp cloth, foil, wax paper or saran.
Butter Fresh Bread Crumbs Hard Cooked Eggs, chopped Parsley, chopped	1 lb. 1 qt. 5 ¾ oz.	3. Brown butter lightly in sautoir. 4. Add bread crumbs and cook until golden brown. 5. Remove from heat; add eggs and parsley and mix. 6. Sprinkle crumb mixture over individual portions of cauliflower when serving.

Sweet Potato Patties with Coconut

YIELD: 50 patties		EACH PORTION: 4 oz. patty
INGREDIENTS	*QUANTITY*	*METHOD*
Sweet Potatoes, A.P.	16 lb.	1. Wash and scrub potatoes. 2. Place on sheet pans. Bake at 350°F. for 45 min. or until tender. (Time will depend on size.)
Butter Sugar Salt Cinnamon	8 oz. 6 oz. 1 oz. 2 tbsp.	3. Cut potatoes and scoop out pulp, discarding skin. Put through food mill. Thoroughly blend all remaining ingredients, except coconut, with sweet potato pulp. 4. Place in clean pan and refrigerate until firm. 5. Using No. 8 ice cream scoop and portion scale, weigh out fifty 4-oz. portions. Form into round, flat patties.
Shredded or Grated Coconut	2 lb.	6. Roll each patty in coconut. Place on brown paper on sheet pan and refrigerate until ready to cook.
Butter	for sauteing	7. Saute lightly in butter, turning when brown. 8. Remove to sheet pans. Finish heating in oven. Bake at 350°F. for 10 to 20 min.

See color picture, p. 188.

Cauliflower

YIELD: 50 portions		EACH PORTION: about 3 oz.
INGREDIENTS	*QUANTITY*	*METHOD*
Cauliflower, frozen or fresh, trimmed Water, boiling, salted Butter, melted Salt Pepper	12½ lb. for cooking 1 lb. to taste to taste	1. Place cauliflower in rapidly boiling salted water. When water returns to boil, reduce heat and cook until just tender. Do not overcook. 2. When cooked drain well, add butter and adjust seasoning. 3. If holding for service, reserve cooking liquor; cool cauliflower in cold running water. Reheat in cooking liquor; finish with butter and seasoning.

NOTE: Frozen vegetables do not require as long a cooking time as most fresh vegetables.

Corn Mexicane

YIELD: 50 portions		EACH PORTION: about 3½ oz.
INGREDIENTS	*QUANTITY*	*METHOD*
Frozen Whole Kernel Corn Green Pepper, chopped fine Butter OR Margarine Pimientoes, chopped fine Salt Pepper	10 lb. 1 pt. 8 oz. 1 7 oz. can to taste to taste	1. Place corn in sauce pan with boiling salted water to cover. 2. When water returns to boil, reduce heat and cook until nearly tender. 3. Saute green peppers in butter or margarine. Drain corn well and combine all ingredients. Saute for a few minutes to blend flavors.

VARIATIONS: Corn O'Brien may be prepared in a similar manner using the same garnish as for Potatoes O'Brien (p. 217).
   There are many varieties for **Corn Saute**, using onions, celery, shallots, scallions and chives. Corn may also be combined with other contrasting vegetables to produce varied and interesting vegetable dishes.

NOTE: Oil or shortening may be used in place of butter or margarine.

Vegetables

Buttered Carrots

YIELD: 50 portions	EACH PORTION: 3½ oz.	
INGREDIENTS	*QUANTITY*	*METHOD*
Carrots, A.P. Butter Salt	12 lb. 6 oz. to taste	1. Peel carrots carefully and slice in 1/8 in. thick, diagonal slices. Cover with salted water and bring to a boil. 2. When water comes to boil, reduce heat and cook until tender but with some crispness. 3. Drain; add butter and adjust seasoning at service time.

VARIATIONS: For **Carrots Vichy**, parboil carrots in soda water; drain well. To complete cooking, saute in butter with 3 oz. sugar. Chopped fresh parsley is added prior to service.

NOTE: Most of the carrots on the market today are young and do not require sugar. However, old carrots will benefit by the addition of a small amount of sugar.

If time permits, cook carrots underdone and hold in carrot liquor off heat. They will finish cooking in their own liquor. Reheat as needed. Adjust seasoning before serving.

Butternut Squash

YIELD: 50 portions	EACH PORTION: about 4 oz.	
INGREDIENTS	*QUANTITY*	*METHOD*
Butternut Squash, A.P. Water, boiling	20 lb. for cooking	1. Peel squash and remove seeds. 2. Cut in uniform pieces and place in large pot. 3. Cover halfway to top of squash with boiling water. 4. Cover pot; simmer for 30 min. or until tender. Do not overcook. Drain well.
Butter, melted Sugar, granulated Salt White Pepper	1 lb. 1 cup 2 tbsp. ½ tsp.	5. Whip in mixer at low speed until well broken up. Increase to medium speed and add all remaining ingredients. Scrape down sides of bowl. 6. Whip until lumps are gone; adjust seasoning. (Overwhipping makes squash excessively watery.) 7. Hold in bain marie.

NOTE: If squash is cooked in steam jacketed kettle, keep cover closed and light steam on for a few minutes after draining. This will evaporate excessive moisture.

Although this squash is generally drier than some of the other winter squashes, adequate measures should be taken to insure a quality product. Cooking in excessive amounts of water, overcooking and overhandling may make a wet squash that is difficult to serve.

Corn on the Cob

YIELD: 50 portions	EACH PORTION: 1 ear	
INGREDIENTS	*QUANTITY*	*METHOD*
Corn Water, boiling, unsalted Butter, drawn	50 ears to cover as needed	1. Divide corn into two separate pots, 25 ears each. Cover with boiling water. Cover pots. 2. When water returns to boil, cook about 4 to 8 min. or until done. Young, fresh corn requires very little cooking time. 3. Older corn may require the addition of a little sugar to replace the sugar content that has turned to starch, but there is no formula to make old corn good. Hold in hot cooking liquor for service, but cook as near to serving time as possible. Dining room personnel should serve generous butter portions on the side.

See color picture, p. 185.

Summer Squash

YIELD: 50 portions	EACH PORTION: about 3 oz.	
INGREDIENTS	QUANTITY	METHOD
Summer Squash (yellow), A. P. Water, boiling, salted	12 lb. for cooking	1. Score squash by running prongs of dinner fork lengthwise along squash. 2. Remove any discolored or undesirable spots and wash well. Dry with clean towel. 3. Cut squash crosswise (in round discs) about 3/8 in. thick. Discard end pieces. 4. Keep squash in original form and line up in rows in lightly buttered hotel pans. Cover half-way up with boiling salted water. 5. Cover pans with clean wet towel; tuck ends of towel inside pan. Simmer on top of range until squash is tender, but still maintains shape. Drain off part of water.
Butter, melted Salt **White Pepper**	1 lb. to taste to taste	6. Butter well and season with salt and pepper. 7. Serve with slotted spoon, being careful to keep squash lined up as it is served. Drain well before putting on plate or in dish. Work one portion of pan at a time. Do not mix the squash.

NOTE: Squash may be cut in pieces and boiled in usual manner, but it is not as appetizing and is usually excessively wet. The method described here demands a little more time in preparation, but makes for much easier service and is a considerably superior product.

Yellow summer squash may be sauteed in the same manner described for Buttered Zucchini (p.193).

It may also be deep fried, using same procedures as for Fried Eggplant (below). This method is also used for Zucchini.

Fried Eggplant

YIELD: 50 portions	EACH PORTION: 3 oz.	
INGREDIENTS	QUANTITY	METHOD
Eggplant, A.P. Bread Flour Egg Wash Bread Crumbs OR Cornmeal	10 lb. 2 lb. 1 qt. 3 lb.	1. Peel eggplant and cut crosswise in ¼ in. slices or cut like french fries. 2. Cover with strong solution of salted ice water to prevent discoloration and maintain crispness. 3. Bread using standard procedure (p. 178). 4. Fry at 350°F. until golden brown and tender. Drain well.

NOTE: Eggplant may be served plain or with Tomato Sauce (p. 318) or other sauces.

Whole Kernel Corn

YIELD: 50 servings	EACH PORTION: 3 oz.	
INGREDIENTS	QUANTITY	METHOD
Frozen Whole Kernel Corn Butter Salt Pepper	10 lb. 8 oz. to taste to taste	1. Place corn in sauce pan with boiling salted water to cover. When water returns to boil, reduce heat and cook until corn is tender (about 2 to 3 min.). Do not overcook. Drain. 2. Add butter and adjust seasoning. Do not add butter until service time.

VARIATIONS: For **Succotash**, combine 5 lb. cooked lima beans with 5 lb. cooked whole kernel corn. Season to taste. Succotash is sometimes creamed. **Old Fashioned Succotash** substitutes shell or horticultural beans for limas.

Vegetables

Scalloped Eggplant and Tomatoes

YIELD: 50 portions	EACH PORTION: about 5 oz.	
INGREDIENTS	*QUANTITY*	*METHOD*
Eggplant, A.P.	5 lb.	1. Wash and peel eggplant. 2. Cut in ½ in. cubes. Cook in boiling salted water about 10 min. or until tender. Drain well.

Tomatoes, canned
Onions, diced fine
Salad Oil
    OR Olive Oil
Bread
Sugar
Salt
Pepper
Sweet Basil
Oregano
Bread Crumbs
    OR Cracker Crumbs
Parmesan Cheese
Butter, melted
	5 qt.
	½ lb.
	6 oz.
	
	1 lb.
	3 oz.
	¾ oz.
	1½ tsp.
	¼ oz.
	½ tsp.
	2 oz.
	
	2 oz.
	2 oz.
		3. Follow entire procedure for Scalloped Tomatoes (p. 207).
		4. Mix eggplant into tomato mixture before placing mixture in casserole and sprinkling with bread crumbs and Parmesan cheese.

Mashed Yellow Turnips

YIELD: 50 portions	EACH PORTION: 3 oz.	
INGREDIENTS	*QUANTITY*	*METHOD*
Turnips, A.P. Potatoes, A.P.	12 lb. 3 lb.	1. Wash and peel turnips and potatoes. Cut uniformly. 2. Cook vegetables separately. Cover with salted water. Bring to boil. Reduce heat and cook about 30 min. or until tender. Drain well.
Butter Sugar White Pepper Salt	8 oz. 4 oz. ½ tsp. 1 tbsp.	3. Rice or mash together in mixing machine. Add remaining ingredients and mix well but do not over-mix. 4. Adjust seasoning and hold in stainless steel bain marie pot for service. Cover with buttered brown paper.

NOTE: To prepare turnips for boiled dinner, peel and cut in ¼ in. thick slices, about 1½ to 2 in. wide. Cook until tender but still holding shape. Drain well.

Quality of turnips changes seasonally. Turnips may sometimes require longer cooking period than potatoes.

Glazed Yellow Turnips and Green Peas

YIELD: 50 portions	EACH PORTION: about 3½ oz.	
INGREDIENTS	*QUANTITY*	*METHOD*
Turnips, yellow, A.P. Butter Sugar, granulated Frozen Green Peas, cooked Salt Pepper	11 lb. 8 oz. 4 oz. 2½ lb. to taste to taste	1. Peel turnips and cut in uniform pieces about ½ in. square. 2. Cook in salted water until nearly tender. Turnips must be kept undercooked. 3. Drain well and saute in butter and sugar until lightly glazed. 4. Add green peas and saute until peas are heated through and turnips are cooked. Season to taste.
See color picture, p. 188.		

Hubbard Squash

YIELD: 50 portions	EACH PORTION: about 4½ oz.	
INGREDIENTS	QUANTITY	METHOD
Hubbard Squash, A.P. Butter Salt White Pepper	22 lb. 1 lb. to taste to taste	1. Cut hubbard squash in halves or quarters, depending on size. (Large pieces are easier to handle.) Remove seeds. 2. Place squash on sheet pan, season and add a little water in bottom of pan to prevent sticking. 3. Bake in preheated oven at 350°F. until squash is soft, about 30 to 45 min. Add additional water if necessary during baking period. 4. Remove from oven and take squash out of shell with large spoon. Put through food mill into large pot or mixing bowl. 5. Add butter and salt and pepper. Blend until smooth and adjust seasoning. 6. Place in clean bain marie pots and keep hot for service.

NOTE: Excessive beating or whipping tends to make this squash more watery. The use of a food mill is suggested to eliminate the beating necessary to make the squash smooth.

Mashed squash that is excessively wet may be placed in buttered baking pans, covered and baked in a slow oven to dry out.

Squash may be cut into portion size pieces and baked, brushed with butter and sprinkled with brown sugar and a small amount of salt, as with Acorn Squash. The squash is then served in the shell.

Baking is the preferred method as it retains more nutritive value and produces a generally superior product. However, squash may be steamed or boiled whole in a short pre-cooking period and cut in pieces to finish cooking. Pulp is then removed from shell and mashed or whipped as suggested above.

Squash may be peeled prior to cooking, cooked and prepared in same manner as Butternut Squash (p. 202). This is an easier way and less time consuming as far as cooks are concerned. However, it does make a wetter product.

Acorn Squash (Des Moines)

YIELD: 50 portions	EACH PORTION: ½ squash	
INGREDIENTS	QUANTITY	METHOD
Acorn Squash, A.P. Butter, melted Salt Sugar, brown	25 (20 lb.) for glaze to taste for glaze	1. Wash and cut squash in half in same direction as ribbing runs. Remove seeds. 2. Butter cut surface lightly. Place on bun pans, or in baking pans with cut side down. 3. Bake at 350° to 375°F. for 30 to 40 min. or until inside (pulp) of squash is quite soft. 4. Turn cut side up. Brush cavity and rim generously with butter. Sprinkle lightly with salt; sprinkle brown sugar evenly over entire cut surface. 5. Replace in oven until sugar is melted and squash is golden brown. Serve hot.

NOTE: Acorn squash may be stuffed with other vegetables or vegetable combinations. It also may be stuffed with sausage or sausage links for a light luncheon plate.

Vegetables

Sweet Potato Croquettes

YIELD: 50 portions		EACH PORTION: 1 large or 2 small, about 5½ oz.
INGREDIENTS	QUANTITY	METHOD
Sweet Potatoes, A.P.	16 lb.	1. Wash and scrub potatoes. Place on sheet pans and bake about 45 min. or until tender (depending on size). 2. Cut potatoes and scoop out pulp, discarding skin. 3. Put through food mill.
Salt Sugar Cinnamon Butter Egg Yolks Cornstarch	1 oz. 6 oz. 2 tbsp. 8 oz. 8 6 oz.	4. Incorporate salt, sugar, cinnamon and butter into potato pulp. 5. Incorporate egg yolks into potato mixture. Blend well. Add cornstarch; mix thoroughly. 6. Place in clean buttered pan or tray. 7. Cover with waxed or greased paper to prevent crusting. 8. Cool slightly, then refrigerate. Chill well.
Breading: Flour Egg Wash: Eggs Milk Bread Crumbs Salad Oil OR Shortening	2 lb. 6 2 qt. 3 lb. to fry	9. When cold, portion with ice cream scoop into 50 or 100 equal portions. Serve 1 or 2, depending on size. 10. Form into cork or cylinder shape and bread, using standard procedure (p. 178). 11. Fry in deep hot fat until golden brown. 12. Drain well and serve hot.

NOTE: If croquettes are not stiff enough, a small amount of dehydrated potato flakes or granules may be added to adjust consistency. Croquettes may be refrigerated after breading to be cooked later.

Potatoes may be boiled or steamed in first step, but baking potatoes produces a dryer product, which is more desirable in preparing croquettes. Sweet potatoes tend to be wetter than white potatoes due to their sugar content.

Sweet potatoes may be breaded with cornflake crumbs for interesting variety. They may also be fried without breading.

Braised Red Cabbage

YIELD: 50 portions		EACH PORTION: 5 oz.
INGREDIENTS	QUANTITY	METHOD
Bacon Fat OR Chicken Fat OR Salad Oil OR Shortening OR Lard Onions, diced fine Sugar, granulated Apples, peeled, cored (½ in. dice) Red Cabbage, shredded coarse Salt Stock or Water	1 lb. 2 lb. 8 oz. 2 lb. 16 lb., A.P. 2 tsp. 1½ qt.	1. Saute onions in fat with sugar until onions are partially cooked. 2. Add apples, cabbage, salt and stock. 3. Cover and simmer about 20 min. or until nearly soft.
Red Wine (optional) Cider Vinegar Salt Pepper	1 pt. 4 oz. to taste to taste	4. Add wine, vinegar and seasonings and cook for 5 min. Adjust seasoning if necessary.

NOTE: White and red cabbage may be braised with many variations and combinations of ingredients, such as salt pork, bacon, ham, onion, garlic, celery seed and various herbs and spices.

Cabbage is sometimes thickened with flour or beurre manie.

When omitting wine, increase cider vinegar to 8 oz.

See color picture, p. 185.

Fresh Beets

YIELD: 50 portions		EACH PORTION: about 4 oz.
INGREDIENTS	QUANTITY	METHOD
Beets, A.P. Butter Salt Pepper	15 lb. ½ lb. to taste to taste	1. Wash beets thoroughly. Trim stems 2 to 3 in. above beets. Retain roots. Place beets in salted water to cover. 2. When water comes to boil, reduce heat and simmer for 45 to 60 min. or until tender. 3. When beets are cooked, strain. Place beets in cold running water until cool enough to handle. Peel and trim. 4. Cut in uniform slices or desired shape. 5. Reheat in butter; add salt and pepper to taste.

Stewed Tomatoes

YIELD: 50 portions		EACH PORTION: about 3 oz.
INGREDIENTS	QUANTITY	METHOD
Onions, diced fine Celery, diced fine Butter Bread Flour	1½ lb. 1 lb. 8 oz. 3 oz.	1. Saute onions and celery in butter until tender. Do not brown. 2. Add flour to sauteed vegetables and make roux. Cook 3 to 4 min. on low heat, stirring constantly.
Tomatoes Sugar Salt Sweet Basil Pepper Thyme	2 No. 10 cans 3 oz. 1½ tbsp. 1 tbsp. 1 tsp. ½ tsp.	3. Drain off half tomato juice and reserve for other use. 4. Combine tomatoes and all spices; bring to boiling. 5. Add juice from tomato-spice mixture to roux mixture gradually, stirring until slightly thickened and smooth. 6. Combine all ingredients and simmer for 10 min. Adjust consistency if necessary. Season to taste with additional salt and pepper.

NOTE: Beurre manie, cornstarch or minute tapioca are sometimes used for thickening this product.

See color picture, p. 185.

Scalloped Tomatoes

YIELD: 50 portions		EACH PORTION: about 3 oz.
INGREDIENTS	QUANTITY	METHOD
Tomatoes Onions, diced fine Butter	2 No. 10 cans 8 oz. 6 oz.	1. Drain off half of the tomato juice and reserve for other use. 2. Saute onions in butter.
Bread Sugar Salt Pepper	1 lb. 4 oz. 1½ tbsp. 1½ tsp.	3. Trim bread and dice in ¼ in. cubes. Toast. 4. Place tomatoes and remaining half of juice, sugar, salt and pepper in sauce pan on range; bring to boiling. 5. Combine onion-butter mixture with toasted bread cubes; mix well. 6. Incorporate bread mixture into tomato mixture; place in lightly greased hotel pan.
Bread Crumbs OR Cracker Meal Parmesan Cheese, grated Butter, melted	2 oz. 2 oz. 2 oz.	7. Top tomato mixture with crumbs and parmesan cheese; drizzle with melted butter. 8. Bake at 375°F. for 30 to 40 min. Top should be nicely browned.

Vegetables

Tomato Rice Pilaf

YIELD: 50 portions		EACH PORTION: 4½ oz.
INGREDIENTS	QUANTITY	METHOD
Butter Onions, chopped fine Rice Chicken Stock, hot Tomatoes, chopped, with juice Salt	12 oz. 8 oz. 4 lb. 1 qt. 1 No. 10 can 2 tsp.	1. Melt butter in 5 to 6 qt. saucepan. 2. Add onions and saute until transparent. 3. Add rice and saute about 5 min. stirring often. 4. Add hot chicken stock, tomatoes and salt. 5. Cover tightly and bake at 350°F. for 18 to 20 min. or until all liquid is absorbed and rice is dry and fluffy. 6. Pilaf may be served in scooped out tomatoes, as shown here.

NOTE: Average solid-to-liquid yields on canned tomatoes provide a total formula base of two parts liquid to one part rice. Variations in tomato pack may sometimes require minor adjustment in formulation.

See color picture, p.185.

Risi Bisi

YIELD: 50 portions		EACH PORTION: about 4½ oz.
INGREDIENTS	QUANTITY	METHOD
Salad Oil Onion, chopped fine Garlic, minced	12 oz. 8 oz. 1 tsp.	1. Saute onion in oil until lightly browned. Add garlic, saute lightly.
Rice, raw Cooked Ham, diced fine Bay Leaf	4 lb. 12 oz. 1	2. Stir in rice, ham and bay leaf. Saute about 5 min., stirring often.
Chicken Stock Salt White Pepper	1 gal. 2 tsp. ½ tsp.	3. Combine rice mixture with stock, salt and pepper; stir well. Bring to a boil. 4. Cover tightly. Bake at 350°F. for 20 to 25 min. or until rice is done. Remove bay leaf.
Green Peas, cooked, drained Pimientoes, drained, diced Mushrooms, cooked, drained, diced	1 pt. 7 oz. 3 oz.	5. Heat peas, pimiento and mushrooms. Add to rice and toss lightly with fork to combine. 6. Cover and heat for 3 to 4 min. longer.

NOTE: Also known as **Rice Valencienne.**

See color picture, p. 188.

Whole Baby Beets in Orange Sauce

YIELD: 50 portions	EACH PORTION: 3 oz., 4 to 5 beets	
INGREDIENTS	QUANTITY	METHOD
Baby Beets, whole, canned (over 100 count)	2 No. 10 cans	1. Drain beets, reserving juice.

Orange Sauce:
    Orange Juice
    Sugar
Vinegar, white
Orange Peel, grated or julienne
Cornstarch
	1½ qt.
	4 oz.
	4 oz.
	2¼ oz.
	3 oz.
		2. Combine beet juice, 1 qt. orange juice, sugar, vinegar and orange peel. Bring to boil.
		3. Mix cornstarch with balance of orange juice and add gradually to hot liquid, stirring until thickened and smooth.
		4. Bring to boil and adjust thickening and seasoning if necessary. Add drained beets and heat.
		5. Hold for service. Acid content will turn beets bright red.

NOTE: Marmalade may be substituted for sugar and orange peel.

See color picture, p. 185.

Vegetable Plate with Poached Egg

YIELD: 50 portions	EACH PORTION: 12 oz. vegetables and egg	
INGREDIENTS	QUANTITY	METHOD
Broiled Tomatoes Frozen Spinach Frozen Cauliflower Fresh Carrots Frozen Peas	50 12 lb. 10 lb. 8 lb. 8 lb.	1. Cook all vegetables according to directions. Drain well and serve piping hot. 2. Arrange on plate in following manner: center each plate with broiled tomato, place mound of spinach at 6 o'clock, carrots at 9 o'clock, peas at 12 o'clock and cauliflower at 3 o'clock. Arrange toast points between vegetables.
Toast Points Eggs, poached	as needed 50	3. Arrange well drained poached egg on bed of spinach.

NOTE: Any other suitable variety of vegetables may be used to make colorful and attractive combinations.

Macedoine of Vegetables

YIELD: 50 portions	EACH PORTION: about 3 oz.	
INGREDIENTS	QUANTITY	METHOD
Mushrooms, diced Butter	8 oz. for sauteing	1. Saute mushrooms in small amount of butter over high heat.
Celery, diced medium Onions, diced medium Pimientoes, drained, diced	1 lb. 12 oz. 1 7-oz. can	2. Saute onions and celery in butter. 3. Combine cooked fresh vegetables and pimientoes.
Mixed Vegetables, frozen Water, boiling, salted Salt Pepper	7½ lb. for cooking to taste to taste	4. Cook in small amount of boiling salted water until tender. (Test lima beans and green beans as they require longest cooking time.) 5. Combine all vegetables, simmer 5 min. Season to taste with salt and pepper.

NOTE: Nearly any reasonable combination of vegetables may be used. Care should be taken that they are contrasting and attractively colored. Vegetables that discolor quickly or bleed, such as beets, should be incorporated a few at a time during service.

Vegetables

Julienne or Alumette Potatoes

YIELD: 50 portions		EACH PORTION: about 5 oz.
INGREDIENTS	QUANTITY	METHOD
Potatoes, A.P.	18 lb.	1. Wash and peel potatoes. Cut into large matchstick sized pieces and soak in ice water to crisp. 2. Drain and dry well. 3. Heat deep fat fryer to 350°F. 4. Fill baskets ½ full and immerse slowly into hot fat. Shake basket frequently to avoid sticking and to obtain even browning. 5. Remove potatoes when golden brown and spread on pans lined with brown paper.
(Since the demand on the deep fry kettle and the time element present a problem in quantity service, Julienne or Alumette potatoes are usually served at small parties.)		
NOTE: These are also called **Shoestring Potatoes**.		

Whipped Potatoes

YIELD: 50 portions		EACH PORTION: about 5 oz.
INGREDIENTS	QUANTITY	METHOD
Potatoes, A.P. Water Salt White Pepper Salt Butter Light Cream, hot Milk, hot	17 lb. to cover 2 oz. to taste to taste 8 oz. 1 pt. as needed	1. Peel and eye potatoes. If large potatoes are used, cut into pieces of uniform size. Keep in cold water until ready to cook. 2. Cover with water and add 2 oz. of salt. Bring to boil and reduce heat. Cook 25 to 30 min. or until tender. 3. Drain well and place in mixing machine with paddle. Break up well and replace paddle with whip. Beat at low speed until well mashed. 4. Add butter; beat. Add cream, blend. Add hot milk until desired consistency, blending well. Beat at medium, then high speed until light and fluffy. Do not overmix.
NOTE: Potatoes may require ricing prior to whipping.		
See color picture, p. 185.		

Potatoes Champs Elysees

YIELD: 50 portions		EACH PORTION: 5 oz.
INGREDIENTS	QUANTITY	METHOD
Potatoes, A.P. Mushrooms, fresh	16 lb. 3 lb.	1. Wash and peel the potatoes; cut julienne style. 2. Wash and clean mushrooms; slice 1/16 in. thick.
Butter, melted Grated Cheese Salt Pepper	for baking 2 lb. to taste to taste	3. Butter the baking pan with melted butter. 4. Place a layer of potatoes about 1 in. thick in the baking pan. Salt and pepper lightly. Add a light layer of mushrooms and sprinkle with grated cheese. 5. Drizzle lightly with melted butter. Continue process, alternating potatoes and mushrooms, until baking pan is filled to the brim. 6. Bake at 350°F. until potatoes are tender and almost all moisture has evaporated. 7. Cut finished potatoes into squares for each portion. Keep warm until service. Brush potatoes with melted butter just before serving.

Potato Croquettes

YIELD: 50 portions		EACH PORTION: 5 oz.
INGREDIENTS		*METHOD*
Same ingredients as for Duchesse Potatoes (p. 212), adding ½ lb. Cornstarch		1. Follow recipe and ingredients for Potatoes Duchesse (p. 212), adding ½ lb. cornstarch. 2. Mix well and spread in buttered pan or tray. Cover with waxed or buttered paper to prevent crusting. 3. Cool, then refrigerate. Chill well. 4. When cold, portion with ice cream scoop into 50 or 100 equal portions (serve 1 or 2 depending on size and shape). Bread, using standard procedure. Fry in deep fat until golden brown. Drain well and serve. (Potatoes may be prepared without breading.)

VARIATIONS: For **Potato Puffs,** use ¾ croquette mixture and ¼ pate a choux. Drop by dessert spoonsful into deep fat, about 350°F. Fry until golden brown and crisp. Serve immediately, four to an order.

For **Potato Cheese Puffs,** incorporate 1½ lb. grated American cheese into potato puff mixture. Proceed as for potato puffs.

NOTE: If croquettes are not stiff enough, a small amount of dehydrated potato flakes or granules may be added to adjust consistency.

Croquettes may be refrigerated after breading to be cooked later.

Care must be taken in selecting frying temperature, depending on temperature of croquettes. (Review Deep Fat Frying Section, pp. 175-179.)

Potatoes Hashed in Cream No. 1

YIELD: 50 portions		EACH PORTION: 5½ oz.	
INGREDIENTS	*QUANTITY*	*METHOD*	
Cream Sauce, light (p. 314) Potatoes, cooked, chopped Salt Pepper	1 gal. 12 lb. to taste to taste	1. Heat Cream Sauce. 2. Add potatoes. Season to taste. 3. Heat for service but do not let mixture boil.	
NOTE: Sherry can be added if desired.			

Potatoes Hashed in Cream No. 2

YIELD: 50 portions		EACH PORTION: 5½ oz.
INGREDIENTS	*QUANTITY*	*METHOD*
Potatoes, A.P. Light Cream Salt Pepper	17 lb. 1 gal. to taste to taste	1. Peel and cut potatoes in quarters. Cook in boiling salted water until about half done. 2. Drain well and chop. Combine partially cooked potatoes and heated cream. Simmer until potatoes are cooked and cream is thickened by potato starch. Season to taste.

Vegetables

Theresa Potatoes

YIELD: 50 portions	EACH PORTION: 1 potato	
INGREDIENTS	QUANTITY	METHOD
Potatoes, A.P. (medium) Onions, small dice Salad Oil OR Margarine White Chicken Stock, hot Salt Pepper Parsley	50 1½ lb. 4 oz. about 1 gal. to taste to taste ¼ bunch	1. Peel and eye potatoes. Shape uniformly as for Potatoes Fondant. 2. Slice 1/8 in. thick, but keep potato together. Place in greased baking pan. 3. Saute onions in oil. Distribute evenly over potatoes. Season. 4. Add stock to partly cover. Cover with buttered paper and bake at 375°F. for ½ hr. Remove paper and finish cooking. Most of liquid should be absorbed. Sprinkle with chopped fresh parsley and serve one potato intact for each serving.
NOTE: Idaho potatoes provide most satisfactory product for this method of preparation because of uniformity of size.		

Potatoes Duchesse

YIELD: 50 portions	EACH PORTION: 5 oz.	
INGREDIENTS	QUANTITY	METHOD
Potatoes, peeled Butter, melted Egg Yolks Salt Pepper Grated Nutmeg (optional)	14 lb. ½ lb. 10 to taste to taste to taste	1. Cook as for Whipped Potatoes (p. 210). Do not overcook as they get soggy. 2. Drain well. Place on the range to permit evaporation of excess moisture. Remove from range and cool slightly. Blend well with butter, egg yolks, salt and pepper. A small amount of nutmeg may be added if desired, but it should not predominate taste. 4. Place potato mixture in pastry bag with star tube and bag out in desired shape on lightly buttered bake sheet. Excess butter will make bagging difficult. Brush lightly with egg wash or slightly whipped egg whites. Brown lightly in oven at 475°F.

Potato Pancakes

YIELD: 50 portions	EACH PORTION: 2 pancakes, each 2½ oz.	
INGREDIENTS	QUANTITY	METHOD
Potatoes, peeled Onions, peeled Lemons, juiced Eggs, whole Salt Pepper Bread Flour Matzo Meal	12 lb. 6 lb. 4 12 ½ tsp. ¼ tsp. 4 oz. 6 oz.	1. Grind or grate potatoes and onions together; add lemon juice to prevent discoloration. 2. Place in a china cap; squeeze liquid content out. Hold liquid, allowing starch to settle to bottom of pot. Pour off liquid and add remaining starch to potatoes and onions in stainless steel bowl. 3. Add eggs, salt and pepper. Mix. Add flour gradually, keep blending; add matzo meal, blend thoroughly.
Salad Oil	4 cups	4. Cover bottom of frying pan with ¼ in. oil. Bring to 325°F., and place level serving spoon of batter in frying pan. When pancake is lightly browned, turn over and brown other side. 5. Finish in oven. Bake at 375°F. until browned and crisp.
NOTE: ¼ cup chopped parsley may be added to batter.		

Potatoes, Hongroise

YIELD: 50 portions		EACH PORTION: about 4 oz.
INGREDIENTS	*QUANTITY*	*METHOD*
Onions, chopped fine Butter Potatoes, peeled, sliced Paprika Salt	6 oz. 8 oz. 12 lb. 2 tbsp. 1½ tbsp.	1. Saute onions in butter for 5 min. 2. Add sliced potatoes and cook 5 min. longer. 3. Add paprika and salt.
Tomatoes, fresh, peeled Stock OR Consomme Parsley, chopped	3 lb. for cooking 1 cup	4. Chop tomatoes coarsely and combine with potatoes. 5. Add stock to barely cover. 6. Cook over low heat until potatoes are done and moisture has been absorbed. 7. Top with chopped fresh parsley for service.

Scalloped Potatoes

YIELD: 50 portions		EACH PORTION: 4 oz.
INGREDIENTS	*QUANTITY*	*METHOD*

Butter
   OR Margarine
Potatoes, peeled, sliced (1/8 in.)
Salt
Pepper
Milk, scalded
   OR Milk and Cream, mixed
	1 lb.
	
	12 lb.
	to taste
	to taste
	about 1 gal.
		1. Butter baking pans. Put a layer of potatoes in bottom and season with salt and pepper. Dot with butter or margarine.
		2. Continue layers until all potatoes are used.
		3. Pour on milk until even with top layer of potatoes.
		4. Cover with greased paper and bake at 350°F. for ½ hr.
		5. Remove paper and continue cooking until potatoes are tender when pierced with a fork.

NOTE: Top should be lightly browned. Heat may be increased during cooking in order to brown, but excessive heat may cause "breaking" or curdling of milk products.

   Light cream sauce is sometimes used.

   Potatoes may be pre-cooked.

   Alternate layers of potatoes with sauteed onions for additional flavor.

Potatoes Fondant

YIELD: 50 portions		EACH PORTION: 1 potato
INGREDIENTS	*QUANTITY*	*METHOD*
Potatoes, peeled, medium Salt White Pepper Butter	50 to taste to taste 1 lb.	1. Shape potatoes to the form and size of a medium egg. 2. Cook potatoes in boiling salted water. Keep slightly undercooked. Drain well. 3. Place in buttered pan. 4. Top with butter and seasonings. Add a little white stock to prevent burning. 5. Bake at 400°F. until tender, covering pan with buttered parchment paper. 6. Brown potatoes when done, if necessary, under broiler.

Vegetables

Franconia Potatoes

YIELD: 50 portions	EACH PORTION: 1 potato	
INGREDIENTS	*QUANTITY*	*METHOD*
Potatoes, A.P. Water, salted Butter, melted OR Margarine, melted Salt Pepper	50 to cover ½ lb. to taste to taste	1. Peel potatoes and trim to uniform size. Cover with salted water and bring to a boil. Reduce heat; cook about 15 min. Remove from heat and drain. 2. Place potatoes in buttered baking pans. Brush with butter and season. 3. Bake at 400°F. for about 45 min.
NOTE: Potatoes should be nicely browned. Turn if necessary during baking.		

Oven Roast Potatoes

YIELD: 50 portions	EACH PORTION: 1 potato	
INGREDIENTS	*QUANTITY*	*METHOD*
Potatoes, A.P. Salad Oil Salt White Pepper	50 1 pt. 2 oz. 2 tbsp.	1. Peel and eye potatoes and shape as for Boiled Potatoes. Keep uniform. Hold in cold water while preparing. Dry all potatoes well with clean towel. 2. Rub with oil. Place in greased baking pan. Season. 3. Bake at 400°F. for 1 hr. or until brown and tender. Turn over halfway through cooking and brush occasionally with oil. Reduce heat if potatoes brown too fast before cooking through.

Potatoes Lorette

YIELD: 50 portions	EACH PORTION: 4½ oz.	
INGREDIENTS	*QUANTITY*	*METHOD*
Potatoes, peeled	12 lb.	1. Cook as for whipped potatoes. Do not overcook.
Pate a Choux based on formula below: Water, hot Shortening Flour, bread Eggs, whole	 1 qt. 1 lb. 1½ lb. 18	2. While potatoes are cooking, prepare Pate a Choux. a. In a saucepan, combine water, shortening, salt. b. Place on range and bring to a good rolling boil. Shortening must be melted. c. Add flour and cook mixture using a wooden spoon until it is smooth and rolls free from side of pan. Mixture should be dry when cooked and not stick to sides of pan. Remove from heat. d. Add two or three eggs at a time to cooked mixture, blending well after each addition of eggs. Continue until all eggs are incorporated.
Salt	1 tsp.	3. Pass cooked potatoes through ricer or food mill. 4. Combine potatoes with Pate a Choux and season to taste. Blend well. 5. With pastry bag and tube, bag out cylinder or cigar-shaped potatoes onto a greased paper. 6. Slide potatoes off paper into deep hot fat (350° to 360°F.). Cook until puffed and brown. Drain on absorbent paper and serve immediately.
VARIATIONS: For **Potatoes Lorette Amandine:** roll Lorette Potatoes in slivered or chopped almonds and fry in deep hot fat. For **Potatoes Dauphine:** add Parmesan cheese to taste before bagging.		
NOTE: Potatoes may be bagged out and refrigerated to be cooked later.		

Kartoffelkloesse (German Potato Dumplings)

YIELD: 50 portions		EACH PORTION: 5 oz. (1 or 2 dumplings)
INGREDIENTS	*QUANTITY*	*METHOD*
Potatoes (peeled and cooked day before use)	15 lb.	1. Put potatoes through food grinder.
Eggs, whole	12	2. Mix potatoes, eggs, cornstarch, parsley and seasonings.
Cornstarch	1 lb.	
Parsley, freshly chopped	1½ oz.	
Salt	to taste	
Pepper	to taste	
Nutmeg	to taste	
Bacon, sauteed, finely ground	8 oz.	3. Blend bacon, croutons and onions.
Bread, finely cubed or diced for croutons, sauteed in bacon fat	12 oz.	4. Make small balls of potato mixture (about size of a golf ball), make a hole in center. Place a teaspoonful of bacon-crouton mixture inside and seal tightly.
Onions, finely chopped, smothered	4 oz.	
Flour	8 oz.	5. Roll in flour and cook in salted boiling water for about 7 min.
Bread Crumbs, fresh (Step No. 6)	2 lb.	6. Roll in bread crumbs previously sauteed in butter.
Butter OR Margarine	1 to 1½ lb.	

Hashed Brown Potatoes

YIELD: 50 portions		EACH PORTION: 4 oz.
INGREDIENTS	*QUANTITY*	*METHOD*
Salad Oil OR Margarine	1 lb.	1. Heat salad oil or margarine in fry pan with beveled lip. When hot, add potatoes to ¾ full. Season lightly with salt and pepper.
Potatoes, cooked, chopped or shredded, refrigerated	12 lb.	2. Cook over high heat several minutes, turning over occasionally until potatoes are heated through.
Salt	to taste	3. Allow potatoes to brown well on bottom. Turn entire mass over, being careful not to disturb the golden crust and brown evenly on the other side.
Pepper	to taste	4. Flip once more and sprinkle with chopped parsley before serving. Serve omelette style with serving spoon.

Baked Idaho Potatoes

YIELD: 50 portions		EACH PORTION: 1 potato
INGREDIENTS	*QUANTITY*	*METHOD*
Potatoes, Idaho, baking	50	1. Wash and scrub potatoes well. Pierce one end with clean fork to allow steam to escape and prevent bursting. This will also make a mealier potato.
		2. Place potatoes on shallow baking pans or sheet pans and bake at 400°F. for 1 hr. or until tender. Test by gently squeezing potato. They should yield to light pressure. Firmness indicates further cooking required.
		3. Score top in criss-cross fashion with sharp knife and open potato by squeezing from near bottom. Generous butter portions should be served by dining room personnel.

NOTE: Idaho potatoes are purchased by count per box. Cooking time will vary depending on size.
Raw potatoes may be placed on a bed of rock salt in a pan during baking to prevent scorching.

Vegetables

Baked Stuffed Potatoes

YIELD: 50 portions	EACH PORTION: 1 potato	
INGREDIENTS	*QUANTITY*	*METHOD*
Potatoes, Idaho baking Butter Salt Pepper Egg Yolks Light Cream or Milk Paprika	50 ½ lb. to taste to taste 5 for mixing as needed	1. Follow procedure for Baked Potatoes, (p. 215). 2. When cooked, remove upper portion of shell by slicing lengthwise. 3. Scoop out potato pulp, reserving shell. 4. Put pulp through ricer and mix with butter and salt and pepper. 5. Work in egg yolks and hot milk or cream. Whip smooth and fluffy to desired consistency. 6. With pastry bag and star tube bag, pipe potato mixture back into shells. 7. Sprinkle with paprika and additional butter and return to oven for about 10 min. or until heated through and nicely colored on top.

VARIATIONS: Potatoes may be sprinkled with parmesan cheese if desired.
For **Potatoes Jackson**, add ½ lb. parmesan cheese to mix.
For **Potatoes Georgette**, add ½ tsp. nutmeg and 1 cup chopped chives.

Potatoes, Rissole

YIELD: 50 portions	EACH PORTION: 4½ oz.	
INGREDIENTS	*QUANTITY*	*METHOD*
Potatoes, A.P. Butter OR Margarine Salt Pepper Parsley, chopped	17 lb. 1½ lb. to taste to taste for garnish	1. Peel and shape potatoes with melon ball cutter or parisienne knife in small oblong or egg shape. Reserve trimmings. 2. Place potatoes in salted water and bring to boil. Reduce heat and simmer about 7 to 8 min. They must be undercooked. 3. Drain well and finish cooking with butter in sautoir in oven at 350°F. until golden brown. Season with salt and pepper and sprinkle with chopped fresh parsley before serving.

NOTE: For quantity service, potatoes may be finished in deep fat fryer.

Potatoes au Gratin

YIELD: 50 portions	EACH PORTION: about 4 oz. potatoes, 4 oz. sauce	
INGREDIENTS	*QUANTITY*	*METHOD*
Potatoes, peeled, diced (3/8 in.) Cheese Sauce (p. 316) Bread Crumbs Paprika Butter, melted	12 lb. 1½ gal. ½ cup 1 tbsp. 2 oz.	1. Cook potatoes as for Delmonico (facing page). Drain well; place in buttered pans. 2. Pour on sauce, mixing well. 3. Mix bread crumbs and paprika; sprinkle over top. Drizzle with melted butter.
		4. Bake at 350°F. for 30 min. or until fully cooked and golden brown. 5. If needed, place low under broiler to brown top before serving.

NOTE: Additional cheese is sometimes sprinkled on top before crumbs. Grated parmesan cheese may also be used. If potatoes are distributed in 2 pans there will be more gratin to improve the appearance of each portion. If potatoes are baked in 1 pan, reduce sauce by ½ gal.

See color picture, p. 188.

Italian Potato Dumplings (Gnocchi Piemontaise)

YIELD: 50 portions	EACH PORTION: 5½ oz.	
INGREDIENTS	*QUANTITY*	*METHOD*
Potatoes, A.P.	15 lb.	1. Scrub potatoes. Place in pot, cover with salted water. Bring to boil, reduce heat and simmer for 30 to 35 min. or until done. 2. Peel and put through ricer or food mill.
Salt Egg Yolks Bread Flour	2 tsp. 6 2 lb.	3. Combine salt, egg yolks and flour in order given. 4. Adjust consistency, adding additional flour, if needed, to make a stiff dough. Roll on floured board in rolls about ¾ in. in diameter. 5. Cut into 1 in. lengths. Toss in flour and mark each with tines of a fork, making four distinct marks. 6. Test poach one gnocchi to check consistency and adjust if required before cooking the entire amount. 7. Drop into boiling salted water and poach 8 to 10 min. As gnocchi cook, pieces rise to the top. 8. Drain well or remove with a strainer when cooked.
Parmesan Cheese Butter, melted Salt Pepper	1 pt. 8 oz. to taste to taste	9. Place in lightly buttered shallow pans and sprinkle evenly with parmesan cheese. Sprinkle lightly with butter and place in oven at 475°F. until top is crusty and nicely browned. Gnocchi may be placed under broiler to finish if desired.
NOTE: Gnocchi may also be served with tomato sauce or its variations. When serving with sauce, mask well with sauce and sprinkle with 8 oz. parmesan cheese, omitting butter.		

Potatoes, O'Brien

YIELD: 50 portions	EACH PORTION: about 4 oz.	
INGREDIENTS	*QUANTITY*	*METHOD*
Bacon, diced Salad Oil OR Margarine Onions, diced fine Green Peppers, diced fine Pimientoes, drained, diced fine Potatoes, cooked, diced	1 lb. 8 oz. 1 lb. 1 lb. 1 7-oz. can 12 lb.	1. Fry bacon in heavy skillet until done but not crisp. Drain off half of the bacon fat. 2. Add oil, onions and green pepper to skillet. Saute until vegetables are tender-crisp. 3. Add pimientoes. Keep warm. 4. Fry potatoes as for Hashed Brown Potatoes (p. 215). Garnish each pan, before serving, with bacon mixture.

Delmonico Potatoes

YIELD: 50 portions	EACH PORTION: 6 oz.	
INGREDIENTS	*QUANTITY*	*METHOD*
Potatoes, peeled, diced (3/8 in.) Green Peppers, small dice Cream Sauce, medium (p. 314) Pimientoes, small dice	12 lb. 1 lb. 1 gal. 1 7 oz. can	1. Cook potatoes in salted water until slightly under-done. Drain well. Allow to cool. 2. Place green peppers in boiling salted water and simmer for 5 min. or until tender. When cooked, drain well and combine with pimientoes and Cream Sauce. 3. Place potatoes in buttered baking pan and cover with sauce, mixing well. 4. Cover with buttered paper and bake at 350°F. for 25 to 30 min. or until potatoes are fully cooked and heated all the way through. (If browned top is desired, omit buttered paper.)

Vegetables

Boiled Potatoes

YIELD: 50 portions	EACH PORTION: 1 potato, 3 to 4 oz.	
INGREDIENTS	QUANTITY	METHOD
Potatoes, A.P. Water, salted	50 (13 to 16 lb.) as needed	1. Peel and eye potatoes carefully. Make 50 uniform portions, trimming to shape when necessary. (Save clean trimmings for future use.) 2. Cover with salted water and bring to boil. Reduce heat; simmer until tender. Drain carefully, being cautious of steam. Potatoes should be dry and mealy. 3. To hold for service, place in hotel pan and cover with wet towel. Keep covered in steam table.

VARIATIONS: For **Parsley Potatoes,** pour or brush ½ lb. melted butter on potatoes and sprinkle with ¾ cup chopped fresh parsley.

For **Boiled Potatoes Parisienne,** scoop balls out of raw potatoes with melon ball cutter or parisienne knife. Reduce cooking time. Do not overcook. (Save trimmings for other use.)

Cottage Fried Potatoes

YIELD: 50 portions	EACH PORTION: about 5 oz.	
INGREDIENTS	QUANTITY	METHOD
Potatoes, peeled, cooked, sliced ¼ in. thick Salad Oil OR Margarine Salt Pepper	15 lb. 1 lb. to taste to taste	1. Heat oil or margarine in fry pan with beveled lip. When hot, add potatoes to ¾ full. Season lightly with salt and pepper. 2. Cook over high heat several minutes, turning over occasionally until potatoes are heated through. 3. Allow potatoes to brown well on bottom. Turn entire mass over, being careful not to disturb the golden crust and brown evenly on the other side. 4. Turn out onto plate. Serve hot. Garnish with parsley, if desired.

NOTE: For **American Fried Potatoes,** slice cooked potatoes thinly and saute as for Hashed Brown or Cottage Fried Potatoes.

Lyonnaise Potatoes

YIELD: 50 portions	EACH PORTION: 5 oz.	
INGREDIENTS	QUANTITY	METHOD
Onions, peeled, sliced thin Oil OR Margarine Potatoes, cooked, sliced or chopped Salt Pepper	3 lb. 1 to 1½ lb. 15 lb. to taste to taste	1. Saute onions in oil or margarine until tender. 2. Proceed as for hashed brown potatoes, using sufficient quantity sauteed onions for each pan as cooked.

NOTE: Chopped fresh parsley is usually used for garnish.

Baked Macaroni and Cheese

YIELD: 50 portions	EACH PORTION: 8 oz.	
INGREDIENTS	*QUANTITY*	*METHOD*
Elbow Macaroni, raw Cheese Sauce (p. 316)	3½ lb. 1½ gal.	1. Cook macaroni until tender (not al dente). Cool and drain well. (See directions for pasta cooking on p. 26.) 2. Prepare Cheese Sauce as indicated in recipe.
Milk, hot Cheddar Cheese, grated or coarsely ground	1 qt. 12 oz.	3. Combine macaroni, Cheese Sauce, milk and cheddar cheese. 4. Place in 2 lightly buttered hotel pans (steam table insert pans). Cover with buttered or lightly oiled brown paper and bake at 350°F. for ½ hr. or until hot and bubbly.

NOTE: For **Baked Macaroni au Gratin**, sprinkle macaroni lightly with mixed bread crumbs, parmesan cheese and paprika. Dot with butter. Cover with buttered brown paper. Bake at 350°F. for about 25 min.; remove paper and bake for 5 to 10 min. longer or until golden brown. Serve piping hot.

Additional Methods of Serving Vegetables

Artichokes, French: boiled, stuffed and baked, fried

Artichokes, Jerusalem: boiled

Asparagus: boiled, in cream au gratin, butter sauce, baked, with cheese, vinaigrette, in salad

Beets: boiled, pickled, Harvard, saute, julienne, relish

Broccoli and **Brussels Sprouts:** boiled, saute, in cream, puree, au gratin

Cabbage: boiled, shredded, braised, creamed, stuffed and baked, cole slaw

Red Cabbage: sauerkraut, Bavarian, braised

Carrots: boiled, glazed, Vichy, julienne, in cream, croquette, loaf puree

Cauliflower: boiled, creamed, saute, fritters, Hollandaise

Celery: boiled, in cream, braised (hearts)

Celery Knob: glazed, braised, puree, in salads, fritters

Corn: on the cob, kernel, in cream, saute, Delmonico, croquette, fritters, custard

Cucumbers: boiled or steamed, in salad, pressed in cream, stuffed and baked

Eggplant: baked, saute, french fried, stuffed and baked

Green Peppers: creole, grilled

Kohlrabi: boiled, creamed, saute

Kale: boiled

Leeks: boiled, braised, in salad

Lima Beans: boiled, creamed, au gratin, Bretonne, bonne femme, puree

Mushrooms: saute, broiled, stewed, in cream, stuffed, croquette, puree

Okra: stewed, with canned tomatoes, in soups

Onions: as seasoning agent, boiled, fried, stuffed and baked, in cream, smothered, grilled, puree

Parsnips: boiled, glazed, fried, fritters, puree

Peas: boiled, in cream, souffle, puree, Paysanne, French

Sorrel: puree

Spinach: boiled, creamed, leaf, croquettes, souffle

String Beans (Green Beans): boiled, in cream, au gratin, in salad, puree

Tomato: stewed, scalloped, fried, baked, jellied, stuffed

Zucchini: boiled, mashed, baked, french fried, puree, deep fried, saute

Techniques for Successful Salads

A salad may be generally defined as any cold dish of meat, poultry, fish, fruit, dairy product or vegetables, served singly or in combination, usually with some form of dressing. There are few exceptions.

Salads are extremely wholesome as fresh fruits and vegetables furnish many essential vitamins and minerals.

Salads are too often neglected or relegated to a minor role and do not receive proper attention. Salads should complement and highlight a meal. They offer excellent opportunities for displaying artistic talent.

Salad Categories

1) Appetizers: such as shrimp, lobster, crabmeat cocktails, fruits, pickled herring, chopped chicken livers, etc. They should not dull or satisfy the appetite but should be appealing and light in character so as to create a stimulating effect on the diner.

2) Accompaniment: a side salad, served with the dinner or as a separate course; a moderate portion that will offer contrast with the rest of the dinner. Preferably not too sweet so as to jade the appetite. Good examples are mixed green salad hearts of lettuce, pear and cottage cheese and pickled beet salads.

3) Main course salads: which, as the name implies, constitute the whole meal. They may be any reasonable combination of meat, poultry, fish, fruit, vegetable, dairy, gelatin or macaroni products. Good examples are: chicken salad with celery or pineapple; fruit salad plate; tomato stuffed with tuna salad, or avocado stuffed with crabmeat or chef's salad.

4) Dessert salads: often sweet in character; composed of fruits, nuts, dairy products, gelatins. May be molded or frozen. Examples: ginger ale salad mold; jellied fruit; strawberry mousse.

These four categories bear reference primarily to individual salads. Further discussion will be devoted to buffet salads and salad bowls for multiple service.

In any type of food preparation the quality of the finished product can be no better than its ingredients. This is particularly true of salads where eye appeal, texture and color contrast and a light, artistic touch are of prime importance. Flavor and harmony of combination require equal consideration.

Basic Principles and Factors Related to Good Salads

1) Quality of ingredients: includes freshness, not only in purchasing, but in preparation.

2) Eye appeal: attractive, appetizing and tasteful in appearance.

3) Simplicity: the basis of real beauty. It is easy to overdo by being too elaborate, too ornate or by over-garnishing. K.I.S. Keep it simple.

4) Neatness: an artist or photographer keeps his picture within a frame. Regard the inner rim of a plate as a picture frame and in setting up or displaying a salad, keep it within the inside rim of the plate.

5) Contrast and harmony: both in color and texture.

6) Proper food combinations: pineapple and coconut go well with chicken, but are not usually combined with tuna. Choose your combinations with care, but also with imagination.

7) All foods should be identifiable: hash has its place, but not in salad preparation.

8) Foods properly chilled: does not mean ice cold. Just as fine wine loses much of its flavor when served too cold, so do salads and other foods.

9) A basic rule in all food preparation: hot foods—hot or warm plates; cold foods—cold plates. Keep a sufficient quantity of plates for service in the refrigerator, replenishing them as they are used. This is particularly important during the warm months.

10) Clean, crisp greens: discussed in detail further in this section.

11) Flavorful, tempting to the palate: in striving for eye appeal, don't lose sight of this factor. Fortunately, the two usually go together.

12) Foods properly drained: water or excess juices will weaken dressings and look sloppy on a plate.

13) Do not overcook foods: destroys color, vitamins and minerals. Remember the rule of eye appeal.

Four Basic Parts

1) Base: usually lettuce or some form of salad green

2) Body: the ingredients that constitute the salad itself

3) Dressing: should bear a direct relationship to the salad

4) Garnish: designed to give contrast and eye appeal to the salad, but not to be so elaborate as to detract from the body

Some form of salad green is nearly always used as a base before placing the body of the salad on the plate. The base serves to keep the salad from looking bare, provides contrast and helps to dress up the salad.

The body, or the ingredients which make up the salad, may be used in an infinite variety of combinations and arrangements. It is the ingredients that are chosen which often give the salad its name.

Dressings are explained in detail in a separate section of this chapter. Dressings are either served separately, placed on, or mixed with, a salad immediately prior to service. This aids in maintaining the crispness and freshness of a salad and prevents a watery or swimming pool effect.

The garnish is the finishing touch to the salad which aids in creating eye appeal through contrast and harmony of color and ingredients. It should be simple enough not to detract from the salad yet contrasting and effective enough to attract the attention of and appeal to the diner. The flavor and texture of the garnish must also be related to the salad.

Salads on the Menu With the exception of banquet service (where a specific salad is listed on the menu), diners are usually given their choice of two or three salads. These salads should offer as much contrast as possible. An example might be: Tossed Garden Salad; Pear and Cottage Cheese Salad with French Fruit Dressing; Cole Slaw Souffle Salad with Sour Cream Dressing. Tossed salads are invariably served with some form of french dressing.

The variety of salads one might offer would depend not only upon cost and availability of ingredients, but upon labor and refrigeration as well. Planning of any menu should take into consideration labor—both number and skill—equipment, work, service and storage areas. Acceptability by the guests is a prerequisite.

Gelatin Salads offer an infinite variety of colorful and popular salads that are economical and easy to make. Containers and molds are available in many different shapes for individual and multiple service.

It is of extreme importance that the correct ratio of gelatin to liquid be observed. Too much gelatin results in a stiff, rubbery product. Too little gelatin produces a soft, sloppy salad.

Basic formula for 1 gal. of gelatin, using flavored gelatin, is: 1 package (24 oz.) of fruit-flavored gelatin per gallon of liquid. The liquid may be part water and part fruit juices. It is a good practice to utilize juices drained from salad fruits in the preparation of gelatin for salads or desserts. This provides additional flavor and nutritional value.

Basic formula for 1 gal. of plain gelatin, using unflavored gelatin, is: 3½ oz. of plain gelatin per gallon of liquid. Gelatin swells or becomes hydrated (the opposite of dehydrated) when placed in liquid. When the liquid is heated to temperatures of 95°F. or over, the gelatin dissolves. Unflavored gelatin should be soaked in cold water prior to its use.

It is desirable to add only sufficient hot liquid to dissolve the gelatin, usually not over one-half of the total amount to be used. The remaining liquid is added cold. This facilitates the forming of the gel. When all hot or boiling liquid is added to the gelatin, more time is required for the gel to cool and set and some flavor may be lost due to high temperatures.

Although basic formulas have been given for gelatin, the actual amount may vary in practice depending on several factors: temperature; length of time gel may set; acid content of other ingredients; sugar content of other ingredients, and whether the gelatin is to be used in a solid or whipped or foamy state.

The gel sets more rapidly at cold temperatures. The longer it takes to set, the stiffer or more rubbery it gets. Vinegars and fruit acids inhibit the action of the gel and some fruits, such as fresh pineapple, cannot be added to gelatin unless they have been boiled.

Excesses of sugar also inhibit the action of the gel. When gelatin is whipped or beaten foamy with a wire whip, its volume increases. As the volume increases, its power to gel decreases. These factors should be taken into consideration when preparing gelatin salads and other gelatin products.

These variations are not as difficult as they sound and practical experience will soon enable an accomplished cook or salad person to judge requirements. Once the requirements are determined, proper measurements should be made, using level volume measurements for small quantities and weight measurements when producing in larger quantities. Ice may be substituted for part of the liquid to speed the formation of the gel.

Salad Greens There are many varieties of salad greens. While the majority of them are available year round, the quality and price will vary with the season and area in which they are grown. Quality and price are generally most favorable when vegetables are in season in your area and are in bountiful supply.

Iceberg or Head Lettuce This is perhaps the most familiar salad green, distinguished by its firm, compact head with light green leaves. Its firm compactness makes it ideal for hearts of lettuce. Head lettuce is also used extensively as a base and as an ingredient in a large variety of mixed salads.

Boston Lettuce The round head has loosely packed, light green leaves that separate easily. It is tender and fragile. Although it is grown year round (in the southern market), its distribution is limited due to its perishable nature.

Bibb Lettuce (Limestone Lettuce) Similar to Boston lettuce in size and shape, but more crisp. Bibb lettuce is not plentiful in the general market.

Escarole Sometimes referred to as broad leaf endive, escarole is a fan-shaped, flat head with broad loose leaves. Darker green than its cousin, chicory, it is rather bitter in taste. The ends are sometimes tough and rubbery and are often discarded.

Chicory Also known as curly endive, chicory comes in a spreadout bunch with thin twisted leaves, curly on the outer edges. Color shades from dark green outside to pale yellow or white in the center. It has a slightly bitter taste. Chicory is used in mixed salads and as a base and garnish for fruits, fruit salads, entrees and for garnishing cold buffet trays.

Romaine has an elongated head with slender, loose, green leaves which are fairly coarse in mature plants. It retains its crispness, is used in mixed green salads.

Belgian Endive A tightly packed, narrow, pointed head, spearlike in character is typical of Belgian endive. Size varies, but averages 4 to 6 in. in length. Its center is pale yellow to white. Since it is grown and shipped mostly in the Atlantic coast area, it is usually expensive. Belgian endive is often served alone with appropriate dressing. It should be split in half lengthwise before cleaning.

Chinese Cabbage Also known as celery cabbage, Chinese cabbage has a long, narrow head with green leaves shading to white in center. It resembles cabbage in taste, but is somewhat milder. Crisp and bitey, it is excellent for mixed salads; also used in Chinese cookery.

Watercress Sometimes used in green salads and soups, watercress is more extensively used as garnish for salads, fruits and main dishes. It has tiny green leaves similar to small clover but fragile, on thin stalks. Watercress is bound together in small bunches. Its taste is peppery and it is highly perishable. Keep refrigerated or iced as part of the garnish mise en place.

Parsley More properly classified as an herb, although used to a considerable extent as a garnish for salads and other dishes, parsley is also used in bouquet garni and as an ingredient in many types of cooking.

Other Salad Ingredients Also used in mixed salads are greens and other vegetables: raw spinach, Swiss chard, red cabbage, radishes, carrots, celery, scallions or green onions, red onions, cucumbers and tomatoes.

Tomatoes are seldom added to a mixed green salad during preparation as their water and acid content tends to wilt the greens and make them soggy. Tomatoes are usually placed on this type of salad as a garnish. An exception to this might be an occasion where the tomatoes are marinated in dressing and added to a salad immediately prior to service, or where greens are not used.

Preparation of Greens Greens are used so extensively in nearly all types of salad preparation that their care and handling is *extremely* important. Proper washing and storage of greens is often a tiresome task but is essential to their use. The following procedures are recommended:

Wash thoroughly several times in large quantity of cold water, separating the leaves to remove all grit and dirt. It may sometimes be necessary to cut lengthwise through the core of some greens in order to remove all traces of dirt or sand.

The core is removed intact from iceberg lettuce very simply by holding the head of lettuce in the palm of one hand, core up, and exerting light pressure against the core with the other hand. It is usually not necessary to cut the core with a knife and it is not recommended to smash the core with force as this often results in bruising and rusting of lettuce.

Excessive handling and cleaning of greens too far ahead of use also results in rusting. After careful washing, the greens should be drained well, removing the greens from the water rather than the water from the greens. This allows grit and dirt to settle to the bottom of the sink or container and not back into

the greens. This technique should be remembered when washing all fruits and vegetables.

Use colanders or wire salad baskets to drain salad greens. After draining and removing as much water as possible, cover the greens with a clean damp cloth or place in plastic bags which are excellent for this purpose, then refrigerate to crisp. Greens should be quite dry before service. The core is not removed from iceberg lettuce when used for hearts as it helps to hold the lettuce together when it is cut into wedges. Greens in a mixed salad should be cut or torn bite size as a convenience to the patron.

Watercress should be separated so that each stalk may be thoroughly washed in the same manner as suggested for other greens. It may be wrapped in towels and stored under refrigeration for short periods of time.

Parsley has better keeping qualities than watercress but loses its bloom if not stored properly. It should be thoroughly washed and stored in a tightly covered glass container under refrigeration. Both watercress and parsley should be drained and dried as well as possible before being placed under refrigeration.

Handling Fruits and Vegetables With little exception, most fresh fruits and vegetables require refrigeration. Unripe fruits, melons and tomatoes may be held at room temperatures until they ripen and then stored under refrigeration.

Bananas should not be refrigerated as this tends to darken them without ripening.

To ripen tomatoes, place them in a dry, dark area out of the sun. Strong sunshine may rot them.

Melons give off a characteristic odor and should not be stored near butter or other products which might absorb their odor or flavor. Once cut, however, melons also absorb odor and should not be stored near strong flavored vegetables, such as cabbage.

Canned fruits and vegetables should be chosen for highest quality and bought by specification for size and count. All canned goods should be stored in a cool dry place and refrigerated unopened for a few hours or overnight prior to service.

Some fresh fruits and vegetables turn dark when cut and exposed to the air. Bananas, apples, pears, peaches, avocados may be sprinkled, brushed, or preferably marinated in liquids of acid content, such as orange juice, grapefruit juice, lemon, lime or pineapple juice or salted cold water. These fruits are usually mild or bland in flavor and the marination not only aids in preventing discoloration, but improves their flavor as well. This is suggested in the course of preparation before the salads are set up for service.

Stainless steel knives, equipment and utensils are best for fresh fruit preparation as they do not stain or discolor foods.

See p. 231 for information on Salad Preparation, Buffet Service, Storage, Garnishes, Salads for Dieters, Green Salads.

SUCCESSFUL SALADS

Know-how of basic salad techniques and a sense of showmanship are prerequisites for the preparation of Caesar Salad at the table. This combination can pay off in high check averages, for the patron is willing to pay for tableside pageantry. Caesar Salad was created from necessity, as were many other famous dishes. One story of its creation tells of a Mexican hotel man, named Caesar, who found himself with an unexpected horde of guests. The patrons held out, the food supply did not. Caesar had left only crates of romaine, eggs and some stale bread. Thus the salad, which the staff was instructed to serve with showmanship as the specialty of the house.

Caesar Salad

Hearts of Lettuce

Fresh Fruit Chantilly

SUMMER SALADS

Appetizing salads give excellent return in dollars and cents

Shredded Carrot and Raisin Salad

Pickled Beet Salad

Orange and Grapefruit Salad

String Bean and Pimiento Salad

Cottage Cheese Jubilee Salad

Cole Slaw

Fruit Slaw

Mixed Green Salad, Herb Dressing

Mikado Salad

Mandarin Orange Waldorf Salad

Cucumber-Onion Salad

Lettuce and Tomato Salad

A skillfully flavored salad dressing that is appropriate in flavor, texture and color to a particular salad is essential to success in salad preparation. Herbs, flavorings, oils and vinegars may be blended in intricate amounts, but should always heighten the flavor and crispness of the greens or other salad ingredients, not drown them. Tested recipes for the three basic dressings—french, mayonnaise and cooked or boiled—variations upon these dressings and popular recipes for salads are included in this section.

Stuffed Prune Salad

Chef's Salad

Pineapple and Cottage Cheese Salad

Tomato Andalouse

Waldorf Salad

Macaroni Salad with Julienne of Ham

MOLDED SALADS

Perfection Salad

Jellied Fruit Mold

Peach and Raspberry Mold

Lime Pear Aspic

Molded Spring Vegetable Salad

Tomato Aspic

Cucumber-Lime Gelatin Mold

Salad Preparation and Service

Preparation When possible, salads should be set up to order, or as few as possible made at one time. Again, the availability of help, number of guests to be served, etc., must be taken into consideration.

Mass production or assembly line techniques of setting up salads are recommended for banquets or where a large number of salads must be made ahead. This calls for advance preparation of all ingredients, including dressings and garnishes.

In the mass production method, a specified number of plates are laid out in a large work area convenient to the person or persons making the salads. The bases, a lettuce cup or whatever green is being used, are placed on all the plates. The body of the salad is then placed on the base. If the salads are to be served immediately, the dressing and garnish may also be put on at this time. If salads are to be refrigerated for later use, the dressing and garnish are put on at time of service.

Buffet Service For buffet service, where large salad bowls and platters or trays are used, the salads should be as attractive as possible. A garnish may be simple but contrasting in its beauty.

Simplicity makes it easier for a patron to focus his attention on a single item and makes for easier service, particularly if a guest is to serve himself. It avoids handling and mixing of a complicated garnish into a salad as it is served, causing an unattractive appearance.

Simplicity also demands less initial labor and time. When several items are displayed for buffet service, the number of pieces alone is enough to call for the guest's attention. Over-garnishing can cause such a profusion of color and ingredients that a guest may have difficulty in identifying the foods. A centerpiece usually dominates the theme and everything should be related but subservient to it.

Salads of the appetizer type are sometimes served in boats or bowls carved from ice. Fruits and fruit salads are often served in watermelon baskets or huge iced bowls. When possible, silver service should be used in buffet work. Silver trays and platters are expensive, however, and all food operations cannot afford to maintain a sufficient number of trays and platters for an entire buffet.

Storage In other areas of quantity food service, salads are often prepared in large numbers. This is especially true of industrial, school and college or hospital feeding. Care must be taken to insure correct refrigeration of these foods in suitable containers.

Stainless steel and crockery aid in holding foods with limited discoloration. Aluminum is not quite as acceptable because it may discolor. Enamel is not recommended as it chips quite easily and the danger of foreign materials in foods is obvious. Mixed green and tossed salads are often stored in plastic bags or plastic barrels of the same type used for storing sugar and flour.

Garnishes for Salads Great stress has been placed upon simplicity in garnishing. This does not prevent full use of the imagination in arranging pleasing and colorful plates. While garnishes should provide contrast, they should also bear relation to the salad they are to be used with.

Vegetable and egg garnishes are usually related to vegetable, macaroni, meat and fish salads; fruit and dairy garnishes with fruit and gelatin salads.

Watercress is used for nearly all types of foods, but parsley seldom accompanies a fruit dish. When contrasting colors and textures in the salad itself appear sufficient, additional garnish is not necessary.

The following is a list of garnishes that are often used.

WITH FRUITS OR GELATIN SALADS:
  Watercress-Mint leaves
  Nuts, halved or chopped
  Strawberries
  Cherries, fresh or green and red maraschino, bing
  Grapes, fresh or canned
  Other fresh and canned fruits including bananas, apples, citrus fruits (fresh), mandarin oranges, kumquats, pineapple, fresh blueberries, melon balls, cooked pitted prunes
  Whipped cream, cream cheese, cottage cheese, sour cream

WITH OTHER SALADS:
  Hard-cooked eggs, slices, wedges, grated, fancy cut
  Parsley, sprigs or chopped
  Carrot curls or sticks
  Radishes, sliced, chopped, rosettes
  Beets, fancy cut
  Pimiento, fancy strips, chopped
  Fluted cucumbers, sliced
  Tomatoes, slices, wedges, cherry tomatoes
  Green peppers, strips or rings
  Olives, ripe, green or stuffed, sliced, chopped
  Pickles, various types: whole, sliced, fanned, sticks
  Lemons, limes, slices, wedges

Salads for Dieters Due to the diet consciousness of the American public, main course salads and salad plates are becoming increasingly popular the year around, although, quite naturally, these foods are featured more extensively during the summer months.

Well meaning dieters often go astray when a simple fruit salad is dressed generously with mounds of rich, whipped cream. This emphasizes the need for many food operations to have on hand some form of low calorie dressing that may be served at a guest's request. Low calorie cheeses may also be served, such as cottage cheese or yoghurt.

Main course salads require a balance in food values as well as contrast in flavor and texture. While cooks and chefs are not expected to be dietitians or nutritionists, they should have some insight into this subject. As an example, avocados are a high fat content food. They are often served stuffed with seafood in which mayonnaise is generally used. Citrus fruits are also often used in combination with avocados. With these food values considered, we also find a contrast in texture and harmony of color that will prove appealing and attractive to most guests. While potato salad, a standard American favorite, is often an accompaniment, it need not always be made with mayonnaise. Mild oil and varied vinegars or chicken stock are sometimes used which lower the fat content. Plain sliced tomatoes, which would not require additional dressing, might be served with this plate.

Sherbets are often served with fruits, as appetizers and main courses. When available, water sherbets are recommended rather than milk sherbets as they are less sweet and lower in fat content. Sugars and fats serve to satisfy the appetite and are not preferred for appetizers.

Green Salads Individual mixed salad bowls are sometimes served as a main course. While they vary in character, the bulk of the salads is nearly always a mixed green or tossed salad. Most of these names are interchangeable: tossed salad, garden salad, mixed green salad. These mainly imply that the ingredients are a blend of raw or cooked vegetables with greens and usually accompanied by some variation of French Dressing.

A mixed green salad by name should contain only mixed greens. However, a menu might read: Tossed Garden Salad Bowl with Julienne of Turkey, Ham and Swiss Cheese. This specifically states what the accompanying ingredients are. A salad of this type is usually referred to as a Chef's Salad.

A menu that is specific in content enables a guest to understand it clearly and know what to expect when he orders. This often avoids confusion and resultant poor relationships.

Caesar Salad

YIELD: 50 portions		
INGREDIENTS	*QUANTITY*	*METHOD*
Romaine Garlic, chopped Salad Oil Bread, cubed	6 lb. 2 tbsp. 12 oz. 12 oz.	1. Wash romaine carefully and cut or break into bite size pieces. Drain as dry as possible. 2. Saute garlic in oil until light brown. Strain and discard garlic. 3. Saute bread cubes in garlic oil until golden brown. Drain and keep warm.
Salad Oil Lemon Juice Salt Black Pepper	1¼ qts. 12 oz. 1½ tbsp. ½ tsp.	4. Make basic French dressing with oil, lemon juice, salt, pepper. Add drained oil from anchovies.
Eggs Parmesan Cheese Anchovy Fillets	12 4 oz. 50	5. Place romaine in bowl and add lightly beaten eggs. Toss lightly, coating well. Add parmesan cheese, tossing lightly again. 6. Arrange portion on chilled salad plate. 7. Dress with 1 oz. dressing just before service time. Garnish with croutons and curled anchovy fillet.
See color picture, p. 223.		

Mixed Green Salad, Herb Dressing

YIELD: 50 portions		EACH PORTION: 2½ oz.
INGREDIENTS	*QUANTITY*	*METHOD*
Lettuce Romaine Chicory Escarole	4 heads 3 heads 3 heads 1 head	1. Wash and clean all greens. Dry well and crisp in refrigerator. 2. Cut or break in bite size pieces and mix together. Return to refrigerator.
Sweet Basil Oregano White Pepper Garlic, minced French Dressing (p. 258)	½ tsp. ½ tsp. ¼ tsp. ¼ tsp. 1 qt.	3. Mix spices and garlic with Basic French Dressing. Just before service time, toss salad lightly with dressing to coat all greens thoroughly. 4. Serve in salad bowl or on chilled salad plate.
See color picture, p. 226.		

Chinese Cabbage Salad

YIELD: 50 portions		EACH PORTION: about 3 oz.
INGREDIENTS	*QUANTITY*	*METHOD*
Chinese Cabbage	9 lb.	1. Split, wash and clean Chinese cabbage. 2. Shred in ¼ in. slices cut crosswise. 3. Arrange on chilled salad plate.
Scallions, chopped French Dressing (p. 258)	3 bunches 1½ qt.	4. Garnish with chopped scallions, including green portion. Serve with French dressing.
NOTE: Cabbage may be tossed with dressing prior to service and finished with scallion garnish.		

Salad Del Monte

YIELD: 50 portions		EACH PORTION: 3 oz. asparagus
INGREDIENTS	*QUANTITY*	*METHOD*
Asparagus, cooked, drained, chilled Lettuce, washed and trimmed Pimientoes	10 lb. 4 heads 1 7-oz. can	1. Arrange asparagus on crisp lettuce or lettuce cups. 2. Decorate with thin strips of pimiento placed diagonally across asparagus.
Hard Cooked Eggs, chopped Parsley, chopped French Dressing (p. 258)	12 1 oz. 1¼ qt.	3. Sprinkle with chopped, hard cooked eggs mixed with chopped fresh parsley. 4. Serve with French dressing.

Mikado Salad

YIELD: 50 portions		EACH PORTION: about 3 oz.
INGREDIENTS	*QUANTITY*	*METHOD*
Rice, raw	2 lb.	1. Cook rice, cool and drain well.
Frozen Peas, cooked Pimientoes, small dice Onions, minced French Dressing (p. 258) Lettuce, washed, cleaned and trimmed	2 lb. 1 7-oz. can 4 oz. about 1 qt. 4 heads	2. Combine all ingredients and chill for at least 1 hr. 3. Portion with No. 16 ice cream scoop, packed firmly. Serve on bed of lettuce.
Watercress	for garnish	4. May be garnished with watercress if desired.
See color picture, p. 226.		

Salads

Chef's Salad with Julienne of Turkey, Ham and Swiss Cheese (recipe below)

Green Bean and Pimiento Salad (recipe top of facing page)

Chef's Salad with Julienne of Turkey, Ham and Swiss Cheese

YIELD: 1 portion		
INGREDIENTS	*QUANTITY*	*METHOD*
Mixed Greens (escarole, romaine, chicory), chopped Turkey, white meat, julienne Ham, julienne Swiss Cheese, julienne Tomato Wedges or Slices	1 pt. ¾ oz. ¾ oz. ¾ oz. 4	1. Place mixed greens in salad bowl. 2. Arrange julienne meat, cheese and tomato wedges over greens.
Blue Cheese, crumbled Watercress French Dressing (p. 258)	1 oz. 1 spray 2 oz.	3. Sprinkle with blue cheese. Place generous bouquet of watercress in center of salad. 4. Serve French dressing in sauce boat on side.
See color picture, p. 228.		

Devilled Egg Salad

YIELD: 50 portions	EACH PORTION: 2 halves on lettuce leaf	
INGREDIENTS	*QUANTITY*	*METHOD*
Hard Cooked Eggs Mustard, dry Worcestershire Sauce Salt Mayonnaise (p. 260)	50 1 tbsp. 1 tsp. ½ tsp. 12 oz.	1. Chill and peel eggs. Slice in half lengthwise and remove yolks. Mash or put through sieve, and combine with all ingredients except lettuce. 2. Mix to smooth paste stiff enough to hold shape when used with pastry bag. Adjust seasoning and consistency. With pastry bag and large star tube, fill cavity of whites of eggs with egg yolk mixture.
Lettuce, washed, cleaned and trimmed Parsley	4 heads for garnish	3. For each portion arrange 2 halves on lettuce leaf and garnish with parsley sprig.

Green Bean and Pimiento Salad

YIELD: 50 portions		EACH PORTION: 3 oz.
INGREDIENTS	QUANTITY	METHOD
Frozen Green Beans	7½ lb.	1. Cook frozen green beans in boiling salted water. 2. Cool thoroughly and drain well.
Onions, finely minced Pimientoes, drained, chopped fine Garlic, finely minced French Dressing (p. 258) Lettuce, washed, cleaned, trimmed	½ lb. 1 7 oz. can 1 tsp. 1 qt. 4 heads	3. Mix all ingredients except lettuce and marinate for at least 1 hr. 4. At service time, drain well and serve on bed of lettuce or lettuce cup on chilled salad plate.

See color picture, p. 225.

Lettuce and Tomato Salad

YIELD: 50 portions		EACH PORTION: 3 tomato slices on lettuce cup with mayonnaise
INGREDIENTS	QUANTITY	METHOD
Tomatoes, ripe, clean Lettuce, washed, cleaned, trimmed Mayonnaise (p. 260) Parsley	9 lb. 4 lb. 1 qt. for garnish	1. Slice tomatoes thinly. 2. Separate lettuce leaves, making as many lettuce cups as possible. Place lettuce portions on cold salad plates. 3. Place 3 slices of tomato, overlapping each other on lettuce base. 4. Dress with 1 tbsp. of mayonnaise for each portion and garnish with sprig of fresh parsley.

NOTE: Portions may be placed on sheet pans and held under refrigeration. They may be plated just prior to service. Do not dress until service time.

See color picture, p. 226.

Antipasto

YIELD: 10 portions		
INGREDIENTS	QUANTITY	METHOD
Lettuce, washed, cleaned, trimmed	1 head	1. Place crisp lettuce cup on chilled salad plate. 2. Shred ¼ cup lettuce and place in center.
Tuna, drained Genoa Salami, sliced Rose Radishes Anchovy Fillet, flat Provalone Cheese, sliced Ripe Olives Celery, pieces or hearts Pimientoes Parsley Oil and Vinegar	1 6½ oz. can 5 oz. 10 10 5 oz. 10 10 pieces 10 strips 10 sprigs to taste	3. Place tuna on shredded lettuce. Arrange remainder of ingredients on lettuce around tuna. In arranging, remember to contrast colors and shapes. 4. Antipasto may be dressed with oil and vinegar or oil and vinegar may be served separately.

NOTE: There are many varied antipasti. The above recipe entails minimum labor and expense while still providing a refreshing and appetizing dish. It is also well suited for quantity production.

For individual service, larger portions and more varied ingredients may be used such as marinated vegetables and other fish and meats. Dressings are nearly always served on the side. Olive oil and wine vinegar (not mixed) are often preferred.

Salads

Tomato Andalouse (recipe below)

Pickled Beet Salad (recipe top of facing page)

Tomato Andalouse

YIELD: 50 portions	EACH PORTION: 1 filled tomato	
INGREDIENTS	*QUANTITY*	*METHOD*
Tomatoes, medium	50	1. Peel tomatoes. Cut off top slice and carefully hollow out tomatoes, reserving pulp for other use.
Celery, julienne Mayonnaise Lettuce, washed, cleaned and trimmed Parsley	2 lb. to moisten celery 4 heads to garnish	2. Mix julienne of celery lightly with enough mayonnaise to moisten. 3. Fill tomato with celery mixture. 4. Serve tomato in crisp lettuce cup, garnish with sprig of parsley.
NOTE: Tomatoes may be cut in quarters almost to bottom and then filled, as in photograph.		
See color picture, p. 229.		

Danish Cucumber Salad

YIELD: 50 portions	EACH PORTION: 3½ oz.	
INGREDIENTS	*QUANTITY*	*METHOD*
Cucumbers Salt Turmeric Water Vinegar	8 lb. 2 tbsp. 2 tsp. 1 qt. 1 qt.	1. Peel cucumbers. Slice about 1/8 in. thick on bias. 2. Mix salt and turmeric until smooth in stainless steel bowl. 3. Add water and vinegar. 4. Add cucumbers and mix well. Refrigerate for 2 to 3 hr., turning over occasionally.
Raisins Sour Cream Onions, grated, with juice Parsley, chopped fine Mayonnaise (p. 260) Lettuce, washed, cleaned, trimmed	½ lb. 1 qt. 2 tbsp. 2 tbsp. 1 pt. 4 heads	5. Plump raisins in hot water, cool, drain well. 6. Combine sour cream, onions and juice, parsley and mayonnaise. 7. Arrange 3 to 4 drained cucumber slices in lettuce cup. 8. Top with generous teaspoon dressing and sprinkle with raisins.

Pickled Beet Salad

YIELD: 50 portions	EACH PORTION: 3 oz.	
INGREDIENTS	*QUANTITY*	*METHOD*
Onion Rings, sliced thinly Beets, sliced Vinegar, cider Salt Sugar, granulated Mixed Pickling Spices in cheesecloth bag Whole Cloves Water, cold (see Step. 3)	1½ lb. 1½ No. 10 cans 8¼ oz. 1 tbsp. 4 oz. 1 tbsp. 6 to cover	1. Combine onions, beets and beet juice 2. Mix vinegar, salt and sugar. Stir until sugar and salt are dissolved. 3. Pour over beets; add spices. Add water to cover if necessary. Marinate overnight.
Lettuce, washed, cleaned and trimmed Parsley	4 heads for garnish	4. Drain well before serving. 5. Serve in lettuce cup with some of onions on top. Garnish with fresh parsley sprig.

NOTE: Julienne beets may also be used. Salad may be made several days ahead. Remove spice bag after first day. Make sure beets remain covered.

See color picture, p. 225.

Garden Salad

YIELD: 50 portions	EACH PORTION: about 4 oz. and dressing	
INGREDIENTS	*QUANTITY*	*METHOD*
Lettuce) Chicory) Variable, depending on Escarole) quality and availability Cucumbers Radishes Carrots (optional) Celery Red Onions	2 lb. 3 lb. 3 lb. 3 lb. 2 bunches 12 oz. ½ bunch 1 lb.	1. Clean, wash, drain and crisp all greens 2. Score cucumbers with a fork, cut in half lengthwise and slice thinly across. Peel cucumbers if waxed. 3. Wash and clean radishes. Slice thinly. 4. Scrub carrots and shred medium on grater. 5. Wash and peel celery. Slice thinly across on bias. 6. Peel red onions. Cut in half. Slice very thin. 7. Cut tomato wedges.
Tomatoes, washed, stems removed Emulsified French Dressing (p. 258)	9 1½ qt.	8. After crisping, combine all ingredients except tomatoes and dressing. 9. Place portion of salad in bowl, dress with Emulsified French Dressing and top with tomato wedge. Dressing may be mixed with salad if serving immediately. Green pepper rings may be used as garnish.

Carrot and Raisin Salad

YIELD: 50 portions	EACH PORTION: about 4 oz.	
INGREDIENTS	*QUANTITY*	*METHOD*
Raisins Water Sugar Salt Lemon Juice	1½ lb. 1 qt. 2 tbsp. 1 tsp. from 1 lemon	1. Combine first 5 ingredients. Cover and simmer 3 to 4 min. Remove from heat and let stand until raisins are plump. Drain well and cool.
Carrots, raw, peeled, shredded Mayonnaise (p. 260) French Dressing (p. 258) Lettuce, washed, cleaned, trimmed Watercress	8 lb. 1 pt. 1 pt. 4 heads for garnish	2. Combine carrots, raisins and blended mayonnaise and French dressing. 3. Serve in lettuce cups with watercress garnish.

See color picture, p. 225.

Salads

Crabmeat Salad in Avocado (recipe below)　　　　　　*Macaroni and Ham Salad (recipe top of facing page)*

Crabmeat Salad in Avocado

YIELD: 20 portions		EACH PORTION: ½ stuffed avocado
INGREDIENTS	*QUANTITY*	*METHOD*
Crabmeat Celery, chopped Mayonnaise Lemon Juice Salt White Pepper	4 lb. 2 lb. about 1 pt. 2 tsp. 1/2 tsp. 1/8 tsp.	1. Clean crabmeat and mix with celery, mayonnaise, lemon juice, salt and pepper. Adjust seasoning if necessary.
Avocados, ripe Grapefruit Juice 　OR Other Acid Medium Lettuce, cleaned, trimmed, crisp Pimientoes Watercress 　OR Parsley	10 6 oz. 2 heads 1 3-3/4 oz. can for garnish	2. Cut avocados in half lengthwise. Trim slightly on bottom to prevent tipping over. Remove stone and dip avocado halves in grapefruit juice or other acid medium to prevent discoloration. 3. Drain well and place on lettuce bed on chilled plate. Place about 5 oz. crabmeat mixture in each avocado half. Garnish with thin strip of pimiento and sprig of parsley or spray of watercress.
NOTE: **Salad** may be further garnished with grapefruit sections and green pepper rings if desired. 　　Salad may be served with saratoga chips or other crisp food, such as potato sticks. Varied types of pickles are also good accompaniment for this dish.		

Hearts of Lettuce

YIELD: 50 portions		EACH PORTION: 3 oz. wedge with dressing
INGREDIENTS	*QUANTITY*	*METHOD*
Lettuce, washed, cleaned, 　trimmed, core intact Thousand Island Dressing (p. 260)	8 lb. 2½ qt.	1. Cut lettuce in 3 oz. wedges, leaving core in to hold lettuce together. 2. Place on cold salad plate and dress with 1½ oz. of Thousand Island dressing.
See color picture, p. 224.		

Macaroni and Ham Salad

YIELD: 50 portions		EACH PORTION: about 5 oz.
INGREDIENTS	*QUANTITY*	*METHOD*
Elbow Macaroni, raw	3 lb.	1. Cook macaroni, drain well.
Ham, cooked, julienne Celery, diced Pimientoes, diced Green Peppers, diced, blanched Onions, chopped fine Lettuce, washed, cleaned, trimmed French Dressing (p. 258)	1½ lb. 1½ lb. 7 oz. 6 oz. 4 oz. 4 heads about 2 qt.	2. Have all ingredients well chilled. 3. Combine all ingredients with French Dressing. 4. Refrigerate for one-half hour before serving. 5. Drain well. Serve in lettuce cup.

NOTE: A small amount of garlic may be incorporated in French Dressing for additional flavor.

See color picture, p. 229.

Potato Salad

YIELD: 50 portions		EACH PORTION: 4½ oz.
INGREDIENTS	*QUANTITY*	*METHOD*
Celery, diced fine Onions, minced Hard Cooked Eggs, chopped medium Pimientoes, diced, drained Mayonnaise (p. 260)	1½ lb. 3 oz. 8 1 7 oz. can about 1 qt.	1. Combine first 5 ingredients and refrigerate 2 to 3 hr. or overnight if possible.
Potatoes, A.P. French Dressing (p. 258) Salt Pepper Lettuce, washed, cleaned and trimmed	12 lb. 5 oz. to taste to taste 4 heads	2. Peel and cut potatoes in ¾ in. cubes. Boil until nearly tender. Keep slightly undercooked. Place pot of potatoes in sink and let cold water run in until potatoes are cool enough to handle, but still warm. 3. Drain very well and toss with French dressing and small amount of salt and pepper. Let stand until cool enough to combine with mayonnaise mixture. 4. Combine all ingredients and adjust seasoning if necessary. 5. Serve in lettuce cup.

NOTE: Potatoes will crush somewhat when mixing. It is important that they are not overcooked to prevent complete masking. Consistency may be adjusted as required.

Belgian Endive

YIELD: 50 portions		
INGREDIENTS	*QUANTITY*	*METHOD*
Belgian Endive	50 pieces	1. Clean and prepare endive. 2. Drain well and refrigerate. Endive must be dry. 3. Cut endive in half lengthwise and arrange both halves cut side up on chilled salad plate.
Pimientoes Blue Cheese Dressing (p. 259)	1 7 oz. can about 2 qt.	4. Garnish with thin strip of pimiento placed diagonally across one end. 5. Dress with 1 oz. of Blue Cheese dressing at opposite end.

Salads

Chiffonade Salad

YIELD: 50 portions		EACH PORTION: 3½ oz.
INGREDIENTS	*QUANTITY*	*METHOD*
Lettuce, washed, cleaned, trimmed	4 heads	1. Line bowl or salad plate with lettuce.
Romaine Chicory Celery Tomatoes Chiffonade Dressing (p.257) Watercress	3 lb. 2 lb. 2 bunches 5 lb. 1½ qt. for garnish	2. Break or cut bite size pieces of washed and cleaned chicory and romaine. 3. Cut julienne of celery in long and short strips. 4. Peel tomatoes and cut in eighths. 5. Place chicory, romaine and julienne of celery on lettuce. 6. Garnish with tomato wedges. Dress with Chiffonade Dressing. Watercress may also be used for garnish.

Stuffed Celery

YIELD: 50 portions		
INGREDIENTS	*QUANTITY*	*METHOD*
Cream Cheese Stuffed Olives, finely chopped, dry	2 lb. 4 oz.	1. Stir cream cheese until smooth. 2. Combine olives and cream cheese.
Celery, (cut in 3 in. pieces) washed Lettuce, washed, cleaned and trimmed	100 4 heads	3. Place celery on tray. 4. Place cream cheese and olive mixture in pastry bag with large star tube. Bag mixture into celery.
Pimientoes Parsley	1 7-oz. can for garnish	5. Line a salad plate with lettuce or lettuce cup and place 2 pieces of celery on top. 6. Garnish with one thin strip of pimiento placed diagonally across celery and sprig of parsley.

NOTE: Blended blue cheese and cream cheese or Roquefort cheese and cream cheese may also be used. Olive juice may be used to soften cream cheese.

Cole Slaw

YIELD: 50 portions		EACH PORTION: 3 oz.
INGREDIENTS	*QUANTITY*	*METHOD*
Cabbage, green, cleaned, trimmed, core out Carrots, finely shredded Onions, finely minced	7 lb. ¾ lb. 4 oz.	1. Shred cabbage very fine. Mix with carrots and onion.
Vinegar Salad Oil Sugar Mustard, dry Salt Cooked Dressing or Mayonnaise (p.260) Lettuce, washed, cleaned, trimmed	12¼ oz. 6 oz. 3 oz. 2 tsp. 1 oz. 1½ pt. 4 heads	2. Mix all other ingredients except lettuce and combine with cabbage mixture. 3. Toss lightly but mix well. 4. Chill thoroughly and serve in center of lettuce cup.

NOTE: For **Mixed Cabbage Slaw**, substitute 3½ lb. red cabbage for ½ the cabbage indicated in the recipe above.

See color picture, p. 226.

Hot German Slaw

YIELD: 50 portions	EACH PORTION: 3 oz.	
INGREDIENTS	QUANTITY	METHOD
Bacon, diced Vinegar, cider	1 lb. 8¼ oz.	1. Saute bacon until lightly browned. Add vinegar and bring to boil.
Cabbage, shredded, E.P. Onions, minced Sugar Salt (variable) Pepper	7 lb. 1 lb. 4 oz. 1 tbsp. ½ tsp.	2. Add bacon mixture to cabbage and onions. 3. Add seasonings and adjust if necessary. 4. Mix well and serve immediately.

Hot German Potato Salad No. 1

YIELD: 50 portions	EACH PORTION: 4½ oz.	
INGREDIENTS	QUANTITY	METHOD
Potatoes, A.P.	12 lb.	1. Cook potatoes in their jackets. Peel and dice while still hot.
Bacon, chopped, raw	1 lb.	2. Fry bacon until crisp.
Vinegar Stock Celery, diced fine Onions, mild, diced fine Parsley, chopped Pepper	8 oz. about 1½ pt. 1 lb. 12 oz. 1 oz. ½ tsp.	3. Combine and heat vinegar and stock. 4. Combine all ingredients. Allow to stand for ½ hr. before serving. 5. May be served hot or cold.
NOTE: Salad seldom requires salt as bacon usually provides enough.		

Hot German Potato Salad No. 2

YIELD: 50 portions	EACH PORTION: 4 ½ oz.	
INGREDIENTS	QUANTITY	METHOD
Potatoes, A.P.	12 lb.	1. Cook potatoes in their jackets. Peel and dice or slice while still hot.
Bacon, chopped, raw Celery, diced fine Onions, mild, diced fine Bread Flour	1 lb. 1 lb. 12 oz. variable	2. Fry bacon until half done. Add celery and onions and finish cooking bacon. 3. Add enough flour to pick up excess grease. Cook for 2 to 3 min.
Vinegar, hot Stock, hot Pepper Parsley, chopped	8 oz. about 1½ pt. ½ tsp. 1 oz.	4. Add hot vinegar and stock gradually, stirring until smooth and thickened. Consistency should be like heavy cream. Adjust if necessary. Add pepper. 5. Combine with potatoes and let stand ½ hr. before serving. May be served hot or cold. Sprinkle with chopped parsley.
NOTE: Salad seldom requires salt as bacon usually provides enough.		

Salads

Kidney Bean Salad

YIELD: 50 portions	EACH PORTION: about 4 oz.	
INGREDIENTS	*QUANTITY*	*METHOD*
Kidney Beans, drained	2 No. 10 cans	1. Drain beans well.

Hard Cooked Eggs
Pickles, sweet or dill, A.P.,
    small dice
Celery, small dice
Onions, chopped fine
Pimientoes
Salt
White Pepper
Mayonnaise
    OR Cooked Dressing
    (p. 260)
	2 doz.
	1 qt.
	
	1 qt.
	4 oz.
	1 7 oz. can
	to taste
	to taste
	to bind
		2. Slice a sufficient number of eggs to provide 50 slices for garnish. Reserve.
		3. Chop balance of eggs. Combine chopped eggs and all other ingredients except egg slices. Mix with mayonnaise to bind. Chill thoroughly.

Lettuce, washed, cleaned, trimmed Parsley	4 heads for garnish	4. Serve in crisp lettuce cup with sprig of fresh parsley and slice of egg for garnish.

Tomato and Cucumber Salad

YIELD: 50 portions	EACH PORTION: about 3 oz.	
INGREDIENTS	*QUANTITY*	*METHOD*
Tomatoes, washed, stems removed Cucumbers, washed Lettuce, washed, crisped Parsley	7 lb. 6 4 heads for garnish	1. Slice tomatoes. 2. Score cucumbers lengthwise with tines of dinner fork. If cucumbers are waxed or old, peel first. Slice cucumbers on bias about 1/8 in. thick. 3. Arrange 2 slices each tomatoes and cucumbers alternately on lettuce bed. 4. Serve with appropriate dressing and garnish with fresh parsley.

Vegetable Salad a la Russe

YIELD: 50 portions	EACH PORTION: about 4 oz.	
INGREDIENTS	*QUANTITY*	*METHOD*
Carrots, cooked Green Beans, cooked Kidney Beans, canned, drained Green Peas, cooked Celery, diced Pimientoes, diced Lima Beans, baby, cooked	2 lb., A.P. 2 lb., A.P. 2 No. 303 cans 2½ lb. 1 lb. 1 7 oz. can. 2½ lb.	1. Dice carrots. 2. Cut string beans in ¾ in. pieces. 3. Drain kidney beans well. 4. Combine all ingredients except mayonnaise. Chill thoroughly.
Mayonnaise (p. 260) Lettuce, washed, cleaned, trimmed	to bind, about 1½ qt. 4 heads	5. Mix vegetables with mayonnaise lightly as needed. Season to taste. Serve in lettuce cup.

NOTE: Other vegetable combinations may be used. Vegetables must not be overcooked. Use only sufficient mayonnaise to bind.

Tomato Stuffed with Tuna Salad

YIELD: 20 portions	EACH PORTION: 1 stuffed tomato	
INGREDIENTS	*QUANTITY*	*METHOD*

Tuna, canned, drained
    and broken up
Celery, diced, E.P.
Mayonnaise (p. 260)
Lemon Juice
Salt
Pepper
	4 lb., 2 oz.
	    can
	2 lb.
	about 1½ pt.
	from ½ lemon
	to taste
	to taste
		1. Combine other ingredients and part of mayonnaise. Add mayonnaise until of proper consistency.

Tomatoes, medium, washed Lettuce, cleaned, trimmed, crisp Watercress OR Parsley	20 2 heads for garnish	2. Remove stem of tomato with small sharp knife. Cut 6 to 9 equal sections (depending on size of tomato) three-quarters through tomato from top of stem end to bottom. Do not cut all the way through. 3. Press sections outward from one another slightly to accommodate salad, filling between each section and in middle. Keep salad flush with tomato edges and wipe if necessary, so that attached tomato wedges are distinct. 4. Place in crisp lettuce cup and garnish with fresh parsley sprig or watercress. Carrot curls, celery sticks, radish roses or fluted cucumbers may also be used.
NOTE: Tomatoes may be peeled prior to use by dipping for a few seconds in boiling water or holding over a hot flame. The skins will peel easily with a sharp knife. Prolonged heating will make tomato soft from partial cooking. Refrigerate tomatoes after peeling so that they will be chilled for service. Various salad fillings may be used.		

Cucumber and Onion Salad

YIELD: 50 portions	EACH PORTION: about 3½ oz.	
INGREDIENTS	*QUANTITY*	*METHOD*
Cucumbers, peeled Onions, peeled	8 lb. 2½ lb.	1. Slice cucumbers and onions paper thin.
Sugar Salt Pepper Vinegar, cider Water, cold Salad Oil	4 oz. 2 tbsp. 2 tsp. 1 qt. 1 pt. 1 pt.	2. Dissolve spices in vinegar and add water and oil, mixing well. 3. Pour over cucumbers and onions, mixing thoroughly. Marinate for 1 hr. and chill thoroughly.
Lettuce, washed, cleaned, trimmed Parsley	4 heads for garnish	4. At service time, drain and place on lettuce leaf. Garnish with parsley sprig.
See color picture, p. 226.		

Salads

Cottage Cheese Jubilee Salad

YIELD: 50 portions		EACH PORTION: 2 oz. and dressing
INGREDIENTS	QUANTITY	METHOD
Cottage Cheese Celery, diced fine Maraschino Cherries, chopped Carrots, raw, peeled, shredded	5 lb. 12 oz. 4 oz. 8 oz.	1. Combine all ingredients except lettuce, dressing and watercress. Add small amount of milk or cream if necessary to moisten.
Lettuce, washed, cleaned, trimmed Honey Lemon Dressing (p. 257) Watercress	about 4 heads about 1½ qt. for garnish	2. Place cottage cheese mixture in crisp lettuce cup using No. 16 ice cream scoop. 3. Serve with 1 tbsp. Honey Lemon Dressing. 4. Garnish with spray of fresh watercress.

See color picture, p. 225.

Avocado Grapefruit Salad

YIELD: 50 portions		
INGREDIENTS	QUANTITY	METHOD
Grapefruit, whole, medium Avocados, ripe	12 6	1. Peel and section grapefruit, removing white membrane. Reserve juice. 2. Cut avocado in half lengthwise. Remove seed and peel. Cut thin slices across and dip in grapefruit juice to prevent discoloration of avocado.
Lettuce, whole, medium, washed, cleaned and trimmed Pimientoes French Dressing (p. 258)	4 heads 1 7 oz. can 1 qt.	3. Alternate avocado and grapefruit sections on lettuce leaf, using 2 grapefruit sections and 3 slices of avocado. 4. Garnish with thin strip of pimiento placed diagonally across salad. 5. At service time, dress with 1 tbsp. dressing.

Summer Fresh Fruit Salad Bowl

YIELD: 6 portions		
INGREDIENTS	QUANTITY	METHOD
Oranges (Cal. No. 126), pared and sliced	9	1. Peel oranges and slice crosswise.
Fresh Pears, washed, cut in quarters, unpeeled Fresh Peaches, washed, peeled, cut in halves Romaine, washed, cleaned, trimmed Red Raspberries Chicory, washed, cleaned, trimmed	3 3 2 heads 1½ pt. 1 head	2. Hold cut pears and peaches in grapefruit or pineapple juice. 3. Place romaine in salad bowl and arrange orange slices, peach half, raspberries and pear quarters with chicory garnishing.

NOTE: Salad may be topped with lemon or orange sherbet.

Many variations of fresh fruit salad bowls and salad plates may be prepared utilizing fresh fruits in season. Other colorful and appetite-stimulating salads may be prepared utilizing canned or frozen fruits.

For a popular main-course **Summer Fresh Fruit Salad Plate** for individual service, use pineapple wedge; slices of cored, unpeeled, red-skinned apple; orange or grapefruit segments or slices; bananas, and melons in season. Garnish with frosted grapes, fresh sweet cherries or fresh berries. Cottage cheese or sherbet provide a nutritive and satisfying addition to this salad. Salad may be garnished with watercress or fresh mint.

YIELD: 50 portions	EACH PORTION: 5½ oz.	
INGREDIENTS	QUANTITY	METHOD
Orange Sections Grapefruit, diced Pineapple, fresh, diced Grapes, seeded, washed Apples, peeled, diced	2 qt. 2 qt. 2 qt. 1 qt. 1 qt.	1. Drain all fruits well and mix together.
Mayonnaise OR Cooked Dressing (p. 260) Whipped Cream	8 oz. 1 pt.	2. Immediately prior to service, combine mayonnaise and whipped cream. Blend with fruits.
Lettuce, washed, cleaned, trimmed Fresh Mint Berries	4 heads to garnish to garnish	3. Serve in lettuce cup and garnish with fresh mint, berries or other appropriate fruit in season.

NOTE: Various fruit combinations may be used. A small amount of sugar may be added to whipped cream if desired.

See color picture, p. 224.

Banana Nut Salad

YIELD: 50 portions	EACH PORTION: ½ banana	
INGREDIENTS	QUANTITY	METHOD
Bananas Acid Fruit Juice	25 to cover	1. Peel bananas and cut in half crosswise. Dip in fruit juice.
Mayonnaise (p. 260) Walnuts, chopped fine	2 qt. 1½ lb.	2. Shake dry and dip in mayonnaise. 3. Roll in finely chopped nuts.
Lettuce, washed, cleaned and trimmed Maraschino Cherries Watercress	4 heads 50 halves to garnish	4. Place on lettuce cup and garnish with maraschino cherry cut in petals like a flower. 5. Place cherry on center of banana with piece of watercress alongside.

NOTE: Equal portions of mayonnaise and whipped cream may be used in place of straight mayonnaise.

See color picture, p. 225.

Blackstone Salad

YIELD: 50 portions		
INGREDIENTS	QUANTITY	METHOD
Oranges Grapefruit Apples, cored Celery Green Peppers, chopped fine Mayonnaise (p. 260)	24 8 3 lb. 1½ lb. 1 lb. to bind	1. Pare and section oranges and grapefruit. 2. Partly peel apples, leaving red skin for color. 3. Chop grapefruit, apples, celery and green peppers. 4. Bind with very small amount of mayonnaise.
Romaine, washed and trimmed Green Pepper Slices Pimientoes	3 heads 1 lb. 1 7 oz. can	5. Spread evenly in 1½ in. wide strip in center of a romaine leaf. 6. Place orange sections on top in a row. 7. Alternate green peppers and pimientoes between orange sections.

YIELD: 50 portions		
INGREDIENTS	QUANTITY	METHOD
Oranges, whole Grapefruit, whole, medium	18 12	1. Pare oranges and grapefruit. Remove white membrane and cut in sections. 2. Save all orange and grapefruit juice for preparation of dressing.
Lettuce, washed, cleaned, trimmed	4 heads	3. Separate lettuce leaves, making as many lettuce cups as possible. 4. Place fruit sections on lettuce bed, alternating fruits and using 2 sections each kind.
Pimientoes, drained Fruit French Dressing (p. 259)	1 7 oz. can 1½ qt.	5. Cut pimientoes in strips and garnish each salad with strip of pimiento placed diagonally across fruit. 6. At service time, garnish with 1 oz. Fruit French Dressing.
See color picture, p. 225.		

Stuffed Prune Salad

YIELD: 50 portions	EACH PORTION: 2 prunes	
INGREDIENTS	QUANTITY	METHOD
Prunes, medium-large, cooked	100	1. Pit prunes.
Cream Cheese Peanut Butter	1½ lb. 4 oz.	2. Blend cream cheese and peanut butter until consistency for bagging. Use small amount of milk or cream if necessary. 3. Place mixture in pastry bag with star tube. Bag mixture into each prune finishing with rosette on top.
Lettuce, washed, cleaned, trimmed Maraschino Cherries, quartered	4 heads 25	4. For each portion, arrange 2 prunes on lettuce bed. 5. Garnish each prune with 1 cherry quarter. 6. Serve with Fruit French Dressing (p. 259) or French Dressing (p. 258).
See color picture, p. 228.		

Salad Alma

YIELD: 50 portions		
INGREDIENTS	QUANTITY	METHOD
Oranges Grapefruit Avocados Pimientoes Green Peppers Romaine, washed, trimmed Pickled Walnuts (variable) French Dressing (p. 258)	18 12 6 1 7 oz. can 1½ lb. about 3 heads 1 jar. 1½ qt.	1. Pare and section oranges and grapefruit. Save juice for Step 2. 2. Cut avocado in half and remove stone. Peel and slice in half moon shape. Dip in citrus juices to prevent avocado from discoloring. 3. Clean peppers and cut in thin strips. 4. On a leaf of romaine, alternate 2 pieces of orange, grapefruit and avocado. Place 1 strip each of pimiento and green pepper crossed on top of fruit. 5. Garnish with 2 slices of pickled walnuts at the end. Serve with French Dressing.
NOTE: Sweet red peppers may be substituted for pimientoes when available.		

YIELD: 50 portions		
INGREDIENTS	QUANTITY	METHOD
Lettuce, washed, cleaned, trimmed Pineapple Slices Cottage Cheese French Dressing (p. 258)	4 heads 50 3 lb. 1½ qt.	1. Separate lettuce leaves, making as many lettuce cups as possible. Place lettuce portions on cold salad plates. 2. Place slice of pineapple in center of each lettuce portion. 3. Place small spoonful (about 1 oz.) cottage cheese in center of each pineapple slice. 4. Dress with 1 oz. of French Dressing. Garnish with watercress if available. Maraschino cherries or pimientoes may also be used.
See color picture, p. 228.		

Diplomat Salad

YIELD: 50 portions	EACH PORTION: about 2½ oz.	
INGREDIENTS	QUANTITY	METHOD
Apples Celery Pineapple, drained weight Mayonnaise (p. 260) Lettuce, washed and trimmed Walnuts, chopped	3½ lb. 1½ lb. 1½ lb. to bind 4 heads 8 oz.	1. Peel apples, leaving red part of skin. Core, dice and marinate in salted ice water or acid juice. 2. Dice celery and pineapple finer than apples. 3. Drain apples well. Dry on clean towel. 4. Combine with mayonnaise to bind. 5. Place individual portions of mixture in lettuce cup. Garnish with chopped walnuts.
NOTE: Apples, celery and pineapple may be julienned. Additional mayonnaise may be bagged on top of salad as part of garnish. If fresh pineapple is used, soak in sugared water overnight.		

Pineapple-Raisin Waldorf Salad

YIELD: 50 portions	EACH PORTION: 2 oz.	
INGREDIENTS	QUANTITY	METHOD
Apples	3½ lb.	1. Pare washed apples partially, leaving portion of red skin. 2. Core and dice. Place in salted cold water or acid juice to prevent discoloration. Juice from canned pineapple may be used.
Raisins	12 oz.	3. Plump raisins in steamer or in hot water. Drain well and dry on clean towels. All ingredients must be dry.
Celery, diced fine Pineapple, canned, diced drained weight Mayonnaise (p. 260)	1½ lb. 12 oz. to bind about 1 pt.	4. Combine apples, raisins, celery and pineapple. Mix with mayonnaise to bind.
Lettuce, washed, cleaned, trimmed Walnuts, chopped	4 heads 8 oz.	5. Serve in lettuce cups and garnish with chopped walnuts.
NOTE: Other fruits may be used for Waldorf variations. Walnut halves may also be used for garnish.		

YIELD: 50 portions	EACH PORTION: ½ pear with 1 oz. cottage cheese and dressing	
INGREDIENTS	QUANTITY	METHOD
Lettuce, washed, cleaned, trimmed Pear Halves Cottage Cheese French Dressing (p. 258)	4 heads 50 3 lb. 1 qt.	1. Separate lettuce leaves and make as many lettuce cups as possible. 2. Drain pear halves and place one for each portion, cut side up, on lettuce leaf. Place small spoonful of cottage cheese on each pear half. 3. Dress with 1 tbsp. dressing and garnish with watercress, if available. Maraschino cherries or pimientoes may also be used for garnish.

Fruit Slaw

YIELD: 50 portions	EACH PORTION: 3 oz.	
INGREDIENTS	QUANTITY	METHOD
Oranges, A.P. Pineapple, diced, drained French Dressing (p. 258) Raisins, washed, plumped and cooled Cabbage, shredded Lettuce, washed, cleaned, trimmed	8 2 No. 303 cans 1 pt. 12 oz. 7 lb. 4 heads	1. Peel and dice oranges. 2. Reserve pineapple and orange juice and add to French dressing. 3. Combine all ingredients except dressing and lettuce. Mix well and chill. 4. Just before serving, toss lightly with dressing. Serve in lettuce cup on chilled salad plate.
See color picture, p. 226.		

Waldorf Salad

YIELD: 50 portions	EACH PORTION: 3 oz.	
INGREDIENTS	QUANTITY	METHOD
Apples, eating, A.P.	7 lb.	1. Wash and pare apples partially, leaving portion of red skin intact. Quarter and core apples and cut into ½ in. cubes. Place apples in cold salted water to prevent discoloration. Fruit juice or other acids may be used to prevent discoloration. Drain well and dry in clean towels.
Celery, large dice Mayonnaise (p. 260) Lettuce, washed, cleaned, trimmed	2 lb. 1 pt. 4 heads	2. Combine with celery and 1 pt. mayonnaise and chill. 3. Serve on lettuce bed.
Mayonnaise Walnuts, coarsely chopped	8 oz. 8 oz.	4. Dress each serving with 1 tsp. of mayonnaise and chopped walnuts.
See color picture, p. 229.		

Mandarin Orange Waldorf

YIELD: 50 portions	EACH PORTION: 3 oz.	
INGREDIENTS	QUANTITY	METHOD
Waldorf Salad Mandarin Oranges, drained Lettuce, washed, cleaned, trimmed	50 portions 1 No. 2½ can 4 heads	1. Prepare Waldorf Salad according to recipe above, omitting walnuts and mayonnaise garnish. 2. Place Waldorf Salad on lettuce leaf, and use 2 sections of mandarin orange to garnish top of each portion.
See color picture, p. 226.		

Drain bing cherries and hold on clean towels. Soften cream cheese with a small amount of milk or cream, add almond extract to taste. Bag cream cheese mixture into cherries.

Place the bing cherries which have been filled with cream cheese mixture and finished with a rosette on top in the pear halves, one cherry for each pear half.

Drain pear halves, reserving syrup to chill for dressing; turn upside down on clean towels or paper towels. Arrange the pear halves cup side up in crisp lettuce cups.

Dress each serving with 1 oz. of the combined pear syrup and orange juice just before service. Garnish with watercress sprigs. Salad plates should be well chilled.

Bing Cherry and Pear Salad

YIELD: 50 portions		EACH PORTION: 1 pear half with cherry and juice
INGREDIENTS	*QUANTITY*	*METHOD*
Bing Cherries, pitted	50	1. Drain bing cherries and hold on clean towels. 2. Reserve juice for other use.
Cream Cheese Almond Extract Milk or Cream	1½ lb. to taste to soften cheese	3. Soften cream cheese using almond extract to taste and small amount milk or cream.
Canned Pear Halves Orange Juice Lettuce, washed, cleaned and trimmed Watercress	50 about 1 pt. 4 heads for garnish	4. Drain pear halves, reserving syrup, and turn upside down on clean towels. 5. Combine pear syrup and orange juice; chill. 6. Place cream cheese mixture in pastry bag with star tube. 7. Stuff each cherry with cheese, finishing with good sized rosette on top. 8. Arrange pear halves cup side up in crisp lettuce cups. 9. Place stuffed bing cherry in each pear half. 10. Dress with 1 oz. chilled juices at service time. 11. Garnish with watercress.

YIELD: 50 portions		EACH PORTION: about 4 oz. and dressing
INGREDIENTS	QUANTITY	METHOD
Lime Gelatin Water	1½ lb. 1 gal.	1. Dissolve gelatin in ½ gal. of hot water. Add ½ gal. of cold water and mix well. Chill until slightly thickened.
Cucumbers, peeled and finely chopped Vinegar, cider Onions, minced fine Salt Lettuce, washed, cleaned, trimmed Sour Cream, whipped creamy	2½ lb. 4 oz. 4 tbsp. 2 tbsp. 4 heads 1 pt.	2. Marinate cucumbers, vinegar, onions and salt. 3. Fold into gelatin and pour in individual molds or hotel pan. Chill until firm. 4. Unmold or cut in desired size and serve on lettuce bed. Dress with 1 tsp. sour cream.

See color picture, p. 230.

Jellied Salad, Rubanne

YIELD: 50 portions		EACH PORTION: about 4 oz. and dressing
INGREDIENTS	QUANTITY	METHOD
Red Colored Gelatin (Raspberry, Cherry, Strawberry Flavors) Water Lemon Gelatin Water Orange Gelatin Water Lettuce, washed, cleaned, trimmed Mayonnaise OR Fruit Salad Dressing	12 oz. ½ gal. 12 oz. ½ gal. 12 oz. ½ gal. 4 heads 1½ qt.	1. Mix flavored gelatins separately, using ½ hot water and ½ cold water. 2. Fill molds or pans 1/3 full with red gelatin. Chill until firm. 3. Chill lemon gelatin until beginning to set. When red gelatin is firm, pour lemon gelatin over it. 4. Chill orange gelatin until beginning to set. When lemon gelatin is firm, pour orange gelatin over it. Refrigerate until firm. 5. Unmold or cut portions and serve in lettuce cup with mayonnaise (p. 260) or Fruit Salad Dressing (p. 258).

NOTE: Any combination of contrasting colors may be used.

Lime Pear Aspic

YIELD: 50 portions		
INGREDIENTS	QUANTITY	METHOD
Lime Gelatin Hot Water Cold Water (see Step 2)) Pear Juice from Pear Halves)	24 oz. ½ gal. to cool	1. Dissolve gelatin in hot water. 2. Add cold water to pear juice to make ½ gal. and add to gelatin mixture. 3. Pour enough in molds or pans to make layer ¼ in. thick. Chill until nearly set. 4. Chill remaining gelatin until partially set.
Pear Halves Maraschino Cherries Lettuce, washed, cleaned, trimmed	50 50 4 heads	5. Arrange pear halves cut side up on nearly firmed gelatin and place a Maraschino cherry in the center of each pear half. Refrigerate to firm so that pear halves will not be disarranged when pouring on balance of gelatin. 6. Pour over balance of gelatin and refrigerate until firm. 7. Unmold or cut so that each pear half is clear and even in each portion. Serve in lettuce cup with appropriate dressing but do not mask fruit.

See color picture, p. 230.

YIELD: 50 portions	EACH PORTION: about 4 oz.	
INGREDIENTS	QUANTITY	METHOD
Peaches, canned, sliced, including syrup Vinegar Sugar Stick Cinnamon Whole Cloves Orange Gelatin Water (see Steps 2 and 3) Salad Greens, washed, cleaned, trimmed	1¾ qt. 1 pt. 24 oz. 1½ oz. 1½ tbsp. 24 oz. to dissolve and cool 4 heads	1. Drain peaches, reserving syrup. Combine peach syrup, vinegar, sugar and spices. Simmer covered 10 min. 2. Strain and add hot water to juice to make ½ gal. 3. Dissolve gelatin in hot liquid, add ½ gal. cold water. 4. Chill until slightly thickened, fold in peaches. Pour into shallow pans. Chill until firm. Cut into squares. 5. Serve on crisp salad greens.

Jellied Bing Cherry Salad

YIELD: 50 portions		
INGREDIENTS	QUANTITY	METHOD
Bing Cherries, canned, whole, pitted Black Cherry Gelatin Hot Water (140° to 160°F.) Cold Water (see Step 1)	2 No. 2 cans 24 oz. ½ gal. as needed	1. Drain cherries, reserving liquid. Add cold water to cherry liquid to make ½ gal. 2. Dissolve gelatin in ½ gal. hot water. 3. Add ½ gal. cold liquid, stir well. Chill until slightly thickened. 4. Chop cherries and fold into thickened gelatin. Pour into individual molds or pans. Chill until firm.
Cream Cheese Milk OR Cream Lettuce, washed, cleaned, trimmed Watercress	2 lb. to soften cheese 4 heads for garnish	5. Soften cream cheese with small amount of milk or cream. Place in pastry bag with star tube. 6. When gelatin is firm, unmold or cut in portions and place in lettuce cup. 7. Bag out cream cheese rosette on each portion.
NOTE: Salad may be garnished with small spray of watercress.		

Ginger Ale Salad

YIELD: 50 portions		
INGREDIENTS	QUANTITY	METHOD
Gelatine Cold Water Pineapple, canned, diced Water and/or Fruit Juice Sugar, granulated Salt Ginger Ale	4 oz. 1 pt. 1½ pt. 1 qt. 8 oz. 1 tsp. 2½ qt.	1. Soak gelatine in cold water. 2. Drain pineapple. Add sufficient water or fruit juice to pineapple juice to make 1 qt. 3. Bring liquid to boil and add sugar and salt. 4. Combine with gelatine and stir mixture until dissolved. 5. Cool and add ginger ale. Chill until mixture starts to thicken.
Apples, diced Lemon Juice Royale Anne Cherries, pitted Celery, diced Lettuce Watercress	1 lb. 4 oz. 1½ pt. 8 oz. 4 heads for garnish	6. Combine apples and lemon juice to prevent discoloration and add flavor. 7. Drain well and fold apples, cherries, pineapple and celery into gelatine mixture. 8. Pour in individual molds or pans and refrigerate until firm. 9. Unmold or cut in portions and serve in crisp lettuce cup with appropriate dressing. Salad may be garnished with spray of fresh watercress.

YIELD: 50 portions		
INGREDIENTS	QUANTITY	METHOD

Raspberry Gelatin
Hot Water (140° to 160°F.)
Cold Fruit Juices
Peaches, sliced, well drained
Frozen Raspberries, thawed
   and drained
Lettuce, washed, cleaned, trimmed
Mayonnaise
   OR Sour Cream Dressing
	24 oz.
	2 qt.
	2 qt.
	1 No. 10 can
	2 lb.
	
	4 heads
	1 qt.
		1. Dissolve the gelatin in hot water. Add cold fruit juices.
		2. Arrange peach slices in molds or salad pans. Pour half the gelatin mixture over the peaches. Chill until firm.
		3. Add raspberries to remaining gelatin and, when it is almost congealed, pour over the first layer. Chill until firm.
		4. Serve on lettuce with Mayonnaise (p. 260) or Sour Cream Dressing (p. 260).

See color picture, p. 230.

Whipped Black Cherry Gelatin, Minted Cream Cheese

YIELD: 50 portions	EACH PORTION: about 3 oz. and dressing	
INGREDIENTS	QUANTITY	METHOD
Black Cherry Gelatin Water or Fruit Juice, hot Water or Fruit Juice, cold	1½ lb. ½ gal. ½ gal.	1. Dissolve gelatin in hot water, add cold water and mix well. Chill until slightly thickened. 2. Place in *cold* mixing bowl and beat at high speed for 5 min. (Gelatin will increase in volume). 3. Pour into individual molds or hotel pan and chill until firm.
Lettuce, washed, cleaned, trimmed Cream Cheese Apple Mint Jelly Watercress	4 heads 2 lb. 4 oz. to garnish	4. Unmold or cut desired shape and serve on lettuce cup or chilled salad plate. 5. Blend cream cheese and jelly until consistency of slightly thickened cream. Dress top of gelatin with generous tablespoon of dressing. May be garnished with watercress.

Perfection Salad

YIELD: 50 portions	EACH PORTION: 4 oz.	
INGREDIENTS	QUANTITY	METHOD
Unflavored Gelatine Water, cold Water, boiling Sugar Salt	5 oz. 1 pt. 3 qt. 1 qt. 2 tbsp.	1. Soak gelatine in cold water. 2. Combine gelatine, boiling water, sugar and salt, mixing until dissolved.
Vinegar, cider Lemon Juice	14¼ oz. 8 oz.	3. Cool and add vinegar and lemon juice. 4. Chill and partly set.
Cabbage, shredded Celery, chopped Green Peppers, chopped Pimientoes, drained, chopped Lettuce, washed, cleaned and trimmed	2 qt. 1½ qt. 4 oz. 1 7 oz. can 4 heads	5. Combine all ingredients and pour into individual molds or pans. Refrigerate until firm. 6. Unmold or cut portions. Serve on lettuce bed.

NOTE: Salad may also be used as garnish for meats and sandwiches.

See color picture, p. 230.

Jellied Fruit Mold, Sour Cream Dressing

YIELD: 50 portions		EACH PORTION: about 4 oz. and dressing
INGREDIENTS	*QUANTITY*	*METHOD*
Fruit Cocktail Raspberry, Strawberry or Cherry Gelatin Water and Fruit Juice	1 No. 10 can 1½ lb. 1 gal.	1. Drain fruit cocktail, reserving juice. 2. Heat ½ gal. water. Dissolve gelatin in hot water. 3. Combine fruit juice with sufficient cold water to make ½ gal. Add to dissolved gelatin mixture. Chill until slightly thickened.
Lettuce, washed, cleaned, trimmed Sour Cream Mayonnaise (p. 260)	4 heads 1 pt. 1 pt.	4. Fold in drained fruit and chill in individual molds until firm. If molds are not available, fill clean hotel pan. 5. Unmold or cut (depending on form) and place on lettuce bed. 6. Dress with 1 tbsp. combined sour cream and mayonnaise.

Molded Spring Vegetable Salad

YIELD: 50 portions		EACH PORTION: about 4 oz.
INGREDIENTS	*QUANTITY*	*METHOD*
Lemon Gelatin Salt Hot Water (140° to 160°F.) Vinegar	20 oz. 2 tbsp. 3½ qt. 6 oz.	1. Dissolve gelatin and salt in hot water. Add vinegar. 2. Chill until slightly thickened.

Chopped Fresh Vegetables (Celery,
  Cucumbers, Tomatoes, Onions)
Salad Greens, washed, cleaned and
  trimmed
	3 qt.
	
	4 heads
		3. Fold peeled and chopped vegetables into slightly thickened gelatin. Chill until firm.
		4. Serve on crisp greens.

See color picture, p. 230.		

Tomato Aspic

YIELD: 50 portions		EACH PORTION: 4 oz.
INGREDIENTS	*QUANTITY*	*METHOD*
Unflavored Gelatine Tomato Juice, cold	6 oz. 1 pt.	1. Soak gelatine in cold tomato juice.
Tomato Juice (see Step 4) Onions, fine diced Carrots, fine diced Sugar, granulated Salt Bay Leaves Cloves, whole	5 qt. 1 lb. ¾ lb. 6 oz. to taste 2 6	2. Combine tomato juice, onions, carrots, sugar, salt, bay leaves and cloves. Simmer mixture for 15 min. Strain. 3. Measure strained liquid and add enough more tomato juice to make 5½ qt. 4. Combine with soaked gelatine and stir until dissolved.
Vinegar Lemon Juice Celery, diced, cooked Lettuce, washed, cleaned and trimmed	4 oz. 4 oz. 1½ pts. 4 heads	5. Cool and add vinegar and lemon juice. Chill until slightly congealed. 6. Fold in cooked diced celery. Pour in individual molds or pans. 7. Chill until firm. 8. Serve in lettuce cup with appropriate dressing.
See color picture, p. 230.		

PREPARING COLE SLAW SOUFFLE SALAD

Shred cabbage finely for Cole Slaw Souffle Salad. Cut large heads of cabbage into quarters for easier handling; smaller heads in half. Hold knife as for slicing and cut fine shreds as in picture at left. Cabbage may also be shredded by machine or manual shredder.

Dissolve lemon flavored gelatin in hot water. The recommended water temperature is 140°F. to 160°F. Stir until all particles of gelatin are dissolved. Add cold water and blend with dissolved gelatin.

Chill gelatin until slightly thickened. This may be done in refrigerator or freezer. For speed, add ice cubes as part of cold water, or place bowl in bed of ice until gelatin is thick.

Add 12 oz. vinegar, 1½ pt. mayonnaise, salt and pepper to thickened gelatin. Beat with a wire whip until smooth and fluffy. Combine remaining ingredients and fold in.

Pour gelatin mixture into individual molds or into hotel pans and chill until firm. Run small knife around edge of molds to loosen gelatin. Unmold and serve on a lettuce bed as shown at right. (Recipe on facing page.)

Cole Slaw Souffle Salad

YIELD: 50 portions		EACH PORTION: 3 oz.
INGREDIENTS	QUANTITY	METHOD
Lemon Flavored Gelatin Water, hot Water, cold	18 oz. 1 qt. 1 qt.	1. Dissolve gelatin in hot water. Add cold water. 2. Chill until slightly thickened.
Cider Vinegar Mayonnaise Salt White Pepper Cabbage, finely shredded Green Peppers, finely chopped Onions, chopped fine Celery Seed	12 oz. 1-1/2 pt. 1-1/2 tsp. 1/4 tsp. 3 qt. 3 oz. 1-1/3 oz. 1-1/2 tsp.	3. Add vinegar, mayonnaise, salt and pepper. Beat until fluffy. 4. Combine remaining ingredients, except lettuce leaves, and fold into gelatin. 5. Pour into pans or individual molds and chill until firm.
Lettuce	4 heads	6. Serve on lettuce bed.

Sunset Salad

YIELD: 50 portions		EACH PORTION: about 4½ oz.
INGREDIENTS	QUANTITY	METHOD
Lemon Gelatin Salt Hot Water and Canned Pineapple Juice (140° to 160°F.) Vinegar	24 oz. 3 tsp. 3½ qt. 4 oz.	1. Dissolve gelatin and salt in hot liquid. 2. Add vinegar and chill until slightly thickened.
Carrots, peeled, grated Crushed Pineapple, canned, drained Salad Greens, washed, cleaned, trimmed	2 qt. 1 qt. 4 heads	3. Combine carrots and pineapple. Fold into gelatin. Chill until firm. 4. Serve on greens.

Salad Dressings

Some type of dressing is employed in the service of nearly all salads. The dressing adds flavor, increases palatability and sometimes serves as a binding agent, garnish and lubricant. (The oil content helps to lubricate bulk vegetables, such as lettuce and other greens, and aids in lubricating the alimentary tract.) Dressings also provide important food values.

There are three basic types of dressings: French dressing, mayonnaise and cooked or boiled dressing.

French dressing and mayonnaise have a basis of oil, while boiled dressing contains no fat or oil other than a small amount of butter.

French Dressing is a temporary emulsion of oil, acids (usually vinegar) and seasonings. An emulsion is a mixture in which the oil particles are held in suspension in their associated liquids. French dressing is a temporary emulsion because the oil and acid usually separate soon after mixing. French dressing may be made a permanent emulsion by adding an emulsifying agent—such as egg yolk—that keeps the oil in suspension.

Salad Oils The quality of the oil used will determine to a great extent the quality of the dressing. This is true also of the other ingredients. There are a number of oils available, such as corn, cottonseed, soybean, peanut and olive.

Olive oil is the most expensive and has a definite characteristic flavor. It may be used singly or in combination with other oils. The other oils, as a group, are more bland in flavor and more suitable for general use.

Olive oil, derived from the pressing of olives, may be purchased in varying quality. The highest quality, termed virgin oil, is from the first pressing of the olives. Some oils are available that contain a percentage of olive oil, the balance usually of vegetable origin.

Vinegars

There are several types of vinegar:
1) Cider vinegar, made by the fermentation of apples
2) White or distilled vinegar, derived from the fermentation of grains. It is colorless and without fruit flavor
3) Wine vinegar, made from white and red grapes
4) Flavored vinegars, which are made by immersing herbs, seeds and other seasonings in any of the above vinegars. (These may be made by utilizing your own collection of seasonings.)
5) Malt vinegar, made from fermented barley and cereals. Not used extensively

Vinegars vary in their acid strength, usually 4 to 5 per cent acid content. The acid content is labeled on the container. Fruit vinegars have a flavor and mellowness that is not found in white vinegar which has a sharper taste. The selection of vinegar is important in the oil and vinegar ratio.

The proportion of oil to vinegar depends on the heaviness of the oil and the sharpness of the vinegar. Ratios are usually 3 or 4 parts of oil to vinegar by volume. Lemon or lime juice may be substituted for part of the vinegar. A variation of french dressing, called fruit French dressing, may be made by substituting fruit juice for a part or all of the vinegar.

Most vegetable oils thicken or clot under refrigeration. French dressing does not normally require refrigeration unless large quantities are prepared and held for storage. If refrigerated, it should be removed prior to service and held at room temperature until restored to its original appearance.

Mayonnaise is a semi-solid emulsion of edible vegetable oils, eggs (whole or yolks), vinegar and/or lemon juice and seasonings. Government regulations state that commercially prepared mayonnaise shall contain not less than 50 per cent vegetable oils and the sum of oil and egg yolks shall be not less than 78 per cent. Some products that employ starch pastes to aid emulsification and do not otherwise comply with standards for mayonnaise are commercially termed salad dressing.

Excellent commercially prepared mayonnaise may be purchased. This eliminates the general preparation of mayonnaise in the kitchen. However, some operations still make their own, and knowledge of the preparation of mayonnaise will prove valuable in emergencies.

Preparation of Mayonnaise that will stand up well and not separate involves certain factors and techniques:

Cold oil is difficult to break up into small fat globules; this affects ease of emulsification. It is recommended that oil and eggs be at room temperature for ease in obtaining emulsification.

An emulsion is more readily achieved when all ingredients are at the same temperature.

Although whole eggs are entirely suitable in the preparation of mayonnaise, egg yolks are a more efficient emulsifying agent because of their ability to hold additional fats. Fresh eggs are superior to aged or frozen eggs for use in mayonnaise. Frozen eggs, upon thawing, are more liquid and a larger quantity is required than of fresh eggs. Egg yolks and dry ingredients (seasoning, such as dry mustard, salt, sugar and white pepper) are beaten together in the initial preparation step, prior to the addition of oil.

Rapid and thorough beating of the eggs and oils in the beginning steps is one of the most important factors in producing the initial emulsion.

The method of adding oil is a deciding factor to the stability of the emulsion. Oil must be added slowly in the beginning and in small quantities. Once the emulsion begins to form, the oil may be added more rapidly and in greater volume, but in quantity not to exceed the volume of emulsion already formed.

The acid or vinegar may be added at various intervals during the mixing alternately with the oil, or when a large percentage of emulsion is formed. Vinegar will thin the emulsion and make it more liquid. It also reduces the intensity of the yellow color of the egg yolks.

Separation may occur if: 1) oil is added too fast; 2) oil is added in too large volume at one time; 3) improper or inefficient mixing methods are used; 4) ingredients are at wrong temperature.

Breaking or separating may be corrected by various methods: 1) starting new with fresh egg yolks; 2) starting new with a small quantity of prepared mayonnaise. It is obvious that re-emulsifying requires additional labor and time. Strict observance of prescribed methods and procedures will lessen the possibility of separation and minimize the necessity of the additional step.

Mayonnaise should be stored in a cool, dry place; but it does not normally require refrigeration unless mixed with other products. A thin film of oil will form on the top of mayonnaise that has been opened and remains exposed to the air. This is not harmful and may be incorporated by simply mixing it with a spoon.

French dressing and mayonnaise provide the basis from which nearly all other dressings are made. These are the mother sauces as applied to salad preparation.

Boiled Dressing is not used extensively and its preparation in the kitchen is somewhat limited. Its use is usually restricted to products that require a degree of tartness, such as some types of cole slaw and potato salad. It is prepared in a double boiler over hot water and is principally composed of eggs, vinegar, seasonings similar to those used in mayonnaise and some liquid. This can be either milk, cream or water. Boiled dressing is usually thickened with flour or cornstarch.

Selection of Dressing The selection of a proper dressing for each kind of salad is essential to success. The dressing should be suitable to the salad in flavor and consistency, in heartiness (which applies to nutritional value and digestibility), and in color and appearance. The amount of dressing should be sufficient to flavor the entire salad, but not excessive enough to make it watery or otherwise alter the desired effect.

Salads of a distinct flavor require mild seasonings. Salads of bland character require more highly seasoned dressings. Fruit French dressings are used only with fruit. Mayonnaise and its variations are used with all types of salads; but since mayonnaise is of a relatively heavy character, the selection of salads with which it is used should be made with care. French dressing and its variations are extremely versatile, although their greatest use is with tossed salads, salad greens and their combinations.

As previously stated, most dressings should be served separately or mixed into the salad just before service. Exceptions to this rule are potato salad, poultry, meat and seafood salads. This type of food gains flavor if mixed and refrigerated a few hours.

Honey Lemon Dressing

YIELD: 3½ pt.		
INGREDIENTS	QUANTITY	METHOD
Honey (Orange Blossom), refined Lemon Juice Salt Paprika	1 qt. 1½ pt. ¾ oz. 1 tbsp.	Combine all ingredients and mix well.
VARIATION: Add 4 oz. sour cream to 8 oz. Honey Lemon Dressing.		

Chiffonade Dressing

YIELD: 3 qt.		
INGREDIENTS	QUANTITY	METHOD
French Dressing (p. 258) Eggs, hard-cooked, small dice Onion, grated Beets, pickled, chopped Parsley, chopped fine	2 qt. 6 4 oz. 12 oz. ¾ oz.	1. Combine all ingredients. 2. Chill before serving. 3. Stir well when serving.

Salad Dressings

Basic French Dressing

YIELD: 1 quart		
INGREDIENTS	QUANTITY	METHOD
Vinegar, cider	8¼ oz.	1. Dissolve seasonings in vinegar. Combine with oil and mix vigorously.
Salt	1 tbsp.	
White Pepper	1½ tsp.	2. Must be well mixed at time of service.
Salad Oil	1½ pt.	

Diet French Dressing

YIELD: 2½ qts.		
INGREDIENTS	QUANTITY	METHOD
Tomato Juice	2 qt.	1. Place egg in bowl, beat well while adding all other ingredients.
Salad Oil	8 oz.	
Lemon Juice	4 oz.	2. Shake well before serving.
Worcestershire Sauce	3 tbsp.	
Liquid Hot Pepper Sauce	¼ tsp.	
Garlic)	½ clove	
Salt) pulverized	to taste	
Egg, whole	1	
Vinegar, cider	2¾ oz.	

Emulsified French Dressing

YIELD: 5 qt.		
INGREDIENTS	QUANTITY	METHOD
Salad Oil	3 qt.	1. Beat eggs until thickened. Add dry ingredients to eggs until well blended.
Cider Vinegar	1½ pts.	
Eggs, whole	3	2. Add oil slowly, when thickened, add a little vinegar. Alternate oil and vinegar until all has been used.
Salt	1 tbsp.	
Garlic	1 tsp.	
White Pepper	1 tsp.	
Sugar	4 oz.	
Dry Mustard	2 tbsp.	
Paprika	2 tbsp.	
Worcestershire Sauce	1 tbsp.	3. Add worcestershire sauce; finish with lemon juice and water.
Lemon Juice	8 oz.	
Water	8 oz.	

Fruit Salad Dressing

YIELD: 2 qt.		
INGREDIENTS	QUANTITY	METHOD
Water	3 oz.	1. Gradually add water to cornstarch and sugar, mixing until smooth.
Cornstarch	3 oz.	
Sugar	14 oz.	
Eggs, beaten	8	2. Add eggs, blend well.
Pineapple Juice	1 pt.	3. Combine fruit juices and heat to boiling point.
Orange Juice	1 pt.	4. Gradually add juices to starch-egg mixture, stirring constantly.
Lemon Juice	½ pt.	5. Cook, over low heat, stirring constantly until thick. Cool.

Fruit French Dressing

YIELD: 1 quart		
INGREDIENTS	*QUANTITY*	*METHOD*
Orange and Grapefruit Juice Salt Sugar Salad Oil	1 pt. 1 tbsp. 2 tsp. 1 pt.	Combine as for Basic French Dressing (formula facing page).

French Dressing Variation

YIELD: 1 quart		
INGREDIENTS	*QUANTITY*	*METHOD*
Vinegar, cider Salt Mustard, dry Sugar White Pepper Salad Oil	8¼ oz. 1 tbsp. 1 tbsp. 1 tsp. ½ tsp. 1½ pt.	1. Combine in the same manner as Basic French Dressing (facing page). The addition of grated onion or a small amount of finely minced garlic is optional.

Additional French Dressing Variations

To make the following dressings, add the ingredients indicated to 1 qt. of Basic French Dressing (facing page).

BAR-LE-DUC DRESSING: Make Basic French Dressing with lemon juice in place of vinegar. Blend in 8 oz. of Bar-le-Duc.

CUCUMBER DRESSING: Add 1½ pt. of grated cucumbers.

CURRANT JELLY DRESSING: Make Basic French Dressing with lemon juice in place of vinegar. Blend in 8 oz. of red currant jelly.

CHEESE DRESSING: Add 1 tsp. prepared mustard and 4 oz. of grated cheese.

CHUTNEY DRESSING: Add 8 oz. of chutney.

GARLIC DRESSING: Add ¼ tsp. garlic powder or ½ tsp. finely mashed garlic.

HAWAIIAN DRESSING: Add 8 oz. each of orange juice and pineapple juice.

HERB DRESSING: Add 1/8 tsp. marjoram, 1/4 tsp. sweet basil, 1 tsp. fresh chopped parsley, and 1/4 tsp. finely mashed garlic.

MINT DRESSING: Add 1 oz. finely shredded mint or blend in 4 oz. mint flavored apple jelly.

OLIVE-FRENCH DRESSING: Add 2 oz. chopped stuffed green olives and 2 oz. chopped, pitted black olives.

ROQUEFORT DRESSING: Add 6 oz. crumbled Roquefort cheese. **BLUE CHEESE DRESSING** may be prepared in the same manner.

Blue or Roquefort Cheese Dressing

YIELD: 3¼ qt.		
INGREDIENTS	*QUANTITY*	*METHOD*
Blue or Roquefort Cheese Mayonnaise (p. 260)	2 lb. ½ gal.	1. Break down cheese in mixing bowl, but do not mash to a paste. 2. Blend in mayonnaise.
Dry Mustard Salt Pepper, White Vinegar, Cider	2 tsp. 1 tsp. 1 tsp. 6 oz.	3. Dissolve dry ingredients in vinegar.
Salad Oil Water, cold	1 pt. 12 oz.	4. Add oil to mayonnaise, beating constantly. 5. Whip in vinegar and dissolved seasonings. 6. Finish with cold water, mixing thoroughly. 7. Store in covered glass or stainless steel container.

NOTE: Be sure to identify this dressing properly on your menu. Dressing may not be called "Roquefort" if Blue Cheese is used.

Mayonnaise

YIELD: 1 qt.		

INGREDIENTS	QUANTITY	METHOD
Egg Yolks	4 yolks	1. Beat egg yolks in bowl.
Sugar	1 tbsp.	2. Mix dry ingredients together and add to eggs in
Salt	2 tsp.	bowl. Beat a few minutes.
Mustard, dry	2 tsp.	3. Add oil slowly at first; when thick, add a small
Salad Oil	1¾ pt.	amount of vinegar. Alternate oil and vinegar until
Vinegar	2 oz.	all has been used. Finish with lemon juice.
Lemon Juice	2 tbsp.	

Mayonnaise Variations

INGREDIENTS	QUANTITY	METHOD
CHANTILLY DRESSING		Fold mayonnaise into whipped cream. Add sugar and
Mayonnaise (formula above)	8 oz.)	nutmeg.
Cream, whipped	8 oz.)	
Sugar	1 tbsp.) 1 pt.	
Nutmeg, grated (optional)	Pinch)	
COMBINATION DRESSING		Blend equal parts of French Dressing and mayonnaise.
French Dressing (p. 258)	) equal parts	
Mayonnaise (formula above)	)	
SOUR CREAM DRESSING		Combine all ingredients.
Mayonnaise (formula above)	1 pt.)	
Lemon Juice	½ lemon) 1½ pt.	
Sour Cream	8 oz.)	

Chicken or Fish Mayonnaise Dressing

YIELD: 1 qt.		

INGREDIENTS	QUANTITY	METHOD
Mayonnaise (formula above)	1½ pt.	1. Combine all ingredients and stir well.
Light Cream	8 oz.	
Onion Juice	1½ to 2 tsp.	
Hot Pepper Sauce	2 oz.	
VARIATION: Add 2 tsp. of chopped chives.		

Thousand Island Dressing

YIELD: 1 qt.		

INGREDIENTS	QUANTITY	METHOD
Mayonnaise (formula above)	1 lb. 2 oz.	Combine all ingredients and mix thoroughly.
Hard Cooked Eggs, chopped	2	
Chili Sauce	7 oz.	
Pickles, sweet, chopped, drained	4 oz.	
Onion, minced	2 tbsp.	
Pimientoes, chopped fine	1½ oz.	
NOTE: There are many variations; chopped stuffed olives, chopped green peppers and parsley can be used.		

Piquante Dressing

YIELD: 1 gal.		
INGREDIENTS	*QUANTITY*	*METHOD*
Vinegar Catsup Salad Oil Salt Dry Mustard Paprika Pepper	1½ pt. 1½ pt. 1¼ qt. 2 tbsp. 2 tbsp. 2 tbsp. 2 tbsp.	1. Combine all ingredients except eggs and onion and whip thoroughly.
Eggs, hard-cooked, finely diced Onion, minced	15 (1½ pt.) 1 medium (8 oz.)	2. Add finely diced hard-cooked eggs and minced onion.

Princess Dressing

YIELD: 1½ qt.		
INGREDIENTS	*QUANTITY*	*METHOD*
Cream Cheese, room temperature Melba Sauce Milk OR Light Cream	1½ lb. 12 oz. 10 oz.	1. Cream the cheese until light and fluffy. 2. Add Melba Sauce, blending well. 3. Add milk or cream gradually, mixing well. Whip to the consistency of light whipped cream.
NOTE: Princess Dressing may be served with fruit or cottage cheese salads and on fresh fruit cups used as appetizers.		

Vinaigrette Dressing

YIELD: 1 qt.		
INGREDIENTS	*QUANTITY*	*METHOD*
French Dressing (variation p. 258) Parsley, chopped Chives, chopped Capers, chopped Pickles, sweet, chopped OR Relish Hard Cooked Egg, chopped	1 qt. 2 tbsp. 2 tbsp. 1 tbsp. 1 tbsp. 1	Combine all ingredients and mix well.
NOTE: Chopped green olives may also be added.		

Chef's Salad Dressing

YIELD: 1 gal.		
INGREDIENTS	*QUANTITY*	*METHOD*
Tarragon Vinegar Cider Vinegar Salt Dry Mustard Sugar White Pepper Salad Oil Garlic, crushed and chopped	4 oz. 12½ oz. 2 tbsp. 2 tbsp. 2 oz. 1 tbsp. 3 qt. 1½ tbsp.	1. Dissolve spices in vinegars. Add oil and garlic and blend well. 2. Stir or shake immediately prior to service.

Salad Dressings

Boiled Dressing

YIELD: 2½ pt.		
INGREDIENTS	*QUANTITY*	*METHOD*
Flour	6 tbsp.	1. Blend flour, sugar, salt, mustard and cayenne.
Sugar	3 tbsp.	2. Add egg yolks and beat until smooth.
Dry Mustard	3 tsp.	3. Add milk, mixing well; add vinegar and lemon juice slowly.
Salt	3 tsp.	
Cayenne Pepper	1/3 tsp.	4. Cook in double boiler over low heat, stirring constantly until thick. Remove from heat and add butter.
Egg Yolks, beaten	6	
Milk	1 qt.	
Vinegar	4 oz.	5. Pour in glass container or stainless steel bowl and cool.
Lemon Juice	2 oz.	
Butter	6 tbsp.	
NOTE: Dressing becomes heavier when cold.		

Green Goddess Dressing

YIELD: 2 qt.		
INGREDIENTS	*QUANTITY*	*METHOD*
Garlic, minced fine	1 tbsp.	1. Place garlic, anchovies, chives, parsley, salt and pepper in stainless steel bowl and mix well.
Anchovies, minced fine	2 oz.	
Chives, minced fine	1 oz.	
Parsley, minced fine (squeeze juice and reserve)	1½ oz. (and juice, see note)	
Salt	2 tsp.	
Pepper, black	½ tsp.	
Lemon Juice	from 2 lemons	2. Add lemon juice and tarragon vinegar, mixing well.
Tarragon Vinegar	2 oz.	
Mayonnaise (p. 260)	1 qt.	3. Add mayonnaise and parsley juice and blend well.
Sour Cream	1 pt.	4. Fold in whipped sour cream.
NOTE: The juice is squeezed from the parsley in order to color the dressing. The dressing will not have sufficient color unless this procedure is used. Green Goddess Dressing is best if made several hours before serving. It should be stored under refrigeration.		

Hot Bacon Dressing

YIELD: 2 qt.		
INGREDIENTS	*QUANTITY*	*METHOD*
Onions, chopped	½ lb.	1. Fry onions and bacon together until onions are clear and bacon is crisp. Drain off fat and reserve.
Bacon, diced	1 lb.	
Water	1 pt.	2. Combine water and vinegar. Heat to boiling. Add sugar, salt and pepper.
Vinegar	1 pt.	
Sugar	½ lb.	
Salt	¼ oz.	
Pepper	½ tsp.	
Cornstarch	2 oz.	3. Blend cornstarch, water and fat from bacon to a smooth paste. Stir into hot liquid. Heat to boiling. Mixture will thicken slightly. Cook about 10 min. Add onion and bacon.
Water	8 oz.	
		4. Pour hot over salad greens or shredded cabbage just before serving.

SOUPS

At almost any point on the globe soup is a flavorful, nutritional mainstay. Thousands of soups, of endless variety, can be prepared from the methods and principles given here, for it is in the addition of meats, vegetables, fruits, seasonings, starch products and garnitures that soups become individual and typically national or regional. Explanation and preparation techniques of the several basic stocks, in addition to many soup formulas, are included in this section.

Bavarian Lentil Soup

Cold Fruit Soup

Washington Chowder

Oxtail Soup a l'Anglaise

Scotch Broth

Gaspacho

Borscht

Chicken Gumbo Creole

Navy Bean

New England Clam Chowder

OUPS

English Beef Broth with Barley

Duck Soup, Parisienne

Jellied Beef Consommé

Cream of Asparagus

Cream of Tomato

Oyster Stew

Chicken Noodle

Shrimp Bisque

BOUILLABAISSE MARSEILLAISE

Probably no single soup holds more fascination for diners than the famous French Bouillabaisse. Because of its amazing number and variety of ingredients and its distinct, succulent aroma, Bouillabaisse deserves service with a flair, and thus contributes to high check averages. Bouillabaisse is one of the best known products of La Provence, France, and its regions bordering the Mediterranean Sea. Many of the fish and small crustacea used in Bouillabaisse are found only in the Mediterranean, so substitutions of fish available in this country must be made. Stand-ins are given in the recipe. As shown here, Bouillabaisse should be served as two separate items, broth and fish. The patron then mixes the two to his taste, usually pouring the broth over toasted slices of french or garlic bread.

Soup as a main course

Techniques for Soup Cookery

Soup may be defined as a liquid food derived from meat, poultry, fish or vegetables. Years ago soup constituted the entire meal; and, because it was hearty and filling and an economical source of food, it became a mainstay in the diet. This is still true in many countries.

Today, in the United States, we generally regard soup as an appetizer or starter preceding the main course. However, many present methods of preparation and variation of ingredients are carry-overs from the earlier era of economic necessity. Although the method by which soup stock is derived may differ, this rule still holds true: good stock is essential in order to produce a tasty, flavorful and nutritious product.

Classification of Soups

There are virtually thousands of soups which may be prepared by a few basic methods and principles. In order to make learning easier and to establish a foundation for soup preparation we will classify soups in the following manner:
1) Clear soups, which include broths and bouillons (pronounced boo-ee-yohng), consommes and vegetable soups
2) Thick soups, which include cream soups, purees, chowders and bisques
3) Special and national soups which comprise both groups

Clear Soups Broths and bouillons are interchangeable terms. They are liquids in which any food, including vegetables, has been boiled or simmered. Originally they were specifically derived from meats, although there have been recent recognized exceptions.

Consommes are clarified bouillons or stocks reduced to increase richness.

Vegetable soups are derived from broths and bouillons and contain all types and varieties of vegetables.

Thick Soups Cream soups are thickened soups with the addition of milk and/or cream. The name denotes the predominant ingredients: cream of asparagus, cream of chicken, cream of fresh vegetables.

Purees are thickened soups without the addition of milk and cream. They are principally derived from legumes (dried peas, beans and lentils) but may be made from any starchy vegetable.

Chowders are derived from fish, shellfish and—more recently—vegetables, although the vegetable chowders would be more aptly termed cream soups. With few exceptions, chowders are made with milk and/or cream and include potatoes.

Bisques are usually derived from shellfish and may be thickened with various preparations. They are named according to their predominant flavor characteristic, such as shrimp bisque or lobster bisque, and should contain no other fish than that for which they are named. They are usually prepared with cream.

Special and National Soups are of great variety and include soups that are both clear and thick. They are Minestrone (Italy), Mulligatawny, (India), Olla Podrida (Spain), Oxtail Soup (England), Pot-au-Feu (France), Scotch Broth (Scotland) and many others.

Potage was originally a classification of soup, but is more commonly interpreted today as meaning simply soup. It is, however, often associated with vegetables (dried and fresh), macaroni products and rice. When used, the term potage precedes its given name as: Potage St. Germain, which is a puree of fresh peas; or Potage Bonne Femme, which is a puree of white beans with vegetables.

Soup Service Most soups should be served piping hot in hot serving dishes. There are a few warm weather soups that are served cold in liquid or jellied form. They include Vichyssoise—a potato soup; tomato madrilene—often served jellied; consommes—served cold or jellied; and foreign specialty soups such as cold borscht and gazpacho. Chilled cups should be used for their service.

When two or more soups are offered on the menu, they should provide as much contrast as possible.

Soups selected for banquet or party service should contrast with the entree or main course. A light soup or consomme suggests a hearty entree, a hearty or heavy soup, a light entree.

Various garnishes are discussed in a later section.

Consomme A consomme is a clear, transparent soup derived from stock, broth or bouillon. The process by which consomme is obtained is termed clarification. The object of clarification is to extract all impurities and fine floating particles from a stock, broth or bouillon and to produce a light, stimulating and extremely clear and transparent soup.

Nearly all consommes are derived from two sources: chicken stock which is used for white consommes and beef stock for others. The various consommes are numerous and are named for additional ingredients that go into their production, historical figures and events, or the accompanying garnish.

Although most consommes are served hot, a few are served cold or jellied as previously explained.

Clarification The process of clarification utilizes three major ingredients:

1) Raw beef and egg whites which contain albumin, a protein that coagulates.

2) Tomatoes or tomato products or lemon juice or vinegar, all of which are acid, which helps the clarification process.

3) Fresh vegetables, herbs and spices which contribute flavor and nutritive values to the finished stock.

Protein (as in egg whites and ground beef) is altered chemically by the application of heat so that it coagulates, much like the clotting of blood, congealing of gelatin or the setting of egg whites, when exposed to heat.

The chemical action of these three ingredients causes a coagulation of the egg white and meat protein, absorbing minute food particles and forming a solid mass, separating it from the remaining liquid. The resultant liquid is said to be clarified. This coagulation or floating mass is called a raft.

Heating to boiling temperature will affect success of clarification. Therefore, it is important that consomme must not boil vigorously, but barely simmer until clarification has been accomplished. Remember that vigorous boiling produces cloudy stocks. If a good strong stock is used as a base, 1 to 1½ hr. is sufficient for clarification.

Time the clarification, starting when the raft is completely formed and floating on top of the stock and the stock has come to a boil. At this point, the heat should be reduced immediately or the stock pot placed in an area of the range where it will barely simmer. Excessive heat will cook the clarification products before they have a chance to do their job. Consomme must always be started with cold stock so the finished product will be clear.

Until the raft begins to form, the stock and other ingredients should be stirred frequently to prevent them from sticking to the bottom of the pot and to keep them in suspension. After the formation of the raft and during the simmering process, no further stirring is necessary.

If the heat is properly regulated, there will be no scorching or burning on the bottom of the stockpot. The slight agitation caused by simmering will keep the foods and food particles in suspension and bring them to the top (the underside of the raft, to which they will adhere).

When clarification has been completed, the consomme should be strained carefully through a double fold of fine cheesecloth, using a china cap. The consomme should not be forced through the china cap, but allowed to drain by its own weight. Forcing may filter particles through the cheesecloth into the strained consomme. This defeats the purpose of clarification. Some of the consomme should be tested for color and the seasoning corrected. It is then held for service with an appropriate garnish.

A stockpot with a spigot (faucet) is preferred for preparing stock and consommes as it facilitates handling and saves time and labor. The spigot allows the stock to be drained easily into sauce pans, measuring or other containers, and avoids heavy lifting and dipping with a sauce pan to transfer the finished product to other containers.

Soup Garnishes The garnishes for soups are many in number and of infinite variety. They may be extremely simple, such as chopped parsley or other herbs, or more complex, such as quenelles of meat, fish or poultry.

The soup is often named for the garnish that accompanies it. Garnish that demands a fresh look or that may get soggy on standing (such as croutons), should be placed on the soup at service time. Croutons are sometimes served on the side. A partial list of commonly used garnishes appears below:

Croutons:	Made from bread, toast, pastry, pate-a-choux. Profiterolles are also made from pate-a-choux. They are miniature cream puffs which may be filled or used plain.
Cereals:	Rice or barley
Cheese:	Cheese balls or grated parmesan. Parmesan floated, served with croutons or on the side
Dairy Products:	Unsweetened whipped cream or sour cream
Meats:	Usually small dice or julienne
Poultry:	Same as meats
Seafood:	Diced or flaked. All foods should be in large enough pieces to be distinguishable
Pastes:	Fine noodles, vermicelli, spaghetti and other fine macaroni products. Filled pastes, such as kreplach and wonton
Vegetables:	Cut in various sizes and shapes from which the name often derives: julienne, brunoise, paysanne. Also printaniere, which refers to spring vegetables

Accompaniments of a crisp character are often served with soup. These may be melba toast, various crackers, pastry or bread sticks, whole grain and shredded wafers, croutons.

Stocks

Stock is the liquid in which meat or meat bones, fish or fish bones or vegetables have been cooked to extract the flavor. Stocks provide the basis for nearly all soups and sauces and are one of the most important ingredients used in food preparation.

Although the number of operations maintaining daily stockpots is decreasing, this is in great part due to lack of adequate personnel and time and increasing labor costs, rather than because stock made in the operation's own kitchen is less good than manufactured bases for stock.

Many houses that formerly did their own butchering now buy prefabricated and portion-controlled meats. This means that they no longer have bones with which to make stock unless they purchase them from their purveyor or packing house. Larger operations that still employ their own butchers have ample bones and trimmings with which to work.

The manufactured bases, such as chicken base or beef base, are used today by most operations, and are also excellent sources to be used to augment or add flavor to stocks made in the kitchen. These bases (primarily derived from specially processed vegetables, spices and seasonings) can be used to advantage very effectively. But whether or not the operation actually makes its own stock, knowledge of the proper procedures to use should be part of the basic training for cooks.

Because the use of bones in preparing stock and the resultant labor involved are expensive compared to the use of bases, proper care and handling of these stocks is essential to justify their use.

Present Day Cooking Methods Many kitchens formerly maintained a constant stockpot. It simmered on the range day and night and was added to or taken from as needed. This practice has largely been replaced by shorter cooking methods which retain considerably more nutritive value and flavor. Many of the same principles are applied to the new short-time method of cooking.

Stocks are started by standard procedure; but in order to maintain more of their food value, vegetables are often added during the cooking process rather than at the beginning. The prime difference is in the reduction of cooking time. Five to six hours is usually sufficient time to obtain desired extractives. Excessive cooking destroys food values and often develops bitter flavor.

Long cooking periods tend to extract more gelatinous properties from bones. Old school cooks felt that this was desirable, and an indication of good stock; but it is now known that this is not the sole indication of quality.

Utilization of leftovers is necessary and beneficial in maintaining good nutritive values and cost control. All types of odds and ends are often added to stocks during the cooking process: roast pork bones, tomato ends or over-ripe tomatoes, other bits of vegetables, bones and meat trimmings. All ingredients must be clean and wholesome to produce a good stock and fulfill the cook's obligation to the eating public.

Stocks should never be salted as they are seldom used in their original form, and their reduction or concentration would make them excessively salty and unpalatable.

Meat bones should be cut with a meat saw in pieces convenient to handle (3 or 4 in. in length); or they may be ordered cut from the purveyor. Small pieces of bone also expose more surface areas to the liquid in which they are cooked, making possible a greater degree of extraction.

Chopping bones with a cleaver often splinters the bones and damages the cutting edge of the cleaver. The splinters are a health hazard and improper use of the cleaver is a danger to fingers and hands.

For instructional purposes let us be concerned with making stock from scratch or the beginning.

Major Stocks There are four major stocks from which most soups, sauces and gravies are made: brown stock, white stock, chicken stock, fish stock.

Beef bones constitute the main ingredient in brown stock, although other types of bones, such as veal, may be used in combination. The bones are browned in the oven prior to the addition of water to impart color and flavor. Vegetables, spices and herbs are used in nearly all stock preparation to impart additional flavor.

White stock, while originally composed primarily of veal bones, may be nearly any combination of beef, veal or poultry bones that have been blanched.

Chicken stock is derived from cooked fowl and poultry. When necessary, chicken parts (backs, wings, necks) may be purchased economically from purveyors.

Fish stock is obtained by poaching fish and/or bones in water. Fish stock or fish fumet (pronounced foomay) often utilizes a mirepoix, wine, vinegar or lemon juice in preparation.

Cooking Stocks It is recommended that stock be brought to a boil and then the heat reduced so that the liquid barely simmers, in order to retain clarity and nutritional value. Scum should be removed periodically as it accumulates. If stock boils vigorously or for extended periods, it becomes cloudy and its use is limited.

Continuing research indicates that flavors are extracted from a meat product whether or not the liquid is hot or cold when the meat product is introduced. The main factor is the time element. Scientific tests now evidence that a sealing in of flavor does not occur because of use of a hot liquid.

All stocks and sauces (with the exception of those that curdle at high heat) should be brought to boiling when finishing whether the product is to be used immediately or stored.

Cooling and Storing Stocks For storage, stock should be cooled as quickly as possible. The following is the recommended procedure for cooling stocks and sauces to be refrigerated:

1) Place pot in an empty sink on bricks or blocks so that cold water may circulate underneath and on all sides.

2) Install an overflow pipe and turn on cold water. Water should flow constantly so that as the water level reaches the top of the overflow and drains off, additional water is added. The constant supply of cold water will bring down the temperature of the contents of the stockpot until it becomes cool enough to refrigerate.

3) If available, ice may be added to the water to hasten the cooling process. Occasional stirring of the stock is recommended so that the heat will be evenly distributed. This is particularly true where a thickening agent has been used, in which case the stock retains the heat longer. The heat sometimes pockets and occasional stirring is necessary to keep an even temperature and reduce the possibility of spoilage.

4) If the water level is higher than the contents of the pot, there is danger of the pot tipping over. Tie the stockpot handle securely to a nearby pipe or fixture.

5) When cooled, remove stock from sink. Refrigerate.

Do not remove the fat that rises to the top when stock cools. Under refrigeration the fat will congeal or harden and form a protective coating on the stock. It is easy to remove fat intact before reheating. The fat may be discarded or saved for preparation of roux.

If it becomes necessary to place the stockpot in the walk-in refrigerator directly from the range, there may be little danger to the stock itself, providing the walk-in can produce the temperature necessary to cool it. However, there are disadvantages. The resultant excessive moisture from steam and the greater demand on the walk-in may result in deterioration of other foodstuffs.

The moisture may condense, forming ice over the blower (fan) which impairs the circulation of air. The strain on an overloaded walk-in can bring the temperature down so that keeping qualities of other foodstuffs may suffer. Whether stock can safely go from stove to walk-in depends on weather, condition of walk-in and compressor and amount and type of food under refrigeration. These points should all be checked. Whenever possible, a precooling process is preferred.

Pots should be refrigerated so that the blower is not blocked and air may circulate freely. Highly perishable foods, such as variety meats, should not be placed too near the stockpots. If warm stocks are placed in the walk-in, they should be vented.

Where adequate refrigeration is not available, it is common practice to vent stocks and other foods for cooling at room temperature. This is practical in cool weather, but becomes a problem during the warm months when foodstuffs may spoil or become poison-producing before they are cooled and refrigerated.

When cooling in this manner, place in the coolest areas possible, preferably near windows or other sources of changing air. The pots should be vented and covered with a clean cloth. All open windows must be adequately screened. Windows that are not screened invite the entry of insects, rodents, squirrels and leave premises open to theft.

Observe all rules of sanitation and health. Remember the rule: *Cool hot foods as quickly as possible. Reheat (to boiling) cold foods as quickly as possible.*

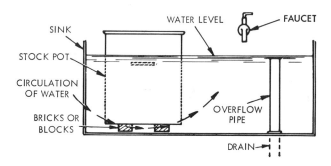

Sachet Bag

INGREDIENTS	QUANTITY	
Tie in Cheesecloth:		
Parsley Stems, chopped	2 tsp.	
Thyme	1 tsp.	
Bay Leaves	2	
Peppercorns, crushed	1 tsp.	
Garlic, chopped or crushed	1 tsp.	
(optional)		
NOTE: This sachet bag is adequate for flavoring about 2½ gal. liquid. Cloves, dill, tarragon stems, and similar items can also be used in sachet bags as required by individual recipes.		

Basic White Stock

YIELD: about 4½ gal.		
INGREDIENTS	*QUANTITY*	*METHOD*
Bones, Veal, Beef or Chicken Water, to cover	25 lb. about 6 gal.	1. Review preparation of stock. Cut bones with meat saw. 2. Wash and rinse all bones in cold water. 3. Place bones in stockpot and cover with cool water. 4. Place on range and bring to a boil. Drain all liquid. Cover bones with cold water again. 5. Bring to a boil. Reduce heat and simmer 3 hr.

Mirepoix:
   Onions, chopped
   Celery, chopped
   Carrots
Bay Leaves
Thyme
Peppercorns, crushed
Cloves, whole
Parsley Stems
	
	2 lb.
	1 lb.
	1 lb.
	3
	1 tsp.
	1 tsp.
	1 tsp.
	from ½ bunch
		6. Add mirepoix, spices, herbs and parsley stems.
		7. Simmer for an additional 3 hr.
		8. Strain through china cap and cheesecloth.
		9. Vent and cool (see facing page). Refrigerate and use as required.

Basic Brown Stock

YIELD: about 4½ gal.		
INGREDIENTS	*QUANTITY*	*METHOD*
Beef Bones	25 lb.	1. Review preparation of stock. Cut bones with meat saw. 2. Place the bones in a large roasting pan and brown in preheated oven at 375°F. 3. Turn bones occasionally to brown uniformly. 4. Remove bones from pan and place in stock pot.
Water, to cover	about 6 gal.	5. Drain fat from pan and reserve 6. Deglaze roast pan with part of water to dissolve crusting. 7. Cover bones with cool water and deglazing liquor and bring to a boil. 8. Reduce heat and simmer 3 hr.

Mirepoix:
   Onions
   Celery
   Carrots
Tomatoes, canned
Bay Leaves
Thyme
Peppercorns, crushed
Cloves, whole
Parsley Stems
	
	2 lb.
	1 lb.
	1 lb.
	½ No. 10 can
	3
	1 tsp.
	1 tsp.
	6
	
		9. Saute vegetables for mirepoix in reserved fat until browned.
		10. Add mirepoix, tomatoes, spices, herbs to stock.
		11. Simmer for an additional 3 hr.
		12. Strain through china cap and cheesecloth.
		13. Vent and cool (see facing page). Refrigerate. Use as required.

NOTE: Veal bones may be substituted for part of the beef bones, when available. Neck and shin bones are generally preferred. Vegetable trimmings and other bones are often used. Skim fat and scum frequently. Do not allow to boil vigorously.

Soups

Court Bouillon

YIELD: 3½ qt.		

INGREDIENTS	QUANTITY	METHOD
Water	7 pt.	1. Combine all ingredients and bring to boil.
Vinegar, cider	8 oz.	2. Reduce heat and simmer ½ hr.
Onions, fine dice	3 oz.	3. Strain and adjust seasoning.
Celery, fine dice	2 oz.	
Carrots, fine dice	2-1/3 oz.	
Salt	1 oz.	
Peppercorns, crushed	1 tsp.	
Parsley Sprigs	5	
Cloves, whole	1/2 tsp.	
Bay Leaf	1	
Lemon, sliced thin	1/2	

Clear Consomme

YIELD: about 3 gal.	**EACH PORTION:** 8 oz.	

INGREDIENTS	QUANTITY	METHOD
Ground Shank Meat, Beef	3 lb.	1. Review clarification process in soup section (p. 267). Grind or chop beef shin meat and vegetables.
Onions, ground or chopped, coarse	2 lb.	
Celery, ground or chopped, coarse	1 lb.	
Carrots, ground or chopped, coarse	1 lb.	
Egg Whites	1½ pt.	3. Blend all ingredients in stock pot and mix well, stirring briskly.
Parsley Stems	10	4. Bring to a slow boil, stirring occasionally. When mixture reaches boiling point, reduce heat and let simmer slowly until the coagulated mass comes to the top. Simmer for 1 to 1½ hr.
Leaf Thyme	½ tsp.	
Cloves	5	
Bay Leaves	3	5. When consomme is clear and full flavored, strain through a fine cheesecloth.
Peppercorns, crushed	1 tbsp.	
Tomatoes, canned	1 qt.	
Brown Beef Stock, cold	4 gal.	

VARIATIONS: To prepare either beef or chicken consomme to be served cold as **Jellied Consomme**, after clarification add 3½ oz. unflavored gelatine to each gal. of prepared consomme. Soak gelatine in cold water before adding to consomme.

For **Chicken Consomme**, substitute chicken stock for beef stock and omit tomatoes. Use 4 oz. lemon juice or vinegar in place of tomatoes.

Breton—Add julienne celery, onions, leeks
Brunoise—Simmer vegetables cut in small dice in small amount of consomme; add before serving
Celestine—Add julienne of thin pancakes
Du Barry—Add flowerettes of cauliflower
Florentine—Add boiled spinach, fine cut thin pancakes
Julienne—Made like Brunoise, but vegetables cut in thin matchlike strips
Printaniere—Add spring vegetables cut in small dice
Royale—Add Custard Royale cut in various shapes (recipe facing page)
Saint Germaine—Add fresh green peas to beef consomme
Tosca—Add boiled small squares of cucumber and peeled tomato, julienne of cooked celery and pearl tapioca

Custard Royale for Consomme

YIELD: 50 portions		
INGREDIENTS	*QUANTITY*	*METHOD*
Milk Eggs Salt Hot Pepper Sauce Worcestershire Sauce	1 qt. 8 to taste dash dash	1. Blend 1 pt. milk, eggs, salt, hot pepper sauce, worcestershire sauce. 2. Boil 1 pt. milk and blend with rest of mixture. 3. Pour about ¼ in. deep in buttered pan. 4. Place pan in sheet pan with boiling water in it. Cover with greased paper. 5. Bake at 250°F. until firm to prevent formation of air holes. 6. Remove from oven when done and place in sheet pan with ice water in it to stop cooking action. Cut in desired shape for garnish.
NOTE: For red color, mix in 4 oz. tomato sauce, add red food color and 2 extra eggs. For green color, put 4 oz. green peas or spinach through fine sieve and add 2 extra eggs.		

Consomme Madrilene

YIELD: 50 portions	**EACH PORTION:** 8 oz.	
INGREDIENTS	*QUANTITY*	*METHOD*
Ground Beef, lean Onions, ground or chopped coarse Celery, ground or chopped coarse Carrots, ground or chopped coarse Egg Whites Parsley Stems Leaf Thyme Cloves Bay Leaves Peppercorns, crushed Tomatoes, canned Chicken Stock, cold	3 lb. 2 lb. 1 lb. 1 lb. 1 pt. 10 ½ tsp. 5 3 10 to 15 2 No. 10 cans 3½ gal.	1. Review clarification process in soup section (p. 267). 2. Grind or chop beef and vegetables. 3. Blend all ingredients but tomatoes and stock in stock pot. Mix well, stirring briskly. Add remaining ingredients. 4. Bring to a slow boil, stirring occasionally. Reduce heat and let simmer slowly until the coagulated mass comes to top. Simmer for 1 to 1½ hr. 5. When consomme is clear and full flavored, strain through a fine cheesecloth.
VARIATIONS: For **Jellied Consomme Madrilene**, add 4 oz. plain gelatine to each gallon. Soak gelatine in cold water before adding to consomme. Because clarification absorbs some red tomato color, pure red food color may be added after clarification is completed. It should be noted that Consomme Madrilene requires more gelatine than many other consommes due to the acidity of the tomatoes.		

Soups

French Onion Soup (recipe top of facing page)

English Beef Broth

YIELD: 50 portions	EACH PORTION: 8 oz.	
INGREDIENTS	*QUANTITY*	*METHOD*
Onions, diced (¼ in.)	2 lb.	1. Clean and wash vegetables thoroughly. Peel onions, carrots and turnips. Scrape celery stalks (no leaves). Cut all vegetables in small dice ¼ in. square.
Celery, diced (¼ in.)	1 lb.	2. Cut beef into small cubes.
Carrots, diced (¼ in.)	1 lb.	3. Heat butter or salad oil in soup pot. Add all vegetables and meat. Smother covered until all vegetables are tender but not colored or browned.
White Turnips, diced (¼ in.)	8 oz.	
Leeks, diced (¼ in.)	1 bunch	
Raw Lean Beef, round or chuck	2 lb.	
Butter	4 oz.	
OR Salad Oil		
Brown Stock (p.271)	2½ gal.	4. Add stock, crushed tomatoes and sachet bag.
Tomatoes, crushed	1 No. 2½ can	5. Bring to a boil, then lower heat and simmer for ½ hr. or until meat is done. Occasionally remove scum and fat with ladle.
Sachet Bag:		
Thyme	1 tsp.	6. Remove sachet bag. Adjust seasoning. Remove excess fat with ladle.
Sage	1 tsp.	7. Add barley and water, blend and simmer 2 to 3 min. Place in bain marie.
Bay Leaf	2	
Allspice	3	
Salt	to taste	
Pepper	to taste	
Cooked Barley, with water	4 oz.	
Worcestershire Sauce	to taste	
Parsley, chopped	to garnish	8. Wash, dry and chop parsley fine. Garnish soup by sprinkling parsley over each cup at time of service.
VARIATION: For **English Lamb Broth**, substitute lamb for beef.		
See color picture, p. 264.		

Beef Soup with Farina Dumplings

YIELD: 50 portions	EACH PORTION: 8 oz.	
INGREDIENTS	*QUANTITY*	*METHOD*
Beef Stock, clear	2½ gal.	1. Place beef stock on range. Bring to boil.
Butter	4 oz.	2. Cream butter; add eggs, farina and salt. Refrigerate 10 min. Remove dumpling mix from refrigerator. Adjust consistency by adding more farina, if necessary.
Eggs, whole	4	3. Drop by ½ teaspoonful into boiling stock. Cover and simmer about 10 to 15 min.
Farina	about 8 oz.	4. Remove to warm part of range and let stand for 5 min. before serving.
Salt	1/8 tsp.	

French Onion Soup

YIELD: 50 portions		EACH PORTION: 8 oz.
INGREDIENTS	*QUANTITY*	*METHOD*
Onions, peeled, sliced fine Butter 　OR Margarine Beef Stock, warm Chicken Stock, warm	8 lb. 8 oz. 1½ gal. 1½ gal.	1. Saute onions in butter in uncovered soup pot until onions begin to brown. Color evenly. 2. Add strained clear stocks, and mix. 3. Bring to boil and reduce heat. Simmer for about 25 min. or until onion flavor is well developed. Avoid over-cooking onion. Remove scum periodically.
Salt Pepper Dry Sherry (optional)	to taste to taste 6 oz.	4. Season to taste. Add sherry. Serve with croutons and parmesan cheese. Croutons may be placed on the soup or served on the side. Parmesan cheese should be served on the side.

CROUTONS FOR ONION SOUP
METHOD I
Make a paste with ½ lb. creamed butter and 6 oz. parmesan cheese. Trim crusts from white bread and spread butter mixture generously over bread. Cut each slice of bread in 4 equal squares. Bake until dry and lightly browned.
METHOD II
Place cut bread on bake sheet and toast one side lightly under broiler. Turn over and sprinkle lightly with melted butter or margarine. Sprinkle generously with parmesan cheese. Sprinkle lightly with paprika and once more with butter. Place in oven and bake until dry and light brown. May be finished under broiler for color. If bread is fresh, keep in warm place so that it will become crisp all the way through.

Oxtail Soup (Clear)

YIELD: 50 portions		EACH PORTION: 8 oz.
INGREDIENTS	*QUANTITY*	*METHOD*
Oxtails, disjointed Mirepoix: 　Onions, coarsely chopped 　Carrots, coarsely chopped 　Celery, coarsely chopped Beef Stock Tomatoes, chopped	10 lb. 1 lb. ½ lb. ½ lb. 2½ gal. 1 No. 10 can	1. Brown the disjointed oxtails in a black pan. Add mirepoix and cook until vegetables are tender. Place in a soup pot with 2 gal. stock and tomatoes. Reserve a few tomatoes diced for garnish. Cook until meat is tender.
Barley, soaked several hours or overnight	½ lb.	2. Cook presoaked barley and rinse in cold water.
Celery, small dice Carrots, small dice Turnips, small dice	2 lb. 2 lb. 2 lb.	3. Bring carrots, turnips and celery to one boil and drain. Place all three together in remaining ½ gal. stock and simmer until vegetables are done.
		4. Remove oxtails, pick meat off bones and cut meat in dice.
Egg Whites Water Tarragon Vinegar	12 8 oz. as needed	5. Skim grease from soup. To clear the soup, beat egg whites with 8 oz. of water, dash of tarragon vinegar and dash of salt until frothy. Add to stock, beating rapidly. Slowly bring to a boil. Remove from heat. Pass through a double cheesecloth.
Sherry Wine Worcestershire Sauce	4 oz. to taste	6. Combine cooked diced vegetables and barley with clarified oxtail stock. 7. Add sherry and worcestershire sauce and hold for service.

Soups

Essence of Celery Celestine

YIELD: 50 portions	**EACH PORTION:** 8 oz.	
INGREDIENTS	*QUANTITY*	*METHOD*

Essence of Celery:
   Egg Whites
   Water
   Chopped Beef
   Onions)
   Carrots)
   Celery)   Coarse grind
   Garlic)
   Peppercorns
   Thyme
   Bay Leaves
   Beef Stock, cold
   Chicken Stock, hot
   Onion, cut in rings and browned
	18 whites
	½ pt.
	2 lb.
	2 lb.
	1 lb.
	3 bunches
	3 cloves
	to season
	to season
	to season
	2 gal.
	2 gal.
	1
		Celery:
		1. Put egg whites in soup pot and beat with salt and water.
		2. Add chopped beef and mix well.
		3. Add raw vegetables and spices.
		4. Stir in cold beef stock, then hot chicken stock. Bring to boil, stirring periodically until the raft starts to form.
		5. Make an opening in raft and add browned onion rings. Simmer for 1 to 1½ hr.
		6. Strain through china cap and cheesecloth.

Celestine:
   Eggs, whole
   Milk
   Salt
   Flour
   Butter, melted
   Parsley, chopped
   Chives, chopped
	6
	1½ pt.
	pinch
	1 lb.
	1½ oz.
		Celestine:
		1. Whip eggs, add milk and salt and mix.
		2. Mix in flour and butter. Add chives and parsley last.
		3. Fry like French Pancakes (p. 121) and cut julienne.
		4. Add 1 generous teaspoon julienne pancakes each serving.

Tomato Bouillon with Rice

YIELD: 50 portions	**EACH PORTION:** 6½ oz.	
INGREDIENTS	*QUANTITY*	*METHOD*
Chicken Stock Tomato Juice Celery, chopped Onion, chopped Sugar Salt	6 qt. 5 qt. 2 lb. 1 lb. ¾ oz. 1 oz.	1. Simmer all ingredients together until vegetables are soft.
Lemon Juice Rice, cooked	4 oz. 1 qt.	2. Strain and add lemon juice. 3. Bring to boil and hold for service. 4. Add cooked rice when serving.
NOTE: Barley or any of the paste products may be substituted for rice.		

Le Pot-au-Feu

YIELD: about 25 portions		EACH PORTION: 8 oz.
INGREDIENTS	*QUANTITY*	*METHOD*
Beef Plate Beef Shank Water	3 lb. 2 lb. 1 gal.	1. Place beef plate and beef shank in medium sized stock pot. Add 1 gal. cold water. Bring to boil. Albumen in the meat will coagulate and come to the surface during boiling. Carefully remove this scum as it forms. Add a small amount of cold water occasionally to retard boiling and facilitate removal of scum. This operation is important for a clear bouillon.
Carrots Turnips Parsnips Onions, stuck with Cloves Whites of Leeks) Celery) tied together Parsley) Salt	6 3 2 2 2 4 1 stalk 1 sprig to taste	2. Add all vegetables except cabbage; add salt. Simmer 2½ to 3 hr. or until tender, removing scum as above. Wipe edge of pot occasionally with piece of wet muslin to remove scum forming there.
Cabbage, cored and blanched	2 heads	3. One hour before serving, place cabbage in a separate deep pan, just large enough to hold it. Moisten with a soup ladle of bouillon and a ladle of fat removed from top of stock pot. Cook until cabbage is tender. 4. At service time, remove stock from heat. Add ½ pt. cold water; let stand a few minutes. Skim off grease which comes to surface. 5. Strain bouillon into large soup tureen. Place the meat in the center of a large platter and arrange all vegetables around it with cabbage at ends. Serve tureen and platter together.

NOTE: Additional vegetables can be cut into batonette shape and used as a garnish in place of vegetable from which flavor and nutrients have been extracted in the broth during the cooking process. These vegetables should be blanched in beef stock for about 15 to 20 min. and be reserved until service.

Petite Marmite

YIELD: 50 portions		EACH PORTION: 8 oz.
INGREDIENTS	*QUANTITY*	*METHOD*
Stewing Chicken, whole OR Fowl, whole Beef, shin meat or chuck Beef Stock Chicken Stock Small Sachet Bag	6 lb. 5 lb. 2 gal. 2 gal. 1	1. Brown chicken and beef in oven at 400°F. Remove and put into beef and chicken stock with sachet bag. Simmer until beef and chicken are tender, 1½ to 2 hr., skimming frequently.
Carrots, batonette* Turnips, batonette Leeks, batonette Cabbage, batonette	100 100 100 100	2. Clean and cut vegetables, separate and place in individual cheesecloths. Place all bags in beef and chicken stock for last half hour of cooking.
Marrow (beef shin and shank bones) Croutons Parmesan Cheese, grated Chervil, chopped	50 slices 50 for croutons for garnish	3. Remove beef and chicken, cool and cut batonette. 4. Remove vegetables from cheesecloth bags. Add to meat in another pot. Reduce stock to 2½ gal. Strain and add to vegetables and meat.
		5. Serve in marmite pots topped with slice of marrow and toasted crouton with parmesan cheese. 6. For marrow, blanch bones in salt water. Slice, then put in ice water until serving time. One piece to an order. Serve with chopped chervil on top.

*Batonette means cut into blocks 1 in. long and ¼ in. wide.
NOTE: Petite Marmite is named after the pot (marmite) it is cooked in.

Chicken Soup

YIELD: 50 portions		
INGREDIENTS	*QUANTITY*	*METHOD*
Onions, small dice Celery, small dice Chicken Stock, hot Salt Pepper Parsley, chopped	1½ lb. 1 lb. 2½ gal. to taste to taste 1½ oz.	1. Add vegetables to hot stock and simmer until tender. 2. Add salt and pepper to taste. 3. Sprinkle parsley over soup at serving time.

NOTE: Soup may be served with various garnishes, such as rice or soup noodles.
   Vegetables may be sauteed before incorporating with stock or broth, if desired.

Chicken Broth with Parsley Dumplings

YIELD: 50 portions		EACH PORTION: 1 bowl broth with 2 dumplings
INGREDIENTS	QUANTITY	METHOD
Chicken Stock	2½ gal.	1. Bring chicken broth to boil and keep hot.
PARSLEY DUMPLINGS Flour Baking Powder Salt Eggs, whole Milk Salad Oil Parsley, chopped	 12 oz. ¾ oz. 1 tsp. 3 10 oz. 2 oz. 1 oz.	**Preparation of Parsley Dumplings** 2. Sift flour, baking powder and salt together. 3. Beat the eggs and combine with the milk and salad oil. 4. Add the liquid mixture and parsley to the dry ingredients, stirring only enough to moisten all ingredients. 5. Drop ½ tsp. at a time on an oiled tray or sheet pan. 6. Place in sectional steamer and steam for 5 min. 7. Add 2 dumplings to each bowl of broth just as it is being served.
NOTE: Soup is to be served immediately. All dumplings may be added to soup.		

Chicken Broth Brunoise

YIELD: 50 portions		EACH PORTION: 8 oz.
INGREDIENTS	QUANTITY	METHOD
Onions Carrots Celery Chicken Stock Salt Pepper	1 lb. 1 lb. ½ lb. 2½ gal. to taste to taste	1. Cut vegetables in small uniform dice, about 1/8 in. square. (Brunoise) 2. Add to the stock. Simmer for 20 min. Season to taste.
NOTE: **Chicken Broth with Egg Drops** as follows: Egg Drops—12 eggs) 1 tbsp. Worcestershire) beat together 1. Pour above mixture through coarse china cap into 2½ gal. boiling chicken broth and shake well while cooking. **Chicken Broth with Rice:** Add 1 qt. cooked rice to 2½ gal. chicken stock.		

Duck Soup, Parisienne

YIELD: 50 portions		EACH PORTION: 8 oz.
INGREDIENTS	QUANTITY	METHOD
Bones from about 12 Roast Ducks Water Onions, coarsely chopped Carrots, coarsely chopped Celery, coarsely chopped Wings, necks and giblets, raw	 3 gal. 2 lb. 1 lb. 1 lb.	1. Brown all bones in oven at 350°F. 2. Transfer to stock pot and add cool water to cover. 3. Bring to boil and reduce to simmering. 4. Add onions, carrots, celery, wings, necks and giblets. Simmer 2 hr.
Carrots, small Parisienne White Turnips, small Parisienne Yellow Turnips, small Parisienne Salt Pepper	1 pt. 1 pt. 1 pt. to taste to taste	5. Strain stock, save giblets. 6. Trim giblets well, slice thin and reserve for garnish. 7. Cook carrots, white and yellow turnips separately. 8. Strain and add giblets and vegetables to stock. 9. Season to taste.
See color picture, p. 265.		

Clear Turtle Soup

YIELD: 50 portions		EACH PORTION: 8 oz.
INGREDIENTS	QUANTITY	METHOD

Clear Beef Consomme
Herb Sachet:
  Sweet Basil
  Marjoram
  Rosemary
  Fennel
  Mint
  Sage
  Allspice
  Thyme
  Bay Leaves
	2½ gal.
	
	½ tsp.
	½ tsp.
	½ tsp.
	½ tsp.
	½ tsp.
	½ tsp.
	½ tsp.
	½ tsp.
	3
		1. Bring clear consomme to light boil in stock pot. Add herb sachet, properly tied in cheesecloth, and simmer 15 min. Taste for flavor and simmer 10 to 15 min. longer if more flavor is desired. Remove sachet.

Green Turtle Meat, canned Salt Pepper Dry Sherry Wine Arrowroot (optional)	2 No. 2½ cans to taste to taste ½ pt. 4 tbsp.	2. Drain turtle meat, add liquid to consomme. Rinse cans with consomme and pour into stockpot. Continue to simmer. Skim scum from consomme. Transfer about 2 qt. to another stockpot. 3. Cut turtle meat into small cubes. Add to the 2 qt. of consomme. Simmer for a few minutes to dissolve all gelatine. Remove turtle meat and add to stockpot. Season to taste with salt and pepper and add sherry wine.

NOTE: In many instances clear turtle soup is lightly thickened with arrowroot diluted with sherry wine.

Clam Broth

YIELD: 50 portions		EACH PORTION: 8 oz.
INGREDIENTS	QUANTITY	METHOD
Clams Salt Cornmeal Ice	½ bushel 1 handful 2 handfuls to cover clams	1. Wash clams in sink full of water; all the clams that float to the top are dead or bad and should not be used. 2. Put clams in pot, sprinkle with handful of salt and 2 handfuls of cornmeal and cover with ice. Refrigerate overnight. 3. In the morning, repeat Step 1.
Celery Water Hot Pepper Sauce Worcestershire Sauce Salt	6 stalks 2½ gal. to taste to taste to taste	4. Put celery on the bottom of the stock pot. 5. Add clams, almost cover with water and season. Let come to boil, then push pot to side of range and let stand 20 min. Remove from range and let stand 30 min. Drain off broth through spigot and let stand for 20 min. 6. Put plate in bottom of pot. Strain broth through cheesecloth into pot. Season to taste.

NOTE: To make **Clam Broth Bellevue:**
use ½ Clam Broth and ½ Chicken Stock; put dash of whipped cream on top just before serving.

Vegetable Soup

INGREDIENTS	QUANTITY	METHOD
YIELD: 50 portions	**EACH PORTION**: 8 oz.	
Onions, medium dice	2 lb.	1. Saute onions, carrots and celery in oil in soup pot until nearly tender. Do not brown.
Carrots, medium dice	1½ lb.	2. Add stock and bring to boil.
Celery, medium dice	1 lb.	3. Add tomatoes and juice. When soup returns to boil, reduce heat and simmer until vegetables are tender, about ½ hr. Remove scum as it rises to top.
Salad Oil	8 oz.	
OR Chicken Fat		
Chicken Stock, hot	2 gal.	
Tomatoes, chopped	1 No. 2½ can	
Cooked Peas	1 pt.	
Salt	to taste	
Pepper	to taste	

NOTE: Cooked peas may be added just prior to service or a heaping teaspoon placed in each cup when serving.
There are many variations of vegetable soup and nearly any combination of vegetables is acceptable.
Paysanne means peasant style and refers primarily to a coarse cut vegetable, 1/4 in. by 1/4 in. by 1/8 in.
Fermiere, which means farmer's wife, has discs of carrots, turnips, celery, potatoes, onions, cabbage.
Brunoise refers to vegetables cut in small dice.

Minestrone Soup

INGREDIENTS	QUANTITY	METHOD
YIELD: 50 portions	**EACH PORTION**: 8 oz.	
Blackeyed Beans	6 oz.	1. Soak beans overnight. Wash, drain and cook in lightly salted water until tender.
OR Other Dried Beans		
Oil	4 oz.	2. Heat oil or render salt pork in a soup pot and add vegetables and garlic. Cover and smother until tender but not browned.
OR Chopped Salt Pork		
Onions, paysanne cut	2 lb.	3. Add crushed tomatoes, stock, salt and pepper.
Celery, paysanne cut	1 lb.	4. Bring to a fast boil, then reduce to simmer and cook for ½ hr. Avoid overcooking of vegetables.
Carrots, paysanne cut	1 lb.	
Green Peppers, paysanne cut	12 oz.	
*Cabbage, paysanne cut	8 oz.	
Garlic, crushed, chopped	6 cloves	
Tomatoes, canned, crushed	1 qt.	
Stock, white	2½ gal.	
Salt	¾ oz.	
Pepper	½ tsp.	
Ditalini	6 oz.	5. Add Ditalini to soup, stir and cook until done.
OR Other Macaroni Product		
Chick Peas	1 No. 303 can	6. Add cooked beans and chick peas. Adjust seasoning. Bring to boil. Remove from heat and keep hot in bain marie.
Pesto	1 lb.	7. Form pesto into small balls and drop into hot soup. Heat until dissolved.
See p. 88		8. Stir well before serving. Grated parmesan cheese may be served with soup. Serve the grated parmesan cheese separately.

*Spinach can be used instead of cabbage.

See preparation pictures, p. 282.

Soups

MINESTRONE SOUP

Make Pesto for Minestrone Soup by combining ground salt pork, parsley and garlic; form into small balls. Drop into hot soup, heat until dissolved. Stir soup well before serving (Recipe p. 88.)

Serve cups or bowls of soup topped with parmesan cheese or offer parmesan cheese at the table. Minestrone is a hearty Italian soup and is usually served with Italian entrees. (Recipe on p. 281.)

Dutch Potato Soup

YIELD: 50 portions	EACH PORTION: 8 oz.	
INGREDIENTS	*QUANTITY*	*METHOD*
Onions, chopped fine	1 pt.	1. Saute onions, celery and carrots lightly in butter.
Celery, chopped fine	1 pt.	2. Add potatoes and stock and boil slowly for 35 to
Carrots, chopped fine	1 pt.	40 min.
Butter	3 oz.	3. Season and sprinkle with chopped parsley when
Potatoes, sliced very thin	1 gal.	serving.
Rich Beef Stock	2½ gal.	
OR Rich Chicken Stock		
Parsley, chopped	for garnish	

Manhattan Clam Chowder

YIELD: 50 portions	EACH PORTION: 8 oz.	
INGREDIENTS	*QUANTITY*	*METHOD*
Clams, chopped	3 qt. OR 2 No. 5 cans	1. If fresh clams are used, place clams and juice in large pot and add water. Bring to boiling point. Remove from heat.
Water	6 qt.	2. Add enough stock to potatoes to cover. Cook
Potatoes, peeled, small dice	1 lb.	diced potatoes in clam stock or water and hold for Step 6.
Salt Pork, ground or chopped fine	12 oz.	3. Render fat from salt pork. Remove remaining pork scraps or strain rendered fat into large soup pot.
Celery, small dice	1 lb.	
Onions, small dice	2 lb.	4. Add diced vegetables to pork fat and saute until
Carrots, small dice	8 oz.	nearly tender. Add minced garlic and saute briefly.
Leeks, small dice	8 oz.	
Peppers, green, small dice	8 oz.	
Garlic, minced	1 tsp.	
Tomatoes, canned, chopped	1 qt.	5. If fresh clams are used, strain stock from clams into vegetables, add tomatoes and sachet bag and simmer slowly for about ½ hr. If using canned clams, use liquid from cans plus fish stock or a combination of fish stock and canned or bottled clam juice or broth.
Sachet Bag:		
Whole Peppercorns	10	
Oregano	1 oz.	
Salt	1½ tbsp.	
White Pepper	½ tsp.	
Worcestershire Sauce (optional)	1 tbsp.	6. Remove sachet bag and add clams and potatoes.
		7. Season to taste and keep hot for service.

NOTE: Manhattan Clam Chowder is also called **Long Island** or **Philadelphia Chowder**.

Cock-A-Leekie Soup

YIELD: 50 portions	EACH PORTION: 8 oz.	
INGREDIENTS	*QUANTITY*	*METHOD*
Fowl Water Mirepoix: Celery, coarsely chopped Onions, coarsely chopped Carrots, coarsely chopped	12 lb. 4 gal. 1 lb. 1 lb. 1 lb.	1. Wash fowl inside and out. 2. Cover fowl with cold water in stock pot. Add mirepoix and simmer until fowl is tender. 3. When fowl is done, remove from pot and cool. 4. Strain stock through china cap and cheesecloth into soup pot. Skim off fat.
Leeks Potatoes Salt Pepper	2 lb. 4 lb. to taste to taste	5. Wash and drain leeks. 6. Cut potatoes and leeks julienne. 7. Add leeks to stock and bring to boil, then add potatoes and cook until done. 8. Cut fowl julienne and add to soup. 9. Season to taste.
Prunes, soaked overnight	1½ lb.	10. Cook prunes in water until tender. 11. Remove pits from prunes, and bring to one boil in chicken stock. 12. Serve prune on side, as garnish.

Chicken Gumbo Creole

YIELD: 50 portions	EACH PORTION: 8 oz.	
INGREDIENTS	*QUANTITY*	*METHOD*
Butter OR Rendered Chicken Fat Onions, diced medium Celery, diced medium	9 oz. 3½ lb. 2 lb.	1. Heat butter or chicken fat in soup pot. Add onions and celery and smother until tender (do not brown).
Chicken Stock Bouquet Garni Tomatoes, crushed	3 gal. 2 No. 2½ cans	2. Add chicken stock, bouquet garni and tomatoes; bring to fast boil, reduce heat. Simmer 30 min.
Green Peppers, diced medium	1½ lb.	3. Blanch green peppers in boiling salted water 5 min. Cook and drain.
Rice Salt Pepper Okra, cut (½ in. long pieces)	6 oz. ¾ oz. ¾ tsp. 1½ lb.	4. Wash rice, drain, add to soup, stir. Add salt and pepper. Cook until rice is done, then add okra and green peppers. Cook 5 min. longer. Remove fat and scum.
Chicken Meat, cooked, diced Hot Pepper Sauce (optional)	1 lb. to taste	5. Check seasoning, remove from heat. Place in bain marie. Add diced chicken.

VARIATION: For **Beef Gumbo Creole**, substitute 1½ lb. cooked, diced beef for chicken and use beef stock in place of chicken stock.

See color picture, p. 264.

Soups

Turkey Creole Soup

YIELD: 50 portions	**EACH PORTION**: 8 oz.	
INGREDIENTS	*QUANTITY*	*METHOD*
Onions, medium dice Celery, medium dice Salad Oil Turkey Stock, hot Tomatoes, chopped medium Rice, raw Sachet Bag	3 lb. 1½ lb. 8 oz. 2 gal. 1½ qt. 6 oz. 1	1. Saute onions and celery in salad oil in soup pot until tender. 2. Add turkey stock and bring to boil. 3. Add tomatoes, rice and sachet bag. When stock returns to boil, reduce heat and simmer about ½ hr. or until rice is cooked.
Green Peppers, medium dice Turkey Meat, diced	1 lb. 8 oz.	4. Blanch green peppers in boiling salted water about 4 min. Drain well and add to soup. Peppers should retain some texture and firmness. 5. Add turkey. Season to taste.
File Powder (optional) Water, cold Hot Pepper Sauce (optional)	2 tsp. 8 oz. to taste	OPTIONAL: Remove soup from heat. Dissolve 2 tsp. file powder in 1 cup cold water. Stir in to soup rapidly to prevent stringing. If soup is too hot when adding file powder, it will become stringy and unpalatable.

VARIATION: For **Turkey Gumbo**, add one No. 2 can okra.

Scotch Broth

YIELD: 50 portions	**EACH PORTION**: 8 oz.	
INGREDIENTS	*QUANTITY*	*METHOD*
Pearl Barley Lamb Stock, boiling	6 oz. 2½ gal.	1. Combine barley and ½ gal. boiling stock. Stir to prevent sticking. Return to boil and simmer for about 1 hr. or until done.
Shoulder Lamb, raw, lean, small dice Onions, cut in small dice (brunoise) Carrots, cut in small dice (brunoise) Celery, cut in small dice (brunoise) Turnip, yellow, cut in small dice (brunoise) Leeks, diced (brunoise) Salt Thyme Pepper, White Worcestershire Sauce Parsley, chopped	2 lb. 2 lb. 1½ lb. 1 lb. 8 oz. 4 oz. 1½ oz. ½ tsp. ½ tsp. to taste to garnish	2. Place all other ingredients in remaining boiling stock. When stock returns to boil, reduce heat and simmer for ½ hr. Avoid overcooking brunoise of vegetables. 3. Combine cooked barley and stock with remainder of soup. Adjust seasoning and hold for service. 4. Serve sprinkled with chopped parsley.

VARIATIONS: For **Lamb Broth Ecoccaise**, eliminate barley. When soup is cooked, stir in rolled oats to thicken. Cook only until glossy and slightly thickened.

NOTE: Cooked lamb meat removed from bones may be substituted for part of raw lamb meat. Add to soup when finished.
  This is a hearty soup containing many vegetables and slightly thickened by the barley.

See color picture, p. 263.

Potage Basque

YIELD: 50 portions		EACH PORTION: 8 oz.
INGREDIENTS	*QUANTITY*	*METHOD*
Cabbage, trimmed, diced fine	3 lb.	1. Place cabbage, salt pork, onions and leeks in 1 gal.
Salt Pork, whole piece	1 lb.	boiling stock and cook together. Cook barley sep-
Onions, diced fine	1 lb.	arately in 1 gal. stock.
Leeks, diced fine	12 oz.	
Stock, chicken or beef, boiling	2 gal.	
Barley, uncooked	1 lb.	
Potatoes, diced (¼ in.)	2 lb.	2. When barley is cooked, add potatoes and cook un-
Cream Sauce, light	1 gal.	til potatoes are tender. Add cream sauce and com-
Tomatoes, chopped, cooked	1 qt.	bine remaining ingredients.
Parsley, chopped fine	1 oz.	3. Remove salt pork and simmer 5 min. Adjust sea-
Celery Leaves, white, chopped fine	1 oz.	soning.
Salt	to taste	
White Pepper	to taste	

Potage Parisienne

YIELD: 50 portions		EACH PORTION: 8 oz.
INGREDIENTS	*QUANTITY*	*METHOD*
Leeks, white only	3 lb.	1. Cut leeks and onions about same size as potatoes.
Onions, peeled	2 lb.	Saute leeks and onions in butter for 3 to 4 min.
Butter	12 oz.	2. Add flour, blending well; add stock and bring to
Flour	1 pt.	boil.
Stock, chicken	3 gal.	3. Add potatoes. Reduce heat and simmer for 45
Potatoes, peeled, cut	8 lb.	min.
(1/16 in. thick, 1/2 in. square)		4. Adjust seasoning if necessary.
Cream, light	1 pt.	5. Add cream just before serving.
Bread, trimmed, diced	½ loaf	6. Saute diced bread in butter until golden brown.
(3/8 in. square)		7. Combine chives with soup for garnish and add
Butter	4 oz.	croutons to individual portions.
Chives, finely cut	4 oz.	

Rice Soup Florentine

YIELD: 50 portions		EACH PORTION: 8 oz.
INGREDIENTS	*QUANTITY*	*METHOD*
Green Onions, chopped	12	1. Saute onions, leeks and garlic in olive oil but do
Leeks, diced	8	not brown.
Olive Oil	8 oz.	2. Julienne spinach, add to above and smother for 10
Garlic	4 cloves	min.
Spinach	4 lb.	
Soup Stock	2¼ gal.	3. Add stock and rice, boil for 20 min. or just until
Rice, raw	14 oz.	rice is cooked.
Waffle Batter (unsweetened)	8 oz.	4. Add cheese to waffle batter and drop batter through
Parmesan Cheese, grated	2 oz.	colander into soup. Bring to a boil, remove from
Salt	to taste	heat. Season and serve.
Pepper	to taste	
Grated Nutmeg	to taste	

Soups

Old Fashioned Cabbage Soup

YIELD: 50 portions		EACH PORTION: 8 oz.
INGREDIENTS	QUANTITY	METHOD
Onions, diced medium Celery, diced small Butter Cabbage, shredded Parsley, chopped	12 oz. 8 oz. 10 oz. 5 lb. 2 tbsp.	1. Saute onions and celery in butter until nearly tender. 2. Add cabbage and chopped parsley and smother 5 min.
Flour Chicken Stock, hot	10 oz. 9 qt.	3. Add flour, blending well. Cook 2 to 3 min. 4. Add stock gradually. Mix smooth. Simmer ½ hr.
Frankfurters, sliced Frozen Peas, cooked Mushrooms, diced small, sauteed Salt Pepper	1½ lb. 2½ lb. 6 oz. 2 tsp. ½ tsp.	5. Add frankfurter slices, cooked peas, mushrooms, salt and pepper. Bring to boil. Reduce heat and simmer 5 min. Hold for service.

Barley and Mushroom Soup

YIELD: 50 portions		EACH PORTION: 8 oz.
INGREDIENTS	QUANTITY	METHOD
Barley Onions, small dice (brunoise) Celery Carrots Leeks Chicken Fat Chicken Stock, double strength Bouquet Garni Mushrooms, diced or sliced Salt Pepper	1 lb. ¾ lb. ½ lb. ½ lb. ¼ lb. ½ lb. 2½ gal. 3 lb. to taste to taste	1. Cook barley in boiling water. 2. Smother brunoise vegetables in chicken fat. 3. Drain barley thoroughly and add to vegetables. 4. Add chicken stock, bring to a boil and simmer. Add bouquet garni. 5. Smother mushrooms in chicken fat. 6. Add mushrooms to soup and complete cooking.

NOTE: To smother, saute in a covered pot slowly. This retains moisture and prevents burning.
For double strength, reduce chicken stock to about ½ volume to increase flavor.

Borscht

YIELD: 50 portions		EACH PORTION: 1 soup cup, 8 oz.
INGREDIENTS	QUANTITY	METHOD
Beets, canned Onions, medium dice Vinegar, cider Sugar, granulated Water	1 No. 10 can. 1 lb. 12¼ oz. 6 oz. 6 qt.	1. Drain beets. Place beet juice, onions, vinegar, sugar and 1 qt. of water in soup pot. Simmer until onions are cooked. 2. Chop or coarse grind beets.
Lemon Juice Salt Pepper	4 oz. to taste to taste	3. When onions are cooked, add balance of water, beets and lemon juice to soup pot. Bring to boil and adjust seasoning. Remove from heat and cool according to standard procedure
Sour Cream	1 pt.	4. Refrigerate overnight.
		5. Serve ice cold in cold cups. Top each portion with a teaspoon of sour cream at service time.

See color picture, p. 263.

Borscht, Polish Style

YIELD: 50 portions		EACH PORTION: 8 oz.
INGREDIENTS	QUANTITY	METHOD
Leeks, white only Onions Celery Fennel Duck Stock Salt (variable) Pepper	1½ lb. 1 lb. 1 lb. 8 oz. 2½ gal. 1½ tbsp. ½ tsp.	1. Cut leeks, onions, celery and fennel in large or coarse julienne. Place leeks, onions, celery and fennel in soup pot. Add duck stock, salt and pepper. Bring to boil. Skim scum on top, cover and simmer until tender.
Beets, cooked, fresh or canned, chopped or ground Cooked Beef) Cooked Duck) Cut in julienne Polish Sausage) Sour Cream	1 qt. 8 oz. 8 oz. 6 oz. 1 pt.	2. If fresh beets are used, wash, cut tops off and cook until tender. Remove skins and grind to obtain a volume of 1 qt. Add beets to the vegetables with the julienne of beef, duck and sausage. 3. Serve sour cream separately.
NOTE: Potatoes are generally used in this recipe, particularly when beef and duck are not available. Ground or finely shredded beets are also served separately with sour cream and not put into soup.		

Olla Podrida (Spanish National Soup)

YIELD: 50 portions		EACH PORTION: 8 oz.
INGREDIENTS	QUANTITY	METHOD
Black-eyed Beans Onions, medium dice Celery, medium dice Garlic, finely minced Salad Oil Rice, raw Saffron, finely crushed Chicken Stock	½ lb. 2 lb. ½ lb. 1½ tbsp. 12 oz. 8 oz. ½ tsp. 2 gal.	1. Simmer black-eyed beans in enough water to cover for about 2 hr. or until cooked. Reserve. 2. Saute onions, celery and garlic in oil in soup pot. 3. Add raw rice and saffron. Saute about 5 min., stirring frequently. 4. Add chicken stock and simmer until rice is cooked.
Sausage (Chorizos) Garbanzos, canned, and juice Chicken, cooked, medium dice Ham, cooked, medium dice	1½ lb. 2 No. 2 cans 12 oz. 1 lb.	5. Poach sausage separately 7 to 8 min. Remove from cooking water and cool. 6. Remove outside casing. Cut sausage lengthwise in 4 equal pieces. Slice across ¼ in. thick. Add to soup. 7. Drain black-eyed beans and add beans and remaining ingredients to soup. Simmer about 10 to 15 min. to blend flavors. 8. Season to taste if necessary. Skim excess grease.
NOTE: Chorizos sausage should be used if available; otherwise use Italian hot sausage. If Chorizos is used, it should be sliced thin.		

Philadelphia Pepper Pot with Spaetzli

YIELD: 50 portions		**EACH PORTION:** 8 oz.

INGREDIENTS	QUANTITY	METHOD
Honeycomb Tripe Chicken Stock, hot	3 lb. 2½ gal.	1. Cut tripe in ½ in. cubes, cover with part of chicken stock; cook slowly until tender.
Butter Onions, medium dice Flour Salt White Pepper Sweet Marjoram	10 oz. 2 lb. 10 oz. 1 tbsp. 1 tsp. 1 tsp.	2. Melt butter in soup pot, add onions, saute until tender. Add flour to make roux and cook 8 to 10 min. but do not brown. 3. Reserve sufficient stock to blanch green peppers and to cook potatoes. Add balance of stock gradually to roux, stirring until slightly thickened and smooth. Add seasonings. When soup reaches boil, reduce heat and simmer.
Green Peppers, medium dice Potatoes, peeled, cut (¼ in. dice)	1 lb. 2 lb.	4. Blanch green peppers in boiling chicken stock for 5 min. 5. Cover potatoes with lightly salted stock and cook until nearly tender. 6. When tripe and potatoes are done, add to soup with water in which they were cooked. 7. Drain blanched green peppers and add to soup. 8. Adjust seasoning and hold for service. 9. Prepare Spaetzli according to recipe below. 10. Spaetzli may be placed in cups or bowls at service time. If soup is to be served in quantity rather than individual service, spaetzli may be placed in soup.

Spaetzli

YIELD: 50 portions		**EACH PORTION:** 2 oz.

INGREDIENTS	QUANTITY	METHOD
Eggs, whole Water Flour Salt Nutmeg	12 1 qt. 3 lb. 2 tsp. 1 tsp.	1. Whip eggs well with wire whip in large mixing bowl (preferably stainless steel). 2. Add water and blend. 3. Add flour, salt and nutmeg and mix until well blended. Do not overmix. 4. Drop spaetzli mixture into a large pot of boiling salted water (about 3 gal.) by holding a colander over the water and working the batter through the holes in the colander. 5. Cook about 3 min. Remove with skimmer and place in pan with generous amount of water, stirring to prevent the spaetzli from sticking together.

NOTE: If spaetzli are to be made in advance of use, they may be removed to cold water to prevent further cooking and to "set" them. They may then be drained and held for service.

New England Clam Chowder

YIELD: 50 portions		EACH PORTION: 8 oz.
INGREDIENTS	QUANTITY	METHOD
Water, warm Clams, raw, minced Salt White Pepper Worcestershire Sauce Potatoes, diced (¼ in.) Salt Pork, ground Onions, diced	4 qt. 2½ lb. frozen, OR 2 No. 5 cans 1½ oz. ½ tsp. 2 tsp. 3½ lb. 1 lb. 2 lb.	1. In a large sauce pan, combine water, clams and seasonings. Bring to a boil. 2. Remove enough of above stock to cover potatoes. Cook potatoes. 3. Place salt pork in heavy soup pot, cook until partially rendered. 4. Add onions, saute until transparent.
Bread Flour Milk, hot Light Cream, hot Butter, melted	8 oz. 2 qt. 1 qt. 2 oz.	5. Add flour, make roux, cook 5 to 6 min. 6. Add clam stock to roux, stir until smooth. 7. Add potatoes, clams, milk and cream. 8. Adjust seasoning and add melted butter.

NOTE: If fresh clams are used, clams in shell must be thoroughly scrubbed and rinsed before cooking. Cover with water and cook 20 to 30 min. Drain, let sand settle to bottom. Rinse clams in cold water and remove from shell. Chop or grind, depending on toughness. Drain broth by pouring carefully from top so that sand and sediment will remain at bottom.

See color picture, p. 264.

New England Fish Chowder

YIELD: 50 portions		EACH PORTION: 8 oz.
INGREDIENTS	QUANTITY	METHOD
Potatoes, diced (¼ in.) Fish Stock, hot Salt Worcestershire Sauce White Pepper	3 lb. 7 qt. 1½ oz. 2 tsp. ½ tsp.	1. Cover potatoes with 1 gal. fish stock and add seasonings. Simmer until potatoes are done.
Salt Pork, ground or diced Butter OR Margarine Onions, sliced Flour	1 lb. 4 oz. 2 lb. 10 oz.	2. Heat salt pork until partially rendered. If salt pork is diced, render fat from pork and discard scraps. Add the butter or margarine and onions and saute until the onions are soft and transparent. 3. Add the flour to make roux, and cook 5 to 6 min. but do not brown. 4. Add the remainder of the stock gradually, stirring until thickened and smooth. Cook 10 min. 5. Add the cooked potatoes and stock. Blend with wooden paddle.
Milk, whole Light Cream Haddock Fillets, skinned, cut (¾ in. chunks) Butter, melted Hot Pepper Sauce (optional)	1 qt. 1 qt. 2 lb. 2 oz. to taste	6. Heat the milk and cream together and combine with chowder base. 7. Adjust seasoning and add fish. Keep hot until fish is cooked (4 to 5 min.). Do not boil. 8. Add 2 oz. butter and hold for service.

NOTE: Special care should be taken to remove all bones and skin from fish.

Soups

Seafood Chowder

YIELD: 50 portions	**EACH PORTION:** 8 oz.	
INGREDIENTS	*QUANTITY*	*METHOD*
Scallops Halibut Shrimp, peeled, deveined 　　(21 to 25 count)	2 lb. 2 lb. 1 lb.	1. Cut scallops ½ in. dice. Cover with 1 qt. water and poach 3 min. Remove from heat and reserve. 2. Cover halibut with 2 qt. water and poach 7 to 8 min. or until cooked but still firm. Reserve. 3. Cut each cleaned shrimp in 4 equal pieces.
Onions Celery Butter Flour Potatoes, small dice Clams 　　(or 1 qt. cooked fresh clams)	2 lb. 8 oz. 1 lb. 12 oz. 1½ lb. 1 No. 5 can	4. Saute onions and celery in butter and add shrimp. Cook about 5 min. or until shrimp are done. 5. Add flour, mixing well. Cook 3 to 4 min. but do not brown. 6. Cook potatoes separately in 1 qt. of water. 7. Add strained halibut stock to roux gradually, stirring until thickened and smooth. 8. Add potatoes and cooking water, clams and clam liquor and scallops with cooking water. 9. Remove bones and skin from halibut, flaking in pieces large enough to identify. Add flaked fish to chowder.
Milk, hot Light Cream, hot Salt Pepper	2 qt. 1 qt. to taste to taste	10. Add combined hot milk and cream. Season to taste.

Oyster Stew (Soup Course)

YIELD: 50 portions	**EACH PORTION:** 6 oz.	
INGREDIENTS	*QUANTITY*	*METHOD*
Milk	2 gal.	1. Scald milk, but do not boil.
Salt Pepper Oysters, shucked, with liquid Butter Paprika	2 oz. 2 tsp. ½ gal. 8 oz. to garnish	2. Add salt and pepper to oysters; cook over low heat until the edges of the oysters begin to curl. 3. Pour scalded milk over oysters. 4. Add butter. 5. Sprinkle top with paprika. Serve immediately.
NOTE: Care should be taken not to overcook oysters; they get tough if heated too long. Serve at once to avoid curdling.		

Potato Chowder

YIELD: 50 portions	**EACH PORTION:** 8 oz.	
INGREDIENTS	*QUANTITY*	*METHOD*
Butter Onions, diced medium Celery, chopped Flour Chicken Stock, hot	1 lb. 3 lb. 12 oz. 8 oz. 6 qt.	1. Melt butter, add onions, celery; saute til tender. 2. Add flour, blending well. Cook 3 to 4 min. but do not brown. 3. Add 3 qt. chicken stock gradually, stirring until slightly thickened and smooth.
Potatoes, peeled, diced (¼ in.) Milk, hot Light Cream, hot Parsley, chopped	3 qt. 2 qt. 1 qt. for garnish	4. Cook potatoes in balance of chicken stock until done. Add potatoes, stock to first mixture; blend. 5. Add hot milk and cream and season to taste. 6. Sprinkle individual servings with chopped parsley at service time.

Vegetable-Tomato Chowder

YIELD: 50 portions		EACH PORTION: 8 oz.
INGREDIENTS	QUANTITY	METHOD
Mixed Frozen Vegetables, cooked and drained	2½ lb.	1. Cook frozen vegetables, reserving cooking water for Step No. 4
Butter Cabbage) Celery) diced fine Onions) Flour	10 oz. 14 oz. 14 oz. 9 oz. 8 oz.	2. Heat butter in sauce pan, smother cabbage, celery and onions until tender but not browned. 3. Stir in flour, continue to cook slowly until roux is well blended (10 min.).
Beef or Chicken Stock and liquid obtained from cooking of frozen vegetables Potatoes, small dice Tomato Sauce Milk, scalded Chopped Parsley Salt Pepper	3 qt. 3 lb. 1 qt. 1 gal. 2 tbsp. to taste to taste	4. Stir in stock and juices of cooked vegetables. Stir until smooth. Add the raw diced potatoes and tomato sauce and continue to cook slowly until potatoes are tender, about 40 min. 5. Add vegetables, scalded milk, chopped parsley, salt and pepper.

Washington Chowder

YIELD: 50 portions		EACH PORTION: 8 oz.
INGREDIENTS	QUANTITY	METHOD
Salt Pork, diced medium Onions, diced medium Flour Salad Oil	8 oz. 8 oz. 6 oz. to thin	1. Partially render diced salt pork in soup pot. 2. Add onions and finish cooking salt pork, browning onions lightly. 3. Add flour to make roux. 4. Add as much oil as necessary for proper consistency. 5. Cook for 3 to 4 min.
Chicken Stock Potatoes (¼ in. dice) Frozen Corn, whole kernel Celery, diced medium Green Peppers, diced Tomatoes, canned, chopped Baking Soda Sugar Salt White Pepper Hot Pepper Sauce Thyme Basil	2 qt. 4 lb. 2½ lb. ¾ lb. 3 oz. 1½ No. 10 cans ¾ oz. 1 tbsp. 1 tbsp. ½ tsp. to taste ¼ tsp. ¼ tsp.	6. Add stock gradually, blending roux well. Stir until smooth and bring to boil. 7. Add potatoes, corn and celery; simmer until potatoes are nearly tender. 8. Add green peppers and cook until tender. 9. Add tomatoes and baking soda. 10. Add seasonings and simmer 5 min. 11. Remove from heat.
Milk	1½ gal.	12. Heat milk and add to above soup mixture and hold for service.

See color picture, p. 263.

Soups

Corn Chowder Maryland

INGREDIENTS	QUANTITY	METHOD
YIELD: 50 portions	**EACH PORTION:** 8 oz.	
Salt Pork	1½ lb.	1. Saute salt pork until lightly brown. Add onions and sweat.
Onions, diced fine	1¾ lb.	2. Add flour, blend to make roux. Cook 5 to 10 min. but do not brown.
Flour	1 lb.	
Chicken Stock	2 gal.	3. Blend in chicken stock. Add sachet bag. Bring to boil.
Sachet Bag:		
Whole Peppercorns	10	
Oregano	1 oz.	
Creamed Corn	4 No. 303 cans	4. Add creamed corn. Bring slowly to boiling, strain through china cap. Put back on range.
Potatoes, diced	4 lb.	5. Add potatoes and cook 15 min.
Corn, cut fresh from cob	4 lb.	6. Add corn; season to taste. Cook until potatoes are just tender.
Heavy Cream, cold	2 qt.	7. Finish with heavy cream. Season.
Salt	to taste	
Hot Pepper Sauce	to taste	

New England Corn Chowder

INGREDIENTS	QUANTITY	METHOD
YIELD: 50 portions	**EACH PORTION:** 8 oz.	
Salt Pork	1 lb.	1. Chop or grind salt pork. Render and strain fat into soup pot. Discard rendered scraps.
Onions, small dice	2 lb.	2. Add onions and saute until tender.
Flour	8 oz.	3. Add flour, mixing well. Cook without browning 3 to 4 min.
Chicken Stock	1 gal.	4. Add chicken stock slowly, stirring until smooth.
Cream Style Corn	2 qt.	5. Add corn.
Potatoes, raw, small dice	2 qt.	6. Cook potatoes separately, drain and add to chowder.
Milk, hot	2 qt.	7. Add hot milk and cream.
Light Cream, hot	1 qt.	8. Season to taste.

Cream of Chicken Soup

INGREDIENTS	QUANTITY	METHOD
YIELD: 50 portions	**EACH PORTION:** 8 oz.	
Onions, medium dice	1 lb.	1. Saute vegetables in butter in sauce pot until nearly tender.
Celery, medium dice	½ lb.	
Carrots, medium dice	½ lb.	2. Add flour to make roux. Cook 8 to 10 min. but do not brown.
Butter	1 lb.	3. Add hot stock gradually, stirring until slightly thickened and smooth.
Bread Flour	12 oz.	
Chicken Stock, hot	2 gal.	4. Add bay leaf and simmer ½ hr.
Bay Leaf	1	5. Bring to boil and pass through food mill. Pass through china cap if necessary.
Milk, hot	2 qt.	6. Add heated milk and cream.
Light Cream, hot	1 qt.	7. Adjust seasoning and add diced chicken. Hold for service.
Chicken Meat, finely diced	6 oz.	

Mulligatawny Soup

YIELD: 50 portions	EACH PORTION: 8 oz.	
INGREDIENTS	*QUANTITY*	*METHOD*

Onions, cut in small dice
Celery, cut in small dice
Chicken Fat
    OR Butter
    OR Margarine
Eggplant, cut in small dice
Green Peppers, cut in small dice
Apples, peeled, small dice
	2 lb.
	1 lb.
	12 oz.
	
	12 oz.
	8 oz.
	1½ lb.
		1. Saute onions and celery in fat in heavy soup pot until tender.
		2. Blanch eggplant separately in boiling salted water 5 min.
		3. Blanch green peppers and apples together in boiling salted water 5 min.

Flour Curry Powder Salt Pepper, white Chicken Stock, hot	10 oz. 3 tbsp. to taste 1 tsp. 1 pt.	4. Add flour, curry powder, salt and pepper to fat and mix well. Cook over low heat 5 to 6 min., do not brown. 5. Add hot chicken stock gradually, stirring until thickened and smooth. Return to boil and add drained eggplant, green peppers and apples. Simmer until vegetables are tender.
Milk, hot Cream, light, hot Rice, boiled Chicken Meat, diced	2 gal. 1½ qt. 12 oz. 8 oz.	6. Blend in scalded milk and cream. 7. Add boiled rice, diced cooked chicken. 8. Adjust seasoning and hold for service.

Cream of Mushroom Soup

YIELD: 50 portions	EACH PORTION: 6 oz.	
INGREDIENTS	*QUANTITY*	*METHOD*
Butter, clarified Onions, chopped fine Mushrooms, washed and chopped fine Flour	1 lb. 1 lb. 2 lb. 12 oz.	1. Saute onions and mushrooms in butter until soft. Do not brown. 2. Add flour. Stir until smooth. Cook 5 min.
Chicken stock, hot Milk, hot Cream, light Salt Pepper	6 qt. 2 qt. 1 qt. to taste to taste	3. Add hot chicken stock gradually, stirring until smooth. Simmer 7 or 8 min. until thickened and smooth. Whip as necessary. 4. Add hot milk and cream and season to taste.

Cream of Tomato Soup (recipe below)

Cream of Tomato Soup

YIELD: 50 portions		EACH PORTION: 8 oz.
INGREDIENTS	*QUANTITY*	*METHOD*

Rind and Fat of Shank of Smoked Ham
Mirepoix:
  Carrots, medium cut
  Celery, medium cut
  Onions, medium cut
  Garlic Cloves, crushed
  Peppercorns
  Parsley Stems
  Bay Leaves
  Whole Clove
	
	1½ lb.
	1 lb.
	1 lb.
	3
	1 tbsp.
	as needed
	3
	1
		1. Fry out fat and rind to lightly brown.
		2. Add mirepoix, reduce heat and cook to allow mirepois to pick up some fat (about 8 to 10 min.). Do not burn.

Flour Stock Canned Tomatoes Tomato Puree	12 oz. 1 gal. 1 No. 10 can 1½ qt.	3. Add flour; stir and blend well. Cook about 3 to 4 min. 4. Add stock, blend; add canned tomatoes and tomato puree. 5. Simmer about 1 hr. and strain well.
Light Cream Sauce OR Light Cream Salt	2 qt. to taste	6. Blend strained base into hot cream sauce and cream gradually while whipping. Adjust seasoning.
See color picture, p. 265.		

Duchess Soup

YIELD: 50 portions		EACH PORTION: 8 oz.
INGREDIENTS	*QUANTITY*	*METHOD*
Carrots, finely chopped or grated Celery, finely chopped Water, boiling	1 qt. 1 qt. 2 qt.	1. Simmer chopped carrots and celery in the boiling water until tender, about 15 min.

Onions, finely chopped
Butter
  OR Margarine
Flour
Milk
Chicken Stock
  OR Bouillon
Sharp American Cheese, diced
	4 oz.
	1 lb.
	
	1½ pt.
	4 qt.
	4 qt.
	
	4 lb.
		2. Saute onion in butter until soft but not brown. Add flour and blend well.
		3. Place over hot water, add milk and chicken stock or bouillon and cook until thickened, stirring constantly. Add cheese and stir until blended. Add cooked vegetables and their cooking water and heat thoroughly.
		4. Serve topped with chopped parsley or watercress and accompanied with toasted bread sticks or crackers.

Cream of Asparagus Soup

YIELD: 50 portions	EACH PORTION: 6 oz.	
INGREDIENTS	QUANTITY	METHOD
Chicken Stock, hot Asparagus, cut Onions, medium dice Bay Leaf	6 qt. 1 No. 10 can 1 lb. 1	1. Bring stock to boil. 2. Add asparagus, onion and bay leaf and simmer ½ hr.
Butter Bread Flour	10 oz. 10 oz.	3. While simmering, melt butter and add flour to make roux. Cook 10 min. over low heat but do not brown. 4. Add cooked roux to stock gradually, stirring until thickened and smooth. 5. Bring back to boil.
Milk, hot Cream, light, hot	2 qt. 1 qt.	6. Heat milk and cream together. 7. Remove cooked base from heat and pass through food mill. 8. Combine strained base and milk and cream. 9. Adjust seasoning and hold for service.

VARIATIONS: Here are some of the cream soup variations.

Cream of Carrot: Follow recipe for Cream of Asparagus substituting 4 lb. of carrots for asparagus and increasing chicken stock to 7 qt. Cut carrots small dice (uniform) for knife practice.

Cream of Cauliflower: Follow recipe for Cream of Asparagus, substituting 4 lb. frozen cauliflower for asparagus and increasing chicken stock to 7 qt.

Cream of Celery: Follow recipe for Cream of Asparagus, substituting 4 lb. of celery for asparagus and increasing chicken stock to 7 qt. Reserve ½ lb. of finely diced, cooked, white celery for garnish.

Cream of Onion: Follow recipe for Cream of Asparagus, substituting 4 lb. of onions for asparagus and increasing chicken stock to 7 qt.

Cream of Spinach: Follow recipe for Cream of Asparagus, substituting 3 lb. frozen spinach for asparagus and increasing chicken stock to 7 qt.

NOTE: Fresh, frozen or canned vegetables may be used according to the season, availability and cost of supplies.

See color picture, p. 265.

Cream of Broccoli Soup

YIELD: 50 portions	EACH PORTION: 8 oz.	
INGREDIENTS	QUANTITY	METHOD
Frozen Broccoli Onions, medium dice Bay Leaf Chicken Stock, hot	2½ lb. ½ lb. 1 7 qt.	1. Heat stock. Add broccoli and onions and bay leaf and simmer for 1 hr.
Butter Flour Milk, hot Cream, light, hot	10 oz. 10 oz. 2 qt. 1 qt.	2. Combine flour and butter to make roux. Cook 8 to 10 min., but do not brown. 3. Add cooked stock to roux gradually, stirring until slightly thickened and smooth. Simmer additional ½ hr. 4. Pass through food mill. 5. Add heated milk and cream. 6. Adjust seasoning and hold for service.

Soups

Cream of Mixed Vegetables

YIELD: 50 portions	EACH PORTION: 8 oz.	
INGREDIENTS	*QUANTITY*	*METHOD*
Chicken Stock Frozen Mixed Vegetables	6 qt. 2½ lb.	1. Bring stock to boil. Add frozen mixed vegetables, return to boil and cook until tender.
Onions Celery Carrots Butter Flour	1 lb. ½ lb. ½ lb. 1 lb. 12 oz.	2. Saute onions, celery and carrots in butter until tender. 3. Add flour to make roux. Cook 10 min. Do not brown. 4. Strain hot stock, reserving cooked frozen vegetables. Gradually whip stock into roux. Simmer ½ hr. 5. Add cooked vegetables.
Milk Light Cream	2 qt. 1 qt.	6. Heat milk and cream together. 7. Add to soup and adjust seasoning.

Creme Bagration

YIELD: 50 portions	EACH PORTION: 8 oz.	
INGREDIENTS	*QUANTITY*	*METHOD*
Onions, medium dice Carrots, medium dice Celery, medium dice Leeks (optional), medium dice Butter Bread Flour Fish Stock (Haddock, Halibut, Cod, etc.)	1 lb. ½ lb. ½ lb. 4 oz. 12 oz. 10 oz. 6 qt.	1. Saute onions, carrots, celery and leeks in butter in soup pot. 2. Add flour to make roux. Mix well and cook 3 to 4 min. but do not brown. 3. Add hot fish stock gradually, stirring until slightly thickened and smooth.
Mushrooms, diced medium Milk, hot Cream, light, hot Fish, cooked Ditalini or Tubetini, cooked	12 oz. 2 qt. 1 qt. 2 lb. 1½ pt.	4. Saute mushrooms separately until tender. Add to soup. 5. Incorporate hot milk and cream. 6. Add cooked fish garnish and ditalini. Adjust seasoning.

NOTE: Other pasta products may be substituted. Various cooked fish may be used for garnish; haddock, halibut, fillet of sole, cod or shrimp.

Cream of Almond Soup

YIELD: 50 portions	EACH PORTION: 6 oz.	
INGREDIENTS	*QUANTITY*	*METHOD*
Almond Paste Almonds, chopped Chicken Stock Butter Flour	¼ lb. 1 lb. 6 qt. 10 oz. 10 oz.	1. Pass almonds through a fine grinder and cook in stock with almond paste for ½ hr. 2. Melt butter in soup pot. Add flour to make roux. Cook for 3 to 4 min., but do not brown. 3. Gradually add stock to roux; blend until smooth. Bring soup just to simmer.
Milk Cream, light Sugar Salt	2 qt. 1 qt. 1 oz. to taste	4. Lower heat, add hot milk and cream. 5. Add sugar, season with salt.

NOTE: Chicken stock is preferable for the preparation of all cream soups, but other white stocks such as beef and veal may be used.

If cream soup breaks from overheating, whip some cold milk or cream into soup.

Creme Monaco

YIELD: 50 portions		**EACH PORTION:** 8 oz.
INGREDIENTS	*QUANTITY*	*METHOD*
Chicken Stock, hot Watercress, washed and cleaned Onions, medium dice Bay Leaf	7 qt. 3 bunches 1 lb. 1	1. Bring stock to boil. 2. Reserve leaves from 1 bunch of watercress for garnish. Simmer balance with onion and bay leaf in stock for 1 hr.
Butter Flour	10 oz. 10 oz.	3. Melt butter and add flour to make roux. Cook 10 min. over low heat but do not brown. 4. Add stock gradually to cooked roux, stirring until thickened and smooth. Bring to boil, lower heat, hold.
Milk Light Cream	2 qt. 1 qt.	5. Heat milk and cream together. 6. Remove cooked base from heat and pass through food mill. 7. Combine strained base, milk and cream and adjust seasoning. 8. Add reserved watercress leaves for garnish and hold.

Peanut Butter Soup

YIELD: 50 portions		**EACH PORTION:** 8 oz.
INGREDIENTS	*QUANTITY*	*METHOD*
Celery, diced medium Onions, diced fine Peppers, green, diced fine Water, boiling	1½ pt. 6 oz. 4 oz. 2 qt.	1. Simmer celery, onions, and green peppers in lightly salted boiling water until tender.
Butter 　OR Margarine Flour Milk, hot	3 oz. 3 oz. 9 qt.	2. Make roux with butter or margarine and flour. Cook lightly but do not brown. 3. Gradually add hot milk to roux; blend until smooth. This will be very thin.
Peanut Butter Sugar Salt	2 lb. 2 tbsp. 3 tbsp.	4. Place in stainless steel double boiler and add peanut butter, sugar and salt. Blend well until smooth. 5. When vegetables are cooked, add them with cooking water to peanut butter mixture. Cook in double boiler until heated and smooth.
NOTE: Servings may be garnished individually with chopped, fresh parsley or chopped peanuts.		

Shrimp Bisque

YIELD: 50 portions	EACH PORTION: 6 oz.	
INGREDIENTS	QUANTITY	METHOD
Court Bouillon: 　Water 　Onion, chopped fine 　Lemon, sliced thin 　Bay Leaf 　Cloves, whole 　Celery, chopped fine	 1 gal. ½ lb. 1 1 3 4 oz.	1. Combine water, onion, lemon, bay leaf, cloves and celery. Simmer for 15 min. 2. Strain liquid into soup pot and bring to boil.
Shrimp, raw, in shell	2½ lb.	3. Add raw shrimp and simmer 5 to 6 min. 4. Remove shrimp from stock (court bouillon) and reserve stock. 5. Cool shrimp in cold water, peel and devein; coarsely chop and reserve.
Butter Flour Paprika	1 lb. 12 oz. 2 tsp.	6. Make a roux with butter, flour and paprika, blending well. Cook 3 to 4 min. Do not burn. 7. Add hot stock slowly, stirring until slightly thickened and smooth.
Milk, hot Cream, light, hot Sherry Wine	2 qt. 1 qt. 4 oz.	8. Add combined hot milk and cream. 9. Add sherry and shrimps. Season to taste. Serve with Profiterolles (p. 403).
See color picture, p. 265.		

Oyster Bisque

YIELD: 50 portions (about 2½ gal.)		
INGREDIENTS	QUANTITY	METHOD
Oysters, shucked, with liquor Water	2 qts. 3 qt.	1. Drain and chop oysters, reserving liquor. 2. Combine oysters, oyster liquor and water. Bring to a boil.
Butter Flour	16 oz. 16 oz.	3. Make roux with butter and flour. Cook 5 min. but do not brown. 4. Gradually whip in all liquid from cooking oysters. Cook until thickened and smooth.
Milk, scalded Cream, light Salt Pepper	4 qt. 2 qt. to taste to taste	5. Add scalded milk, whipping as necessary. Cook until thickened and smooth. 6. Add oysters and simmer 5 min. Add cream and season to taste. Hold for service.
NOTE: If using aluminum cookware, be careful not to bang sides and bottom with whip. This causes discoloration of the product. 　Oyster bisque may be garnished with tiny Profiterolles (p. 403) or a teaspoon of unsweetened whipped cream.		

Puree Fresh Green Pea

YIELD: 50 portions		EACH PORTION: 8 oz.
INGREDIENTS	QUANTITY	METHOD
Onions, medium dice Salad Oil Flour Chicken Stock, hot Frozen Peas	1 lb. 10 oz. 8 oz. 2 gal. 5 lb.	1. Saute onions in oil in stock pot until tender. 2. Add flour and blend well. Cook 3 to 4 min. without browning. 3. Add 1 gal. chicken stock gradually, stirring until slightly thickened and smooth. 4. Cook peas in remainder of chicken stock until soft. 5. Put peas and stock through food mill and add to thickened chicken stock. 6. Reserve a few peas to use as garnish when serving.

Puree of Split Pea

YIELD: 50 portions		EACH PORTION: 8 oz.
INGREDIENTS	QUANTITY	METHOD
Ham Shanks (if available) Split Peas, yellow or green, quick-cooking Bay Leaves Water, hot OR Stock, hot	3 3 lb. 2 3 gal.	1. Put ham shanks, split peas and bay leaves in 2 gal. of water or stock and bring to boil. Reduce to simmer.
Salt Pork, fine dice or ground Onions, medium dice Celery, medium dice Flour Salt Pepper	1 lb. 2 lb. 1 lb. 6 oz. to taste to taste	2. Saute salt pork until some of the fat is rendered. 3. Add onions and celery and cook until nearly tender. 4. Add flour to make roux. Cook 5 to 6 min. 5. Add remaining gallon liquid gradually, stirring until slightly thickened and smooth. 6. Add peas and ham shank mixture. 7. Simmer 1 hr. or until peas are soft. 8. Pass through food mill and china cap. 9. Adjust seasoning and consistency. Remove meat from ham shanks and use for garnish.

NOTE: For other purees, dried beans and lentils may be substituted. Soak beans overnight. Follow same procedure.

Boula Boula

YIELD: 50 portions		EACH PORTION: 1 bouillon cup, 8 oz.
INGREDIENTS	QUANTITY	METHOD
Frozen Peas Beef Stock Clear Turtle Soup, canned	2½ lb. 2 gal. 2 No. 2½ cans	1. Defrost raw peas and put through meat grinder. 2. Add beef stock and turtle soup to make a thin puree. Bring to boil and simmer gently 30 min.
Turtle Meat, canned Sherry Wine Brandy Whipped Cream	1 No. 2½ can 8 oz. 4 oz. 1 qt.	3. Strain. Dice turtle meat and add to soup with sherry wine and brandy 10 min. before serving time. 4. Serve in bouillon cups or ovenproof casseroles. Garnish with whipped cream. Glaze cream by placing the serving dish under broiler for a few seconds.

NOTE: The whipped cream may also be sprinkled with grated parmesan cheese, if desired. Place serving dish under the broiler just long enough to delicately brown the cheese.
Boula Boula may be prepared from turtle soup of previous day.

Soups

Puree of Black Bean Soup

YIELD: 50 portions		**EACH PORTION**: 8 oz.
INGREDIENTS	*QUANTITY*	*METHOD*
Black Turtle Beans	3 lb.	1. Wash and soak the beans overnight in refrigerator.
Salt Pork	6 oz.	2. Saute salt pork in a thick soup pot.

Mirepoix:
    Onions
    Carrots
    Celery
Stock, light
	
	1 lb.
	½ lb.
	½ lb.
	2½ gal.
		3. Add the mirepoix and smother for 10 min.
		4. Add the drained beans and sweat for 5 min.
		5. Add stock.

Burgundy Wine Salt Pepper Lemon Eggs, hard cooked	1 pt. to taste to taste 50 slices 50 slices	6. Bring to a slow boil and cook until the beans are done. 7. Pass the soup through a food mill. Place back on the range and bring back to a boil. 8. Pass through a fine china cap. 9. Finish with the burgundy wine. Season to taste. 10. Lay a round slice of lemon, peeled, over a slice of hard-boiled egg and place in bottom of each soup bowl. Pour soup in and serve.

Potage Parmentier

YIELD: 50 portions		**EACH PORTION**: 8 oz.
INGREDIENTS	*QUANTITY*	*METHOD*
Potatoes, peeled, sliced Leeks, white only, finely sliced Onions, finely sliced Butter Flour	6 lb. 2 bunches 2 lb. ½ lb. ½ lb.	1. Wash, peel and slice potatoes. Keep in fresh water. 2. Wash, clean, trim, slice onions and leeks. 3. Heat butter in soup pot. Add sliced onions and leeks. Saute slowly stirring occasionally. Cook until tender (do not brown). Add flour and continue to cook for 3 or 4 min. Stir frequently.
Chicken Stock, hot Salt Pepper	2 gal. to taste to taste	4. Add half the stock, stirring well; bring soup to a boil, then reduce to simmering. Simmer 8 to 10 minutes until thickened and smooth. 5. Drain water from potatoes. Cook potatoes in remaining stock until tender. 6. Combine cooked potatoes and stock with thickened onion and leek mixture. Puree through food mill; strain through fine china cap. Season to taste.
NOTE: Cream of Leek and Potato Soup may be made by adding 2 qt. scalded light cream.		

Potato and Leek Puree

YIELD: 50 portions		**EACH PORTION**: 8 oz.
INGREDIENTS	*QUANTITY*	*METHOD*
Potatoes, peeled, sliced thin Onions, diced fine White part of Leeks, washed well, sliced thin Chicken Stock, hot Parsley, chopped	5 lb. 2 lb. 3 lb. 2 gal. 2 oz.	1. Combine all ingredients except parsley and bring to boil. Reduce heat and simmer about 1 hr. or until ingredients are soft. 2. Puree through food mill and season to taste. 3. Sprinkle each portion with chopped parsley when serving.
NOTE: Consistency may be adjusted with small amount of roux or beurre manie if desired.		

Vichyssoise

YIELD: 50 portions (about 2½ gal.)	EACH PORTION: 8 oz.	
INGREDIENTS	*QUANTITY*	*METHOD*
Potatoes, peeled, sliced thin Onions, sliced thin Leeks, white portion only, sliced thin Bay Leaf Peppercorns, white, crushed Chicken Stock	6 lb. 2 lb. 1 lb. 1 ½ tsp. 4 qt.	1. Combine potatoes, onions, leeks, bay leaf, pepper-corns and chicken stock in heavy sauce or soup pot. Simmer covered until thoroughly cooked. 2. Put through fine food mill and cool.
Cream, light, very cold Chives Salt Hot Pepper Sauce	4 qt. 2 oz. to taste to taste	3. To finish for service, add very cold cream, chopped chives and season to taste.

NOTE: If any graininess remains from potatoes, soup may be put through a china cap before adding chives.
Soup should be served in chilled cups.
The base may be prepared and stored under refrigeration, adding cream and chives at time of service. The base, without cream, should keep for several days if properly refrigerated.

Potage Faubonne

YIELD: 50 portions	EACH PORTION: 8 oz.	
INGREDIENTS	*QUANTITY*	*METHOD*
Navy Beans	3 lb.	1. Pick through beans and soak overnight in cold water. 2. Bring beans to boil; drain and reserve.
Onions, medium dice Celery, medium dice Leeks, medium dice Ground Salt Pork Chicken Stock, hot Sachet Bag: Whole Peppercorns Oregano	1 lb. ½ lb. ½ lb. ½ lb. 2½ gal. 10 1 oz.	3. Smother onions, celery and leeks in salt pork in heavy soup pot. 4. Add the 2½ gal. hot stock, beans and sachet bag. Simmer until beans are soft.
Salt Pepper Hot Pepper Sauce Worcestershire Sauce Leeks, julienne Chicken Stock	to taste to taste to taste to taste 1 pt. 1 qt.	5. Remove sachet bag and pass mixture through food mill. Then pass through fine china cap. Return to range and season. 6. Bring julienne of leeks to boil in the 1 qt. stock; cook until leeks are tender. Add leeks and stock to soup.

Puree Mongole

YIELD: 50 portions	EACH PORTION: 8 oz.	
INGREDIENTS	*QUANTITY*	*METHOD*
Puree of Green Split Pea Stock, hot Tomato Puree Frozen Peas, cooked Carrots, cooked, small dice Corn, whole kernel, cooked	1½ gal. 3 qt. 2 qt. 1 pt. 1 pt. 1 pt.	1. Combine puree of peas, stock and tomato puree. 2. Add garnish of cooked vegetables.

NOTE: Equal portions of puree of split pea and tomato soup may also be used.

Soups

Potage Potiron

YIELD: 50 portions	EACH PORTION: 8 oz.	
INGREDIENTS	QUANTITY	METHOD

Salt Pork
Mirepoix:
   Onions
   Carrots
   Leeks
   Celery
Sachet Bag
Chicken Broth
Potatoes, sliced (¼ in. thick)
Pumpkin
	¾ lb.
	
	1 lb.
	1 lb.
	8 oz.
	4 oz.
	1
	2 gal.
	6 lb.
	6 lb.
		1. Dice salt pork and saute in soup pot. Add mirepoix, smother 10 min.
		2. Add sachet bag, stock and potatoes.
		3. Clean pumpkin, remove skin and add pulp to the stock.
		4. When pumpkin and potatoes are cooked, pass through a food mill.
		5. Put back on range and bring to a boil.

Light Cream	1 qt.	6. Pass through a china cap and then add the light cream. Season with salt and pepper to taste.

Cold Strained Gumbo

YIELD: about 25 portions	EACH PORTION: 8 oz.	
INGREDIENTS	QUANTITY	METHOD
Onions, chopped Celery, chopped Green Peppers, chopped Garlic Butter Chicken Broth Rice, raw	1 pt. 1 pt. 4 oz. 1 tsp. ¼ lb. 3 qt. 8 oz.	1. Saute onions, celery, green peppers and garlic in butter. 2. Add chicken broth and rice and cook for 30 min.
Tomatoes, chopped Okra Tomato Puree	1½ pt. 1½ pt. 8 oz.	3. Add chopped tomatoes, okra and tomato puree and cook for 30 min. Strain through coarse sieve and add salt and pepper to taste.
NOTE: This is not a clear soup, but is full bodied and will have rice and vegetable particles in suspension.		

Navy Bean Soup

YIELD: 50 portions	EACH PORTION: 8 oz.	
INGREDIENTS	QUANTITY	METHOD
Navy Beans OR Pea Beans	3 lb.	1. Soak beans overnight in cold water to cover.
Onions, large dice Celery, large dice Carrots, large dice Leeks, large dice Pesto (p. 88) Tomatoes, large dice Chicken Stock, hot Beef Stock, hot	1½ lb. 1¼ lb. 1 lb. ½ lb. 8 oz. 1½ qt. 1¼ gal. 1¼ gal.	2. Smother diced vegetables in pesto 10 min. then add tomatoes. 3. Add chicken and beef stock. Simmer until vegetables are soft.
Chives, chopped Whites of Celery, chopped Salt Hot Pepper Sauce	2 tbsp. 2 tbsp. to taste to taste	4. Cook beans al dente in 6 qt. water and drain. Add ¾ of beans to the stock and vegetables. Pass remaining ¼ beans through a food mill. Add to soup as a thickening agent. 5. Add the chopped chives and whites of celery. 6. Season to taste with salt and hot pepper sauce.
See color picture, p. 264.		

Bavarian Lentil Soup

YIELD: 50 portions	EACH PORTION: 8 oz.	
INGREDIENTS	*QUANTITY*	*METHOD*
Ham Fat Butter Carrots, small dice (brunoise) Onions, small dice (brunoise) Celery, small dice (brunoise) White Turnips, small dice (brunoise) Leeks, small dice (brunoise) White Vinegar Beef Stock Chicken Stock	¼ lb. ½ lb. 2 lb. 1 lb. 1 lb. ½ lb. ¼ lb. 4 oz. 1 gal. 1 gal.	1. Melt ham fat and butter in soup pot. 2. Add vegetables and smother. Add vinegar, salt and pepper. 3. Add beef and chicken stock. Bring to boil.

Lentils
Sachet Bag:
    Whole Peppercorns
    Oregano
Frankfurters, sliced thin
Worcestershire Sauce
Salt
Pepper
	3 lb.
	
	10
	1 oz.
	2 lb.
	to taste
	to taste
	to taste
		4. Bring lentils to one boil in water to cover. Wash and drain, add to soup. Add sachet bag.
		5. Add frankfurters, skim off fat, season to taste and cook until done.

See color picture, p. 263.		

Potage Garbure

YIELD: 50 portions	EACH PORTION: 8 oz.	
INGREDIENTS	*QUANTITY*	*METHOD*
Butter Carrots) Leeks) Onions) finely minced Turnips) Small Cabbage) Celery)	8 oz. 2 lb. 1 lb. 1 lb. 1 lb. 1 lb. 8 oz.	1. Melt butter in the sauce pan and smother the vegetables for 10 min.
Chicken Stock Salt Pepper	2½ gal. to taste to taste	2. Add chicken stock and cook for another hr.; 1 lb. sliced potatoes may be added. 3. When cooked, pass through a sieve, bring to a thorough boil. Season and serve with Cheese Toast.

CHEESE TOAST		
YIELD: 50 portions	EACH PORTION: 2 ½-in. strips	
INGREDIENTS	*QUANTITY*	*METHOD*
Soft Butter Parmesan Cheese Bread Slices, trimmed	½ lb. ½ lb. 25	1. Mix butter and cheese until well blended. 2. Spread mixture on slices of bread. 3. Cut bread in strips ½ in. wide. 4. Place on sheet pan and brown in oven at 350°F.

Soups

Knickerbocker Bean Soup

YIELD: 50 portions	EACH PORTION: 8 oz.	
INGREDIENTS	QUANTITY	METHOD
Navy Beans OR Pea Beans	2 lb.	1. Pick over and wash beans. Soak 3 to 4 hr. or overnight. Drain.
Salt Pork, ground Onions, small dice Carrots, small dice Chicken Stock	4 oz. 1 lb. 8 oz. 2½ gal.	2. Combine beans with salt pork, 3 oz. of onion, carrots and 2 gal. of stock. 3. Bring to boil. Reduce heat and simmer 2½ to 3 hr. or until beans are tender.
Potatoes, peeled, diced (¼ in. square)	1½ lb.	4. Cook potatoes in remaining stock until tender.
Bacon, diced	4 oz.	5. Saute bacon and remainder of onions until onions are lightly browned and bacon is cooked.
Tomatoes, canned Parsley Salt Pepper	½ No. 10 can 1 oz. to taste to taste	6. Combine all ingredients. Bring to boil and remove from fire. Adjust seasoning.

Canadian Pea Soup

YIELD: 50 portions	EACH PORTION: 8 oz.	
INGREDIENTS	QUANTITY	METHOD
Salt Pork, small dice Carrots) Leeks) Celery) diced Onions) Turnips) Whole Yellow or Green Peas	1 lb. 1½ lb. ¾ lb. ¾ lb. ¾ lb. ¾ lb. 4 lb.	1. Brown salt pork and add vegetables, smother. 2. Add peas.

White Stock
Bouquet Garni:
  Parsley Stalks
  Bay Leaves
  Thyme
  Whole Peppercorns
  Crushed Garlic
	3 gal.
	
	15
	2
	1 tsp.
	10
	2
		3. Add stock and put in bouquet garni. Bring to boil and let simmer.

Cooked Ham, diced Jelly from Ham	2 lb. 1 lb.	4. Add ham and ham jelly about ½ hr. before soup is finished. 5. Add salt and pepper to taste.

Bouillabaisse (recipe below)

Bouillabaisse

YIELD: 10 portions

INGREDIENTS	QUANTITY	METHOD
Fresh Firm Fish (red fish, red snapper, halibut, black or striped bass)	3 lb.	1. Trim, clean, wash and cut fish in 4 oz. pieces. Wash lobsters, cut in 8 pieces each, crack claws. Remove stone bag and black vein.
Lobsters (1½ lb. each)	2	
Olive Oil	4 oz.	2. Pour oil into brazier or rondeau. Add onions, leeks, tomatoes, garlic and seasonings.
Onions, julienne	1 pt.	3. Arrange lobster and fish over vegetables. Cover and simmer for 8 to 10 min., or until the juices have been extracted.
Leeks (white part) julienne		
Tomatoes, peeled, seeded, cubed	6	
Garlic, crushed	3 cloves	
Parsley, chopped coarsely	2 oz.	
Saffron	1 tsp.	
Bay Leaf	2	
Thyme, fresh	1 sprig	
Salt	2 tbsp.	
Pepper, freshly ground	½ tsp.	
Water	2½ qt.	4. Add water and white wine. Cover and bring to a fast boil. Lower heat and boil gently for 15 to 20 min. To serve, place thin slices of dry French bread in soup plates. Remove the fish and lobster pieces to a platter. Stir the juices, pour juices over the bread and serve hot. Fish and lobster pieces may be eaten with the soup.
White Wine, dry	1 pt.	
See color picture, p. 266.		

Oxtail Soup a l'Anglaise

YIELD: 50 portions	**EACH PORTION**: 8 oz.	

INGREDIENTS	QUANTITY	METHOD
Oxtail, cut in 1 in. pieces Brown Beef Stock	6 lb. 2½ gal.	1. Brown oxtails in oven at medium heat, saving grease. 2. Transfer browned bones to stock pot and add beef stock. 3. Bring to boil, reduce heat and simmer 3 to 4 hr. or until meat is tender enough to remove from bone easily. Hold stock for Step No. 7.
Barley, dry	6 oz.	4. Cook barley separately in water to cover for about 2 hr. or until done.
Turnips, medium dice Onions, medium dice Carrots, medium dice Celery, medium dice Leeks, medium dice Flour	1 lb. 2 lb. 1 lb. 12 oz. 6 oz. 4 oz.	5. Strain reserved grease into stock pot and saute remaining vegetables except tomatoes and parsley. Add small amount of oil if necessary. 6. Add bread flour and mix thoroughly. Cook to a light brown for 3 to 4 min. 7. Add hot stock gradually, stirring until smooth. Simmer 15 to 20 min.
Tomatoes, chopped	1½ pt.	8. Add tomatoes. 9. Add barley with barley water.
Parsley, chopped Sherry or Madeira Wine	1½ oz. 6 oz.	10. Remove meat from bones, cut in dice and add to soup. 11. Season to taste and add wine. Sprinkle with chopped parsley at service.

See color picture, p. 263.

Mock Turtle Soup

YIELD: 50 portions	**EACH PORTION**: 8 oz.	

INGREDIENTS	QUANTITY	METHOD

Small Calf's Head
Brown Stock
Lemons
Salt
Pepper
Bouquet Garni:
    Parsley
    Thyme
    Bay Leaf
Mirepoix:
    Carrots, peeled, cut fine
    Onions, cut fine
    Celery, washed, cut fine
	4 to 6 lb.
	3 qt.
	4
	to taste
	to taste
	
	1 sprig
	½ sprig
	¼
	
	½ lb.
	½ lb.
	4 oz.
		1. Bone calf's head. Place meat in sauce pan, fill with cold water and wash meat until water is clear.
		2. Place calf's head meat in sauce pan, cover with water, add a little salt and bring to boil. Cook for 5 to 10 min. Place under cold water faucet and cool.
		3. When meat is cold, remove from water; trim all parts that are not edible. Cut the remaining parts into ¼ in. squares. Return meat to sauce pan.
		4. Cover with 1 qt. of brown stock, the juice of 4 lemons, salt, pepper and bouquet garni. Add the vegetable mirepoix. Place on heat, bring to boil, reduce heat and simmer until meat is tender. Skim scum frequently with skimmer.

Basic Brown Sauce or Espagnole Eggs, hard cooked Lemons Sherry Wine	2 gal. 8 8 10 oz.	5. Put the remaining brown stock in soup pot, add the Brown Sauce, bring to a boil and stir. Check seasoning and consistency—should not be too thick. Use the juices in which the calf's head was cooked to thin, if needed. Remove the bouquet garni. Add the meat and mirepoix to soup. 6. Peel and cut hard cooked eggs in small cubes. Add to soup. Peel and cut lemons removing membranes and seeds. Cut lemons in small cubes and add to soup. Add dry sherry wine. Place soup in bain marie; serve.

Gaspacho (Also see p. 384)

YIELD: 32 portions		EACH PORTION: 8 oz.
INGREDIENTS	QUANTITY	METHOD
Cucumbers, large, peeled, minced Salt Tomatoes Pimientoes Green Onions, minced	12 4 oz. 2½ qt. 8 oz. 12	1. Mash cucumber; add salt. Let stand several min. 2. Add tomatoes, pimientoes and onions.
Vinegar Olive Oil Garlic, minced Sugar Cumin Salt Pepper	4 oz. 4 oz. 2 cloves 1½ tbsp. ¼ tsp. to taste to taste	3. Mix together vinegar, oil, garlic, sugar, cumin, salt and pepper. Let stand for several minutes. Add to cucumber mixture.
Consomme Water Chives, chopped	2½ qt. 1¼ qt. for garnish	4. Combine all ingredients. 5. Chill well and garnish with chopped chives.

See color picture, p. 263.

Jellied Tomato Soup

YIELD: 50 portions		EACH PORTION: 8 oz.
INGREDIENTS	QUANTITY	METHOD
Tomatoes, chopped, with juice Celery, chopped Onions, chopped Stock, beef or chicken	2 No. 10 cans 4 lb. 2 lb. 5 qt.	1. Simmer tomatoes, celery, onions and stock for 15 min.
Sugar Salt Cloves, ground White Pepper	3 oz. ¾ oz. 2 tsp. 1 tsp.	2. Add sugar, salt, cloves and pepper and simmer 15 min. more.
Gelatine Lemon Juice	7 oz. 8 oz.	3. Soak gelatine in small amount of cold water. 4. Remove soup from heat. 5. Stir in gelatine until dissolved. 6. Add lemon juice and adjust seasoning. 7. Strain and chill. 8. Cut loosely by stirring and serve in chilled cups.

NOTE: Place small amount in sauce or small dish and refrigerate to test consistency before chilling entire batch. (Gelatine often varies in power.) Add small amount of yellow and red coloring if necessary.

Soups

Cold Fruit Soup

YIELD: 24 portions	EACH PORTION: 5 oz.	
INGREDIENTS	*QUANTITY*	*METHOD*
Water Sugar, granulated Sweet Pitted Cherries, drained Peaches, canned, sliced, drained Maraschino Cherries, drained, quartered Mandarin Orange Segments and Syrup Raisins, seedless Juice of Lemons	1 qt. 12 oz. 8 oz. 8 oz. 6 oz. 1 11-oz. can 3 oz. 3	1. Bring water to a boil and stir in sugar until dissolved. 2. Add pitted cherries, peaches, maraschino cherries, mandarin oranges with syrup, raisins and lemon juice. Return to boil, reduce heat and barely simmer while completing remaining procedure.
Orange Juice Water, cold Cornstarch	1½ qt. 8 oz. 1½ oz.	3. Bring orange juice to a boil in a separate pot. 4. Blend cornstarch and cold water and add to orange juice, beating lightly until thickened and smooth. 5. Combine with first mixture and blend well, being careful not to mash or break fruit. Bring to a boil and remove from fire. 6. Pour into a clean container, and when partially cooled, refrigerate. Serve in chilled bouillon cups.
See color picture, p. 263.		

Chilled Tea-House Orange Soup

YIELD: 40 portions	EACH PORTION: 5 oz.	
INGREDIENTS	*QUANTITY*	*METHOD*
Orange Juice Pineapple Juice Cloves	4 qt. 1½ qt. 24	1. Combine orange juice, pineapple juice and cloves. Bring to boil.
Sugar Cornstarch	14 oz. 3 oz.	2. Mix sugar and cornstarch, add a little cold juice and mix well. Add to remainder of hot juice and cook until thickened, stirring constantly.
Lemon Juice Mint Leaves	1 qt. for garnish	3. Cool and add lemon juice. Chill thoroughly. 4. Serve in chilled bouillon cup; use mint leaf garnish.

Welsh Rarebit

YIELD: 50 portions	EACH PORTION: 6 to 7 oz.	
INGREDIENTS	*QUANTITY*	*METHOD*

Cream Sauce:
  Flour
  Butter
  Milk
	
	½ lb.
	½ lb.
	1 gal.
		1. Make Cream Sauce.
		2. Strain through china cap.

Sharp Cheddar Cheese, shredded
Ale
  OR Beer
Stock
  OR Milk
Paprika
Worcestershire Sauce
Mustard, dry
Salt
	10 lb.
	1 qt.
	
	1 qt.
	
	1 tbsp.
	4 oz.
	¾ oz.
	to taste
		3. Add cheese, ale, stock and spices.
		4. Cook slowly at low temperature until cheese is melted.
		5. Season to taste.
		6. Serve over toast placed on bottom of shirred egg dish.
		7. Sprinkle with paprika; serve piping hot.

VARIATIONS: Buck or Golden Buck Rarebit is a Welsh Rarebit with a poached egg added. **Yorkshire Buck Rarebit** is a Welsh Rarebit with a slice of broiled ham or crisp bacon and a poached egg.

Sauces, Thickening Agents

A sauce is a fluid dressing for meat, poultry, fish, desserts and other culinary preparations. Sauces enhance the flavor and appearance of the food they accompany. They may also add nutritional value.

A sauce may present contrast in flavor, color and consistency. It should not, however, prevail over the food with which it is associated. It should be so prepared that it forms a part of the food it accompanies.

In most cases a sauce should be of proper consistency to flow readily and provide a coating for the food but not thick or heavy enough to saturate the food or cause difficulty in digestion.

A sauce must not mask or cover the flavor of a dish. Poor meat or poultry cannot be disguised by a sauce.

It is essential that the seasoning be correct so that the food product will not be flavorless or excessively flavored. Seasoning is an art learned only through experience, and extreme care must be exercised in the use of spices and herbs until this knowledge is mastered.

Many sauces are derived from the same basic stocks that are used in soup making. Sauce stocks are often reduced in volume by boiling to increase their strength.

Categories of Sauces

There are thousands of sauces varying in name and content. They fall into two basic categories: warm sauces and cold sauces.

The warm sauces comprise the largest group and are served with all types of food. The cold sauces are served with both hot or cold food and include various butter preparations that are often associated with shellfish.

The warm sauces are derived from a few leading sauces that are used as a basis for nearly all others. The leading sauces are sometimes referred to as mother sauces. Sauces that are derived from them are termed small sauces.

The leading sauces are:
1) Espagnole or Brown
2) Bechamel or Cream
3) Tomato Sauce
4) Veloute (chicken or fish)
5) Hollandaise

Espagnole or Brown Sauce is made from brown stock and brown roux and is used extensively in the preparation of all types of meat and poultry dishes.

Bechamel or Cream Sauce, while originally prepared from veal stock, is a term now used interchangeably with cream sauce. It is derived from milk and/or cream with the addition of white roux. This sauce is used with all types of vegetables and creamed dishes, including soups, fish, poultry, dairy and macaroni products. While white sauce is made of roux and milk, the term cream sauce is often used interchangeably.

Tomato Sauce is prepared from tomato products, white stock, seasonings and roux. It is used with various meat, poultry, fish, vegetable and macaroni dishes. It is also used for producing other products with a tomato character.

Veloute Sauce may be either chicken, veal or fish, although chicken is the usual ingredient. A veloute is derived from stock with the addition of light roux and is associated with the product from which it is derived. Fish veloute is specifically derived from a fumet (an essence or rich fish stock or court bouillon in which fish has been cooked). The term fumet is also used for reduced stocks derived from game.

Hollandaise Sauce Although hollandaise is not a basic sauce as such, it is included here because many of the drawn butter sauces are prepared in the same manner. Other sauces are derived from hollandaise, and it is used in combination with various culinary preparations to obtain a variety of sauces popular in fine eating establishments.

Hollandaise and its derivatives must be handled with extreme caution. Because of their high butter and egg content, these sauces must never be exposed to high heat because they will curdle.

The temperature at which they must be held (not over 180°F.) is a natural and prolific breeding ground for bacteria which thrive and multiply best under these conditions. These sauces should be made only in very small quantities and should not be held over from one meal to another. Maximum retention time should not exceed 1½ hr. Practice proper sanitation procedures and avoid danger of food poisoning.

Stainless steel cookware must be used for preparation of hollandaise sauce, as aluminum discolors eggs.

Hollandaise and its derivatives are often used with fish, vegetables and eggs.

Meat Glaze or glace de viande is a gelatinous reduction of brown stock. This quality is due to the gelatinous content of the bones used in preparing brown stock. It is used to strengthen the flavor and consistency of sauces and other culinary preparations. It is also used to coat special dishes before serving, to improve their flavor and appearance.

Meat glaze is made by reducing brown stock in a large sauce pan or pot on the range. The stock should be allowed to simmer slowly and then be transferred to smaller sauce pans or pots as it reduces. The pot should be selected to hold the amount of stock used. At each change it should be carefully strained.

Each successive reduction will become heavier in consistency. The heat should be reduced as the product becomes heavier so that it will not burn. If heavy-bottom pots are available, their use is recommended.

When sufficiently reduced, the glaze should be thick enough to coat a spoon. It should be cooled and stored for future use and should be tightly covered to prevent dehydration or drying out. It may be kept for an indefinite period without spoilage. When small amounts are made, it does not require refrigeration.

It should now become clear why salt is not used in preparing stock. As the liquid is reduced by evaporation, its salt content remains the same and the finished product would be disagreeable to taste.

Demi-Glace Sauce is obtained by reducing a combination of equal quantities of espagnole and brown stock to half. It is used with small brown sauces.

Thickening Agents Roux (pronounced roo) is a thickening agent used in making sauces, soups and gravies. It is composed of flour and fat, such as butter, margarine, shortening, chicken fat, oil or rendered meat drippings and cooked.

The fat is used in a liquid state and mixed with flour in a definite ratio, usually equal proportions by weight. The ratio will vary at times as flour is not always the same, and different fats have different absorption qualities. There are minor exceptions to this ratio, notably in the preparation of cream soups. Bread flour is preferred for the preparation of roux.

Types of Roux There are two main types of roux: pale or light roux for use in light or white sauces and brown roux for preparing brown sauces. The degree to which roux is cooked depends upon its intended use. White roux requires only enough cooking to remove the taste of raw starch. Brown roux requires more cooking to obtain the brown color which also imparts some flavor.

The type of roux and intensity of the heat will further determine the cooking time. It may be cooked in a heavy pan on top of the range or baked in a slow oven. Frequent stirring will prevent scorching and burning. Hot cooked roux should be the consistency of moist sand and have a somewhat nutty odor.

Roux is a stock item that is often prepared and kept on hand for general use. Properly prepared roux has excellent keeping qualities and does not require refrigeration if not prepared too far in advance.

Cooking Roux In proper preparation, roux must be cooked prior to its introduction in a sauce, soup or gravy. This eliminates an uncooked or raw flour-starch flavor that often accompanies products made with uncooked roux.

If a product is finished to the desired consistency with raw roux and placed in the steamtable or bain marie, it will continue to cook under the influence of heat. As the roux cooks in the product, it alters the consistency, often thickening the product to a point requiring dilution which results in a less pronounced and often weakened flavor.

Roux may also be overcooked. Starch undergoes a breakdown when exposed to high or prolonged heat. This is particularly true when brown roux is made. Brown sauces may occasionally thin down when exposed to prolonged time in the steamtable because of the breakdown of the flour starch in the roux. Generally speaking, 5 to 15 minutes should be sufficient cooking time for most roux. Proper cooking procedures will result in products of uniform and lasting consistency with smooth velvety texture.

Smooth sauces and gravies may be obtained when roux and liquid are of different temperatures. The cool roux may be combined with hot stock or cool stock may be combined with hot roux. This procedure may be followed when time is not an important factor and when sufficiently heavy sauce pans are available in which products may undergo prolonged cooking and extremes of temperature without scorching. The process requires time for the roux and liquid to equalize temperatures and to reach the boiling point.

The sauce must be stirred constantly with a wire whip and brought to a boil to fully incorporate the ingredients, to kill bacteria and to produce a smooth velvety texture. The longer cooking process exposes the sauce to danger of scorching and burning if thin pans are used and the product is not stirred continuously.

When Time Is Short If time is an important factor and sauce pans of a suitable nature are not available, an equally smooth sauce may be obtained when both roux and liquid are hot, providing the necessary precautions are taken. The stock must be added to the roux in small quantities, stirring with a wire whip to smoothness before additional stock is incorporated. In reverse, small quantities of roux may be added to boiling liquid if the same precautions are taken. The advantage of this method is that the full thickening power of the roux is immediately obtained.

In either method, care must be taken that roux does not settle in rounded areas of a pan that are not easily reached by a whip.

Flavor While thickening is one of its main functions, the roux is also in a great part responsible for the ultimate flavor of a finished product. In frying and sauteing, fats and oils are often selected because of their delicate flavor—olive oil in Italian cooking, peanut oil in Chinese cooking. This is also true in the preparation of roux.

The type of fat or oil selected must relate to its intended use. Chicken fat, although relatively bland in character, has a flavor of its own and greatly enhances the flavor of chicken veloute, fricassee sauce and cream sauce. (Chicken fat is also used extensively in Jewish cooking.) Sausage fats have a strong and definite flavor and are not in general use. However, sausage fat is excellent for preparing country gravy to be served with sausage. Butter and margarine are recommended for general use.

It is necessary here to differentiate gravies from sauces by the definition that all gravies are derived from meat or poultry juices extracted in dry heat methods of cookery. The predominant flavor of a gravy should be the same as the meat from which it is made.

The roux used in the thickening of gravies should be derived, at least in part, from the meat or poultry, with which it is associated. Fat drippings are used in preparing the roux in many instances, each separate gravy being thickened with its own roux, prepared specifically for the particular purpose—turkey-fat roux for turkey gravy, pork-fat roux for pork gravy, etc.

Cornstarch is a thickening agent which, when mixed with water, juice or stock and subjected to heat, provides a glossy semi-clear finish to a product. It is used extensively in preparing many sweet sauces served with meats and poultry and in the preparation of some dessert sauces. It is also used in Chinese cookery.

Cornstarch should be blended smooth in an adequate amount of cold liquid and added to boiling or near boiling liquid, stirring or beating to prevent lumping and scorching. A cornstarch solution may be added to cold liquids and then heated, but this method is most often used with dairy products and in baking. Cornstarch mixes most easily when the dry is added to the wet.

When uncooked, cornstarch sauces will appear cloudy and opaque, but they become clear and glossy when cooked. Cornstarch sauces, like all other sauces and gravies, excluding those containing butter and eggs, should be brought to a boil before removing from heat.

Whitewash Another thickening agent that is sometimes used is called whitewash. It is composed of flour and water and resembles whitewash in color and consistency. It adds nothing beneficial beyond thickening, as its flavor can be no different than its ingredients. Its general use is not recommended.

Beurre Manie (pronounced burr-mahnyay), or manie butter, is used for a quick thickening agent in some of the small sauces. Four ounces of softened butter is mixed with 3 oz. of sifted flour and kneaded until well combined. It is pinched off in tiny balls about the size of a pea and dropped into near boiling sauce and mixed smooth. The sauce to which the butter is added should boil only long enough to cook the flour and eliminate what might otherwise be a disagreeable raw flavor. If the sauce boils too long or too vigorously, it will break or separate.

Liaison (pronounced lee-ay-zohn) is a mixture of cream and beaten egg yolks that is added to soups and sauces to improve color, increase flavor, improve texture and bind them together. The finished product must be held under 180°F. or the eggs will curdle.

For this reason a liaison is usually added at the last minute to reduce the possibility of the eggs curdling. Part of a soup or sauce is whipped into a liaison gradually until all of the mixture is incorporated. By adding a small portion of hot sauce or soup to the cold liaison, the temperature of the eggs is not increased too markedly at one time. If the liaison is to be added to the soup or stock, the product must be sufficiently cooled to prevent curdling of the eggs.

A rule of thumb ratio is three parts of cream to one part of eggs by weight. Weight measurement is more accurate than volume. As this form of liaison is expensive, its use is prohibitive in many operations. It is used primarily in establishments where menu prices are above average and most items are cooked to order.

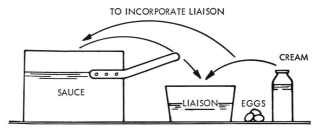

To incorporate liaison:
1) Remove sauce from heat.
2) Correct seasoning and strain if necessary.
3) Combine beaten egg yolks and cream.
4) Whip small amounts of sauce into liaison gradually until certain that eggs will not curdle.
5) Incorporate liaison-sauce mixture with balance of sauce.
6) Hold for service.

Raw Potatoes are sometimes used as a thickening agent in puree soups and are cooked with legumes. The starch from the potatoes is the major thickening factor. Potato starch settles to the bottom of a soup crock if it stands for long periods of time. A small amount of roux is often added to prevent this separation.

Other Thickening Agents Oatmeal, rice and other farinaceous or mealy products are sometimes used as thickening agents. Fresh bread crumbs or raspings are also employed in white sauces such as horseradish sauce.

Arrowroot, which has an action much like that of cornstarch, but produces a clearer finished product, was much in use years ago but is seldom used today. Newer products have been introduced, particularly in the baking area, that produce the same results at considerably less expense.

Brown Sauce (Espagnole)

YIELD: 5 qt.		
INGREDIENTS	QUANTITY	METHOD
Onions, medium dice Celery, medium dice Carrots, medium dice Butter, OR Margarine OR Other Fat Agent Bread Flour	1 lb. ½ lb. ½ lb. 10 oz. 10 oz.	1. Saute all vegetables in butter or fat in heavy sauce pot until onions are transparent. 2. Add flour and cook 10 min.
Brown Stock, hot (p. 271) Tomato Puree Bay Leaf, whole Salt Pepper	5 qt. 8 oz. 1 to taste to taste	3. Add hot Brown Stock and Tomato Puree, stirring until slightly thickened and smooth. 4. Add bay leaf, salt and pepper and cook 1½ hr. 5. Adjust flavor and consistency. 6. Strain and hold for service.

Robert Sauce

YIELD: 1 qt.		
INGREDIENTS	QUANTITY	METHOD
Shallots, chopped Butter Mustard, dry White Wine	1 oz. 3 oz. 1 tbsp. 10 oz.	1. Saute the shallots lightly in butter. Add the mustard, blending well. 2. Add wine and reduce by 1/3.
Espagnole (above) Lemon Juice Sugar, granulated	1 qt. 2 tbsp. 1 tsp.	3. Add the Espagnole and simmer about 20 min. Add lemon juice and sugar. 4. Strain and adjust seasoning.

Bordelaise Sauce

YIELD: about 1 qt.		
INGREDIENTS	QUANTITY	METHOD
Red Wine Shallots, chopped fine Peppercorns, finely ground Thyme Bay Leaf, small Brown Sauce (top of page) Butter	4 oz. 2 1/2 tsp. 1/8 tsp. 1 1 qt. 4 oz.	1. Reduce wine with shallots, pepper, thyme and bay leaf by boiling for several minutes. 2. Add the Brown Sauce; simmer ½ hr. 3. Finish with butter. Strain through fine cheesecloth.
Marrow, diced or slices	1 lb.	4. Poach marrow in boiling water for 3 min. 5. Remove marrow with skimmer and add to sauce.
NOTE: This sauce is generally served on beef tenderloin, filet mignons or sirloin steak.		

Sauce Chateau

YIELD: about 12 oz.		
INGREDIENTS	QUANTITY	METHOD
White Wine Shallots, chopped Thyme Bay Leaf Salt Pepper	4 oz. 2 1 pinch 1 to taste to taste	1. Reduce white wine with chopped shallots, thyme, bay leaf, salt and pepper by boiling for several minutes.
Brown Sauce (p.312) Maitre d'Hotel Butter	1 pt. 4 oz.	2. Add the Brown Sauce. Reduce to at least half its quantity. 3. Strain through fine cheesecloth. Add the Maitre d'Hotel butter.

Mushroom Sauce

YIELD: about 1 gal.		
INGREDIENTS	QUANTITY	METHOD
Mushrooms, washed and sliced Shallots, finely chopped Butter, melted	2 lb. 3 tbsp. 1 lb.	1. Saute mushrooms and shallots together in butter in sauce pot.
Bread Flour	9 oz.	2. Stir in flour to make roux. Cook 10 min., stirring constantly.
Brown Stock, hot (p. 271) Burgundy Wine Salt	1 gal. 4 oz. to taste	3. Add hot stock and stir until slightly thickened and smooth. 4. Add wine. Salt to taste. Bring to boil and remove from range.
		5. If holding for service, spread small amount melted butter over top to prevent formation of skin.

Cider Sauce

YIELD: 1 pt.		
INGREDIENTS	QUANTITY	METHOD
Cider Brown Sauce (p. 312) Chopped Shallots Cloves Bay Leaf Salt Pepper	1 pt. 1 pt. 2 2 1 to taste to taste	1. Bring cider to a boil; add the Brown Sauce, chopped shallots, cloves and bay leaf. 2. Simmer gently until volume is reduced about half. Season to taste with salt and pepper. 3. Strain through fine cheesecloth.
NOTE: This sauce is generally served with ham.		

Sauces

Barbecue Sauce

YIELD: 2 gal.		
INGREDIENTS	*QUANTITY*	*METHOD*
Onions, minced Garlic, minced Salad Oil Bread Flour Brown Stock, hot (p. 271)	6 oz. 2 tbsp. 8 oz. 6 oz. 3 qt.	1. Saute onions and garlic in oil in sauce pot. 2. Add flour to make roux. Stir until well blended. 3. Add hot stock, stirring smooth.
Sugar Mustard, dry Black Pepper Vinegar, cider Tomato Sauce or Puree Lemon Juice Worcestershire Sauce Barbecue Spice or Chili Powder Salt	4 oz. 1 tbsp. 2 tsp. 8¼ oz. 2 qt. from 3 lemons 8 oz. 1 tbsp. to taste	4. Dissolve sugar, mustard and pepper in vinegar. 5. Add Tomato Sauce, vinegar mix and lemon juice to brown sauce. 6. Add worcestershire sauce and barbecue spice to chili powder. Simmer 30 min. Add salt and adjust seasoning.
NOTE: Barbecue Sauce is used for preparing barbecued meat or poultry.		

White Sauce No. 1 (Light)

INGREDIENTS for:	*1 gal.+*	*3 gal.+*	*5 gal.+*	*METHOD*
Butter OR Margarine Bread Flour Milk Salt	6 oz. 6 oz. 1 gal. 1 tbsp.	1 lb. 1 lb. 3 gal. 3 tbsp.	1 lb. 12 oz. 1 lb. 12 oz. 5 gal. 2 oz.	1. Melt butter in thick-bottomed sauce pot. Stir in flour to make a roux. Cook over low heat, stirring constantly for 8 to 10 min. Do not allow roux to brown. 2. Heat milk to boiling. Stir into roux gradually, beating briskly until sauce is thickened and smooth. 3. Simmer for 5 min. stirring occasionally. Bring to a boil. 4. Strain through china cap.

NOTE: To hold White Sauce in bain marie, spread a little melted butter over top of sauce to keep a skin from forming. This light White Sauce is generally prepared for use in creamed vegetables.
Cream Sauce: Use cream or cream and milk mixture as desired.

White Sauce No. 2 (Medium)

INGREDIENTS for:	*1 gal.+*	*3 gal.+*	*5 gal.+*	*METHOD*
Butter OR Margarine Bread Flour Milk Salt	8 oz. 8 oz. 1 gal. 1 tbsp.	 1 lb. 8 oz. 3 gal. 3 tbsp.	2 lb. 10 oz. 2 lb. 10 oz. 5 gal. 2 oz.	Same as White Sauce No. 1

White Sauce No. 3 (Heavy)

INGREDIENTS for:	*1 gal.+*	*3 gal.+*	*5 gal.+*	*METHOD*
Butter OR Margarine Bread Flour Milk Salt	12 oz. 12 oz. 1 gal. 1 tbsp.	2 lb. 2 lb. 3 gal. 3 tbsp.	3 lb. 6 oz. 3 lb. 6 oz. 5 gal. 2 oz.	Same as White Sauce No. 1

Egg Sauce

YIELD: 1 gal.		
INGREDIENTS	QUANTITY	METHOD
Cream Sauce, medium (facing page) Hard Cooked Eggs, small dice Chopped Chives) Chopped Parsley) optional	1 gal. 12 1 tbsp. 1 tbsp.	1. Follow recipe for medium Cream Sauce. Adjust seasoning. 2. Dice hard cooked eggs and combine with Cream Sauce. Stir gently.

Mustard Sauce

YIELD: about 1 gal.		
INGREDIENTS	QUANTITY	METHOD
Cream Sauce, medium (facing page) Prepared Mustard	1 gal. 1 pt.	1. Combine hot Cream Sauce with prepared mustard and blend well. 2. Keep warm for service.

NOTE: To substitute dry mustard for prepared mustard, add ½ cup dry mustard and juice of 2 lemons or ¼ cup vinegar to 1 gal. of Cream Sauce.

Cardinal Sauce

YIELD: 1 gal.		
INGREDIENTS	QUANTITY	METHOD

Shrimp, cooked, peeled and
    cleaned, chopped fine
    OR Lobster Meat, cooked
Butter
	1 lb.
	
	1 lb.
		1. Saute shrimp or lobster meat in butter in sauce pan.

Paprika	1 tsp.	2. Sprinkle in paprika.
Bread Flour	8 oz.	3. Add flour and blend well. Cook 5 to 6 min. but do not brown.
Milk, hot Light Cream, hot	2½ qt. 1 qt.	4. Add hot milk and cream gradually, stirring until thickened and smooth.
Sauterne Wine Lemon Juice Salt White Pepper	4 oz. from 2 lemons to taste to taste	5. Add wine and lemon juice. Adjust seasoning.

Lobster Coral, forced
    through a fine wire sieve
    (optional)
	4 oz.	6. The coral should be sprinkled on top of sauce at serving time as a garnish.

Sauces

Cheese Sauce

YIELD: 1 gal.		
INGREDIENTS	*QUANTITY*	*METHOD*
Milk Cheddar Cheese, cubed American Cheese, cubed Paprika Mustard, dry Worcestershire Sauce Salt	3 qt. 1 lb. 1 lb. 2 tsp. 2 tsp. 1 tbsp. 1 tsp.	1. Combine milk, cheeses, paprika, mustard, Worcestershire and salt in top of double boiler. 2. Heat until cheese is melted and milk begins to form a skin on top.
Butter Bread Flour	6 oz. 6 oz.	3. Prepare roux with butter and flour. Cook 4 to 5 min. but do not brown. 4. Add roux to milk-cheese mixture, a small amount at a time, whipping until smooth. 5. Cook mixture until thickened and smooth. Then cook for 10 to 15 min. longer. 6. Bring almost to boil, remove from heat. 7. Strain through china cap.

Mornay Sauce

YIELD: 1 gal.		
INGREDIENTS	*QUANTITY*	*METHOD*
Bread Flour Butter, melted Milk, whole, hot Egg Yolks) Liaison Light Cream) Salt Parmesan Cheese Butter, cold, broken in small pieces	12 oz. 12 oz. 3 qt. 8 4 oz. to taste 4 oz. 6 oz.	1. Review liaison procedure in section on Thickening Agents (p. 311). 2. Stir flour into melted butter to make roux. Cook 6 to 8 min. but do not brown. 3. Add hot milk and stir until slightly thickened and smooth. 4. Beat egg yolks and cream together to make a liaison. 5. Whip small amounts of hot milk mixture into liaison gradually. Slowly whip egg mixture into remaining hot milk mixture. 6. Season with salt. 7. Cook just 1 min. Do not overheat. 8. Remove from heat. Add parmesan cheese, stirring to incorporate. 9. Add cold butter broken in small pieces, stirring until fully blended. 10. Reserve in warm place for service.
NOTE: Overheating or extended period of heat will "break" this sauce.		

Mock Hollandaise Sauce

YIELD: 2 qt.		
INGREDIENTS	*QUANTITY*	*METHOD*
Butter Flour Milk	½ lb. ¼ lb. 1½ qt.	1. Melt ¼ lb. butter; add flour to make a roux. Heat the milk and add to the roux. Follow procedure as recipe for Cream Sauce (p. 314).
Egg Yolks Lemon Juice Salt Cayenne Pepper	9 yolks 4 oz. to taste to taste	2. Beat the egg yolks thoroughly and add very slowly to the Cream Sauce, mixing continuously. 3. Melt the remaining ¼ lb. butter; add slowly to the sauce. Add lemon juice. 4. Season with salt and very lightly with the cayenne pepper; pass through fine cheesecloth, add egg color if necessary and adjust thickening. 5. Place in bain marie ready for service. (Treat as for Hollandaise Sauce, p. 321.)

Horseradish Sauce

YIELD: 1 gal.		
INGREDIENTS	QUANTITY	METHOD
Cream Sauce, medium (p. 314) Prepared Horseradish	1 gal. 1 pt.	Combine hot Cream Sauce and prepared horseradish.
NOTE: Excessive heat or extended periods of heat tend to break down sauce.		

Basic Sauce Veloute

YIELD: about 1 gal.		
INGREDIENTS	QUANTITY	METHOD
Butter OR Margarine Bread Flour Stock (chicken), hot Seasoning	10 oz. 10 oz. 1 gal. according to stock	1. Melt butter in sauce pan, stir in flour to make a smooth roux. Cook roux slowly for 5 to 6 min.; do not brown. 2. Slowly whip in stock until thickened and smooth. Check seasoning. Continue to cook sauce for 30 min. 3. Strain and reserve for intended usage.
VARIATIONS: With the addition of cream, the above sauce becomes **Supreme Sauce**. With the addition of egg yolks and lemon juice, it becomes **Sauce Allemande**.		
NOTE: Veloute may also be prepared with fish stock or veal stock but then would be specifically identified as *fish veloute*, etc.		

Sauce Poulette

YIELD: 1 gal.		
INGREDIENTS	QUANTITY	METHOD
Butter Shallots, chopped fine Fresh Mushrooms, washed, sliced fine Chicken Veloute (recipe above) Light Cream, scalded Salt Pepper Parsley, chopped	4 oz. 1 oz. 2 lb. 3 qt. 8 oz. to taste to taste ¾ oz.	1. In sauce pan, melt butter, add shallots; smother until tender (do not brown). 2. Add mushrooms, cook until tender. 3. Stir in Chicken Veloute. Continue to simmer sauce for 20 min. stirring frequently. 4. Incorporate cream and bring to boil. 5. Season to taste with salt and pepper. Add parsley.

Hongroise Sauce

YIELD: about 2 gal.		
INGREDIENTS	QUANTITY	METHOD
Butter Onions, chopped very fine Flour Paprika	8 oz. 4 oz. 8 oz. 1-1/3 oz.	1. In sauce pan heat butter, add onions, cook slowly until tender (not colored). 2. Stir in flour and paprika. Cook roux slowly while stirring, 8 to 10 min.
Chicken Stock, hot Tomato Paste Salt Pepper	1-1/2 gal. 4 oz. to taste to taste	3. When roux is ready, stir the chicken stock and the tomato paste in with wire whip. Season to taste with salt and pepper, continue to cook for 25 min. Stir frequently.
Cream, scalded	3/4 qt.	4. Strain through china cap and cheesecloth. Add scalded cream.

Sauces

Tomato Sauce No. 1

YIELD: 5 qt.		
INGREDIENTS	*QUANTITY*	*METHOD*
Garlic, chopped fine	1 tbsp.	1. Saute garlic in melted butter until garlic is lightly
Butter, melted	12 oz.	browned.
Onions, chopped fine	1 lb.	2. Add onions and celery; saute until soft.
Celery, chopped fine	8 oz.	3. Add flour to make roux; stir until well blended.
Bread Flour	6 oz.	Cook 5 min.
Brown Stock, hot (p. 271)	3 qt.	4. Add Brown Stock. Stir until slightly thickened and
Tomatoes, peeled	1 qt.	smooth.
Tomato Puree	2 qt.	5. Add peeled tomatoes, tomato puree and spices.
Bay Leaves	2	6. Simmer for 1½ hr.
Thyme, ground	1 tsp.	7. Strain. Adjust seasoning.
Peppercorns, crushed	1 tsp.	
Cloves, whole	3	
Salt	to taste	

Tomato Sauce No. 2

YIELD: about 2½ gal.		
INGREDIENTS	*QUANTITY*	*METHOD*
Skin of Salt Pork	½ lb.	1. Saute salt pork skins in brazier.
Mirepoix:		2. Add mirepoix and sweat.
Onions, coarsely chopped	8 oz.	3. Add tomatoes, tomato puree, salt and sugar.
Celery, coarsely chopped	4 oz.	4. Add netural stock, browned bones and sachet bag.
Carrots, coarsely chopped	4 oz.	5. Cover and bake at 300°F. for 1 hr.
Leeks, coarsely chopped	2 oz.	
Sachet Bag:		
Thyme	2 tsp.	
Bay Leaf	4	
Garlic Cloves, crushed	5	
Parsley Stems	15	
Peppercorns, whole	10	
Tomatoes	1½ No. 10 cans	
Tomato Puree	1 No. 10 can	
Salt	3 oz.	
Sugar	1½ oz.	
Neutral Stock	½ gal.	
Veal and Pork Bones, browned	2½ lb.	
		6. Skim frequently.
		7. Remove bones and put sauce through food mill.
		8. Vent and refrigerate.

Spaghetti Sauce

YIELD: 2 gal.

INGREDIENTS	QUANTITY	METHOD
Salad Oil Onions, finely chopped Celery, finely chopped Green Peppers, finely chopped Garlic, minced	1 pt. 2 lb. ½ lb. 2 oz. 5 tbsp.	1. Saute onions, celery, and green peppers in salad oil for about 10 min., stirring frequently. 2. Add garlic and cook for about 2 min. longer.
Italian Tomatoes, crushed Tomato Puree Sweet Basil Leaves, crushed Oregano Leaves, crushed Bay Leaves Salt	2 No. 10 cans 1 No. 10 can 2 tsp. 2 tsp. 2 to taste	3. Add tomatoes, puree and seasonings. 4. Simmer uncovered for 2 hr. 5. Remove from fire and puree sauce through fine food mill. 6. Season with salt and hold for service.

NOTE: To make Meat Sauce for Spaghetti: use basic sauce above and add 2 lb. of lightly sauteed ground beef, drained of excess fat.

Spanish Sauce for Spanish Omelette

YIELD: 1½ gal.

INGREDIENTS	QUANTITY	METHOD
Onions, cut (1 in. long, ¼ in. wide) Celery, cut straight across (1/8 in. wide) Mushrooms, sliced Garlic, minced Salad Oil	2 lb. 1 lb. 1 lb. 1 tbsp. 8 oz.	1. Saute onions, celery, mushrooms in salad oil until tender. 2. Add garlic and saute 2 min. longer.
Tomatoes, canned, chopped medium Tomato Puree Thyme Bay Leaves	1 No. 10 can 1½ qt. 1 tsp. 2	3. Add tomatoes, puree and spices. Simmer uncovered, 1½ hr. stirring often.
Green Peppers, cut (1 in. long, ¼ in. wide) Salt Okra (optional) Stuffed Green or Black Pitted Olives, sliced	1 lb. to taste 1 No. 303 can 8 oz.	4. Blanch green peppers in boiling salted water for 5 min. Drain well. 5. When sauce has cooked 1½ hr., remove bay leaves, add green peppers and simmer 15 min. 6. Remove from heat and adjust seasoning. 7. Add okra and its juice and sliced olives.

NOTE: The sauce should be thick when finished so that it will not flow when enclosed in an omelette.

Milanaise Sauce

YIELD: 1 qt.   **EACH PORTION:** 2 oz. sauce and garnish

INGREDIENTS	QUANTITY	METHOD
Mushrooms, julienne Butter Tongue, julienne, cooked Ham, julienne, cooked Basic Spaghetti Sauce, hot (above)	5 oz. 2 tbsp. 5 oz. 5 oz. 1 qt.	1. Saute mushrooms in butter. Add mushrooms, tongue and ham to hot tomato sauce. 2. Individual serving consists of: 2 oz. sauce, 1 oz. julienne ham, 1 oz. julienne tongue, 1 oz. julienne mushrooms.

NOTE: If used over a side dish, decrease julienne garnish by one-half.

Sauces

Creole Sauce

YIELD: 1 gal.		
INGREDIENTS	*QUANTITY*	*METHOD*
Salad Oil Onions, coarsely chopped Celery, cut across (1/8 in. wide) Garlic, fresh, minced	8 oz. 1½ lb. 1 lb. 1 tsp.	1. Heat oil in sauce pot. 2. Add onions, celery and garlic. Saute until nearly cooked (about 15 min.).
Tomatoes, canned, chopped Tomato Puree Bay Leaf Black Pepper Thyme	1 No. 10 can 1 qt. 1 ½ tsp. ½ tsp.	3. Add tomatoes, puree and seasonings. Cook slowly 1½ hr.
Green Peppers, coarsely chopped Hot Pepper Sauce (optional)	1 lb. to taste	4. In boiling salted water, blanch green peppers for 5 min. Drain well. 5. When sauce is cooked, remove bay leaf. 6. Add green peppers and simmer 15 min. 7. Adjust seasoning and hold for service.

Creole Sauce-Louisiana

YIELD: about 1 gal.		
INGREDIENTS	*QUANTITY*	*METHOD*
Salad Oil 　OR Butter Green Onions, sliced fine Celery, sliced fine Green Peppers, sliced fine Garlic, chopped	6 oz. 10 oz. 8 oz. 10 oz. 1 clove	1. In sauce pot heat oil or butter; in it smother onions, celery, green peppers and garlic until tender, but not browned.
Tomatoes, canned Tomato Puree Sugar Salt Pepper Thyme Hot Pepper Sauce	3 qt. 1 qt. 3 tbsp. 3 tbsp. 1 tsp. ½ tsp. few dashes	2. Add tomatoes and tomato puree, sugar, salt, pepper, thyme and hot pepper sauce. Stir; bring to a boil, reduce heat to simmering and cook for 1½ hr.
Cornstarch Water	2 oz. 4 oz.	3. Check seasoning and correct, if necessary. Blend cornstarch with cold water and stir into sauce. Cook until clear and thickened.
VARIATIONS: A variety of Creole Sauces are served and prepared with olives, mushrooms, anchovies and okra or gumbo file.		

Hollandaise Sauce No. 1

YIELD: 1½ qt.		

INGREDIENTS	QUANTITY	METHOD
Egg Yolks Water, cold	12 2 oz.	1. Whip egg yolks and water together in stainless steel bowl. 2. Place bowl over pot of boiling water (like a double boiler) making sure that bottom of bowl *does not* touch water. (This results in overcooking.) 3. Whip yolks lightly until cooked to a soft peak. Stir *down* from edges and *up* from bottom of bowl. 4. Remove from range.
Clarified Butter, warm Lemon Juice Cayenne Pepper Salt	2½ lb., A.P. from 2 lemons to taste to taste	5. Slowly pour butter into eggs, whipping lightly to blend. 6. Add lemon juice, cayenne pepper and salt if needed. 7. Do not overheat. FOLLOW SANITATION AND HOLDING PROCEDURES for Hollandaise on next page.

Hollandaise Sauce No. 2

YIELD: 1 qt.		

INGREDIENTS	QUANTITY	METHOD
Butter	1 lb.	1. Melt butter in small sauce pan and clarify.
Peppercorns, crushed Cider Vinegar Water, cold	6 3 oz. 1/4 cup	2. Crush peppercorns finely with bottom of sauce pan. Place crushed peppercorns in sauce pan; add vinegar. Bring to boil and reduce. Remove from heat; allow to cool.
Egg Yolks Salt Cayenne Pepper Lemon Juice	6 3/4 tsp. 1/8 tsp. from 1/2 lemon	3. Add egg yolks and water, beat vigorously with wire whip. Place sauce pan in bain marie or in a large sauce pan with boiling water (not a double boiler). Continue to whip egg yolks until they foam up and thicken to form a soft peak. 4. When the substance of the egg yolks is like a cooked soft custard, remove from bain marie. Begin to whip in the clarified butter, adding it by degrees with ladle until all is added. 5. Season with salt, cayenne pepper and lemon juice. 6. Strain through cheese cloth. Reserve in warm place for immediate usage.

Additional Information on Hollandaise

NOTE: Hollandaise Sauce is one of the few sauces that cannot be successfully refrigerated to retard bacteria growth or boiled to kill organisms. This is because refrigeration hardens the butter in the sauce and causes the mixture to become solid, while overheating the sauce coagulates the eggs and causes the mixture to become lumpy.

When Hollandaise is being prepared, and later in serving it or adding it to other sauces, follow these **Sanitation and Holding Procedures:**

1) Use only fresh eggs and fresh butter.

2) Sterilize all equipment, such as wire whip, spoons, pots and other materials by scalding.

3) Serve all of the sauce within 1½ hr. after it is prepared—*never hold sauce any longer.*

4) Never add leftover Hollandaise Sauce to new batch of freshly prepared sauce.

In the primary reduction of crushed pepper and water, white or tarragon vinegar may be added in the reduction.

Hollandaise Sauce may be added to Mornay Sauce to obtain glazed sauce under the salamander, used in fish or delicate poultry sauce.

Other Variations:

Anchovy butter or paste may be added to Hollandaise sauce.

Double Hollandaise: double the amount of egg yolks.

Mock Hollandaise: half Veloute or Cream Sauce No. 2; half Hollandaise Sauce.

Grimod: Hollandaise Sauce with saffron.

Mousseline: whipped cream in equal proportion added to Hollandaise Sauce.

Maltaise: grated orange peel and orange juice reduction.

Figaro: Hollandaise with reduction of tomato puree and poached fine julienne of celery.

Bearnaise Sauce

YIELD: 1½ qt.		
INGREDIENTS	*QUANTITY*	*METHOD*
Shallots, minced Peppercorns, crushed Tarragon Vinegar*	2 oz. 1 tsp. 1 cup	1. Place shallots, peppercorns and tarragon vinegar in small sauce pot. Cook to reduce slowly until liquid is nearly evaporated. Do not scorch. 2. Place residue in cheesecloth; press or squeeze all moisture or liquid into small pot.
Hollandaise Sauce (p. 321)	1½ qt.	3. Prepare Hollandaise, *omitting* lemon juice. Finish with the reduction liquid as a substitute for the lemon juice. Stir in well. 4. Add teaspoon of finely chopped tarragon leaves if available. Finely chopped parsley may be substituted.
*Cider vinegar with 1 tbsp. tarragon leaves may be substituted for tarragon vinegar.		
NOTE: FOLLOW SANITATION AND HOLDING PROCEDURES FOR HOLLANDAISE SAUCE (above).		

Hot Glaze Royal Sauce

YIELD: 2½ qt.		
INGREDIENTS	*QUANTITY*	*METHOD*

Cream Sauce No. 3 (p. 314), hot
Liaison:
   Egg Yolks
   Light Cream
Hollandaise Sauce (p. 321)
Whipped Cream, unseasoned
	1 pt.
	
	5
	4 oz.
	1 qt.
	1 pt.
		1. Combine hot Cream Sauce and Liaison (p. 311).
		2. Add Hollandaise Sauce to hot Cream Sauce mixture.
		3. Fold in whipped cream.

Maitre d'Hotel Butter

YIELD: 25 oz.		
INGREDIENTS	*QUANTITY*	*METHOD*
Butter	20 oz.	1. Work butter until soft.
Salt	½ tsp.	2. Add seasonings and parsley.
White Pepper	to taste	3. Stir in lemon juice and heat slowly.
Parsley, fresh, chopped	1½ oz.	
Lemon Juice	3 oz.	
NOTE: Maitre d'Hotel Butter may be refrigerated in same manner as Anchovy Butter.		

Anchovy Butter

YIELD: about 1¼ lb.		
INGREDIENTS	*QUANTITY*	*METHOD*
Anchovy Fillets	24	1. Pound or chop anchovy fillets to paste.
Butter, softened	1 lb.	2. Work into butter.
		3. Make ¾ in. round, pipelike roll. Wrap in waxed paper and refrigerate.
		4. Cut off in desired amounts as needed.

Sweet and Sour Sauce

YIELD: 1 qt.		
INGREDIENTS	*QUANTITY*	*METHOD*
Chicken Stock	1 qt.	Follow instructions for Chinese "White" Sauce (p. 353).
Vinegar	1 oz.	
Sugar	2 tbsp.	
Salt	1 tsp.	
White Pepper	¼ tsp.	
Cornstarch	6 tbsp.	
NOTE: Starch is increased because of acid content of sauce.		

Cocktail Sauce

YIELD: about 1 qt.		
INGREDIENTS	*QUANTITY*	*METHOD*
Chili Sauce	1 pt.	Combine all ingredients. Chill.
Tomato Catsup	¾ pt.	
Prepared Horseradish (see Note)	4 oz.	
Lemon Juice	3 tbsp.	
Salt	1 tsp.	
Worcestershire Sauce	1 tsp.	
Hot Pepper Sauce	1 dash	
NOTE: If milder sauce is desired, omit hot pepper sauce. The quantities of horseradish will vary according to strength.		

Sauces

Cumberland Sauce

YIELD: 5 qt.		
INGREDIENTS	QUANTITY	METHOD
Currants Hot Water	12 oz. 1 gal. for cooking	1. Put currants in hot water to cover in a sauce pan; simmer slowly until currants are swelled and soft.
Oranges Lemons	2 2	2. Peel a very thin layer of skin (the zest) from the oranges and lemons. The skins should be free of any membrane or white part. 3. Cut skins in a very fine julienne ¾ in. long. Poach in hot water to cover for 20 min. Drain, discarding the water.
Cornstarch Cold Water	6 oz. 1 pt.	4. Dissolve cornstarch in 2 cups of cold water. Add gradually to currant mixture, stirring to prevent lumps. Cook until transparent.
Brown Sugar	12 oz.	5. Squeeze the juice from the 2 oranges and 2 lemons. 6. Add orange and lemon juice to currant mixture. Incorporate brown sugar; stir until dissolved.
Currant Jelly Port Wine Salt	4 oz. 4 oz. to taste	7. Pour 1 pt. of the liquid from the sauce into a bowl; whip in the currant jelly. Then return this to the sauce. 8. Add port wine. Season to taste with salt. 9. Stir in the julienne of lemon and orange peel.

Raisin Sauce

YIELD: 50 portions		
INGREDIENTS	QUANTITY	METHOD
Raisins, seedless Demi-Glace Sauce Orange Juice Lemon Juice Brown Sugar Vinegar, cider	12 oz. 3 qt. from 2 oranges from 2 lemons 1 lb. 3 tbsp.	1. Put raisins in a sauce pot with 3 qt. Demi-Glace Sauce. Add remaining ingredients and simmer slowly until soft.
NOTE: When served with sugar baked ham, deglaze pan ham was cooked in and strain into raisin sauce.		

Tartar Sauce

YIELD: about 1 gal.		
INGREDIENTS	QUANTITY	METHOD
Dill Pickles, finely chopped and squeezed dry Onions, finely chopped Stuffed Green Salad Olives, finely chopped Mayonnaise (p. 260) OR Boiled Dressing (p. 262)	1 qt. 1 pt. 8 oz. 2½ qt.	1. Mix all ingredients together until well blended.
		2. Store in glass jar or stainless steel container. Cover. Keep in refrigerator

International Cuisine

This section, developed from material presented to advanced students at the Culinary Institute of America, is a response to the growing interest in foreign food. These unique menus adapt well for special occasion promotions. Menus for 11 International dinners feature dishes from some 20 countries and the recipes needed to prepare them. Many dishes are pictured as portioned for service; suggestions for varying their presentation are included.

England

GIBLET SOUP

GOLDEN BUCK

ROAST LEG OF LAMB WITH MINT SAUCE

POACHED HADDOCK WITH PARSLEY SAUCE

ROAST FILET OF BEEF, LONDON HOUSE

CHEDDAR CHEESE-BREAD AND BUTTER PUDDING

ROAST POTATOES

BUTTERED CARROTS

BOILED LEEKS

Roast Leg of Lamb with Mint Sauce

YIELD: 8 to 10 portions	**EACH PORTION:** 4 to 5 oz. meat with 1½ to 2 oz. mint sauce	
INGREDIENTS	*QUANTITY*	*METHOD*
Lamb Leg, bone in, roast-ready (6 to 8 lb.) Salad Oil Salt Pepper	1 as required to taste to taste	1. Rub surface of lamb leg with oil. Sprinkle with salt and pepper. 2. Roast for about 1 hr. in preheated 375°F. oven. Start with fat side down; roast for ½ hr. Turn and complete cooking. Allow roast to rest before carving. Slice thin.
Mint Sauce (see below)	about 12 oz.	3. Serve with Mint Sauce.
MINT SAUCE		
YIELD: 12 oz.		
Water Vinegar (cider) Sugar Mint Leaves, chopped	8 oz. 4 oz. 2 oz. 2 tbsp.	1. Bring water, vinegar and sugar to a boil in a small saucepan. Remove from heat. 2. Add mint leaves. Allow to steep for several min. 3. Reheat before serving. (May also be served cold.) Serve on the side.

Boiled Leeks

METHOD
1. Wash leeks in cold water. Trim well and cut about 4 in. lengths, using white portion and reserving green portion for other kitchen use. 2. Tie 2 or 3 pieces together, depending on size, and cook in boiling salted water. 3. Remove from water and drain well. Remove string, and serve with butter and chopped parsley.

Carrots with Butter

METHOD
1. Scrub or lightly peel young carrots. Cut as desired. 2. Cook in minimum amount of boiling salted water. A small amount of sugar may be added if desired. 3. Prior to service, drain remaining water. Butter carrots well, and sprinkle with chopped fresh parsley.

Giblet Soup

YIELD: 25 portions	EACH PORTION: 1 soup cup, 8 oz.	
INGREDIENTS	*QUANTITY*	*METHOD*
Chicken Giblets, raw Water	2½ lb. 1 gal.	1. Wash, clean and prepare giblets for cooking. Simmer in 1 gal. of water for about ½ hr. Remove from heat. Strain and reserve stock. Trim giblets, retaining edible portion. Slice thin in fairly uniform pieces, about 3/8 in. each. Reserve.
Butter Onions, minced Flour Chicken Stock Salt White Pepper Nutmeg (optional) Rice, boiled or steamed	4 oz. 6 oz. 3 oz. see Method to taste to taste to taste 10 oz.	2. Saute onions in butter. Do not brown. Add flour and cook, stirring to prevent scorching or coloring. 3. Add reserved stock gradually, stirring or whipping as it thickens. Add sufficient chicken stock to make 1 gal. (to compensate for loss during cooking of giblets). Season. Bring to a boil. Add sliced giblets. Maintain low, simmering temperature and cook slowly until giblets are tender. 4. Adjust seasoning and consistency as required. Add boiled rice as garnish or place 1 tsp. of hot rice in each soup cup at time of service.

Golden Buck

YIELD: 1 portion		
INGREDIENTS	*QUANTITY*	*METHOD*
Cheddar Cheese, grated or fine chopped Ale Dry Mustard/Cayenne Pepper Salt	3½ oz. 1½ oz. to taste to taste	1. Combine cheese, ale and seasonings. Heat in heavy pan over low fire until cheese is melted. Whip smooth and adjust seasoning.
Crouton, sliced Soft Poached Egg	1 1	2. Place a toasted, sliced crouton in the bottom of a warm shirred egg dish or casserole. 3. Place the poached egg on the crouton. Top with the rabbit. Garnish as desired; serve at once.
NOTE: A small amount of stabilizing agent may sometimes be required, depending on the type of cheese. A small amount of chicken veloute, cream sauce, cornstarch, etc. may be added.		

Poached Haddock with Parsley Sauce

YIELD: 10 portions	EACH PORTION: 7 to 8 oz. with sauce	
INGREDIENTS	*QUANTITY*	*METHOD*
Haddock Fillets Butter Court Bouillon	5 lb. see Method as required	1. Skin haddock fillets. Cut fillets in 7 to 8 oz. portions. 2. Butter a suitable pan. Place fish portions in pan and cover the fish half-way with hot court bouillon. 3. Cover with buttered paper and simmer until fish is cooked. Do not overcook.
Parsley Sauce (see note)	1 qt.	4. Drain well and place portions on hot plates or platters. Serve with parsley sauce. (Reserve fish stock for other kitchen use.)
NOTE: Court Bouillon: To each quart of basic court bouillon, add about 1 tbsp. of chopped fennel. Parsley Sauce: To each quart of basic white sauce, add 2 oz. of lemon juice and 1 oz. of chopped fresh parsley. Adjust consistency with cream as desired.		

England

Roast Filet of Beef, London House

YIELD: 7 to 8 portions		EACH PORTION: 2 slices, about 6 oz. with 2 oz. sauce
INGREDIENTS	QUANTITY	METHOD
Tenderloin of Beef, whole, trimmed Pate de Foie Gras Truffles	about 3½ to 4 lb. 14 to 16 oz. as desired	1. After trimming and preparing filet for roasting, carefully cut tenderloin lengthwise, terminating the cut about ¾ in. from the outside edge so that it may be opened, butterfly-style, but remains in one piece. 2. Form the pate in cigar shape and place strip full length of tenderloin. Sprinkle with truffles as desired. 3. Fold the open flap over, closing the tenderloin, so that it now appears in its original shape. Tie securely with butcher's twine. 4. Roast in a hot oven for about ½ hr. The internal temperature of the meat should register about 135° F. when removing meat from oven. 140°F. is rare for beef. Carry-over heat should bring doneness to medium-rare for service.
Sauce Perigueux*	about 1½ pt.	

*Perigueux Sauce is a Madeira Sauce (p. 58) with chopped truffles. A finer distinction may be drawn by the use of diced truffles. The sauce then becomes Perigourdine.

NOTE: Substitutions may be made for foie gras to reduce costs. A number of pates and/or terrines may be used. It is important, however, that they have a low fat and/or gelatin content, so as to retain proper consistency during cooking.

Cheddar Cheese—Bread and Butter Pudding

YIELD: 2 portions (side orders)		
INGREDIENTS	QUANTITY	METHOD
Butter	see Method	1. Butter two small straight-sided casseroles.
Bread, white Paprika	1 to 2 slices see Method	2. Cut two croutons from the bread (same size as top of casserole). 3. Butter the croutons and sprinkle with paprika. Reserve.
Egg, whole Milk Cheddar Cheese, sharp, chopped fine Salt White Pepper Dry Mustard	1 4 oz. 1-1/2 oz. 1/4 tsp. to taste 1/8 tsp.	4. Beat the egg. Add the milk, mixing well. 5. Blend in cheese and seasonings. 6. Pour mixture in casseroles. Place crouton on top.
		7. Bake in oven at 350°F. about 20 min. Custard should test wet in center as carry-over heat will cause it to cook a bit more after removing from oven. Serve at once in casserole.

Roast Potatoes

	METHOD
	1. Peel potatoes; shape with a paring knife, reserving edible trimmings for other use. 2. Blanch in boiling salted water. Drain well; dry potatoes. Rub with oil, season with salt and pepper. Roast in 400°F. oven until golden brown.

Holland-Belgium

WATERZOOI
(CHICKEN SOUP)

**HOLLANDSE GEKOOKTE TARBOT,
GEKLOPTE BOTER SAUS**
(POACHED TURBOT, HOLLANDAISE)

GESTOOFDE KONIJIV MET PRUIMEN
(STEWED RABBIT WITH PRUNES)

BLINDE VINKEN
(BRAISED BEEF ROULADES)

VLAAMS GESTOOFDE OSSELAPPEN
(CARBONADE OF BEEF, FLAMANDE)

GESTOOFDE WITLOF, IN BRUINE BOTER
(BELGIAN ENDIVE SAUTE)

PATATTENVLA
(POTATO PIE)

Blinde Vinken (Braised Beef Roulades)

YIELD: 16 portions		EACH PORTION: 1 roulade with vegetables and sauce
INGREDIENTS	*QUANTITY*	*METHOD*
Boneless Steaks, bottom round, (¼ in. thick, 8 oz.) Prepared Mustard Black Pepper Thyme, ground	16 2 oz. 1 tsp. ¼ tsp.	1. Flatten the slices of bottom round to about ¼ in. thickness. Spread each piece with prepared mustard and sprinkle with black pepper and thyme.
Slab Bacon (3/8 in. strip), blanched Dill Pickle (3/8 in. strip) Mirepoix for braising	16 16 1 pt.	2. Place a strip of blanched bacon and a strip of pickle on each steak; roll each steak firmly around the bacon and pickle and tie securely. Brown lightly in a heavy pan or brazier. Remove the roulades and reserve. Saute the mirepoix.
Dark Beer Tomato Puree Espagnole	2 pt. 8 oz. 2 qt.	3. Deglaze the pan with the beer. Reduce halfway and add the tomato puree and espagnole (make sure sauce is fairly reduced), and return the roulades to the sauce. Cover and braise about 1 hr. or until tender.
Vegetables for garnish: Carrots, brunoise Celery, brunoise Onions, brunoise	4 oz. 4 oz. 4 oz.	4. Cook the brunoise vegetables separately in a small amount of lightly salted water. 5. When meat is cooked, place roulades in a clean pan and strain the sauce over the roulades. Adjust seasoning and consistency. 6. Drain the brunoise vegetables and add to the sauce. Serve with a generous portion of vegetables and sauce on top.

Turbot with Geklopte Boter Saus (Poached Turbot Hollandaise) (recipe below)

Patattenvla (Potato Pie) (recipe top of facing page)

Geklopte Boter Saus (Poached Turbot Hollandaise)

YIELD: 1 portion per pound, as purchased	EACH PORTION: Luncheon 6 to 7 oz. Dinner 8 to 10 oz.

Turbot is a European flatfish similar to the American halibut in appearance but more delicate in flavor.
PREPARATION
   1. Two cutting methods may be employed:
      2 cutting methods may be employed:
      a) full cut steaks (troncons)
      b) boneless fillets
   To cut full-cut steaks it is necessary to cut through the center bone at right angles to the length of the fish. Average portion yield is 1 portion per pound (head on, untrimmed). Portion weight, raw, cut, trimmed, to average 12 oz.
   To cut fillets, run knife down length of center bone, in similar manner to filleting flounder or sole. This procedure will yield 4 separate fillet pieces. (If filleting, reserve bones and head for fish stock.)
   Remove the skin and cut fish crosswise into desired portion sizes.
TO POACH
   1. Butter a shallow pan. Place portions in pan. Do not overcrowd.
   2. Pour hot court bouillon over fish. Cover and simmer gently until cooked. Do not overcook.
FOR SERVICE
   Remove fish portion(s) from court bouillon. Drain carefully and place on warm plate. To be accompanied with boiled potatoes. Garnish fish with lemon and parsley or watercress. Serve Hollandaise Sauce on the side. Fish should be served free of bone and skin.

COURT BOUILLON
   Prepare a basic court bouillon, using a 4 to 1 ratio of water and milk; e. g. 1 qt. of water to 8 oz. of milk.

Gestoofde Witlof, in Bruine Boter (Belgian Endive Saute)

YIELD: 10 portions	EACH PORTION: 1 Endive	
INGREDIENTS	*QUANTITY*	*METHOD*
Belgian Endive Salt Sugar	10 1 oz. 1 oz.	1. Trim endive, cutting out stalk at butt end. Do not separate leaves. 2. Blanch briefly in boiling water or blanch with a little sugar and salt. Keep undercooked.
Flour Butter	4 oz. 4 oz.	3. Drain well; dredge in flour. 4. Saute golden brown in butter.

Patattenvla (Potato Pie)

YIELD: about 25 portions	EACH PORTION: 1 square (4½ oz.)	
INGREDIENTS	*QUANTITY*	*METHOD*
Potatoes, peeled	5 lb.	1. Boil potatoes. Drain well and puree with food mill.
Egg Yolks Sour Cream Butter Salt White Pepper Nutmeg Chives, chopped	5 1 pt. 6 oz. to taste to taste to taste 1 oz.	2. Add egg yolks, sour cream and one-half of the butter. Reserve balance. Add seasoning and chives. Adjust consistency as desired.
Edam Cheese, grated Bread Crumbs, fresh	1 lb. 2 oz.	3. Place mixture in lightly buttered "hotel" pan. Sprinkle with cheese and bread crumbs. Finish with reserved butter. 4. Bake in oven preheated to 400°F. until top is golden brown.
NOTE: For a la carte service, portion in small ramekins or casseroles and bake as required.		

Gestoofde Konijiv Met Pruimen (Stewed Rabbit with Prunes)

YIELD: 7 portions	EACH PORTION: 3 pieces with prunes and sauce	
INGREDIENTS	*QUANTITY*	*METHOD*
Rabbits, skinned and dressed (average weight: 2¼ to 2½ lb.) Flour Lard OR Oil	3 for dredging about 4 oz.	1. Clean rabbit thoroughly, removing sinews and tendons. Cut into seven pieces as shown in the diagram. Trim well and reserve trim, bones, etc. 2. Dredge rabbit pieces in flour. Shake off excess flour and saute rabbit pieces in lard or oil in heavy brazier until light brown. Remove rabbit; keep warm.
Shallots, diced Mirepoix, fine	1 oz. 1 pt.	3. Add trim and bones, shallots and mirepoix and saute lightly in same pan in which rabbit was cooked.
White Wine Espagnole Salt Pepper Thyme Bayleaf	1 qt. 2 qt. 2 tsp. ¾ tsp. ½ tsp. small piece	4. Add wine, espagnole, seasoning and rabbit pieces, and braise, covered, about 1 hr. or until tender.
Pitted Prunes, soaked* Red Currant Jelly	½ lb. (dry weight) 4 oz.	5. Remove rabbit and place in a clean pan. Strain and skim sauce; adjust consistency. Pour over rabbit and add the prunes and currant jelly. Simmer about 5 min. and adjust seasoning. Serve with prunes and sauce.
*NOTE: Prunes may be soaked in water or wine, as desired.		

Holland — Belgium

Waterzooi (Chicken Soup)

YIELD: 25 portions	EACH PORTION: 1 soup cup, 8 oz.	
INGREDIENTS	*QUANTITY*	*METHOD*
Fowl, eviscerated (about 5 lb.) Water Salt Pepper Thyme Bay Leaf Garlic	1 5 qt. 1 tbsp. ½ tsp. ¼ tsp. small piece equivalent of ½ tsp.	1. Cook fowl in water with spices. When fowl is cooked, remove from stock and cool. Remove meat from bones. Reserve meat. 2. Strain stock.
Butter Flour	4 oz. 4 oz.	3. Prepare a roux from the butter and flour. Add the hot stock gradually, stirring smooth. Simmer about 15 min. Adjust consistency and flavor as desired. Quantity should be 1 gal. Adjust.
Carrots, julienne Leeks Celery, julienne Potatoes, peeled, julienne Onions Parsley	4 oz. 4 oz. 4 oz. 8 oz. 4 oz. to garnish	4. Smother the vegetables with a small amount of butter. Add to soup and simmer until vegetables are tender. Do not overcook the vegetables. 5. Cut chicken meat into bite size strips and add to the soup. When serving, sprinkle with chopped, fresh parsley.

NOTE: In Holland and Belgium, this soup is considered a "solid" food, a main course item, rather than a soup.

Vlaams Gestoofde Osselappen (Carbonnade of Beef Flamande)

YIELD: 10 portions	EACH PORTION: 8 to 10 oz. meat with sauce	
INGREDIENTS	*QUANTITY*	*METHOD*

Boneless Steaks, from
    bottom round
Flour
Shortening
    OR Substitute
	10 (8 to 10 oz.)
	
	for dredging
	about 4 oz.
		1. Flatten the steaks to about ½ in. thickness with a meat mallet.
		2. Dredge in flour and saute in a heavy brazier until well browned. Remove and reserve steaks.

Onions, peeled, diced Beer	2 lb. 3 pt.	3. Saute the onions in the same pan as steaks. When onions are golden brown, add the beer. Bring to high heat, deglazing the pan. Reduce the beer to ½ volume.
Espagnole Brown Stock	1 qt. 1 qt.	4. Add the espagnole and brown stock. Blend well, adjusting the consistency as desired.
Tomato Puree Salt Pepper Small Bouquet Garni (of Parsley, Thyme and Bayleaf)	4 oz. 1 tbsp. 1 tsp.	5. Add the balance of ingredients. Simmer briefly, and make flavor adjustments as required. 6. Return the steaks to the pan. Cover and braise until meat is tender. 7. Transfer steaks to a clean pan. Strain sauce and add to steaks. Cover and keep warm for service.

NOTE: In Belgium steaks are cooked very soft (fork-tender).

Potato Croquettes (II)

YIELD: 25 portions		EACH PORTION: about 4 oz.
INGREDIENTS	*QUANTITY*	*METHOD*
Potatoes, peeled Egg Yolks	5 lb. 8	1. Boil potatoes in salted water until potatoes are cooked. Drain well and dry. Pass the potatoes through a fine food mill. Incorporate egg yolks while potatoes are still very hot.
Butter Salt White Pepper Nutmeg	6 oz. to taste to taste to taste	2. Add balance of ingredients. When mixture is cool enough to handle, form into desired shapes. Dusting the work bench or board with a little flour or cornstarch will make working easier. After forming croquettes, refrigerate covered for at least an hour while they firm up.
Breading		3. Bread the croquettes, using standard breading procedures.
Oil	for deep frying	4. Deep fry as needed at a thermostat setting of 375°F. It is suggested that a sample test croquette be breaded and fried before making up the entire batch in the event that an adjustment in consistency or flavor is desired.
NOTE: Potato quality varies considerably in terms of water, sugar, starch content. Potatoes should be cooked, but very dry and mealy. Cooking time to be adjusted on this basis.		

Austria-Germany

CONSOMME MIT GRIESSNOCKERL
(CONSOMME WITH SEMOLINA DUMPLINGS)

KIRSCHEN KALTSCHALE
(COLD CHERRY SOUP)

WIENER SAFT GULASCH
(VIENNESE BEEF GOULASH)

ZWIEBELROSTBRATEN
(VIENNESE STYLE BRAISED MINUTE STEAK)

WIENER SCHNITZEL
(VIENNESE STYLE BREADED VEAL CUTLET)

BRATWURST UND EISBEIN MIT SAUERKRAUT
(BRATWURST AND PIG KNUCKLES WITH SAUERKRAUT)

POMMERISCHE MASTGANS
(ROAST GOOSE WITH APPLES AND PRUNES)

GEDUNSTETES ROTKRAUT IN ROTWEIN
(BRAISED RED CABBAGE IN RED WINE)

EINGMACHTE ERBSEN
(VIENNESE STYLE GREEN PEAS)

KARTOFFEL SALAD
(POTATO SALAD)

BRATKARTOFFEL
(PANFRIED POTATOES)

Consomme Mit Griessnockerl (Consomme with Semolina Dumplings)

YIELD: 15 portions	**EACH PORTION:** 1 consomme cup with 2 dumplings	
INGREDIENTS	*QUANTITY*	*METHOD*
CONSOMME (see p. 272)	3 qt.	

GRIESSNOCKERL

YIELD: 30 dumplings

Butter Eggs, whole Salt Nutmeg White Pepper	4 oz. 2 1 tsp. ½ tsp. ¼ tsp.	1. Cream the butter. Beat the eggs with the seasoning and blend with the butter, a little at a time, beating well.
Semolina	8 oz.	2. Stir in semolina, mixing thoroughly. Consistency may require some adjustment. Semolina varies considerably; size of eggs, etc. A small amount of water may be added, if necessary. 3. Cover and store in the refrigerator for a minimum of 20 min. 4. Make a test dumpling and poach lightly to see if seasoning or consistency requires adjustment. 5. Using two teaspoons, make small shaped dumplings and poach, covered, in lightly salted water about 10 min.
Chives	to garnish	6. Place 2 dumplings in consomme cup at service time; pour in hot consomme and sprinkle with chopped chives.

Zwiebelrostbraten (Viennese Style Braised Minute Steak)

YIELD: 6 portions		EACH PORTION: 8 oz. with onions and juice
INGREDIENTS	QUANTITY	METHOD
Sirloin Steaks (8 oz.) Salt Pepper Flour Lard OR Oil	6 to taste to taste for dredging 2 oz.	1. Flatten the steaks and season with salt and pepper. (The steaks should be very thin.) Dredge the steaks in flour and saute lightly on both sides in hot lard or oil. Remove the steaks and reserve.
Onions, sliced thin	12 oz.	2. Place the onions in the same pan in which the steaks were sauteed. Saute, coloring well, but keep fairly crisp. Remove half the onions and reserve for service.
Vinegar, white Beef Stock	1 oz. 1 pt.	3. Deglaze the pan with the vinegar and place the steaks back in the pan with the onions. Add about half the beef stock and simmer about 1 hr. Add stock periodically as required, turning the steaks if necessary. 4. Serve each Rostbraten with a little of the juice-onion mixture and top with the reserved, crisply sauteed onions. Roast potatoes are usually served with this dish.

NOTE: Today's travelers may frequently find that the Zwiebelrostbraten on many Austrian menus may not be braised or "roasted" but sauteed only. The American influence has caused some restaurants to change their procedures because few Americans enjoy well-done steaks. The sauteed steak is not true Zwiebelrostbraten but may appear on some menus as such.

Bratwurst Und Eisbein Mit Sauerkraut (Bratwurst and Pig Knuckles with Sauerkraut)

YIELD: 10 portions		EACH PORTION: 1 pig's knuckle and 1 bratwurst on sauerkraut
INGREDIENTS	QUANTITY	METHOD
Slab Bacon, diced (3/8 in.) Onions, medium dice	½ lb. 1 lb.	1. Render slab bacon. Add diced onions and saute. 2. Add sauerkraut, water, vinegar, spices and potatoes, blending well. Add pig knuckles. Simmer slowly, covered, until pig knuckles are tender and moisture has been reduced.
Sauerkraut Water Vinegar Juniper Berries Caraway Seeds Salt Sugar Bay Leaf Potatoes, raw, grated Pigs' Knuckles	1 No. 10 can 1 qt. 4 oz. ½ tsp. ½ tsp. 1 tsp. 1 tbsp. small piece 2 lb. 10	3. Separately cover the bratwurst with boiling water and let stand for 10 min. 4. Remove bratwurst from water; drain well and dip in milk and flour. Panfry in lard or oil until they are brown and crisp. 5. Arrange pig's knuckle and bratwurst link on a mound of sauerkraut for each portion. Usually served with bread dumplings or boiled potatoes.

Bratwurst
Milk and Flour
 	
Oil for Frying
	10
	See Method,
	  step 5
	See Method,
	  step 5	

NOTE: "Eisbein" is actually a cured ham-hock; cured pig knuckles are served as a substitute.

Pommerische Mastgans

YIELD: 6 portions	EACH PORTION: 2 pieces with gravy	
INGREDIENTS (A)	QUANTITY	METHOD
Goose (8 to 9 lb., dressed)	1	1. Prepare goose for stuffing by removing all fat and traces of viscera. Clean thoroughly.
Apples (firm, cooking-type) Prunes, dried Salad Oil Salt White Pepper Rosemary	1 lb. 6 oz. for rubbing to taste to taste to taste	2. Wash apples. Cut apples in quarters. Stuff goose with apples and prunes. Truss firmly. Oil surface of goose lightly and rub in spices. 3. Place, breast up, in pan with a rack in preheated oven at 400°F. for 10 min., then reduce to 350°F. 4. Roast for 1½ hr., basting occasionally.
INGREDIENTS (B)		
Mirepoix Brown Stock	6 oz. 1 pt.	5. Remove pan from oven. Pour off goose fat and reserve. Remove rack. Add mirepoix and place goose breast side down on mirepoix. Return to oven and complete roasting. Increase temperature if required to achieve crispness of skin. *Approx. additional roasting time: 1 to 1½ hr. Total roasting time: 2½ to 3 hr.* 6. When roasting is completed, reserve goose for service in a warm place. Deglaze pan with brown stock. Simmer mirepoix; strain and adjust seasoning and consistency. CARVING GOOSE FOR SERVICE 1. Cut and remove trussing twine. Remove and discard fat-soaked apples and prunes. 2. Remove legs. Disjoint; cut thigh in 2 portions....... straight along the bone. This method should yield 6 pieces. 3. Remove breasts, cutting straight along breastbone. Cut each breast (on the bias) into 3 equal portions. Serve 1 piece of leg and 1 piece of breast per portion. SERVING SUGGESTIONS Serve with braised red cabbage and fresh applesauce. Serve slightly thickened gravy on the side; about 2 oz. per portion.

Wiener Schnitzel (Viennese Style Breaded Veal Cutlets)

YIELD: 6 portions	EACH PORTION: 6 to 8 oz. cutlet	
INGREDIENTS	QUANTITY	METHOD

Veal Cutlets, leg (6 to 8 oz. each)
Breading:
    Flour
    Strong Egg Wash
    Fresh Bread Crumbs
Lard
    OR Oil
	6
	
	about 4 oz.
		1. Flatten cutlets to about ¼ in. thickness. Season as desired and bread them, using standard procedures. Use fresh bread crumbs only. Fry in hot oil over medium heat until nearly done and golden brown.

Butter	about 4 oz.	2. Transfer to a clean pan with hot butter and cook lightly until butter is absorbed.

NOTE: Wiener Schnitzel are usually served with lemon wedges and mixed salad. They are not served with a sauce unless specifically identified as a different method of preparation on the menu.

Kirschen Kaltschale (Cold Cherry Soup)

YIELD: 12 portions		EACH PORTION: 1 soup cup
INGREDIENTS	*QUANTITY*	*METHOD*
Sour Cherries, with juice Water Red Wine Lemon Juice Sugar Whole Cloves Stick Cinnamon	1 qt. ¾ to 1 qt. 1 pt. 2 oz. 4 oz. 2 or 3 small piece	1. Reserve 12 cherries for garnish. Reserve 2 oz. of water. 2. Place balance of cherries, water, wine, lemon juice, and spices in a suitable pot; bring to boil. Reduce heat and simmer briefly.
Cornstarch Lemon Slices, thin	2 tsp. 12	3. Mix cornstarch with 2 oz. of water. Add to simmering soup, stirring well. The soup should be of a thin consistency, but the cornstarch will aid in achieving a fine sheen. Strain through cheesecloth, removing cloves and cinnamon stick. Adjust seasoning. Chill well. Serve in chilled cups with cherry and lemon slice garnish.
NOTE: Some flavoring adjustment may be necessary, depending on tartness of cherries, etc. Although not in the original formulation, a small amount of orange juice aids in bringing out the flavor.		

Kartoffel Salat (Potato Salad)

YIELD: 15 portions		EACH PORTION: 5 oz.
INGREDIENTS	*QUANTITY*	*METHOD*
Potatoes	5 lb., A.P.	1. Cook potatoes in their jackets. Peel and slice thin while potatoes are still warm.
Onions, finely diced Salad Oil Vinegar, white Beef Stock, hot Salt Black Pepper	1 lb., A.P. 6 oz. about 8 oz. 6 oz. to taste to taste	2. Combine all ingredients except potatoes, reserving part of the vinegar. 3. Add sliced potatoes and mix carefully so that potatoes will retain reasonable shape. Adjust seasoning; add balance of vinegar as desired. 4. Marinate for several hours under refrigeration but do not serve too cold.
NOTE: Small, oblong-shaped potatoes are preferred for uniform slicing.		

Eingemachte Erbsen (Viennese Style Green Peas)

YIELD: 15 portions		EACH PORTION: 4 oz.
INGREDIENTS	*QUANTITY*	*METHOD*
Butter Flour Beef Stock, hot	3 oz. 2 oz. 1 pt.	1. Prepare a light roux with the butter and flour. Add hot beef stock, stirring smooth. Simmer for 10 min.
Sugar Salt Black Pepper Green Peas, (frozen) cooked Parsley, chopped	2 oz. ½ tsp. ¼ tsp. 2½ lb. 1 oz.	2. Add balance of ingredients, mixing well. Return to a boil; remove from heat and serve.

Wiener Saft Gulasch (Viennese Beef Goulash)

YIELD: 12 portions		
INGREDIENTS	*QUANTITY*	*METHOD*
Onions, sliced or diced Lard OR Salad Oil	4 lb. 4 oz.	1. Saute onions in lard in heavy brazier, browning the onions well.
Vinegar, white Paprika (Hungarian) Marjoram, powdered Garlic, fine mince Caraway Seeds, powdered Bayleaf Lemon Zest, grated Salt	2 oz. about 4 tbsp. 1 tsp. 2 tsp. 1 tsp. small piece 1 tbsp. to taste	2. Add vinegar, deglazing lightly. Add balance of ingredients, *except meat,* blending well.
Beef Chuck, cubed	5 lb.	3. Add meat. Cover and simmer slowly until meat is tender. If moisture content is too low, a small amount of beef stock or water may be added.
NOTE: In Austria, the goulash is usually served with bread dumplings or spaetzli.		

Gedunstetes Rotkraut in Rotwein (Braised Red Cabbage)

YIELD: 15 to 20 portions	EACH PORTION: about 4 oz.	
INGREDIENTS	*QUANTITY*	*METHOD*
Margarine OR Substitute (e.g. goose fat) Onions, peeled, diced	3 oz. 4 oz.	1. Saute onions in margarine or fat agent.
Sugar Lemon Juice OR Cider Vinegar	3 oz. 2 oz.	2. Add sugar and brown lightly. Add lemon juice or vinegar similar to deglazing process.
Red Cabbage, peeled, cored, shredded Apples, peeled, cored, diced Red Wine Salt Pepper Powdered Cloves Stick Cinnamon	4 lb. ½ lb. 1 pt. to taste to taste about ½ tsp. 1 small piece	3. Add cabbage, apples, wine and seasoning. Mix thoroughly. 4. Cover and simmer until cabbage is cooked but still has some crispness. 5. Remove cinnamon stick; adjust seasoning.
NOTE: A small amount of flour, or "whitewash," may be added to bind cabbage lightly.		

Bratkartoffeln (Panfried Potatoes)

	METHOD
	1. Small potatoes are cooked in their jackets, peeled and cut in half lengthwise. 2. They are then panfried in lard or butter until golden brown and crisp.

Switzerland

CONSOMME DIABLOTIN

KÄSE SOUFFLE OR SOUFFLE FROMAGE
(CHEESE SOUFFLE)

KÄSE FONDUE

ZÜRICHER GESCHNETZELTES
(SWISS STYLE SHREDDED VEAL)

SAURE LEBER
(SHREDDED LIVER IN SOUR CREAM SAUCE)

BERNER SCHLACHTPLATTE
(SWISS STYLE BUTCHER PLATE)

BROT KNOEDEL
(BREAD DUMPLINGS)

GEDÜNSTETER KOCHSALAT
(BRAISED LETTUCE)

ROESTI POTATOES
(SWISS STYLE HASH BROWN POTATOES)

SPAETZLI
(NOODLE PRODUCT USED FOR GARNISHING
AND AS POTATO SUBSTITUTE)

Consomme Diablotin

YIELD: 30 to 35 portions	EACH PORTION: 1 soup cup with Diablotin	
INGREDIENTS	*QUANTITY*	*METHOD*
CONSOMME Consomme (p. 272)	1½ gal.	

DIABLOTINS
  Heavy Cream Sauce, hot
  Egg Yolks
  Swiss Cheese, grated
  Salt
  Cayenne Pepper
	8 oz.
	4
	1 lb.
	to taste
	to taste
		1. Heat Cream Sauce; remove from fire and blend in the egg yolks gradually. Add cheese and seasonings.

French Bread	See Step 2	2. Cut French bread in thin slices and toast one side only. 3. Spread cheese mixture on the untoasted side and place under the broiler (or salamander) to glaze. Use immediately. Place 1 or 2 Diablotins, depending on size, in the soup at time of service.
NOTE: Various forms of croutons are sometimes served on the side.		

Switzerland

Berner Schlachtplatte (Swiss Style Butcher Plate)
(recipe below)

Kase Fondue
(recipe top of facing page)

Berner Schlachtplatte (Swiss Style Butcher Plate)

YIELD: 12 portions		EACH PORTION: 9 to 10 oz. assorted meat plus sauerkraut
INGREDIENTS	*QUANTITY*	*METHOD*

Shortribs, beef, lean, trimmed
Sausage, smoked (kielbasi type)
Marrow Bones, sliced
   (about ½ in. thick)
Stock (see Method, Step 1, a, b and c)
	4 lb.
	1 lb.
	12
	
	as required
		1. Do the following:
		   a. Cook shortribs separately in seasoned stock.
		   b. Cook sausage separately in seasoned stock.
		   c. Poach bones with marrow in stock.

Onion, medium dice Salad Oil OR Rendered Bacon Fat Sauerkraut Wine, white Potato, raw, peeled, grated Juniper Berries Caraway Seeds Salt Pepper	4 oz. 2 oz. 3 lb. 1 pt. 4 oz. 2 tbsp. 2 tbsp. to taste to taste	2. Saute onion until transparent. Combine onion, sauerkraut, wine, grated potato, juniper berries, caraway seeds, salt and pepper. Place in large roast pan or brazier.
Smoked Pork Loin Slab Bacon Pigs' Knuckles, cured	4 lb., A.P. 1 lb., A.P. 6	3. Place smoked ribs, slab bacon and pigs' feet on top of sauerkraut. Cover pan and cook in preheated oven at 375°F. for about 1½ hr. or until meats are tender. For platter service, place sauerkraut on platters. Slice and/or cut meats and arrange on top of sauerkraut. Add marrow bones; garnish with parsley. Serve with boiled potatoes or Brot Knoedel (p. 344). For individual service, follow above procedure, dividing product in 12 reasonably uniform portions.

NOTE: The amounts of meat indicated are primarily guidelines. Much depends on trim, as purchased specifications, etc. Individual product portions (e.g. slab bacon) should be small, as total product served is substantial.

Kase Fondue

YIELD: 6 portions	EACH PORTION: 8 oz.	
INGREDIENTS	*QUANTITY*	*METHOD*
Garlic Clove, crushed	1	1. Rub a suitable earthenware casserole with the garlic clove.
White Wine Emmenthaler, chopped fine Gruyere, chopped fine	1 pt. 1 lb. 1 lb.	2. Heat wine in casserole. 3. Put the cheese in the casserole and place over moderate heat. Stir occasionally as the cheese melts. Do not overheat or cook.
Salt Cayenne Pepper Kirschwasser	to taste to taste 1 oz.	3. When the cheese is melted, add seasoning and kirschwasser, blending well. Adjust seasoning as desired.

NOTE: The fondue may be prepared in the kitchen, or at tableside over a low flame. Care must be taken not to over-heat cheese.

Small pieces of French bread are served separately and guests are provided with fondue forks with which to spear the bread and dunk it into the fondue.

There are many variations of cheese-based fondues. Some employ thickening agents such as flour or cornstarch.

Spaetzli

YIELD: 6 portions		
INGREDIENTS	*QUANTITY*	*METHOD*
Eggs, whole Water	3 8 oz.	1. Beat eggs thoroughly in a mixing bowl. 2. Add water blending well.
Flour Salt Nutmeg White Pepper	10 to 12 oz. 1/2 tsp. 1/4 tsp. 1/8 tsp.	3. Add balance of ingredients, beating smooth. It is suggested that you begin with 10 oz. of flour and add additional flour if necessary. 4. Drop the spaetzli into rapidly boiling, salted water using special machine (see note) and cook for about 3 min. or until the spaetzli rise and float on the surface. The water should not stop boiling. 5. As the spaetzli rise to the surface of the water, remove them with a skimmer or slotted spoon and place in cold water to stop cooking. Drain well, cover them with a clean, damp cloth, and reserve in a dry place for further preparation.
		6. For service, saute the spaetzli lightly in butter in a hot pan. They may be served immediately from the pan, or baked for 5 to 10 min. (additional time) at 360°F. for additional color and moisture balance.

NOTE: If a spaetzli machine is not available, the spaetzli may be passed through a colander placed over the pot of water. Force the dough through the holes in the colander using the back of a spoon.

Caution: The colander must be kept 8 to 10 in. from the boiling water so that the dough will not cook in the colander.

Switzerland

Zuricher Geschnetzeltes (Swiss Style Shredded Veal)

YIELD: 5 to 6 portions		EACH PORTION: 5 to 6 oz. with mushrooms and sauce.
INGREDIENTS	*QUANTITY*	*METHOD*
Veal Leg, thinly sliced Butter, clarified	2 lb. 2 to 3 oz.	1. Shred the veal and saute in clarified butter over high heat, coloring well. Do not overcook. Remove veal and reserve in a warm place.
Shallots, chopped Mushrooms, sliced Wine, white, dry Demi-glaze	2 oz. 1 pt. 8 oz. 4 oz.	2. Cook shallots in same pan the veal was cooked in. Add mushrooms and saute lightly. 3. Deglaze with the wine; add demi-glaze and reduce half-way.
Cream Salt White Pepper Butter	8 oz. to taste to taste 1 oz.	4. Add cream and seasoning and cook over medium heat, reducing liquid to the consistency of cream. A small amount of cornstarch may be used for thickening, if necessary. 5. Immediately prior to service, place veal in the sauce with the mushrooms and heat thoroughly but do not boil. Finish with a piece of fresh butter, stirring well.
NOTE: May be accompanied by Gruyere Risotto or Spaetzli.		

Geduensteter Kopfsalat (Braised Lettuce)

Romaine or Boston Lettuce is suggested.	
	METHOD
	1. Clean and trim lettuce. Blanch in lightly salted, boiling water. 2. Cool and remove the lettuce from the water. Lettuce may be cut in half lengthwise or used whole, depending on size. Squeeze all water from each piece, individually. 3. Grease or butter suitable baking dish and sprinkle with fine mirepoix. Place ball-shaped lettuce on the bed of mirepoix. Season, and add white stock to a level about half-way up the lettuce. Place in a medium oven and cook for about ½ hr. or until done, basting as required.
NOTE: Strips of bacon may be placed on each piece of lettuce before baking if additional flavor is desired.	

Kase Auflauf or Souffle au Fromage (Cheese Souffle)

YIELD: 6 appetizer portions	EACH PORTION: 5 oz.	
INGREDIENTS	QUANTITY	METHOD
Milk	12 oz.	1. Butter an 8 in. souffle dish carefully and dust it with flour. 2. Bring the milk to a boil.
Butter Flour Cornstarch	3 oz. 2 oz. ½ oz.	3. In a separate pan, prepare a light roux with the butter, flour and cornstarch. Do not color. 4. Add the hot milk gradually, whipping until smooth and thick.
Egg Yolks	6	5. Remove from the heat and let cool a little. Incorporate the egg yolks one or two at a time, mixing well.
Swiss Cheese, grated Salt Cayenne Pepper	4 oz. to taste to taste	6. Add the cheese and seasoning, blending well.
Egg Whites	6	7. Beat the egg whites to a medium peak. Fold one-half the egg whites into the mixture. Then carefully fold in the balance of the egg whites. 8. Fill the souffle dish to within 1 in. of the rim, adding a collar if necessary. Bake in a 350° to 375°F. oven about 35 to 40 min.

Saure Leber (Shredded Liver in Sour Cream)

YIELD: 5 portions	EACH PORTION: about 6 oz. with sauce	
INGREDIENTS	QUANTITY	METHOD
Calves' Liver, trimmed, deveined Salad Oil Salt Pepper Marjoram	2 lb. 2 oz. to taste to taste to taste	1. Shred liver and saute in hot oil over a brisk fire. Color well but *do not overcook*. Remove liver from pan; season liver and reserve in a warm place. Discard oil.
Butter Onions, medium dice Vinegar Veal Gravy OR Brown Sauce	2 oz. 1 pt. 1 oz. 1 pt.	2. Saute onions in butter in the same pan. 3. Add vinegar and veal gravy and simmer about 5 min.
Sour Cream	8 oz.	4. Add sour cream, blending well. Reheat but do not boil. 5. Place the liver back in the sauce, mixing well. Serve immediately.

Brot Knoedel (Bread Dumplings)

YIELD: 10 to 14 dumplings	EACH PORTION: 1 or 2 dumplings	
INGREDIENTS	*QUANTITY*	*METHOD*

Onions, finely diced
Butter
  OR Substitute
 	
Hard Rolls
  OR French-Italian type
  Bread* (fine dice) about
Parsley, fresh, chopped
Flour
	4 oz.
	2½ oz.
	
	1¼ lb.
	
	1¼ lb.
	1 oz.
	2½ oz.
		1. Saute onions in butter until lightly browned. Cool slightly and blend with diced hard bread and parsley. Sprinkle flour over the surface of the mixture and blend lightly.

Eggs, whole, beaten Milk Salt White Pepper Nutmeg	3 12 oz. 1 tsp. ¼ tsp. ½ tsp.	2. Combine eggs, milk and seasonings. Pour over the bread mixture and blend all ingredients, lifting bread mixture lightly in a folding action to keep mixture as light and fluffy as possible. 3. Cover and refrigerate for at least ½ hr. before using. Prior to cooking, adjust consistency and seasoning. TO PREPARE: Wet hands and form dumplings size of a small orange, about 2½ in. diameter. Place in lightly salted boiling water and simmer, covered, for 10 to 15 min.
*NOTE: Bread should be day old or more and fairly dried out.		

Roesti Potatoes (Swiss Style Hash Brown Potatoes)

	METHOD
	Roesti potatoes are a form of hashed brown potatoes. The day prior to use, cook fairly large potatoes, keeping them underdone. To prepare, grate the potatoes coarsely and pan fry until very crisp. Minced onions are optional. The potatoes should be as dry and as mealy as possible to produce a superior product.
NOTE: Preparations vary regionally; adding bacon, onions, eggs, parsley, chives.	

Jewish

CHICKEN OR FLAISHIG ZOOP MIT KREPLACH
(CHICKEN OR BEEF BROTH WITH KREPLACH)

FLAISH KNISHES
(MEAT KNISHES)

GEFILTE FISH

CHICKEN MIT ZOOP AND KNAIDLACH
(CHICKEN IN THE POT, MATZO BALLS)

BROOST GEDEMPT MIT CIDER
(POT ROAST WITH CIDER)

HOLISHKES
(MEAT FILLED CABBAGE)

KASHA VARNITSHKES
(BUCKWHEAT GROATS WITH MACARONI)

MEHREN-TZIMMES MIT FLOMMEN
(CARROT-PRUNE TZIMMES)

KISHKE
(STUFFED DERMA)

POTATO LATKES
(POTATO PANCAKES)

LUKSHEN KUGEL
(NOODLE PUDDING)

Chicken Mit Zoop and Knaidlach (Chicken in the Pot, Matzo Balls)

YIELD: 5 to 6 portions	EACH PORTION: 1 soup dish with vegetables and matzo balls	
INGREDIENTS	*QUANTITY*	*METHOD*
Chicken, whole (about 3½ lb.) Carrots, coarsely chopped Onions, coarsely chopped Celery, coarsely chopped Parsnips, coarsely chopped Salt Pepper, white Bayleaf	1 4 oz. 4 oz. 2 oz. 2 oz. 1 tbsp. ¼ tsp. small piece	1. Clean chicken well. Place in a deep saucepot and boil about 15 min. Add vegetables and seasonings and simmer for 35 to 40 min. or until chicken is tender. 2. Remove chicken from the pot. Disjoint, remove all bones and sinews and cut into portion pieces. Skim surface of soup, leaving a minor amount of fat.
Matzo Balls (see below) Chives, chopped OR Parsley, chopped	garnish	3. Place chicken pieces in soup dishes and serve with vegetables and matzo balls. Sprinkle with chopped chives or parsley.

Matzo Balls

YIELD: 16 oz.		
INGREDIENTS	*QUANTITY*	*METHOD*
Eggs, whole Chicken Fat OR Salad Oil Stock Matzo Meal Salt Pepper	4 2 oz. 2 oz. ½ pt. to taste to taste	1. Beat eggs. Add rendered chicken fat or oil, stock and seasonings. Stir in matzo meal, mixing well. Cover and refrigerate for at least ½ hr. 2. Form small balls with the mixture and poach, covered, in lightly-salted water or stock. Test one dumpling and adjust seasoning if necessary before poaching the entire mixture.

Jewish

Chicken or Flaishig Zoop Mit Kreplach (Chicken or Beef Broth with Kreplach)

YIELD: 50 portions	EACH PORTION: 8 oz. broth with 1 Kreplach	
INGREDIENTS	*QUANTITY*	*METHOD*
Chicken OR Beef Broth	2½ gal.	Bring broth to a boil and hold for service.
NOODLE DOUGH Flour Eggs, whole Water, cold	½ lb. 2 2 to 3 tsp.	Blend ingredients thoroughly. Knead until smooth. Cover with a damp towel and let dough rest for ½ hr.
FILLING Chicken, cooked, boneless Eggs, whole Parsley, minced Onion Juice	½ lb. 1 1 tbsp. 1 tsp.	Mix all ingredients. Adjust seasoning. Refrigerate until needed.

PREPARATION OF KREPLACH
1. Roll noodle dough very thin. Cut into 1½ in. squares.
2. Place about ½ tsp. of filling slightly off center of square of dough as shown in the diagram.
3. Brush lower edges of dough lightly with water. Fold dough over filling and press edges firmly.
4. Place in boiling salted water or stock. Simmer for 10 to 15 min. Kreplach should be done when they rise to the surface.
   Remove to a clean pan with a little stock and keep warm for service.
   Serve with clear broth.

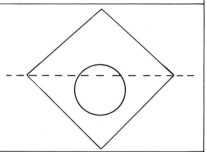

NOTE: May also be served with gravy for lunch.

Mehren-Tzimmes Mit Flommen (Carrot-Prune Tzimmes)

YIELD: 20 to 25 portions	EACH PORTION: 3½ to 4 oz.	
INGREDIENTS	*QUANTITY*	*METHOD*
Carrots, diced Water	5 lb., A.P. see Method	1. Prepare carrots. Barely cover with lightly salted water. Cook, covered, until carrots are nearly tender. Drain and reserve cooking liquor and carrots.
Flour Margarine OR Chicken Fat	4 oz. 4 oz.	2. Make a roux with the flour and margarine or chicken fat.
Honey OR Brown Sugar Pitted Dried Prunes	½ pt. 1 lb.	3. Add the cooking liquor gradually, whipping mixture smooth. Add honey (or brown sugar) and simmer briefly. 4. Place carrots and prunes in a buttered baking pan and pour sauce over them. 5. Bake at 350°F. about ½ hr.

Broost Gedempt Mit Cider (Pot Roast with Cider)

YIELD: 20 to 24 portions	**EACH PORTION:** 4 to 5 oz. with broth	
INGREDIENTS	*QUANTITY*	*METHOD*
A) MARINADE 　Cider 　Molasses 　Garlic, minced 　Bay Leaf 　Ginger, ground 　Allspice, ground	 2 qt. 2 oz. 2 tsp. medium piece ¼ tsp. ¼ tsp.	1. Prepare marinade by combining all ingredients under "Marinade." Marinate beef overnight under refrigeration.
B) Chuck 　OR Brisket of Beef 　Flour 　Salad Oil 　OR Shortening	10 lb. to dredge to brown meat	2. Remove meat from marinade. Dry well; dredge in flour and brown on all sides in hot oil in small brazier.
C) Carrots, chopped 　Celery, chopped 　Onions, chopped	½ lb. ½ lb. 1 lb.	3. Pour off all fat. Add marinade and vegetables to meat and simmer, covered, about 2 hr. Test meat for doneness and adjust cooking time as required. Remove meat from pot and reserve in warm place. 4. Strain broth and adjust seasoning. Slice beef, serving about 2 to 3 slices per serving. Serve with a small amount of reduced broth.

Gefilte Fish

YIELD: 12 dumplings	**EACH PORTION:** 1 dumpling with gelatinized fish stock	
INGREDIENTS	*QUANTITY*	*METHOD*
Stock		1. Use bones and edible fish trimmings to prepare stock.
Pike, boneless, skinless 　OR Carp, boneless, skinless Onion, diced	1½ lb. 5 oz.	2. Chop fish and diced onions into a paste or pass twice through the fine plate of a chopper.
Eggs, whole Matzo Meal Salt White Pepper	2 3 tbsp. 1½ tsp. ¼ tsp.	3. Combine fish mixture, eggs, matzo meal, and salt and pepper. Divide mixture into 12 equal portions and shape into eliptical dumplings.
Carrots, sliced Onions, sliced	3 oz. 5 oz.	4. Test poach a small dumpling for seasoning and consistency before poaching total formulation. 5. Poach the dumplings, covered, in fish stock with the carrots and onions. Cooking time may vary with size and procedure. 　Suggestion: Cook dumplings 10 to 15 min. Remove pot from heat. Leave covered. Allow dumplings to cool. They will continue to cook until heat diminishes substantially. 6. When sufficiently cool, refrigerate and chill well. Place a piece of carrot on the top of each dumpling and serve a small amount of the gelatinized fish stock. Traditionally accompanied by horseradish, or beet horseradish.

NOTE: Varying combinations of pike, carp, and white fish may be used. Pike and carp are superior to whitefish.
Bread may be substituted for matzo meal if desired. If using bread, soak one trimmed slice in water and squeeze dry but keep light and fluffy. Grind with fish and onions.

Potato Latkes (Potato Pancakes)
(recipe below)

Lukshen Kugel (Noodle Pudding)
(recipe top of facing page)

Potato Latkes (Potato Pancakes)

YIELD: 12 portions	EACH PORTION: 2 Latkes, 2½ oz. each	
INGREDIENTS	QUANTITY	METHOD
Potatoes, peeled Onions, peeled	3 lb. 8 oz.	1. Grate potatoes. Squeeze out liquid so that potatoes will be relatively dry. Place in mixing bowl. 2. Grate onions into potatoes.
Eggs, whole Matzo Meal Salt Salad Oil	4 4 oz. 1 tsp. for frying	3. Add eggs, matzo meal and salt. Blend all ingredients well, but do not overmix. 4. Drop by spoonful into well oiled hot skillet. Brown well on both sides. For crisper pancakes, increase amount of oil. Drain well prior to serving.

VARIATIONS:

   A) Use same mixture. Place in lightly oiled, shallow baking pan. Bake at 375°F. for about 45 min., or until cooked and well browned. Cut into portion-size squares.

   B) Place mixture in lightly oiled muffin pans. Bake as above.

NOTE: Care must be exercised to keep oil absorption to a reasonable minimum.

   If mixture is not to be used immediately, a small amount of lemon juice may be added to retard discoloration of potatoes.

   As the starch quantity of potatoes varies, minor adjustments in consistency of the mixture may be required. A small amount of potato starch or flour may be added to tighten up the mixture if it is excessively loose prior to cooking.

Lukshen Kugel (Noodle Pudding)

YIELD: 24 side portions		**EACH PORTION**: about 4 oz.
INGREDIENTS	*QUANTITY*	*METHOD*
Noodles, medium to broad	2 lb.	1. Cook noodles until tender but still firm. Cool, drain well and place in mixing bowl.
Chicken Fat, rendered, OR Substitute Egg Yolks Sugar Cinnamon Nutmeg Salt Raisins	8 oz. 12 yolks 1 lb. about ½ tsp. about ½ tsp. 1 tsp. 1 lb.	2. Add melted chicken fat or substitute, egg yolks and seasonings. Blend well. Incorporate raisins.
Egg Whites	12 whites	3. Beat egg whites to a medium peak. Fold into noodle mixture and place in lightly oiled casserole or baking dish. 4. Bake, uncovered at 350°F. about 40 min.
NOTE: Noodle Pudding is frequently served as a side dish on the Sabbath, or with holiday poultry. It is also a popular buffet item.		

Holishkes (Meat Filled Cabbage)

YIELD: 12 portions		**EACH PORTION**: 2 rolls with sauce
INGREDIENTS	*QUANTITY*	*METHOD*
Cabbage	3 to 4 large heads	1. Core cabbage and blanch for 10 to 12 min. in boiling, salted water. Remove, cool, and separate large leaves; reserve for formula. Use inside of the cabbage for other kitchen production.
Chopped Beef Rice, raw Onions, minced Carrots, grated Salt Pepper Eggs, whole	3 lb. 2 oz. ½ lb. 2 oz. 2 tsp. ½ tsp. 3	2. Mix beef, rice, vegetables, seasonings and eggs. Blend thoroughly, but keep mixture as light as possible. 3. Scale 2 oz. portions of meat mixture. Place on flattened cabbage leaves, folding ends of cabbage leaves to the center and rolling securely but not too tight. The mixture (with the rice) will expand. Prepare 24 units.
Lemon Juice Brown Sugar Tomato Puree Water	4 oz. 6 oz. 6 oz. 1½ pt.	4. Butter a baking pan and place cabbage rolls close together in the pan. 5. Combine the balance of ingredients. Add additional water to barely cover cabbage rolls, if required. 6. Cover and bake for 45 to 50 min. at 350°F. Remove cover and bake for about 20 additional min. Serve cabbage rolls with a small amount of sauce.
NOTE: There are many variations of filling and sauce ingredients, often with subsequent menu term changes, but procedures remain, basically, the same.		

Jewish

Kishke (Stuffed Derma)

YIELD: about 1½ lb.		

INGREDIENTS	*QUANTITY*	*METHOD*
Flour Beef Suet, chopped Carrot, grated Onion, grated Salt Pepper Matzo Crumbs	6 oz. 6 oz. 5 oz. 5 oz. 1/4 tsp. 1/8 tsp. 4 oz. by weight	1. Combine ingredients as listed, mixing well.
Sausage Casing	as required	2. Stuff casings. Do not pack too tight as the mixture expands as it cooks. If the casings are packed too full they are likely to burst during cooking. 3. Tie casings securely. Rinse clean and place in rapidly boiling, salted water for 1 min. Remove from water and drain well. 4. Stuffed kishke may be poached or roasted. Kishke may be roasted with poultry such as duck, chicken, etc., or it may be roasted separately with onions and chicken fat. After poaching, refrigerate until needed. Slice when cold and reheat in a heavy pan or on a griddle. Cooking time varies with size of casing and density of product. Average roasting time at moderate temperatures (about 350°F.) is 1½ to 2 hr. Average poaching time is 1 to 1½ hr.

Kasha Varnitshkes (Buckwheat Blended with Bow Tie Macaroni)

YIELD: 12 to 15 portions		

There are several forms of kasha, but kasha is generally interpreted to mean buckwheat groats. Groats are available in this country in a number of particular sizes, varying from fine to whole.

Kasha Varnitshkes are a combination of cooked buckwheat groats and cooked, square, or bow-tie macaroni, heated together with onions browned in chicken fat, nyah fat, or oil.

INGREDIENTS	*QUANTITY*	*METHOD*

Nyah Fat
   OR Chicken Fat
   OR Salad Oil
Onions, minced
	2 oz.
	
	2 oz.
		1. Saute onion in nyah fat or substitute until brown.

Buckwheat Groats, coarse Eggs, whole	1 pt. 2	2. Combine groats and eggs and stir into onions.
Water, boiling Salt Pepper	1 qt. 2 tsp. ¼ tsp.	3. Add 1 qt. of boiling water, salt and pepper. Cover and cook over low heat about 10 min. Remove cover and cook for an additional 5 min. Kasha should be full grained, but grains should be reasonably separated as with rice pilaf.
Bow-Tie Macaroni, cooked al dente	½ lb., A.P.	4. Combine with cooked bow-tie macaroni, folding in carefully. Place in pan and bake at 375°F. about 15 min.
NOTE: For plain kasha, eliminate macaroni.		

Flaish Knishes

YIELD: 20 portions	EACH PORTION: 2½ oz. each	
INGREDIENTS	*QUANTITY*	*METHOD*
DOUGH		
Margarine	8 oz.	1. Rub margarine and flour together until the mixture is mealy.
Flour	12 oz.	2. Dissolve salt in boiling water. Stir into flour-margarine mixture, blending well. Cool if necessary. Wrap well to prevent drying. Refrigerate overnight.
Water, boiling	8 oz.	
Salt	¼ tsp.	
FILLING		
(A variety of fillings may be used. The following formulation is a useful guide.)		
Onions, minced	2 oz.	1. Saute onions lightly in margarine. Add meat and complete cooking. Cool.
Margarine	3 oz.	
OR Nyah Fat		
OR Substitute		
Ground Beef and/or Liver (or combination)	12 oz.	
Egg, whole, shelled	1	2. Pass mixture through medium plate of food chopper. Add seasonings and egg. Adjust seasoning as required. Refrigerate until needed.
Salt	to taste	
Pepper	to taste	
Chicken Cracklings, small pieces	20	

Preparation:

1. Flour board or benchtop well. Roll dough about 1/8 in. thick. Brush with oil. Cut in uniform 3½ in. squares or cut in circles with dough cutter.

2. Place a generous No. 100 scoop, or its equivalent, of filling off-center of the square or circle. Place a piece of crackling on top of mixture. Fold opposite edges of dough and seal firmly.

3. Prepare an egg wash. Place knishes on ungreased baking sheet and brush with wash. Sprinkle lightly with sesame seeds. Bake in preheated oven at 400°F. about 20 min. or until crust is well baked and golden brown.

Quantity Production Meat Knishes:

For preparing large quantities, knishes are frequently made "strudel style;" that is, in long rolls that may be cut to portion size as desired. The individual portion cuts may be baked *as is* . . . or formed with the hands to shapes shown at upper right in picture of Potato Latkes, p. 348.

The Orient

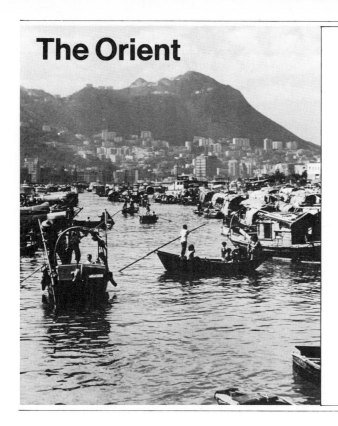

WON TON SOUP

JAPANESE CLAM SOUP

CHINESE TWICE-COOKED PORK

FRIED RICE BASIC, AND EGG GARNISH

WON TON

CHINESE EGG ROLLS

LOBSTER SAUCE

FRIED BONELESS CHICKEN WINGS IN SAUCE

CLAM SAUCE
(FOR FRIED BONELESS CHICKEN WINGS)

**BASIC "WHITE" SAUCE
AND BASIC "DARK" SAUCE**

BATTER FOR BUTTERFLY SHRIMP

CHINESE MUSTARD

DUK SAUCE

BEEF WITH PEA PODS (SNOW PEAS)

BARBECUED SPARERIBS

SA-NWIN-MA-KIN
(SEMOLINA OR FARINA PUDDING)

GINGER-ORANGE SAUCE

Won Ton Soup

YIELD: 10 portions		EACH PORTION: 1 soup cup
INGREDIENTS	*QUANTITY*	*METHOD*
Chicken Stock, clear	1-1/2 qt.	1. Bring stock to low boil. Add scallions, cooked meat, salt and pepper. Simmer 2 to 3 min., adjust seasoning as desired.
Scallions, finely sliced (tops included)	2 oz.	
Cooked Meat (preferably pork), fine julienne	4 oz.	
Salt	1/2 tsp.	
Pepper, white	1/8 tsp.	
Won Ton, cooked, heated	10	2. Place 1 heated won ton, a piece of shrimp and a small leaf of spinach in each cup. Add 1 tsp. of julienne egg to each dish. Add piping hot soup and serve immediately.
Shrimp, cooked, sliced in half lengthwise, (whole shrimp)	5	
Spinach, fresh, blanched	4 to 5 oz., A.P.	
Pancake Omelette, one-egg, fine julienne	1	

NOTE: See separate formula for Won Ton.
   Won Ton may be boiled, similar to ravioli, and held for service in soup or stock, etc.

Japanese Clam Soup

YIELD: 10 portions	EACH PORTION: 1 soup bowl or cup	
INGREDIENTS	*QUANTITY*	*METHOD*
Dried Mushrooms	1/4 oz.	1. Wash mushrooms in cold water. Drain well.
Bamboo Shoots	2 oz.	2. Chop mushrooms. Julienne Bamboo shoots.
Snow Peas (pea pods), stemmed	10 pieces	3. Place mushrooms, bamboo shoots and snow peas in
Chicken Stock, boiling	1-1/2 qt.	boiling stock. Simmer about 4 min.
Sherry Wine OR White Wine	2 oz.	4. Add all remaining ingredients. Bring soup back to a boil and remove from heat.
White Pepper	1/8 tsp.	
Salt	1/4 tsp.	Adjust seasoning and serve in heated bowls or cups.
Japanese Baby Clams (and juice)	1 10-1/2 oz. can	Garnish with lemon slices.
Lemon Slices, very thin	10	

Basic "White" Sauce

YIELD: 1 qt.		
INGREDIENTS	*QUANTITY*	*METHOD*
Chicken Stock	1 qt.	1. Reserve 4 oz. of chicken stock. Place the balance in a saucepan and bring to a boil.
Sugar	1 tsp.	2. Combine reserved cool stock, sugar, salt and pepper, and cornstarch.
Salt	1 tsp.	3. Reduce heat and add cornstarch mixture to hot stock, stirring until thickened and smooth.
White Pepper	¼ tsp.	Use as required.
Cornstarch	4 tbsp.	

NOTE: This basic sauce is relatively bland in flavor, but this is compensated for by the seasoning and flavor achieved in the preparation of other ingredients with which it is combined.

Basic "Dark" Sauce

Follow the formulation for "White" Sauce, adding 1 tbsp. of bead molasses and 2 tbsp. of soy sauce to the chicken stock.

Batter for Butterfly Shrimp

YIELD: 1 pt.		
INGREDIENTS	*QUANTITY*	*METHOD*
Eggs, whole, beaten	2	1. Combine eggs and beer.
Beer	12 oz.	
Flour, bread	12 oz.	2. Add dry ingredients all at once. Mix smooth. Adjust consistency as required. Moisture content of flour may vary. If batter is heavy, adjust with a small amount of milk. If batter is too thin, adjust with cornstarch.
Salt	¼ tsp.	
Pepper, white	¼ tsp.	
Allspice	¼ tsp.	
Ginger Root, grated	¼ tsp.	Do not overmix.
Baking Powder	½ tsp.	
Cornstarch	for dredging	**Frying Procedure** Dredge shrimp lightly in cornstarch. Shake off excess, dip shrimp in batter and immerse directly into deep fat. Fry at about 360°F. Serve immediately with appropriate sauce.

Oriental

*Lobster Sauce
(recipe below)*

*Fried Boneless Chicken Wings in
Sauce (recipe top of facing page)*

Lobster Sauce

(Contains no lobster, but is so named because of its association with the lobster dish.)		
YIELD: 1½ qt.		
INGREDIENTS	*QUANTITY*	*METHOD*
Peanut Oil Garlic, minced fine Pork, very lean, ground coarse (¼ in. plate)	1 tbsp. 2 tsp. 1 lb.	1. Heat oil in pan. (Optional: stir-fry small piece of ginger root and discard.) Add pork and garlic. Stir well. Cook about 3 to 4 min. stirring as required.
Egg, beaten Stock, chicken, hot Bead Molasses Soy Sauce	1 28 oz. 1 tbsp. 2 tbsp.	2. Add beaten egg, scrambling well into mixture. (See * below.) 3. Add hot stock, molasses, and soy sauce.
Stock, chicken, cold Cornstarch	4 oz. 1½ oz.	4. Mix cornstarch and cold stock. Incorporate with sauce mixture, stirring well until thickened.
Scallions, raw, sliced	2 oz.	5. Add scallions (and shrimp or other product). Simmer briefly, adjust seasoning and serve. *The egg is sometimes added to the hot stock mixture which results in a "threading" of the eggs with an entirely different appearance than if adding the egg at Step 3. Either procedure is acceptable.

FOR LOBSTER, CANTONESE; or LOBSTER, CHINESE STYLE:
   Black beans are sometimes included in the lobster sauce formulation but are an optional ingredient. Cooked black beans may be partly mashed, sauteed lightly in oil, and the sauce added.
   Cut live lobsters in pieces, removing undesirable portions. Saute pieces lightly in oil, until all of the shell pieces are red. Add a small amount of water or stock, cover, and steam for 4 to 5 min. Remove cover; add lobster sauce. Simmer briefly to marry flavors and ensure that lobster is cooked.
FOR SHRIMP IN LOBSTER SAUCE:
   Two alternate procedures:
   A) Saute cleaned, butterflied shrimp in small amount of garlic oil until nearly done. Add lobster sauce and simmer lightly until shrimp is cooked and flavor developed. Do not overcook.
   B) Clean and butterfly shrimp. Marination optional. Dip shrimp in cornstarch, strong eggwash, and cornstarch. Fry in deep oil (about 360° to 375°F.) until golden brown but not fully cooked. Finish in lobster sauce until shrimp is cooked and flavor is developed.

NOTE: Minor additional thickening of sauce may develop if held very long, due to cornstarch-egg breading. Adjust as required. Should be prepared to order.

Fried Boneless Chicken Wings in Sauce

YIELD: 8 portions		EACH PORTION: 4 pieces with 4 oz. sauce
INGREDIENTS (A)	QUANTITY	METHOD
Chicken Wings (pieces) fried (see instructions for boning chicken wings)	32 (16 wings)	
INGREDIENTS (B) SAUCE Cornstarch Sugar Chicken Stock	1½ oz. ½ tsp. 1 qt.	1. Mix cornstarch and sugar with 4 oz. of cold stock. Reserve.
Dried Mushrooms Garlic, minced fine Soy Sauce	1 oz. 1 tsp. 2 oz.	2. Combine all other sauce ingredients. Bring to a boil. 3. Reduce heat slightly. Mix cornstarch well and add to stock, stirring until mixture is thickened. Adjust flavor and consistency as desired.
INGREDIENTS (C) Peanut Oil Ginger, fresh	3 oz. small piece	1. Heat oil in suitable pot. Saute ginger until lightly browned. Remove and discard ginger.
Onions, peeled, sliced coarsely Green Peppers, cleaned, trimmed, (cut ½ in. strips)	½ lb., A.P. 1½ lb., A.P.	2. Cook peppers and onions in ginger-flavored oil. Cook over high heat, stirring (or tossing) to prevent browning. Cook about 3 min. 3. Combine sauce and vegetables. Cover and simmer briefly. Vegetables should be cooked but peppers, particularly, should maintain some crispness. Add fried chicken pieces. Simmer briefly to marry. Serve in casserole; 4 chicken pieces per portion, with about 4 oz. sauce.

Instructions for Boning Chicken Wings

Chicken wings may be boned raw (prior to cooking).

Cut the joints as shown in the diagram, reserving the wing tip for stock, if desired.

The two usable wing pieces may be used boneless or with a single bone. A single bone is frequently left in when frying chicken wings to be used as hors d'oeuvre. This provides a "handle" to make service easier for guests.

The wing should be completely boned when incorporated with a sauce.

To bone the wings, cut the "knob" of the bones so that the meat can be freed from the bones.

Hold a single wing between the thumb and forefinger of each hand.

Place one end of the wing on the bench. Peel the meat down from the bone. A towel is helpful to keep your fingers from slipping. When the meat has been peeled down, hold the bone(s) in one hand and the meat in the other. . .and pull them apart. If they do not separate easily, cut the meat from the bone with a sharp knife.

For Clam Sauce recipe, see p. 363.

Oriental

Beef with Pea Pods (Snow Peas) (recipe below)   *Chinese Twice-Cooked Pork (recipe top of facing page)*

Beef with Pea Pods (Snow Peas)

YIELD: 4 portions	EACH PORTION: 6 oz.	
INGREDIENTS	QUANTITY	METHOD
Peanut Oil Beef Tenderloin Slices Garlic, minced fine	1 oz. 1 lb. ¼ tsp.	1. Heat peanut oil. Add beef slices and cook briefly over high heat.
Snow Peas, trimmed, ready-to-cook	½ lb.	2. Add garlic and snow peas and saute lightly.
Basic Dark Sauce	1 pt.	3. Add sauce. Adjust seasoning as desired. Serve immediately.

Chinese Mustard

YIELD: about 8 oz.		
INGREDIENTS	QUANTITY	METHOD
Dry Mustard Salt Sugar Vinegar	4 tbsp. ¼ tsp. ½ tsp. 1 tbsp.	1. Combine mustard, salt, sugar and vinegar, blending well.
Water, boiling	4 oz.	2. Add hot water and blend smooth.

Duk Sauce

YIELD: about 1 qt.		
INGREDIENTS	QUANTITY	METHOD
Apricots, dried	½ lb.	1. Cook apricots until tender. Drain well.
Plums, purple, pitted	1 No. 2½ can	2. Drain plums and reserve liquid.
Molasses Ginger, fresh, grated Honey	1 tsp. ¼ tsp. 3 oz.	3. Puree apricots and plums. Add molasses, grated ginger and honey. Mix well and adjust consistency with the liquid from the plums. Use additional water if necessary.

Chinese Twice-Cooked Pork

YIELD: 15 to 18 appetizer portions		
INGREDIENTS	*QUANTITY*	*METHOD*
MARINADE Chicken Stock Beet Juice Sherry Wine Soy Sauce Molasses Garlic, fine mince Ginger, fresh, crushed Red Food Coloring (Quantities may be increased as required using about same ratios as above)	8 oz. 4 oz. 4 oz. 4 oz. 3 oz. 1 tbsp. 1 small piece ¼ tsp.	1. Combine all marinade ingredients in small pot. Bring marinade to a boil; simmer for 5 min. Remove from heat and cool.

PORK
Pork tenderloins, lean, trimmed
   (9 to 10 oz. each)
   OR
Boneless, trimmed pork loin may be substituted for pork tenderloin. Only the "eye" of the loin should be used. Use equal weight. Increase in cooking time required as mass increases.
Honey
	6
	
	as required
		2. Marinate pork tenderloins for 3 to 4 hr.
		3. Place pork and marinade in covered pot on range. Bring to a boil. Reduce heat and simmer for 15 min.
		4. Remove pork and place on rack in a roasting pan. Pour sufficient marinade in bottom of pan to create moisture as meat cooks.
		5. Roast in preheated oven at 400°F. for 15 to 20 min., or until meat is tender. Brush with honey and cook an additional 5 min. Do not overcook.

Service: Cut thin, diagonal slices and serve with hot mustard and duk sauce accompaniment.		

Sa-Nwin-Ma-Kin (Semolina or Farina Pudding)

YIELD: 20 portions	**EACH PORTION**: about 5 oz.	
INGREDIENTS—A	*QUANTITY*	*METHOD*
Semolina OR Farina Coconut Milk Milk Salt Sugar* *If sweetened coconut milk is used, reduce sugar accordingly.	16½ oz. 1 qt. 1 qt. 1½ tsp. 14 oz.	1. Combine ingredients under "A." Mix well and let stand for ½ hr.
INGREDIENTS—B		
Butter	4 oz.	2. Place over medium heat and bring to a boil. Add butter, (B) stirring well. Reduce heat and cook until thickened. Remove from heat. Cool slightly.
Dates, pitted, chopped	5½ oz.	3. Add dates to mixture.
Egg Whites Almonds, sliced, toasted	4 4 oz.	4. Beat egg whites to medium peak. Fold in egg whites. 5. Place half the mixture in a well-buttered pan or casserole. Sprinkle half the almonds on top. 6. Place remaining mixture in the pan and top with balance of almonds. 7. Bake in moderate oven about 45 min. Cool before serving. May be topped with a variety of sauces as desired. See formula for Ginger-Orange Sauce p 362.

Won Ton

Won ton skins are prepared from the same basic dough as egg roll skins. It is impractical to make them when they are available in your area. They may be purchased in Chinese grocery stores and in Chinese noodle factories. There are about 75 won ton skins per lb. of noodle dough. Egg roll skins may be cut in four equal segments if won ton skins are not available. They may be frozen (raw) if well wrapped. They must be thoroughly defrosted prior to use in order that they are pliable.

Nearly any variety of filling may be used. Filling is usually meat, fish or poultry based, however, and seldom contains vegetables in the ratio used for egg rolls.

A basic noodle dough formula for won ton appears below. The formulation is sufficient for about 80 skins. The yield is slightly in excess of a pound.

WON TON SKINS

INGREDIENTS	QUANTITY	METHOD
Flour Salt Eggs, whole, beaten	16 oz. 2 tsp. 2	1. Sift flour and salt into a mixing bowl. 2. Blend eggs into flour-salt mixture.
Water, cold	1½ to 2 oz.	3. Add cold water and knead mixture thoroughly until smooth. Wetting the hands and shaking off excess water may be helpful during the kneading process. 4. Cover the dough with a clean, damp cloth or towel. Allow to rest about ½ hr., preferably under refrigeration. 5. Roll paper thin, maintaining a square or rectangular shape to reduce necessity for excessive rerolling of dough. 6. Cut into 2½ to 3 in. squares. There are several methods of filling and folding the won ton. They may be prepared in the manner indicated below.

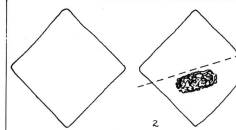 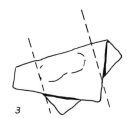

2   3   4   REVERSE SIDE

		METHOD
		1. Place won ton wrapper on board or bench in position shown. (Same as for egg rolls.) 2. Place a small amount of filling on the lower section. Note dotted line to indicate where wrapper is to be folded. 3. Fold wrapper so that opposite points do not meet—a little bit off center. 4. Fold left and right sides toward center, crossing them, and press firmly to seal.

NOTE: Won ton skins may also be used for miniature egg rolls for hors d'oeuvres. The won ton may also be fried and served as an hors d'oeuvre. As indicated in prior formulations, the flour-moisture content may require adjustment due to variations in flour.

When rolling the dough and/or stacking the skins—a light dusting of flour or cornstarch is suggested.

Chinese Egg Rolls

YIELD: 25 units		

Egg roll skins may be purchased from a Chinese grocery store or noodle factory. They are packed 16 egg roll skins to a pound and are available in a 5-lb. pack. They must be used while fresh and pliable. They become stiff and crack as they dry out.

INGREDIENTS	*QUANTITY*	*METHOD*
FILLING Celery, sliced thin (including tops) Cabbage, white, sliced thin Water	2 lb. 2 lb. (see method)	1. Cook celery and cabbage separately in boiling, salted water. Cook celery about 5 min. after water returns to boil (after adding celery). Cook cabbage about 3 min. on same basis. Test products. They should retain crispness. (They will continue to cook during cooling). 2. Cool in running water. Drain well. Press water out of celery and cabbage. They should be very dry. A potato ricer works reasonably well for this purpose.
Bean Sprouts, fresh, blanched Water Chestnuts, chopped Bamboo Shoots, chopped Pork, cooked, chopped fine Shrimp, cooked, chopped fine Scallions, fine slice White Pepper Salt Monosodium Glutamate (or sugar) Soy Sauce Garlic Powder	1 pt. 4 oz. by weight 4 oz. by weight ½ pt. ½ pt. 4 oz. ¼ tsp. ½ tsp. ½ tsp. 1 oz. ¼ tsp.	3. Combine all ingredients, mixing well. Adjust seasoning as desired. Mixture should be thoroughly cool before using.

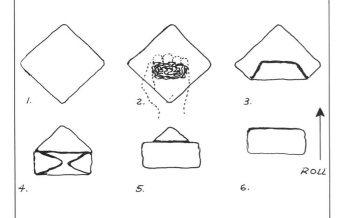

To Prepare Rolls:

Practice is required to prepare well-shaped egg rolls. Initial preparation feels awkward, but skill increases rapidly as practice continues.

Place an egg roll skin on a bench or board as shown in the diagram.

Curl your fingers around a small amount of filling, compressing the filling lightly.

Place the filling on the lower section of the egg roll skin.

Fold the lower section up and over the filling, tucking the tip of the egg roll skin well around the filling.

Begin to roll the filled skin away from you.

Fold the left and right edges in, as shown in the diagram.

Roll *firmly* to assure that there are no air pockets. Roll all the way up.

NOTE: A dab of water or egg will aid in securing the top "flap." The roll must be fairly compact and well sealed.
Fry at 360° to 375°F. until a light golden brown.
Cool and refrigerate.
At service time, re-fry until thoroughly heated and crisp.
Serve with hot mustard and duk sauce.

Chao-Tse

YIELD: 50 to 60 units		
INGREDIENTS	*QUANTITY*	*METHOD*

DOUGH
    Water, cold
    Salt
    Salad Oil
    Bread Flour
	
	1 pt.
	2 tsp.
	2 oz.
	2 lb.
		1. Mix all ingredients. If using machine, mix about 7 to 8 min. If hand mixing, knead well after initial mixing. Let dough rest for 15 to 20 min. before using.
		2. Form dough in long, uniform cylinder, about 1¼ in. in diameter.
		3. Pinch off pieces of dough, rolling thinly to form a circle of about 2½ in. in diameter.
		4. Hold rolled dough piece in palm of hand (left hand if righthanded). Place about 1 heaping tsp. of filling in center of dough. Fold to make a semicircle, pressing the edges with finger to form a tight seal. Continue until all dough is used. See Filling formulation below.

NOTE: Some adjustments in flour content may be required, as flour may vary from time to time. A light dusting of flour is suggested when rolling the dough.

CHAO-TSE MAY BE STEAMED, BOILED OR FRIED:

Steaming Method

Place dumplings on an open rack over boiling water. It is suggested that cheesecloth be placed on the rack and the dumplings placed on the cheesecloth. When water is boiling well and steam is formed, cover tightly, adjusting heat to maintain steam. Cook about 20 min.

Boiling Method

Bring water or stock to boil. Gently add dumplings. Do not overload. Dumplings will sink to the bottom. As the dumplings cook, they will rise to the surface. When dumplings rise, add sufficient cold water to stop boiling. Dumplings will sink to bottom. Bring to a boil again. When dumplings rise to surface the second time, they should be ready for service.

Frying Method

Fry "raw dough" dumplings in deep oil to cover (as with egg rolls). Fry golden brown. Make an initial test dumpling to "get the feel." Serve piping hot with duk sauce and mustard.

SAUCES FOR STEAMED AND BOILED DUMPLINGS		
Number 1 Soy Sauce Distilled Vinegar Water	 4 oz. 2 oz. 4 oz.	1. Combine all ingredients.
Number 2 Mustard, prepared Salad Oil Sugar Soy Sauce Distilled Vinegar	 1 tbsp. 1 tbsp. ½ tsp. 4 oz. 2 oz.	1. Combine all ingredients. Blend well.
Number 3 Peanut Butter Garlic Powder Sherry Wine Soy Sauce Cider Vinegar Water	 2 heaping tbsp. ¼ tsp. 2 oz. 4 oz. 2 oz. 2 oz.	1. Blend all ingredients in order. Adjust consistency as required.

Continued on facing page.

Chao-Tse *(Cont.)*

FILLING FOR CHAO-TSE		
YIELD: 50 to 60 units (See Chao-Tse formulation)		
INGREDIENTS	*QUANTITY*	*METHOD*
Pork, minced fine 　　OR Beef, minced fine 　　OR Shrimp, minced fine	1 lb.	1. Combine all ingredients, mixing well. Mixture should be paste-like in consistency but not "wet." 2. Adjust consistency and seasoning. Use as desired.
Ginger Root, fresh, grated	½ tsp.	
Salt	½ tsp.	
Pepper	¼ tsp.	
Soy Sauce	2 tbsp.	
Garlic Powder	¼ tsp.	
Celery 　　OR Cabbage, cooked, finely 　　　　minced	1 lb.	
Scallions, sliced 　　(including tops)	2 oz.	
NOTE: Be sure that celery or cabbage is quite dry. All moisture should be pressed out before combining with other ingredients. 　　Nearly any variety of filling or combination of ingredients may be used. The above formulation is to serve as a guideline, but substitutions may be made depending on product availability, etc.		

Barbecued Spareribs

YIELD: Variable. (Rule of thumb for hors d'oeuvre, about ½ to ¾ lb., raw, per portion. Small spareribs preferred.)		
INGREDIENTS	*QUANTITY*	*METHOD—MARINADE*
MARINADE 　　Soy Sauce	1 pt.	1. Combine all ingredients, mixing well. Use as required.
Sherry Wine	4 oz.	
Stock	8 oz.	
Catsup	4 oz.	
Garlic, minced to nearly a paste	1 tsp.	
Pepper	¼ tsp.	
Sugar	1 tbsp.	
Ginger, fresh, minced	1 tsp.	
		To Prepare Ribs: 1. Trim most of fat from spareribs, leaving only sufficient fat for flavor during cooking. Cut rib piece in half, parallel to the bone, for ease of handling. Cut part-way in other sections to expose greater surface area to marinade. 2. Place ribs in boiling water. Simmer about 25 to 30 min. 3. Remove from water. Place ribs in suitable pan and marinate overnight, if possible. 4. Remove from marinade. Place ribs on rack in pan in oven preheated to 350° to 375°F. Roast about 1 to 1½ hr., basting occasionally with marinade and turning as required.
Honey	4 oz.	5. About ½ hr. before cooking time is completed, brush with a mixture of equal parts of honey, soy sauce, and oil. Brush ribs well, and cook about 15 min. on each side. **For Service:** 　　Cut in single rib pieces, parallel to the bone.
Soy Sauce	4 oz.	
Salad Oil	4 oz.	

Chicken Macadamia (Sweet and Sour Chicken)

YIELD: 4 portions		
INGREDIENTS	QUANTITY	METHOD
Chickens (about 3½ lb. each) Cornstarch Macadamia Nuts, unsalted, coarse chopped	2 sufficient to dredge chicken 1-1/3 oz.	1. Completely bone chicken. Cut chicken in moder- ate, uniform-size pieces, not to exceed 3/4 in.
MARINADE		
Salad Oil Soy Sauce Brandy Onions, grated Pepper, white Monosodium Glutamate OR Sugar	4 oz. 4 oz. 1 oz. 1-1/3 oz. 1/2 tsp. 1/2 tsp.	2. Combine all marinade ingredients. 3. Place chicken in marinade for 1/2 hr., turning once. Keep breast-leg meat separate at all times.
BATTER		
Ginger, fresh Eggs, whole Water Flour Cornstarch Salad Oil	small piece 2 4 oz. 2 oz. 1 oz. to brown	4. Prepare batter by rubbing bowl with fresh ginger. Place eggs in bowl; beat well. Add water and mix. Blend in flour and cornstarch. Mix smooth but do not overmix. 5. Drain chicken well. Dredge in cornstarch. Place in batter. 6. Remove from batter, draining excess. Fry lightly in hot oil to color. Complete cooking in preheated 350°F. oven. Place white and dark meat in individual casseroles or serving dishes. Mask with sauce and sprinkle with macadamia nuts. (See formula for sauce below).
SAUCE FOR CHICKEN MACADAMIA.		
Water	4 oz.	1. Reserve ¼ cup water. Mix with cornstarch.
Cornstarch Vinegar Soy Sauce Sherry Sugar, brown Red Pepper, sweet, chopped cooked	2 tbsp. 2 oz. 2 tbsp. 1 oz. 2 tbsp. 1-1/3 oz.	2. Separately, in a small pan, combine balance of wa- ter, vinegar, soy sauce, sherry and sugar. Bring to boil. Reduce heat and stir in water-cornstarch mix- ture, stirring until thickened. Adjust consistency if desired. Remove from heat and stir in red pep- per. Serve as indicated.
NOTE: Other ingredients may be added as desired; e. g. pineapple chunks, green peppers, water chestnuts, etc.		

Ginger-Orange Sauce

YIELD: about 1¼ qt.		
INGREDIENTS	QUANTITY	METHOD
Orange Juice Sugar	1½ pts. 8 oz.	1. Combine juice and sugar. Bring to a boil.
Water Cornstarch	8 oz. 3 tbsp.	2. Reduce heat. Combine water and cornstarch and add to juice-sugar mixture, stirring until lightly thickened.
Candied Ginger, chopped fine Orange Zest, fine julienne, blanched	1 tbsp. 3 tbsp.	3. Remove from heat. Stir in ginger and orange zest. Serve warm.

Clam Sauce (for Fried Boneless Chicken Wings)

YIELD: about 1 qt.		
INGREDIENTS	*QUANTITY*	*METHOD*
Onions, chopped fine Peanut Oil Garlic, minced	1 lb. as required 1 tbsp.	1. Saute onions in small amount of oil. Add garlic.
Cornstarch Water	1 tbsp. 1 pt.	2. Add cornstarch, mixing well. Add water and juice from clams, stirring until mixture is slightly thickened.
Japanese Baby Clams Pepper, white	1 10½-oz. can ¼ tsp.	3. Add pepper and clams. Reheat and adjust seasoning as desired. Combine with hot, fried chicken wings and serve immediately.

Fried Rice, Basic and Egg Garnish

YIELD: 8 to 10 portions		
This is a variation of the Chinese method, but is particularly effective for buffet service when there are a number of dishes to prepare.		
INGREDIENTS	*QUANTITY*	*METHOD*
Salad Oil Celery, chopped fine Onions, sliced fine Garlic, minced Rice	4 oz. ½ lb. ½ lb. 1 tbsp. 1 lb.	1. Heat oil in pan. Add celery and saute lightly for 3 to 4 min. Add onions and garlic. Add rice, mixing well and saute until all oil is absorbed.
Chicken Stock, boiling Soy Sauce Caramel Coloring Sugar Black Pepper	1½ pt. 3 oz. 1 tbsp. ½ tsp. ½ tsp.	2. Add balance of ingredients, blending well. Bring to boil. Reduce heat to low. Cover and cook until all liquid is absorbed. Finish with cover off to be sure rice is quite dry. Spread on sheet pan to cool. Service: stir-fry with additional desired ingredients. Any combination of firm fish, meat, poultry, vegetables may be used. Example: blanch 1½ cups of fresh bean sprouts in a small amount of oil. Mix the cold cooked rice (above) with ½ cup of cooked, chopped shrimp; 1 cup cooked, slivered or chopped pork; 1 cup sliced scallions; ½ cup of egg garnish (see formula for egg garnish below). Stir-fry until well blended and heated.
EGG GARNISH (for use with Fried Rice) Eggs, whole Salt Pepper Sherry Wine OR Water Salad Oil	 2 to taste to taste 2 tsp. as required	1. Beat eggs, seasoning and wine (or water) together. 2. Place small amount of oil in a 6 in. sautoir. Heat the oil and pour in half of egg mixture. Turn pan so mixture flows over entire surface. Cook only until well set. Remove from pan and cool. Repeat, using balance of egg mixture. 3. Roll "pancakes" and cut in fine julienne strips. Cut in half and separate strips with fingers. *Alternately*—the raw egg may be stirred into very hot fried rice and scrambled through the mixture.

Italy Rome-Naples

STRACCIATELLA
(EGG AND CHEESE SOUP)

**RISOTTO CON LE CALAMARI
ALLA NAPOLITANA**
(RISOTTO OF SQUID ALLA NAPOLITANA)

SCAMPI GRIGLIA PESCATORA
(GRILLED SCAMPI)

LASAGNA DI CARNEVALE NAPOLITANA
(SPECIALTY OF NAPLES,
SERVED DURING PRE-LENTEN SEASON)

SPAGHETTI CON VONGOLE
(SPAGHETTI WITH CLAMS)

**SCALOPPINE DI VITELLO ALLA BOLOGNESE
FINOCCHI BRASATI CON BURRO**
(BRAISED FENNEL KNOBS IN BUTTER)

SPINACI ALLA ITALIANA
(SPINACH SAUTEED WITH ONIONS AND GARLIC)

POLENTA NAPOLITANA

Stracciatella (Eggs and Cheese Soup)

YIELD: 22 to 24 portions	EACH PORTION: 6 oz. soup	
INGREDIENTS	*QUANTITY*	*METHOD*
Chicken Stock, clear	1 gal.	1. Reserve 8 oz. of cold chicken stock. Bring the balance of the stock to a slow boil.
Eggs, whole Parmesan Cheese, grated Farina or Semolina Salt White Pepper Nutmeg	8 4 oz. 4 oz. to taste to taste to taste	2. Combine the eggs, cheese, farina and spices. Add the cold stock, mixing well. Pour the mixture into the boiling soup, stirring continuously. 3. Simmer briefly to cook. Adjust seasoning. Serve immediately. Optional garnish: shredded spinach, rice.

Spinaci Alla Italiana (Spinach Sauteed with Onions and Garlic)

YIELD: 10 to 12 portions	EACH PORTION: about 3 oz.	
INGREDIENTS	*QUANTITY*	*METHOD*
Spinach, frozen*	3 lb.	1. Cook thawed spinach in a small amount of boiling salted water. Drain and cool. Do not overcook.
Onions, minced Olive Oil Garlic, minced Salt Pepper Nutmeg (optional) *Thaw the spinach under refrigeration.	3 oz. 2 oz. 1 tbsp. 2 tsp. ¾ tsp. to taste	2. Saute the onions in olive oil. Add the garlic and spinach and saute lightly. Season to taste and serve very hot.
NOTE: Fresh spinach may be substituted when available, using about double the amount of frozen spinach, by weight.		

Lasagne Di Carnevale Napolitana (Specialty of Naples, Served during Pre-Lenten Season)

YIELD: 24 portions	**EACH PORTION:** about 8 oz.	

INGREDIENTS	QUANTITY	METHOD
Ricotta Cheese	2 lb.	1. Combine the ricotta cheese, one-half of the parmesan cheese, the spices and seasonings and eggs, mixing well. Taste, and adjust seasoning.
Parmesan Cheese, grated	8 oz.	
Salt	2 tsp.	
Black Pepper (fresh ground preferred)	1 tsp.	
Basil	1 tsp.	
Oregano	½ tsp.	
Eggs, whole	4	
Italian Sweet Sausage, cooked	1 lb., A.P.	2. Remove the skin from the cooked sausages and chop the meat.
Italian Meat Sauce	2 qt.	3. Place a thin layer of sauce in the bottom of a full-size steam table insert or similar pan.
Lasagna Noodles, boiled, drained	2 lb., A.P.	4. Arrange a layer of well-drained (undercooked) noodles in the pan.
Mozzarella, sliced thin	1 lb.	5. Spread a layer of the ricotta mixture on top of the noodles.
		6. Sprinkle part of the meat on top of the noodles.
		7. Add sauce, a layer of sliced mozzarella, and sprinkle with parmesan cheese.
		8. Continue to layer until all materials are used, finishing with a layer of lasagna noodles, a little meat sauce, and a layer of mozzarella.
		9. Bake covered at 375°F. about 45 min.
		10. Remove cover; bake 5 to 10 min. longer.
		11. Remove from oven and allow to set up before cutting.

Spaghetti Con Vongole (Spaghetti with Clams)

YIELD: 15 portions	**EACH PORTION:** 5 to 6 oz.	

INGREDIENTS	QUANTITY	METHOD
CLAM SAUCE		1. Scrub clams thoroughly in clean water. Place clams in a pot with one-half the oil, all of the garlic, and one-half the wine. Steam clams, covered, until the clams open.
Small Hardshell Clams	about 2 doz.	
Olive Oil	8 oz.	
Garlic, coarse chopped	2 tbsp.	2. Remove the clams. Strain broth carefully and reserve.
White Wine, dry	12 oz.	3. Remove the clams from the shells. Chop as required. (We do not have the same small clams that might be used in Italy.)
Onions, sliced	12 oz.	4. Saute onions in balance of oil. Add balance of wine and reduce. Add tomatoes, seasonings, and reserved clam broth.
Tomatoes, peeled, chopped	2½ to 3 lb., A.P.	5. Simmer about 20 to 25 min. Adjust seasoning and consistency. Sauce may be "tightened" up with a small amount of cornstarch if necessary.
Salt	to taste	
Red Pepper	to taste	
Chili Peppers, optional	small amount	6. Add clams and reheat but do not continue to cook.
Parsley	for garnish	
Spaghetti	2½ lb.	7. Serve immediately over hot spaghetti. (Review cooking procedure for spaghetti p. 26.) Sprinkle with chopped parsley.

NOTE: Parmesan cheese may be served on the side if desired.

Scaloppini Di Vitello Alla Bolognese (recipe below)   *Polenta Napolitana (recipe top of facing page)*

Scaloppini Di Vitello Alla Bolognese

YIELD: 4 portions		EACH PORTION: 3 scaloppini with ham and cheese
INGREDIENTS	QUANTITY	METHOD
Veal, thin-sliced (scaloppini) Flour Olive Oil	1¼ lb. sufficient to dredge veal about 2 oz.	1. Dredge the veal pieces lightly in flour, shaking off excess. Saute quickly in olive oil 2. Transfer to individual heat-proof dishes or small casseroles.
Marsala Wine Stock Ham, thin-sliced (Parma or Prosciutto) Parmesan Cheese, grated	2 oz. 2 oz. about 4 oz. about 2 tbsp.	3. Deglaze the saute pan with Marsala. Add stock. Distribute equally over the veal in the 4 dishes. 4. Place a piece of ham on top of each veal slice. Sprinkle with parmesan cheese. 5. Place in hot oven to heat and color. Do not overcook. Serve with risotto.

NOTE: For the above use, the veal pieces should be about 2 in. or slightly more in diameter and weigh about 1½ oz. each. Three pieces should weigh 4½ to 5 oz.

   The ham should be cut to correspond to the approximate size and shape of the veal pieces.

Polenta Napolitana

YIELD: 15 portions		EACH PORTION: 6 oz. polenta plus garnish
INGREDIENTS	*QUANTITY*	*METHOD*
Water Salt Cornmeal	5 pt. 1 tsp. 1 lb.	1. Combine water, salt, and cornmeal. Cook in a heavy pot or double boiler over moderate heat for about ½ hr. Stir occasionally. When sufficiently cooked, mixture should come away from sides of pan when stirred with spoon.
Sausages, Italian, sweet Pork Cracklings (ciccioli) Parmesan, grated Olive Oil Mozzarella, chopped Pecorino, grated	1 lb. ½ lb. 2 oz. by weight for pan 1 lb. 2 oz.	2. When cornmeal is cooking, prick sausages lightly with a fork and place in heavy skillet or pan with a small amount of water. Panfry on top of range or complete cooking in oven. Do not overcook. 3. When sausage is cooked, remove from pan to cool. Slice and reserve. Combine fat from pan with cornmeal mixture for flavor. Add parmesan, pork cracklings. 4. Wet a suitable pan with cold water and place polenta mixture in pan. Cool and refrigerate. When cold, slice ¼ in. thick. 5. Brush a 1/3 size steam table pan with olive oil. Place a layer of polenta slices in bottom of pan. Next, place a layer of sliced sausages, mozzarella and pecorino. Continue, using all product. Make top layer polenta. Bake in preheated oven at 375°F. for ½ hr. Cut in squares or rectangles for service.

Scampi Griglia Pescatora (Grilled Scampi)

Scampi is the plural of the Italian "scamp," meaning prawn. Dublin Bay Prawns and the French Langoustines are a similar type crustacean. Shrimp are frequently substituted for scampi on many menus, but correctly speaking scampi are a specific type of crustacean. Basically, most formulations for scampi can easily substitute shrimp, miniature spiny lobster tails, etc. Menu terminology should, of course, agree with the product.	**Procedure:** 1. Split the tails from the inside, keeping the back of the shell intact. Clean and wash them. 2. Brush with butter, season with garlic, salt; sprinkle with a little parsley, fresh bread crumbs and paprika. 3. Broil to order. Finish in the oven.

NOTE: Seasoned butter may be made up and kept under refrigeration to be used as needed.

Risotto Con Le Calamari Alla Napolitana (Risotto of Squid Alla Napolitana)

YIELD: 8 portions		
INGREDIENTS	*QUANTITY*	*METHOD*
SQUID		
Squid	2 lb.	1. Clean squid, removing ink sac, and cut in ½ in. slices.
Olive Oil	3 oz.	
White Wine, dry	8 oz.	2. Saute in a small amount of hot oil. Deglaze the pan with white wine; remove from the heat and reserve.
Green Peppers, julienne	1 pt.	3. In a separate pan, saute the onions and green peppers in the balance of the olive oil. Add remaining ingredients except butter, parmesan cheese and scallions and simmer about 20 min.
Onions, small dice	2 oz.	
Tomatoes, canned, drained well	1 pt.	
Garlic, minced fine	2 tsp.	
Basil	½ tsp.	4. Adjust seasoning and add squid and wine. Keep hot but do not boil. Additional cooking is not suggested.
Oregano	½ tsp.	
Pepper	¼ tsp.	
Salt	2 tsp.	5. Combine the risotto and squid (see separate formula for risotto). Carefully mix in the butter and parmesan cheese.
Butter	2 oz.	
Parmesan Cheese, grated	2 oz.	
Scallions, sliced	2 oz.	Sprinkle with finely sliced scallions when serving.
RISOTTO (FOR SQUID)		
Olive Oil	3 oz.	1. Saute the shallots or scallions in olive oil in a heavy saucepan.
Shallots, cut fine	2 oz.	
OR Scallions, cut fine		2. Add the rice and saute until rice is transparent and all oil is absorbed.
Rice, white (NOT converted)	1 pt.	
White Stock, hot	1 qt.	3. Add the stock gradually, in three or four stages, stirring frequently during cooking.
OR Chicken Stock, hot		4. Cook until rice is done, and all moisture has been absorbed.

Finocchi Brasati Con Burro (Braised Fennel Knobs in Butter)

YIELD: (See note below)		
INGREDIENTS	*QUANTITY*	*METHOD*
Fennel Knobs, small	6	1. Clean and trim fennel knobs. Cook in boiling, salted water until nearly tender.
		2. Drain well, dry and cut into sections, cutting away the hard core.
Butter	6 oz.	3. Butter a pan and arrange the cut sections in the pan.
Lemon Juice	2 oz.	4. Sprinkle with lemon juice, the parmesan cheese, and the balance of the butter.
Parmesan Cheese, grated	4 oz.	
White Stock	about 12 oz.	5. Pour the stock into the pan from the side so that the cheese, etc., is not disturbed.
		6. Place in oven and bake at 375°F. for 20 to 30 min. until golden brown.
NOTE: General yield is 4 to 5 portions per lb. This is from fennel that has been trimmed of leaves, stalks, etc. as above.		

Italy Lombardy

ZUPPA PAVESE
(ITALIAN EGG SOUP)

SALTIMBOCCA ALLA ROMANA
(VEAL SCALOPPINE WITH HAM AND SAGE)

PICCATA MILANESE
(PAN FRIED VEAL SCALLOPS
WITH MACARONI AND MILANESE GARNISH)

CHICKEN CACCIATORE

CASONSEI DI BERGAMO
(RAVIOLI BERGAMO STYLE)

RISOTTO ALLA MILANESE
(RICE COOKED IN SAFFRON STEEPED STOCK
WITH ONIONS AND CHEESE)

RISI BISI
(RICE PILAF WITH PEAS, HAM AND MUSHROOMS)

FRITTO MISTO
(MIXED FRY OF MEAT, VARIETY MEATS, VEGETABLES)

VERZADA
(WHITE CABBAGE WITH PORK SAUSAGE)

MELANZANE ALLA PARMIGIANA
(BAKED EGGPLANT IN SAUCE WITH PARMESAN CHEESE)

PAPRICHE STUFATE
(STEWED SWEET PEPPERS)

Zuppa Pavese (Italian Egg Soup)

YIELD: 16 portions	EACH PORTION: 1 soup plate with bread slice and egg	
INGREDIENTS	*QUANTITY*	*METHOD*
Chicken Stock, seasoned	1 gal.	1. Bring chicken stock to a boil. Reduce heat, but keep very hot.
Italian Bread Slices Butter	16 sufficient to saute bread	2. Saute bread slices golden brown. Reserve in a warm, dry, place.
Eggs, whole Parmesan Cheese, grated Chives, chopped	16 for garnish for garnish	3. *Lightly* poach eggs and keep warm. (See note below.) 4. Place bread slices in soup plates. Place an egg on each bread slice. Pour very hot soup over the egg and garnish with cheese and chives. Serve immediately.

NOTE: The original formulation follows the procedure of placing raw eggs on the croutons in the soup plates and pouring the boiling hot soup over them. For most American tastes, the egg does not reach an acceptable state of doneness using this method. In using the above procedure, however, care should be taken in the initial poaching to *just set the egg* so that when the boiling soup is poured over the egg it will not be overcooked.

Risi Bisi (Rice Pilaf with Peas, Ham and Mushrooms)

See recipe p. 208.

*Chicken Cacciatore
(recipe below)*

*Casonsei Di Bergamo (Ravioli Bergamo Style)
(recipe top of facing page)*

Chicken Cacciatore

(The following suggested procedure is a modification of an original formulation, in that the chicken is prepared and served boneless.)

YIELD: 4 oz. portions   **EACH PORTION:** ½ chicken, 4 oz. sauce

INGREDIENTS	QUANTITY	METHOD
Chicken, eviscerated, (2½ lb. each) Flour Olive Oil Onions, medium dice	2 sufficient to dredge about 6 oz. 4 oz.	1. Bone chicken completely, disjointing legs and cutting each breast into two equal pieces. Reserve. 2. Saute onions in small amount of olive oil. When cooked, remove from pan and reserve. 3. Dredge chicken in seasoned flour and saute in balance of oil over medium heat. 4. Color chicken well, but do not cook fully. 5. Remove chicken from pan and reserve. Deglaze pan with wine. Reduce to half volume. Add demi-glaze and simmer for 5 min.
Wine (may be white or red) Tomatoes, fresh, peeled, seeded, diced Mushrooms, cleaned, whole, small or sliced Garlic, mashed with salt Demi-glaze Oregano, crushed to powder Basil, crushed to powder Salt Pepper	1 pt. 2 lb., A.P. 1 lb., A.P. 1 tbsp. 1 pt. ½ tsp. 1 tsp. to taste to taste	6. Combine wine mixture, tomatoes, mushrooms, onions, spices and seasonings. 7. Place chicken in pans or individual cocottes, using equal portion of breast and leg meat. Distribute sauce. Cover and bake in preheated oven at 375°F. about ½ hr. or until chicken is tender.
GARNISH: Chopped Parsley Grated Lemon Peel	 2 tsp. ½ tsp.	**For Service** Sprinkle with chopped parsley, grated lemon peel. **Optional** Pan-fried croutons.

Casonsei Di Bergamo (Ravioli Bergamo Style)

INGREDIENTS	QUANTITY	METHOD
YIELD: 6 portions		
DOUGH Flour, bread Salt Eggs, whole Olive Oil	1 qt. (about 1 lb.) ½ tsp. 4 to 5 see Method 4	1. Sift flour and salt. Make a "well" in the flour. 2. Add 4 eggs; mix well and determine by consistency if an additional egg is required. 3. Knead the mixture thoroughly until very smooth. 4. Brush surface with olive oil; cover with a clean, damp cloth and allow to rest. The pasta should rest for about 1 hr. to "strengthen" or lose some of its elasticity. Be sure that it does not dry out.
FILLING Butter Onions, fine dice Pork, ground, very lean Garlic, minced fine	3 oz. 2 oz. 8 oz. 1 tsp.	1. Saute onions lightly in butter. Add pork and garlic, complete cooking. Cool slightly.
Parsley, chopped Bread Crumbs Parmesan Cheese, grated Stock, cool Eggs, whole Salt Pepper	1 oz. 1 oz. 2 oz. 2 oz. 2 to taste to taste	2. Combine all ingredients, mixing well. Form a small "test" ball and bake. Taste, adjusting seasoning and consistency, if required. 3. It is suggested that mixture chill. The aspects of time and temperature allow mixture to set up, and reduce potential sanitation problems when working with the material at room temperature.
		Preparing the Ravioli: 1. Lightly dust board or bench with flour. 2. Roll the dough in a large rectangle; it should be no more than 1/16 in. thick. 3. Trim evenly. Using a pastry bag with plain tube, pipe filling on one-half of the paste. Filling should be about the size of a small marble and be spaced about 1½ in. apart. 4. When one-half of the paste is completed, carefully fold the other half over to cover. Avoid creating air pockets. If a few air pockets result, force them to the side carefully using your fingers. Seal firmly. Using a serrated pastry wheel, cut in between each line of filling, cutting down and across. 5. Separate them and place on a lightly floured tray (one layer). 6. Poach in gently simmering salted water about 5 min. Water should continue to simmer. If simmering should be reduced, figure time from when simmering starts again. It is important to keep the ravioli *underdone*. They will be subject to further cooking as they will be lightly sauteed in butter for service.

NOTE: Egg yolks produce a more tender paste product than whole eggs. Whole eggs are used in this formulation to produce a firm enough product to hold its shape through the sauteing process, etc.

Risotto Alla Milanese (Rice Cooked in Saffron Steeped Stock with Onions and Cheese)

Use procedure for Risotto (with squid, p. 368), using butter and onions. Steep saffron in stock to cook rice. Fold in additional butter and Parmesan cheese when rice is cooked.
Veal marrow is sometimes included in the formulation.

Piccata Milanese (Pan Fried Veal Scallops with Macaroni and Milanese Garnish)

YIELD: 10 portions		EACH PORTION: 3 veal cutlets, each 1½ oz.
INGREDIENTS	*QUANTITY*	*METHOD*

PICCATA
    Small Veal Scallops
    Flour
	3 lb.
	sufficient to dredge
		1. Trim and flatten veal scallops. Dredge in flour.

Eggs, whole, beaten Parmesan Cheese, grated Fresh Bread Crumbs	about 6 4 oz. 2 oz.	2. Mix eggs, parmesan cheese, and bread crumbs. 3. Dip each cutlet in the egg-cheese mixture. 4. Panfry on both sides until golden brown. Serve on bed of macaroni, prepared Milanese, as described below.

MACARONI (MILANESE)
    Macaroni, cooked
       OR Ziti, cooked
       OR Other Pasta, cooked
    Italian Tomato Sauce, hot
GARNISH:
    Julienne of Combined Ham,
       Tongue, Mushrooms, Truffles
	1 lb., A.P.
	
	1 qt.
	
	½ pt.
		1. Cook macaroni, al dente, and drain well.
		2. Combine with sauce and garnish and mix. Top with veal scallops.

NOTE: The Milanese garnish may be sauteed and blended with the macaroni, or with the tomato sauce.		

Saltimbocca Alla Romana (Veal Scaloppine with Ham and Sage)

YIELD: 4 portions		EACH PORTION: 3 pieces with wine jus
INGREDIENTS	*QUANTITY*	*METHOD*
Veal, thin-sliced, scaloppini (1½ oz. each) Prosciutto Ham, thin-sliced Sage Leaves Butter, clarified	1¼ lb. about 4 oz. 12 sufficient to saute meat	1. Flatten the scaloppini very thin. On each slice place a sage leaf and piece of ham. Secure with a toothpick. 2. Saute on both sides in clarified butter. It is suggested that the ham side be very lightly sauteed.
White Wine, dry Salt Pepper Veal Jus (optional)	4 oz. to taste to taste 2 oz.	3. Deglaze the pan with white wine. Add the veal jus, if desired, and reduce. Adjust seasoning. 4. Place scaloppini on each plate, overlapping slightly. Pour over the wine-jus reduction and serve immediately.
NOTE: For the above use, the veal pieces should be about 2 in. in diameter. Three pieces (per portion) should weigh 4½ to 5 oz., raw, ready-to-use. Ham slices should be cut to correspond to the size of the veal slices. Some formulations suggest folding the veal over the prosciutto and sage and securing with a toothpick before cooking, which is also an acceptable procedure.		

Fritto Misto (Mixed Fry of Meat, Variety Meats and Vegetables)

The term, fritto misto, suggests an assortment of fried foods. The French term is Friture, Italienne. Fritto Misto may be a luncheon dish, but is more frequently considered in the hors d'oeuvres category.

Fritto Misto may be prepared from a number of ingredients, but particularly utilizes some of the variety meats such as: brains, sweetbreads, etc., and vegetables.

Some products may be fried raw; others may require blanching prior to frying.

Fritto Misto employs a number of preparation methods and may be fried in a batter, floured only, prior to frying, or breaded. Products may be deep fried, pan fried or sauteed.

Products may include: veal, pork, beef or variety meats; vegetables such as: zucchini, mushrooms, eggplant, cauliflower, broccoli, etc.

They should be prepared to order. Tomato Sauce is sometimes served on the side.

Melanzane Alla Parmigiana

INGREDIENTS	QUANTITY	METHOD
YIELD: 20 to 24 small portions		
Eggplant Salt	6 lb. as required	1. Peel eggplant. Hold peeled eggplant in salted or acidulated water while peeling the others. Drain well and slice lengthwise, about ¼ in. thick. 2. Arrange on a bake sheet and sprinkle with salt. Allow to drain for 10 to 11 min. Salt will draw moisture from the eggplant. Follow the same procedure with the other side. Be sure to remove all salt. Press the eggplant firmly with a clean towel to remove as much moisture as possible.
Sauce (tomato or meat) Prosciutto, julienne Parmesan Cheese, grated Butter	1½ pt. 6 to 8 oz. 4 oz. see Step 4	3. Place a thin layer of sauce in a suitable bake pan. 4. Arrange a layer of eggplant slices. Make several layers of ingredients (as with Lasagna), covering eggplant with prosciutto, sauce and parmesan cheese. Dot surface with butter and bake in a moderate oven about 1 hr. Allow to rest briefly after removal from the oven prior to service.

NOTE: The texture of eggplant may vary considerably at different times of the year, and depending on the quality of the eggplant. Soft-flesh or spongy eggplant should be sauteed lightly prior to incorporating with other ingredients.

Papriche Stufate (Stewed Sweet Peppers)

INGREDIENTS	QUANTITY	METHOD
YIELD: 12 to 15 side portions	**EACH PORTION:** about 4 oz.	
Italian Sweet Peppers, A.P.	2 lb.	1. Wash, clean and core peppers, discarding core and seeds, etc.
Olive Oil Garlic Clove, whole	4 oz. 1	2. Saute garlic in hot oil until brown. Remove and discard garlic.
Tomatoes, peeled and chopped Salt Pepper Parsley, chopped	2 lb. to taste to taste for garnish	3. Cut peppers in strips and saute in oil for 3 to 4 min. Add tomatoes and seasonings and simmer to marry flavors. Peppers should retain some "bite." May be served hot or cold. Garnish with parsley.

Verzada (White Cabbage with Pork Sausage)

INGREDIENTS	QUANTITY	METHOD
YIELD: 16 portions	**EACH PORTION:** about 3 oz. cabbage and 2 sausages	
Cabbage, trimmed Butter Onions, sliced	4 lb. 2 oz. 12 oz.	1. Trim cabbage; core and shred coarsely. Wash and drain. 2. Saute onions in butter in large, heavy pot or brazier. Add cabbage.
Pork Belly, diced Vinegar Salt Pepper Sausage (pork, small link) OR Sausage, Italian, hot or mild Parsley, chopped	6 oz. 1 oz. to taste to taste 32 2 lb. as garnish	3. Add pork belly, vinegar, salt and pepper and mix well. 4. Prick sausages with a fork and place on top of cabbage. 5. Cover and simmer about 1 hr. Serve each portion with a garnish of 2 sausages and sprinkle with fresh chopped parsley.

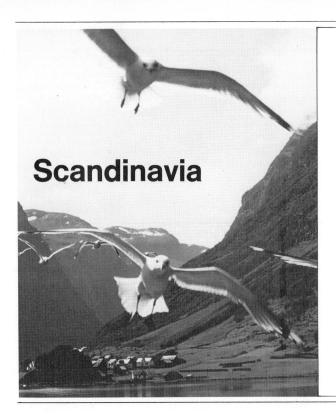

Scandinavia

BERGENS FISKESUPPE
(FISH SOUP)

CREPES SUEDOISE
(APPETIZER CREPES)

SILLGRATIN
(HERRING AND POTATO CASSEROLE)

PYTT I PANNA
(SWEDISH ROAST MEAT HASH)

BIFF À LA LINDSTRÖM
(BEEF LINDSTROM)

FRIKADELLER
(DANISH MEAT PATTIES)

PLOMMONSPACKAD FLASKKARRE
(SWEDISH ROAST PORK STUFFED WITH
PRUNES AND APPLES)

BRUNEDE KARTOFLER
(CANDIED BROWNED POTATOES)

SMORDAMPETE NYPOTETER MET PERSILLE
(NEW POTATOES WITH PARSLEY)

SURSÖTE RÖDBETER MET KUMMEL
(SWEET-SOUR BEETS WITH CARAWAY)

PINAATTIO HUKAISET
(SPINACH PANCAKES)

Bergens Fiskesuppe (Bergen Fish Soup)

YIELD: 3 qt.		EACH PORTION: 1 soup cup
INGREDIENTS	*QUANTITY*	*METHOD*
Fish Fumet, hot Carrots, peeled, finely chopped Parsnips, peeled, finely chopped Potatoes, peeled, finely chopped Onions, peeled, finely chopped Leeks, finely chopped Salt Pepper Halibut, boneless	½ gal. 2 oz. 1 oz. 4 oz. 4 oz. 4 oz. to taste to taste 1 lb.	1. Add vegetables to fish fumet; season, and cook for 15 min. 2. Cut fish in medium dice and add to the soup. Simmer about 5 min.; adjust seasoning and remove soup from heat.
Egg Yolks Water Sour Cream Parsley, chopped	2 yolks 4 oz. about 6 oz. sufficient for garnish	3. Combine egg yolks and water. Stir in liaison carefully so that fish will not be broken up. Serve in hot cups with a teaspoon of sour cream; sprinkle with freshly chopped parsley.
NOTE: Cod or haddock may be substituted for halibut. Additional caution is required, however, as cod and haddock are not as firm fleshed as halibut.		

Smordampete Nypoteter Met Persille (New Parsley Potatoes)

See Boiled Poatatoes, p. 218.

Plommonspackad Flaskkarre (Swedish Roast Pork Stuffed with Prunes and Apples)

YIELD: (See Method, Step No. 9)		
INGREDIENTS	*QUANTITY*	*METHOD*
Pork Loin (about 12 to 14 lb.) Prunes, pitted Apple, tart (peeled, large dice) Salt Pepper Ginger Mirepoix, fine Brown Stock Cornstarch	1 8 to 10 1 apple to taste to taste to taste 12 oz. 1½ pt. see "Method"	1. Prepare the pork loin, removing all bones except the rib bones (remove chine bones, blade, etc.). 2. Force a clean steel *lengthwise* through the loin, making a small "channel" in which to insert the prunes and apple. 3. Place the prunes and pieces of apple in the cavity, alternating prunes and apples. Push them all the way in with the steel but do not pack them too tight. 4. Tie the roast and season with salt, pepper and ginger. Roast in moderate oven, fat side up. 5. When meat is about half-cooked, pour off the fat and add the mirepoix. 6. Finish cooking the meat. When meat is cooked, remove from pan and keep warm. 7. Pour off additional fat and brown mirepoix. Add the brown stock; deglaze the pan and simmer the mirepoix about 10 min. 8. Strain the jus and remove any excess fat. Adjust seasoning and thicken with a small amount of cornstarch. 9. Serve one rib cut per portion, with 1½ oz. jus.
NOTE: Base average portion yield on 12 oz. per person A.P.		

Sillgratin (Herring and Potato Casserole)

YIELD: 12 appetizer portions		
INGREDIENTS	*QUANTITY*	*METHOD*
Salt Herring, medium size	3	1. Soak herring overnight. Skin and fillet fish.
Onions, sliced Butter	1 lb. 2 oz.	2. Saute onions in butter.
Potatoes, sliced Pepper Bread Crumbs Butter, melted	2 lb. to taste about 2 oz. 2 oz.	3. In a suitable baking dish, place a layer of potatoes, then salt herring, a layer of onions, and finish with a layer of potatoes. Sprinkle small amount of pepper on each layer. 4. Sprinkle with bread crumbs and melted butter. 5. Bake about 1 hr. at 375°F.

Pinaattio Hukaiset (Spinach Pancakes)

YIELD: 15 small pancakes		
INGREDIENTS	*QUANTITY*	*METHOD*
Milk Butter, melted Flour	12 oz. 1 oz. 4¼ oz.	1. Combine milk, butter and flour in a mixing bowl.
Eggs, whole, beaten Sugar Spinach, cooked, pureed Salt Pepper	2 ½ tsp. ½ lb. to taste to taste	2. Add balance of ingredients, blending well. 3. Make a test pancake and adjust seasoning as desired. 4. For each pancake, place about 1 oz. of spinach mixture (by volume) in a well buttered saute pan. Cook on both sides, turning once.

Crepes Suedoise (Appetizer Crepes) Specialty of Grand Hotel in Stockholm (recipe below)

Frikadeller (Danish Meat Patties) (recipe top of facing page)

Crepes Suedoise (Appetizer Crepes) Specialty of Grand Hotel in Stockholm

YIELD: 5 portions		EACH PORTION: 2 crepes
INGREDIENTS	QUANTITY	METHOD
Crepes, small (about 6 in. diam.) (see p. 413) FILLING Smoked Salmon, chopped Eggs, hard-cooked, chopped Dill, fresh, minced Butter, melted Bread Crumbs, fresh	10 6 oz. 4 eggs 1 tbsp. about 2 oz. about 2 oz.	1. Combine salmon, eggs and dill. Adjust seasoning as desired. 2. Divide mixture into 10 equal portions. Place mixture in each of 10 trimmed crepes and roll carefully, bringing in ends before completing roll. 3. Place 2 crepes each in individual casseroles. Brush each crepe with melted butter and sprinkle lightly with fresh crumbs. 4. Heat in preheated oven at 375°F. to 400°F., lightly browning crumbs. Do not dry out. Serve with Dill Sauce (see below).
DILL SAUCE Prepare about 1 pt. Sauce Supreme (p.317). Flavor with chopped fresh dill.		

Biff a la Lindstrom (Beef Lindstrom)

YIELD: 12 to 14 portions		EACH PORTION: 2 patties
INGREDIENTS	QUANTITY	METHOD
White Bread, trimmed Cream Ground Beef Boiled Potatoes, finely diced Cooked Beets, finely chopped Onions, diced (sauteed) Capers, finely chopped Salt Pepper Eggs, whole	6 slices 8 oz. 4 lb. 1 pt. ½ pt. ½ pt. 1 oz. to taste to taste 6	1. Cut trimmed bread in small dice and soak in cream. 2. Combine all ingredients, mixing carefully but uniformly. 3. Shape into small patties about 4 to 5 oz. 4. Panfry over medium heat. This is a popular Smorgasbord item but may be used for individual service. May be accompanied with lingon berries or fried egg garnish.

Brunede Kartofler (Candied Browned Potatoes)

YIELD: 4 to 6 portions		
INGREDIENTS	QUANTITY	METHOD
Potatoes, raw, Parisienne cut Sugar Butter Salt Pepper	1 qt. 4 oz. 2 oz. to taste to taste	1. Blanch potatoes in boiling, salted water for 3 to 4 min. Drain. 2. Caramelize sugar lightly in a sautoir. Add butter and potatoes. Saute potatoes until done, seasoning as desired.

Frikadeller (Danish Meat Patties)

YIELD: 6 portions	EACH PORTION: 2 patties	
INGREDIENTS	*QUANTITY*	*METHOD*
Pork, ground Veal, ground Flour Soda Water (sparkling club soda)	12 oz. 12 oz. 1½ oz. 12 oz.	1. Blend ground meats and flour. 2. Add soda water gradually, mixing lightly until all liquid is absorbed.
Eggs, whole, beaten Onions, minced Salt Pepper Butter	2 3 oz. to taste to taste 4 oz.	3. Add balance of ingredients, mixing carefully. 4. Refrigerate for at least 1 hr. to firm the mixture. 5. Shape into small oblong patties about 3½ oz. each. Saute in butter. Frikadeller are traditionally served with boiled potato, with pickled beet salad as a separate accompaniment.

Pytt I Panna (Swedish Roast Meat Hash)

YIELD: 5 to 6 portions		
INGREDIENTS	*QUANTITY*	*METHOD*
Potatoes, raw, peeled, small dice	20 oz.	1. Panfry the potatoes until they are cooked.
Onions, diced Butter Cooked Leftover Roast 　(Veal or Beef), diced Salt Pepper Eggs, fried or poached Gherkins	10 oz. 4 oz. 20 oz. to taste to taste for garnish see Method	2. In a separate pan, saute the onions in butter until they are cooked and lightly browned. 3. Add the meat to the onions. Mix well and cook until meat is thoroughly heated. Season with salt and pepper. 4. Mix meat, onions, and potatoes. Adjust seasoning if required. Serve with fried or poached egg and small gherkins (each portion).

Sursote Rodbeter Met Kummel (Sweet-Sour Beets with Caraway)

YIELD: 25 portions	EACH PORTION: 3½ oz.	
INGREDIENTS	*QUANTITY*	*METHOD*
Rosebud Beets	1 No. 10 can	1. Drain beets. Reserve beets. Place beet juice in saucepan over medium heat, reserving 8 oz. to dissolve cornstarch. Adjust liquid content as necessary to make 1 qt. Bring beet juice to a boil.
Sugar Salt Cornstarch	6 oz. 2 tsp. 3 oz.	2. Combine sugar, salt, cornstarch and reserved beet juice. Add to beet juice, stirring constantly until mixture is thickened and smooth.
Butter 　OR Margarine Vinegar Caraway Seeds 　OR Cumin	2 oz. 6 oz. 1 tbsp.	3. Add butter, vinegar, beets and caraway seeds. 4. Heat thoroughly and adjust seasoning before serving.

Middle East

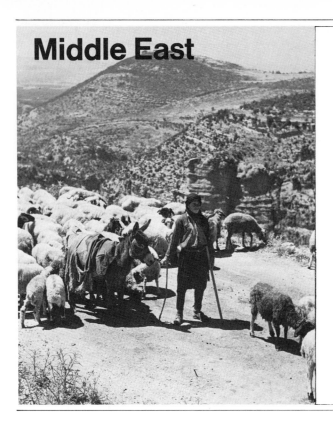

BEURRECKS ALA TURQUE
(APPETIZER-HORS D'OEUVRE)

MOUTABEL
(EGGPLANT APPETIZER)

SOUPA AVGOLEMONO
(EGG AND LEMON SOUP)

RISHTA ADDIS
(LENTIL SOUP)

PAKISTANI CHAPLI KEBAB
(PAKISTANI STYLE LAMB PATTIES)

SAYADIYA
(ORIENTAL FISH PILAF)

SHISH TAOUK
(ARABIC CHICKEN BROCHETTES)

CURRY OF LAMB

SHISH KEBAB VARIATIONS

MASHI WARAK
(STUFFED GRAPE LEAVES)

MASHI KUSSA
(STUFFED MARROW SQUASH)

PILÂVI ZEYTINLI
(PILAF WITH LEEKS)

PEARL BARLEY WITH PINE NUTS

Moutabel (Eggplant Appetizer)

YIELD: 1½ qt.		
INGREDIENTS	*QUANTITY*	*METHOD*
Eggplant, whole Tahini Paste (sesame seed paste)	about 3 lb. 4 oz.	1. Bake eggplant until the eggplant is quite soft and the skin is darkened and wrinkled. 2. Cool the eggplant under running water. Remove the skin and as many of the seeds as possible. 3. Pass the eggplant through a food mill and work in the sesame seed paste a little at a time.
Onions, grated Garlic, paste Salt Pepper Olive Oil Lemon Juice	1 oz. 1 tsp. 2 tsp. ½ tsp. 8 oz. 3 oz.	4. Add the grated onion, garlic and spices, and gradually add the oil and lemon juice. 5. Refrigerate, covered, for an hour or more. Adjust seasoning or add more oil and/or lemon juice, if desired. Mixture should be well chilled prior to service.
GARNISH (Variable): Black Olives Tomato Wedges Hot Peppers Sweet Peppers, etc.		6. Serve as an appetizer and garnish as indicated.

Beurrecks ala Turque (Appetizers — Hors d'Oeuvre)

Basically, Beurrecks ala Turque are an appetizer-hors d'oeuvre consisting of gruyere cheese and bechamel sauce wrapped in a thin noodle paste, breaded and fried.

Thin crepes are sometimes substituted for noodle paste, but noodle paste appears to have been indicated in early formulations.

The following formulation makes sufficient filling for 30 to 35 small Beurrecks, but actual size may be determined by personal preference.

FILLING

INGREDIENTS	QUANTITY	METHOD
Cheese, Gruyere, diced small Bechamel Sauce, very heavy, cool Pepper, cayenne	1 lb. 1 pt. ½ tsp.	1. Combine all ingredients, mixing well. Cover and refrigerate until quite firm. 2. Divide the chilled mixture into uniform portions. Form each portion into cigar shape. Wrap each portion in thin noodle paste. 3. Bread a l'anglaise (flour, egg wash, bread crumbs). Fry at 375°F. and serve immediately.

Soupa Avgolemono (Egg and Lemon Soup)

YIELD: 25 to 30 cups	**EACH PORTION**: 1 soup cup, 8 oz.	
INGREDIENTS	QUANTITY	METHOD
Chicken Stock Rice	1¼ gal. 6 oz.	1. Bring chicken stock to a boil. Stir in rice and cook until nearly tender. 2. Remove from heat.
Eggs, whole, beaten Lemon Juice Salt Pepper Turmeric	6 4 oz. 1 tsp. ¼ tsp. ½ tsp.	3. Combine eggs, lemon juice and seasonings. 4. Stir a small amount of soup into the liaison (egg-lemon juice mixture). After tempering liaison, add to the soup, whipping well. Adjust seasoning, if necessary.
Chives Chicken Meat, cooked, julienne	for garnish 1 pt.	5. Place a teaspoon of chicken in each soup cup and add the soup. Sprinkle a few chives in each cup.

Sayadiya (Oriental Fish Pilaf)

YIELD: 4 portions	**EACH PORTION**: 1 fillet	
INGREDIENTS	QUANTITY	METHOD
*Fish Fillets (about 6 oz. each) Lemon Juice Salt White Pepper Milk Flour Salad Oil	4 1 oz. to taste to taste 2 oz. sufficient to dredge fish about 3 oz.	1. Season fish fillets with lemon juice, salt and pepper. Dip in milk; dredge in flour. Shake off excess and saute in oil over medium heat.
Tomato Slices (about ¼ in. thick) Onion Slices (about 1/8 in. thick) Pilaf (rice) Pine Nuts, toasted (Yogurt)	12 12 4 portions 1-1/3 oz.	2. Lightly saute tomato and onion slices. 3. Arrange pilaf on a platter(s). Place fish fillet on top of rice. Place alternating slices of tomato and onion on top of fish, using three slices each tomato and onion per portion. Sprinkle with pine nuts. Garnish with parsley or watercress. Serve yogurt as accompanying side dish.

*Firm-flesh fish, such as bass. Sole or similar type fish may also be used.

Middle East

Shish Taouk (Arabic Chicken Brochettes)
(recipe below)

Curry of Lamb
(recipe on facing page)

Shish Taouk (Arabic Chicken Brochettes)

YIELD: 8 portions	**EACH PORTION:** 1 skewer	
INGREDIENTS	*QUANTITY*	*METHOD*
MARINADE Olive Oil Lemon Juice Parsley, chopped Garlic Cloves, crushed Salt Pepper	1 pt. 4 oz. 1 tbsp. 3 to taste to taste	1. Combine all marinade ingredients.
Chickens (about 2½ lb. each)	4	2. Bone chicken. Cut in uniform pieces, not to exceed ¾ in. Marinate overnight. Turn chicken pieces (in marinade) at least once.
Mushroom Caps (or white truffles)	32	3. Remove chicken from marinade. Drain well. Place on skewers using 4 mushroom caps (or truffle pieces) per skewer. 4. Broil, using medium heat. 5. Serve on a bed of rice pilaf. Garlic butter optional.
NOTE: Any suitable "broiling" method may be used: open fire-charcoal, gas, electricity, etc. Care must be taken not to overcook or dry out chicken. The skewer may be removed in the kitchen when plating, or removed by the waiter or watiress in the dining room.		

Rishta Addis (Lentil Soup)

YIELD: 2 gal.	**EACH PORTION:** 1 soup cup, 8 oz.	
INGREDIENTS	*QUANTITY*	*METHOD*
Olive Oil Onions, fine dice Garlic, minced	3 oz. 2 lb., A.P. 2 tsp.	1. Saute onions in olive oil. Add garlic and saute lightly.
Lamb Stock Lentils Salt Pepper Coriander Fine Noodles, (vermicelli) cooked Scallions, fine slice	2 gal. 1 pt. 2 tsp. ½ tsp. ½ tsp. ½ lb., A.P. 4 oz.	2. Add stock, lentils and seasoning. Cook until lentils are tender. 3. Adjust seasoning as required. Arrange vermicelli and scallions in each cup before adding soup.

Curry of Lamb

YIELD: 8 to 9 portions	EACH PORTION: 4 oz. cooked meat with 4 oz. sauce	
INGREDIENTS	*QUANTITY*	*METHOD*
Lamb Shoulder, boneless, defatted, cubed Lamb Stock (derived from bones)	3 lb. 3 qt.	1. Pre-cook cubed lamb in stock about 45 minutes. Skim surface of simmering stock periodically. 2. Remove meat from stock. Place in brazier or other suitable pan and cover with a clean, damp towel; reserve. Strain stock and reserve.
Salad Oil Onions, diced Mirepoix Apples, cored, diced Bananas, peeled, diced	4 oz. 4 oz. 8 oz. 6 oz. 2 (each)	3. In a heavy pot, saute onions and mirepoix in salad oil. Add apples and bananas. Cook briefly.
Flour Curry Powder	3 oz. 4 tbsp.	4. Combine flour and curry powder. Incorporate with fruits and vegetables. Cook lightly, stirring frequently.
Cumin Seed Fennel Seeds Sugar, brown Coconut, grated Orange and Lemon Zest Cloves, whole	1 tbsp. 1 tsp. 2 tbsp. 4 tbsp. 1 tbsp. 2	5. Add balance of ingredients, stirring well. 6. Incorporate hot stock gradually, stirring well, until all stock is incorporated. Simmer until vegetables and fruits are well cooked and have lost their identity. 7. Pass sauce through a food mill into a clean pot. Adjust flavor and consistency. 8. Pour sauce over cubed pre-cooked lamb. Cover and cook in preheated oven at 375°F. until lamb is tender. Stir occasionally.

Service:
Serve with rice and relishes as desired.
Curry may be served in individual casseroles or may be plated.
Relishes may vary from a single, simple chutney to a variety of cooked, candied and/or pickled fruits and vegetables.
Single portion casserole service suggestion: about 8 oz. by volume.

Pakistani Chapli Kebab (Pakistani Style Lamb Patties)

YIELD 10 patties	EACH PORTION: 5 oz.	
INGREDIENTS	*QUANTITY*	*METHOD*
Onions, fine dice Salad Oil Garlic, minced	2 oz. 1 oz. 1 tsp.	1. Saute onions in oil. Add garlic and saute briefly. Cool.
Bread, white, trimmed Lamb, lean, ground Eggs, whole, beaten Pine Nuts, sauteed (or toasted) Tahini Paste (sesame seed paste) Parsley, chopped Salt Pepper Coriander Cumin Seed Fennel Seed	3 slices 3 lb. 2 2 oz. 1 tbsp. 1 tbsp. 1 tsp. 1/2 tsp. 1/4 tsp. 1/8 tsp. 1/8 tsp.	2. Break or cut bread in pieces. Soak to soften. Squeeze out all excess water. 3. Combine all ingredients. Blend well but keep mixture as light and fluffy as possible. 4. Shape into patties. May be refrigerated until needed. Broil or cook on griddle.

Mashi Warak (Stuffed Grape Leaves)

YIELD: 30 units		
INGREDIENTS	*QUANTITY*	*METHOD*
Onions, fine dice Oil Garlic, minced	1-1/3 oz. 1 oz. 1 tsp.	1. Saute onions in oil. Add garlic and saute lightly. Cool.
Lamb, ground Rice, soaked in cold water Parsley, chopped Salt Pepper Turmeric Cumin Seeds Fennel Seeds Cinammon, ground Pine Nuts, toasted Eggs, whole, beaten	1 lb. 4 oz. 1 tbsp. 1 tsp. 1/4 tsp. 1/8 tsp. 1/4 tsp. 1/4 tsp. 1/4 tsp. 1 oz. 2	2. Mix with lamb and rice. Add seasonings, pine nuts and eggs and mix well, but keep as light as possible. 3. Make a test portion and adjust seasoning, as desired.
Grape Leaves, poached (about 2 in. x ¾ in.) Lamb Stock, hot Lemon Juice	30 1 gal. 4 oz.	4. Divide lamb mixture into equal portions. Place in grape leaves and roll tightly into cigar shape, folding in ends. 5. Place a large plate in the bottom of a pot or brazier. Arrange the stuffed grape leaves on the plate and cover with another plate. Add lamb stock and lemon juice. 6. Cook about 1 hr. or until the grape leaves are soft and lamb and rice are cooked.
Garlic Butter Mint, chopped	see Method see Method	For service, brush with a little garlic butter and sprinkle lightly with chopped, fresh mint.

Mashi Kussa (Stuffed Marrow Squash)

METHOD
1. Core very small marrow squash (Zucchini) lengthwise, with an apple corer. Do not cut all the way through. Leave sufficient solid end to hold in filling. 2. Stuff the cavity with the same lamb mixture as for Mashi Warak, using *cooked* rice in the formulation in place of raw rice. 3. Arrange in a baking dish and top with hot tomato sauce. 4. Bake, covered, about 1 hr. or until the squash are tender but still hold their form.

Shish Kebab Variations

FOR BASIC SHISH KEBAB, see p. 70.

Shish kebab may be served in several ways. Pilaf is a usual accompaniment for table service. The skewers may be removed in the kitchen, or by the waitress or captain in the dining room.

Swordlike skewers are sometimes used for showmanship in hotels and specialty restaurants, and merchandising may include flaming the Shish Kebab at table, etc.

In the Middle East it is served in the form of a sandwich, placing the cooked meats and/or vegetables between Arabic or Syrian bread.

Syrian bread is available in many supermarkets in the United States. It is a lean dough bread; thin and flat, like a large pancake. It stales rapidly and is tough and rubbery when stale.

A number of kebab variations appear below:

KEBAB BIL BATINJAN
Lamb and eggplant pieces. Grilled and garnished with onions and tomatoes.
KEBAB HALABI
Prepared with Kifta. Kifta is minced lamb, similar to Chapli Kebab. See recipe p. 381.
KEBAB MASHWI
Lamb kebabs, grilled onions and tomatoes.
KEBAB MUSHAKAL
Pieces of cubed lamb and balls of Kifta (or Chapli Kebabs) grilled on a skewer.

Pearl Barley with Pine Nuts

YIELD: 15 portions **EACH PORTION:** about 5 oz.

INGREDIENTS	QUANTITY	METHOD
Olive Oil	3 oz.	1. Saute onions. Add nuts and saute until nuts are light brown.
Onions, minced	1 pt.	2. Add barley. Saute until all oil is absorbed.
Pine Nuts	2 oz.	3. Add spices and stock. Cover and bake for 40 to 45 min. in a slow oven (300°F).
Barley, pearl	1 pt.	Stir chives in lightly (with a fork) before serving.
Salt	2 tsp.	
Pepper	½ tsp.	
Stock, white, hot	2 qt.	
Chives, chopped	1 oz.	

NOTE: Cashew nuts may be substituted for pine nuts if desired.

Pilavi Zeytinli (Pilaf with Leeks)

YIELD: 10 to 12 portions **EACH PORTION:** about 4½ oz.

INGREDIENTS	QUANTITY	METHOD
Salad Oil	2 oz.	1. Saute leeks in oil. Add rice and coat evenly, stirring well.
Leeks, white only, sliced	1 pt.	
Rice	1 pt.	
Stock, white, hot	28 oz.	2. Add hot stock and seasoning.
Salt	1 tsp.	3. Cover and bake about 20 min. at 350° to 375°F.
Pepper	¼ tsp.	

Spain-South America

Gazpacho (Cold Fresh Vegetable Soup) *(Also see p. 302)*

YIELD: 25 portions	EACH PORTION: 8 oz.	
INGREDIENTS	*QUANTITY*	*METHOD*
Onions, peeled	1 lb.	1. Place all ingredients except tomato juice in a food chopper or blender. Chop very fine. Ingredients should be well blended (the eggs aid emulsion).
Green Peppers, washed, trimmed	1 lb.	
Cucumbers	1-1/2 lb.	
Tomatoes	1-1/2 lb.	2. Add the tomato juice, operating the machine only until the juice is blended with other ingredients. Adjust seasoning and refrigerate, covered, until soup is well chilled.
Garlic, minced	2 tbsp.	
Salt	2 tsp.	
Pepper	1/4 tsp.	
Cayenne Pepper	1/4 tsp.	**Service**
Thyme	1/8 tsp.	Make a separate garnish of diced tomatoes, cucumbers, and green peppers. Place a heaping teaspoon of garnish in each cup or bowl before serving.
Savory	1/8 tsp.	
Tomato Puree	8 oz.	
Wine Vinegar	4 oz.	
Olive Oil	12 oz.	
Lemon Juice	2 oz.	
Eggs, whole	5	
Tomato Juice	1-1/2 pt.	

NOTE: Trimmed, white bread is sometimes incorporated in the soup to aid emulsion; or a small round of bread is sometimes placed in the cup prior to service.

Hot pepper sauce may be added to the soup, but caution should be exercised to achieve general acceptance.

Additional tomato juice, strong beef consomme or clam juice may be used for a lighter consistency.

Enchiladas

Enchiladas are rolled or folded tortillas filled with a variety of cooked meat and cheese fillings. They are served hot with a spicy sauce and sometimes sprinkled with chopped onions and grated cheese.

ENCHILADA SAUCE—Mole Colorado

YIELD: about 1½ pt.

INGREDIENTS	QUANTITY	METHOD
Olive Oil Onions, minced Garlic, minced	2 oz. 4 oz. 2 tsp.	1. Saute onions in olive oil. Add garlic and saute briefly.
Flour Chili Powder Salt Allspice Vinegar Pimientoes, chopped Tomatoes, well-drained Ham Trimmings	1 tbsp. 2 tbsp. 1½ tsp. ½ tsp. 1 tbsp. 1 7-oz. can 1 pt. 2 oz.	2. Combine flour and seasonings, then add all ingredients to onions, stirring well. 3. Simmer sauce for 35 to 40 min. or until quite thick, stirring occasionally. 4. Adjust seasoning and pass the sauce through a food mill. Use as required.

Seviche Del Peru (Appetizer of Marinated Fish)

Seviche is a South American appetizer consisting of any raw, firm-fleshed fish marinated in lemon or lime juice and seasonings. Onions, scallions, green peppers, etc. may be included.

A basic procedure appears at right:

Slice very thin or julienne fish such as: red snapper, halibut, bass, scallops, etc. Place in a casserole and cover with blended lemon and lime juice, pepper and a small amount of oil. Marinate for two to three days under refrigeration. Serve very cold and garnish with scallions, olives and slices of avocado. If desired, a small amount of thinly-sliced onion may be marinated with the fish. The fish and marinade should be "turned over" two or three times during the marination period to ensure uniform seasoning and marination.

Garbanzos (Chick Peas)

YIELD: 18 to 20 portions   **EACH PORTION:** about 4 oz.

INGREDIENTS	QUANTITY	METHOD
Chick Peas Garlic, whole clove, large Olive Oil Salt Pepper Tomato Juice Water (see right)	2 lb. 1 4 oz. 1 tbsp. 1 tsp. 1 qt. 1 pt.	1. Simmer all ingredients gently until the chick peas are tender. The chick peas should be soft but still retain their shape. Add additional water as required until beans have absorbed maximum moisture. 2. Remove garlic and adjust seasoning before serving.

NOTE: Chick peas are somewhat international in nature, and are used in various forms in a number of countries.

Matambre

YIELD: 3 2-flank or 6 1-flank steaks

The flank steak is a flat, oval shaped muscle obtained from the inside flank. It should be practically free of fat for use in this formulation. Average trimmed weight will approximate 1½ lb.

PREPARING THE MEAT

The flank must be butterflied by placing it flat on a cutting board and slitting it horizontally in the direction of the grain. The steak, knife and cutting board will be in the same plane.

The steak should be cut full length and nearly full depth, terminating the cut about ½ in. from the edge of the meat so that the meat will remain in 1 piece.

As the cut is made, peel back the top flap so that the steak is open and flat. Pound it lightly to achieve uniform thickness.

Marinate for 3 or 4 hr. at room temperature, or overnight under refrigeration.

PREPARING THE ROLL

A) For a small slice (as served), 2½ in. diameter: Place the opened steak on a board or bench, with the smallest end toward you and the grain running away from you. Proceed as indicated.

B) For a large slice (as served): Place 1 steak, cut-side up, on a cutting board, with the wide end of the steak nearest you, grain side away from you. Place the second steak cut-side up, so that the smaller end overlaps the small end of the first steak by 2 in. Pound the overlapping ends together, flattening them slightly for improved uniformity. The grain should be running the same way in both steaks and the resultant shape should resemble a rectangle.

INGREDIENTS	QUANTITY	METHOD
FILLING (Sufficient for 3 2-flank Matambre rolls, or 6 single-flank rolls.) Bread Crumbs, fresh Eggs, hardcooked, chopped coarse Whole Kernel Corn, cooked, drained Marinade	1 qt. 12 oz. 12 oz. as required	1. Combine crumbs, eggs and corn. Add sufficient marinade to moisten. Adjust seasoning. Reserve balance of ingredients for later preparation.
Flank Steaks Spinach, fresh, washed, drained Carrot Strips, lightly cooked (approx. "finger-size" diameter; length: width of Matambre roll) Onions, raw, thin-sliced Cilantro, chopped Salt Pepper	6 (about 1½ lb.) 1 lb. about 8 oz., raw, peeled 8 oz. 2 oz. to taste to taste	2. Place a portion of crumb mixture ¼ in. thick over the surface of the open flanks. Spread mixture uniformly to within 1 in. of the flank end furthest away, but spread the mixture fully to the sides. 3. Place spinach on top of the crumb mixture. Place carrot strips on top of the spinach, about 2 in. apart as in the photograph. Put a light layer of onions on top. Sprinkle liberally with freshly chopped cilantro. Crushed chili or finely minced chili peppers are optional. Season to taste.
		4. Roll firmly, beginning with the edge nearest you and rolling away from you. Roll jelly-roll fashion into a compact cylinder. A small amount of filling will come out of the ends because of the pressure. Tie securely with butcher's twine. A single length of twine is suggested rather than tying each circle of twine separately. Two alternate methods of cooking may be employed: The Matambre may be covered with simmering stock and poached, or it may be treated in the following manner: a. Brown the roll under the broiler or in a heavy pan on top of the range. b. Place the browned meat in a casserole or covered pan with sufficient stock to come about one-third of the way up the roll. c. Cover the pan and place in oven preheated to 375° F. for about 1 hr. or until Matambre is cooked. (After ½ hr., turn Matambre and check doneness.)

Continued on facing page.

Matambre *(Cont.)*

TO SERVE HOT: Remove from cooking utensil and allow Matambre to set up for 10 to 15 min. to facilitate slicing. Reduce cooking liquor and season as desired. Cut Matambre in ¼ in. slices across the grain. Serve with reduced pan juices.

TO SERVE COLD: Remove from heat. Place Matambre in clean pan with sufficient weight on top to compress lightly. Complete cooling in this manner, preferably under refrigeration. When cold, slice as above and serve on chilled plate. May be accompanied by a spicy sauce.

Guacamole (Cold Avocado Dip)

YIELD: about 1½ qt.

INGREDIENTS	QUANTITY	METHOD
Tomatoes, fresh, peeled	1 lb.	1. Mash tomatoes in a blender or pass through a food chopper.
Avocados, large, ripe	6	
Green Chili	1 4-oz. can	2. Add all other ingredients and mash to a heavy puree.
Lemon Juice	2 oz.	3. Adjust seasoning and refrigerate until well chilled.
Lime Juice	1 oz.	
Onion, grated	2 oz.	
Olive Oil	2 oz.	
Salt	1½ tsp.	
Pepper	¼ tsp.	

NOTE: A further seasoning adjustment may be required prior to service after flavors have "married." The mixture should be spicy but not uncomfortably hot.

Tamales de Cerdo y de Res

YIELD: 8 to 10 each   **EACH PORTION:** 3 to 4 pieces

INGREDIENTS	QUANTITY	METHOD
Beef, lean, diced (about ¼ in.)	½ lb.	1. Combine beef, pork, enchilada sauce in a heavy pot. Cook over medium heat until meat is nearly done. Add pinto beans and seasonings and complete cooking. Meat should be tender and mixture reasonably dry or "heavy" in consistency.
Pork, lean, diced	½ lb.	
Enchilada Sauce	8 oz.	
Pinto Beans, cooked	2 oz.	
Chili Powder	dash	
Salt	to taste	2. Cool and reserve. Meanwhile, soak corn husks in hot water to make them pliable.
Corn Husks (Mexican, dried)	3 oz.	
TAMALE MIXTURE		
Masa Harina	8 oz.	3. Mix Masa Harina with water, lard, baking powder and salt. Beat smooth and fluffy.
Water	12 oz.	
OR Stock, warm		
Lard	3 oz.	
Baking Powder	½ tsp.	
Salt	¼ tsp.	
Olives, small, pitted	10 each	

TO ASSEMBLE
1. Place one or two corn husks on cutting board or bench. Husks should be about 5 in. wide.
2. Place about 2 generous tbsp. of masa mixture on corn husk and spread over lower 2/3 of corn husk, leaving 1 in. of space on each side.
3. Place about 1 generous tbsp. of meat mixture in center of upper half of spread masa mixture. Top with olive.
4. Fold corn husk-masa mixture over meat so that edges of masa fit together fairly uniformly. Fold back "empty" corn husk flap and sides. Turn with loose flap down.
5. Steam flap-side down for about 40 to 50 min. Remove from heat. Serve 3 to 4 pieces per appetizer portion.
   Serve additional enchilada sauce on the side.

Platano Asado (Plantain)

Platanos (plantain) are a banana-like fruit of a tropical tree. They are less sweet than bananas and of high starch content. They must be cooked to be eaten. They may be baked, deep fried, sauteed and cooked in a number of different ways. They are frequently peeled and baked in the oven until done, or sliced quite thin and cooked in deep oil as for potato chips.

Frijoles Refritos (Re-Fried Beans)

Simmer pinto beans in water with a small piece of salt pork. Drain the beans well. Mash them and fry in hot bacon fat or lard, turning them frequently with a spatula.

Frijoles Refritos are used hot and cold and for filling tacos, etc.

Empanadas

YIELD: 35 to 40 Empanadas

There are many forms of empanadas, including a variety of fillings and several types of pastry. Two formulations for pastry are given below. Any of the varieties may be portioned for luncheon size or used as hors d'oeuvres. Very small "empanadas" are termed empanadillas. They may be served with a spicy sauce or plain.

INGREDIENTS	QUANTITY	METHOD
PASTRY A (Masa base) Masa Harina (corn flour)	1 qt.	1. Place the masa harina in a bowl.
Water, boiling Enchilada Sauce Lard Salt	1½ pt. 4 oz. 2 oz. 1 tsp.	2. Combine the other ingredients and heat until shortening melts. 3. Work water-sauce-shortening mixture into the masa harina, kneading smooth. 4. Cover and chill. Follow standard dough holding procedures.
		TO FILL 1. Break off bits of dough about the size of a No. 30 ice cream scoop. 2. Make into balls and flatten on parchment paper or similar. 3. Place 2 tbsp. filling (recipe follows) slightly off center. Place a wedge of egg and piece of olive on top of filling; fold dough over the filling, bringing the paper up and over, matching the edges of the dough. 4. Pinch edges together firmly. Bake at 400°F. until nicely browned.
PASTRY B Shortening (well chilled) Flour Salt Cold Water	4 oz. 1¼ lb. 1 tsp. 9 to 10 oz.	1. Follow standard procedures for preparing pie dough. Rub shortening into flour. Keep fairly coarse. 2. Dissolve salt in water and work into flour and shortening. 3. Let rest briefly.
		TO FILL 1. Roll dough out on lightly floured board or bench. (Same basic procedure as for pie preparation.) 2. Cut 5 in. circles with dough cutter. 3. Wash dough lightly. Place 2 tbsp. filling (recipe follows) on dough. Place a wedge of egg and a piece of olive on top of filling. Fold edges over and seal firmly. Shape as desired. Bake at 400° F. until pastry is golden brown. Empanadas may be washed with milk or egg wash prior to baking to improve color.

Continued on facing page.

Empanadas *(Cont.)*

FILLING FOR EMPANADAS		
YIELD: 18 to 20 portions	**EACH PORTION**: 2 tbsp.	
Onions, minced Olive Oil Garlic, minced Meat, coarse ground or fine dice	2 oz. 2 oz. ¼ tsp. ¾ lb.	1. Saute onions in olive oil. Add garlic and meat. Saute to brown meat.
Enchilada Sauce	8 oz.	2. Add enchilada sauce and cook until meat is tender. Keep moist.
Black Pepper Salt Chili Powder (optional) Parsley, chopped	¼ tsp. ½ tsp. ¼ tsp. 2 tbsp.	3. Blend parsley and seasonings together. 4. Remove meat mixture from heat and add blended seasonings. Adjust flavor as desired.
Eggs, hard-cooked Pitted Olives, any variety	2 2 oz.	5. Reserve eggs and olives for filling empanadas. Cut each egg lengthwise into 6 wedges. Slice olives.
NOTE: Filling may be cooled and refrigerated and held for later use, or may be used immediately if empanadas are to be baked immediately.		

Mole Pablano Con Pollo

YIELD: 6 to 8 portions		
INGREDIENTS	*QUANTITY*	*METHOD*
Salad Oil Onions, minced Green Peppers, minced Almonds, chopped fine Sesame Seeds Garlic, minced	for frying 4 oz. 3 oz. 1 tbsp. 1 tsp. 2 tsp.	1. Saute onions and peppers in oil. Add almonds and sesame seeds, browning lightly. Add garlic and saute briefly.
Tomatoes, canned, drained Enchilada Sauce Peanut Butter Chicken Stock Cinnamon, ground Thyme Coriander Seeds Cloves, ground Chili Powder Ginger, ground Salt Anise Seeds Toasted Bread Cubes	1/2 pt. 1 qt. 1 tbsp. 1 pt. 1/2 tsp. 1/8 tsp. 1/2 tsp. 1/8 tsp. 1/2 tsp. 1/8 tsp. 1 tbsp. 1/4 tsp. 2 oz.	2. Add all other ingredients (except chicken and chocolate). Mix well and simmer about 1 hr.
Chicken, eviscerated, cleaned (about 3 lb. each), cut for frying Salad Oil Chocolate, bitter	2 for frying 1 oz.	3. While sauce is simmering fry chicken in hot oil in heavy pan. Cook chicken to half-done stage. 4. Pass cooked sauce through coarse plate of food mill. 5. Pour sauce over chicken and cook, covered, until chicken is tender. Remove from heat and stir in chocolate.

Paella

YIELD: 8 portions		
INGREDIENTS	QUANTITY	METHOD
Chicken, eviscerated, cleaned (3 lb.) Olive Oil	1 for frying	1. Cut chicken in small pieces. 2. Fry on both sides in hot oil in paella pan or other suitable pan until nearly done. Remove chicken from pan and reserve.
Onions, minced Chorizo, sliced Green Peppers, diced Garlic, minced Rice, raw (not converted)	4 oz. 4 oz. 2 oz. 1 tbsp. 1 pt.	3. Saute onions in same pan, adding additional oil as necessary. Add chorizo, green peppers, and saute briefly. 4. Add garlic and rice and saute until rice is shiny.
Tomatoes, canned, drained, chopped Pimientoes, drained, chopped Green Olives, pitted Garbanzos, cooked, drained Clam Juice Salt Pepper	8 oz. 3½ oz. 2 oz. 12 oz. 8 oz. 2 tsp. ½ tsp.	5. Add tomatoes, pimientoes, olives, clam juice and garbanzos. Stir well to achieve uniform mixture. Adjust seasoning. 6. Push mixture aside in several places in pan and add chicken pieces.
Saffron, ground or pounded mortar-pestle Chicken Stock, hot	½ tsp. 1 qt.	7. Add saffron to stock, mixing well. 8. Pour boiling stock over the mixture in the pan. Shake the pan gently to distribute products evenly. 9. Cover pan and simmer for 10 min.
Shrimps, peeled, deveined, raw Mussels OR Small Clams, in the shell	½ lb. 24	10. Add shrimp and clams. Bake, covered, in a moderate oven for an additional 10 to 15 min. 11. Remove cover and cook for an additional 5 min. 12. Prepare uniform portions for service.
NOTE: Paella should retain some moisture. The rice should be reasonably firm but not dried out. Paella is prepared with a variety of ingredients, usually relating to product availability in a specific area. Any reasonable product additions and substitutions can be made.		

Calabacitos Con Queso (Squash with Cheese)

YIELD: 16 to 20 portions	EACH PORTION: about 4½ oz.	
INGREDIENTS	QUANTITY	METHOD
Lard OR Bacon Fat Scallions, sliced	4 oz. 4 oz.	1. Saute scallions lightly in lard or bacon fat
Tomatoes, well-drained Salt Pepper Zucchini, washed, sliced	1 qt. 1 tbsp. 1 tsp. about 3 lb. A.P.	2. Add all ingredients (except cheese), blending well. 3. Simmer, partially covered, until squash is tender. Adjust seasoning.
Cheese (Jack cheese or similar), diced	4 oz.	4. Remove from heat and stir in cheese. Cover and let cheese melt. Serve immediately.
		Alternate Method Undercook squash. Place squash-tomato mixture in baking pan. Sprinkle with the cheese (do not incorporate). Bake at 375°F. for 10 min. or until heated through.

Tacos

YIELD: about 24 units		

INGREDIENTS	QUANTITY	METHOD
Tortillas, fried ("sandwich" shaped)	24	A. 1. Combine cooked meat or fish, pinto beans, cheddar cheese, enchilada sauce and chili powder. It is suggested that the chili powder be mixed separately with the sauce before being incorporated with the other ingredients to ensure uniformity of seasoning.
A. Cooked Meat OR Fish	1½ pt.	
Cooked Pinto Beans, drained	1½ pt.	2. Allow mixture to set, and flavors to marry. The "hotness" of the chili is often more pronounced after setting.
Cheddar Cheese, shredded	1 pt.	
Chili Powder	½ tsp.	
Enchilada Sauce, cold	1 pt.	Adjust seasoning as required. Mixture should be moist but hold together reasonably well. A small amount of oil may be added if desired.
Salad Oil	see Method	
B. Tomatoes, peeled, diced	1½ pt.	B. 1. Combine tomatoes, jack cheese, scallions and lettuce.
Jack Cheese, shredded	1½ pt.	
Scallions, chopped	3 oz.	2. Place a small amount of mixture "A" in each warm taco shell. Top with mixture "B" and serve immediately.
Lettuce, shredded	see Method	

NOTE: A variety of fillings may be used for tacos. The above is simply a guideline.

Tortillas take many forms and are used for a number of purposes. Fresh tortillas are preferable to canned or frozen. To prepare tortillas for tacos, slide the flat tortillas into hot oil and fry until crisp. They soften and become pliable when first put in hot oil but crisp rapidly. They must be formed while still pliable and then fried crisp.

Tacos "machines" are available in which fresh tortillas may be placed in the desired U-form (while still pliable) and the entire unit immersed in deep frying oil, cooking them all at once. The unit is then removed from the oil and opened; the tacos removed and kept warm or served immediately.

Sancocho de Colombia (Chicken and Pork Stew with Vegetables)

YIELD: 50 portions	**EACH PORTION:** 8 oz.	

INGREDIENTS	QUANTITY	METHOD
Water, hot	2½ gal.	1. Place fowl in pot with water. Bring to a boil and simmer for about 1 hr.
Fowl, eviscerated (about 5 lb.)	2	
Pork Shoulder, trimmed, diced	3 lb.	2. Add pork, onions, garlic and seasonings. Simmer until fowl is cooked. Remove fowl from heat and cool. Skin and bone fowl; cut in small pieces and reserve.
Onions, small dice	4 oz.	
Garlic, minced	1 tsp.	
Salt	2 tbsp.	
Pepper	½ tsp.	3. Pork should be nearly tender when fowl is cooked. Test for doneness and proceed as below.
Savory	1 tsp.	
Cayenne Pepper	¼ tsp.	
Yucca Root, medium dice	3 lb., A.P.	4. Add diced yucca root and simmer for ½ hr. Add platano and zucchini and cook until all ingredients are tender. Adjust seasoning if necessary.
Platano, medium dice	3 lb., A.P.	
Zucchini, skin on, medium dice	3 lb., A.P.	5. Add cooked chicken meat. Reheat and serve as desired.

How to Set Up a Buffet Table

Whether the arrangement is simple or elaborate, food on the buffet table should be dramatically displayed. Effective food display will help provide the lavish note enjoyed by patrons when eating out, while at the same time the food service operator will be able to take advantage of the economy in serving personnel which buffet meals offer.

When planning a buffet dinner, it's a good idea to set up a separate dessert table which will help to keep patrons moving and lessen congestion. Another way to keep the buffet line in motion is to set up separate tables for water, glasses, forks, spoons, butter, napkins, condiments or relishes.

Decorative nonfood items can be employed to further enhance the lavish impression created by the food. Ice carvings — the traditional buffet table decoration — can be used to hold flowers or food and thus serve a dual purpose. Arranged with the platters of food, relishes and garnishes can add much to the decor. Radishes, potatoes, turnips or beets make attractive flowers. Arrangement of the relishes on the plate will also add to the general attractiveness of the table.

Decorated hams — as well as turkeys, chickens and fish — colorful salad molds and special care in developing maximum color contrasts for all foods to be placed on the buffet table will heighten eye appeal. Pimiento, chopped hard cooked eggs, colorful gelatin, contrasting fruits and many other garnishes will assure maximum attraction for buffet specialties.

Colorful trays, bowls, and chafing dishes also help to dramatize buffet foods. And, of course, gleaming silver, cutlery, accessories and lighted candles will add the finishing touch of elegance to the table (see color pictures, pp. 108, 109).

For detailed information on setting up all types of buffets, see *The Professional Chef's Art of Garde Manger* by Frederic H. Sonnenschmidt and Jean F. Nicolas and *The Professional Chef's Book of Buffets* by George K. Waldner and Klaus Mitterhauser.

*Dessert Section which follows
Prepared for The Culinary Institute of America
By Joseph Amendola, then Bakery Chef*

DESSERTS

A meal's perfect ending is its dessert. Many food operators have built enviable reputations by concentrating on dessert favorites from Baked Alaska to delicate Bavarian Cream. Typical of the variety available to the menu maker are the desserts shown on the following pages.

THE PROFESSIONAL CHEF

Baked Alaska Grand Success

Kahlua Parfait

Ice Cream Bombe

Peppermint Ice Cream Coupe

Cantaloupe Alaska

Planning Desserts

Remember that desserts are long-profit items, and are worthy of all the time and effort that can be put into them. The number and kinds of desserts featured will, of course, depend upon the type of operation. Wise menu planners set up a definite dessert pattern for daily use.

If desserts are to have continuing appeal, a pleasing variety must be featured. While it is important to serve the specialty of the house, and a few other stand-bys daily, variety is necessary to maintain high sales.

In planning desserts, consider the demands those chosen will make on the production department. Try to combine those requiring little effort or hard work with those demanding elaborate preparation.

You should know the individual cost of every dessert on your menu and base the size of the portion and the selling price on it. Although it is possible to have a much better mark-up on desserts than on entrees, don't reduce dessert volume by setting the price too high.

Dramatizing desserts is important to increasing profits. Presenting desserts to customers with style and flair — perhaps from a dessert cart or through a display near the entrance of the dining room — will increase sales.

Desserts shown at left:
(1) Charlotte Russe; (2) Charlotte Royale; (3) Pate Dome; (4) Bavarian Cream; (5) Apple Strudel; (6) Rice Imperatrice; (7) Lady Locks; (8) Meringue Swan Chantilly; (9) Swiss Chocolate Pie; (10) Rice Imperatrice; (11) Pithivier; (12) Peach Conde; (13) Fruit Tartlettes.

CREAM PUFF PASTE VARIATIONS

Turban

Croquenbouche

Cream Puff Swan

French Doughnuts

Banana Surprise

Honey Bee Hive

Techniques for Successful Desserts

The modern pastry chef and baker realize that they must offer many variations in their desserts in order to attract new patrons. Although fancy pastries are usually referred to as french pastries, many nations have contributed hundreds of popular variations to these popular desserts.

Some pastries and desserts are known in the trade as standard types. They may be greatly improved by developing variations and creating special names for them for use in the hotels and restaurants where they originate.

The best quality of ingredients obtainable must be used for these delicious pastries. Patient craftsmanship is necessary for a fine finished product.

Originality and ingenuity plus careful selection of a variety of pastries and desserts have created an enviable reputation for many hotels and restaurants.

To Achieve Best Results In order to achieve the best results in today's baking, the baker should be knowledgeable in several areas.

There are primarily four basic areas to consider in the art of baking: ingredients, equipment, formulas and methods, skill and craftsmanship.

Ingredients Only the very best ingredients will result in a good wholesome product. First of all, there should be an understanding of the ingredients.

Flour, for example, is the backbone of most baked products. There are different types of flour: hard wheat and soft wheat. It is essential to choose the right flour for the product. Hard wheat flour is referred to as bread flour and is used in combination with yeast products. Soft wheat flour refers to pastry or cake flour and is used in baking powder or chemically leavened products.

While the above is usually the rule with the flours, there are of course occasional exceptions to the rule. To help the beginner gain a thorough understanding of ingredients, there are many good technical books on the market. In Joseph Amendola's *The Bakers Manual* and *Understanding Baking* there are excellent sections on ingredients.

Knowing the tolerance in the temperature of yeast is another important point. The following table will serve as a guide:

> *38°F.—retarding point of yeast*
> *80°F.—normal for dough temperature*
> *138°F.—thermal death point*

The table above shows how different temperatures affect the yeast bacteria. At 38°F. it is inactive, at 80°F. it is functioning normally, and at 138°F. it does not function at all, but dies and no gases are being produced.

Equipment There are a number of major articles of equipment used in a bakeshop: mixers, ovens, ranges, refrigerators, pans of all sizes. The proper loading of an oven can make a big difference. It determines whether there is a loss of heat and also the recovery of that heat to the predetermined selection of degree.

If a great number of products are to be loaded into a preheated oven, a slightly higher degree should be used from the start to compensate for the load. This is especially true when the products to be baked come from a freezer or retarder box.

The position of the pans or products in the oven is also very important. They must be placed so that heat can circulate properly, resulting in more uniform finished products.

To get best results from mixers, consideration should be given to the size of bowl, attachments used, etc. A good technical manual will show the proper use of the fine equipment available today. These manuals should be in every baker's library.

Formulas and Methods Bakers may be compared to pharmacists, for a pastry chef must, in a way, fill a prescription. The flour mills, yeast companies and bakery supply firms all have fine research laboratories which prepare excellent formulas. If these are followed, results will be excellent. Weighing the ingredients in quantity baking is very important in obtaining uniform results.

The formula sheet gives speed, cost and control of the product, and also the yield. The advantages of this type of sheet are that it:

- Gives name of product.
- Gives information for method used.
- Lists ingredients and the order of their incorporation.
- Gives specific weights in pounds or ounces.
- Gives the ingredient costs per pound.
- Provides room to give extended cost of each and every ingredient plus total cost of batch.
- Gives total weight of a finished batch.
- Gives scaling weight, instructions, yield of product.
- Gives baking temperature.
- Gives cost per ounce of product.
- Gives cost per pound of product.
- Provides space for remarks.

This type of sheet is used in the formulas in this section. It is recommended that this standard form be used for all formulas used in baking.

Skill and Craftsmanship Two of the most important factors in skill and craftsmanship are a love of baking and the right kind of experience. The proper teaching of a novice will result in a fully experienced baker. Some products are easy to make, and little experience is necessary. However, there are many products that require great skill and patience for best results. Many of us learn through trial and error, and experience is, of course, our best teacher.

Techniques for Ice Cream Desserts

Ice cream is one of the nation's favorite desserts. Coupes, parfaits, mousses, oven-browned ice cream desserts and bombes are only a few of the many desserts which can be made with ice cream. And because elaborate-appearing ice cream desserts are often easy to prepare, they will not put undue strain on the production department.

Here is a collection of ice cream dessert variations which will glamourize any menu.

Baked Alaska Cut a thin layer of sponge cake (p. 419). Add a block of ice cream and cover each side with sponge cake. Cover the whole area with a thick layer of meringue. Brown in oven.

Baked Alaska Grand Success Cut out center of an 8-in. sponge cake, fill cavity with well drained bing cherries (canned). Top with layer of ice cream, add the piece cut from center of cake. Cover with meringue, making pyramid effect. Brown and top with apricot halves. (See color picture, p. 393.)

Cantaloupe Alaska Cut cantaloupe in two. Remove seeds. Fill cavity with ice cream. Top with meringue. Brown meringue and serve. (See color picture, p. 393.)

Orange Surprise Place a small piece of sponge cake on the bottom of an orange rind cup. Add a scoop of ice cream. Cover with meringue. Brown.

Coconut Tropical Dessert Use half shell of a coconut with a paper cut as a liner. Start with fruit as a base (sliced banana or pineapple, etc.). Add ice cream. Top with meringue and brown; or top with whipped cream and shredded coconut or macadamia nuts.

Fresh Pineapple Delight Quarter fresh pineapple. Remove core. Add small piece of sponge cake (p. 419). Top with ice cream. Cover with meringue. Brown. This dessert also can be made with a pear half instead of pineapple.

Parfaits Add fruit to parfait glass first. Then add ice cream, packing it in firmly. Top with whipped cream. Parfaits can be made with a wide variety of flavors of fruits and liqueurs.

Coupes Pat ice cream into dessert glass first. Top with a circle of whipped cream. Add fruit or sauce to center of circle. Coupes can also be made in a wide variety of flavors.

Peach Melba Using a piece of sponge cake as a base, add a scoop of ice cream, half a peach, melba sauce and whipped cream. Top with sliced almonds.

Chocolate Ice Cream Cups To chocolate shell cups, add ice cream, whipped cream and top with nuts.

Pear Helene Top sponge cake with ice cream, pear half, chocolate sauce and toasted sliced almonds.

PREPARING BAKED ALASKA GRAND SUCCESS

STEP 1:
To make Baked Alaska Grand Success, cut center out of an 8-in. sponge cake (p. 419). Fill the cavity with well-drained bing cherries. Kirsch may be added for flavoring.

Fruit Mousse A fruit flavored mousse should be garnished with the same fruit used as puree in the recipe.

Snow Princess Top sponge cake (p. 419) with a scoop of ice cream and place a small doll (the princess) in the center of the ice cream. Add whipped cream around the base of the sponge cake. Garnish with cherries.

Meringue Ice Cream Glace Top Meringue Shells (p. 409) with a scoop of ice cream and sauce.

Banana Surprise Make a Cream Eclair (p. 402) into the shape of a banana. Split eclair in half. Add pastry cream or ice cream and half a banana. Top the Banana Surprise with Chocolate sauce and nuts. (See color picture, p. 396.)

Lady Finger Ice Cream Top sponge cake with ice cream and place Lady Fingers (p. 420) around the ice cream. Top with whipped cream and cherry. Garnish with sauce around base.

Appareil a Bombe is a base made for Mousse or Biscuit (bisque) Glace. It consists primarily of egg yolks, sugar and water and is prepared as follows:

1. Mix 3 lb. sugar and 1 lb. water and cook at 240°F. until it reaches the soft ball stage.

2. Place 24 egg yolks in a mixer and beat with a whip at medium speed.

3. Pour cooked sugar and water mixture slowly on top of eggs while they are being beaten and beat until cold. When a creamy consistency has been reached, remove from mixer and place in refrigerator until ready for use. This paste will keep for a week or longer under refrigeration.

4. When ready to use base in making Mousses, Biscuits Glace, etc., fold ½ lb. of base mixture into

STEP 2:
Top sponge cake and cherries with a layer of hard ice cream. On top of the layer of ice cream, place the piece of sponge cake previously cut from the center of the cake.

STEP 3:
Cover the entire dessert with meringue, swirling around the sides. Since the center slice of sponge cake is smaller than the base, you will have a pyramid effect.

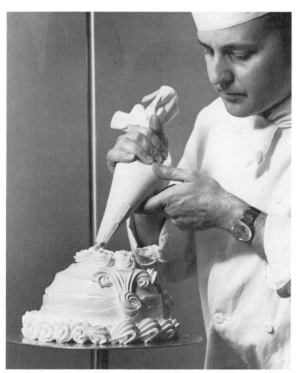

STEP 4:
Top the pyramid with additional meringue, using a pastry tube to build it up. Edges of meringue swirls will brown to provide a contrast with the glossy white of the meringue.

STEP 5:
Place Baked Alaska in the oven long enough to brown the meringue. Top with apricot halves. Baked Alaska Grand Success is shown in color on p. 293.

each quart of whipped cream. Add liquor, fruit, etc., as needed for specific dessert.

Biscuit Tortoni To the basic mixture (see directions above), add 1 oz. rum or brandy and 4 oz. crushed macaroons. Mix together and fill tortoni cups. Use a star tube. Sprinkle with crushed macaroons, top with a maraschino cherry and freeze.

Mousse Mousses are frozen whipped ice cream desserts of various flavors. The identifying flavor (Chocolate, Strawberry, Mocha, etc.) is added to the base and whipped cream mixture. It is then put in brick type molds and frozen. For serving, cut into slices or serve as larger pieces decorated with whipped cream and fruits and topped with a sauce.

Biscuits Glace are made from the same basic mixture as mousses. These desserts are frozen in paper souffle cups or cases and are served in the same containers in which they are frozen. The dessert is usually decorated to harmonize with the flavor of the mixture.

Ice Cream Bombes Originally Ice Cream Bombes were spherical or dome shaped, hence the name Bombe.

Today, however, Ice Cream Bombes vary in shape, but their contents remain basically the same.

The traditional method of making Ice Cream Bombes is to place the mixture in a mold and freeze it in ice and rock salt. However, today's advanced freezing facilities make this unnecessary.

Although any shape mold may be used, spherical shaped molds have an interesting and attractive appearance. Two attractive shapes of bombe molds are shown in picture at left.

To make an Ice Cream Bombe, line the mold with ice cream, ice, sherbet, mousse, fruit or nuts and candy or a combination of two or three of these ingredients. Freeze.

Unmolding Bombes To unmold Ice Cream Bombes, dip the mold quickly into hot water. Dry the mold and place upside down on a cold platter. Remove mold.

Slicing and Serving Bombes An Ice Cream Bombe should be garnished and served immediately after unmolding. The bombe is usually topped with whipped cream. Additional garnishing is determined by the ingenuity of the chef.

To slice Ice Cream Bombes use a silver knife dipped in hot water.

Strawberry Bombe Mask a bombe mold with strawberry ice cream. Make a second lining of lemon ice. Fill with strawberries which have previously been soaked in kirsch. Freeze.

Bombe Carmen Mask a bombe mold with vanilla ice cream about ½ in. thick. Fill the center with a raspberry mousse. Freeze.

Ice Cream Bombes

Traditional Ice Cream Bombes are made in spherical or dome-shaped molds as shown at right. Many different shaped molds are now available, however. Decoration is only limited by the chef's ingenuity.

Mousses, Biscuits Glace, Biscuit Tortoni

Variations of appareil a bombe mixture include: Chocolate and Strawberry Mousse Hearts, top left and right; Neapolitan Mousse, center; Chocolate-Vanilla, Coffee-Walnut and Mocha Biscuit Glace, lower left; Biscuit Tortoni, lower right.

Techniques for
Eclair and Cream Puff Paste Desserts

Eclair and Cream Puff Paste (Pate a Chou)

METHOD	INGREDIENTS	LB.	OZ.	COST PER LB.	COST
1. Bring to a good rolling boil.	Water or Milk Shortening or Butter Salt	2 1	 ½		
2. Combine with Step 1; blend. Cook until the mixture is smooth and rolls free from side of pot. Remove from heat.	Bread Flour	1	8		
3. Add slowly until a medium stiff paste is obtained. Blend well after each addition of eggs.	Eggs (variable—about 24)	2	8		
Total					
Scaling Instructions		**Cost Per Oz.**			
Baking Temperature: 400°F. for a good half hour.		**Cost Per Lb.**			
Remarks: Paper may be used on pans, or they may be lightly greased.					

Precautions
1. Make sure that the shortening and water are brought to a good rolling boil.
2. Improper cooking of Step 1. (Be sure shortening is melted.)
3. Mixture in Step 2 should be dry when cooked and not stick to pot.
4. Consistency of mix is very important. Common mistakes are using too many eggs or using too few eggs.
5. Incorrect addition of eggs must be avoided. (Add only 2 or 3 at a time, blending in well after each addition.)
6. Shell must not be removed from oven until it is completely dry or it will collapse.

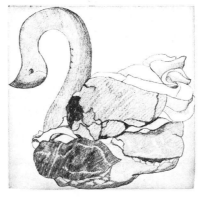

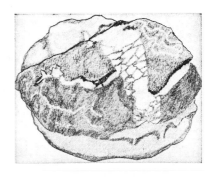

Polka Tart

1. Roll out pie crust or pastry dough about ⅛ in. thick. Cut a circle about 8 in. in diameter for a large tart, 3 in. in diameter for an individual tart.

2. Place dough on a baking sheet lined with baking paper. Using a plain tube, dress out a rim of Cream Puff Paste (p. 401) around the edge.

3. Bake at 400°F. for about 30 min. or until golden brown. Cool; fill with Pastry Cream (p. 411).

4. Place a generous amount of granulated sugar on top of Pastry Cream. Caramelize the sugar by pressing a red hot poker on top of the pastry.

Cream Puff Swan

1. Using a pastry bag and tube with a ¼-in. opening, form the head and neck of the swan from Cream Puff Paste (p. 401). Paste should be dressed out to form a question mark.

2. Using a Cream Puff Shell (see directions at right), cut off the top third. Then cut this into two pieces to be used as wings.

3. Fill the remainder of the Cream Puff Shell with whipped cream or Pastry Cream (p. 411). Place wing, neck and head in position in the filling. Dust with confectioner's sugar.

Cream Puff Shells, Baskets

1. Using a plain ½-in. tube and pastry bag, dress out Cream Puff Paste (p. 401) onto paper-lined or lightly greased baking pans. Puffs should be about 2 in. in diameter when dressed out. Space well apart to permit uniform baking.

2. Bake at 400°F. for about 30 min. or until dry and golden brown. Cool.

3. Fill with Pastry Cream (p. 411), whipped cream, a combination of both or ice cream. Frost with your favorite icing or top with sauce.

4. Cream Puff Baskets are made by removing the top of the Cream Puff Shell, filling and inserting handle as shown in the illustration below. (Handles should be dressed out using a pastry tube with a ¼-in. opening. Make them in the shape of a ring.)

5. Cream Puff Fantasies are made in the same manner as Cream Puff Baskets, except that three smaller circles are inserted into the filling rather than the one large circle which acts as the handle of the basket.

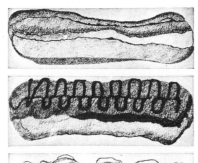

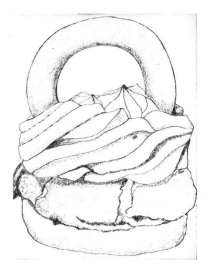

French Doughnuts

1. Heat fat in a kettle to 375°F.

2. Cut a piece of heavy paper to one-half the size of the kettle.

3. Fill pastry bag with Cream Puff Paste (p. 401). Using a star tube, dress out rings 2½ to 3 in. in diameter on the heavy paper. Keep rings well apart.

4. Take paper in both hands and insert it into the kettle of hot fat (paper side up). The rings will drop off into the fat.

5. Allow doughnuts to fry for about 10 min., or until golden brown on one side. Then flip over and allow the other side to brown. Remove from fat and drain well.

6. French Doughnuts may be split and filled with jam or Pastry Cream (p. 411) or iced with a plain flat icing.

Eclairs

1. Line a baking sheet with paper or grease it lightly.

2. Fill a pastry bag with Cream Puff Paste (p. 401). Using a plain ½-in. tube, dress out fingers 3 to 4 in. in length. Space well apart.

3. Bake at 400°F. for about 30 minutes or until dry. Cool.

4. Fill with Pastry Cream, whipped cream or a combination of both. (Ice cream may also be used.) Ice with flavored fondant or top with sauce.

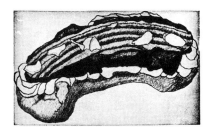

Banana Surprise

1. Make a curved Eclair Shell (facing page). Split shell in two. Each shell makes two desserts.

2. Fill shell with Pastry Cream (p. 411) or ice cream.

3. Cut a banana into four quarters and place on top of filling.

4. Top Banana Surprise with chocolate sauce and sprinkle with toasted sliced almonds.

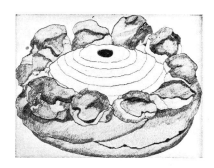

St. Honore

1. Dress out 15 1-in. Cream Puff Shells (facing page) and bake.

2. Roll out pie crust or pastry dough to about ⅛ in. thick. Cut a circle 8 in. in diameter. Place dough on a sheet pan lined with paper.

3. With a plain tube, dress out a rim of Cream Puff Paste (p. 401) around the edge of the pastry. (Use the same technique as for Polka Tart, facing page.)

4. Bake at 400°F. for about 30 min. or until dry and golden brown. Cool.

5. Dip the small Cream Puff Shells (Step No. 1) into caramelized sugar and place on the rim of the larger baked circle. Affix with additional caramelized sugar.

6. Fill the center of the pastry with a Bavarian Cream (p. 420) or Pastry Cream (p. 411).

7. Garnish with cherries and serve.

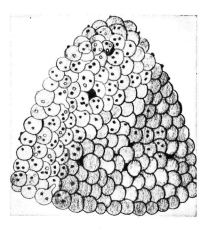

Honey Bee Hive

1. Line a baking sheet with paper. Using a ½-in. plain tube and pastry bag, dress out ¼-in. balls of Cream Puff Paste (p. 401) onto pan.

2. Bake in 400°F. oven for 15 to 18 min. until dry. Cool.

3. Dip these small puffs into a mixture of 4 parts honey and 1 part granulated sugar boiled together.

4. Arrange puffs on a platter, stacking them in the shape of a bee hive.

5. Sprinkle with nonpareils.

Note: Also used to garnish soups.

Beignet Souffle

1. Heat fat to 370°F. Dress Cream Puff Paste (p. 401) onto paper.

2. Place balls in deep fat using the same technique as for French Doughnuts, (p. 402). (If preferred, Cream Puff Paste can be dropped by the spoonful directly into the hot fat.)

3. Fry in hot fat until golden brown on all sides. Serve with Sabayon Sauce or dust with confectioner's sugar.

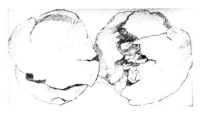

Profiterolles (Hors d'Oeuvre Puffs)

1. Using a plain tube, dress out 1-in. balls of Cream Puff Paste (p. 401).

2. Bake at 400°F. for about 20 min. or until dry. Cool.

3. Split shells and fill with whipped cream, Pastry Cream (p. 411), Bavarian Cream (p. 420) or any comparable mixture.

4. Frost with flavored fondant icing. Garnish with nuts, fruits, etc.

Note: The famous **Profiterolles au Chocolat** are filled with ice cream or whipped cream and served with a thin chocolate sauce.

The puffs may also be filled with savory mixtures and served as cocktail hors d'oeuvres.

Turban

1. Trace a 6- to 8-in. circle on a paper-lined baking sheet.

2. Using a plain pastry tube, dress out a circular band of Cream Puff Paste (p. 401) about 1½ in. thick.

3. Brush with egg wash. Sprinkle with raw sliced almonds.

4. Bake at 400°F. for about 30 min. or until dry. Cool.

5. Split the ring horizontally. Fill with whipped cream or Pastry Cream (p. 411). Place top back on ring and dust with confectioner's sugar.

Techniques for Puff Paste Desserts

Figure 1

Figure 2

Figure 3

Figure 4

Figure 5

Figure 6

Puff Paste is a rolled pastry from which a wide variety of flaky and fine-tasting products are made.

No other baked product is quite like puff paste. It contains no sugar or leavening agent, yet it rises to eight times its original size. This is due to the process of rolling alternate layers of fat and dough. (There are often well over 1000 layers.) A product which is only ¼ in. high before baking will sometimes rise to over 2 in. with hundreds of fine flakes. A finished puff paste is tender and crisp.

Some bakers feel that the addition of cream of tartar helps the dough to rise. However, properly made puff paste will rise without the addition of cream of tartar to help it.

Rules for Preparing Puff Paste

Great care must be taken in preparing and rolling puff paste or the finished product will not be up to standard. The following rules should be observed:

1. Scale and prepare dough strictly according to formula (below).

2. When butter or puff paste shortening is rolled into the dough, it must be the same consistency as the dough. Poor dough will result if one is stiffer than the other.

3. In warm climates or bake shops, dough should be kept under refrigeration after it is rolled.

4. Care must be taken to make sure every particle of the puff paste shortening or butter is evenly distributed through the dough. All end corners should be folded squarely.

Puff Paste Dough

METHOD	INGREDIENTS	LB.	OZ.	COST PER LB.	COST
1. Make into a dough. Remove from mixer. Round into a ball shape. Allow to stand 15 to 20 min.	Bread Flour Salt Butter Eggs (5 eggs) Cold Water	5 2	 1 8 8 4		
2. Roll Step 1 into Step 2. Directions for this process are given below.	Butter or Puff Paste	5			
Total Yield: about 100					
Scaling Instructions				Cost Per Oz.	
Baking Temperature: 350° to 375°F. for 20 to 25 min.				Cost Per Lb.	

ROLLING IN AND FOLDING PUFF PASTE

1. Roll the dough following the direction of the four corners (Figure 2). Leave the center somewhat thicker.

2. Place shortening in center (Figure 2) and lap over the four sides. (Figure 3). Flatten with a rolling pin by gently pounding dough (Figure 4).

3. Roll out again about ½ in. thick and twice as long as it is wide.

4. After brushing off all excess flour, fold both ends toward middle and then double again (Figure 5).

5. Allow the dough to stand in a cool place or put in the refrigerator for at least 20 to 30 minutes.

6. Repeat the rolling process four times. On the final roll, make a "three-way fold." (Figure 6).

5. All excess flour should be brushed off before folding dough.

6. A minimum of 20 to 30 min. should be allowed before folding.

7. If paste is left over from the preceding day, it will require additional rolling before being cut. Otherwise dough will not develop properly during baking.

8. After dough is cut, it should stand for 20 to 30 min. before baking. This prevents excessive shrinkage.

9. Puff paste should be baked until it is dry and crisp.

Cream Slices

1. Roll out a piece of Puff Paste (p. 404) ⅛ in. thick. Brush entire surface with water. Sprinkle with sliced almonds or filberts.

2. Using a pastry wheel, cut dough into 2- by 4-in. oblongs.

3. Place on sheet pans and allow to stand 30 min. Bake at 375°F. for 20 to 25 min.

4. After baking, split in two. Fill with whipped cream. Dust with confectioner's sugar.

Cheese Sticks

1. Give two turns to a 1-lb. piece of Puff Paste (p. 404). Dust between folds with 2 oz. grated cheese mixed with salt and paprika.

2. Roll out to about ⅙ in. thick into strips 1 in. wide.

3. Roll these strips into twisted sticks. Place on wet sheet pans. Allow to stand 30 min.

4. Bake at 375°F. for 20 to 25 min. After baking, cut into strips 4 in. in length. Serve.

Napoleons

1. Roll 1½ lb. Puff Paste scraps (p. 404) very thin. Roll to the size of a baking pan.

2. Place on pan and allow to stand for 30 min. Prick all over to prevent blistering while baking.

3. Bake at 375°F. for 20 to 25 min.

4. After baking, cut into three strips. Place one on top of the other with vanilla-flavored Pastry Cream (p. 411) between layers.

5. Frost the top with one or more flavors of fondant icing.

6. When fondant is dry, cut into bars about 4 in. wide and 2 in. long.

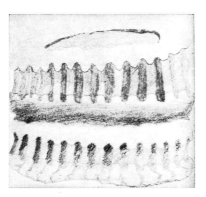

Patty Shells

1. Roll out a piece of Puff Paste dough (p. 404) to about ⅛ in. thick.

2. Using a 3-in. scalloped edge cutter, cut out rounds. Place rounds on a clean wet baking pan.

3. Roll out another piece of Puff Paste dough to ¼ in. thick. Be sure thickness is uniform.

4. Using the same cutter as before, cut into rounds. Then using a 2-in. scalloped edge cutter, cut a hole in the center of each round.

5. Wash the first rounds with water. Then carefully place the rings cut from the second rounds on top of the washed rounds.

6. Wash with an egg wash. Allow to stand for at least 30 min.

7. Bake at 375°F. for 20 to 25 min.

Note: Greased paper placed over the top of the patty shells before they are baked prevents them from toppling over.

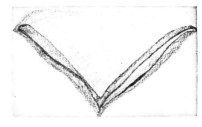

Turnovers

1. Roll out Puff Paste dough (p. 404) ⅛ in. thick. Cut into 5-in. squares.

2. Wash surface of squares with water; fold cornerwise to form triangle. (Filling may be put into these turnovers before folding or they may be baked without filling.)

3. Allow to stand about 30 min.

4. Bake at 375°F. for 20 to 25 min.

5. If baked without filling, turnovers may be split with a knife and filled with a variety of fruit fillings.

Vol-au-Vent

1. Follow directions for Patty Shells given at left. Vol-au-Vent is merely a large Patty Shell, somewhat thicker in proportion to its diameter.

2. A top crust for the shell can be made from the center cut from the second round.

3. Top crust is more attractive if it is scored before baking. Pattern for scoring is shown above.

Cream Horns (Lady Locks)

1. Roll Puff Paste (p. 404) into a strip about 15 in. wide and 48 in.

Desserts

long. When the rolling is completed, pastry should be no more than ⅛ in. thick.

2. Cut into strips about ¼ in. wide. Wash surface with water. Roll each strip on a cream horn tin, starting the strip on the small end of the tin and following a diagonal direction. When the tin is covered, roll the horns in granulated sugar. Place in baking pans.

3. Allow to rest before baking to reduce shrinkage.

4. Bake at 375°F. until lightly browned. Remove tins from the baked horns. Fill with marshmallow filling or whipped cream.

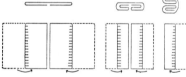

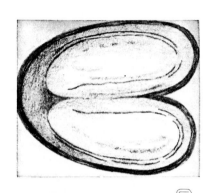

Palm Leaves (Pig's Ears)

1. Sprinkle work bench with granulated sugar. Roll out a 1-lb. piece of Puff Paste dough (p. 404) to ⅛ in. thick; sprinkle top with sugar.

2. Fold dough toward the center from both ends; repeat a second time. (See diagram above.)

3. Cut in ¼ in. slices. Place on solid sheet pan; allow to stand 15 to 20 min.

4. Bake at 400°F. Turn over when half done to color both sides. (This also aids in caramelizing the sugar.)

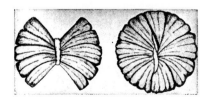

Butterflies

1. Roll out scraps of Puff Paste dough (p. 404). Layer 2 or 3 flat pieces of dough one on top of the other.

2. Brush a narrow strip down the center of each layer with water. Make an impression with rolling pin.

3. Cut into ½ in. pieces perpendicular to the impression. Give piece a half twist (with cut side up). Lay a small (¼- by 2-in.) piece across the center of twisted piece to form body.

4. Allow to stand 15 to 20 min. Bake at 400°F. Turn over when half done to color both sides.

Pinwheels

1. Roll out a piece of Puff Paste dough (p. 404) to ⅛ in. thick. Cut into ¼-in. squares.

2. Make four incisions in each square. Use a sharp knife. These incisions are made at each corner and reach to within 1 in. of the center (see first diagram above).

3. Brush the center of each square with egg wash. Fold each corner to the center (see second diagram); press firmly. This forms the pinwheel from which this pastry gets its name.

4. Brush the surfaces with egg wash. Place a dab of fruit preserves in the center of each pinwheel.

5. Place on pans. Allow to stand for a few minutes. Bake at 350°F. for about 20 to 25 min.

Apple Strudel—Made in Puff Paste

1. Roll out Puff Paste (p. 404) paper thin into a 6- by 24-in. sheet. Place on a paper-lined solid sheet pan.

2. Add sponge cake crumbs to apple filling mixture, using enough to absorb excess liquid.

3. Place apple mixture (p. 413) in center of dough. Brush edges

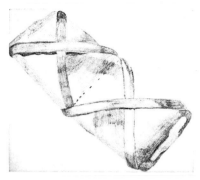

with egg wash.

4. Roll out a cover (the same size as bottom). Fold in half lengthwise. Cut to ⅔ the width.

5. Cover apple mixture with second piece of dough; trim excess and seal well with fingers.

6. Brush surface with egg wash.

7. Allow to stand 20 min. Bake at 375°F. for 20 to 25 min.

Note: For variation, cherries, blueberries or your favorite fruit filling may be used.

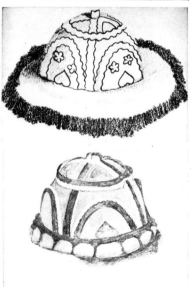

Pate Dome

1. Roll out Puff Paste dough (p. 404) to ¼ in. thick. Cut out one 8-in. circle for base and one 10-in. circle for top.

2. Wash entire surface of the

bottom round with water.

3. Roll and ball up parchment paper into round dome shape. Cover with aluminum foil. Place in center of washed bottom round. (See illustration on facing page).

4. Cover with the 10-in. round of dough.

5. Seal bottom securely. Notch entire outer bottom edge with paring knife.

6. Roll out scraps of Puff Paste dough. Cut a ¼-in. circular band for around the bottom. Cut another ¼-in. circular band and place about 2 in. from top. (This piece acts as cutting guide for the finished product.)

7. Cut four ¼-in. strips and place on dome to divide it into quarters. Cut out desired designs and place within the quarters. (See facing page.) Wash the entire surface. Allow to stand 30 min. Bake at 375° F. for 20 to 25 min.

Note: *After* pate has baked about 10 min., one or two small cuts can be made to allow moisture to escape.

Fleurons

1. Roll out trimmings from Puff Paste dough (p. 404) ¼-in. thick.

2. Cut out pieces with a crescent cutter as in diagram (at right).

3. Brush surface with egg wash.

4. Allow to stand on a baking sheet pan in the refrigerator for 20 min.

5. Bake at 375°F. about 15 min.

6. Use to garnish fish dishes and certain vegetable purees.

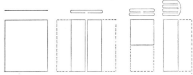

Four Fingers

1. Roll out a rectangle of Puff Paste dough (p. 404) using sugar to roll out instead of flour.

2. Mark the center lengthwise and fold the sides to the center. Next mark the center crosswise and fold along this line. (See diagram above.) Fold once again along the original center and press together.

3. Slice and bake as for Palm Leaves (facing page).

4. Fingers may be sandwiched in pairs with butter cream.

Pithivier

1. Roll out Puff Paste (p. 404) to ¼ in. thick. Cut out two 8-in. rounds. Wash entire surface of one round with water.

2. Place a mound of frangipane in the center of this round. Cover with second round and secure bottom.

3. Roll out scraps of Puff Paste dough to ¼ in. thick. Cut out a ¼ in. circular band 8 in. in diameter. Place this ring around the bottom of the frangipane-filled rounds. Cut small slits all around bottom.

4. Brush surface with egg wash.

5. Cut a swirl design all around the mound with small paring knife.

6. Allow to stand for 30 min.; bake at 375°F. for 20 to 25 min. (If Pithivier becomes too brown, it may be covered with greased brown paper.)

7. Remove from oven when baked. Sprinkle liberally with powdered sugar and return to oven for glazing. (See picture below).

Techniques for Preparing Meringue Desserts

Meringues are made principally from egg whites, sugar and flavoring. The glamorous meringue inspires still another group of exquisite dessert specialties.

A meringue is often thought of as a difficult item to make. However, if the formula (below) is followed closely and the basic rules are applied, no difficulty should be encountered and results should be excellent.

It is very important to make sure that all utensils used are clean and free from grease. There should be no traces of yolk with the egg whites, and no traces of flour must come in contact with the meringue mixture. There are many variations of meringue shells. These are given on the following pages.

Rules for Making Meringues

1. Make sure all utensils are free from fat and flour.
2. Use a minimum of handling.
3. Have oven preheated to desired temperature. Meringues should go into oven at once.
4. It is preferable to use paper lined pans.
5. It is essential that the product be baked dry without browning.

Meringue Shells — Basic Formula

METHOD	INGREDIENTS	LB.	OZ.	COST PER LB.	COST
1. Whip together to a stiff peak.	Egg Whites Granulated Sugar Flavoring (to taste)	1 1			
2. Fold into above mixture, using a minimum amount of motion.	Granulated Sugar	1			
Total Yield: 50 shells					
Scaling Instructions: tube into desired shapes		**Cost Per Oz.**			
Baking Temperature: bake dry (about 1 hr.) at 250°F.		**Cost Per Lb.**			
Remarks: For variation, 4 oz. granulated nuts or chocolate bits or melted chocolate may be folded in.					

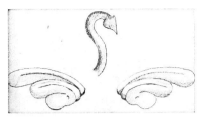

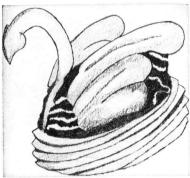

Swans, Baskets, Initials

1. Line a baking sheet with paper. Fit a pastry bag with a plain ¼ in. pastry tube and fill with Meringue mixture (recipe, facing page).

2. Dress out Meringue in the shape of question marks to form heads and necks of swans. (See illustration.)

3. To form the wings make both left and right as shown.

4. For base of swan, use an oval meringue nest (column at far right). Let Meringues dry in oven at 250°F. for about 1 hr. Then fill base with ice cream or pink colored whipped cream. Affix meringue head and wings with chocolate or icing.

5. For baskets, make rings or horseshoe shapes for the handle. As a base for the basket use a round nest (column at far right) filled with whipped cream or ice cream.

6. Initials or numerals may be made and used as decorations for cakes and desserts. After dressing

out initials or numerals, dry in oven at 250°F. for about 30 min.

Meringue Torte

1. Line a baking pan with paper. Trace three circles about 8 in. in diameter each. Fit a pastry bag with a plain round tube and fill with Meringue mixture (recipe, facing page).

2. Spiral the meringue on the paper, outlining and filling in the circles.

3. Dry out in oven at 250°F. for about 1 hr. Cool and remove from paper.

4. To serve, alternate layers of meringues with ice cream, whipped cream, fruit or a combination.

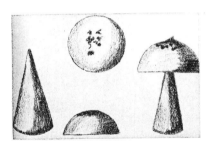

Meringue Mushrooms

1. Line a baking sheet with paper. Fit a pastry bag with a ⅜ in. round tube and fill with Meringue mixture (recipe, facing page).

2. Dress out several stems about 2 in. high. Also dress out an equal number of 1-in. round caps.

3. Sprinkle caps with cocoa powder or cinnamon.

4. Bake at 250°F. for about 30 min. Cool. Affix caps to stems with chocolate icing. Mushrooms may be served as a garnish for ice cream or as a petit four.

Meringue Glacé

1. Line a baking pan with paper.

Fit a pastry bag with a star tube and fill with Meringue mixture (recipe, facing page). Dress out rosettes or ovals.

2. Sprinkle with fine granulated sugar, and follow instructions for Meringue Shells (below).

3. To serve, press a meringue rosette or oval on each side of a scoop of ice cream. Garnish with whipped cream.

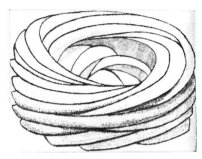

Meringue Nest or Shells

1. Line a baking sheet with paper. Using a pastry bag and a plain ⅜ in. pastry tube filled with Meringue mixture (recipe, facing page), dress out round or oval nests 3 to 4 in. in diameter and about 1 in. high. Space apart on the sheet pan.

2. Sprinkle these shells with fine granulated sugar.

3. Bake at 250°F. for about 1 hr. (Meringues will peel freely from paper when dried out sufficiently. Meringues of this type should dry out without browning.)

4. To serve, fill with fruit, whipped cream or Mousse (p. 400). Garnish with whipped cream or sauce.

Schaum Torte

1. Line a baking pan with paper. Trace four 8-in. circles.

2. Fit a pastry bag with a plain ⅜ in. tube and fill with Meringue mixture (recipe, facing page).

3. Completely cover one circle with meringue using a spiral effect.

4. Outline two of the circles with meringue about 1½ in. wide and 1 in. thick.

5. On the final circle press out a ring of Kisses (p. 410) with a star tube. Each kiss must touch the one next to it. This will form a wreath of Meringue Kisses.

6. Dry in oven at 250°F. for about 1 hr. Cool and remove from paper.

7. Place the solid meringue circle on a cool serving platter.

8. Place the two outlined circles

on top of the solid circle.

9. Fold 1 pt. sliced strawberries which have been soaked in liqueur into 1 pt. heavy cream that has been whipped.

10. Fill the meringue shell with this mixture and place the wreath of Meringue Kisses on top. Garnish with a whole strawberry.

Meringue Pie Shell

1. Butter and flour a pie pan.

2. Fit a pastry bag with a ⅜ in. plain tube and fill with Meringue mixture (p. 408). Starting from the center of pie plate, spiral the meringue all the way to the side and top of pie plate. Make Meringue about ¾ in. thick.

3. Dry out in oven at 250°F. for about 1½ hr. Loosen from paper and cool.

4. There are many interesting and attractive fillings which may be used for this shell. A favorite is a Tart Lemon Filling (p. 420) which contrasts with the sweet meringue.

Meringue Kisses

1. Fit a pastry bag with a star tube; fill with Meringue mixture (p. 408).

2. Dress out small, interesting shapes. (As a variation, fold granulated nuts or chocolate into Me-

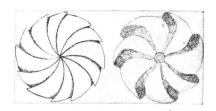

ringue Mixture before dressing out.)

3. Dry in oven at 250°F. for about 25 min.

Meringue Variations

In addition to the variations already described, meringues can be made into many other shapes including: round, oval, boats, hearts, shamrocks, animals and cookies.

Many different fillings may be used. Among the most popular are: whipped cream, ice cream, fruit fillings or Tart Lemon Filling (p. 421).

The Orange Tree

The tree itself is sculptured from ice, and this type of dessert centerpiece is generally referred to as a sockel.

The sockel enables a dessert to be served in a most attractive manner. It is especially effective on a buffet table as it adds height to the display.

The oranges used in this sockel are the Orange Surprise Dessert described on p. 398. Sockels may also be made from rice, bread, cake, farina, etc., and are usually a shaped base serving as an elevation for the dessert.

More information on ice sculpturing may be found in *Ice Carving Made Easy*, by Joseph Amendola.

Basic Pastry Cream

METHOD	INGREDIENTS	LB.	OZ.	COST PER LB.	COST
1. Bring to a boil.	Milk Sugar	1	12 3		
2. Mix together and add to hot milk and sugar, stirring continuously until mixture comes to a boil. Remove from heat.	Sugar Egg Yolks Cake Flour Cornstarch Milk		3 3 1½ 1 4		
3. Stir into above mixture.	Butter Vanilla (to taste)		½		
Total Yield :					
Scaling Instructions	Cost Per Oz.				
Baking Temperature	Cost Per Lb.				

Variations: Chocolate Filling: Add 1½ oz. of melted chocolate to Step 3.
Banana Cream Filling: Slice into filling approximately 1 banana per pie.
Coconut Cream Filling: Add 2 oz. of coconut per pie to mixture. Top with whipped cream.

PASTRY CREAM (Creme Patissiere, also known as Custard Cream)

Pastry cream is a cream which plays an important part in the making of pastry. For this reason it is very important that it should be well made. Smoothness and flavor are of special importance, and therefore great care must be taken during the mixing and boiling process.

Milk should be scalded with ½ of the sugar. The egg yolks must be well beaten with the rest of the sugar, flour and cornstarch, until absolutely smooth. When milk is scalded, a part of the milk should be mixed with the egg mixture and then added to the first mixture and boiled together, stirring continuously with a whip to prevent the cream from burning, and at the same time to insure a thorough mixing and obtaining a smooth cream.

Add the butter when cream is removed from the heat. This is also the time for adding the vanilla or flavoring.

Never allow your sugar and eggs to stand without mixing. If you do, the sugar will curdle the eggs. Small hard lumps will form. . . you will find that it is necessary to strain your mixture before using. In this way you will lose about ¼ of the value of the eggs, and the cream will be grainy instead of smooth. Therefore, it is very important that the sugar and eggs should be mixed immediately.

Pastry Cream should be cooled as fast as possible in a shallow pan (rather than a heavy pot) and refrigerated.

There are four precautions that can be taken to prevent a heavy skin from forming on the top of the cream.

1. Stir the cream occasionally as it cools to prevent a skin from forming.

2. After removing cream from heat, place in a shallow pan to cool and top with small pats of butter. This will melt and form a protective coating.

3. Sprinkle top of the cream with granulated sugar while cooling. This will melt and give a syrupy protective coating.

4. Place waxed paper or cellophane over the top of the cream, cutting some small holes in the paper for steam to escape while cooling.

Most important, always keep refrigerated until use.

Variations

Whipped cream may be folded into cold Pastry Cream for added richness.

Meringue may be folded into hot Pastry Cream for a fluffier, lighter cream.

A small amount of gelatin may be dissolved and mixed with either of the above variations to give more body.

For other variations, chocolate, coffee, fruit or any liqueur can be mixed in.

Apple Strudel Dough (recipe below)

Apple Strudel Dough

METHOD	INGREDIENTS	LB.	OZ.	COST PER LB.	COST
1. Mix into a smooth dough. Shape into a ball and brush with vegetable oil. Let dough relax for ½ hr. Spread dough on a 36 in. by 36 in. cloth and stretch thin and transparent (like tissue paper). This dough will make a 30 in. by 30 in. square.	Bread Flour Pastry Flour Salt Egg (1) Shortening Water		5 3 1/8 1/4 4		
2. Brush entire surface with butter; egg wash bottom.					
3. Spread filling leaving 2 in. on each side. Fold ends under. Roll like jelly roll. Cut in half **and** place on paper lined pan. Brush with butter.	(See recipe on facing page)				
Total Yield: 25 servings					
Scaling Instructions		**Cost Per Oz.**			
Baking Temperature: 400°F. for 45 min.		**Cost Per Lb.**			
Remarks: Serve with whipped cream.					
See color picture, p. 394					

Crepes — Basic Recipe

METHOD	INGREDIENTS	LB.	OZ.	COST PER LB.	COST
1. Mix and blend eggs and water. Add salt.	Whole Eggs (8) Water (1 qt.) Salt	2	½		
2. Gradually add corn-starch and flour. Blend well	Cornstarch (1 cup) Flour (1 cup)		4 4		
3. Add to mixture in Step 2. Blend	Butter, melted		4		

4. Heat an ungreased pan. Ladle in batter, rolling and turning pan so entire surface is thinly covered. Saute without coloring. Turn. Set other side without coloring.

5. Place a small amount of granulated sugar in pan. Allow to caramelize while pressing with back of a spoon. Add 2 pats butter and juice or rind of 1 lemon. Add Crepes. Baste with liquid and fold. De-glaze pan with brandy. Flame. Pour over plated Crepes.

Total Yield: 20 servings

Remarks: A mix of 1 qt. liquid makes about 60 Crepes. To store, cover with waxed paper or foil and refrigerate. If Crepes tend to stick while sauteing, pan may be wiped occasionally with a cloth dipped in melted butter. Use just enough to produce a light coating. This should be done only when absolutely necessary.

Variations

Suzette—Basic orange, flamed with Grand Marnier liqueur and cognac.

Rose-Mary—Basic orange with peach, red cherries; flamed with Curacao.

Cinzano-Kirsch—Basic lemon-orange, flamed with Cinzano and Kirsch.

Cafola—Basic coffee with grated sweet chocolate, flamed with Creme de Cacao and Kahlua (coffee liqueur).

Copacabana—Basic coffee with hazlenut puree, flamed with Kahlua.

Bresilienne—Basic coffee, flamed with Creme de Cacao or Kahlua.

Hawaienne—Basic orange with pineapple cubes.

Georgina—Stuffed with diced pineapple, flamed with Curacao.

Normande—Stuffed with stewed apples, diced, flamed with Calvados.

Napolitaine—Stuffed with a little orange marmalade, flamed with Curacao.

Maltaise—Orange-lemon, flamed with Curacao.

Marcelle—Basic crepe, lightly stuffed with chestnut puree, flamed with Maraschino.

Jeanette—Basic crepe, stuffed with a little hazelnut butter, flamed with Maraschino.

Parisienne—Stuffed with diced Lady Fingers marinated in Curacao, flamed with Maraschino.

Suchard—Basic crepe with chocolate, flamed with Creme de Cacao.

Sicilienne—Basic crepe with lemon, flamed with any fruit liqueur (lemon-flavored if possible).

San Juan—Basic crepe, flamed with rum.

Summertime—Basic crepe; add lemon, orange or any fruit flavored sherbet.

Virgin Islands—Basic crepe, banana and rum.

Apple Filling for Strudel

METHOD	INGREDIENTS	LB.	OZ.	COST PER LB.	COST
1. Melt butter. Add remaining ingredients. Steam. Remove from heat.	Apples, No. 10 can Brown Sugar Butter Cinnamon (1 tsp.) Raisins	7 1	8 8		
2. Add to ingredients in Step 1.	Cake, cubed or diced, toasted		12		

Total Yield: 25 servings

Scaling Instructions	Cost Per Oz.
Baking Temperature	Cost Per Lb.
Remarks: Use with Strudel Leaves	

Torte de Ricotta (of Italian Cheese) (recipe below)

Torte de Riccota (of Italian Cheese)

METHOD	INGREDIENTS	LB.	OZ.	COST PER LB.	COST
1. Rub through fine sieve.	Riccotta Sugar	1	8 4		
2. Mix; add to ingredients in Step 1.	Salt Vanilla (to taste) Citron (diced fine)		1/8 1 1		
3. Add gradually to ingredients above.	Eggs (4) Brandy Toasted Almonds		1 4		
4. Make lattice top and bake.					
5. Dust with confectioner's sugar.					
Total Yield: 8 to 10 servings (1 pie or cake)					
Scaling Instructions: Pour into 8-in. cake pan or 10-in. pie pan lined with cookie dough	**Cost Per Oz.**				
Baking Temperature: 350°F. for about 45 min.	**Cost Per Lb.**				

Rice Imperatrice (recipe below)

Rice Imperatrice

METHOD	INGREDIENTS	LB.	OZ.	COST PER LB.	COST
1. Dissolve gelatin in hot water. Pour ½ in. on bottom of mold to be used. Allow to set.	Water, hot (1 pt.) Raspberry Flavored Gelatin	1	4		
2. Place these ingredients in a pot and simmer for about 10 min. Allow to cool and set.	Blanched (cooked) Rice Milk (1 qt.) Salt Vanilla (to taste) Gelatin, unflavored Sugar	2 2	½ 1 8		
3. Whip cream and fold in with mixture that has been set (Step 2).	Heavy Cream (1 qt.)	2			
4. Fold in with above mixture, (Step 3) and pour into mold or form which has the gelatin on bottom.	Maraschino Cherries chopped		8		
5. Place in refrigerator until set. Unmold by setting forms in warm water and place on serving plates.					
Total Yield: 30 servings					
Scaling Instructions		Cost Per Oz.			
Baking Temperature		Cost Per Lb.			

See color picture, p. 395.

Fruit Conde
(recipe below)

Strawberries a la Ritz (Fraises a la Ritz)
(recipe top of facing page)

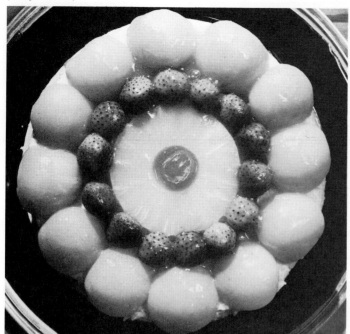

Fruit Conde

METHOD	INGREDIENTS	LB.	OZ.	COST PER LB.	COST
1. Place ingredients in a pot and simmer for about 10 min. Allow to cool and set.	Milk (1 pt.) Blanched Rice Salt Sugar Gelatin, unflavored	1 1	¼ 4 ½		
2. Whip cream and fold into mixture that has been set (Step 1). Add nesselrode mixture. Place this mixture in a large or small Charlotte mold. Refrigerate until mixture is set.	Heavy Cream, whipped (1 pt.) Nesselrode Mixture	1	6		
3. When set, unmold on a dish; place assorted fruit on top of rice mixture. Brush top of fruit with a hot Apricot Sauce and serve.					
Total Yield: 15 servings					
Scaling Instructions	Cost Per Oz.				
Baking Temperature	Cost Per Lb.				
See color picture, p. 395.					

Strawberries a la Ritz (Fraises a la Ritz)

METHOD	INGREDIENTS	LB.	OZ.	COST PER LB.	COST
1. Put well-sugared strawberries in a bowl. Pour the Anisette liqueur over them. Leave in refrigerator for 1 or 2 hr. until well chilled.	Strawberries (1 qt.) Sugar (to sweeten) Anisette (¼ cup)				
2. Blend sugar, flour and eggs together. Slowly dilute with boiling milk and cook for a few minutes. Stir constantly until mixture boils. (This preparation must be smooth.) Let cool.	Flour Sugar Eggs (4) Boiling Milk (1 qt.)	2	3 8		
3. Add well-beaten cream and gently mix in strawberries and juice (Step 1).	Heavy Cream (1 cup)		8		
Total Yield: 8 servings					
Scaling Instructions		Cost Per Oz.			
Baking Temperature		Cost Per Lb.			
Remarks: Add a little red coloring if necessary to give mixture a pink color. A few large strawberries can be arranged as a garnish on top. Serve very cold.					

Fancy Butter Cookies (Spritz)

METHOD	INGREDIENTS	LB.	OZ.	COST PER LB.	COST
1. Rub together.	Almond Paste Confectioner's Sugar	1	8 8		
2. Add eggs gradually to obtain a smooth batter.	Eggs	1			
3. Add and whip until light.	Shortening and Butter	2			
4. Add and mix until smooth. Do not overmix.	Cake Flour	3			
5. Tube out to form various shapes.					
Total Yield: 24 doz. cookies					
Scaling Instructions		Cost Per Oz.			
Baking Temperature: 375°F. for about 10 to 12 min.		Cost Per Lb.			

Desserts

Angel Food Cake (recipe below)

Charlottes (recipe top of facing page)

Angel Food Cake

METHOD	INGREDIENTS	LB.	OZ.	COST PER LB.	COST
1. Beat about 5 min. at high speed	Egg Whites Vanilla (to taste)	2			
2. Blend together. Add gradually to ingredients in Step 1. Beat until mixture forms a wet peak.	Sugar Cream of Tartar Salt	1	¼ ¼		
3. Sift and blend. Add to the ingredients in Step 2 and fold in.	Sugar Cake Flour	1	13		
Total Yield: 48 servings					
Scaling Instructions: Scale about 14 oz. to an 8-in. angel cake pan		**Cost Per Oz.**			
Baking Temperature: 350°F. for 25 min.		**Cost Per Lb.**			
Remarks: Precautions should be taken not to overbeat this mixture and to fold in Step 3 after it is thoroughly mixed. Otherwise these cakes will collapse and the volume will be smaller. Turn the cake upside down after removing from the oven. Allow to cool before removing from the pans.					

Charlottes

Charlotte Russe
1. Trim the required number of Lady Fingers (p. 420) and line the bottom of a plain Charlotte mold with the Lady Fingers.
2. Line the sides of the mold with Lady Fingers.
3. Place Bavarian Cream mixture (see formula p. 420), in the center of the mold. Allow to set in refrigerator.
4. Unmold on a cold dish and decorate with whipped cream. (Charlotte Russe can also be prepared in individual molds or portions.)

VARIATIONS: Charlotte Royale and Strawberry Charlotte (recipes below) are two of the several varieties of Charlottes that can be prepared.

Charlotte Royale
1. Line a round bowl with sliced jelly rolls.
2. Fill with Bavarian Cream mixture (see formula p. 420).
3. Chill in refrigerator.
4. Unmold and decorate with whipped cream.

Strawberry Charlotte
1. Line the bottom of a plain Charlotte mold with strawberry jelly.
2. Line the sides with Lady Fingers (p. 420).
3. Fill the center with a Strawberry Bavarian cream mixture (see formula p. 420).
3. When set, unmold the Charlotte on a cold dish and decorate or garnish with whipped cream and strawberries.

NOTE: Peach, raspberry, apricot or any other fruit can be used in place of strawberry to make other fruit-flavored Charlottes.

See color pictures p. 394.

American Sponge Cake

METHOD	INGREDIENTS	LB.	OZ.	COST PER LB.	COST
1. Place in sheet pan and heat.	Sugar	6			
2. Add to sugar and beat to lemon color for about 10 min. at high speed.	Whole Eggs Egg Yolks Vanilla or Lemon Extract (to taste) Salt	4	8 8 1		
3. Heat until butter is melted.	Milk Butter	2	8 8		
4. Sift together and blend. Fold in with above alternately with milk. Mix as little as possible.	Cake Flour Baking Powder	4	8 2		
Total Yield: 100 servings					
Scaling Instructions:	Cost Per Oz.				
Baking Temperature: 375°F. for 15 to 18 min.	Cost Per Lb.				

Bavarian Creams (recipe below)

Lemon Angel Filling (recipe bottom of facing page)

Bavarian Creams

METHOD	INGREDIENTS	LB.	OZ.	COST PER LB.	COST
1. Heat.	Milk (1 qt.)	2			
2. Beat together. Add to milk (Step 1). Do not boil. Cool.	Egg Yolks (6) Sugar Gelatin, unflavored		8 ½		
3. Whip cream and fold into above mixture (Step 2) after it has cooled and started to thicken.	Heavy Cream, whipped (1 pt.)	1			
4. Place in a mold or cup and allow to set until firm. Unmold and serve with sauce.					
Total Yield: 15 servings					
Scaling Instructions		Cost Per Oz.			
Baking Temperature		Cost Per Lb.			

Lady Fingers

METHOD	INGREDIENTS	LB.	OZ.	COST PER LB.	COST
1. Whip egg whites. Add sugar gradually until a stiff meringue is made.	Egg Whites (16) Sugar Vanilla (to taste)	1 1			
2. Whip and add to stiff meringue. Fold in.	Egg Yolks (16)		10		
3. Sift and fold in.	Bread Flour	1			
Total Yield: 100 Lady Fingers					
Scaling Instructions		Cost Per Oz.			
Baking Temperature: 375°F. to 400°F. for 7 to 8 min.		Cost Per Lb.			

*Linzer Torte or
Slices (recipe below)*

Linzer Torte or Slices

METHOD	INGREDIENTS	LB.	OZ.	COST PER LB.	COST
LINZER DOUGH 1. Cream together.	Butter Sugar	1 1			
2. Add gradually.	Eggs		8		
3. Add and mix into a dough.	Lemon Rind (1) Nutmeg Cinnamon Nut Powder Pastry Flour	 1 3	 1/8 1/8		
3. Refrigerate before rolling.					
Total Yield: 50 servings					
Scaling Instructions	Cost Per Oz.				
Baking Temperature	Cost Per Lb.				

Lemon Angel Filling

METHOD	INGREDIENTS	LB.	OZ.	COST PER LB.	COST
1. Simmer ingredients for 30 minutes. Remove from heat. Cool.	Lemon Juice Egg Yolks (8) Sugar Salt Gelatin		5 6 12 ¼ ¼		
2. Fold into mixture in Step 1.	Heavy Cream, whipped (1 qt.)	2			
3. Fill pie shells with filling.	two 9-in. Meringue Pie Shells (p. 408)				
4. Decorate top of pie with chocolate shavings.	Chocolate Shavings (p. 422)				
Total Yield: for two 9-in. pies					
Scaling Instructions	Cost Per Oz.				
Baking Temperature	Cost Per Lb.				

Desserts

Chocolate Shavings or Curls

METHOD	INGREDIENTS	LB.	OZ.	COST PER LB.	COST	
1. Melt to approximately 100°F. Cool to 85°F.	Chocolate Coating					
2. Spread out on tray or marble slab. Continue cooling until chocolate becomes firm.						
3. Using a small rake (see photo), rake up chocolate into shavings and curls.						
Total Yield:						
Scaling Instructions		Cost Per Oz.				
Baking Temperature		Cost Per Lb.				

Remarks: Chocolate shavings and curls make a very effective garnish for pies, cakes, ice cream, etc.
For **Chocolate Curls**, follow Step 1 above. Then spread a thin coating of the chocolate, about 5 or 6 in. wide, on a marble slab. When this cools and sets, lightly rub top of chocolate with the palm of the hand. Hold a french knife at 45° angle, and cut in 1 in. strips, pushing up and forward so chocolate curls.

Croquembouche

The Croquembouche is an arrangement of filled and carmel coated cream puffs piled up in a pyramid shape. The base for the pyramid may be a circle of nougat or pastry.

To make a Croquembouche, like the one pictured here, first make about 60 1-in. cream puffs. (The number of cream puffs needed will vary depending on the size of the finished Croquembouche.) Cool; fill puffs with Pastry Cream (p. 411).

Prepare a circle of nougat or pastry to serve as the base of the arrangement. (Directions for making nougat below.)

Dip 1 filled cream puff at a time into hot caramel syrup and place in a circle around inside of the nougat or pastry. Place a second circle of puffs on top of the first layer, positioning second row of puffs between those in the first row like this,

oo second layer
ooo first layer.

Continue to build the pyramid, using 6 to 9 layers of puffs and making each circle slightly smaller than the one underneath it.

The ornamental top and the triangle around the bottom in the picture are made of nougat candy. (See below for directions.) The design can be varied.

To Make Nougat: Combine 1 lb. granulated sugar with juice of ¼ lemon; cook syrup in sauce pan until golden brown. Remove from heat and add 12 oz. warm sliced almonds. (Sesame seeds may be substituted for sliced almonds.) Spread mixture on an oiled marble slab, roll out with lightly oiled rolling pin and cut with a lightly oiled knife (or cutters) to desired shapes. To keep nougat from becoming cool while working, place in a warm (250°F.) oven. After cutting into desired shapes, allow to cool and harden.

To hold pieces of nougat in place, use caramelized sugar, dipping the pieces in it, then putting them in place and holding them in position until set. After all pieces of the desired decoration have been assembled, add small dots of royal icing as the finishing touch.

For the Croquembouche that is shown here, the crown was assembled separately, then set on the top of the pyramid before serving. The crown decoration was made of small triangular nougat shapes cut and cooled over a lightly oiled rolling pin. A 4-in. circle and a 2-in. circle were then cut out of the nougat and the triangular pieces were then affixed by the method described above.

Basic
Menus

The following Basic Menus are used for teaching during the student's first year at the Culinary Institute of America. As far as possible, menus have been planned to present an appetizing combination of soup, salad, vegetable and entree. However, greatest emphasis has been placed on selection of items which will give the student the widest experience in preparing a variety of popular dishes. Formulas for all items on the Basic Menus and many of the Related Subjects are given in this book.

SET. NO. 1	RELATED SUBJECTS

Puree of Split Pea Soup aux Croutons (p. *299*)
Chopped Beef Steak Pattie (p. *50*),
   Mushroom Sauce (p. *313*)
Baked Idaho Potato (p. *215*)
Buttered Green Peas (p. *194*)
Lettuce and Tomato Salad (p. *235*),
   Mayonnaise (p. *260*)

    Salisbury Steak, Smothered Onions
    French Fried Onion Rings (p. *179*)
    Baked Individual Meat Loaf

Fresh Vegetable Soup (p. *281*)
Rolled Braised Shoulder of Lamb, Mint Jelly (p. *75*)
Whipped Potato (p. *210*), Sauteed Zucchini (p. *190*)
Hearts of Lettuce (p. *238*) with Thousand Island
   Dressing (p. *260*)

    Roast Stuffed Shoulder of Lamb (p. *69*)

Scotch Broth (p. *284*)
Chicken Fricassee with Buttered Noodles (p. *118*)
Corn on the Cob (p. *202*)
Pineapple and Cottage Cheese Salad (p. *247*)
   French Dressing (p. *258*)

    Lamb Broth, Ecoccaise (p. *284*)
    Curried Chicken with Rice and Chutney (p. *116*)
    Chicken Tetrazzini (p. *129*)

Cream of Chicken Soup (p. *292*)
Baked Stuffed Pork Chop, Glazed Apple (p. *84*)
Delmonico Potatoes (p. *217*)
Buttered Green Beans (p. *198*)
Jellied Fruit Mold (p. *253*), Sour Cream Dressing
   (p. *260*)

    Broiled Pork Chop
    Breaded Pork Chop
    Breaded Pork Tenderloin

New England Clam Chowder (p. *289*)
Broiled Mackerel, Anchovy Butter (p. *153*)
French Fried Potatoes (p. *181*)
Cauliflower au Gratin (p. *200*)
Cole Slaw (p. *240*)

    Mackerel Buena Vista
    Tinker Mackerel

SET NO. 2	RELATED SUBJECTS

Minestrone (p. *281*)
Spaghetti (p. *27*) with Meat Balls (p. *53*)
    Sauce (p. *319*)
Fried Eggplant (p. *203*)
Mixed Green Salad (p. *233*), Mild Garlic
    Dressing (p. *259*)
	Baked Stuffed Green Peppers
	Spaghetti al Burro (with butter)
	Spaghetti Parmesan
	Spaghetti (p. *27*), Milanaise (p. *319*)

Puree of Yellow Split Peas aux Croutons (p. *299*) Ham Steak Hawaiian (p. *82*) Sweet Potato Patties with Coconut (p. *201*) Shredded Cabbage with Celery Seeds (p. *199*) Whipped Black Cherry Gelatin, Minted Cream Cheese (p. *252*)	Broiled Ham Steak, Sherried Peach Half Fried Fingers of Ham, Sweet Pepper Relish Banana Fritters
Cream of Asparagus Soup (p. *295*) Roast Chicken with Giblet Sauce (p. *125*) Potatoes au Gratin (p. *216*) Hubbard Squash (p. *205*) Orange and Grapefruit Salad (*246*), French Dressing (p. *258*)	Boneless Baked Stuffed Chicken, Leg Stuffed Breast of Chicken
Vegetable Soup, Paysanne (p. *281*) Beef Pot Pie with Dumpling (p. *50*) Whole Baby Beets in Orange Sauce (p. *209*) Green Bean and Pimiento Salad (p. *235*), French Dressing (p. *258*)	Individual Beefsteak Pie with Vegetables (p. *45*) Beef Shortcake
New England Fish Chowder (p. *289*) New England Codfish Cakes with Fried Egg (p. *153*) Diced Fresh Carrots and Peas (p. *194*) Baked Macaroni and Cheese (p. *219*) Fruit Slaw (p. *248*)	Codfish Puffs for Hors d'Oeuvre Escalloped Hamburger and Macaroni

SET NO. 3	RELATED SUBJECTS
Puree of Dry Lima Beans (p. *299*)	
Baked Hamburger Loaf (p. *48*)	Baked Vienna Loaf
Mushroom Sauce (p. *313*)	Baked Swedish Meat Cakes
American Fried Potatoes (p. *218*)	Baked Beef and Rice Loaf
Mashed Yellow Turnips (p. *204*)	
Waldorf Salad (p. *248*)	
Consomme Brunoise (p. *272*)	
Chicken Pot Pie (p. *126*)	Chicken Pot Pie with Dumplings (p. *117*)
Hashed Brown Potatoes (p. *215*)	Chicken Tetrazzini (p. *129*)
English Green Peas (p. *194*)	
Pear and Cottage Cheese Salad (p. *248*)	
Chicken Gumbo Creole (p. *283*)	
Breaded Veal Cutlet (p. *96*), Tomato Sauce (p. *318*)	Scallopine of Veal Marsala (p. *99*)
Shells, Parmesan	Various cuts related to veal leg
Whole Kernel Corn (p. *203*)	Macaroni Products (p. *26*)
Avocado-Grapefruit Salad (p. *244*),	
French Dressing (p. *258*)	
Broiled Grapefruit au Sherry (p. *16*)	
Old Fashioned Beef Stew (p. *55*)	Dumpling variations
Cucumber-Lime Salad (p. *250*), Sour Cream Dressing	Potted Beef with Mushrooms
(p. *260*)	
Manhattan Clam Chowder (p. *282*)	
Broiled Salmon Steak (p. *157*), Maitre	
d'Hotel Butter (p. *323*)	Poached Salmon (p. *152*), Egg Sauce (p. *315*)
Boiled Potatoes Parisienne (p. *218*)	Hollandaise Sauce (p. *321*)
Buttered Lima Beans (p. *197*)	Bearnaise Sauce (p. *322*)
Shredded Lettuce (p. *238*), Piquante	
Dressing (p. *261*)	

SET NO. 4	RELATED SUBJECTS
Navy Bean Soup (p. *303*) Roast Round of Beef au Jus (p. *60*) Oven Roast Potatoes (p. *214*) Succotash (p. *203*) Devilled Egg Salad (p. *234*)	Discussion natural gravies Discussion Top Round, Bottom Round and Steamship Round

Cream of Broccoli Soup (p. *295*)
New England Boiled Dinner (p. *59*) or
New York Boiled Dinner (p. *59*) with
   Parsley Potato, Carrots, Beets, Turnips,
   Cabbage, Boiled Onion (Optional)
Mixed Green Salad, Herb Dressing (p. *233*)
	Boiled Beef (p. *151*) with Horseradish
	   Sauce (p. *317*)
	Boiled Corned Brisket (p. *51*)
	Grey Cure vs. Jewish Corned Beef (p. *59*)

English Beef Broth with Barley (p. *274*) Chicken a la King (p. *121*) Potatoes Fondant (p. *213*) Buttered Asparagus (p. *194*) Tomato Aspic Salad (p. *253*)	French Pancakes Stuffed with Creamed Chicken (p. *121*) Brunswick Stew
Consomme Celestine (p. *272*) Pan Fried Hash (p. *58*) with Poached Egg (p. *21*) Buttered Carrots (p. *202*) Cucumber and Onion Salad (p. *243*)	Hash Variations: Roast Beef Hash Corned Beef Hash Red Flannel Hash
Cream of Tomato Soup (p. *294*) Fried Deep Sea Scallops (p. *180*) Tartar Sauce (p. *324*) Julienne Potatoes (p. *210*) Spinach Vinaigrette (p. *197*) Mandarin Orange Waldorf Salad (p. *248*)	Scallops, Saute Broiled Scallops en Brochette Baked Scallops en Coquille

SET NO. 5	RELATED SUBJECTS
Cream of Mixed Vegetable Soup (p. *296*) London Broil (p. *61*), Bordelaise Sauce (p. *312*) Lyonnaise Potatoes (p. *218*) Cauliflower Polonaise (p. *200*) Banana Nut Salad (p. *245*)	Braised Beef Flank, Jardiniere
Cream of Spinach Soup (p. *295*) Boiled Corned Spareribs (p. *83*) or Barbecued Fresh Spareribs (p. *82*) Potato Gnocchi (p. *217*) Sauerkraut (p. *194*) Salad Alma (p. *246*)	Sweet and Sour Spareribs Gnocchi variations (p. *217*)
Fresh Fruit Cup (p. *17*) Chicken Chow Mein with Chinese Vegetables (p. *123*) Garden Salad (p. *237*), Emulsified French Dressing (p. *258*)	Chicken Chop Suey, Steamed Rice Subgum Chop Suey Chinese Vegetables

Chicken Consomme (p. *272*)
Lamb Chop Mixed Grill (p. *77*)
   (Calves Liver, Sausage Link, Bacon Strip,
   Baked Tomato, Mushroom Cap)
Potato Croquette (p. *211*)
Blackstone Salad (p. *245*)
	Preparing Liver for Service
	Blanching Bacon (p. *23*)
	Baked Little Link Sausage

Corn Chowder, Maryland (p. *292*) Baked Stuffed Shore Haddock, Creole Sauce (p. *150*) Duchesse Potatoes (p. *212*) Lima Beans, Forestiere (p. *196*) Chiffonade Salad (p. *240*)	Fillet of Haddock, Meuniere (p. *158*) Fried Haddock, Cape Style Baked Haddock, Cheese Sauce

SET NO. 6	RELATED SUBJECTS
Puree Mongole (p. *302*) Boiled Picnic Shoulder with Cabbage (p. *85*) Boiled Pork Shoulder with Spinach (p. *85*) Small Whole Boiled Potatoes (p. *218*) Stuffed Celery (p. *240*)	Roast Boneless Pork Shoulder Beet Greens (p. *199*)
French Onion Soup au Crouton (p. *275*) Irish Lamb Stew No. 1 (p. *70*) Arabian Peach Mold (p. *251*)	Lamb Patties (p. *75*) Fricassee of Lamb
Puree of Lentils (p. *299*) Roast Duckling a l'Orange (p. *115*) Candied Sweet Potatoes (p. *193*) Pearl Onions (p. *198*) Belgian Endive (p. *239*), Blue Cheese Dressing (p. *259*)	Salmis of Duckling, Brown Rice (p. *115*) Apple, Celery and White Rice Stuffing Prune and Rice Stuffing
Duck Soup, Parisienne (p. *279*) Roast Loin of Pork, Applesauce (p. *83*) Potatoes Hashed in Cream (p. *211*) Buttered Kale (p. *199*) Mixed Green Salad (p. *233*), Green Goddess Dressing (p. *262*)	Braised Pork Tenderloin, Sauce Robert (p. *312*) Roast Boneless Pork Loin (p. *83*)
Cream of Mushroom Soup (p. *293*) Fried Fillet of Sole, Tartare (p. *150*) Cottage Fried Potatoes (p. *218*) Corn Mexicane (p. *201*) Pickled Beet Salad (p. *237*)	Poached Fillet of Flounder, Cardinal Sauce Fillet of Sole, Veronique

SET NO. 7	RELATED SUBJECTS
Puree of Black Bean Soup (p. *300*) Broiled Hip Steak or Rump Steak (p. *52*), 　French Fried Onion Rings (p. *179*) Potatoes O'Brien (p. *217*) Swiss Chard (p. *199*) Tomato and Cucumber Salad (p. *242*), Herb 　Dressing (p. *233*)	Breakdown of Hip: First Steak Cuts Second Steak Cuts Swiss Steaks
Consomme Florentine (p. *272*) Veal Cutlet, Holstein (p. *100*) Rotini (p. *26*), Milanaise (p. *319*) Italian Green Beans (p. *198*) Lime Pear Aspic (p. *250*)	Wiener Schnitzel
Seafood Cocktail (p. *16*) Cream of Asparagus Soup (p. *295*) Vegetable Plate with Poached Egg (p. *209*) Perfection Salad (p. *252*)	Vegetable Plate Variations
Philadelphia Pepperpot Soup (p. *288*) Hungarian Veal Goulash (p. *95*) with 　Spaetzli (p. *288*) Brussels Sprouts (p. *198*) Danish Cucumber Salad (p. *236*)	Brown Veal Stew Fricassee of Veal (p. *95*)
Creme Bagration (p. *296*) Seafood Newburg in Pattie Shell (p. *167*) Shoestring Potatoes (p. *210*) French Green Peas (p. *197*) Diplomat Salad (p. *247*)	En Casserole, Toast Points, Toast Cups, Seafood Pie with Potato Chip Topping

SET NO. 8	RELATED SUBJECTS
Puree of Fresh Green Peas (p. *299*)	
Roast Tender Ham (p. *86*), Raisin Sauce (p. *324*)	Cumberland Sauce (p. *324*)
Sweet Potato Croquettes (p. *206*)	Champagne Sauce
Green Bean Panache (p. *199*)	Cider Sauce (p. *313*)
Fresh Fruit Chantilly (p. *245*)	

Oxtail Soup a l'Anglaise (p. *306*)
Roast Young Tom Turkey, Giblet Gravy (p. *120*)   Braised Turkey Wings
Whipped Potato (p. *210*)   Braised Giblets with Vegetables
Butternut Squash (p. *202*)
Salad Del Monte (p. *233*)

Turkey Creole Soup (p. *284*)   Plain Omelette
Omelette Variations (p. *22*)   Spanish Omelette (p. *319*)
Potatoes Lorette (p. *214*)   Ham or Bacon Omelette
Creamed Peas and Celery (p. *199*)   Fresh Tomato Omelette
Stuffed Prune Salad (p. *246*)   Souffle

Mulligatawny Soup (p. *293*)
Turkey Croquettes (p. *127*)   Turkey Turnover
    Supreme Sauce (p. *317*) or Ham Croquettes   Ham Cutlet
    (p. *87*), Cream Sauce (p. *314*)
Potatoes Hongroise (p. *213*)
Macedoine of Vegetables (p. *209*)
Chinese Cabbage (p. *233*), French Dressing (p. *258*)

Shrimp Bisque (p. *298*)
Broiled Swordfish Steak Maitre d'Hotel (p. *152*)   Baked Swordfish, Creole Sauce
French Fried Potatoes (p. *181*)   Fried Fingers of Swordfish, Tartare
Carrots Vichy (p. *202*)
Cole Slaw Souffle (p. *255*)

SET NO. 9	RELATED SUBJECTS
Potato and Leek Puree (p. 300) Saute Tenderloin Tips with Fresh Mushrooms in Sauce (p. 47) Potato Puffs (p. 211) Spinach Timbales (p. 195) Kidney Bean Salad (p. 242)	Filet Mignon Open Tenderloin Steak Sandwich Larded Tenderloin of Beef
Antipasto (p. 235) Braised Shortribs of Beef (p. 44) Rissole Potatoes (p. 216) Scalloped Eggplant and Tomatoes (p. 204) Carrot and Raisin Salad (p. 237)	Boiled Shortribs Relation to Rib
Creme Monaco (p. 296) Avocado Stuffed with Crabmeat Salad (p. 239) or Tomato Stuffed with Tuna Salad (p. 243) Saratoga Chips (p. 182) Green Peas Forestiere (p. 196) Ginger Ale Salad (p. 251)	Stuffed Avocado, Neptune Crab Louis

Borscht (p. 286)
German Sauerbraten No. 1 (p. 64) with
    Potato Pancakes (p. 212)
Braised Red Cabbage (p. 206)
Garden Salad (p. 237), Olive French
    Dressing (p. 259)
	Borscht Variations (p. 287)

Potato Chowder (p. 290)
Assorted Seafood Platter (p. 165)
Tomato Rice Pilaf (p. 208)
Broccoli, Hollandaise (p. 195)
Mixed Cabbage Slaw (p. 240)
	Fisherman's Platter, sometimes called
	    Seafood Combination Plate; contains
	    Scallops, Clams, Sole, Shrimp, Crabcakes

SET NO. 10	RELATED SUBJECTS
Dutch Potato Soup (p. *282*) Swiss Steak, Jardiniere (p. *55*) Theresa Potatoes (p. *212*) Corn O'Brien (p. *201*) Tomato Andalouse Salad (p. *236*)	Swiss Steak in Tomato Sauce (p. *56*) Potted Swiss Steak, Smothered Onions (p. *63*)
Vegetable Soup, Fermiere (p. *281*) Yankee Pot Roast of Beef (p. *47*) Oven Roast Potatoes (p. *214*) Potato Pancakes (p. *212*) Acorn Squash (p. *205*) Sunset Salad (p. *255*), Cream Dressing (p. *260*)	Boiled Fresh Beef (p. *51*), Mustard Sauce (p. *315*) Braised Beef, Jardiniere
Seafood Chowder (p. *290*) Summer Fresh Fruit Salad Bowl (p. *244*) Vegetable Salad a la Russe (p. *242*)	Salad Variations: Fresh Fruit Salad with Sherbet Fresh Fruit Salad Bowl Fruit Salad with Cottage Cheese
Little Neck Clams (p. *162*) French Lamb Stew (Navarin of Spring Lamb) (p. *73*) Rice Pilaf (p. *208*) Jellied Bing Cherry Salad (p. *251*)	Curry of Lamb with Rice and Chutney (p. *72*)
Oysters on the Half Shell (p. *163*) Broiled Halibut Steak (p. *155*), Maitre d'Hotel Butter (p. *323*) Rice Croquettes (p. *183*) Stewed Tomatoes (p. *207*) Hot German Slaw (p. *241*)	Baked Halibut au Gratin Baked Halibut Casserole en Bordure Baked Halibut with Lobster Newburg Sauce

SET NO. 11	**RELATED SUBJECTS**

Barley and Mushroom Soup (p. *286*)
Grilled Minute Sirloin Steak (p. *49*)
Baked Stuffed Potato (p. *216*)
Green Peas with Tiny Pearl Onions (p. *197*)
Caesar Salad (p. *232*)

Relation to Rib and Hind Quarter
Accompanying Sauces: Bearnaise (p. *322*), etc.

Shrimp Cocktail (p. *16*)
Roast Leg of Lamb, Mint Jelly (p. *76*)
Boulangere Potatoes (p. *76*)
Glazed Yellow Turnip with Peas (p. *204*)
Macaroni and Ham Salad (p. *239*)

Boneless Lamb Leg
Preparation of Leg for:
Shashlik
Shish Kebab (p. *70*)

Jellied Beef Consomme (p. *273*)
Chicken Cacciatore (p. *122*)
Risi Bisi (p. *208*)
Horticultural Beans with Onion (p. *196*)
Molded Spring Vegetable Salad (p. *253*)

Broiled Half Chicken (p. *125*)
Arroz con Pollo (p. *119*)
Pollo a la Valenciana

Tomato Bouillon with Rice (p. *276*)
Roast Rib of Beef au Jus (p. *57*)
Yorkshire Pudding (p. *57*)
Franconia Potatoes (p. 214)
Cauliflower, Polonaise (p. *200*)
Pineapple-Raisin Waldorf (p. *247*)

Boneless Rib
Rib Eye
Steaks

Oyster Bisque (p. *298*)
Brook Trout, Meuniere (p. *157*)
Corn Fritters (p. *180*)
Summer Squash (p. *203*)
Peach and Raspberry Mold (p. *252*)

Broiled Brook Trout
Pan Fried Brook Trout
Escalloped Oysters

SET NO. 12	RELATED SUBJECTS
Cream of Onion Soup (p. 295) Ragout of Beef, Francaise (p. 59) Kartoffelklosse (p. 215) Garden Salad (p. 237)	Casserole of Potted Beef, Family Style Smothered Beef and Onions
Olla Podrida (p. 287) Cold Boiled Turkey with Potato Salad (p. 239) Baked Zucchini (p. 193) Jellied Salad Rubanne (p. 250), Sour Cream Dressing (p.260)	Turkey Club Sandwich, Potato Chips, Pickles Fresh Turkey Salad in Lettuce Cup, Tomato Wedges
Jellied Consomme Madrilene (p. 273) Breast of Chicken, Eugenie (p. 131) or Chicken Maryland (p. 117), Corn Fritter (p. 180) Scalloped Potatoes (p. 213) Green Beans, Amandine (p. 198) Cottage Cheese Jubilee Salad (p. 244), Honey Lemon Dressing (p. 257)	Breast of Chicken, Virginienne Sous-Cloche Boneless Stuffed Chicken Leg
Consomme Royale (p. 272) Roulade of Beef (p. 53) Hot German Potato Salad (p. 241) Braised Celery (p. 196) Bing Cherry and Pear Salad (p. 249)	Roulade Variations: Breakdown of Bottom Round Preparation of Beef for Roulades
Vichyssoise (p. 301) Lobster Variations (pp. 165, 168, 169) Cheese Potato Puffs (p. 211) Mikado Salad (p. 233)	Background Lobster Broiled, Baked Stuffed, Thermidor, Hot and Cold Boiled

Advanced Menus

The following menus are used for teaching during the student's second year at the Culinary Institute of America. Formulas for all soups and entrees, as well as many of the salads and vegetables, (see Basic Menus, pp. 423 to 434) are given in this book.

SET NO. 1

Vegetable Soup, Brunoise (p. 281)
Broiled Chopped Beef Steak (p. 50)
   Bordelaise Sauce (p. 312)
Baked Idaho Potatoes
Green Peas
Hearts of Lettuce, Thousand Island
   Dressing

Chicken Broth, Egg Drops (p. 279)
Breaded Veal Cutlet, Saute Gruyere
   (p. 96)
Rotelle Macaroni, Milanaise
Green Beans, au Beurre
Grapefruit and Orange Salad,
   Maraschino

Cream of Spinach Soup (p. 295)
Broiled Spring Chicken (p. 125)
Potatoes au Gratin
Corn on the Cob
Cucumber and Onion Salad, Vinegar
   Dressing

Stuffed Egg and Celery with Blue
   Cheese (p. 240)
Boiled Beef Dinner (p. 59)
Jellied Fruit Mold

New England Clam Chowder (p. 289)
Boiled Halibut with Maitre d'Hotel
   Butter or Tarragon Butter
French Fried Potatoes
Cole Slaw

SET NO. 2

Puree of Green Split Pea Soup
   (p. 299)
Baked Spanish Meat Loaf (p. 48)
Oven Roast Potatoes
Cauliflower au Gratin
Mixed Greens, Chiffonade Dressing

Gaspacho (p. 302)
Veal Chops, Saute Italienne (p. 98)

Noodles, Parmesan
Peas, Forestiere
Panama Salad

Cream of Asparagus Soup (p. 295)
Braised Shoulder of Lamb, Bretonne
   (p. 74)
Shredded Lettuce, Green Goddess
   Dressing

Lamb Broth, Ecoccaise (p. 284)
Roast Young Tom Turkey, Giblet Gravy
   (p. 120)
Whipped Potatoes
Buttered Squash
Pear and Cottage Cheese Salad,
   Princess Dressing

Vichyssoise (p. 302)
Salmon Variation (pp. 152, 157)
Rice Croquettes (p. 183)
Buttered Baby Limas
Perfection Salad

SET NO. 3

Beef Gumbo Creole Soup (p. 283)
Boneless Roast Loin of Pork (p. 83)
Franconia Potatoes
Zucchini au Beurre
Melba Salad

Broiled Grapefruit (p. 16)
Irish Lamb Stew No. 3 (p. 71)
Doctor Salad

Consomme St. Germaine (p. 272)
Roast Young Duckling, Bigarade (a
   l'Orange) (p. 115)
Potatoes Brabant
Buttered Broccoli
Tossed Salad, French Dressing

Polish Borscht (p. 287)
Braised Short Ribs of Beef (p. 44)
Parsley Pearl Potatoes
Peas and Carrots

Fruit Salad in Aspic

Cream of Mushroom Soup (p. 293)
Fisherman's Plate, Tartar Sauce
   (p. 165)
Potatoes Julienne
Baked Tomato Parmesan
Caesar Salad

SET NO. 4

Petite Marmite (p. 278)
Shish Kebab (p. 70)
Rice Pilaf
Diplomat Salad

Potage Parmentier (p. 300)
Baked Ham, Cider Sauce (p. 84)
Scalloped Apples
Buttered Spinach
Fresh Vegetable Salad

Potage Faubonne (p. 301)
Chickenburgers (p. 127), Sauce
   Chateau (p. 313)
Potatoes O'Brien
Buttered Cauliflower
Caprice Salad

Chilled Fruit Cup (p. 17)
Beef Rouladen in Burgundy Sauce
   (p. 45)
Potato Fondante
Fresh Beet Greens
Tomato Aspic with Julienne of Celery

Long Island Clam Chowder (p. 282)
Baked Smoked Cod (p. 151) with
   Border of Duchesse Potatoes
Green Beans au Beurre
Pickled Beet Salad

SET NO. 5

Puree of Yellow Split Pea aux Croutons
   (p. 299)
London Broil (p. 61),

Advanced Menus

Bordelaise Sauce (p. 312)
Delmonico Potatoes
Buttered Fresh Carrots
Grapefruit and Cheese Salad

Potage Garbure (p. 301)
Pork Chop, Fermiere (p. 85)
Potatoes Parisienne
Cottage Cheese Jubilee Salad

Minestrone Soup (p. 281)
Chicken Chasseur (p. 124)
Potatoes Croquette
French Green Beans
Cucumber and Pineapple Gelatin Salad

Consomme Florentine (p. 272)
Braised Round of Beef, Jardiniere
  (p. 47)
Whipped Potatoes
Brussels Sprouts
Salad Alice

Cream of Tomato Soup (p. 294)
Fillet de Sole Marguery (p. 149)
Pomme de Terre Nature
Spinach Timbale
Mexican Cole Slaw

SET NO. 6

Rice Soup, Florentine (p. 285)
Calves Liver, Saute (p. 97)
Scalloped Potatoes
Fried Eggplant
Beatrice Salad

Bavarian Lentil Soup (p. 303)
Holstein Schnitzel (p. 100)
Noodles Gratinee
Harvard Beets
French Endive, Mild Garlic Dressing

Vegetable Soup, Fermiere (p. 281)
Chicken Tetrazzini (p. 129)
Tossed Salad

Duchess Soup (p. 294)
Roast Rib of Beef, au Jus (p. 57)
Yorkshire Pudding
Rissole Potatoes
Mashed Hubbard Squash
Heart of Palm, French Dressing

Cream of Celery Soup (p. 295)
Fillet of Haddock, Meuniere (p. 158)
Long Branch Potatoes
Scalloped Tomatoes
Peach and Cottage Cheese Salad,
  Fruit French Dressing

SET NO. 7

Dutch Potato Soup (p. 282)
Scallopine of Veal Marsala (p. 99)
Spaghetti al Burro
Deep Fried Zucchini
Lettuce and Tomato Salad

Mock Turtle Soup (p. 306)
Argentine Lamb Chops (p. 74)
Theresa Potatoes
Corn O'Brien
Salad Jeanette

Baked Grapefruit au Rum (p. 16)
Chicken a la King (p. 121)
Baked Rice
Cardinal Salad

Philadelphia Pepperpot Soup
  (p. 288)
Braised Beef a la Mode, Parisienne
  (p. 62)
Chinese Cabbage, Roquefort Dressing

Corn Chowder, Maryland (p. 292)
Baked Oyster Variations (p. 164)
Saratoga Chips
Whole Beets in Orange Sauce
Jellied Waldorf Salad

SET NO. 8

Canadian Pea Soup (p. 304)
Roast Leg of Lamb, Boulangere
  (p. 76)
Broccoli, Polonaise
Chiffonade Salad

Beef Broth with Barley (p. 274)
Chicken Pot Pie with Tender Crust
  (p. 126)
Cranberry Gelatin Salad

Chicken Broth with Rice (p. 279)
Swiss Steak in Sour Cream (p. 51)
Potato Puffs
Baked Eggplant
Knickerbocker Salad

Consomme Royale (p. 272)
Gulyas (Hungarian Goulash,(p. 95)
Potatoe Pancake
Ideal Salad, Sour Cream Dressing

Clam Broth (p. 280)
Lobster Newburg, Classical (p. 166)
Cottage Fried Potatoes
Peas, Paysanne
Molded Spring Vegetable Salad

SET NO. 9

Cream of Vegetable Soup (p. 296)
Roast Top Round of Beef, au Jus
  (p. 60)
Gnocchi Piemontaise
Green Beans
Pineapple and Cream Cheese Salad

Consomme Tosca (p. 272)
Navarin of Spring Lamb (p. 73)
Mixed Garden Salad, Herb Dressing

Barley and Mushroom Soup (p. 286)
Estouffade of Duckling (p. 133)
Baked Stuffed Potato
Corn Mexicane
Blackstone Salad

Potage Mulligatawny (p. 293)
Pizzaola Sauce with Shrimp
  (p. 168)
Mixed Garden Vegetables
Melon in Season

Oyster Stew (p. 290)
Crab Cake Maryland (p. 170)
Hashed in Cream Potatoes
Glazed Carrots and Onions
Salad Romaine

SET NO. 10

Potage Garbure (p. 301)
Beef a la Deutsch (p. 49)
Cheese-Potato Croquette
Cauliflower Polonaise
Fruit Cup

Cold Fruit Soup (p. 308)
Fricassee of Turkey Wings (p. 118)
Whipped Potato
Green Peas and Corn Panache
Devilled Egg Salad

Consomme Printaniere (p. 272)
Entrecote Bercy (p. 58)
Buttered Asparagus
Chilled Stuffed Tomato, Julienne
  of Celery

Potage Potiron (p. 302)
Roast Native Capon, Chestnut Stuffing
  (p. 129)
Glazed Yams
Braised Celery
Whipped Raspberry Gelatin with
  Minted Cream Cheese

Clam Broth (p. 280)

Baked Cod, Bella Vista (p. 149)
French Fried Potatoes
Creamed Mixed Vegetables
Orange Ambrosia

SET NO. 11

Cream of Celery aux Croutons
(p. 295)
Broiled Hip Steak, Bordelaise (p. 52)
American Fried Potatoes
Braised Spinach
Health Salad

Beef Consomme with Noodles
(p. 272)
Breast of Chicken, Hongroise
(p. 122)
Sweet Potato Croquettes
Buttered Asparagus
Lorenzo Salad

Consomme Madrilene (p. 273)
Creamed Lamb a l'Indienne (p. 69)
Baked White Rice
Swiss Chard
Jellied Grapefruit and Celery Salad

Navy Bean Soup (p. 303)
Veal Paprika with Sauerkraut (p. 100)
Spaetzli Saute
Carrot and Raisin Salad

New England Fish Chowder (p. 289)
Fillet of Flounder, McBain (p. 156)
Timbale of Elbow Macaroni
Fried Julienne of Eggplant
Mixed Cabbage Slaw

SET NO. 12

Potage Basque (p. 285)
Baked Stuffed Spareribs (p. 86)
Gnocchi Romaine
Braised Lettuce
Jellied Orange Cole Slaw

Consomme du Barry (p. 272)
Arroz con Pollo (p. 119)
Julienne Buttered Beets
Mixed Garden Salad

Cream of Chicken Soup (p. 292)
Sweet and Sour Stuffed Cabbage
(p. 54)
Potatoes Anna
Green Beans with Pimientos
Hawaiian Salad

Potage Parisienne (p. 285)
Turkey Mushroom Pie with
Cornbread Topping (p. 124)

Asparagus Vinaigrette
Fruit Salad

Chilled Fruit Cup (p. 17)
Dumpling of Pike, Venetian Sauce
(p. 151) or Gefilte Fish
Baked Rice a la Grecque
Lima Bean Panache
Hearts of Lettuce, Russian Dressing

SET NO. 13

Chicken Gumbo Creole (p. 283)
Tournedos Rossini (p. 63)
Potatoes Victoria
Brussels Sprouts, Forestiere
Marinated Tomato and Cucumber
Salad

Creme Monaco (p. 296)
Poulet Roti Farci (p. 130)
Candied Sweet Potato
Glazed Pearl Onions with Peas
St. Regis Salad

Cock-A-Leekie (p. 283)
Welsh Rarebit (p. 308)
Omelette Variations
Corn Fritter
Asparagus Polonaise
Macaroni Salad with Julienne of Ham
and Green Pepper

Tomato Bouillon with Rice (p. 276)
Sauerbraten No. 2 (p. 65)
Potato Latkes
Braised Red Cabbage
Stuffed Celery

Vegetable-Tomato Chowder (p. 291)
Shrimp and Rice, Louisiana Style
(p. 166)
New Peas
Tropical Salad

SET NO. 14

Cream of Almond Soup (p. 297)
Minute Sirloin Steak, Maitre d'Hotel
(p. 49)
Potato Pascal
Spinach, Country Style
Hearts of Lettuce, Blue Cheese
Dressing

Jellied Beef Consomme (p. 272)
Chicken Marengo (p. 119)
Potatoes Olivette
Buttered Green Beans
Candlestick Salad

Beef Soup with Farina Dumplings

(p. 274)
Bacon or Ham and Eggs, Country Style
(pp. 21, 23)
Cottage Fried Potatoes
Zucchini and Yellow Summer Squash
Medley
Indian Salad

Cream of Asparagus Soup (p. 295)
Chicken Stew, Family Style (p. 123)
Fedora Salad

Washington Chowder (p. 291)
Fillet of Sole Bonne Femme (p. 154)
Gnocchi Parisienne
Cole Slaw Mexicaine

SET NO. 15

Creme Bagration (p. 296)
Osso Bucco (p. 101)
Lyonnaise Potatoes
Buttered Spinach
Salad Bretonne

Old Fashioned Cabbage Soup
(p. 286)
Poulet a la Kiev (p. 126)
Sweet Potato Puff
Broccoli Hollandaise
Pineapple and Carrot Salad

Chicken Noodle Soup (p. 278)
Epigramme of Lamb (p. 73)
Potatoes O'Brien
Asparagus, Mornay
Jellied Fruit Salad

Essence of Celery, Celestine (p. 276)
Blanquette of Veal a l'Ancienne
(p. 97)
Pommes Saute
Corn Saute au Paprika
Long Island Salad

Cider Shrub (p. 16)
Coquilles St. Jacques, Mornay
(p. 161)
Souffle Potatoes
French Green Peas
Lettuce and Asparagus Salad

SET NO. 16

Chicken Broth with Parsley Dumplings
(p. 279)
Beef Stroganoff (p. 46)
Home-made Noodles
Kidney Bean Salad

Jellied Tomato Soup (p. 307)
Braised Oxtails Jardiniere (p. 61)

Whipped Potatoes
Braised Savoy Cabbage
Waldorf Salad

Oxtail Soup Anglaise (p. 306)
Coq-au-Vin Champenois (p. 101)
Baked Brown Rice
Baby Lima Beans au Beurre
Spring Garden Salad

Cream of Cauliflower (p. 295)
Frog Legs, Provencale (p. 154)
Polenta
Baked Acorn Squash
Jellied Salad Rubanne

Bouillabaisse Marseillaise (p. 305)
Whitefish, Variations (p. 158)
Potatoes, Jackson
Stewed Tomatoes
German Cole Slaw

SET NO. 17

Cream of Onion Soup (p. 295)
Roast Sirloin of Beef au Jus (p. 56)
German Fried Potatoes
Green Beans Nicoise
Lorraine Salad

Chicken Gumbo Creole (p. 283)
Rock Cornish Game Hen Variations
   (pp. 128, 130)
Wild Rice
Mixed Green Vegetable Compote
Celery Salad

Little Neck Clams, Cocktail Sauce
   (p. 162)
Sweetbread Variations (p. 91)
Rice Valencienne
Carrot Timbale
Banana Nut Salad

Le Pot au Feu (p. 277)
Orange Waldorf Salad

Oysters on the Half Shell (p. 162)
Baked Fillet of Sole en Papillote
   (p. 147)
Minute Potatoes
Buttered Summer Squash
Chatelaine Salad

SET NO. 18

Peanut Butter Soup (p. 297)
Beef Tenderloin Wellington and
   Variations (p. 52)

Minted Green Peas
Carrots Vichy
Fruit Slaw

Clear Green Turtle Soup,
   Cheese Straws (p. 280)
Chicken Saute a la Pierre (p. 134)
Potatoes Lorette
Buttered Peas
Salad Alma

Boula Boula (p. 299)
Chef's Salad with Julienne of Turkey,
   Ham and Swiss Cheese (p. 234)
Swiss Salad Bowl
Potatoes Alumette

Knickerbocker Bean Soup (p. 304)
Boneless Stuffed Chicken with Rice
   (p. 135)
Fresh Vegetable Garniture
Lettuce and Asparagus Salad

Chilled Tea-House Orange Soup
   (p. 308)
Lobster Variations (p. 169)
Choice of Allumette, Julienne,
   French Fried or Gaufrette Potatoes
Asparagus, Butter Aspic
Cucumber Lime Aspic

Spices, Herbs, Seasonings

Name	Description and Source	Uses
Allspice	Dried berry of pimento (not pimiento) tree, grown in West Indies. Flavor resembles blend of cinnamon, nutmeg and cloves, hence the name.	Used whole in pickling, stews, soups, preserved fruit, boiling fish, spicing meat and gravy. Ground allspice is used to season pot roasts, baked goods, apple butter, conserves, catsup, mincemeat.
Anise	Dried seed of plant belonging to celery family. From Spain, Netherlands, Mexico	Sprinkled on coffee cake, sweet rolls, cookies; in sweet pickles; flavoring cough syrups, licorice products, some candies, in chocolate cake icing, in anisette liqueur.
Apple Pie Spice	Predominantly cinnamon but also cloves, nutmeg and other sweet spices.	Use in any food in which cinnamon or nutmeg might be used effectively.
Barbecue Spice (or Seasoning)	Paprika and such other seasonings as chili powder, garlic and cloves, with salt and sugar.	Basic seasoning for marinades and basting sauces, also in meat casseroles, egg and cheese dishes, dressings.
Basil Leaves (or Sweet Basil)	Belongs to mint family; one of the best known of herbs. Grown in Europe and U.S.	Famous in tomato dishes; bean, mock turtle and potato soups; good in potato, spaghetti, egg dishes, steaks, salads, venison, wild duck.
Bay Leaves	Dried leaves of edible laurel. From Turkey and Portugal.	Famous in pickled beets, stocks, stews, gravies, relishes, spiced vinegar or marinades, in meats, as sauerbraten, etc.
Bell Pepper Flakes (or Sweet Pepper)	Dehydrated from sweet green and red peppers.	In salads, sauces, soups, stews, sandwich fillings, Spanish rice, creoles.
Caraway Seed	Dried pungent seeds from herb of the carrot family. From Holland and Poland.	In rye bread, baked goods, kraut, cabbage, potatoes, roast pork, goose, cheese, cake, cookies, in Aquavit, a Scandinavian liquor.
Capers	Low growing shrub of the Mediterranean. Green flower buds and young berries of shrub are pickled.	In fish, chicken, potato, green salad. Sauces for fish, lamb, mutton, heart, cold tongue, and as garnish.
Cardamom Seed	Belongs to ginger family. Seeds enclosed in small pod. Seed and pod may be ground together, or only seeds are ground. Put seeds between folds of muslin and pound to powder. From Guatamala and India.	Seeds in pod used in pickling; ground cardamom adds delectable flavor to Danish pastry, coffee cake, fancy rolls. Bruised seeds in coffee are delicious.
Cassia Bark	From cassia tree. Grown in Malaya, China. Resembles cinnamon flavor. Called Chinese cinnamon.	For pickling, preserving. Ground in combination with allspice, nutmeg, clove. Used in mincemeat.
Cassia Buds	Dry unripe fruit of cassia tree.	Pleasing sweet pickling spice.
Cayenne (See Red Pepper)		

This chart was prepared by the Culinary Institute of America; some of the basic data was adapted from material supplied by the American Spice Trade Assn., New York City.

Name	Description and Source	Uses
Celery Flakes	Dehydrated from vegetable celery.	In soups, cream sauces, salads, dips, stuffings, dressings.
Celery Seed (also Salt)	Pungent seed from plant botanically different from garden celery. From India.	Croquette mixtures, stews, slaw, potato salad, salad dressing, pickles, cheese, fish, meat spreads, in stocks and consomme.
Chervil Leaves	Aromatic herb of carrot family, like parsley but more delicate.	Salads, soups, egg and cheese dishes; as a garnish for cold buffet food items.
Chili Peppers	A fine satiny surfaced red pepper. Grown in Mexico and Southwest U. S.	Used to make chili powders for chili con carne, tamales, pickles, cooking dried beans. Both green and ripe peppers pickled and used to make hot sauces.
Chili Powder	A blend of chili peppers, cumin seed, oregano, garlic powder, salt, etc.	Most widely used in chili con carne. Also used in cocktail sauces, gravies, stews, appetizers.
Chives	Grows indoors or outdoors from small onion-like bulbs. Has mild, onion-like flavor. Also available freeze dried.	Adds color and flavor to cottage and cream cheese, egg and potato dishes, soups, salads, dips.
Cinnamon	Bark from various trees of the cinnamon family varying in color from tan to reddish brown.	To flavor pickles, preserves, fruits, hot drinks and for after-dinner coffee. Ground cinnamon used in baked goods, puddings, cake, mincemeat.
Cinnamon Sugar	Blend of ground cinnamon and sugar.	For sprinkling on buttered toast, upper crusts of fruit pies, baked apples, sugar cookies.
Cloves	Nail-shaped dried flower bud of the clove tree. Rich and pungent in flavor. From Madagascar, Tanzania, Indonesia.	Whole cloves in baked ham, stocks, pickling and drinks. Ground cloves in cakes, cookies, conserves, desserts and marinades.
Coriander Seed	Bible-time aromatic herb of carrot family. Flavor like lemon peel and sage. From Morocco, Rumania, Argentina.	Spicy seeds used in curry powder, oriental candy, pickles, meat products and frankfurters.
Cumin or "Comino" Seed	Member of carrot family. An Italian and Mexican favorite. Aromatic seeds with bitter warm flavor. From Iran, India, Lebanon.	In chili powder; cookies, egg and cheese dishes, sauerkraut, soup, meat, rice, pickles, sausage, hot tamales.
Curry Powder	Blend of spices from India. By varying proportions of 16 spices, different flavored curries are produced. Contains turmeric, ginger, red pepper, cumin, coriander, etc.	Used to make curries of meat, fish, eggs, chicken; curry sauce and for flavoring gravies. Adds Oriental touch to rice, veal, shrimp, chicken dishes.
Dill Weed	Herb of carrot family with aromatic leaves, seeds and stem. Grows widely in Europe and U. S.	In sauces for potatoes, beans, fish, lamb, veal.

Name	Description and Source	Uses
Dill Seed	Dried tiny fruit of dill plant. Pleasant pungent flavor. From India.	Good in pickles and to garnish split pea and lentil soup.
Fennel Seed	From plant of carrot family. Aromatic, resembles anise and dill, but has distinct flavor of its own. From India, Argentina.	Popular with Italians and Scandinavians for rolls, rye bread, other baked goods, bean and lentil soup.
File (Gumbo File)	A powder made from dried tender sassafras leaves. It thickens and flavors.	Used in Creole cookery in place of okra to thicken gumbos.
Garlic	Potent flavored bulb of onion family. Flavor either very popular or unpopular. Enjoyable if used with discretion. (Also available as powder, salt, instant minced and chopped.)	Used to enrich flavor of salad dressings, meats, many cooked vegetables, bread, pastas and particularly in dishes from the Mediterranean.
Ginger	Dried root of subtropical plant grown in China, Japan, India, British West Indies. Warm in flavor.	Cracked root used in pickles, preserves, chutney. Ground root in cake, gingerbread, cookies, puddings, soups, pot roasts; Chinese ginger.
Horseradish	A large-leaved perennial herb. Grows below the surface of the ground. White-fleshed pungent roots. (Also available ground or powdered.)	Grated: used as an appetizer condiment; horseradish sauce; grated and added to cocktail sauce.
Italian Seasoning	An herb and red pepper blend which gives Italian characteristic flavor to a wide range of foods.	Used in pizza, spaghetti sauces, salads, cheese souffles.
Juniper Berries	Dried berries of evergreen shrub, with warm pungent flavor.	Used sparingly for epicure's touch in roast venison, lamb, duck, goose, sauerkraut and some stews. Also in gin which gives it its flavor.
Lemon Pepper	A nippy blend of black pepper and dehydrated lemon.	For broiled meats, poultry and seafood. Good, too, in tossed green salads.
Mace	Lacy covering on inner shell holding nutmeg. Nutmeg tree grows in East and West Indies.	Ground mace good with chocolate. Used in pound and other yellow cake, oyster stew, spinach. Whole in pickling, preserving and fish sauces.
Marjoram Leaves	One of the best known herbs; belongs to mint family. Grown mostly in Europe. Potent in flavor.	Good pounded into veal, used in meat, potato, spinach, cheese, egg and fish dishes; chicken or green vegetable salads. Season poultry stuffings, sausage, stews, soups.
Mint (Leaves or Flakes)	A widely grown herb with a delightfully cool, pungent flavor.	Popular in sauce or jelly with roast lamb. Also as edible garnish on carrots, peas, beets.
Mixed Pickling Spice	Whole spices, usually includes mustard seed, bay leaves, red pepper, cinnamon, allspice, ginger.	Used in pickling and preserving meats and to season vegetables, relishes, sauces. Good in stews and soups.

Name	Description and Source	Uses
Mixed Vegetable Flakes	Includes onion, celery, sweet red and green pepper and carrot flakes.	For use in soups, sauces, stews, casseroles and stuffings. Rehydrate with 2/3 as much water and let stand 10 minutes.
Mono Sodium Glutamate	Neutral salt of glutamic acid which is one of twenty-odd amino acids—the building blocks of all proteins. Is extracted from wheat protein and sugar beets.	Used to heighten flavor in meat, poultry, fish and vegetable dishes.
Mustard Seed	Seed of mustard plant grown in England, Europe, Canada and the U. S. Prepared mustard is ground seed blended with other spices and vinegar.	Whole seed in pickles, boiled with beets, cabbage, sauerkraut. Smart salad garnish. Ground mustard flavors sauces, gravies. Prepared mustard in salad dressing, on ham, frankfurters, cheese.
Nutmeg	Kernel of fruit of the Nutmeg tree. Grown in Dutch East Indies and British West Indies. One of the oldest known spices.	Traditional flavoring for baked custard and other desserts. Also used in cream soups, sauces, stews, vegetables such as spinach.
Onions (Powder, salt, instant minced, chopped, sliced)	From sweetly pungent varieties of onions.	Powder and salt wherever onion flavor is called for. Minced, chopped, etc., when particles should be visible.
Oregano Leaves (or Leaf Oregano)	Is wild marjoram. Has a pleasing, pungent fragrance. From Greece, Mexico, Japan.	Widely used in Mexican and Italian dishes; in meat stews, dried beans, lentils, pizza.
Paprika	A red pepper grown in Spain, U. S. and Hungary. Method of grinding determines ultimate flavor. Spanish milder than Hungarian. Rich in Vitamin C.	Used for color and mild flavor. In fish, shellfish, vegetable and egg dishes and and in salad dressing.
Parsley	Widely grown useful herb. Also available dried.	To season and garnish soups, stews, salads, potatoes, stuffings.
Pepper, Black and White	Black pepper is dried small, immature berries of climbing vine. White pepper is mature berries with hulls removed. From Indonesia, India and Brazil.	Used whole in pickling, soups, gravies and meats. Used ground in most meat, vegetable, fish and egg dishes.
Pimiento	Ripe fleshy fruit of a sweet pepper plant. Packed in small cans in its own viscous juice.	Used for spots of brilliant color, mild flavor in soups, stews, salads; as garnish for green vegetables like asparagus, green beans.
Poppy Seed	Tiny seeds of poppy plant—about 900,000 seeds to the pound. Imported from Holland, Rumania, Turkey, Poland.	Used whole as topping for breads and cookies; as filling for Kolachy; in cookies and cake. Garnish for noodles.
Poultry Seasoning	A mixture of several spices as sage, pepper, marjoram, savory, thyme, onion powder and celery salt.	Used in poultry, pork, veal and fish stuffings; to season meat loaf, dumplings, biscuit, crusts for meat and poultry pies.

Name	Description and Source	Uses
Pumpkin Pie Spice	Ground blend of cinnamon, nutmeg, ginger, cloves.	Perfect for pumpkin pie, but use it also for fruit desserts, apple pies and sweet yellow vegetables.
Red Pepper	Whole ground or crushed pods of hot red peppers including "Cayenne." From Japan, Africa, Mexico, Turkey, U. S.	Used sparingly to season meats, fish, egg dishes, mayonnaise and other sauces.
Rosemary Leaves	Belongs to mint family. Grown in Southern Europe and U. S. Dry, needle-like leaves. Used for flavoring.	Delicious in tomato and egg dishes; soups, fish, roast lamb, pork, beef and duck. Improves stuffings, vegetable and cheese dishes when combined with sage. In biscuit and muffin mixtures.
Saffron	Dried stigmas of a species of purple crocus. Grown in Mediterranean region.	Used primarily in Spanish and Italian foods for yellow color as well as flavor in yellow rice, breads, cakes and pea soup.
Sage	The most familiar of herbs. Dried leaf of shrub belonging to the mint family. Grown in Yugoslavia and Albania.	Powerful in flavor. Used to season stuffings, sausage, veal and pork dishes, beans, tomatoes and fresh cheese.
Savory Leaves	Grown principally in Southern France. Has a clean balsam fragrance.	Good in boiled fish. Known as the "bean herb." Fine flavor for peas, beans, lentils, fresh or dried; in stuffing, meat balls, croquettes, meat sauces, gravies, egg dishes.
Seafood Seasoning	A ground blend of savory herbs and pungent spices especially handy when seasoning seafood.	In fish and seafood sauces, chowders, stuffings, breadings.
Seasoned Pepper	Black pepper, sweet pepper flakes and other spices.	Convenient seasoning for dozens of meats, poultry, fish, salads and sauces.
Seasoned Salt	Mixed herbs and spices with salt.	Use as an alternate for part or all of the salt. Added to meat, poultry and egg dishes and in stuffings and sauces.
Sesame Seed (or "Benne")	From pods within blossoms of a plant grown in Central America and U. S. Hulled seeds are pearly white with toasted almond flavor.	Baked on rolls, breads and buns to give rich, nutty flavor to crusts. Used in Jewish candy, Halvah. Sesame oil is used in commercial flour mixtures and Chinese stir-fry cooking.
Shallots	Small type onion producing large clusters of small bulbs. Also available freeze dried.	Used like garlic to flavor meats, poultry, sausage, head cheese, pickles.
Shrimp Spice or Crab Boil	Whole spices with emphasis on red peppers, bay leaves, whole peppercorns and mustard.	Add to cooking water for seafood.
Sorrell	Belongs to dock family. Long slender leaves used fresh have pleasant acid flavor.	Shredded and added to lettuce, makes lemon juice or vinegar unnecessary. Also in some soups.

Name	Description and Source	Uses
Soy Sauce	Made from soy beans by a long curing process.	Used in many Chinese and Japanese dishes.
Tabasco*	Made by macerating fresh picked, small hot Mexican peppers, salting and curing 3 years, blending with vinegar, straining, bottling. Produced in Avery Islands.	Used to season egg dishes, gravies, marinades, salad dressings, sauces, sea foods, poultry and soups.
Tarragon Leaves	Related to wormwood family. Has aromatic leaves of a slightly bitter flavor. From California, France, Yugoslavia.	Adds excitement to fish, egg and chicken dishes, lobster thermidor, fish sauces, beets, spinach, aspics, Bernaise Sauce and variations.
Thyme Leaves	Grown principally in Spain and Southern France. The No. 2 of American favorite herbs.	An essential in the famous New Orleans cuisine. Present in the French Bouquet Garni. Excellent seasoning for Manhattan Clam Chowder, lamb, meat soups, stews. Good on vegetables such as carrots, peas, egg plant, escalloped, onions, also in stuffings, stocks and consomme.
Turmeric	Root of plant belonging to ginger family. Bright yellow with rich appetizing aroma, and a rather sharp, mustardy flavor. From India and Jamaica.	Often combined with mustard for pickling and used in meat and egg dishes. An ingredient of curry powder.

*trade name

Metric Conversions

Although Congress sanctioned the usage of the international metric system in the United States more than 100 years ago, the metric system has only recently begun to make its presence felt in the United States. An official, but not necessarily complete, change from pounds and quarts to grams and liters by 1981 was recommended by the Secretary of Commerce, and the Congress has been presented with several bills that would make conversion to the metric system an actuality. It is likely, however, that much discussion and examination of the effect that such conversion would have on commerce will take place before implementation of the plan. Even without official use of the metric system in the United States, food service personnel should be aware of and knowledgeable about the metric system for the following reasons:

1. The possibility of American-trained Chefs working abroad.

2. The possibility of eventual United States conversion to the international metric system.

3. The purchase of merchandise canned elsewhere with metric weight or measures on label.

4. Translation of recipes prepared outside of the United States where metric measurements have been used.

5. Use of foreign-produced equipment where metric measurement has to be converted.

The metric system is based on the measurement known as the *Meter,* officially defined as the wavelength of a specific color of light, and the approximate equivalent of one yard. Metric measurements are broken down by the decimal system, as is the U.S. dollar. For example:

100 centimeters = 1 meter
100 centiliters = 1 liter

This is actually easier to use and convert than the common American measures where 12 inches equal a foot and 16 ounces equal a pint.
Basic definitions for the metric system are:
1. milli: 1/1000th of, as a millimeter equals 1/1000th of a meter
2. centi: 1/100th of, as a centimeter equals 1/100th of a meter
3. deci: 1/10th of, as a decimeter equals 1/10th of a meter
4. kilo: 1000 times, as a kilometer equals 1000 meters

Weights

The *Kilo,* or kilogram (kg), has 1000 grams and is the standard metric weight unit. It is the *exact* equiv-

alent of 2.205 American pounds. Conversions for recipes are:

GRAMS		OUNCES	GRAMS		OUNCES		OUNCES		GRAMS
1	=	0.035	60	=	2.10		1	=	28.35
2	=	0.07	70	=	2.45		2	=	56.70
3	=	0.11	80	=	2.80		3	=	85.05
4	=	0.14	90	=	3.15		4	=	113.40
5	=	0.18	100	=	3.50		5	=	141.75
6	=	0.21	200	=	7.00		6	=	170.10
7	=	0.25	300	=	10.50		7	=	198.45
8	=	0.28	400	=	14.00		8	=	226.80
9	=	0.32	500	=	17.50		9	=	255.15
10	=	0.35	600	=	21.00		10	=	283.50
20	=	0.70	700	=	24.50		11	=	311.85
30	=	1.05	800	=	28.00		12	=	340.20
40	=	1.40	900	=	31.50		13	=	368.55
50	=	1.75	1000	=	35.00 (2.205 lb.)		14	=	396.90
							15	=	425.25
							16	=	453.59

Liquid Measure

The *Liter* (l) has 1000 milliliters (ml) and is the standard metric unit for liquid volume. The liter is commonly divided into tenths (deciliters or dl) and hundreths (centiliters or cl). One liter is the *exact* equivalent of 1.057 American quarts. Conversions for recipes are:

FLUID OUNCES		CENTILITERS	CENTILITERS		FLUID OUNCES
1	=	2.96	1	=	0.34
2	=	5.92	2	=	0.7
3	=	8.87	3	=	1.0
4	=	11.83	4	=	1.4
5	=	14.79	5	=	1.7
6	=	17.74	6	=	2.0
7	=	20.70	7	=	2.4
8	=	23.66	8	=	2.7
9	=	26.62	9	=	3.0
10	=	29.57	10	=	3.4
11	=	32.53	20	=	7.0
12	=	35.48	30	=	10.0
13	=	38.44	40	=	14.0
14	=	41.40	50	=	17.0
15	=	44.36	60	=	20.0
16	=	47.32	70	=	24.0
			80	=	27.0
			90	=	30.0
			100	=	34.0
			(liter)		

A major advantage of the metric system is that liquid volume and weights are related. One liter of water equals 1 kilo or 1000 grams.

Other metric measures that one should be familiar with are:

100 centimeters (1 meter) = 39⅜ inches
1 centimeter = ⅜ inch
2½ centimeters = 1 inch

Temperatures

An illustration of the relationship between Fahrenheit (°F) and Centigrade (°C) temperatures is included below:

Exact conversions can be found by using the following formulas or chart:

$$C = \frac{5}{9}(F-32)$$

$$F = \frac{9}{5}C+32$$

CENTIGRADE		FAHRENHEIT	FAHRENHEIT		CENTIGRADE
301.5°	=	575°			
			572°	=	300°
			554°	=	290°
288°	=	550°			
			536°	=	280°
274°	=	525°			
			518°	—	270°
260°	=	500°	500°	=	260°
			482°	—	250°
246°	=	475°			
			464°	=	240°
232°	=	450°			
			446°	=	230°
			428°	=	220°
218.5°	=	425°			
			410°	—	210°
204.5°	=	400°			
			392°	=	200°
190°	=	375°	375°	=	190°
			356°	=	180°
176.5°	=	350°			
			338°	=	170°
					Caramel
163°	=	325°			
			320°	=	160°
157°	=	315°			
			302°	=	150°
149°	=	300°			
140.5°	=	285°			
					Hard Crack Stage
			284°	=	140°
138°	=	280°			
					Crack Stage
135°	=	275°			
					Small Crack Stage
132°	=	270°			
			266°	=	130°
129.5°	=	265°			
					Hard Ball Stage
126.5°	=	260°			

CENTIGRADE		FAHRENHEIT	FAHRENHEIT		CENTIGRADE
124°	=	255°			
121°	=	250°			Ball Stage
			248°	=	120°
118.5°	=	245°			
115.6°	=	240°			Soft Ball Stage
113°	=	235°			
			230°	=	110°
107°	=	225°			
100°	=	212°	212°	=	100°
93.5°	=	200°			Water boils
			194°	=	90°
88°	=	190°			
82°	=	180°			
			176°	=	80°
76.5°	=	170°			
71.0°	=	160°			
			158°	=	70°
65.5°	=	150°			
60°	=	140°	140°	=	60°
54.5°	=	130°			
			122°	=	50°
49°	=	120°			
43.5°	=	110°			
			104°	=	40°
37.5°	=	100°			
32.2°	=	90°			
			86°	=	30°
26.7°	=	80°			
21.1°	=	70°			
			68°	=	20°
15.6°	=	60°			
10°	=	50°	50°	=	10°
4.4°	=	40°			
0°	=	32°	32°	=	0°
−1.1°	=	30°			Water freezes
−6.6°	=	20°			
			14°	=	−10°
−12.2°	=	10°			
−17.8°	=	0°			
			−4°	=	−20°
−23.3°	=	−10°			
−28.9°	=	−20°			
			−22°	=	−30°
−34.4°	=	−30°			
−40.0°	=	−40.0°	−40.0°	=	−40.0°

Glossary

*Fr. = word of French origin.

Aging: A term applied to meat held at a temperature of 34 to 36 degrees F. Tough connective tissues are broken down through the action of enzymes thereby increasing tenderness.

Agneau: (an-yo') (Fr.) Lamb.

à la: (ah-lah) (Fr.) According to the style of, such as: a la Francaise or according to the French way.

à la Bourgeoise: (ah-lah-boor-jwahz') (Fr.) Family style. See Bourgeoise.

à la Broche: (ah-lah-brosh') (Fr.) Cooked on a spit over or in front of an open fire. See Brochette.

à la Carte: (ah-lah-cart') (Fr.) Foods prepared to order: each dish priced separately.

à la King: Foods served in a white cream sauce which contains mushrooms, green peppers and often pimientos.

à la Mode: (ah-lah-mod') (Fr.) Usually refers to ice cream on top of pie, but may be other dishes served in a special way. See Beef a la Mode.

à la Provencale: (ah-lah-pro-vahn-sal') (Fr.) Dishes with garlic and olive oil. See Provencale.

à la Russe: (Fr.) The Russian way.

Allemande Sauce: (ah-le-mahnd) White, reduced veloute, egg yolks and cream.

Allumette Potatoes: (all-eu-met') (Fr.) Cut like large matches, similar to Shoestring Potatoes and Pommes Paille.

Amandine: (Fr.) Made with or garnished with almonds.

Andalouse, à l': (ahn-dah-loose') Prepared the Andalusian (Spain) way. Consomme and Potage: Tomatoes and rice. Garnish: Tomatoes, rice, eggplant, red peppers. Sauce: Mayonnaise with tomatoes and red peppers. Spanish onions, cucumbers, tomatoes, eggs, oil-vinegar.

Anglaise: (ahn-glayz') (Fr.) In the English style.

A. P.: As Purchased.

Appareil: Mixture of different elements for preparation for a dish. (i.e. Chicken Croquette mixture.)

Argenteuil: (ahr-zhahn-toy') (Fr.) Consomme: With asparagus. Poached or scrambled eggs with asparagus tips. Garnish: Asparagus points with Hollandaise.

Aspic: (as'-pick) (English) Clear meat, fish or poultry jelly.

au Gratin: (oh-grah-tan') (Fr.) Food covered with a sauce sprinkled with crumbs or cheese and baked.

au Jus: (oh-zhue') (Fr.) (Literal: with juice) Served with natural juices or gravy.

au Lait: (oh-lay') (Fr.) With milk.

au Naturel: (oh-nah-tue-rel') (Fr.) Plainly cooked. See Nature.

aux Croutons: (Fr.) With bread cut in small dice and fried in butter. (See Croutons.)

Avocado, also Avocat: Alligator pear. Brownish or purple berry filled with pulp-like marrow, from Southern California, tropical America and West Indies.

Bain Marie: (Fr.) Double boiler insert or steam table.

Baking: To cook by hot moist heat, usually in an oven.

Bar le duc: (bahr-le-duek') (Fr.) Famous jam made of red currants.

Bard: To wrap poultry, game or fish with thin slices of fat or salt pork.

Baste: To moisten or spoon over a food product with stock, drippings, or fat while cooking.

Barley, Pearl: Polished barley.

Batter: Mixture of flour and liquid of a consistency that can be stirred.

Bean Sprouts: Mung beans from China. Sprouts are tiny and green when used for the preparation of Chinese dishes.

Béarnaise: (bay-ahr-nayz') (Fr.) Name of sauce derived from Hollandaise Sauce. Contains egg yolks, butter, tarragon and seasoning. Also name of a region in France.

Beating: Regular lifting and stirring motion to bring mixture to smooth texture and often for the purpose of incorporating air into the mixture.

Béchamel: (bay-shah-mel') (Fr.) A rich cream sauce or white sauce.

Beef Stroganoff: Tenderloin of beef sauteed with sauces and enriched with sour cream.

Beef, Dried: Soaked in brine and then smoked and dried.

Beurre: (burr) (Fr.) Butter.

Beurre Noir: (burr-nwahr') (Fr.) Butter cooked to a dark brown to which capers and a dash of vinegar are added.

Beurre Noisette: (burr-nwah-zet) Hazelnut butter achieved by melting butter until it turns lightly brown.

Bind: To cause to cohere, unite, or hold together, such as bind a croquette mixture. (Often with egg yolks or a liaison.)

Bisque: (bisk) (Fr.) Thick cream soup or puree, usually of shellfish, bivalves and crustaceans.

Bisque Ice Cream: High butter-fat content ice cream with dried macaroons or sponge cake crumbs.

Blanc: (blahn) (Fr.) White.

Blanch: 1. To boil in water and cool before cooking or freezing, to cleanse and maintain color. 2. To partially cook as with broiled bacon. 3. To dip in boiling water to remove skins from tomatoes, fruits and nuts, etc.

Blanquette d'Agneau: (blahn-ket-dahn-yo') (Fr.) Stewed, blanched lamb with white sauce. Usually shoulder and breast.

Blending: Thoroughly mixing two or more ingredients.

Blue Cheese: See Cheese, Blue.

Blinis: Russian buckwheat pancakes. Usually served with caviar.

Boeuf: (buff) (Fr.) Beef.

Boiled Dressing: Cooked dressing for salads.

Bonne Femme, à la: (bun-fam') (Fr.) Potage: With potatoes, leeks, carrots, onions. Fish: With onions, chopped parsley, shallots, mushrooms and white wine.

Bordure: (bohr-dur') (Fr.) With a Duchesse potato border, used in garnishing.

Borscht: (bohrsht) (Russian) A Russian or Polish soup made with beets and duck. Sour cream is often added.

Bouchée: (boo-shay') (Fr.) Small meat pattie or pastry shell filled with meat, poultry or lobster. Sometimes filled with fruits.

Bouillabaisse: (boo-yah-bays') (Fr.) Fish soup-stew (French Provencal).

Bouillon: (Fr.) A liquid obtained basically from the simmering of beef, veal, or fowl and vegetables in water.

Boulangère: (Literal: Bakers Wife) (boo-lahn-zhair') (Fr.) A style of cooking potatoes beneath roasting meat.

Bouquet Garni: (boo-kay-garnee') (Fr.) A bouquet of fresh herbs tied together, immersed in a liquid, and removed before the dish is served. Tied in a cheese or muslin cloth-sachet bag.

Bouquetière: (boo-k-tyair') (Fr.) With a variety of vegetables in season arranged around the dish or platter of meat, poultry or fish.

Bourgeoise: (boor-jwahz') (Fr.) Plain, family style.

Bourguignonne: (boor-guee-nyohng) Pertaining to Burgundy wine flavored sauces and a garnish of lardons, mushrooms, and pearl onions.

Brazier: Heavy duty stewing pan with tightly fitting cover. Both round and square in shape.

Breading: To roll in bread crumbs or other breading agent before cooking.

Breton: (Fr.) Refers to items which contain or are garnished with beans. Brittany region of France.

Brine: Liquid of salt and vinegar for pickling.

Brioche: (bree-osh') (Fr.) A sweet dough roll of French origin containing yeast and eggs.

Broche: (Fr.) Metal or wood spit used to suspend and turn meat during roasting. See Brochette.

Brochette: (bro-shet') (Fr.) Meat broiled and served on a skewer. A metal pin to hold meat in place. See a la Broche.

Brunoise: (brun-wahz') (Fr.) Cut in fine dice.

Buffet: Display of ready to eat hot and cold foods. Often self-service from table of assorted foods.

Café: (kah-fay) (Fr.) Coffee.

Calorie: The heat required to raise 1 gram of water 1 degree centigrade.

Calories: Fuel value in food. A unit expressing the heat-producing or energy-producing value of food. 1 calorie = 3.968 B.T.U.

Calavo: Trade name for California Avocados.

Canadian Bacon: Trimmed, pressed, smoked loin of pork. Lean.

Candying: Cooking fruit in heavy syrup until transparent; then drain and dry.

Canapé: (kah-nay-pay') (Fr.) An appetizer. Always prepared on a base, such as bread, toast or crackers.

Canard: (kah-nahr) (Fr.) Duck.

Cannelon: (kan-ay-lohn) (Italian) Pasta or crepe stuffed with meat or cheese and served with a tomato or meat sauce.

Capon: (kah-pohn') Castrated poultry noted for its tenderness and delicate flavor.

Cardinal Sauce: Bechamel with shrimp or lobster coral and lemon juice.

Casaba Melon: Lemon yellow skin, white meat, large oval shape, season September to April.

Caviar (ka-vee-are') Eggs or roe of fish, grey and black, usually sturgeon. Seasoned. Caviar from salmon is red.

Cayenne Pepper: Hot seasoning. Red and pungent in powder form, now used in liquid form. Hot pepper sauce.

Celestine Consommé: (say-less-teen) (Fr.) Consomme with sliced unsweetened pancakes.

Cèpes: (sep) (Fr.) Species of mushrooms.

Champignons: (shahm-pee-nyohn) (Fr.) Mushrooms.

Chanterelles: (shahn-tee-rels) (Fr.) Species of mushrooms.

Chantilly Cream: (shahn-tee-yee') (Fr.) Vanilla whipped cream.

Chantilly Sauce: (shahn-tee-yee') (Fr.) Hollandaise sauce with whipped cream.

Chasseur: (shah-seur') (Fr.) (Literal: Hunter Style) Items prepared and served in a tomato sauce with mushrooms, wine, etc.

Chateaubriand: (shah-toh-bree-ahn') (Fr.) Thick double tenderloin steak broiled or sauteed and then sliced. The name of a French author and a great gourmand.

Chaud: (show) (Fr.) Hot.

Chaud-froid: (show-fro-ah') (Fr.) Cold sauces usually bechamel or a veloute with the addition of gelatine used to mask cold food platters for buffets.

Cheese, Blue: Similar to Roquefort in appearance but made of cow's milk instead of sheep's milk.

Chef: (shef) (Fr.) Chief of kitchen.

Chemiser: (shi-miz-ai) (Fr.) To coat with chaud-froid or aspic.

Chiffonade: (shee-fohn-ahd') (Fr.) Shredded vegetables or meats used in soups or salads, or as garnishings. Also dressing: Shredded and chopped vegetables in French Dressing base.

China Cap: A cone shaped strainer or sieve. Also referred to as a "chinois" (French).

Ciseler: (Fr.) To cut, to make an incision in the skin of fish and meat so that it will not crack during cooking.

Clarify: To make clear, by adding a clarifying agent which removes suspended particles such as in the preparation of consommé.

Cloche, sous: (Fr.) Under bell, usually glass.

Cobbler: (Drink) Liquor, sugar, sliced fruit and mint. Fruit dessert. Cobbler Deep Dish Fruit Pies.

Cocotte: (Fr.) Small earthen cooking ware. Oeufs En Cocotte (Eggs in Cocotte).

Coddling: Cooking just below boiling point. Coddled Eggs.

Colbert Sauce: Shallots, butter, claret, brown gravy, butter, lemon.

Compote: (kom-pot') (Fr.) A stewed fruit or combination of fruits; sometimes applied to a stew of birds.

Concasser: (Fr.) To chop coarsely. A coarse mince.

Condiments: Seasonings and appetizing ingredients added to food.

Consommé: (kahn-so-may') (Fr.) A strong, clear, sparkling broth clarified and enriched by the addition of lean chopped beef, egg whites and aromates which coagulate and are removed after clarification.

Coquille: (koh-kee) (Fr.) Shell.

Copper: Metal cooking unit, stationary, heated with steam jacket.

Court Bouillon: (Fr.) Literally, short broth. A preparation of vinegar or wine, water and savory herbs in which fish is cooked.

Cover Charge: Fixed fee for table service independent of the charge for food.

Crecy: (Fr.) Items composed of, or garnished with carrots.

Crêpe: (krep) (Fr.) Thin pancakes.

Crêpes Suzette: Thin french pancake served with rich butter, citrus and brandy sauce.

Cresson: (kray-sohn) (Fr.) Watercress.

Croquette: (kro-ket) (Fr.) A food product or combination of food products, usually breaded and deep fried.

Croutons: (kroo-tohn') (Fr.) Small pieces of fried or toasted bread used in soups.

Cuisine: (kwee-zeen') (Fr.) Art of cookery, cookery, also kitchen.

Cumberland Sauce: Orange and lemon peel julienne and juice, currant jelly, port wine and ground ginger.

Curry: East Indian dish. Was originally a stew. Now referred to with mixing of pungent curry seasoning.

Curry Powder: A mixture of powdered spices.

Deglaze: To moisten a roast pan or saute pan with wine, vinegar, stock or water in order to dissolve the caramelized drippings so that they might be incorporated into the sauce.

Dejeuner: (day-zhoe-nay) (Fr.) Lunch or mid-day meal. Petit Dejeuner—breakfast.

Demi: (de-mee) (Fr.) Half.

Demi-glace: (de-mee-glahs) (Fr.) A reduced espagnole sauce.

Diable: Devilled.

Diced: Cut in small squares.

Dindonneau: (dan-doh-noh) (Fr.) Young turkey.

Drawn butter: Melted butter.

Dredging: Coating with dry ingredients (as flour).

Drippings: The fat and juice which drops from roasting meat.

Dry: As applied to a beverage meaning a low percentage of sugar. As with vin sec—dry wine.

Du Barry (Fr.) Garnish of cauliflower.

Duchesse Potatoes: Mashed with eggs and squeezed through a pastry tube.

Dugléré: (du-glay-ray) (Fr.) With onions, shallots and tomatoes.

Dusting: Sprinkling with flour or sugar.

Ecossaise: (Fr.) Scottish style.

Eggplant: Large, purple, pear-shaped vegetable.

Glossary

Eggs a la Goldenrod: White sauce with chopped whites of eggs poured over toast. Hard cooked yolks pressed through sieve and sprinkled on top.

Eggs Benedict: (bay-nay-dick'). Poached and served with ham or tongue with hollandaise sauce on a toasted muffin.

Eminré: (ay-man-say') (Fr.) Cut fine.

Emincé of Beef: (ay-man-say') (Fr.) Thin slices of meat.

en Bordure: (en-bohr-dur') (Fr.) In a Duchesse Potato Border.

en Brochette: (ahn-broh-shet) (Fr.) On a skewer. See a la Broche.

en Casserole: (ahn-kahs-rol') (Fr.) Food served in the same dish in which it was baked. A fireproof dish and cover.

Enchiladas: Mexican. Tortillas covered with sauce of grated cheese, spices, etc.

en Chemise: (Fr.) With their skins. Usually potatoes. Mashed with a chaud-froid or aspic.

en Coquille: (ahn-koh-kee') (Fr.) In the shell. As with oysters on the half shell.

E. P.: Edible Portion.

Epigramme: (eh-pee-grahm') (Fr.) Small cuts of lamb, meats, poultry and game cooked, cooled, bread crumbed and fried.

Escoffier: (ays-koh-fee-ay) Name of famous French chef, master of modern classical cuisine. Also trade name for bottled sauce—Escoffier Sauce.

Espagnole Sauce: Basic brown sauce, see recipe in text, p 312.

Farce: (fahrs) (Fr.) Stuffing. Forcemeat.

Farci: (Fr.) Stuffed.

Farina: The coarsely ground inner portion of hard wheat.

Farinaceous: Consisting of or made of meal or flour.

Fermière: (fair-mee-air') (Fr.) With discs of carrots, turnips, onions, potatoes, celery, cabbage. Farmer's style.

Filet: (fee-lay) (Fr.) May be tenderloin of beef, mutton, veal or pork without bone. Boned fish are also called fillets.

    Filet: French

    Fillet: English

Finnan Haddie: Smoked haddock.

Fleuron: (Flurr-ohn) (Fr.) Puff paste baked in crescent shape used as a garnish, usually with fish in white wine sauce.

Florentine: (floor-ahn-teen). Literally, as prepared in Florence. With spinach.

Foie-gras: Foie d'oie: (fwah grah) (Fr.) (fwah dwah) Fatted goose liver, most often from the Strasbourg region of France.

Fondantes, Potatoes: Oval shaped, partially cooked by boiling, reshaped in towel and finished in oven.

Fondue: (fohn-du') (Fr.) Melted Swiss Cheese dish. See Welsh Rabbit.

Forcemeat: Chopped meats and seasoning used for stuffing.

Forestiere: (Fr.) Garnished with mushrooms.

French Lamb Chops: Made by scraping the meat and fat from the bones of rib chops a little distance from the end. Broiled over high heat.

Fricassée: (Fr.) In modern usage, applies to a method of preparing poultry and sometimes veal in a white sauce.

Frizzling: Cooking in small amount of fat until crisp.

Froid: (frwa) (Fr.) Cold.

Fromage: (froh-mahzh') (Fr.) Cheese.

Fumet: (foo-meh) (Fr.) A concentrated broth of fish, game and/or vegetables.

Garbanzo: (gar-ban-tho) Chick peas. Spanish national dish.

Garde-Manger: (guard-mon-zhay) (Fr.) Cold meat department, larder or person in charge of it. Larder cook.

Garnish: To embellish foods; to decorate. Also a noun, referring to a foodstuff being used to garnish.

Garniture: (gar-nee-tur) French for garnish.

Gastric: (gas-treek') Cooking term for a mixture of white wine or vinegar, crushed pepper, shallots and spices.

Gateau: (gah-toh) (Fr.) Cake.

Gaufres: (goh-fr) (Fr.) Wafers.

Gaufrette Potatoes: (goh-fret) French fried potatoes in waffle form.

Gefilte Fish: Jewish favorite. Literally, stuffed fish. Today in dumpling form.

Gherkins: Small cucumbers (a few days old). Usually pickled.

Giblets: Liver, heart and trimmings from poultry.

Glaze: A semi-transparent or glossy coating. To cover with same.

Gnocchi: Italian for light dumplings.

Gourmet: (goor-may) (Fr.) Connoisseur of food and drinks.

Gratin, au: (grah-tan) (Fr.) Sprinkled with cheese or buttered crumbs and baked brown.

Gratinée: (Fr.) To brown, usually by topping an item with crumbs, cheese, etc.

Gruyère: (grue-yair') Swiss cheese, also made in France and elsewhere. More tart and with smaller holes than the cheese commonly called Swiss Cheese.

Guava: Tropical fruit: Apple or pear shaped, acid sweet flavor. Made into jams and jellies.

Gumbo: (Soup) Chicken, onions, okra, green peppers and tomatoes.

Haché: (hah-shay) (Fr.) Hashed; minced.

Haricots Verts: (ah-ree-coh-vair') (Fr.) Small green string beans.

Hasenpfeffer: German rabbit stew.

Heifer: A young female cow that has not had a calf.

Herb Bouquet: Mixed herbs tied and used for seasoning.

Hongroise, à la: (ohn-grwahs') Prepared in Hungarian way. Onions, sour cream and paprika. Garnish: With red and green peppers, cabbage and leeks.

Hors d'oeuvre: (ohr-duh-vr) (Fr.) Small relishes or appetizers. Served as first course of the meal. See Antipasto, Assiette Parisienne. A foretaste.

Hush Puppies: Southern deep fat fried dish of corn meal, baking powder, milk, onion, seasoning.

Hydrogenated Fat: Fat treated with hydrogen to maintain stable consistency.

Indian Pudding: Slow baked dessert of corn meal, milk, brown sugar, eggs, raisins and seasoning.

Infusion: Liquid obtained from steeping a food, spice, flower or plant. A wide variety of herb infusions are consumed in Europe for therapeutic purposes.

Johnny Cake: Bread from yellow corn meal, eggs, milk.

Julienne: (zhu-lee-en') (Fr.) Potatoes: cut in long slices thinner than for French fries and served very crisp. Soup: Clear soup with thin strips of vegetables. Meats, Poultry and Vegetables: Cut in narrow 1½ inch strips.

Junket: Brand name of dessert of flavored curdled milk and rennet.

Jus: (zhue) (Fr.) Juice; usually refers to juices from meat. See au Jus.

Karo: Corn syrup, light or dark.

Kasha: Buckwheat groats.

Kippered Herring: Dried or smoked herring.

Kitchen Bouquet: Trade name for bottled gravy coloring and flavoring.

Kosher: (meat) Meat sold within 48 hours after butchering in accordance with prescribed Hebrew religious laws. Or style of cooking adhering to Jewish dietary restrictions.

Kumquats: Gold-orange colored, small, oval citrus fruit.

Lait: (lay) (Fr.) Milk.

Lambs' Sweetbreads: Ris d'Agneau, French.

Langouste: (lahn-goost) (Fr.) Crawfish.

Larding: Strips of salt pork inserted into meat with a special larding needle.

Lardons: (Fr.) Strips of salt pork used for larding and as a garnish. Also, julienne of bacon.

Leek: Small onion-like plant, used as a vegetable or aromatic seasoning.

Legumes: (lay-gyoom) (Fr.) Vegetables. Also refers to such dried foods as beans, peas and lentils.

Lentil: Flat seed somewhat like peas. Used for soups and garnishes. Brown and yellow. Esau sold his birthright for a pottage of lentils (Genesis).

Liaison: (lee-ay-zohn) A binding agent for sauces, usually cream and egg yolks.

Lychee Nut: (Chinese) Small hard shell dried nut.

Lyonnaise Potatoes: (Fr.) Sliced and sauteed with slices of onions.

Mace (seasoning): Outer shell of nutmeg.

Macedoine: (mah-say-dwan) (Fr.) Mixture usually of fruit or vegetables. Macedoine de fruits: Fruit salad.

Madrilène Soup: (mah-dree-lain') Clear consomme with tomato, highly seasoned, served jellied or hot.

Maggi: Brand name for Swiss liquid seasoning.

Maître d'Hôtel: (mai-tre-doh-tel') (Fr.) Head of catering department; head of food service.

Maître d'Hôtel, à la: (mai-tre-doh-tel') Sauce: Yellow sauce. Butter Sauce, lemon juice, parsley, salt, pepper. Butter: Mixture of lemon juice, butter, parsley, salt, pepper.

Manhattan Clam Chowder: With tomatoes, vegetables and quahog clams.

Maraschino: (mah-rahs-kee'noh) Italian cherry cordial. Also cherries.

Marengo, à la: Sauteed Veal (or chicken) with mushrooms, tomatoes, olives and olive oil. Named after the Battle of Marengo, fought by Napoleon and his troops.

Bone Marrow: Soft tissue from the inside or cavity of bones.

Vegetable Marrow: A member of the squash family.

Marsala: Pale golden, semi-dry, Italian wine from Sicily.

Masking: To cover completely (usually with a sauce

or aspic).

Mate: (mah-tay) South American Paraguay tea.

Matelotes: (mah-te-lot) Fish stewed with wine, onions and seasoning. Fish Stews.

Melba: Vanilla ice cream, raspberry jelly or sauce and whipped cream served with peach or pear.

Melba Toast: Very thin white bread baked in oven until golden brown and very crisp.

Menthe: (Fr.) Mint.

Menthe, Creme de: (krem-de-mahnt') Peppermint cordial.

Melting: Making liquid by application of heat.

Menu: (men-u) or (may-nu). Bill of fare.

Meringue: (may-rang) Paste made of egg whites and sugar, souffled.

Meunière, à la: (me-nee-air) (Fr.) Fish: Dipped in flour, sauteed in butter, served with brown butter and lemon, sprinkled with parsley.

Mignon Filets: Small tender filets usually from beef, pork, lamb and veal tenderloins.

Milanaise: (Fr.) Garnish consisting of julienne of ham, tongue, mushrooms and truffles. Literally, as prepared in Milan, Italy.

Minced: Chopped or ground fine.

Mincing: Chopping in less regular parts, similar to grinding.

Minestrone: (mee-nay-stroh-nay) Vegetable soup with a macaroni product and cheese.

Mirepoix: (mere-eh-pwah) (Fr.) Mixture of onions, carrots, celery used to flavor stocks, soups, sauces, stews, pot roasts and roast meat and poultry in marinades.

Mixing: Uniting two or more ingredients.

Mongol Soup: Tomatoes, split peas, julienne vegetables.

Morilles: (mo-riy) (Fr.) Morels, a species of mushrooms.

Mornay: (Fr.) A cheese sauce; cream sauce with the addition of cheese and a liaison.

Mortadella: Italian pork and beef sausage.

Mousse: (moose) (Fr.) Frozen dessert of whipped cream, flavoring and sweetening. May also be hot or cold buffet food made with meat, fish and poultry products.

Mouton: (moo-tohn) (Fr.) Mutton.

Mozzarella: Soft Italian cheese made of milk, shaped in rounds.

Mushroom Sauce: Brown or white sauce, fat, flour, stock, sliced mushrooms, seasoning and with the addition of wine.

Navarin: (nah-vah-rahn') (Fr.) Stew of mutton with onions, celery, carrots, turnips, tomatoes, peas and cut green beans. See Ragout.

Noir: (nwar) (Fr.) Black.

Nouilles: (noo-ee) (Fr.) Noodles: Narrow strips of dried dough, resembling macaroni, used in soups and garnishes.

Oeuf: (uff) (Fr.) Egg.

Okra: Vegetable pods. Used in soups, gumbos. Also served as a vegetable.

Ovaltine: Brand name for a flavored malt and milk powder for milk drinks.

Over-Run: Increased volume produced by whipping in air as in ice cream.

Oysters, Blue Points: Name of oysters from certain Atlantic Coast waters.

Pain: (pan) (Fr.) Bread.

Pan Broiling: Cooking uncovered in a hot skillet. Fat is poured off in cooking.

Palm Hearts: Hearts of young palms. A canned product.

Panache: (pah-nash') (Fr.) Several kinds of mixed birds, fruits, vegetables, usually with contrasting colors.

Papaya: Tropical fruit, the juice of which yields an enzyme used as a meat tenderizer.

Papillote: (pah-pee-oht) (Fr.) Cooked in parchment paper or foil to seal in flavors.

Paprika: Dried and powdered or ground ripe fruit of various kinds of peppers. Used as seasoning and for color.

Parboiling: Boiling for a short period to partially cook.

Parisienne Potatoes: Parisian potatoes made with a small round scoop. Browned, boiled or steamed.

Parmentier: (parmahn-tee-ay) Soup: Potato Soup. A French 18th century alchemist who introduced the potato to France.

Parmesan: Hard, sharp cheese grated for soups, toppings and souffiees.

Parsley: An herb used largely for garnishing.

Pasteurized Milk: Milk held 140 degrees F. for 30 minutes to destroy potentially harmful microbes.

Pastry Bag: Cone bag with metal tip at small end. Used to decorate cakes.

Paysanne: (pay-sahn) (Fr.) (Literal: Peasant Style) Vegetables cut into regular square shapes.

Paupiette: (poh-pee-et') (Fr.) Stuffed rolled thin slices of meat, fish and poultry braised.

Peche: (pesh) (Fr.) Peach.

Petit: (puh-tee) (Fr.) Small.

Petit Dejeuner: (puh-tee′-day-zhuh-nay′) Breakfast.

Petite Marmite: (puh-teet-mahr-meet′) (Fr.) A strong consomme with beef, chicken and vegetables. The name of the earthenware pot it is cooked in.

Petits-Fours: (puh-tee-foor′) (Fr.) Small cakes and cookies generally served with desserts.

Petits Pois: (puh-tee-pwa) (Fr.) Small green peas.

Picnic Ham: Lower end of hog shoulder.

Piece de Resistance: (pee-es-de-ray-zee-stahns′) (Fr.) Main dish.

Pilau: (pee-loh′) Rice sauteed with onions and moistened with white stock. Also spelled pilaf and pilaw.

Pimiento: Red sweet Spanish pepper pod.

Piquant: (pee-kahn′) (pee-kahnt′) Flavored, highly seasoned. A piquant sauce is delightfully pungent.

Pistachio Nuts: Small, pale green inside. Thin hard shell. Tropical.

Plank: A board made of hard wood. Also to cook and serve on a board or plank, usually with an elaborate garnish of vegetables. As with planked steak, fish and poultry.

Poaching: Cooking in water that bubbles lightly. Simmering at 205°F.

Poisson: (pwah-sohn) (Fr.) Fish.

Poivrade (Sauce): (pwav-rahd′) A brown peppery sauce.

Polonaise: (poh-loh-nayz) (Literal: Polish) Garnish consisting of fresh bread crumbs browned in butter, chopped hard cooked egg, beurre noir and chopped parsley.

Pommes de Terre: (pom-de-tair) (Fr.) Potatoes. Literal translation—apples of the earth.

Popovers: Individual, quick, puffed-up, batter rolls of milk, flour and eggs.

Postum: Coffee substitute made of cereal.

Potage: (poh-tahzh′) (Fr.) Soup, usually thickened.

Pot-au-feu: (pot-oh-fe′) (Fr.) Meat broth with meats and various vegetables.

Potiron: (poh-tee-rohn′) (Fr.) Pumpkin.

Potpourri: (poh-poo-ree′) (Fr.) Mixture.

Poulet: (poo-lay) (Fr.) Chicken.

Portion Control: Control of size and weight of individual portions.

Poulette Sauce: Allemande sauce with sliced mushrooms and chives or parsley.

Prefabricated: Refers to meat, and associated products trimmed and cut; often to specification of purchaser.

Printanière: (prahn-tahn-yair) (Fr.) Garnish of spring vegetables cut in small dice.

Profiterolles: Small balls of pate-a-choux used for a garnish.

Pullman Bread: Sandwich bread.

Purée: (pu-ray) (Fr.) Pulp or paste of vegetable or fruit. Thick soup.

Quahaug: (kwah-hawg) Atlantic Coast round clam.

Quenelles: (kay-nel′) (Fr.) Dumplings.

Ragôut: (rah-goo) (Fr.) Thick savory stew. See Navarin.

Raisins: (ray-san) Dried grapes on the vine.

Ramekins: Food baked in shallow baking china or shallow baking dish itself.

Rasher of Bacon: (English) A slice of bacon.

Reduce: To reduce volume by cooking or simmering.

Rendering: Freeing fat from connective tissues by heat.

Rice, Brown: Rice with hulls on. Before polishing.

Ris de Veau: (Ree-de-Voh) (Fr.) Veal sweetbreads (thymus gland).

Rissole: (ree-soh-lay′) (Fr.) Browned.

Rissolé Potatoes: (Pommes rissolees) Cut into shape of an egg and browned. Cooking finished in the oven.

Riz: (ree) (Fr.) Rice.

Roasting: Cooking in the oven—dry heat.

Robert Sauce: (sauce ro-bair′) Brown sauce. Onions, flour, stock, lemon juice. French mustard, white wine.

Roe: Mass of fish eggs. Single fish egg. Female—hard roe, Male—soft roe.

Romaine: (ro-main′) Long, narrow crisp-leaved Roman lettuce, inner leaves are light in color. Long-leaved cos lettuce.

Rôti: (ro-tee) (Fr.) Roast.

Rouge: (roozh) (Fr.) Red.

Roulade: (Fr.) A rolled piece of thin meat.

Roux: (roo) (Fr.) Equal parts of fat and flour cooked; used to thicken sauces and gravies. Light-blonde and dark roux.

Rusks: Light bread or biscuit, sometimes twice baked.

Russian Dressing: Mayonnaise, lemon juice, chili sauce and Worcestershire sauce and chopped pimientos.

Sabayon: (sah-bah-yohn) (Fr.) Dessert—Egg dish served in glasses. Whipped egg yolks, vanilla, sugar, sherry, white wines.

Saffron: Seasoning. Deep orange dried part of purple crocus. To color and flavor rice, national dishes and saffron cakes.

Sage: Leaves of an herb. For seasoning.

Salamander: A broiler-like stove with heat from above and a shelf below. Open front so that dishes can be put on lower shelf for glazing.

Salami: (sah-lah'-mee) Sausage of pork, beef, red wine, highly seasoned.

Salmagundi: Mixture, usually refers to pickled meat, fish, onions, vegetables and seasoning.

Salmis: A type of sauce or ragout made from partially cooked game. Leftovers can be utilized for this preparation.

Sauté: To cook quickly in a small amount of fat.

Searing: Browning surface of meat by intense heat, under the broiler, on top of the range and in an oven.

Sec: (sek) (Fr.) Dry as with vin sec—Dry Wine.

Semolina: Flour high in gluten that is made from durum wheat.

Serviette: (Fr.) A table napkin.

Shad: Fish of the herring family.

Shallots: Vegetables of the onion family (Echalotes, French).

Shaslik of Lamb: (Brochette of Lamb) Lamb seasoned and broiled on a skewer.

Shirred Eggs: (Oeufs au Plat) Baked in cooking china, shirred egg dishes, with butter.

Shoestring Potatoes: Like French fried, but cut very thin. See Allumette, Paille.

Simmering: Slow cooking at just below boiling point from 205°F. to 210°F. As poaching.

Sizzling Steak: Steak served on aluminum platter which has been heated so that the steak and juices sizzle.

Skewering: To fasten meat, poultry, fish or vegetables on long pin during cooking.

Skim: Using a skimmer or ladle, to remove scum or grease accumulated on the surface of a stock, soup or sauce.

Smorgasbord: (smur-goes-board) Swedish tidbits or appetizers usually arranged on large table.

Smother: To cook vegetables in covered kettle until tender.

Soirée: (swah-ray) (Fr.) Evening party.

Sole: (sohl) Flat white fish common to Europe. Dover Sole. Also flat fish from the Pacific Coast of the United States.

Sommelier: (soh-meh-lyay') (Fr.) Wine waiter.

Soufflé: (soo-flay) Light puffed baked custard, consisting of a sauce and eggyolk mixture to which a puree or flavoring is added and into which stiffly beaten egg whites are gently folded.

Soufflé Potatoes: (soo-flay) Potato slices puffed up like little pillows.

Sous Cloche: (su-klush) (Fr.) Under bell, usually glass.

Soy Sauce: Made from soy beans. Brown. For flavoring Chinese foods.

Spanish Rice: With onions, tomatoes, green peppers and saffron.

Sparkling Burgundy: Bright ruby sparkling wine.

Spit: A pointed rod to hold meat or poultry for roasting in front of fire.

Split: 6 oz. size bottle.

Spumoni: (spoo-mah-nee). Fancy Italian ice cream.

Squab: Young pigeon.

Steaming: Cooking in steam in an enclosed chamber.

Steeping: To soak in liquid below boiling point to extract flavor or color, as for tea.

Steer: A young castrated beef animal.

Sterilizing: Destroying bacteria and microorganisms by boiling water, heat or steam.

Stew: Cooking in liquid or sauce with accompanying vegetables and meat.

Stewed Fruit: Simmering fruit in a sweetened liquid.

Stirring: Mixing food in circular motion.

Stock: The liquid in which meat, poultry, fish or vegetables have been cooked. Brown or white.

Sub Gum: (Chinese) Base of many Chinese dishes. Bamboo shoots, water chestnuts, fresh mushrooms.

Suet: Hard protective fat in beef, veal, mutton and lamb around the kidneys.

Suisse, a la (swees) Swiss style.

Sweetbreads: Thymus gland of calf or lamb.

Swiss Chard: Green tender leaf vegetable prepared like spinach.

Tabasco: Brand name for hot red pepper sauce.

Table d'Hôte: (tahbl-doht) (Fr.) Fixed price meal.

Tartare Steak: Raw hamburger steak seasoned and garnished.

Tasse: (tahss) (Fr.) Cup.

Tea, Black: (India, Java, Ceylon) Leaves are fermented.

Tea, Green: Mostly from Japan, unfermented.

Tea, Oolong: (Formosa) Semi-fermented.

Tea, Orange Pekoe: Pekoe refers to downy appearance of underside and ends of leaf buds.

Terrine: (Fr.) An earthenware jar used for the making of pate and potted meats. Served cold.

Tête: (tet) (Fr.) Head.

Thyme: An herb for flavoring.

Timbale: (tahm-bahl) (Fr.) Mold for baking.

Timbale: (Fr.) A small pie crust baked; mold filled with chicken, fish, vegetables or cheese.

Tortillas: Mexican flapjacks or griddle cakes made from corn.

Tournedos: (Fr.) Small slices taken from the heart of the filet of beef.

Tripe: The inner lining of the beef stomachs.

Truffles: Fungus, like mushrooms, grown underground; a seasoning and garnish. Grown mostly in N.E. Italy and S.W. France. (Fr.) Truffe.

Try Out: To cook fat until oil is out (as in making lard). Render.

Turkish Coffee: (Cafe turque). Strong, sweet coffee, made of equal amounts of pulverized coffee and sugar.

Tutti Frutti: (too'-tee-froo'-tee). Mixture of fruit as in ice cream.

Veal Birds: Thin slice of veal rolled around seasoned stuffing. May be stewed or cooked in covered casserole.

Veloute: (vel-oo-teh) (Fr.) Soup: A cream soup to which a liaison is added in addition to a puree of the desired garnish. Sauce: A thick, creamy sauce made by adding veal stock (and milk) to a bland roux.

Vermicelli: Long thin threads of pasta. Like spaghetti but finer.

Vert: (vair) (vairt) (Fr.) Green.

Viande: (vee-ahnd') Meat.

Vichyssoise: (Literal: As prepared in Vichy, France) A cream soup of potato and leeks, pureed.

Vin: (van) (Fr.) Wine.

Vitamins: Growth producing, health protective elements of food.

Vol-au-vent: (vohl-oh-vahn') (Fr.) Case made of puff pastry in which meat or poultry is served, usually covered with a crust lid.

Waldorf Salad: Celery, apples, nuts, whipped cream and mayonnaise on a bed of lettuce.

Washington Pie: Cake with raspberry or loganberry jam between layers.

Waterless Cooker: Cooking utensils of heavy metal in which foods are cooked in their own juices with tight fitting covers as in pressure cooking.

Welsh Rabbit: Cooked cheese, butter, beer, eggs flavored with Worcestershire sauce and spices. (Fr.—Fondue a l'Anglaise.)

Whipping: Rapid beating to increase volume of mixing air.

Wild Rice: Northern watergrass seed—served with game, not a true rice.

Won Ton: Noodle paste stuffed with ground chicken or pork and served in Chinese soup.

Yams: A tuber much like sweet potatoes. From the Southern United States and West Indies, South America and tropical countries.

Yorkshire Pudding: A batter of eggs, flour, milk and salt, baked with beef drippings and served with roast beef. Replaces bread when served.

Zabaglione: Italian for Sabayon but with Marsala wine. It is served in glasses with lady fingers and eaten with a spoon.

Zucchini: (tsoo-kee-nee) Italian squash.

Zwieback: (tsvee-bahk) Hard crispy German biscuit. Twice toasted.

Item	1 Tablespoon Ounces	1 Cup (Standard) Ounces	1 Pint Lb.	1 Pint Oz.	1 Quart Lb.	1 Quart Oz.
Allspice	1/4	4				
Apples, fresh diced					1	
Applesauce		8	1			
Bacon, diced, raw			1			
Bacon, diced, cooked					1	8
Baking Powder	1/2	6		12	1	8
Baking Soda	1/2	6	1		2	
Barley, pearl		8	1		2	
Bread Crumbs, dry		4		8	1	
Bread Crumbs, moist		2		4		8
Butter		8	1		2	
Cabbage, shredded or chopped						12
Carrots, diced, raw					1	3
Celery, chopped, raw				8	1	
Celery Seed	1/6	2-2/3				
Cheese, American, ground		5		10	1	4
Cheese, shredded		4		8		
Cheese, cottage		8	1			
Chocolate, grated	1/4	4		8	1	
Chocolate, melted		8	1		2	
Cinnamon, ground	1/4	3-1/2				
Cloves, ground	1/4	4				
Cloves, whole	1/6	2-2/3				
Cocoa	1/4	3-1/2		6-1/2		
Coconut, shredded		2-3/4		5-1/2		
Coconut, grated		2-1/2		5		
Cornflakes						4
Cornmeal				10-1/2	1	5
Cornstarch	1/3	5-1/3			1	5
Cracker Crumbs						10-1/2
Cranberries, raw				8	1	
Currants, dried		5-1/3			1	5
Curry Powder	1/4	3-1/2				
Egg, whites, (approx.)		8	1		2	
Eggs, whole (without shells)		8	1		2	
Egg, yolks		8	1		2	
Extracts (variable)	1/2					
Farina		6-1/4		12-1/2	1	9
Flour, bread (sifted)		4-1/4		8-1/2	1	1
Flour, cake (sifted)		3-7/8		7-3/4		15-1/2
Gelatin, flavored		5-3/4		11-1/2	1	6
Gelatin, unflavored		5-1/2		11	1	5
Ginger	1/2	3-3/4				

AND MEASURES OF COMMON FOODS

Item	1 Tablespoon	1 Cup (Standard)	1 Pint		1 Quart	
	Ounces	Ounces	Lb.	Oz.	Lb.	Oz.
Hominy Grits		6		12	1	8
Honey		11	1	6	2	12
Legumes:						
Beans, kidney, dry				12-1/2	1	9
Beans, lima, dry				13	1	10
Beans, white, dry				14	1	12
Lettuce, broken or shredded						8
Mace	1/4					
Mayonnaise		8	1		2	
Milk, liquid, whole		8-1/2	1	1	2	2
Molasses		12	1	8	3	
Mustard, ground	1/4	3-1/4				
Nuts, ground		4-1/4		9-1/2	1	3
Nuts, pieces		4		8	1	
Nutmeg, ground	1/4	4-1/4				
Oats, rolled		3		6		12
Oils, cooking or salad		8		16	2	
Onions, dehydrated, flakes		2-1/2		5		10
Onions, chopped		4		8	1	
Paprika	1/4	4				
Parsley, chopped		3		6		
Peanut Butter		9	1	2	2	4
Pepper, ground	1/4					
Peppers, green, chopped		4		8	1	
Pimientos, drained, chopped		7		14		
Potatoes, cooked, diced (approx.)				12-1/2	1	9
Prunes, dry		5-1/4		10-1/2	1	5
Raisins, seedless		5-1/2		11	1	6
Rice, raw		8	1		2	
Sage	1/8					
Salt	1/2	8				
Seasoning, poultry	1/4					
Sugar:						
Brown (firmly packed)		7		14	1	12
Confectioners		4-3/4				
Granulated		8	1		2	
Syrup, corn		11	1	6	2	12
Tapioca, granules		6-1/4		12-1/2	1	9
Tapioca, pearl		5-1/4		10-1/2	1	6
Tea		2-3/4		5-1/2		
Vinegar		8-1/4	1	1/2	2	1
Water		8	1		2	

Bibliography

Amendola, Joseph. *Practical Cooking and Baking for Schools and Institutions.* New York: Ahrens, 1971.

———, and Lundberg, Donald. *Understanding Baking.* Boston: Cahners Books, 1970.

American Spice Trade Assn. *Food Service Seasoning Guide.* New York: American Spice Trade Assn., 1969.

Bogart, L. Jean. *Nutrition and Physical Fitness.* Philadelphia: W. B. Saunders, 1955.

Brodner, Joseph, ed. *Profitable Food and Beverage Operation.* New York: Ahrens, 1962.

Bryan, Arthur H., and Bryan, Charles G. *Bacteriology, Principles and Practice.* College Outline Series. New York: Barnes and Noble, 1969.

Ceserani, Victor. *Practical Cookery.* London: Edward Arnold, 1967.

Coffee Brewing Institute, Inc. *Publication No. 14.* New York, n.d.

Coffman, James P. *Introduction to Professional Food Service.* Boston: Cahners Books, 1968.

Dahl, Crete. *Food and Menu Dictionary.* Boston, Mass.: Cahners Books, 1972.

Escoffier, Auguste. *The Escoffier Cookbook.* New York: Crown Publishers, 1969.

Escoffier, Auguste. *Basic Elements of Fine Cookery.* New York: Crescent, 1941.

———. *Ma Cuisine.* London: Paul Hamlyn, 1965.

———. *A Guide to Modern Cookery.* London: W. Heinemann, 1907.

Fellows, Charles. *A Selection of Dishes and the Chef's Reminder.* Chicago: John Willy, Inc., 1944.

Folsom, LeRoi. *Instructors Guide for the Teaching of Professional Cooking.* Boston: Cahners Books, 1967.

Forster, August. *American Culinary Art.* New York: Athens, 1958.

Gancel, J. *Gancel's Culinary Encyclopedia of Modern Cooking, 12th ed.* New York: Radio City Book Store, 1969.

Heath, Ambrose. *Madam Prunier's Fish Cookery Book.* New York: Dover Publications, 1939.

Hering's Dictionary of Classical and Modern Cookery. New York: Radio City Bookstore, 1970.

Kotschevar, Lendal H. *Quantity Food Production.* 3rd ed. Boston: Cahners Books, 1974.

———, and Lundberg, Donald. *Understanding Cooking.* Amherst, Mass.: University of Massachusetts Bookstore, 1965.

Levie, Albert. *The Meat Handbook.* Westport, Ct.: Avi, 1967.

Lowe, Belle. *Experimental Cookery.* New York: John Wiley, 1955.

Montagne, Prosper. *Larousse Gastronomique.* New York: Crown Publishers, 1961.

Moyer, William C. *Blue Goose Buying Guide for Fresh Fruits and Vegetables.* Fullerton, Calif.: Blue Goose, Inc., 1971.

National Livestock and Meat Board. *Ten Lessons on Meat.* Chicago: National Livestock and Meat Board, 1943.

Pellaprat, H. P. *Modern French Culinary Art.* London: Virtue, 1969.

Ranhofer, Charles. *Epicurean.*

Richardson, Treva. *Sanitation for Foodservice Workers.* Boston: Cahners Books, 1973.

Saulnier, L. *Cookery Repertory (Le Repertoire de la Cuisine).* London: Leon Joeggi.

Shircliffe, Arnold. *Principles of Cookery.* Great Lakes, Ill.: Naval Air Training, 1943.

Shircliffe, Arnold. *Edgewater Beach Hotel Salad Book.* Evanston, Ill.: John Willy, Inc., 1948.

Smith, Henry. *The Master Book of Poultry and Game.* London: Spring Books, n.d.

Smith, Henry. *The Master Book of Soups.* London: Spring Books.

Sonnenschmidt, Frederic, and Nicolas, Jean F. *Professional Chef's Art of Garde Manger.* Boston: Cahners Books, 1973.

Time-Life. *Time-Life Series, Foods of the World.* New York: Time-Life Books.

U.S. Department of Health, Education, and Welfare. *Food Service Sanitation Manual.* Washington, D.C.: Government Printing Office, 1962.

———. *Quantity Food Preparation, A Curriculum Guide. Circ. No. 526.* Washington, D.C.: Government Printing Office, 1962.

Waldner, George K., and Mitterhauser, Klaus. *Professional Chef's Book of Buffets.* Boston: Cahners Books, 1968.

Welch, John M. *A Basic Course in Quality Food Preparation.* The Florida Restaurant Research and Development Foundation with the cooperation of the Florida Light and Power Co., 1959.

Index

Photo credit p. 345:
Architect: A. Epstein Sons, Inc.